THE INTERPERSONAL
COMMUNICATION BOOK

THE INTERPERSONAL COMMUNICATION BOOK

EIGHTH EDITION

Joseph A. DeVito

*Hunter College
of the City University of New York*

An imprint of Addison Wesley Longman, Inc.

New York • Reading, Massachusetts • Menlo Park, California • Harlow, England
Don Mills, Ontario • Sydney • Mexico City • Madrid • Amsterdam

Senior Acquisitions Editor: Deirdre Cavanaugh
Developmental Editor: Cathlynn Richard
Supervising Developmental Editor: Dawn Groundwater
Editor-in-Chief: Priscilla McGeehon
Supplements Editor: Tom Kulesa
Text Design and Project Management: Interactive Composition Corporation
Cover Designer: Kay Petronio
Art Studio: Interactive Composition Corporation
Photo Researcher: Karen Koblik
Full-Service Production Manager: Eric Jorgensen
Manufacturing Manager: Hilda Koparanian
Electronic Page Makeup: Interactive Composition Corporation
Printer and Binder: RR Donnelley & Sons Company
Cover Printer: Coral Graphic Services, Inc.

For permission to use copyrighted material, grateful acknowledgment is made to the copyright holders on pp. 486, which are hereby made part of this copyright page.

Library of Congress Cataloging-in-Publication Data

DeVito, Joseph A., 1938–
    The interpersonal communication book / Joseph A. DeVito. -- 8th ed.
      p. cm.
    Includes bibliographical references and index.
    ISBN 0-321-01302-6
    1. Interpersonal communication.   I. Title.
    BF637.C45D49 1997   97-18770
    302.2--dc21   CIP

ISBN 0-321-01302-06
12345678910—DOW—00999897

To my Uncle Louis for his wisdom and his caring.

CONTENTS IN BRIEF

Contents in Detail   ix
Preface   xix

PART ONE	Interpersonal Communication Preliminaries	2

1. Universals of Interpersonal Communication   4
2. Axioms of Interpersonal Communication   26
3. Culture in Interpersonal Communication   46
4. The Self in Interpersonal Communication   68
5. Apprehension and Assertiveness   90
6. Perception in Interpersonal Communication   106
7. Listening in Interpersonal Communication   130
8. Effectiveness in Interpersonal Communication   152

PART TWO	Messages: Verbal and Nonverbal	172

9. Universals of Verbal and Nonverbal Messages   174
10. Verbal Messages: Principles and Pitfalls   192
11. Verbal Messages: Barriers to Interaction   208
12. Nonverbal Messages: Body and Sound   226
13. Nonverbal Messages: Space and Time   246
14. Messages and Conversation   264

PART THREE	Interpersonal Relationships	284

15. Universals of Interpersonal Relationships   286
16. Relationship Development and Involvement   300
17. Relationship Deterioration and Dissolution   314
18. Relationship Maintenance and Repair   332
19. Power in Interpersonal Relationships   350
20. Conflict in Interpersonal Relationships   370
21. Friends and Lovers   396
22. Primary and Family Relationships   416

Handbook of Experiential Learning Vehicles   435
Glossary of Interpersonal Communication Concepts and Skills   469
Photo Acknowledgments   486
Bibliography   487
Index   506

CONTENTS IN DETAIL

Preface   **xix**

| PART ONE | Interpersonal Communication Preliminaries | 2 |

Unit 1   Universals of Interpersonal Communication   4

The Nature of Interpersonal Communication   6
A Dyadic (Relational) Approach to Interpersonal Communication   ◆
A Developmental Approach to Interpersonal Communication
The Elements of Interpersonal Communication   10
Source-Receiver   ◆   Encoding-Decoding   ◆   Competence   ◆   Messages   ◆
Channel   ◆   Noise   ◆   Context   ◆   Purpose   ◆   Effects   ◆   Ethics
Culture and Interpersonal Communication   19
The Relevance of Culture   ◆   The Aim of a Cultural Perspective
Summary: Unit in Brief   25

Unit 2   Axioms of Interpersonal Communication   26

Theory and Research in Interpersonal Communication   28
Theory in Interpersonal Communication   ◆   Research in Interpersonal
Communication
Interpersonal Communication Is a Transactional Process   31
Interpersonal Communication Is a Process   ◆   Elements Are Interdependent
Interpersonal Communication Is Inevitable, Irreversible, and Unrepeatable   32
Inevitability   ◆   Irreversibility   ◆   Unrepeatability
Interpersonal Communication Is a Process of Adjustment   34
Communication Accommodation
Interpersonal Communication Is a Series of Punctuated Events   37
Relationships May Be Viewed as Symmetrical or Complementary   37
Interpersonal Communications Have Content and Relationship Dimensions   40
Implications of Content and Relationship Dimensions
Summary: Unit in Brief   45

Unit 3   Culture in Interpersonal Communication   46

The Nature of Culture   48
How Cultures Differ   50

Individual and Collective Orientation ◆ High- and Low-Context Cultures ◆ Power Distances

Theories of Culture and Communication   57
Language Relativity ◆ Uncertainty Avoidance ◆ Maximizing Outcomes ◆ Culture Shock

Intercultural Communication   61
The Nature of Intercultural Communication ◆ Principles of Intercultural Communication

Summary: Unit in Brief   67

Unit 4   The Self in Interpersonal Communication   68

Self-Concept   70
Others' Images of You ◆ Social Comparisons ◆ Your Own Interpretations and Evaluations

Self-Awareness   71
The Four Selves ◆ Increasing Self-Awareness

Self-Esteem   74
Attack Your Self-Destructive Beliefs ◆ Engage in Self-Affirmation ◆ Seek Out Nourishing People ◆ Work on Projects that Will Result in Success

Self-Disclosure   77
Factors Influencing Self-Disclosure ◆ Rewards of Self-Disclosure ◆ Dangers of Self-Disclosure: Risks Ahead ◆ Self-Disclosure Guidelines

Summary: Unit in Brief   89

Unit 5   Apprehension and Assertiveness   90

Speaker Apprehension   92
The Nature of Speaker Apprehension ◆ Theories of Speaker Apprehension and Its Management ◆ Empowering Apprehensives

Assertiveness   100
Principles for Increasing Assertiveness

Summary: Unit in Brief   105

Unit 6   Perception in Interpersonal Communication   106

The Perception Process   108
Sensory Stimulation Occurs ◆ Sensory Stimulation Is Organized ◆ Sensory Stimulation Is Interpreted-Evaluated

Attribution   110
Attribution Processes ◆ Attribution Errors

Perceptual Processes   120

Implicit Personality Theory ◆ The Self-Fulfilling Prophecy ◆ Perceptual Accentuation ◆ Primacy-Recency ◆ Consistency ◆ Stereotyping

Increasing Accuracy in Interpersonal Perception   126

Reducing Uncertainty ◆ Checking Perceptions ◆ Perceiving Critically

Summary: Unit in Brief   129

Unit 7   **Listening in Interpersonal Communication**   **130**

The Listening Process   132

Receiving ◆ Understanding ◆ Remembering ◆ Evaluating ◆ Responding

Listening, Culture, and Gender   138

Culture and Listening ◆ Gender and Listening

Effective Listening   141

Participatory and Passive Listening ◆ Empathic and Objective Listening ◆ Nonjudgmental and Critical Listening ◆ Surface and Depth Listening

Active Listening   146

Purposes of Active Listening ◆ Techniques of Active Listening

Summary: Unit in Brief   151

Unit 8   **Effectiveness in Interpersonal Communication**   **152**

Skills About Skills   154

Mindfulness ◆ Flexibility ◆ Cultural Sensitivity ◆ Metacommunicational Ability

A Humanistic Model of Interpersonal Effectiveness   158

Openness ◆ Empathy ◆ Supportiveness ◆ Positiveness ◆ Equality

A Pragmatic Model of Interpersonal Effectiveness   166

Confidence ◆ Immediacy ◆ Interaction Management ◆ Expressiveness ◆ Other-Orientation

Summary: Unit in Brief   171

PART TWO   Messages: Verbal and Nonverbal   **172**

Unit 9   **Universals of Verbal and Nonverbal Messages**   **174**

The Interaction of Verbal and Nonverbal Messages   176

Meanings and Messages   176

Meanings Are in People ◆ Meanings Are More Than Words and Gestures ◆ Meanings Are Unique ◆ Meanings Are Both Denotative and Connotative ◆ Meanings Are Context-Based

Message Characteristics   180

Messages Are Packaged ◆ Messages Are Rule-Governed ◆ Messages Vary in Directness ◆ Messages Vary in Believability ◆ Messages and Metacommunication

Summary: Unit in Brief   191

Unit 10   Verbal Messages: Principles and Pitfalls   192

Disconfirmation and Confirmation   194

Racism ◆ Sexism ◆ Heterosexism ◆ Racist, Sexist, and Heterosexist Listening

Excluding Talk and Inclusion   202

The Principle of Inclusion

Talking About Self or Others and Balance   203

The Principle of Balance

Criticism, Praise, and Honest Appraisal   205

The Principle of Honest Appraisal

Summary: Unit in Brief   207

Unit 11   Verbal Messages: Barriers to Interaction   208

Polarization   210

Correcting Polarization

Intensional Orientation   212

Cultural Identifiers ◆ Correcting Intensional Orientation

Fact-Inference Confusion   215

Pragmatic Implication ◆ Correcting Fact-Inference Confusion

Allness   217

Correcting Allness

Static Evaluation   219

Correcting Static Evaluation

Indiscrimination   219

Ethnocentrism ◆ Correcting Indiscrimination

Summary: Unit in Brief   225

Unit 12   Nonverbal Messages: Body and Sound   226

Communication Through Body Movement   228

Facial Communication   230

Facial Management Techniques ◆ The Facial Feedback Hypothesis ◆ The Influence of Context and Culture

Eye Communication   233
    Eye Contact Functions ♦ Eye Avoidance Functions ♦ Pupil Dilation

Touch Communication   236
    The Meanings of Touch ♦ Touch Avoidance ♦ Who Touches Whom Where:
    Gender and Cultural Differences

Smell Communication   240
    Attraction Messages ♦ Taste Messages ♦ Memory Messages ♦ Identification
    Messages

Paralanguage and Silence   241
    Paralanguage ♦ Silence

Summary: Unit in Brief   245

Unit 13   Nonverbal Messages: Space and Time   246

Spatial Messages   248
    Theories About Space

Territoriality   252
    Signaling Ownership ♦ Signaling Status

Artifactual Communication   253
    Space Decoration ♦ Color Communication ♦ Clothing and Body Adornment ♦
    Artifacts and Culture: The Case of Gifts

Temporal Communication   258
    Cultural Time ♦ Psychological Time ♦ Time and Status

Summary: Unit in Brief   263

Unit 14   Messages and Conversation   264

The Conversational a Process   266
    Opening ♦ Feedforward ♦ Business ♦ Feedback ♦ Closing ♦
    Reflections on the Five Stages of Conversation

Conversational Management   270
    Initiating Conversations ♦ Maintaining Conversations ♦ Closing
    Conversations

Conversational Problems: Prevention and Repair   280
    Preventing Conversational Problems: The Disclaimer ♦ Repairing
    Conversational Problems: The Excuse

Summary: Unit in Brief   283

PART THREE   Interpersonal Relationships   284

Unit 15   Universals of Interpersonal Relationships   286

Advantages and Disadvantages of Interpersonal Relationships   288
Advantages of Interpersonal Relationships ◆ Disadvantages of Interpersonal Relationships

Stages in Interpersonal Relationships: Development to Dissolution   290
Contact ◆ Involvement ◆ Intimacy ◆ Deterioration ◆ Repair ◆ Dissolution ◆ Movement Among the Stages

Summary: Unit in Brief   299

Unit 16   Relationship Development and Involvement   300

Theories of Relationship Development   302
Attraction Theory ◆ Reinforcement Theory ◆ Social Exchange Theory ◆ Equity Theory

Developing Relationships: The First Encounter   310

Summary: Unit in Brief   313

Unit 17   Relationship Deterioration and Dissolution   314

The Nature of Relationship Deterioration   316
The Stages of Deterioration ◆ The Strategies of Disengagement ◆ The Negatives and the Positives

Some Causes of Relationship Deterioration   318
Unrealistic Beliefs about Relationships ◆ Excessive Intimacy Claims
Third-Party Relationships ◆ Relationship Changes ◆ Undefined Expectations
Sex-Related Problems ◆ Work-Related Problems ◆ Financial Difficulties

Communication Patterns in Relationship Deterioration   323
Withdrawal ◆ Decline in Self-Disclosure ◆ Deception ◆ Evaluative Behaviors

What the Theories Say About Relationship Deterioration and Dissolution   326

If the Relationship Ends   328
Break the Loneliness-Depression Cycle ◆ Take Time Out ◆ Bolster
Self-Esteem ◆ Remove or Avoid Uncomfortable Symbols ◆ Seek Support ◆
Avoid Repeating Negative Patterns

Summary: Unit in Brief   331

Unit 18   Relationship Maintenance and Repair   332

Relationship Maintenance   334
Reasons for Maintaining Relationships ◆ Maintenance Behaviors ◆
Interpersonal Maintenance and Rules

What the Theories Say About Maintenance 340

Relationship Repair 340
General Relationship Repair Strategies ◆ Solo Relationship Repair

Relationships in Cultural Context 347

Summary: Unit in Brief 349

Unit 19   Power in Interpersonal Relationships   350

Principles of Power 352
Some People Are More Powerful Than Others ◆ Some People are More
Machiavellian than Others ◆ Power Can Be Increased or Decreased
Power Follows the Principle of Less Interest ◆ Power Has a Cultural
Dimension ◆ Power Is Frequently Used Unfairly

Bases of Power 359
Referent Power ◆ Legitimate Power ◆ Reward Power ◆ Coercive Power
Expert Power ◆ Information or Persuasion Power

Communicating Power 363
Speaking Power ◆ Nonverbal Power ◆ Listening Power

Empowering Others 365

Compliance Gaining and Compliance Resisting 366
Compliance-Gaining Strategies ◆ Compliance-Resisting Strategies

Summary: Unit in Brief 369

Unit 20   Conflict In Interpersonal Relationships   370

The Nature of Conflict 372
Myths About Conflict ◆ The Negatives and Positives of Conflict ◆ Content
and Relationship Conflicts ◆ Conflict and Culture

A Model of Conflict Resolution 377
Define the Conflict ◆ Examine Possible Solutions ◆ Test the Solution ◆
Evaluate the Solution ◆ Accept or Reject the Solution

Conflict Management Strategies 380
Avoidance and Fighting Actively ◆ Force and Talk ◆ Blame and Empathy
Silencers and Facilitating Open Expression ◆ Gunnysacking and Present
Focus ◆ Fighting Below and Above the Belt ◆ Face-Detracting and Face-
Enhancing Strategies ◆ Verbal Aggressiveness, Verbal Abuse, and
Argumentativeness ◆ Dealing with Unfair Conflict Strategies

Before and After the Conflict 393
Before the Conflict ◆ After the Conflict

Summary: Unit in Brief 395

Unit 21   Friends and Lovers   **396**

Friends   398
   The Nature of Friendship ◆ The Needs of Friendship ◆ Stages and
   Communication in Friendship Development ◆ Cultural Differences in
   Friendship ◆ Gender Differences in Friendship
Lovers   406
   The Nature of Love ◆ Types of Love ◆ Cultural Differences in Loving
   Gender Differences in Loving
Summary: Unit in Brief   415

Unit 22   Primary and Family Relationships   **416**

Primary Relationships and Families: Nature and Characteristics   418
   Defined Roles ◆ Recognition of Responsibilities ◆ Shared History and Future ◆
   Shared Living Space ◆ Established Rules
Types of Relationships   422
   Traditionals ◆ Independents ◆ Separates
Communication Patterns in Primary Relationships and Families   426
   The Equality Pattern ◆ The Balanced Split Pattern ◆ The Unbalanced Split
   Pattern ◆ The Monopoly Pattern ◆ Reflections on Types and Patterns of
   Primary Relationships
Improving Communication Within Primary Relationships and Families   430
   Empathic Understanding ◆ Self-Disclosures ◆ Openness to Change
   Fair Fighting ◆ Reasonableness
Summary: Unit in Brief   433

Handbook of Experiential Learning Vehicles   **435**

Glossary of Interpersonal Communication Concepts and Skills   **469**

Photo Acknowledgments   **486**

Bibliography   **487**

Index   **506**

SPECIALIZED CONTENTS

MEDIA & TECHNOLOGY BOXES

1. Interpersonal Communication: Face-to-Face vs. Computer (Unit 2)   35
2. Outing (Unit 4)   79
3. Censorship in Cyberspace (Unit 6)   113
4. Talk Radio (Unit 7)   147
5. Effective Computer Communication (Unit 8)   159
6. Emoticons (Unit 9)   179
7. Learning the Jargon (Unit 10)   204
8. The Spiral of Silence (Unit 12)   244
9. The Rules of Netiquette (Unit 14)   276
10. Parasocial Relationships (Unit 15)   294
11. Developing Relationships Online (Unit 16)   310
12. Online Relationship Communication (Unit 18)   341
13. New Directions (Unit 22)   423

INTERPERSONAL ETHICS BOXES

1. Interpersonal Ethics and Choice (Unit 1)   20
2. Lying (Unit 9)   186
3. Fear and Emotional Appeals (Unit 11)   221
4. Censoring Messages and Interactions (Unit 17)   324
5. Gossip (Unit 21)   407
6. A Personal Ethic of Interpersonal Communication (Unit 22)   428

Self Test Boxes

1. What Do You Believe About Interpersonal Communication? (Unit 1)   7
2. What Do You Know about Research? (Unit 2)   29
3. What Are Your Cultural Beliefs and Values? (Unit 3)   49
4. How Willing to Self-Disclose Are You? (Unit 4)   80
5. How Apprehensive Are You? (Unit 5)   93
6. How Assertive Are You? (Unit 5)   103
7. How Accurate Are You at People Perception? (Unit 6)   112

8.   How Good a Listener Are You? (Unit 7)   134

9.   How Flexible in Communication Are You? (Unit 8)   156

10. Are You a High Self-Monitor? (Unit 8)   169

11. [When] Is Lying Unethical? (Unit 9)   187

12. How Confirming Are You? (Unit 10)   194

13. Can You Distinguish Facts from Inferences? (Unit 11)   216

14. Do You Avoid Touch? (Unit 12)   238

15. What Time Do You Have? (Unit 13)   261

16. How Satisfying Is Your Conversation? (Unit 14)   267

17. What Do You Believe about Relationships? (Unit 17)   320

18. How Committed Are You? (Unit 18)   336

19. How Machiavellian Are You? (Unit 19)   353

20. How Verbally Aggressive Are You? (Unit 20)   387

21. How Argumentative Are You? (Unit 20)   391

22. What Kind of Lover Are You? (Unit 21)   409

23. How Romantic Are You? (Unit 21)   414

24. Perceptions of Relationships (Unit 22)   424

PREFACE

This eighth edition of *The Interpersonal Communication Book* has provided the opportunity and the challenge to bring interpersonal communication into the twenty-first century and at the same time make it more accessible to those who are totally new to this exciting and growing field. It is truly an honor to write a preface to a text that has proven so popular with students and teachers over the last 20 years. The many revisions have enabled me to fine tune a presentation of interpersonal communication that keeps pace with the rapid research advances in the field and meets the ever-changing needs of today's students.

The philosophical foundation of the text continues to be the notion of choice. Choice is central to interpersonal communication because the speaker, listener, and communication analyst are constantly confronted with choice points at every stage of the communication process. The text provides readers with worthwhile options in a wide variety of interpersonal situations and discusses the theory, research, and evidence bearing on these communication choices. As a result, after completing this text, the reader should be better equipped to make more reasoned, more reasonable, and more effective communication decisions.

The Text

This text is a complete learning package that provides students with the opportunity to learn about the research and theory in interpersonal communication and to practice the skills necessary for effective interpersonal interaction.

The unit divisions of the previous editions have been retained. Students continue to favor their brevity and their clear and limited focus, making them easier to read and review. As in the previous edition, the units are grouped into three parts: Preliminaries, Messages, and Relationships.

Each unit opens with **Unit Topics** and **Unit Objectives** to give the reader an overview of what to expect in the unit. In addition, the Unit Opener contains suggestions for experiential learning vehicles or exercises, contained in the Handbook at the back of the book, that will help illustrate and personalize the concepts of the unit. The **Summary: Unit in Brief** charts at the end of each unit highlight and review the major issues considered. The questions for **Thinking Critically** in the margins invite responses to a variety of issues concerning both the theory and research and the skills and applications of interpersonal communication. **Experiential vehicles** appear at the end of the text in a Handbook of Experiential Vehicles in Interpersonal Communication. A combined **Glossary of Concepts and Skills** appears at the end of the text.

Thirteen **Media and Technology** and six **Interpersonal Ethics** boxes are integrated throughout the text. Twenty-four **Self-Tests** are positioned throughout the text to promote more active involvement. These features are explained in more detail below and are identified in the specialized table of contents on page **xvii**.

What's New in the Eighth Edition

This eighth edition is a significant revision, so the major changes and improvements (and there are many) should be noted:

1. **Cultural aspects** of interpersonal communication are given much greater attention than in the previous edition. Because of the growing importance of culture in interpersonal communication, an entire unit (Unit 3, Culture in Interpersonal Communication) is now devoted to culture and is presented early in the text as one of the foundation concepts for understanding interpersonal communication. In addition, major sections throughout the text elaborate on culture in connection with the specific topic discussed. These include the following:
   - an introduction to culture and interpersonal communication (the relevance of culture, the aim of a cultural perspective) (Unit 1)
   - culture as an influencing factor in self-disclosure (Unit 4)
   - culture and speaker apprehension (Unit 5)
   - culture and listening (Unit 7)
   - cultural sensitivity as a skill of interpersonal competence (Unit 8)
   - culture and directness (Unit 9)
   - racism, sexism, heterosexism (Unit 10)
   - cultural identifiers, ethnocentrism (Unit 11)
   - the influence of culture on facial communication, cultural differences in touching, and cultural differences and silence (Unit 12)
   - color and culture, gifts and culture, cultural time (displaced-diffused, monochronism-polychronism, the social clock) (Unit 13)
   - conversational taboos, conversational maxims and culture (peaceful relations, self-denigration, politeness) (Unit 14)
   - equity and culture (Unit 16)
   - relationships in a cultural context (Unit 18)
   - conflict and culture (Unit 20)
   - cultural differences in friendship, cultural differences in loving (degree of love, romantic experiences and attitudes, romantic breakups) (Unit 21)

2. **Media and technology** boxes, a new feature of this edition, relate the concepts of interpersonal communication to a world heavily influenced by both traditional media and new computer technologies. The boxes address the following issues:

   Interpersonal Communication: Face-to-Face vs. Computer (Unit 2)
   Outing (Unit 4)
   Censorship in Cyberspace (Unit 6)
   Talk Radio (Unit 7)
   Effective Computer Communication (Unit 8)
   Emoticons (Unit 9)
   Learning the Jargon (Unit 10)
   The Spiral of Silence (Unit 12)
   The Rules of Netiquette (Unit 14)
   Parasocial Relationships (Unit 15)
   Developing Relationships Online (Unit 16)
   Online Relationship Communication (Unit 18)
   New Directions (Unit 22)

3. **Interpersonal ethics** is covered differently in this edition. A series of 6 ethics boxes distributed throughout the text replace the ethics unit. The use of boxes permits closer coordination of the ethic and specific unit topics and serves to emphasize that ethics is a part of all interpersonal transactions. For those who prefer reading all the ethics material as a single unit, each box contains a note identifying the location of the next ethics box.

4. **Research and theory** is given greater coverage and attention. Recent research findings support just about every topic considered and reflect the changes that have taken place in the field of interpersonal communication over the last ten years. This research emphasis is also reflected in the marginal questions that focus on seeking answers on a wide variety of issues. A new section, Theory and Research in Interpersonal Communication, including a new self-test, has been added and appears in Unit 2.

5. **Critical thinking** has been emphasized even further in this edition. Additional questions and numerous specific sections throughout the text focus on critical thinking as it relates to interpersonal communication, for example: perception (Unit 3), listening (Unit 4), effectiveness (Unit 6), language barriers (Unit 12), and nonverbal communication (Units 10, 13, and 14). Questions for thinking critically about the contents of the unit have been revised and updated and now appear in the margins. These questions focus on evaluating principles and suggestions, synthesizing material covered in the unit, and furthering the understanding of research and theory.

6. Some **organizational changes** have been made.

   In Part One the new unit on culture appears as Unit 3. The effectiveness unit, formerly Unit 6, appears as Unit 8 following the units on the self. The three units on the self have been recast into two more manageable units (Units 4 and 5). And the ethics unit (Unit 5 in the previous edition), as already noted, has been reconceived into integrated boxes. The organization of this first part, then, is as follows:

   1. Universals of Interpersonal Communication
   2. Axioms of Interpersonal Communication
   3. Culture in Interpersonal Communication
   4. The Self in Interpersonal Communication
   5. Apprehension and Assertiveness
   6. Perception in Interpersonal Communication
   7. Listening in Interpersonal Communication
   8. Effectiveness in Interpersonal Communication

   The organization of Part 2 remains as in the previous edition:

   9. Universals of Verbal and Nonverbal Messages
   10. Verbal Messages: Principles and Pitfalls
   11. Verbal Messages: Barriers to Interaction
   12. Nonverbal Messages: Body and Sound
   13. Nonverbal Messages: Space and Time
   14. Messages and Conversation

   The organization of Part 3 remains the same except that the unit on dysfunctional relationships has been eliminated. Important sections of that unit, however, have been incorporated elsewhere in the text. The discussion of sexual harassment (formerly in a box in the dysfunctional relationship unit), in slightly reduced form, now appears in the unit on Power (Unit 19). The discussion of verbal abuse and verbally abusive relationships appears in the unit on Conflict (Unit 20), integrated more closely with the concepts of verbal aggressiveness and argumentativeness. Part 3, then, is as follows:

15. Universals of Interpersonal Relationships
16. Relationship Development and Involvement
17. Relationship Deterioration and Dissolution
18. Relationship Maintenance and Repair
19. Power in Interpersonal Relationships
20. Conflict in Interpersonal Relationships
21. Friends and Lovers
22. Primary and Family Relationships

7. **Self-tests,** so popular in previous editions, have been increased to 24. New self-tests include research in interpersonal communication, cultural beliefs and values, the ethics of lying, interpersonal flexibility, relationship commitment, and Machiavellianism. A complete list of self-tests appears in the Specialized Tables of Contents on pages xvii–xviii.

8. **Experiential vehicles,** formerly at the ends of units, have been reconfigured to make them more useful. Those experiences that can be done alone and that are closely connected with understanding the principles of interpersonal communication have been integrated into the text. Those experiences that are best completed in groups or with the class as a whole have been placed at the end of the text in a Handbook of Experiential Vehicles in Interpersonal Communication. The unit openers identify the vehicles most closely related to the concepts of the unit. In addition, the Handbook is prefaced by a chart that identifies the units for which the vehicles seem most appropriate.

9. **A Glossary of Concepts and Skills** integrates the two glossaries of the previous edition. This new integrated glossary provides both definitions of key terms and, where appropriate, the corresponding skills (*in italics*).

10. Other material has been updated, expanded, or substantially revised; by unit, the most notable are these:

    1. A new section on Culture in Interpersonal Communication (including the relevance of culture and the aim of a cultural perspective) introduces the importance of culture and establishes it as a major theme in this edition; the discussion of feedback has been expanded to include person versus message focus and a corresponding interactive visual (Figure 1.2); a new visual for the purposes of interpersonal communication (Figure 1.3) has been created.

    2. A new section on Theory and Research in Interpersonal Communication with a brief self-test now prefaces the axioms of interpersonal communication; a new figure explaining the transactional view of interpersonal communication (Figure 2.1) has been added; communication accommodation has been added to the discussion of the process of adjustment axiom; the material on communication being culture-specific has been repositioned and now appears in Unit 3.

3. A new unit on the nature of culture, how cultures differ, theories of culture and communication, and intercultural communication has been added to this first part of the text to introduce cultural concepts and a cultural perspective that recur throughout the book.

4. This new unit combines in more streamlined form self-concept, self-awareness, self-esteem, and self-disclosure and new material on cultural influences on self-disclosure. The box on facilitating self-disclosure has been deleted but appears in the third edition of *Messages: Building Interpersonal Communication Skills*.

5. Theories of speaker apprehension (cognitive restructuring, systematic desensitization, and skill acquisition) and cultural influences on speaker apprehension have been added; a clearer identification of assertive communications has been developed; the section on how apprehension and assertiveness begin has been deleted.

6. Discussion of attribution has been restructured and the stability factor has been deleted; more attention is paid to errors of attribution, for example, the fundamental attribution error is now included, and the discussion of perception checking has been repositioned and placed in the expanded section on increasing perceptual accuracy.

7. A major section on Listening, Culture, and Gender has been added; new tables on problem-causing ways of responding (Table 7.2) and on critical listening pitfalls (Table 7.3) have been added.

8. A new self-test on communicator flexibility (from Matthew Martin and Rebecca Rubin) and new cultural perspectives have been added.

9. Gender and cultural differences in directness have been added.

10. A new section on disconfirmation through listening has been added; the principles of criticism and the discussion of inclusive language have been expanded.

11. A new table on the assumptions about the world and about language now prefaces the discussion of barriers (Table 11.1); a major section on cultural identifiers and reprinted guidelines from The Lighthouse, Inc. "What Do You Do When You Meet a Blind Person?" have been added; and a discussion of pragmatic implication has been added as a part of the fact-inference discussion.

12. The discussion of the facial feedback hypothesis has been enlarged a bit; cultural differences and silence has been expanded and updated; and a discussion of smell has been added.

13. Discussion of color communication has been updated and given a cultural emphasis; discussions of monochronism and polychronism and the social clock have been added to the discussion of cultural time; and a new section on "Artifacts and Culture: The Case of Gifts" has been added.

14. The discussion of politeness theory has been expanded; a new table on the functions of backchanneling cues has been added as has new material on the best types of excuses.

15. Major new sections on the disadvantages of interpersonal relationships and on culture and interpersonal relationships have been added; the visual on the stages of relationships has been revised (Figure 15.1); and the stage talk box has been repositioned in the Handbook (Vehicle No. 16).

16. The discussion of equity and its cultural variations has been updated and "The First Encounter" section has been reworked and streamlined.
17. The discussion of unrealistic beliefs about relationships has been integrated into the discussion of causes of relationship deterioration and research on deterioration has been updated.
18. A new self-test on commitment (from Mark Knapp and Eric Taylor) has been added and the discussion of maintenance behaviors has been streamlined.
19. A new discussion with a self-test on Machiavellianism has been added; other new sections include empowering others and communicating power (verbally, nonverbally, and through listening).
20. New discussions on conflict and culture, the issues people argue about, the factors influencing the choice of conflict management strategies, and face-detracting and face-enhancing strategies have been added; the section on conflict management strategies now integrates aggressiveness, verbal abuse, and argumentativeness.
21. New discussions include cultural differences in both friendship and love and love and personality; love and communication and romanticism are both integrated into the discussion of love.
22. New material has been added on shared living space as a defining feature of family; a new section on rules in the family and the role of culture in establishing these rules has been added; and the relationship between equality and equity has been clarified.

The Pedagogy

In this edition, I have increased efforts to make the text even more interactive than previous editions. Some examples of this emphasis are:

- **Unit opening grids** combine the major topics covered in the text (the major headings in the unit) and their corresponding objectives to give a clearer picture of both the theoretical and the applied dimensions of interpersonal communication.
- **Integrated interactive discussions** that ask readers to reflect on their own interpersonal communication and relationships appear throughout the text and in every unit.
- **24 self-tests**, approximately one per unit, ask students to assess their communication behaviors or beliefs (many with instructions for analyzing their own responses so they can see how their behaviors compare with those of other groups). The 24 self-tests are integrated throughout the book.

- **Questions for thinking critically** about the contents of each unit appear in the margins and should prove useful for stimulating discussion and for extending and applying the principles to other areas.
- **Captions** for photos, tables, and figures have been extended beyond what is customary practice; the captions draw more focused attention to the visuals and better integrate them into the text.
- **Experiential vehicles** (several new to this edition) in the appendix, Handbook of Experiential Vehicles, provide opportunities to work actively with the concepts discussed in the text.

◆ **Summary: Unit in Brief** charts highlight and review the major issues considered in each chapter.
◆ **Learning aid notes** appear next to the first appearance of each of the major pedagogical features and explain their purpose and how to get the most value out of them.

Ancillaries

To enhance the teaching and learning experiences in interpersonal communication, a variety of ancillaries are available with this textbook for the instructor and student.

ANCILLARIES FOR THE INSTRUCTOR

Interpersonal Communication Video

Designed especially for use with this edition, a video of eight interpersonal episodes coordinated with the text material, has been prepared by Professors Jean Civikly-Powell and Tom Jewell of the University of New Mexico. With segments written and performed by students from the University of New Mexico, the video covers concepts such as perception, ethics, self-disclosure, sexual harassment and dysfunctional relationships.

This video comes with a guide containing suggestions for using and coordinating the video with the text.

Instructor's Manual/Test Bank

The **Instructor's Manual/Test Bank** written by Marquita L. Byrd of San Jose State University provides suggestions for teaching the course, sample syllabi, chapter outlines and summaries, additional class exercises and experiences, suggestions for using the text's Experiential Vehicles, additional references, over 100 transparency masters, and over 700 test questions including multiple choice, true-false and essay.

Interpersonal Communication TestGen EQ

Our print test bank is available digitally through Longman's TestGen-EQ with QuizMaster-EQ. This fully networkable testing software is available in Windows and Macintosh versions. TestGen-EQ's friendly graphical interface enables instructors to easily view, edit, and add questions, transfer questions to tests, and print tests in a variety of fonts and forms. Search and sort features let the instructor quickly locate questions and arrange them in a preferred order including an ability to print the same test with questions in different order and multiple choice alternatives in different order. QuizMaster-EQ enables instructors to create and save tests and quizzes using TestGen-EQ so students can take them on a computer network. Instructors can set preferences for how and when tests are administered. QuizMaster-EQ automatically grades the exams and allows the instructor to view or print a variety of reports for individual students, classes, or courses.

Transparencies

In addition to the more than 100 transparency masters included in the Instructor's Manual, Longman is pleased to offer for the first time with this book, a package of 74 full color transparencies. These transparencies reproduce many of the figures and tables from the text and include content summaries to facilitate instructor's lecture presentation and to use as lecture outlines. Included in this transaprency packet is a convenient grid developed by the author which offers suggestions for using transparencies in the classroom and how to best integrate them with the text material.

ANCILLARIES FOR THE STUDENT

Studying Communication

A booklet—*Studying Communication*—can be packaged with this edition. Written by the author, this booklet introduces the student to the field of communication and to the way research is conducted—topics that we have too long neglected. In addition, it contains a variety of practical suggestions for helping the student get the most out of the course and the text and covers, for example, how to read a textbook, how to take a test, and how to write a paper in communication.

Brainstorms

Also available is a brief creative thinking booklet subtitled, "How to Think More Creatively About Communication or About Anything Else." Also written by the author, this booklet integrates creative thinking into the introductory communication course and thus complements the critical thinking emphasis in the text. **Brainstorms** introduces the creative thinking process (its nature, values, characteristics, and stages) and its relationship to communication (or anything else). The discussion of each tool includes its purposes, the specific techniques to follow in using the tool, and at least one exercise or application to get started using the tool. Creative thinking sidebars and relevant quotations add to the interactive pedagogy. Guides for coordinating the creative thinking tools with the topics of the textbook are provided as well.

The Interpersonal Challenge 3

This highly interactive game has been expanded and streamlined and is keyed to the eighth edition. The game now contains 200 questions covering such topics as perception, interpersonal relationships, ethical dilemmas, and intercultural communication. Instructions for playing the game have been completely revised; as a result, the game will play faster and more smoothly with small groups in and out of the classroom.

Instructors should contact their local Longman sales representative to request an examination copy of any of these ancillaries or to find out more about our packaging options. One or more of the student ancillaries listed above can be packaged with the eighth edition of *The Interpersonal Communication Book* for a discount.

You may also request examination copies of this matieral and learn about additional Longman Communications titles by visiting us at our web site: http://longman.awl.com

Acknowledgments

I would like to express my appreciation to the many instructors and specialists who carefully reviewed the seventh edition text and the several manuscript revisions for this eighth edition:

Kimberly Batty-Herbert, Clovis Community College
Brian R. Betz, State University of New York College at Oswego
Judy Carter, Amarillo College
Alexia Fussell, Northeast Louisiana University
Elizabeth E. Grant, Southern Illinois University at Edwardsville
Theresa Hest, North Dakota State University
Dorothy W. Ige, Indiana University Northwest
Larry Leslie, University of South Florida
Kenna J. Reeves, Emporia State University
Lesa Stern, Southern Illinois University at Edwardsville
Carol L. Tarantola, University of Wyoming

In addition, I wish to thank the many people who reviewed earlier editions and whose reviews continue to prove valuable with each revision. Thank you, H. Ablomowicz, A. Abrams, Leonard Barchak, Ernest Bartow, Ronald Bassett, Charles Berger, Bernard Brommel, Marquita Byrd, Matt Campbell, Sumitra Chakrapani, James Chesebro, Ronald Coleman, Mark Comadena, Dan Crary, Hal Dalrymple, John Daly, Sue DeWine, Robert Dick, Susan Doyle, Steve Duck, Paul Feingold, Mary Anne Fitzpatrick, Fran Franklin, Jerry Ferguson, David Fusani, Rex Gaskill, Jane Goodale, Elizabeth Graham, Donna R. Hall, James Hasenauer, Katherine Hawkins, Michael Hecht, Randy Hirokawa, Christine Hirsch, Thomas Jewell, James Johnston, Virginia Katz, Marilyn Kelly, Lynne Kelly, Catherine Konsky, Cheris Kramarae, Robert E. Looney, Prestonburg, Thomas Mader, Terri Main, Janet McKenney, Sandra Metts, Bert Miller, Larry Miller, Paul Mongeau, Michelle Neaton, Carolyn Offutt, George B. Ray, Helen Sands, Jeff Ringer, Leonard Robuck, Charles Rossiter, Kristi A. Schaller, William Schenck-Hamilton, Stuart Sigman, Alan Sillars, Dennis Smith, Ralph Smith, Ted Spencer, Jim Towns, Laurel Vartabedian, Dennis Weeden, Ralph Webb, Paul Westbrook, Ethel Wilcox, Jerry Windsor, Deanna Womak, W. Gill Woodall, and Christopher Zahn. I also wish to thank the many people at Longman who contributed greatly to the final product. I especially wish to thank Deirdre Cavanaugh, Communication Editor, Dawn Groundwater, supervising developmental editor, Cathy Richard, development editor, Karen Koblik, photo researcher, and Sally Steele, text designer, for applying their unique talents to this book. I also wish to thank the people at Interactive Composition Corporation, especially Bill Mahaffey, project coordinator, and C.R. Batten, copyeditor, for easing the transition from manuscript to finished book.

Joseph A. DeVito
jdevito@shiva.hunter.cuny.edu

PART

1

Interpersonal Communication Preliminaries

PART CONTENTS

1. UNIVERSALS OF INTERPERSONAL COMMUNICATION

2. AXIOMS OF INTERPERSONAL COMMUNICATION

3. CULTURE IN INTERPERSONAL COMMUNICATION

4. THE SELF IN INTERPERSONAL COMMUNICATION

5. APPREHENSION AND ASSERTIVENESS

6. PERCEPTION IN INTERPERSONAL COMMUNICATION

7. LISTENING IN INTERPERSONAL COMMUNICATION

8. EFFECTIVENESS IN INTERPERSONAL COMMUNICATION

APPROACHING INTERPERSONAL COMMUNICATION

In approaching your study of interpersonal communication, keep the following in mind:

◆ The study of interpersonal communication involves both research and theory on the one hand and applications and skills on the other. Seek both to increase your understanding of the theory and to improve your skills.

◆ Effective interpersonal communicators are not born effective; rather, effectiveness comes through learning and experience. Whatever your present level of skills, you can improve your effectiveness in a wide variety of interpersonal situations by applying the principles discussed here.

◆ Principles of effectiveness vary with the context of communication, especially the cultural context. What works in one culture may not work in another; what proves effective with one group of people may prove ineffective with another. Try, therefore, to see your interpersonal communications within a context.

◆ The principles and skills discussed throughout this book relate directly to your everyday interactions. Personalize what you are learning; identify examples from your own interactions that illustrate the ideas considered here.

◆ Interpersonal communication—like other disciplines—has its own vocabulary. The new vocabulary will help you highlight significant ideas and think more clearly about your own interpersonal interactions.

UNIT

1

Universals of Interpersonal Communication

Unit Topics	Unit Objectives
	After completing this unit, you should be able to:

The Nature of Interpersonal Communication
A Dyadic (Relational) Approach to
    Interpersonal Communication
A Developmental Approach to Interpersonal
    Communication
	1. Define *interpersonal communication* using a dyadic (relational) definition
	2. Define *interpersonal communication* using a developmental definition

The Elements of Interpersonal Communication Source-Receiver Encoding-Decoding Competence Messages Channel Noise Context Purpose Effects Ethics	3. Diagram the model of interpersonal communication presented in this unit and label its parts 4. Define the following elements of interpersonal communication: *source-receiver, encoding-decoding, competence, message, channel, noise, context, purpose, effect,* and *ethics*
Culture and Interpersonal Communication The Relevance of Culture The Aim of a Cultural *Perspective*	5. Explain the role of culture in interpersonal communication

---

EXPERIENTIAL LEARNING VEHICLES

Vehicle No. 2, "Matching Pairs," p. 441, provides an opportunity to analyze communication and especially intercultural communication. Useful as ice breakers are Nos. 3, "I'd Prefer to Be," pp. 442–443, and 12, "Who?" pp. 452–453. No. 15, "Giving and Taking Directions," pp. 456–458, can be used to illustrate the process of communication.

Learning Aid Note

*Each unit begins with a two-part grid to give you an overview of the unit. The **unit topics** are identified on the left and the corresponding objectives or goals on the right. Before beginning the unit, get a general idea of what the unit covers by reading down the left-hand column. Then, focus on the **unit objectives;** these are the goals that you should be able to accomplish after you complete the various sections of the unit. When you complete the unit, return to these objectives to see if you can accomplish each one. If not, then re-read the relevant sections.*

*At the end of this grid is a note on the **experiential learning vehicles,** which identifies one or more experiences that are especially appropriate for the content of this unit and that are included at the end of the text in the Handbook of Experiential Learning Vehicles. If you have the opportunity, try working with these experiential vehicles; they will help you experience and personalize the concepts discussed in the unit.*

Interpersonal communication is something you do every day:

- making friends
- asking for a date
- applying for a job
- responding to a compliment
- being an empathic listener

- giving instructions to new workers
- persuading a friend to go bowling
- developing new relationships
- maintaining and repairing relationships
- dissolving relationships

Understanding these interactions is an essential part of a liberal education. Much as an educated person must know geography, history, science, and mathematics, you need to know the how, why, and what of communication. It is simply a significant part of the world. Moreover, interpersonal communication is an extremely practical art, and your effectiveness as a friend, relationship partner, coworker, or manager will depend on your competence or skill in interpersonal communication.

Understanding the theory and research in interpersonal communication and mastering its skills go hand in hand. The more you know about interpersonal communication, the more insight you will gain about what works and what does not work. This greater knowledge will increase your abilities to apply the principles to unique situations. The more skills you have within your arsenal of communication strategies, the greater will be your options for communicating in any situation. Also, because of these added options, the likelihood is greater that you will be successful.

Realize, too, that interpersonal communication skills are essential to your own empowerment. The ability to communicate successfully in interpersonal situations gives you the power to achieve your goals—to make friends, to establish and maintain successful relationships, to climb the organizational ladder, to adjust to new and different situations, to interact effectively with people from cultures different from your own, and so on. So important is this ability that the U.S. Department of Labor identifies interpersonal skills as one of the five essential skills for a nation and an individual to be economically competitive (*New York Times,* July 3, 1991, A17).

In this book, the emphasis is on your understanding of interpersonal communication: its theories and research and its practical skills. Theory research and skills are considered together as we progress through the elements of interpersonal communication, the ways verbal and nonverbal messages operate in interpersonal encounters, and the ways relationships develop and are maintained, repaired, and even dissolved.

As a preface, examine your assumptions about interpersonal communication by taking the accompanying self-test.

The Nature of Interpersonal Communication

Interpersonal communication can be defined in a variety of ways. One way is to define it by the number of people communicating and their relationship to each other. This we call the dyadic or relational definition. Another way is to define it as a developmental process where communication begins as impersonal and becomes more and more personal as the interactions increase in frequency and intimacy. This we call the developmental definition. Let's look at each.

What Do You Believe About Interpersonal Communication?

Self Test

Respond to each of the following statements with *T* if you believe the statement is usually true or *F* if you believe the statement is usually false.

_____ 1. The more you communicate, the better at it you will be.

_____ 2. Opening lines such as "Hello, how are you?" or "Fine weather today" or "Have you got a light?" serve no useful interpersonal purpose.

_____ 3. In your interpersonal communications, a good guide to follow is to be as open, empathic, and supportive as you can be.

_____ 4. When verbal and nonverbal messages contradict each other, people believe the verbal message.

_____ 5. The best guide to follow when communicating with people from other cultures is to ignore the differences and treat the other person just as you'd treat members of your own culture.

_____ 6. It is better to reveal your feelings than to keep them bottled up.

_____ 7. Effective interpersonal communicators do not rely on "power tactics."

_____ 8. Fear of speaking is detrimental and must be eliminated.

_____ 9. When there is conflict, your relationship is in trouble.

_____10. Couples who communicate a great deal are more likely to stay together than couples who communicate significantly less.

Thinking Critically About Beliefs About Interpersonal Communication

All ten statements are false. For example, in reference to No. 1, consider the problems created and aggravated by using and learning unproductive communication patterns. In reference to No. 2, consider what your typical conversation would look like without these "openers" and also consider the information they convey. In reference to No. 3, be suspicious of all principles that tell you to always do any one thing. As you read this book, you'll discover why all ten statements are false and some of the problems that can arise if you act as if these misconceptions are true.

A Dyadic (Relational) Approach to Interpersonal Communication

In a dyadic or relational definition, **interpersonal communication** is communication that takes place between two persons who have an established relationship; the people are in some way "connected." Interpersonal communication would thus include what takes place between a son and his father, an employer and employee, two sisters, a teacher and a student, two lovers, two friends, and so on.

You could argue that it is impossible to have dyadic (two-person) communication that is not interpersonal. Invariably, there is some relationship between two people who are interacting. Even the stranger who asks directions of a neighborhood resident has an identifiable relationship with the resident as soon as the first message is sent. This interpersonal (but nonintimate) relationship will then influence how the two individuals interact with each other.

Dyadic Primacy   Even when you have triads (groups of three people), dyads (two-person relationships) are still primary; dyads are always central to interpersonal relationships (Wilmot 1987). Consider, for example, the following situation: Al and Bob (a dyad) have been roommates for their first two years of college. Expenses have increased, and so they ask Carl to join them and become a third roommate. Now a triad exists. But the original dyad has not gone away; in fact, now there are three dyads: Al and Bob, Al and Carl, and Bob and Carl. Al and Bob

Learning Aid Note

Throughout this text you'll encounter a variety of self-tests (25 in all) which ask you to pause and reflect on your own communication thoughts and behaviors. In working with these self-tests, focus on the statements in the test, on the issues they raise, and on the thoughts they help generate rather than on the number you get "right" or "wrong." The scores you get are much less important than the insights they help you gain about your own communication patterns.

are ballplayers and interact a lot about sports. Al and Carl are both studying communication and talk about their classes. Bob and Carl belong to the same religious club and frequently discuss the club's activities. At times, of course, all three interact, but even then the topic of conversation will determine who talks primarily to whom. If the topic is sports, Al and Bob will primarily address each other; Carl will be a kind of outsider. When the topic is classes, Bob is the outsider.

You can observe **dyadic primacy** in almost every large group (Wilmot 1987). If you examine families, workers in a factory, neighbors in an apartment house, or students in class, for example, you will find that each large group breaks down, at some times, into a series of dyads. The specific dyad formed naturally depends on the situation, and dyads will probably change over time. As in the case of Al, Bob, and Carl, different dyads will form, depending on the nature of the interaction.

Dyadic Coalitions   A **dyadic coalition** is a two-person relationship formed for achieving a mutually desired benefit or goal (Wilmot 1987). In groups larger than two, dyadic coalitions are frequently formed. Coalitions—whether in the family, among friends, or at work—may be productive or unproductive. Two workers may form a coalition to develop a program for improving worker morale. Two teachers may undertake research together. The result of these coalitions will benefit not only the individuals involved but also, eventually, all members of the group. At other times, coalitions are unproductive. The grandparent who develops a coalition with the grandchild against the child's parent may cause all sorts of family difficulties; parental resentment and jealousy, as well as guilt for the child, are just a few possibilities. A parent, especially during relationship difficulties, may form a coalition with one of the children. This often results in alienating the left-out partner and preventing the child from benefiting from a close relationship with that parent.

Dyadic Consciousness   In addition to what you do and say, your interpersonal relationships depend on what you think about your relationship. As your relationship develops, a **dyadic consciousness** emerges; you begin to see yourself as part of a pair, a team, a couple. It is almost as if a third party enters the picture. No longer is it just you and the other person; it is now you, the other person, and the relationship. As the relationship becomes more involved, this third party takes on greater importance. Often individuals sacrifice their own desires or needs for the well-being of "the relationship."

A Developmental Approach to Interpersonal Communication

In the developmental approach, communications are viewed as existing on a continuum ranging from impersonal at one end to intimate at the other. Interpersonal communication occupies a broad area on this continuum. Interpersonal communication is distinguished from impersonal communication by three factors (Miller 1978).

Psychological Data   In interpersonal interactions, people base their predictions about each other (to some degree) on psychological data—that is, the ways in which a person differs from the members of his or her group. In impersonal encounters, people respond to each other chiefly as members of the class or group

Can you identify any primary dyads in your extended family? What functions do these dyads serve? What dyadic coalitions are you currently a member of? Why were these coalitions formed? Have they served productive purposes?

Have you ever been a part of a dyadic coalition? What was its purpose? Its effect?

Learning Aid Note
*Throughout this text the questions that are normally at the end of the unit are positioned in the margins; in this way they can be better coordinated with the text discussion. These questions focus on a variety of thinking skills: (1) **Self-analysis questions** ask you to analyze yourself as an interpersonal communicator and a relationship partner (friend, colleague, parent) and encourage you to personalize the material; (2) **Application questions** ask you to apply the concepts and principles discussion in one context to another context (for example, how might the skills of effective conversation be used in resolving interpersonal conflict); (3) **Evaluation questions** ask you to make judgments about the principles and theories presented; and (4) **Discovery questions** (the last question in each unit) ask you to consider ways in which you would go about finding answers to a variety of questions, to put on the researcher's hat and figure out how you might conduct research to answer the questions.*

Do men and women behave similarly in regard to dyadic primacy, coalitions, and consciousness? For example, do men and women develop dyadic consciousness at the same time in a relationship? Do they define it in the same way? Do they have different expectations on the basis of dyadic consciousness? Are men and woman equally likely to form dyads? To form dyadic coalitions?

to which each belongs. For example, initially you respond to a particular college professor as you respond to college professors in general. Similarly, the college professor responds to you as he or she responds to students generally. As your relationship becomes more personal, however, both of you begin to respond to each other not as members of groups but as unique individuals. Put differently, in impersonal encounters, the social or cultural role of the person governs your interaction, while in personal or interpersonal encounters, the psychological uniqueness of the person tells you how to interact.

This general move from social data to psychological data is true in the United States and in most European cultures. In many Asian and African cultures, however, the individual's group membership is always important; it never recedes into the background. Thus, in these cultures, one's group membership (one's social data)—even in the closest intimate relationships—is always important, often more important than one's individual or psychological characteristics (Moghaddam, Taylor, and Wright 1993).

Explanatory Knowledge In impersonal relationships, you can do little more than **describe** a person or a person's way of communicating. As you get to know someone a bit better, you can **predict** his or her behavior. If you get to know the person well, you'll become able to **explain** the behavior. The college professor, in

How would you describe your relationship with your best friend or romantic partner in terms of the three characteristics of interpersonal communication noted in the developmental definition: Predictions are based on psychological data, interactions are based on explanatory knowledge, and interactions are based on personally established rules? How does this relationship differ from, for example, the relationship you have with one of your college instructors?

an impersonal relationship, may be able to describe, say, your lateness and perhaps also predict that you will be five minutes late to class each Friday. In an interpersonal situation, however, the professor can go beyond these levels to explain the behavior—in this case, give reasons why you are late.

Personally Established Rules   In impersonal situations, the rules of interaction are set down by social norms. Students and professors behave toward one another—in impersonal situations—according to the social norms established by their culture and society. However, as the relationship between student and professor becomes interpersonal, the social rules no longer totally regulate the interaction. Student and professor begin to establish rules of their own largely because they begin to see each other as unique individuals rather than merely as members of a particular social group.

These two approaches to interpersonal communication—the dyadic and the developmental—are not as separate as they may at first appear. Both help explain what interpersonal communication is, each giving a different perspective to this important form of human behavior. The developmental definition emphasizes the types of interactions that are most significant to people—the more intimate types of relationships that make a substantial difference in your life. The dyadic or relational definition presents an extremely broad view of interpersonal communication while emphasizing that the interactants are—in some ways, at least—connected. An additional perspective on interpersonal communication may be gained by looking at the major divisions or areas of the field as identified in Table 1.1.

Metaphors—figures of speech in which one concept is used in place of another—are powerful tools for gaining different perspectives on a concept (DeVito 1996b). Can you explain interpersonal communication in terms of such metaphors as these: a seesaw, ball game, flower, ice skates, microscope, television sitcom, work of art, long book, rubber band, or software program?

The Elements of Interpersonal Communication

The model presented in Figure 1.1 is designed to present communication, not as a linear sequence where communication goes from person 1 to person 2 to person 1 to person 2 and on an on. Rather it is designed to reflect the circular nature of interpersonal communication where both persons send messages simultaneously. Each of the concepts in the model and discussed here may be thought of as a universal, in that it is present in all interpersonal communication acts.

Source-Receiver

Interpersonal communication involves at least two persons. Each person formulates and sends messages (source functions) and also perceives and comprehends messages (receiver functions). The hyphenated term **source-receiver** emphasizes that both functions are performed by each individual in interpersonal communication.

Do you talk to your instructor differently than you talk to your friends? Can you identify ten differences?

Who you are, what you know, what you believe, what you value, what you want, what you have been told, what your attitudes are, and so on all influence what you say, how you say it, what messages you receive, and how you receive them. Each person is unique; each person's communications are unique.

Table 1.1	The Areas of Interpersonal Communication and Relationships

This is not intended as a formal outline of the field but rather as a guide for identifying some of the important areas under the general topic of interpersonal communication and relationships. The six areas of interpersonal communication are not independent but interact and overlap. For example, interpersonal interaction is a part of all the other areas; similarly, intercultural communication can exist in any of the other areas. The related academic areas suggest the close ties among the fields of study.

General Area	Selected Topics	Related Academic Areas
Interpersonal interaction: Communication between two people	Characteristics of effectiveness Conversational processes Self-disclosure Active listening Nonverbal messages in conversation Online interaction	Psychology Education Linguistics Counseling
Health communication: Communication between health professional and patient	Talking about AIDS Increasing doctor-patient effectiveness Communication and aging Therapeutic communication	Medicine Psychology Counseling Health care
Family communication: Communication within the family system	Power in the family Dysfunctional families Family conflict Heterosexual and homosexual families Parent-child communication	Sociology Psychology Family Studies Social Work
Intercultural communication: Communication among members of different races, nationalities, religions, genders, and generations	Cross-generational communication Male-female communication Black-Hispanic-Asian-Caucasian communication Prejudice and stereotypes in communication Barriers to intercultural communication The Internet and cultural diversity	Anthropology Sociology Cultural studies Business
Business and organizational communication: Communication among workers in an organizational environment	Interviewing strategies Sexual harassment Upward and downward communication Increasing managerial effectiveness Leadership in business	Business Management Public relations Computer science
Social and personal relationships: Communication in close relationships, such as friendship and love	Relationship development Relationship breakdown Repairing relationships Gender differences in relationships Increasing intimacy Verbal abuse	Psychology Sociology Anthropology Family studies

Encoding-Decoding

Encoding refers to the act of producing messages—for example, speaking or writing. **Decoding** refers to the act of understanding messages. By sending your ideas via sound waves, you are putting these ideas into a code, hence *en*coding. By translating sound waves into ideas, you are taking them out of a code, hence *de*coding. Thus, speakers and writers are called **encoders**, and listeners and readers **decoders.** The hyphenated term **encoding-decoding** is used to emphasize that the

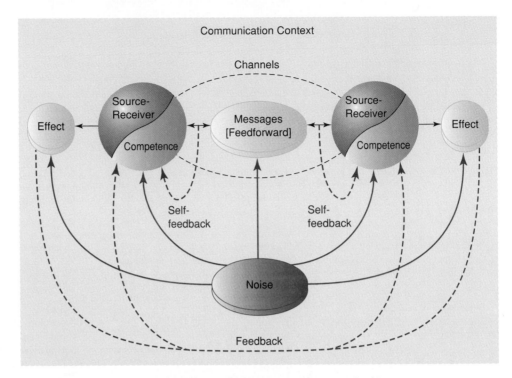

Figure 1.1   A Model of Some Universals of Interpersonal Communication
After you read the section on the elements of interpersonal communication, you may wish to construct your own model of the process. In constructing this model, be careful that you do not fall into the trap of visualizing interpersonal communication as a linear or simple left-to-right, static process. Remember that all elements are interrelated and interdependent. After completing your model, consider, for example: (1) Why is it important to speak of a source-receiver rather than a source and a receiver? Why is it important to speak of encoding-decoding rather than encoding and decoding? (2) Could your model also serve as a model of intrapersonal communication? A model of small group, public, or mass communication? (3) What elements or concepts other than those noted here might be added to the model?

two activities are performed in combination by each participant. For interpersonal communication to occur, messages must be encoded and decoded. For example, when a parent talks to a child whose eyes are closed and whose ears are covered by stereo headphones, interpersonal communication does not occur because the messages, verbal and nonverbal, are not being received.

Competence

Your ability to communicate effectively is your **interpersonal competence** (Spitzberg and Cupach 1989). For example, your competence includes the knowledge that in certain contexts and with certain listeners one topic is appropriate and another is not. Knowledge about the rules of nonverbal behavior—for example, the appropriateness of touching, vocal volume, and physical closeness—is also part of your competence. In short, interpersonal competence includes knowing how to adjust your communication according to the context of the interaction, the person with whom you are interacting, and a host of other factors discussed throughout this text.

You learn communication competence much as you learn to eat with a knife and fork—by observing others, by explicit instruction, by trial and error, and so on. Some have learned better than others, though, and these people are generally the ones with whom you find it interesting and comfortable to talk. They seem to know what to say and how and when to say it.

Not surprisingly there is a positive relationship between interpersonal competence on the one hand and success in college (Rubin and Graham 1988) and job satisfaction (Wertz, Sorenson, and Heeren 1988) on the other. So much of college and professional life depends on interpersonal competence—from meeting and interacting with other students, teachers, or colleagues; to asking and answering questions; to presenting information or argument—that you should not find this connection surprising. Interpersonally competent people also suffer less from anxiety, depression, and loneliness (Spitzberg and Cupach 1989). Interpersonal competence enables you to develop and maintain meaningful relationships, which help reduce anxiety and depression that may come from fear of not having friendships and love relationships.

A major goal of this text and your course is to explain the nature of interpersonal competence to improve your own skills. By improving your competence, you will have a greater number of options available to you. It is much like learning vocabulary: the more words you know, the more ways you have for expressing yourself. This interdependence of theory and skills goes like this:

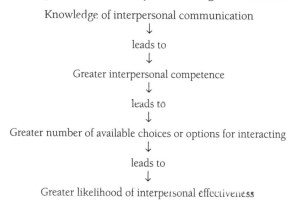

Knowledge of interpersonal communication
↓
leads to
↓
Greater interpersonal competence
↓
leads to
↓
Greater number of available choices or options for interacting
↓
leads to
↓
Greater likelihood of interpersonal effectiveness

What characters in television sitcoms or dramas do you feel demonstrate superior interpersonal competence? What characters demonstrate obvious interpersonal incompetence?

Messages

In interpersonal communication, messages—signals that serve as stimuli for a receiver—must be sent and received. Messages may be auditory (hearing), visual (seeing), tactile (touching), olfactory (smelling), gustatory (tasting), or any combination. Note that interpersonal communication does not have to be oral; you communicate by gesture or touch, for example, as well as by sound.

The clothes you wear communicate to others and, in fact, to yourself as well. The way you walk communicates, as does the way you shake hands, cock your head, comb your hair, sit, smile, or frown. These signals are your interpersonal communication messages.

Interpersonal communication need not occur face-to-face. It can take place by telephone, through prison cell walls, or through videophone hookup. Increasingly, it is taking place through computers as the Media and Technology box in Unit 2 shows. Note, too, that messages need not be intentionally sent. You also communicate through a slip of the tongue, a lingering body odor, or a nervous twitch.

Messages may refer to the world, people, and events as well as about other messages. Messages that are about other messages are called **metamessages** and represent many of your everyday messages, for example: "Do you understand?" "Did I say that right?" "What did you say?" "Is it fair to say that. . . ?" "I want to be honest." "That's not logical." Two particularly important types of metamessages are feedback and feedforward.

Feedback Messages   Throughout the interpersonal communication process, you exchange **feedback**—messages sent back to the speaker concerning reactions to what is said (Clement and Frandsen 1976). Feedback tells the speaker what effect he or she is having on listeners. On the basis of this feedback, the speaker may adjust, modify, strengthen, de-emphasize, or change the content or form of the messages.

Feedback may come from yourself or from others. When you send a message—say, in speaking to another person—you also hear yourself. That is, you get feedback from your own messages: you hear what you say, you feel the way you move, you see what you write.

What kinds of feedback can you observe in the typical college class-room?

In addition to this self-feedback, you get feedback from others. This feedback can take many forms. A frown or a smile, a yea or a nay, a pat on the back or a punch in the mouth are all types of feedback.

Feedback can be looked upon in terms of five important dimensions: positive-negative, person focused-message focused; immediate-delayed; low monitoring-high monitoring, and critical-supportive. To use feedback effectively, then, you need to make educated choices along these dimensions (Figure 1.2).

Positive-Negative   Feedback may be positive—as when you compliment or pat someone on the back for a good job—or negative—as when you criticize what the speaker has said or when reveal your negative reaction with a facial expression or gesture. Positive feedback tells the speaker that he or she is on the right track and should continue communicating in essentially the same way. Negative feedback tells the speaker that something is wrong and that some adjustment should be made. For example, a puzzled look from the listener may suggest that the speaker clarify a term or explain a concept in greater detail.

Positive	___:___:___:___:___:___:___	Negative
Person Focused	___:___:___:___:___:___:___	Message Focused
Immediate	___:___:___:___:___:___:___	Delayed
Low Monitoring	___:___:___:___:___:___:___	High Monitoring
Supportive	___:___:___:___:___:___:___	Critical

Figure 1.2   Five Dimensions of Feedback
Interpersonal relationships can also be described in terms of the types of feedback that each partner gives and can be positioned on these scales. This "feedback model of relationships" would characterize close or intimate relationships toward the left side of the scales, involving feedback that is strongly positive, person focused, immediate, low in monitoring, and supportive. Acquaintance relationships might involve feedback somewhere in the middle of these scales. Relationships with those you dislike would involve feedback close to the right side of the scales, for example, negative, message focused, delayed, highly monitored, and critical. And, of course, as the relationship changes, the types of feedback also change. How accurately do you think this model describes interpersonal communication in relationships?

Person focused-Message focused   Feedback may center on the person ("you're sweet," "You have a great smile"). Or it may center on the message ("Can you repeat that number?" "Your argument is a good one").

Immediate-Delayed   In interpersonal situations, feedback is often sent immediately after the message is received; you smile or say something in response almost simultaneously with your receiving the message. In other communication situations, however, the feedback may be delayed. Instructor evaluation questionnaires completed at the end of the course provide feedback long after the class began. When you applaud or ask questions of a public speaker, the feedback is delayed. In interview situations, the feedback may come weeks afterward. In media situations, some feedback comes immediately through, for example, Nielsen ratings, and other feedback comes much later through viewing and buying patterns.

Low Monitoring-High Monitoring.   Feedback varies from the spontaneous and totally honest reaction (low-monitored feedback) to the carefully constructed response designed to serve a specific purpose (high-monitored feedback). In most interpersonal situations, you probably give feedback spontaneously; you allow your responses to show without any monitoring. At other times, however, you may be more guarded, as when your boss asks you how you like your job or when your grandfather asks what you think of his new earring.

Supportive-Critical   Supportive feedback accepts the speaker and what the speaker says and occurs, for example, when you console another, encourage him or her to talk, or otherwise confirm the person's definition of self. Critical feedback, on the other hand, is evaluative; it's judgmental. When you give critical feedback (whether positive or negative), you judge another's performance, as in, for example, coaching someone learning a new skill.

Feedforward Messages   Feedforward is information you provide before sending your primary messages (Richards 1951). Feedforward reveals something about the messages to come. Examples of feedforward include the preface or table of contents of a book, the opening paragraph of a chapter, movie previews, magazine covers, and introductions in public speeches. Feedforward may serve a variety of functions, for example: (1) to open the channels of communication, (2) to preview the message, (3) to disclaim, and (4) to altercast.

To Open the Channels of Communication   In his influential essay "The Problem of Meaning in Primitive Languages," the anthropologist Bronislaw Malinowski (1923) coined the phrase phatic communion to refer to messages that open the channels of communication rather than communicate information. Phatic communion is a perfect example of feedforward. It is information that tells you that the normal, expected, and accepted rules of interaction will be in effect. It tells you another person is willing to communicate.

To Preview the Message   Feedforward messages frequently preview other messages. They do so in a variety of ways. Feedforward may, for example, preview the content ("I'm afraid I have bad news for you"), the importance ("Listen to this before you make a move"), the form or style ("I'll tell you all the gory details"), and the positive or negative quality of subsequent messages ("You're not going to like this, but here's what I heard").

To Disclaim   The disclaimer is a statement that aims to ensure that your message will be understood and will not reflect negatively on you. Disclaimers, which try to persuade the listener to hear your message as you wish it to be heard, are discussed in greater depth in Unit 15.

To Altercast   Feedforward is often used to place the receiver in a specific role and to request that the receiver respond to you in terms of the assumed role. This process, known as altercasting, asks the receiver to approach your message from a particular role or even as someone else (Weinstein and Deutschberger 1963; McLaughlin 1984). For example, you might ask a friend, "As an advertising executive, what would you think of corrective advertising?" This question casts your friend in the role of advertising executive (rather than parent, Democrat, or Baptist, for example). It asks your friend to answer from a particular perspective.

Channel

The communication **channel** is the medium through which messages pass. The channel acts as a bridge connecting source and receiver. Communication rarely takes place over only one channel; two, three, or four channels are normally used simultaneously. For example, in face-to-face interaction, you speak and listen (vocal-auditory channel), but you also gesture and receive signals visually (gestural-visual channel), and you emit odors and smell those of others (chemical-olfactory channel). Often you touch one another, and this touching also communicates (cutaneous-tactile channel).

Another way to think about channels is to consider them as the means of communication: for example, face-to-face contact, telephone, e-mail and snail mail, film, television, radio, smoke signal, fax, or telegraph.

Noise

Noise enters into all communication systems, no matter how well designed or technically sophisticated. **Noise** is anything that distorts or interferes with message reception. Three main types of noise are physical, psychological, and semantic.

Physical noise interferes with the physical transmission of the signal or message. Sunglasses, the screech of a passing car, the hum of a computer, a speaker's lisp, or a bad phone connection may all be viewed as physical noise because they interfere physically with the transmission of signals from one person to another.

Psychological noise refers to any form of psychological interference that can lead to distortions in the reception and processing of information. Biases and prejudices, closed-mindedness, and stereotyping are examples of psychological noise.

Semantic noise occurs when the receiver does not decode the meanings intended by the sender. An extreme form of semantic noise occurs between people speaking different languages. A more common form is created when you use jargon or technical and complex terms not understood by your listener, or when the listener assigns meanings different from those you intend (as would frequently be the case with ambiguous or highly emotional terms).

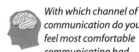
What kinds of feedforward can you find in this book? Are these feedforward messages helpful to you as you read the text? What kinds of feedback messages can you find in this book? Are these helpful? What additional feedforward and feedback messages would you find useful in a textbook? In a lecture? How important do you think the concepts of feedforward and feedback are?

With which channel of communication do you feel most comfortable communicating bad news? Communicating good news? Gossiping?

You cannot eliminate noise completely, but you can reduce its effects. Making your language more precise, acquiring the skills for sending and receiving non-verbal messages, and improving your perceptual, listening, and feedback skills are just a few of the ways in which you can effectively combat the effects of noise.

 What kinds of noise have you experienced today? Can you identify at least one example of each of the three types discussed here?

Context

Communication always takes place in a **context** which influences the form and content of your messages. At times this context is not obvious or intrusive; it seems so natural that it is ignored, like background music. At other times the context dominates, and the ways in which it restricts or stimulates your messages are obvious. Compare, for example, the differences among communicating in a funeral home, in a football stadium, in a quiet restaurant, and at a rock concert. The context of communication has at least four dimensions, all of which interact and influence each other.

The **physical dimension** is the tangible or concrete environment in which communication takes place—the room, hallway, or park, the boardroom or the family dinner table. The size of the space, its temperature, and the number of people present in the physical space would also be part of the physical dimension.

The **temporal dimension** refers not only to the time of day and moment in history but also to where a particular message fits into the sequence of communication events. For example, a joke about illness told immediately after the disclosure of a friend's sickness will be received differently than the same joke told in response to a series of similar jokes.

The **social-psychological dimension** includes, for example, status relationships among the participants, roles and games that people play, norms of the society or group, and the friendliness, formality, or gravity of the situation.

Communication also has a **cultural dimension** (Unit 3). When you interact with people from different cultures you may each follow different rules of communication. This can result in confusion, unintentional insult, inaccurate judgments, and a host of other miscommunications. Similarly, communication strategies or techniques that prove satisfying to members of one culture may prove disturbing or offensive to members of another.

Purpose

Interpersonal communication serves a variety of purposes, for example, to learn, to relate, to influence, to play, and to help.

Interpersonal communication enables you to **learn**, to better understand the external world—the world of objects, events, and other people. Although a great deal of information comes from the media, you probably discuss and ultimately "learn" or internalize information through interpersonal interactions. In fact, your beliefs, attitudes, and values are probably influenced more by interpersonal encounters than by the media or even formal education.

Most important, however, interpersonal communication helps you learn about yourself. By talking about yourself with others, you gain valuable feedback on your feelings, thoughts, and behaviors. Through these communications, you also learn how you appear to others—who likes you, who dislikes you, and why.

Interpersonal communication helps you **relate**. One of the greatest needs people have is to establish and maintain close relationships. You want to feel loved and liked, and in turn you want to love and like others. Such relationships help to alleviate loneliness and depression, enable you to share and heighten your pleasures, and generally make you feel more positive about yourself.

Very likely, you **influence** the attitudes and behaviors of others in your interpersonal encounters. You may wish them to vote a particular way, try a new diet, buy a new book, listen to a record, see a movie, take a specific course, think in a particular way, believe that something is true or false, or value some idea—the list is endless. A good deal of your time is probably spent in interpersonal persuasion.

Talking with friends about your weekend activities, discussing sports or dates, telling stories and jokes, and, in general, just passing the time are **play** functions. Far from frivolous, this purpose is an extremely important one. It gives your activities a necessary balance and your mind a needed break from all the seriousness around us. Everyone has an inner child, and that child needs time to play.

 Can you identify how you used each of the five purposes of interpersonal communication in the last four hours?

Therapists of various kinds serve a helping function professionally by offering guidance through interpersonal interaction. But everyone interacts to **help** in everyday interactions: you console a friend who has broken off a love affair, counsel another student about courses to take, or offer advice to a colleague about work. Success in accomplishing this helping function, professionally or otherwise, depends on your knowledge and skill in interpersonal communication.

The purposes of interpersonal communication can also be viewed from two other perspectives (see Figure 1.3). First, purposes may be seen as motives for engaging in interpersonal communication. That is, you engage in interpersonal communication to satisfy your need for knowledge or to form relationships. Second, these purposes may be viewed in terms of the results you want to achieve. That is, you engage in interpersonal communication to increase your knowledge of yourself and others or to exert influence or power over others.

Interpersonal communication is usually motivated by a combination of factors and has a combination of results or effects. Any interpersonal interaction, then, serves a unique combination of purposes, is motivated by a unique combination of factors, and can produce a unique combination of results.

Effects

Every communication act has **effects**. Even when effects cannot be observed (which may be most of the time), it is assumed that for every interpersonal communication act there are effects, somewhat as "for every action there is a reaction." Just as you cannot not communicate, you cannot not be affected by the messages you receive.

Ethics

 What types of interpersonal communications would you consider unethical? Why? What ethical principles do you think should govern interpersonal communication?

Because communication has consequences, interpersonal communication also involves **ethics**, the rightness or wrongness of a communication act (cf. Jaksa and Pritchard 1994; Johannesen 1990). Communication choices need to be guided by ethical considerations as well as by concerns with effectiveness and satisfaction. The ethical dimension of communication is complicated by the fact that it is so closely interwoven with your own philosophy of life—heavily influenced by the culture in which you were raised—that it is difficult to propose universal guidelines. Notwithstanding this difficulty, ethics is included as a universal of interpersonal communication and is presented in this text in "Interpersonal Ethics" boxes, (see page 20).

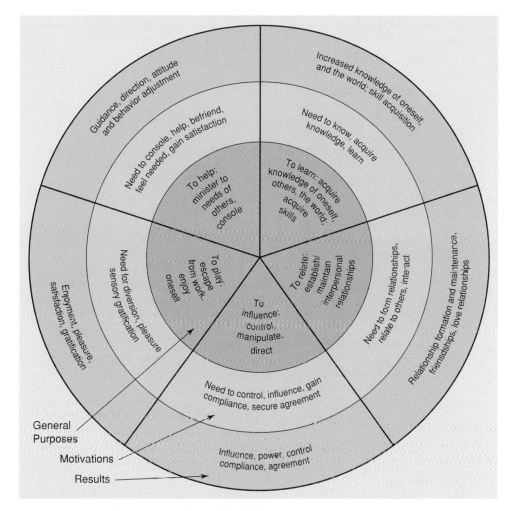

Figure 1.3   Why You Engage in Interpersonal Communication
The innermost circle contains the general purposes. The middle circle contains the motivations. The outer circle contains the results that you might hope to achieve by engaging in interpersonal communication. A similar typology of purposes comes from research on motives for communicating. In a series of studies Rubin and her colleagues (Rubin, Fernandez-Collado, and Hernandez-Sampieri 1992; Rubin and Martin 1994; Rubin, Perse, and Barbato 1988; Rubin and Rubin 1992; Graham 1994; and Graham, Barbato, and Perse 1993) have identified six primary motives for communication: pleasure, affection, inclusion, escape, relaxation, and control. How do these compare to the five purposes discussed here?

Culture and Interpersonal Communication

A walk through any large city, many small towns, and through just about any college campus will convince you that the United States is largely a collection of lots of different cultures (see Figure 1.4). These cultures coexist somewhat separately but also with each influencing each other. This coexistence has led some researchers to refer to these cultures as cocultures (Shuter 1990; Samovar and Porter 1991; Jandt 1995). Here are a few random facts to further support the

Learning Aid Note

As explained on page 18, these ethics boxes focus on just a few of the many ethical issues relevant to interpersonal communication and are designed to raise questions rather than answer them. This first box introduces the nature of ethics in the context of choice. Subsequent boxes, which may be read as you encounter them or in sequence as an entire unit on ethics, and their locations are as follows: Lying (Unit 9), Fear and Emotional Appeals (Unit 11), Censorship (Unit 17), and Gossip (Unit 21). The last ethics box, Personal Interpersonal Ethics (Unit 22), asks that you describe your own ethical system for interpersonal communication.

INTERPERSONAL ETHICS

INTERPERSONAL ETHICS AND CHOICE

One way to distinguish ethical from unethical messages is with the notion of choice. The underlying assumption is that people have a right to make their own choices. Interpersonal communication is ethical to the extent that it facilitates a person's freedom of choice by presenting that person with accurate information. Communication is unethical to the extent that it interferes with the individual's freedom of choice by preventing the person from securing information relevant to the choices he or she will make. Unethical communications, therefore, are those that force a person (1) to make choices he or she would not normally make or (2) to decline to make choices he or she would normally make, or both. The ethical communicator provides others with the kind of information that is helpful in making their own choices.

You have the right to information about yourself that others possess and that influences the choices you will make. Thus, for example, you have the right to face your accusers, to know the witnesses who will be called to testify against you, to see your credit ratings, and to know what Social Security benefits you will receive. On the other hand, people do not have the right to information that is none of their business such as information about whether you and your partner are happy or argue a lot or receive food stamps.

At the same time that you have the right to information bearing on your own choices, you also have the obligation to reveal information that you possess that bears on the choices of your society. Thus, for example, you have an obligation to identify wrongdoing that you witness, to identify someone in a police lineup, to notify the police of criminal activity, and to testify at a trial when you possess pertinent information. This information is essential for society to accomplish its purposes and to make its legitimate choices.

Similarly, the information presented must be accurate; obviously, reasonable choices depend on accuracy of information. Doubtful information must be presented with qualifications, whether it concerns a crime that you witnessed or things you have heard about others.

You also have the right to remain silent; you have a right to privacy, to withhold information that has no bearing on the matter at hand. Thus, for example, your previous relationship history, affectional orientation, or religion is usually irrelevant to your ability to function as a doctor or police officer, for example, and may thus be kept private in most job-related situations. If these issues become relevant—say, you are about to enter a new relationship—then there *may* be an obligation to reveal your relationship history, affectional orientation, or religion, for example.

In a court, of course, you have the right to refuse to incriminate yourself, to reveal information about yourself that could be used against you. But you do not have the right to refuse to reveal information about the criminal activities of others. Priests, psychiatrists, and lawyers, for example, are often exempt from this general rule if the information was revealed in confession or if the accused individual was a patient or client.

In this ethic based on choice, however, there are a few qualifications that may restrict your freedom. The ethic assumes that persons are of an age and mental condition that allows free choice to be reasonably executed and that the choices they make do not prevent others from doing likewise. A child 5 or 6 years old is not ready to make certain choices, so someone else must make them. Similarly, some people with mental disabilities need others to make certain decisions for them.

The circumstances under which you are living also can restrict free choice. For example, persons in the military will at times have to give up free choice and eat hamburger rather than steak, wear uniforms rather than jeans, and march rather than stay in bed. By entering the armed forces, one waives, at least partially, the right to make one's own choices. Furthermore, the choices made must not prevent others from making their legitimate choices. You cannot permit a thief to steal, because in granting that freedom you would be imposing on the rights of potential victims. Similarly, certain information may be restricted because it could be potentially dangerous to society. Thus, for example, information on how to construct bombs, most would agree, is information that the average citizen does not have a right to know.

Think about this approach to ethics as you consider the questions raised in future ethics boxes as well as ethical dilemmas you face every day. Is the notion of choice helpful? Is it consistent with your own feelings about what is right and what is wrong? Would you add additional qualifications?

[The next ethics box appears in Unit 9, page 186, and deals with lying.]

Statistical Portrait of the Nation

The top 10 categories that people claimed as their ancestry in the 1990 Census.

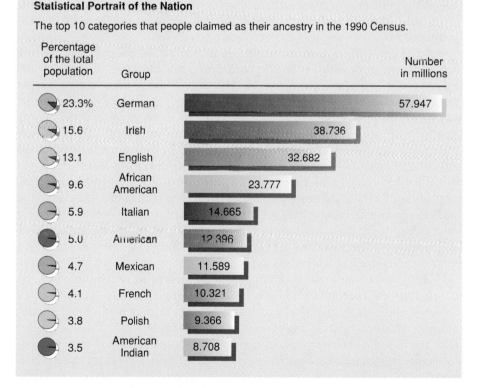

Percentage of the total population	Group	Number in millions
23.3%	German	57.947
15.6	Irish	38.736
13.1	English	32.682
9.6	African American	23.777
5.9	Italian	14.665
5.0	American	12.396
4.7	Mexican	11.589
4.1	French	10.321
3.8	Polish	9.366
3.5	American Indian	8.708

Figure 1.4   Ancestry of United States Residents
With immigration patterns changing so rapidly, the portrait illustrated here is likely to look very different in the coming years. For example, by the year 2030, it is predicted that the United States population will be 73.6 percent white, 12 percent African American, 10.2 percent Hispanic, and 3.3 percent Asian American. By the year 2050 it is predicted that the percentages will be: 52.8 percent white, 24.5 percent Hispanic, 13.6 percent African American, and 8.2 percent Asian American (figures projected by the Census Bureau and reported in New York Times, *March 14, 1996, p. A16). To what factors might you attribute these projections? What will your own state, city, or town look like in 2030? In 2050? That is, in what ways will it resemble or differ from the predictions for the nation as a whole?*

importance of culture generally and of intercultural communication in particular (*Time,* December 2, 1993, p. 14):

♦ Over 30 million people in the United States speak languages other than English in their homes.
♦ In the school systems of New York City, Fairfax County, Virginia, Chicago, and Los Angeles over 100 languages are spoken.
♦ Over 50% of the residents of such cities as Miami and Hialeah in Florida, Union City in New Jersey, and Huntington Park and Monterey Park in California are foreign born.
♦ The foreign born population of the United States in 1990 totaled almost 20 million, approximately 8% of the total United States population.
♦ 30% of the United States Nobel Prize winners (since 1901) were foreign born.

The Relevance of Culture

There are lots of reasons for the cultural emphasis you will find in this book. Most obviously, perhaps, are the vast demographic changes taking place throughout the United States. Whereas at one time the United States was largely a country populated by Europeans, it is now a country greatly influenced by the enormous number of new citizens from Latin and South America, Africa, and Asia. And the same is even more true on college and university campuses throughout the United States. With these changes have come different interpersonal customs and the need to understand and adapt to new ways of looking at communication.

As a people we have become increasingly sensitive to cultural differences. American society has moved from an assimilationist perspective (people should leave their native culture behind and adapt to their new culture) to one that values cultural diversity (people should retain their native cultural ways). And, with some notable exceptions—hate speech, racism, sexism, homophobia, and classism come quickly to mind—we are more concerned with saying the right thing and ultimately with developing a society where all cultures can coexist and enrich each other. At the same time, the ability to interact effectively with members of other cultures often translates into financial gain, increased employment opportunities, and job advancement prospects.

Today, most countries are economically dependent on each other. Our economic lives depend on our ability to communicate effectively across different cultures. Similarly, our political well-being depends in great part on that of other cultures. Political unrest in any part of the world—South Africa, Eastern Europe, and the Middle East, to take a few examples—affects our own security. Intercultural communication and understanding seem now more crucial than ever.

The rapid spread of communication technology has brought foreign and sometimes very different cultures right into your living rooms. News from foreign countries is commonplace. You see nightly—in vivid color—what is going on in remote countries. Technology has made intercultural communication easy, practical, and inevitable. Daily, the media bombard you with evidence of racial tensions, religious disagreements, sexual bias and, in general, the problems caused when intercultural communication fails. And, of course, the Internet has made intercultural communication as easy as writing a note on your computer. You can now just as easily communicate by e-mail with someone in Europe or Asia, for example, as you can with someone in another city or state.

Still another reason is that interpersonal competence is specific to a given culture; what proves effective in one culture may prove ineffective in another. For example, in the United States corporate executives get down to business during the first several minutes of a meeting. In Japan, business executives interact socially for an extended period and try to find out something about each other. Thus, the communication principle influenced by U.S. culture would advise participants to get down to the meeting's agenda during the first five minutes. The principle influenced by Japanese culture would advise participants to avoid dealing with business until everyone has socialized sufficiently and feels well enough acquainted to begin negotiations. Giving a birthday gift to a close friend would be appreciated by many, but among Jehovah's Witnesses, for example, this act would be frowned upon since they do not celebrate birthdays (Dresser 1995). Neither principle is right and neither is wrong. Each is effective within its own culture, and ineffective outside its own culture.

In what ways would interpersonal communication between two persons from the same culture and two persons from widely different cultures differ? In what ways would they be the same?

The Aim of a Cultural Perspective

Because culture permeates all forms of communication, it is necessary to understand its influences if you are to understand how communication works and master its skills. As illustrated throughout this text, culture influences

Do your college courses integrate a multicultural perspective? How is this reflected in your textbooks? What would be the ideal multicultural curriculum for your college? Is this also reflected in the media, for example, in newspapers, magazines, and television? Are your local media more or less "culturally integrated" than the national media?

Another way of looking at the "interculturalization" of the United States is to look at the international visitors. For example, 12,029,000 visitors came from ten countries in 1993. (That's more people than any state in the United States except for California, New York, Texas, and Florida. It's also more people than the total population of such countries as Cuba, Denmark, Ecuador, Finland, Greece, Haiti, and Israel.) Japanese visitors lead the list with over 3 million, followed closely by the United Kingdom, which also sends over 3 million. Germany is next with almost 2 million, followed by (in order) France, Italy, Australia, Brazil, Venezuela, Spain, and Argentina. The ever-present visitors exert influence on residents as residents influence them. Have you ever been a part of this influence process?

How would you go about answering such questions as the following?

◆ *Are interpersonal communication skills related to relationship success? To occupational success?*

◆ *Are competent communicators less anxious?*

◆ *How does the physical context influence communication?*

◆ *How is effective teaching related to the use of feedback and feedforward?*

◆ *Is knowledge about communication related to the ability to communicate effectively? That is, are those who know more about communication more effective communicators than those who know less?*

Learning Aid Note

Each unit ends with a summary. In a "return to objectives" the major topics and objectives of the unit (identified in the unit opener) are phrased as questions. Try answering these questions before reading the summary table and before moving on to the next unit. These general questions are followed by a table summarizing the major concepts covered in the unit. These tables are no substitutes for reading the unit, but will prove useful in at least two ways. First, these tables summarize what you have just read and will help you review the material and test your knowledge before an examination, for example. Second, these tables will help you to see the contents of the unit as a whole. They will help you see the forest as well as the individual trees. The boldface terms are the key terms covered in the unit and are also defined in the glossary at the end of the text.

communications of all types (Moon 1996). It influences what you say to yourself and how you talk with friends, lovers, and family in everyday conversation. It influences how you interact in groups and how much importance you place on the group versus the individual. It influences the topics you talk about and the strategies you use in communicating information or in persuading. And it influences how you use the media and in the credibility you attribute to them.

A cultural emphasis helps distinguish what is universal (true for all people) from what is relative (true for people in one culture and not true for people in other cultures) (Matsumoto 1994, 1996). The principles for communicating information and for changing listeners' attitudes, for example, will vary from one culture to another. If you're to understand communication, then you need to know how its principles vary and how the principles must be qualified and adjusted for cultural differences.

And of course this cultural understanding is needed to communicate effectively in the wide variety of intercultural situations. Success in interpersonal, small group, or public speaking—on your job and in your social life—will depend in great part on your understanding of and your ability to communicate effectively with persons who are culturally different from yourself.

This emphasis on culture does not imply that you should accept all cultural practices or that all cultural practices are equal (Hatfield and Rapson 1996). For example, cock fighting is a part of the culture of a number of countries but you need not find this acceptable or equal to a cultural practice in which animals are treated kindly. Consider this case in point (*Time,* December 2, 1993, p. 61). Assume you are a judge and the following case is presented to you: A Chinese immigrant killed his wife in New York because he suspected her of cheating. A "cultural defense" was offered, essentially claiming that infidelity in a Chinese marriage so shames a man that he is uncontrollable in his anger. Would this cultural defense have influenced your judgment? What actually happened was that the judge, influenced by an anthropologist's testimony that infidelity is so serious in Chinese culture that it pushed him to commit the crime, sentenced him to five years probation.

Further, a cultural emphasis does not imply that you have to accept or follow even the practices of your own culture. For example, even if the majority in your culture find cock fighting acceptable, you need not agree with or follow the practice. You can reject the political philosophy of your country or the religion in which you were raised. Of course, going against your culture's traditions and values is often very difficult. But, it is important to realize that culture influences, it does not determine your values or behavior. Often, for example, personality factors (your degree of assertiveness, extroversion, or optimism, for example) will prove more influential than culture (Hatfield and Rapson 1996).

As demonstrated throughout this text, cultural differences exist throughout the interpersonal communication spectrum—from the way you use eye contact to the way you develop or dissolve a relationship (Chang and Holt 1996). But these should not blind you to the great number of similarities existing among even the most widely separated cultures. Close interpersonal relationships, for example, are common in all cultures though they may be entered into for very different reasons. Further, when discussing differences remember that these are usually questions of degree rather than all-or-none. Thus, most cultures value honesty but some cultures give it greater emphasis than others. The advances in media and technology and the widespread use of the Internet, for example, are influencing cultures and cultural change and are perhaps homogenizing the different cultures, lessening the differences and increasing the similarities.

The cultural emphasis in this text will be seen in two ways. First, cultural issues are integrated into the text as they are appropriate. For example, when discussing self-disclosure or the meanings of nonverbal gestures, we also consider how different cultures view these forms of communication. Second, a complete unit (Unit 3) is devoted to the role of culture in interpersonal communication and introduces intercultural communication where the theories and principles of this rapidly growing area of human communication are discussed.

Summary	U N I T I N B R I E F

A RETURN TO OBJECTIVES:

In this unit we tried to answer three basic questions about interpersonal communication: (1) What is interpersonal communication and how can it be defined using a dyadic and a development perspective? (2) What are its essential elements of interpersonal communication? (3) What is the role of culture in interpersonal communication?

Definitions of Interpersonal Communication	Elements of Interpersonal Communication	Culture in Interpersonal Communication
Dyadic (Relational): Communication between two or a few connected individuals. **Developmental:** Two-person communication based on psychological data, explanatory knowledge, and personally established rules.	**Source-receiver:** The sender and receiver of messages. **Encoding-decoding:** The act of putting meaning into verbal and nonverbal messages and deriving meaning from such messages. **Competence:** The knowledge of and ability to use appropriately one's communication system. **Messages:** The signals that serve as stimuli for a receiver; metamessages are messages that refer to other messages. **Feedback messages:** Messages that are sent back by the receiver to the source in response to other messages. **Feedforward messages:** Messages that preface other messages and ask that the listener approach future messages in a certain way. **Channel:** The medium through which messages pass. **Noise:** The physical, psychological, or semantic interference that distorts a message. **Context:** The physical, social-psychological, temporal, and cultural dimensions in which the communication act takes place. **Purpose:** The reason for the interpersonal interaction. **Effects:** The consequences of communication. **Ethics:** The moral dimension of communication.	**Culture** is an inevitable part of all interpersonal communications and will greatly influence what works and what doesn't work. A cultural emphasis argues for an understanding of cultural differences and a sensitivity to them; it does not mean that you have to agree with or follow any specific cultural beliefs or practices.

UNIT

2

Axioms of Interpersonal Communication

Unit Topics	Unit Objectives
	After completing this unit, you should be able to:
Theory and Research in Interpersonal Communication Theory in Interpersonal Communication Research in Interpersonal Communication	1. Explain the nature and purposes of theory and research in interpersonal communication
Interpersonal Communication Is a Transactional Process Interpersonal Communication Is aProcess Elements Are Interdependent	2. Explain the transactional nature of interpersonal communication
Interpersonal Communication Is Inevitable, Irreversible, and Unrepeatable Inevitability Irreversibility Unrepeatability	3. Explain why communication is inevitable, irreversible, and unrepeatable and the implications of these qualities
Interpersonal Communication Is a Process of Adjustment Communication Accommodation	4. Explain the nature of interpersonal communication adjustment and the theory of communication accommodation
Interpersonal Communication Is a Series of Punctuated Events	5. Explain punctuation in interpersonal communication
Interpersonal Relationships May Be Viewed as Symmetrical or Complementary	6. Distinguish between symmetrical and complementary relationships
Interpersonal Communications Have Content and Relationship Dimensions Implications of Content and Relationship Dimensions	7. Distinguish between the content and relationship dimensions of interpersonal communication

---

EXPERIENTIAL LEARNING VEHICLES

Vehicle No. 1, "Analyzing an Interaction," pp. 437–440, illustrates each of the axioms discussed here. No. 24, "The Television Relationship," pp. 467–468, can also be used to illustrate these foundation principles.

In this unit, we continue to explore the special nature of interpersonal communication by first introducing the nature of theory and research and then explaining some of the basic axioms or principles that are common to all or most interpersonal communication situations.

Theory and Research in Interpersonal Communication

Before you begin reading this section, try taking the self-test, "What Do You Know About Research?" It will help clarify some essential concepts in understanding the research that you'll encounter in this text as well as in other courses.

Throughout this book and throughout your course you'll encounter a wide variety of theories and research findings on interpersonal communication. These theories and research findings constitute what we know about interpersonal communication. They tell us how interpersonal communication works as well as what works effectively. Thus, from these theories and research findings you not only come to understand how interpersonal communication works but you can also derive skills for achieving greater interpersonal effectiveness. Here we look first at theory and then at research.

Theory in Interpersonal Communication

A theory is simply a generalization that explains how something works—gravity, DNA identification, interpersonal attraction, or communication, for example. In academic writing the term is usually reserved for a well-established system of knowledge about how something works or how things are related. The theories you'll encounter will vary from those concerned with explaining how communication (in general) operates (for example, a theory that explains communication as a transactional process) to those concerned with more specific areas (for example, how we are attracted to some people and not to others, how communication works when relationships deteriorate, or how self-disclosure operates in friendship). In reading about these theories, you may well ask yourself, "Why should I learn this? Of what value is this material to me?" Here are a few answers to these very legitimate questions (Griffin 1991; Infante, Rancer, and Womack 1993; Littlejohn 1996).

Theories help you understand how interpersonal communication works. Theories provide general principles that help you understand a great number of specific events—how and why these events occur and how they are related to each other. As one communication theorist puts it, "A good theory synthesizes the data, focuses our attention on what's crucial, and helps us ignore that which makes little difference" (Griffin 1991, p. 4).

Interpersonal communication theories also help you predict future events. The theories summarize what has been discovered in the past and can therefore offer a reasonable prediction for events in the future. For example, based on the theories of interpersonal conflict resolution, you would be able to predict which conflict strategies will prove effective and which will prove ineffective in resolving differences. Of course, these theories will not provide correct answers 100

Self Test   **What Do You Know About Research?**

The following statements are designed to raise important issues about the research process and particularly how research should be interpreted. Mark each statement T if you feel it is generally true and accurate; mark F if you feel it is generally false and inaccurate.

_____1. When one event (B) regularly and consistently follows another event (A) we can say that A causes B or that B results from A.

_____2. It's important to know the results of research because they will apply to you at some point in your life.

_____3. Results from research conducted 20 years ago are generally of only historical interest.

_____4. If the same results emerge from lots of different research studies, we can be pretty sure that the findings are valid.

_____5. The only really worthwhile research findings are those that are found on the basis of experimental research in which all variables are carefully controlled and which are analyzed with the best statistical techniques.

Thinking Critically About Research

Statement 1 is false and raises the often confused difference between correlation and causation. When two things occur together (for example, B consistently and reliably accompanies A) it does not mean that one causes the other; in many instances a third variable, C, might be causing both A and B; that is, both A and B may result from C. For example, let's say that fear of communication and low self-disclosure are observed together in a large number of people; those who have great fear of communication also reveal little of themselves and, conversely, those who have little fear of communication reveal a great deal about themselves. Can you conclude that the level of communication fear determines the amount of self-disclosure? The answer is no; a third factor, say self-esteem, may actually cause both the fear of communication and the level of self-disclosure.

Statement 2 is false. Research results, at least in the humanities and social sciences such as communication, are true in a statistical sense; that is, they apply to, say, 95 percent of the population. You may be in the 5 percent to which the results do not apply. Further, you may be different in crucial respects from the participants sampled in the research study, so the results may not apply to you because of these differences between yourself and the sample surveyed. The vast cultural differences that we are just beginning to understand, for example, make it extremely unlikely that research findings obtained from say "students at a large Midwestern University" will apply to the farm workers in Guatemala.

Statement 3 is also false. Although our research methods today are a lot better than they were 20 years ago, the time during which a research study was conducted is not sufficient reason to consider one worthless and one worthwhile. There were a lot of worthwhile research studies done 20 years ago and a lot of worthless studies done yesterday. It depends on the study and on the changes that may have taken place over the 20 years. For example, a study conducted on power in the heterosexual relationship 20 years ago would have to be examined in light of the tremendous changes that have taken place in our attitudes toward men and women and in sexual equality generally. Other things being equal (though of course other things are never really equal), the more recent study will prove the more useful. To complicate matters even more, you need to consider the particular area of research. For example, certain findings reported from experiments in chemistry will probably remain true for many years; the interactions of carbon and hydrogen, for example, are not likely to change. On the other hand, certain findings on the frequency and causes of divorce, the role of technology in interpersonal relationships, or the reasons relationships are maintained will vary considerably over time.

Statement 4 involves a confusion between validity and reliability—two concepts that are crucial for understanding research findings—and is also false. Reliability refers to the consistency of results. It is a measure of how consistently a particular relationship or result is found in research. Validity, on the other hand, is a measure of the extent to which an instrument or test measures what it claims to measure. For example, intelligence tests are extremely reliable and you will obtain essentially the same results on repeated testing. The validity issue, however, is different and asks "Does the intelligence test really measure intelligence?" Thus, for example, we can measure your degree of romanticism with a simple pencil and paper test and get essentially the same results on repeated testing. But, it is quite another issue to claim that the test really measures what we would consider "romanticism". Consistency of findings does not mean that the test is valid; only that it is reliable. Actually, both are important. We want tests and research instruments generally to be both reliable and valid.

Statement 5 is also false although not everyone would agree with this. The assumption made in this text is that all research methods are useful for different purposes. Historical research is useful for certain questions, survey research is useful for other questions, and experimental research is useful for still other purposes.

percent of the time; but they will offer useful generalizations that are likely to be correct more often than not.

Interpersonal communication theories also help generate research. For example, if a theory predicts that verbal aggressiveness will lead to physical violence this suggests to the researcher a variety of important questions that can be subjected to study (Infante, Rancer, and Womack 1993). For example, the research might ask, "What types of verbal aggressiveness lead to physical violence?" "Are men or women more likely to become physically violent after being verbally aggressive?" "Can we reduce the likelihood of physical violence by teaching people to become less verbally aggressive?" In serving this research-generating function, theories add to our knowledge of interpersonal communication.

Theories do not, however, reveal truth in any absolute sense (Littlejohn 1996).Rather, theories reveal some degree of accuracy, some degree of truth. In the natural sciences such as physics and chemistry, theories have extremely high accuracy. If you mix two parts of hydrogen to one part of oxygen, you will get water—every time you do it. In the social and behavioral sciences (communication, sociology, psychology), the theories are far less accurate in describing the way things work and in predicting how things will work. One communication theorist offers this summary guidance: "Because a theory does not reveal truth, does not mean that it fails to communicate a kind of truth. An insight or useful way of classifying or explaining events is a kind of truth. Just don't make the mistake of believing too hard in one theory because every theory has its limits" (Littlejohn 1996, p. 361).

How would you state a theory that explains what makes for a successful friendship? A theory that explains effective teaching? A theory that explains the relationship between satisfaction and performance in an organization?

Research in Interpersonal Communication

Usually on the basis of some theory and its predictions—though sometimes from a simple desire to answer a question—research is conducted (Clark 1991). It is conducted so that we can learn more about how interpersonal communication works. These learnings and research findings are reported throughout this text. These findings are also used to develop the principles of more effective interpersonal interaction. Research, for example, often tells us what interpersonal strategies work and what strategies don't work. Understanding the research process will help you to better appreciate how we learn about communication as well as better understand the findings, conclusions, and principles that are developed on the basis of research.

Sometimes the questions are totally theoretical: How do listeners deal with ambiguous messages? Sometimes they are extremely practical, even urgent— How can children best resist drugs? Often, of course, practical implications are drawn out of "purely theoretical" research and theoretical insights are drawn out of "purely applied" research.

It is the research, then, that enables you to answer questions about people's interpersonal communication behavior and helps advance truth about an important aspect of human experience. Let us say that you find that total honesty in your romantic relationship is effective and that it creates a strong bond between the two of you. How useful is that "finding" to other couples? On the one hand, it may be very useful because all couples might respond as you and your partner do.

Or, it may be of limited usefulness if your relationship is unique and unlike all other relationships. Research tries to answer these types of questions. With the proper statistical tests, research can tell you how likely it is that total openness will prove effective in other relationships as well.

Now that the nature of theory and research in interpersonal communication is clear we can explore some of the basic axioms or principles that are common to all or most interpersonal encounters. These axioms are largely the work of the transactional researchers Paul Watzlawick, Janet Helmick Beavin, and Don D. Jackson, presented in their landmark *Pragmatics of Human Communication* (1967; Watzlawick 1977, 1978). Together with the concepts already presented (Unit 1), these axioms complete the characterization of what interpersonal communication is and how it works.

These axioms, although significant in terms of explaining theory, also have very practical applications. They provide insight into such day-to-day issues as the following:

How is research a part of your academic life? Your professional life? What types of research would you be especially likely to conduct over the next few years?

◆ Why do disagreements so often center on trivial matters and yet seem so difficult to resolve?

◆ Why are you never able to mind read—to know exactly what another person is thinking?

◆ How does communication express power relationships?

◆ Why do you and your partner often see the causes of arguments very differently?

Interpersonal Communication Is a Transactional Process

A transactional perspective views interpersonal communication as (1) a process (2) whose elements are *inter*dependent. Figure 2.1 explains visually this transactional view and distinguishes it from two earlier views of how interpersonal communication works.

Interpersonal Communication Is a Process

Interpersonal communication is best viewed as an ever-changing and circular process. Everything involved in interpersonal communication is in a state of flux: you are changing, the people you communicate with are changing, and your environment is changing. Sometimes these changes go unnoticed, and sometimes they intrude in obvious ways. But they are always occurring.

The process of communication is circular: each person serves simultaneously as a speaker *and* a listener, an actor *and* a reactor. Interpersonal communication is a mutually interactive process.

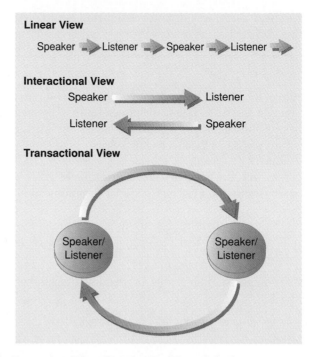

Figure 2.1   The Transactional View of Interpersonal Communication
The top figure represents a linear view of communication, in which the speaker speaks and the listener listens. The middle figure represents an interactional view, in which speaker and listener take turns speaking and listening; A speaks while B listens and then B speaks while A listens. The bottom figure represents a transactional view, in which each person serves simultaneously as speaker and listener; at the same time that you send messages, you are also receiving messages from your own communications and also from the reactions of the other person(s).

Elements Are Interdependent

What implications are there to the principle of transactionalism for your everyday communications with your friends and family?

The elements in interpersonal communication are *inter*dependent. Each element—each part of interpersonal communication—is intimately connected to the other parts and to the whole. For example, there can be no source without a receiver; there can be no message without a source; there can be no feedback without a receiver. Because of interdependency, a change in any one element causes changes in the others. For example, you are talking with a group of fellow students about a recent examination, and your teacher joins the group. This change in participants will lead to other changes—perhaps in the content of what you say, perhaps in the manner in which you express it. But regardless of what change is introduced, other changes result.

Interpersonal Communication Is Inevitable, Irreversible, and Unrepeatable

Interpersonal communication cannot be prevented (it is inevitable), cannot be reversed (is irreversible), and cannot be repeated (is unrepeatable). Let's look briefly at each of these qualities and their implications.

Inevitability

Often communication is thought of as intentional, purposeful, and consciously motivated. In many instances it is. But in other instances you are communicating even though you might not think you are or might not even want to communicate. Consider, for example, the new editorial assistant sitting at the desk with an "expressionless" face, perhaps staring out the window. Although this assistant might say that she or he is not communicating with the manager, the manager may derive any of a variety of messages from this behavior—for example, the assistant lacks interest, is bored, or is worried about something. In any event, the manager is receiving messages even though the assistant might not intend to communicate. In an interactional situation, all behavior is potentially communication. Any aspect of your behavior may communicate if the other person gives it message value. On the other hand, if the behavior (for example, the assistant's looking out the window) goes unnoticed, then no communication would have taken place (Watzlawick, Beavin, and Jackson 1967; Motley 1990a, 1990b; Bavelas 1990; Beach 1990).

What implications does the principle that communication is inevitable have for you today?

The axiom of inevitability has generated lots of controversy (Motley 1990a, 1990b; Bavelas 1990; Beach, 1990). Some assumed that this axiom meant that all behavior communicates; therefore, you cannot not communicate since you cannot behave. But, the original intention of this axiom was that all behavior in an interactional situation communicates; therefore, if you are interacting with another person, all your behavior communicates something. A more reasoned view is that, in general, communication in an interactional situation is inevitable, because you are always behaving; but the behavior must be perceived in some way by the other person for this behavior to be considered communication. What arguments could you advance to support or refute any of these notions?

Further, when in an interactional situation, your responses all have potential message value. For example, if you notice someone winking at you, you must respond in some way. Even if you do not respond openly, that lack of response is itself a response and it communicates (assuming it is perceived by the other person).

Irreversibility

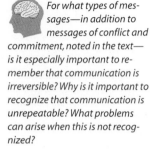

For what types of messages—in addition to messages of conflict and commitment, noted in the text—is it especially important to remember that communication is irreversible? Why is it important to recognize that communication is unrepeatable? What problems can arise when this is not recognized?

The processes of some systems can be reversed. For example, you can turn water into ice and then reverse the process by melting the ice. Moreover, you can repeat this reversal of ice and water for as long as you wish. Other systems, however, are irreversible. In these systems, the process can move in only one direction; it cannot go back again. For example, you can turn grapes into wine, but you cannot reverse the process and turn the wine back into grapes.

Interpersonal communication is irreversible. What you have communicated remains communicated; you cannot *uncommunicate*. Although you may try to qualify, negate, or somehow reduce the effects of your message, once it has been sent and received the message itself cannot be reversed.

In interpersonal interactions (especially in conflict), you need to be especially careful that you do not say things you may wish to withdraw later. Similarly, commitment messages, such as "I love you," must be monitored lest you commit yourself to a position you may be uncomfortable with later.

Unrepeatability

How does the principle of unrepeatability operate in the classroom? In your home? On your job?

In addition to being inevitable and irreversible, interpersonal communication is also unrepeatable. The reason is simple: everyone and everything are constantly changing. As a result, you can never recapture the exact situation, frame of mind, or relationship dynamics that defined a previous interpersonal act. For example, you can never repeat the experience of meeting a particular person for the first time, comforting a grieving friend on the death of his or her mother, or resolving a specific conflict.

You can, of course, try again, as when you say, "I'm sorry I came off so forward; can we try again?" But notice that even when you say this, you do not erase the initial impression. Instead, you try to counteract the initial (and perhaps negative) impression by going through the motions once more. In doing so, you try to create a more positive impression, which you hope will lessen the original negative effect.

Interpersonal Communication Is a Process of Adjustment

Interpersonal communication can take place only to the extent that the parties communicating share the same system of symbols. This is obvious when dealing with speakers of two different languages. Your communication with another person will be hindered to the extent that your language systems differ. This princi-

MEDIA & TECHNOLOGY

INTERPERSONAL COMMUNICATION: FACE-TO-FACE VS. COMPUTER

Interpersonal communication does not have to take place face-to-face; much is currently taking place via computer—through e-mail, chat lines, and Usenet newsgroups. Consider some of the differences.

In face-to-face communication you communicate both verbally and non-verbally; your words are supplemented by facial expressions, body movements, and variations in vocal volume and rate, for example. When you communicate through a keyboard your message is communicated primarily with words. This does not mean, however, that you cannot communicate emotional meanings with a keyboard; in fact, some researchers have argued that using diagrams, pictures, and varied type faces enable you to communicate messages that are rich in emotional meaning (Lea and Spears 1995). Similarly, you can use emoticons (see the Media and Technology box in Unit 9). But, basically, your message is communicated with words. Because of this, sarcasm, for example, is difficult (but not impossible) to convey unambiguously with just words whereas in face-to-face communication you might wink or smile to indicate that you are not being serious and should not be taken literally.

Another obvious difference is that in face-to-face communication the individuals are usually clearly identified. In computer mediated communication, however, you may remain anonymous. You may also pose as someone you are not—a person of another sex or race, or someone who is significantly older or younger that you really are, or as someone of significantly different status (Saunders, Robey, and Vaverek 1994). In face-to-face communication your physical self—the way you look, the way you are dressed—greatly influences the way in which your messages will be interpreted. In computer mediated communication your physical self is communicated through your own descriptions. Although you may send photos of yourself via computer, you can also send photos of others and claim they are of yourself. There is, in short, much greater opportunity for presenting yourself as you want to present yourself when communicating via computer.

When you communicate face-to-face you are both in essentially the same physical environment. In computer mediated communication you may both be in drastically different environments; one of you may be on a beach in Greece while another is in an office in Manhattan.

In face-to-face communication you can monitor the reactions, the feedback, of the other person as you are speaking. In computer mediated communication that feedback will come much later and is likely to be more clearly thought out and perhaps more closely monitored.

Face-to-face communication is evanescent; it fades after you have spoken. There is no trace of your communications outside of the memories of the parties involved or of those who overheard your conversation. In computer mediated communication the messages are written and may be saved, stored, and printed. This difference is especially important with messages of commitment or conflict.

Do the differences between face-to-face and computer mediated communication influence what you say and how you receive what others say?

p. 79

Learning Aid Note

Throughout this text you'll come across Media and Technology boxes. These are designed to highlight some of the connections between the media and the new technologies, on the one hand, and face-to-face interpersonal communication, on the other. This first box introduces some differences between the two forms; subsequent boxes focus more on specific issues of importance in understanding interpersonal communication and relationships. Each box ends with a note identifying where the next box appears so that you can read these in sequence if you wish. The last box (in Unit 22) asks that you write your own media and technology box; so keep this in mind as you read the text and these boxes.

ple takes on particular relevance when you realize that no two persons share identical symbol systems. Parents and children, for example, not only have very different vocabularies but also, even more important, have different meanings for some of the terms they have in common. Different cultures and social groups, even when they share a common language, often have greatly differing nonverbal communication systems. To the extent that these systems differ, communication will not take place.

Part of the art of interpersonal communication is learning the other person's signals, how they are used, and what they mean. People in close relationships—either as intimate friends or as romantic partners—realize that learning the other person's signals takes a long time and, often, great patience. If you want to understand what another person means—by a smile, by saying "I love you," by arguing about trivial matters, by self-deprecating comments—you have to learn their system of signals. Furthermore, you have to share your own system of signals with others so that they can better understand you. Although some people may know what you mean by your silence or by your avoidance of eye contact, others may not. You cannot expect others to decode your behaviors accurately without help.

What practical insights does the principle of adjustment offer? Put differently, what problems would arise in communication if the influence of adjustment was not recognized?

This principle is especially important in intercultural communication, largely because people from different cultures use different signals and sometimes the same signals to signify quite different things. Focused eye contact means honesty and openness in much of the United States. But, that same behavior may signify arrogance or disrespect in Japan and many Hispanic cultures if engaged in by a youngster with someone significantly older.

Communication Accommodation

An interesting theory largely revolving around adjustment is communication accommodation theory. This theory holds that speakers will adjust to or accommodate to the speaking style of their listeners to gain, for example, social approval and greater communication efficiency (Giles, Mulac, Bradac, and Johnson 1987). For example, when two people have a similar speech rate, they seem to be more attracted to each other than to those with dissimilar rates (Buller, LePoire, Aune, and Eloy 1992). Speech rate similarity has also been associated with greater immediacy, sociability, and intimacy (Buller and Aune 1992). Also, the speaker who uses language intensity similar to that of listeners, is judged to have greater credibility that the speaker who used intensity different from that of listeners (Aune and Kikuchi 1993). Still another study found that roommates who were has similar communication attitudes (both were high in communication competence and willingness to communicate and low in verbal aggressiveness) were highest in roommate liking and satisfaction (Martin and Anderson 1995).

Do you accommodate to the interpersonal style of a person you want to impress? Do you notice others accommodating to your style?

As illustrated throughout this text, communication characteristics are influenced greatly by culture (Albert and Nelson 1993). Thus, the communication similarities that lead to attraction and more positive perceptions are likely to be present in *intra*cultural communication but absent in many *inter*cultural encounters. This may present an important (but not insurmountable) obstacle to intercultural communication.

Interpersonal Communication Is a Series of Punctuated Events

Communication events are continuous transactions. There is no clear-cut beginning and no clear-cut end. As participants in or observers of the communication act, you segment this continuous stream of communication into smaller pieces. You label some of these pieces causes or stimuli and others effects or responses.

Consider an example: A married couple is at a party. The husband is flirting with another woman, and the wife is drinking. Both are scowling at each other and are obviously in a deep nonverbal argument. In later recalling the situation, the husband might observe that the wife drank, so he flirted with the sober woman. The more she drank, the more he flirted. The only reason for his behavior (he says) was his anger over her drinking. Notice that he sees his behavior as a response to her behavior. In recalling the same incident, the wife might say that she drank when he started flirting. The more he flirted, the more she drank. She had no intention of drinking until he started flirting. To her, his behavior was the stimulus and hers was the response; he caused her behavior. Thus, the husband sees the sequence as going from drinking to flirting, and the wife sees it as going from flirting to drinking. This example is depicted visually in Figure 2.2.

This tendency to divide communication transactions into sequences of stimuli and responses is referred to as **punctuation** (Watzlawick, Beavin, and Jackson 1967). Everyone punctuates the continuous sequences of events into stimuli and responses for convenience. Moreover, as the example of the husband and wife illustrates, punctuation usually is done in ways that benefit the person and are consistent with his or her self-image.

Understanding how another person interprets a situation, how he or she punctuates, is a crucial step in interpersonal understanding. It is also essential in achieving empathy (feeling what the other person is feeling). In all communication encounters, but especially in conflicts, try to see how others punctuate the situation.

How do you punctuate the events leading up to your successes and your failures? Has punctuation ever been used against you? Have you ever used punctuation against someone else? What effects did this have?

Relationships May Be Viewed as Symmetrical or Complementary

Interpersonal relationships can be described as either symmetrical or complementary (Bateson 1972; Watzlawick, Beavin, and Jackson 1967). In a **symmetrical** relationship, the two individuals mirror each other's behavior (Bateson 1972). If one member nags, the other member responds in kind. If one member is passionate, the other member is passionate. If one member expresses jealousy, the other member also expresses jealousy. If one member is passive, so is the other. The relationship is one of equality, with the emphasis on minimizing the differences between the two individuals.

Note, however, the problems that can arise in this type of relationship. Consider the situation of a couple in which both members are very aggressive. The aggressiveness of one person fosters aggressiveness in the other, which fosters increased aggressiveness in the first individual. As this cycle escalates, the aggressiveness can no longer be contained, and the relationship is consumed by the aggression.

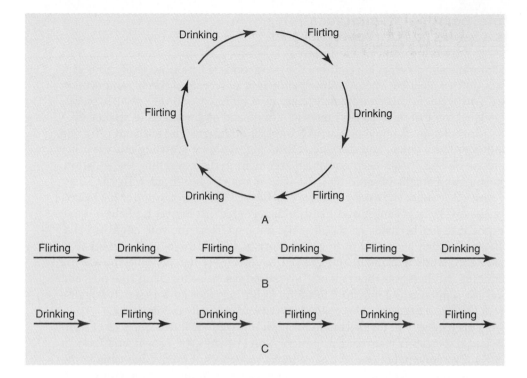

Figure 2.2   Punctuation and the Sequence of Events.
Figure 2.2 (A) shows the actual sequence of events as a continuous series of actions with no specific beginning or end. Each action (drinking and flirting) stimulates another action, but no initial cause is identified. Figure 2.2 (B) shows the same sequence of events as seen by the wife. She sees the sequence as beginning with the husband's flirting and her drinking behavior as a response to that stimulus. Figure 2.2 (C) shows the same sequence of events from the husband's point of view. He sees the sequence as beginning with the wife's drinking and his flirting as a response to that stimulus. Try using this three-part figure, discussed in the text, to explain what might go on when a supervisor complains that workers are poorly trained for their jobs and when workers complain that supervisors don't know how to supervise.

In a **complementary** relationship, the two individuals engage in different behaviors. The behavior of one serves as the stimulus for the other's complementary behavior. In complementary relationships, the differences between the parties are maximized. The people occupy different positions, one superior and the other inferior, one passive and the other active, one strong and the other weak. At times, cultures establish such relationships—for example, the complementary relationship between teacher and student or between employer and employee.

Early marriages are likely to be complementary relationships where each person tries to complete himself or herself. When these couples separate and form new relationships, these new ones are more likely to be symmetrical and involve a kind of reconfirmation of their own identity (Prosky 1992). Generally, research finds that complementary couples have a lower marital adjustment level than do symmetrical couples (Main and Oliver 1988; Holden 1991).

An interesting perspective on complementary and symmetrical relationships can be gained by looking at the ways in which these patterns combine to exert control in a relationship (Rogers-Millar and Millar 1979; Millar and Rogers 1987; Rogers and Farace 1975). Nine patterns are identified; three deal with symmetry (similar-type messages), two deal with complementarity (opposite-type messages), and four are transitional (neither similar- nor opposite-type messages).

In **competitive symmetry**, each person tries to exert control over the other (symbolized by an upward arrow ↑). Each communicates one-up messages (messages that attempt to control the behaviors of the other person):

PAT: Do it now.↑
CHRIS: I'll do it when I'm good and ready; otherwise, do it yourself.↑

In **submissive symmetry**, each person communicates submission (symbolized by a downward arrow ↓); the messages are one-down (messages that indicate submission to what the other person wants):

PAT: What do you want for dinner?↓
CHRIS: Whatever you'd like is fine with me.↓

In **neutralized symmetry**, each person communicates similarly. However (as symbolized by a horizontal arrow →), neither person communicates competitively (one-up) or submissively (one-down):

PAT: Jackie needs new shoes.→
CHRIS: And a new jacket.→

In **complementarity**, one person communicates the desire to control (one-up), and the other person communicates submission (one-down):

PAT: Here, honey, do it this way.↑
CHRIS: Oh, that's great; you're so clever.↓

In another type of **complementarity**—the reverse of the pattern above—the submissive message (one-down) comes first and is followed by a controlling (one-up) message:

PAT: I need suggestions for teaching this new course.↓
CHRIS: Oh, that's easy; I've taught that course for years.↑

Transition Patterns do not involve stating the opposite of the previous message; communicators do not respond to a competitive message with submission or to a submissive message with competition. There are four possible transition patterns:

1. A competitive message (one-up) is responded to without either another competitive message or a submissive message:

PAT: I want to go to the movies.↑
CHRIS: There certainly are a lot of choices this weekend.→

2. A submissive message (one-down) is responded to without either another submissive message or a competitive message:

PAT: I'm just helpless with tools.↓
CHRIS: Lots of people have difficulty using a router.→

3. A transition message (one-across) is responded to with a competitive (one-up) message:

PAT: We can do the job many different ways.→
CHRIS: Well, here's the right way.↑

4. A transition message (one-across) is responded to with a submissive (one-down) message:

PAT: We can do the job many different ways.→
CHRIS: Whatever way you do it is fine.↓

These nine patterns were presented to illustrate one way of looking at the concepts of complementarity and symmetry. It's a particularly interesting one, however, and you can apply it to gain considerable insight into your own friendship, love, and family relationships and communication.

Interpersonal Communications Have Content and Relationship Dimensions

Communications usually refer to the real world, to something external to both speaker and listener. At the same time, they refer to the relationship between the parties. For example, a judge may say to a lawyer, "See me in my chambers immediately." This simple message has both a content aspect, which refers to the behavioral response expected (namely, that the lawyer will see the judge immediately), and a relationship aspect, which says something about the relationship between the judge and the lawyer and, as a result of this relationship, how the communication is to be dealt with. Even the use of the simple command shows that there is a status difference between the two parties. This difference can perhaps be seen most clearly if you imagine the command being made by the lawyer to the judge. Such a communication appears awkward and out of place because it violates the normal relationship between judge and lawyer.

In any two communications, the content dimension may be the same, but the relationship aspect may be different, or the relationship aspect may be the same and the content dimension different. For example, the judge could say to the lawyer, "You had better see me immediately" or "May I please see you as soon as possible?" In both cases, the content is essentially the same; that is, the message about the expected behavioral response is the same. But the relationship dimension is quite different. The first message signifies a definite superior-inferior relationship; the second signals a more equal relationship, one that shows respect for the lawyer.

Think about your own relationships in terms of these concepts and this perspective.
For a starter, consider:
- Can you identify a relationship you have that makes use of one major pattern? What part do you play? Are you comfortable with this pattern?
- Can you identify a general pattern that you use in many or most of your relationships? How satisfied are you with this customary pattern of expression?
- Can you identify relationships you have that began with one pattern of communication and shifted over the years to another pattern? What happened?
- Do these patterns have anything to do with the degree of relationship satisfaction you experience? For example, do you derive greater satisfaction from a relationship that relies on one pattern than you do from a relationship that relies on another pattern?

Can you give a personal example of a communication difficulty you experienced because of the failure to distinguish between content and relationship messages?

Similarly, at times the content may be different but the relationship is essentially the same. For example, a daughter might say to her parents, "May I go away this weekend?" or "May I use the car tonight?" The content of the two questions is clearly very different, but the relationship dimension is essentially the same. It clearly reflects a superior-inferior relationship in which permission to do certain things must be secured.

In a typical conversation, say with an acquaintance at school or work, do you focus more on the content or more on the relationship? Does this focus usually work for you? That is, does it contribute to your conversational effectiveness?

Implications of Content and Relationship Dimensions

The major implications of these content and relationship dimensions center on conflict and its effective resolution. Many problems between people result from failure to recognize the distinction between the content and the relationship dimensions of communication. For example, consider the couple arguing over the fact that Pat made plans to study with friends during the weekend without first asking Chris if that would be all right. Probably both would agree that to study over the weekend is the right decision. Thus, the argument is not primarily concerned with the content level. It centers on the relationship level; Chris expected to be consulted about plans for the weekend. Pat, in not doing so, rejected this definition of their relationship. Similar situations occur when one member of a couple buys something, makes dinner plans, or invites a guest to dinner without first asking the other person. Even though the other person might have agreed with the decision, the couple argue because of the message communicated on the relationship level.

Let me give you a personal example. My mother came to stay for a week at a summer place I had. On the first day, she swept the kitchen floor six times, although I repeatedly said that it did not need sweeping, that I would be tracking in dirt and mud from outside, and that all her effort was just wasted. But she persisted, saying that the floor was dirty and should be swept. On the content level, we were talking about the value of sweeping the kitchen floor, but on the relationship level we were talking about something quite different: we were each saying, "This is my house." When I realized this (although, I confess, only after considerable argument), I stopped complaining about sweeping a floor that did not need sweeping. Not surprisingly, she stopped sweeping.

Consider the following interchange:

DIALOGUE	COMMENTS
HE: I'm going bowling tomorrow. The guys at the plant are starting a team.	*He focuses on the content and ignores any relationship implications of the message.*
SHE: Why can't we ever do anything together?	*She responds primarily on a relationship level, ignores the content implications of the message, and expresses her displeasure at being ignored in his decision.*
HE: We can do something together anytime; tomorrow's the day they're organizing the team.	*Again, he focuses almost exclusively on the content.*

This example reflects research findings that men generally focus more on the content while women focus more on the relationship dimensions of communication (cf. Pearson, West, and Turner 1993; Wood 1994). Once you recognize this difference, you may be better able to remove a potential barrier to communication between the sexes by being sensitive to the orientation of the opposite sex. Here is essentially the same situation but with the added sensitivity:

DIALOGUE	COMMENTS
HE: The guys at the plant are organizing a bowling team. I'd sure like to be on the team. Would it be a problem if I went to the organizational meeting tomorrow?	*Although focused on content, he is aware of the relationship dimensions of his message and includes both in his comments—by acknowledging their partnership, asking if there would be a problem, and expressing his desire rather than his decision.*
SHE: That sounds great, but I was hoping we could do something together.	*She focuses on the relationship dimension but also acknowledges his content orientation. Note, too, that she does not respond as though she has to defend her emphasis on relationship aspects.*
HE: How about your meeting me at Pizza Hut, and we can have dinner after the organizational meeting?	*He responds to the relationship aspect—without abandoning his desire to join the bowling team—and incorporates it into his communications.*
SHE: That sounds great. I'm dying for pizza.	*She responds to both messages, approving of his joining the team and their dinner date.*

Arguments over the content dimension are relatively easy to resolve. Generally, you can look up something in a book or ask someone what actually took place. It is relatively easy to verify disputed facts. Arguments on the relationship level, however, are much more difficult to resolve, in part because you may not recognize that the argument is in fact a relational one. Once you realize that, you can approach the dispute appropriately and deal with it directly.

Have you had an argument that focused on relationship rather than content issues? How did the argument develop? At what point did you recognize that it was a relationship (rather than a content) argument? How was it resolved?

In introducing these axioms, it was noted that they would provide insight into a number of practical issues. How would you use the axioms to describe what is happening in each of the following situations? These scenarios are, of course, extremely brief and are written only as aids to stimulate you to think more concretely about the axioms. Note too that the objective is not to select the one correct axiom (each scenario can probably be described by reference to several axioms) but to make use of an opportunity to think about the axioms in reference to specific situations.

Which of the axioms covered in this unit do you think is most useful for thinking about interpersonal communication?

1. A couple, together for 20 years, argues constantly about the seemingly most insignificant things—who takes the dog out, who does the shopping, who decides where to go to dinner, and so on. It has gotten to the point where they rarely have a day without argument and both are seriously considering a separation.

How would you go about finding answers to the following questions:

◆ *Are the students in your class who are in symmetrical relationships happier than those who are in complementary relationships?*

◆ *Will persons from high-context cultures adapt more easily to a low-context culture than persons from low-context cultures would adapt to a high-context culture?*

◆ *Will persons from cultures with the same context orientation (either high or low) develop stronger and more lasting relationships than will persons from cultures with different context orientations?*

◆ *Will knowledge of these axioms of interpersonal communication have any impact on the number of conflicts a couple has? On the speed with which the conflicts are resolved?*

2. Pat and Chris are a couple who hurt each other regularly. When one makes a negative comment, the other responds with an even more negative comment which is followed by a still more negative one, and so on. This frequently results in extremely serious conflicts. On the other hand, when things are good, they are very good.

3. In the heat of a big argument, Harry said he didn't want to see Peggy's family ever again. "They don't like me, and I don't like them," he said. Peggy reciprocated and said she felt the same way about his family. Now, weeks later, there remains a great deal of tension between them, especially when they find themselves with one or both families.

4. Grace and Mark are engaged to be married and are currently new executives at a large advertising agency. Recently, Grace made a presentation, which was not received positively by the other members of the team. Grace feels that Mark—in not defending her proposal—created a negative attitude and actually encouraged others to reject her ideas. Mark says that he felt he could not defend her proposal because others in the room would have believed his defense was motivated by their relationship and not by his positive evaluation of her proposal. He concluded it was best to say nothing.

5. Margo has just taken over as vice president in charge of sales for a manufacturing company. Margo is extremely organized and refuses to waste time on nonessentials. In her staff meetings, she is business only. Several top sales representatives have requested to be assigned to other VPs. Their reason: they feel she works them too hard and doesn't care about them as people.

Summary ▪ U N I T I N B R I E F

A RETURN TO OBJECTIVES:

In this unit we explained the role of theory and research in interpersonal communication and several axioms or principles, focusing on these basic questions: (1) What is a theory and what functions do theory and research play in interpersonal communication? (2) What is meant by a transactional view of interpersonal communication and how does this differ from a linear and an interactional view? (3) What is meant by interpersonal communication being inevitable, irreversible, and unrepeatable and what are the implications of these qualities? (4) How does adjustment (and communication accommodation) operate in interpersonal communication? (5) What role does punctuation play in interpersonal communication? (6) How do symmetrical and complementary relationships differ from each other? (7) How do content and relationship dimensions of communication differ and what are the implications of these differences?

Axioms	Implications
Theory and research in interpersonal communication: The generalizations about interpersonal communication and the evidence bearing on them.	Through theory and research we learn how interpersonal communication works and from this can derive principles for achieving more effective interpersonal interaction.
Transactional process: Interpersonal communication is a process, an ongoing event, in which the elements are interdependent.	Communication is constantly occurring; do not assume there are clear-cut beginnings or endings. All communication elements are always changing; do not expect sameness. Look, too, for mutual interaction among elements.
Inevitability, irreversibility, and unrepeatability: When in an interactional situation, you cannot *not* communicate; you cannot *un*communicate; and you cannot repeat exactly a specific message.	Seek to control as many aspects of your behavior as possible. In listening seek out nonobvious messages. Beware of messages you may later wish to take back, for example, conflict and commitment messages.
Adjustment: Communication depends on participants sharing the same system of signals and meaning; generally, people move in the direction of imitating or echoing the interpersonal behavior of the other.	Expand common areas, and learn each other's system of signals to increase interpersonal effectiveness; share your own system of signals with significant others.
Punctuation: Everyone separates communication sequences into stimuli and responses on the basis of his or her own perspective.	View punctuation as arbitrary, and adopt the other's point of view to increase empathy and understanding.
Symmetrical and complementary relationships: Interpersonal interactions may stimulate similar or different behavior patterns, and relationships may be described as basically symmetrical or complementary.	Develop an awareness of symmetrical and complementary relationships. Avoid clinging rigidly to behavioral patterns that are no longer useful and mirroring another's destructive behaviors.
Content and relationship dimensions: All communications refer both to content and to the relationships between the participants.	Seek out and respond to relationship messages as well as content messages.

UNIT 3

Culture in Interpersonal Communication

Unit Topics	Unit Objectives
	After completing this unit, you should be able to:
The Nature of Culture	1. Explain *culture, enculturation,* and *acculturation* and their relationship to interpersonal communication
How Cultures Differ Individual and Collective Orientation High- and Low-Context Cultures Power Distances	2. Distinguish between collectivist and individualistic orientation, low- and high-context cultures, and high and low power distances
Theories of Culture and Communication Language Relativity Uncertainty Avoidance Maximizing Outcomes Culture Shock	3. Explain the theories of culture and communication discussed in this unit
Intercultural Communication The Nature of Intercultural Communication Principles of Intercultural Communication	4. Define intercultural communication and explain the general principles for increasing effectiveness in intercultural communication

EXPERIENTIAL LEARNING VEHICLES

Vehicle No. 2, "Matching Pairs," p. 441, provides an interesting view of intercultural communication and especially of the barriers to it. Vehicle No. 19, "Male and Female," p. 463, offers an opportunity to discuss sexual stereotypes and misconceptions. Vehicles No. 17, "Interpersonal Relationships in Songs and Greeting Cards," p. 460–461, No. 18, "Mate Preferences," p. 461–463, and No. 21, "Power Plays," p. 464, illustrate cultural differences and similarities.

Culture (introduced briefly in Unit 1) is a part of every interpersonal communication act. As such it needs to be examined in depth. In this unit we focus on the nature of culture, the ways in which cultures differ, some theories explaining the connection between culture and communication, and intercultural communication—communication between members of different cultures.

The Nature of Culture

Culture refers to the relatively specialized lifestyle of a group of people—consisting of their values, beliefs, artifacts, ways of behaving, and ways of communicating. Included in "culture" would be all that members of a social group have produced and developed—their language, modes of thinking, art, laws, and religion.

Culture is passed on from one generation to the next through communication, not through genes. Thus, culture does not refer to color of skin or shape of eyes since these are passed on through genes, not communication. Culture does refer to beliefs in a supreme being, to attitudes toward success and happiness, and to the values placed on friendship, love, family, or money since these are transmitted through communication.

Culture is not synonymous with race or nationality. However, members of a particular race or country are often taught similar beliefs, attitudes, and values. And this similarity makes it possible to speak of "Hispanic culture" or "African American culture." But, lest we be guilty of stereotyping, recognize that within any large culture—especially a culture based on race or nationality—there will be enormous differences. The Kansas farmer and the Wall Street executive may both be German American but they may differ widely in their attitudes and beliefs and in their general lifestyle. In some ways the Kansas farmer may be closer in attitudes and values to the Chinese farmer than to the suit.

Culture is transmitted from one generation to another through **enculturation,** a process by which you learn the culture into which you are born (your native culture). Parents, peer groups, schools, religious institutions, and government agencies are the main teachers of culture. One new instrument for spreading culture is the Internet. Because the Internet, although worldwide, is so dominated by the United States and by the English language and idiom, the culture of the Internet is dominated by the culture of the United States. "Some countries," notes one media watcher, "already unhappy with the encroachment of American culture—from jeans to Mickey Mouse to movies and TV programs—are worried that their cultures will be further eroded by an American dominance in cyberspace" (Pollack 1995, D1).

A different process of learning culture is **acculturation,** the process by which you learn the rules and norms of a culture different from your native culture. Through acculturation, your original or native culture is modified through direct contact with (or exposure to) a new and different culture. For example, when immigrants settle in the United States (the host culture), their own culture becomes influenced by the host culture. Gradually, the values, ways of behaving, and beliefs of the host culture become more and more a part of the immigrants' culture. At the same time, of course, the host culture changes too as it interacts with the immigrants' culture. Generally, however, the culture of the immigrant changes more. The reasons for this are that the host country's members far outnumber the

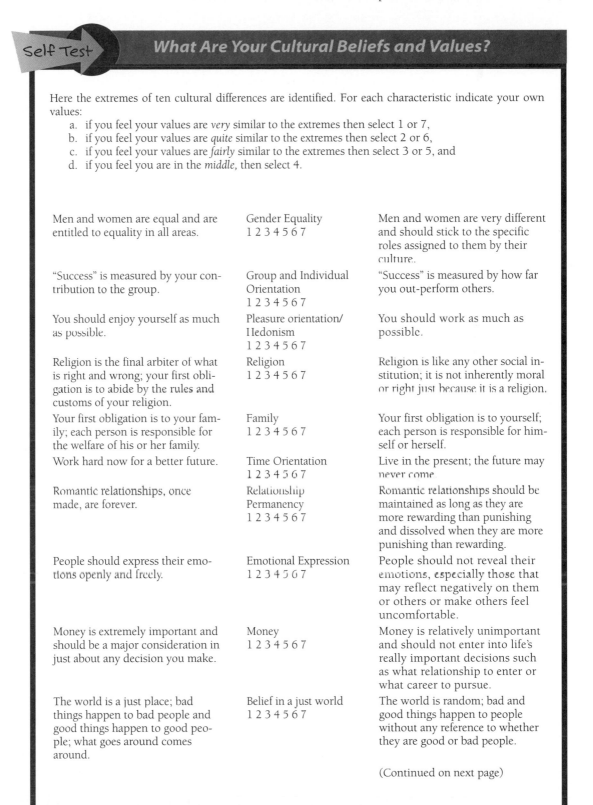

Self Test

What Are Your Cultural Beliefs and Values?

Here the extremes of ten cultural differences are identified. For each characteristic indicate your own values:

    a. if you feel your values are *very* similar to the extremes then select 1 or 7,
    b. if you feel your values are *quite* similar to the extremes then select 2 or 6,
    c. if you feel your values are *fairly* similar to the extremes then select 3 or 5, and
    d. if you feel you are in the *middle,* then select 4.

Men and women are equal and are entitled to equality in all areas.	Gender Equality 1 2 3 4 5 6 7	Men and women are very different and should stick to the specific roles assigned to them by their culture.
"Success" is measured by your contribution to the group.	Group and Individual Orientation 1 2 3 4 5 6 7	"Success" is measured by how far you out-perform others.
You should enjoy yourself as much as possible.	Pleasure orientation/ Hedonism 1 2 3 4 5 6 7	You should work as much as possible.
Religion is the final arbiter of what is right and wrong; your first obligation is to abide by the rules and customs of your religion.	Religion 1 2 3 4 5 6 7	Religion is like any other social institution; it is not inherently moral or right just because it is a religion.
Your first obligation is to your family; each person is responsible for the welfare of his or her family.	Family 1 2 3 4 5 6 7	Your first obligation is to yourself; each person is responsible for himself or herself.
Work hard now for a better future.	Time Orientation 1 2 3 4 5 6 7	Live in the present; the future may never come.
Romantic relationships, once made, are forever.	Relationship Permanency 1 2 3 4 5 6 7	Romantic relationships should be maintained as long as they are more rewarding than punishing and dissolved when they are more punishing than rewarding.
People should express their emotions openly and freely.	Emotional Expression 1 2 3 4 5 6 7	People should not reveal their emotions, especially those that may reflect negatively on them or others or make others feel uncomfortable.
Money is extremely important and should be a major consideration in just about any decision you make.	Money 1 2 3 4 5 6 7	Money is relatively unimportant and should not enter into life's really important decisions such as what relationship to enter or what career to pursue.
The world is a just place; bad things happen to bad people and good things happen to good people; what goes around comes around.	Belief in a just world 1 2 3 4 5 6 7	The world is random; bad and good things happen to people without any reference to whether they are good or bad people.

(Continued on next page)

Thinking Critically About Cultural Beliefs, Values, and Communication

This test was designed to help you explore the possible influence of your cultural beliefs and values on communication. Research shows that your cultural values will influence your interpersonal communications (as demonstrated throughout this text) as well as your decision making, assessments of coworkers, teamwork, trust in others, the importance you place on cultural diversity in the workplace, and your attitudes toward the role of women in the workplace, for example (Stephens and Greer 1995; Bochner and Hesketh 1994). If you visualize communication as involving choices, as noted in Unit 1, then these beliefs will influence the choices you make, how you communicate, and how you listen and respond to the communications of others. For example, your beliefs and values about gender equality will influence the way in which you communicate with and about the opposite sex. Your group and individual orientation will influence how you perform in work teams and how you deal with your peers at school and at work. Your degree of hedonism will influence the kinds of interactions you engage in, the books you read, the television programs you watch. Your religious beliefs will influence the ethical system you follow in communicating. Review the entire list of ten characteristics and try to identify one *specific* way in which each characteristic influences your communication.

 Social Darwinism or cultural evolution holds that much as the human species evolved from lower life forms to Homo sapiens, cultures also evolve. Consequently, some cultures may be considered advanced and others primitive. Most contemporary scholars reject this view because the judgments that distinguish one culture from another have no basis in science and are instead based on individual values and preferences as to what constitutes "civilized" and what constitutes "primitive." Cultural relativism, on the other hand, holds that all cultures are different but that no culture is either superior or inferior to any other (Berry, Poortinga, Segall, and Dasen 1992). This view is today generally accepted and guides the infusion of cultural materials into contemporary textbooks on all academic levels. What do you think of these positions?

immigrant group and the media is largely dominated by and reflects the values and customs of the host culture.

The acceptance of the new culture depends on a number of factors (Kim 1988). Immigrants who come from cultures similar to the host culture will become acculturated more easily. Similarly, those who are younger and better educated become acculturated more quickly than do the older and less well-educated. Persons who are risk takers and open-minded have greater acculturation potential. Also, persons who are familiar with the host culture prior to immigration—whether through interpersonal contact or media exposure—will be acculturated more readily.

Before exploring further the role of culture in communication, consider your own cultural values and beliefs by taking the accompanying self-test. This test illustrates how your own cultural values and beliefs may influence your interpersonal communication in the messages you send and in the messages you receive.

How Cultures Differ

There are at least three major ways in which cultures differ that are especially important for communication. Following Hofstede (1983, 1997) Gudykunst (1991), and Hall and Hall (1987) we discuss collectivism and individualism, high and low context, and power distances.

Individual and Collective Orientation

Cultures differ in the extent to which they promote individual values (for example, power, achievement, hedonism, and stimulation) versus collectivist values (for example, benevolence, tradition, and conformity). As you can see from Table 3.1, people from the United States have a decided preference for individual values (Kapoor, Wolfe and Blue 1995).

One of the major differences between these two orientations is in the extent to which an individual's goals or the group's goals are given precedence. Individual and collective tendencies are, of course, not mutually exclusive; this is not an all-or-none orientation but rather one of emphasis. You probably have both tendencies. Thus, you may, for example, compete with other members of your basketball team for most baskets or most valuable player award (and thus emphasize individual goals). At the same time, however, you will—in a game— act in a way that will benefit the entire team (and thus emphasize group goals). In actual practice both individual and collective tendencies will help you and your team each achieve your goals. Yet, most people and most cultures have a dominant orientation; they are more individually oriented or more collectively oriented in most situations, most of the time.

In some instances, however, these tendencies may come into conflict. For example, do you shoot for the basket and try to raise your own individual score or do you pass the ball to another player who is better positioned to score and thus benefit the team as a whole? You make this distinction in popular talk when you call someone a team player (collectivist orientation) or an individual player (individualistic orientation).

In an individualistic-oriented culture members are responsible for themselves and perhaps their immediate family. In a collectivist culture members are responsible for the entire group.

Success, in an individualistic culture, is measured by the extent to which you surpass other members of your group; you would take pride in standing out from

Consider how cultural differences underlie answers to such questions as:

◆ *Should Christian Science parents be prosecuted for preventing their children from receiving life saving treatment such as blood transfusions? Some states, such as Connecticut and Arizona, grant Christian Scientists special rights in this regard. Should this special treatment be adopted by all states? Should it be eliminated?*

◆ *Should immigration be expanded or limited?*

◆ *Should same sex marriages be legalized?*

◆ *Should cock fighting be permitted or declared illegal in all states as "cruelty to animals?" (Some people argue that this is a part of their culture and should be permitted even though it is illegal in most of the United States. In five states and Puerto Rico, cock fighting is legal.)*

◆ *Should safe sex practices be taught in the schools? (Recall that President Clinton fired Joycelyn Elders from her position as the United States Surgeon General for suggesting that masturbation be discussed in the schools.)*

Do you think that couples with similar ratings (on the cultural differences scale) stay together longer than couples with dissimilar ratings? Do you think couples with similar ratings have fewer and less severe conflicts than couples with dissimilar ratings? How would you go about getting evidence to support (or refute) your prediction?

Table 3.1	**Individualistic and Collectivist Countries**

The countries are listed in order; thus the United States scored highest on individual orientation, Australia next highest, and so on. Similarly, Guatemala scored highest on collectivist values, Ecuador next highest, and so on. With a few notable exceptions, the individualistic countries are wealthy and the collectivist countries are poor. Japan and Hong Kong—scoring somewhere in the middle—are, of course, wealthier than many of the 10 highest scoring countries. Countries listed together (for example, the Netherlands and New Zealand) had the same score. These rankings come from the research of Hofstede (1983; 1997) and Hatfield and Rapson (1996).

Cultures Scoring Highest on Individualistic Orientation	**Cultures Scoring Highest on Collectivist Orientation**
1. United States	1. Guatemala
2. Australia	2. Ecuador
3. Great Britain	3. Panama
4. Canada, the Netherlands	4. Venezuela
5. New Zealand	5. Colombia
6. Italy	6. Indonesia, Pakistan
7. Belgium	7. Costa Rica
8. Denmark	8. Peru
9. Sweden, France	9. Taiwan
10. Ireland	10. South Korea

In this age of multiculturalism, how do you feel about Article II, Section 1 of the United States Constitution? The relevant section reads: "No person except a natural born citizen, or a citizen of the United States, at the time of the adoption of this Constitution, shall be eligible to the office of President."

the crowd. And your heroes—in the media, for example—are likely to be those who are unique and who stand apart. In a collectivist culture success is measured by your contribution to the achievements of the group as a whole; you would take pride in your similarity to other members of your group. Your heroes, in contrast, are more likely to be team players who do not stand out from the rest of the group's members. Not surprisingly, advertisements in individualistic cultures emphasize individual preferences and benefits, independence, and personal success; advertisements in collectivist cultures emphasize group benefits, family integrity, and group harmony (Han and Shavitt 1994).

In an individualistic culture you are responsible to your own conscience and responsibility is largely an individual matter; in a collectivist culture you are responsible to the rules of the social group and responsibility for an accomplishment or a failure is shared by all members. Competition is fostered in individualistic cultures while cooperation is promoted in collectivist cultures.

In an individualistic culture you might compete for leadership in a small group setting and there would likely be a very clear distinction between leaders and members. In a collectivist culture leadership would be shared and rotated; there is likely to be little distinction between leader and members. These orientations will also influence the kinds of communication members consider appropriate in an organizational context. For example, individualistic members will favor clarity and directness while collectivists will favor "face-saving" and the avoidance of hurting others or arousing negative evaluations (Kim and Sharkey 1995).

Distinctions between in-group members and out-group members are extremely important in collectivist cultures. In individualistic cultures, where the person's individuality is prized, the distinction is likely to be less important.

High- and Low-Context Cultures

Cultures also differ in the extent to which information is made explicit, on the one hand, or is assumed to be in the context or in the persons communicating, on the other. A high-context culture is one in which much of the information in communication is in the context or in the person—for example, information that was shared through previous communications, through assumptions about each other, and through shared experiences. The information is thus known by all participants but it is not explicitly stated in the verbal message. A low-context culture is one in which most of the information is explicitly stated in the verbal message. In formal transactions it would be stated in written (or contract) form.

 How would you learn whether men and women differ in their preference for explicit communications, despite their high- or low-context orientation?

To appreciate the distinction between high and low context, consider giving directions ("Where's the voter registration center?") to someone who knows the neighborhood and to a newcomer to your city. To someone who knows the neighborhood (a high-context situation) you can assume that she or he knows the local landmarks. So, you can give directions such as "next to the laundromat on Main Street" or "the corner of Albany and Elm." To the newcomer (a low-context situation), you could not assume that she or he shares any information with you. So, you would have to use only those directions that even a stranger would understand, for example, "make a left at the next stop sign" or "go two blocks and then turn right."

Is communication between these two women intercultural? Some people would argue that because these are two middle class women born and raised in the same United States city, they are from the same culture. Others would claim that because one is African American and one is European American, they were raised differently (with different beliefs, values, and experiences) and therefore can be said to be of different cultures. What do you think?

High-context cultures are also collectivist cultures (Gudykunst, Ting-Toomey, and Chua 1988; Gudykunst and Kim 1992). These cultures (Japanese, Arabic, Latin American, Thai, Korean, Apache, and Mexican are examples) place great emphasis on personal relationships and oral agreements (Victor 1992). Low-context cultures are also individualistic cultures. These cultures (German, Swedish, Norwegian, and American are examples) place less emphasis on personal relationships and more emphasis on the verbalized, explicit explanation and, for example, on the written contracts in business transactions.

The characteristics of both individual-collective and high and low context cultures discussed here are summarized in Table 3.2.

Members of high-context cultures spend lots of time getting to know each other interpersonally and socially before any important transactions take place. Because of this prior personal knowledge a great deal of information is shared by the members and therefore does not have to be explicitly stated. Members of low-context cultures spend a great deal less time getting to know each other and hence do not have that shared knowledge. As a result everything has to be stated explicitly.

This difference between high-and low-context orientation is partly responsible for the differences observed in Japanese and American business groups (alluded to in Unit 1). The Japanese spend lots of time getting to know each other before conducting business, whereas Americans get down to business very

Recently, the United States Department of Education issued guidelines (recommendations that are not legally binding on school boards) covering the types of religious communications and activities public schools may permit (New York Times, August 26, 1995, pp. 1, 8). Among the permitted activities are: student prayer, student-initiated discussions of religion, saying grace, proselytizing that would not be considered harassment, and the wearing of religious symbols and clothing. Among the forbidden activities: prayer endorsed by teachers or administrators, invitations to prayer that could constitute harassment, teaching of a particular religion (rather than about religion), encouraging (officially or through teaching) either religious or anti-religious activity, and denying school facilities to religious groups if the same facilities are provided to non-religious groups. What do you think of these guidelines? If you were a member of a local school board, would you vote to adopt or reject these guidelines? How do your cultural beliefs influence your view of these guidelines?

Table 3.2	Differences in Individual (Low-context) and Collective (High-context) Cultures

In every culture there will of course be variations in each of these characteristics. View these, therefore, as general tendencies rather than absolutes. Further, increased mobility, changing immigration patterns, and exposure to media from different parts of the world will gradually decrease the differences between these two orientations. [This table is based on the work of Hall (1983) and Hall and Hall (1987) and the interpretations by Gudykunst (1991) and Victor (1992).]

Individual (Low-Context) Cultures	Collective (High-Context) Cultures
Your own goals are most important	The group's goals are most important
You are responsible for yourself and to your own conscience	You are responsible for the entire group and to the group's values and rules
Success depends on your surpassing others	Success depends on your contribution to the group
Competition is emphasized	Cooperation is emphasized
Clear distinction is made between leaders and members	Little distinction is made between leaders and members; leadership would normally be shared
In-group versus out-group distinctions are of little importance	In-group versus out-group distinctions are of great importance
Information is made explicit; little is left unsaid	Information is often left implicit and much is often omitted from explicit statement
Personal relationships are less important; hence, little time is spent getting to know each other in meetings and conferences	Personal relationships are extremely important; hence, much time is spent getting to know each other in meetings and conferences
Directness is valued; face-saving is a relatively minor consideration	Indirectness is valued and face-saving is a major consideration

quickly. The Japanese (and other high-context cultures) want to get to know each other because important information is not made explicit. They have to know you so they can read your nonverbals, for example (Sanders, Wiseman, and Matz 1991). Americans can get right down to business because all important information will be stated explicitly.

To high-context cultural members what is omitted or assumed is a vital part of the communication transaction. Silence, for example, is highly valued (Basso 1972). To low-context cultural members what is omitted creates ambiguity. And to this person this ambiguity will be eliminated by explicit and direct communication. To high-context cultural members ambiguity is something to be avoided; it is a sign that the interpersonal and social interactions have not proved sufficient to establish a shared base of information (Gudykunst 1983).

When this simple difference is not understood, intercultural misunderstandings can easily result. For example, the directness characteristic of the low-context culture may prove insulting, insensitive, or unnecessary to the high-context cultural member. Conversely, to the low-context member, the high-context cultural member may appear vague, underhanded, or dishonest in his or her reluc-

How would you describe the culture in which you were raised in terms of high-context and low-context? Have you ever encountered communication differences as a result of differences in context?

tance to be explicit or engage in communication that a low-context member would consider open and direct.

Another frequent source of intercultural misunderstanding that can be traced to the differences in high- and low-context can be seen in face-saving (Hall and Hall 1987). High-context cultures place a great deal more emphasis on face-saving. For example, they are more likely to avoid argument for fear of causing others to lose face whereas low-context members (with their individualistic orientation) will use argument to win a point. Similarly, in high-context cultures criticism should only take place in private. Low-context cultures may not make this public-private distinction. Low-context managers who criticize high-context workers in public will find that their criticism causes interpersonal problems and does little to resolve the original difficulty that led to the criticism in the first place (Victor 1992).

Members of high-context cultures are reluctant to say no for fear of offending and causing the person to lose face. And so, for example, it is necessary to be able to read in the Japanese executive's yes when it means yes and when it means no. The difference is not in the words used but in the way in which they are used. It is easy to see how the low-context individual may interpret this reluctance to be direct—to say no when you mean no—as a weakness or as an unwillingness to confront reality.

Power Distances

In some cultures power is concentrated in the hands of a few and there is a great difference in the power held by these people and by the ordinary citizen. These are called high power distance cultures; examples are Mexico, Brazil, India, and the Philippines (Hofstede 1982). In low power distance cultures, power is more

Recently, the Emma Lazarus poem on the Statute of Liberty was changed. The words in brackets were deleted:

Give me your tired, your poor,
    Your huddled masses yearning to breathe free, . . .
    [The wretched refuse of your teeming shore]
    Send these, the homeless, tempest-tost to me
    I lift my lamp besides the golden door.

Harvard zoologist Stephen Jay Gould, commenting on this change, notes that with the words omitted, the poem no longer has balance or rhyme and, more important, no longer represents what Lazarus wrote (Gould 1995). "The language police triumph," notes Gould, "and integrity bleeds." On the other hand, you could argue that calling immigrants "wretched refuse" is insulting and degrading and that if Lazarus were writing today, she would not have used that phrase. How do you feel about this? Would you have supported the deletion of this line?

evenly distributed throughout the citizenry; examples include Denmark, New Zealand, Sweden, and to a lesser extent the United States. These differences impact on interpersonal communication and relationships in a variety of ways. Before reading these descriptions, think about your own culture and how power was distributed. Would you consider it a high or a low power distance culture? Then, consider the interpersonal differences discussed below and see if these descriptions are consistent with your own experiences. Also, as you go through these differences recognize that the differences between high and low power distance cultures are matters of degree. Characteristics are not in one culture and absent in the other but are in both, but present to different degrees.

For example, friendship and dating relationships will be influenced by the power distance between groups (Andersen 1991). In India (high power distance), for example, friendships and romantic relationships are expected to take place within your cultural class; in Sweden (low power distance), a person is expected to select friends and romantic partners on the basis—not of class or culture—but of individual factors such as personality, appearance, and the like.

In low power distance cultures you are expected to confront a friend, partner, or supervisor assertively; there is in these cultures a general feeling of equality which is consistent with acting assertively (Borden 1991; Morrison, Conaway, and Borden 1994). In high power distance cultures, direct confrontation and assertiveness may be viewed negatively, especially if directed at a superior.

 How would you learn whether people living in high and low power distance cultures differ in their level of happiness?

In high power distance cultures you are taught to have great respect for authority and generally people in these cultures see authority as desirable and beneficial; challenges to authority are generally not welcomed (Westwood, Tang, and Kirkbride 1992; also see Bochner and Hesketh 1994). In low power distance cultures, there is a certain distrust for authority; it is seen as a kind of necessary evil that should be limited as much as possible. This difference in attitudes toward authority can be seen right in the classroom. In high power distance cultures there is a great power distance between students and teachers; students are expected to be modest, polite, and totally respectful. In low power distance cultures students are expected to demonstrate their knowledge and command of the subject matter, participate in discussions with the teacher, and even challenge the teacher, something many high power distance culture members wouldn't even think of doing. The same differences can be seen in patient-doctor communication. Patients from high power distance cultures are less likely to challenge their doctor or admit that they don't understand the medical terminology than are patients in low power distance cultures.

High power distance cultures rely more on symbols of power. For example, titles (Dr., Professor, Chef, Inspector) are more important in high power distance cultures. Failure to include these in forms of address is a serious breach of etiquette. Low power distance cultures rely less on symbols of power and less of a problem is created if you fail to use a respectful title (Victor 1992). But, even in low power distance cultures you may create problems if, for example, you call a medical doctor, police captain, military officer, or professor Ms. or Mr.

Also, in the United States, two people quickly move from Title plus Last Name (Mr. or Ms. Smith) to First Name (Joe or Deirdre). Similarly, in low power distance cultures less of a problem is created if you are too informal or if you presume to exchange first names before sufficient interaction has taken place. In high power distance cultures too great an informality—especially between those differing in power—would be a serious breach of etiquette. Again, in even the lowest power distance culture, you may still create problems if you call your English professor Pat.

Theories of Culture and Communication

A number of attempts have been made to explain the interaction of culture and communication, to formulate a theory of culture and communication. Here are several. Although none provides a complete explanation, each gives us some understanding of how some part of culture interacts with some part of communication.

Language Relativity

The general idea that language influences thought and ultimately behavior got its strongest expression from linguistic anthropologists. In the late 1920s and throughout the 1930s, the view was formulated that the characteristics of language influence the way you think (Carroll 1956; Fishman 1960; Hoijer 1954; Miller and McNeill 1969; Sapir 1929). Since the languages of the world differ greatly in semantics and syntax, it was argued that people speaking widely different languages would also differ in how they viewed and thought about the world. This view became known as the **linguistic relativity hypothesis.**

Subsequent research and theory, however, did not support the extreme claims made by linguistic relativity researchers (Pinker 1994). A modified hypothesis seems currently supported: The language you speak helps to highlight what you see and how you talk about it. For example, if you speak a language that is rich in color terms (English is a good example) you will find it easier to highlight and talk about nuances of color than will someone from a culture which has fewer color terms (some cultures distinguish only two, three, or four parts of the color spectrum). But, this does not mean that people see the world differently; only that their language helps (or doesn't help) them to focus on certain variations in nature and makes it easier (or more difficult) to talk about them. Nor does it mean that people speaking widely differing languages are doomed to misunderstanding each other. Translation enables us to understand a great deal of the meaning in a foreign language message. And, of course, we have our communication skills, we can ask for clarification, for additional examples, for restatement. We can listen actively, give feedforward and feedback, use perception checking.

Language differences do not make for very important differences in perception, thought, or behavior. Difficulties in intercultural understanding are more often due to ineffective communication than to differences in languages.

Uncertainty Avoidance

Cultures differ greatly in their attitudes toward uncertainty and in how they deal with it. These attitudes and ways of dealing with uncertainty have consequences for interpersonal communication and relationships.

Some cultures do little to avoid uncertainty and have little anxiety about not knowing what will happen next; uncertainty to them is a normal part of life and is accepted as it comes. Members of these cultures are not threatened by unknown situations. Other cultures do much to avoid uncertainty and have great anxiety about not knowing what will happen next; uncertainty is seen as threatening and

Krowll has just come to your college from another galaxy. Krowll asks for your help in learning the rules of your culture, especially those rules concerning interpersonal interaction. For example, Krowll isn't quite sure about the following four issues: (1) Is it considered correct to interrupt someone who is speaking, and if so when is it permissible? (2) How do you begin a conversation with someone you have never met before? (3) How long do you maintain eye contact when talking with someone? How long do you maintain eye contact when listening to someone? (4) What do you do with your hands and feet when you are sitting in a chair talking with someone? Would these rules differ depending on whether Krowll is male or female? What interpersonal communication rules can you give Krowll for dealing with these four communication situations?

Table 3.3	Uncertainty Avoidance and Culture

The suggestion offered with Table 3.2 applies here as well. There are wide differences within each culture as well as between cultures. These rankings are based on average scores obtained by members of these cultures. The countries are listed in order: Greece had the weakest uncertainty avoidance score (they don't worry about uncertainty), Portugal was second weakest, Guatemala third, and so on. Singapore had the strongest uncertainty avoidance score (they worry a great deal about uncertainty), Jamaica was second, Denmark third, and so on. Countries listed together had the same score.

Weak Uncertainty Avoidance, Little Anxiety	Strong Uncertainty Avoidance, Lots of Anxiety
Greece	Singapore
Portugal	Jamaica
Guatemala	Denmark
Uruguay	Sweden
Belgium, Salvador	Hong Kong
Japan	Ireland
Yugoslavia	Great Britain
Peru	Malaysia
France, Chile, Spain, Costa Rica, Panama, and Argentina	India
Turkey and South Korea	Philippines
Mexico	United States

something that must be counteracted. Table 3.3 presents the countries that have the greatest anxiety over or feel most threatened by uncertainty and those that have the lowest anxiety.

The potential for communication problems when people come from cultures with different attitudes toward uncertainty can be great. Here are just a few examples. The manager from a weak uncertainty avoidance culture will accept workers who work only when they have to and will not get too upset when workers are late. The manager from a strong uncertainty avoidance culture will expect workers to be busy at all times and will have little tolerance for lateness.

Parents from these different cultural orientations will raise their children differently. The parent from the weak uncertainty avoidance culture will want the child raised with few and lenient rules on what, for example, is "dirty and taboo." The parent from the strong uncertainty avoidance culture will want the child raised with very rigid rules.

Members from weak uncertainty avoidance cultures feel that aggression and emotions should not be revealed; members from strong uncertainty avoidance cultures feel that such emotions have their place and may be legitimately revealed in the appropriate setting.

Because weak uncertainty avoidance cultures have great tolerance for ambiguity and uncertainty, they minimize the rules governing interpersonal and business communication and relationships (Hofstede 1997; Lustig and Koester 1996). Members who do not follow the same rules as the majority of the culture are easily and readily tolerated. Some may even encourage different approaches and perspectives. Strong uncertainty avoidance cultures (having little tolerance for

Geert Hofstede (1997, p. 119), who conducted much of the cultural research reported here, claims that those cultures which have strong uncertainty avoidance believe "What is different, is dangerous." Weak uncertainty avoidance cultures believe "What is different, is curious." Does your experience support this distinction?

uncertainty) create very clear-cut rules for interaction. Persons who break these rules are not readily accepted.

Students from weak uncertainty avoidance cultures appreciate freedom in education and prefer vague assignments without specific timetables. These students will want to be rewarded for creativity and will easily accept the teacher's (sometimes) lack of knowledge. Students from strong uncertainty avoidance cultures prefer highly structured learning experiences where there is very little ambiguity—specific objectives, detailed instructions, and definite timetables. These students expect to be judged on the basis of the right answers and expect the teacher to have all the answers all the time (Hofstede 1997).

Maximizing Outcomes

In intercultural communication—as in all communication—you try to maximize the outcomes of your interactions (Sunnafrank 1989). You try to gain the greatest rewards while paying the least costs. For example, you probably interact with those you predict will contribute to positive results; for example, you seek conversations that will prove satisfying, enjoyable, exciting, and so on. Because intercultural communication is difficult and positive outcomes may seem unlikely (at least at first), you may avoid it. And so, for example, you talk with the person in class who is similar to rather than different from you. However, extending and stretching yourself may actually result in greater satisfaction in the long run.

Also, consider that when you have positive outcomes, you continue to engage in communication and increase your communications. When you have negative outcomes, you begin to withdraw and communicate less. The implication here is obvious: Don't give up easily, especially in intercultural settings.

Since intercultural communication may be new or different from your usual communications, you will probably be more mindful, more consciously aware of it (Gudykunst 1989; Langer 1989). This has both positive and negative consequences. On the positive side, this increased awareness probably keeps you more alert. It prevents you from saying things that might appear insensitive or inappropriate. On the negative side, it leads to guardedness, lack of spontaneity, and lack of confidence.

In your mindful state you probably make predictions about which types of communication will result in positive outcomes; you try to predict the results of, for example, the choice of topic, the positions you take, the nonverbal behaviors you display, the amount of talking versus listening that you do, and so on. You then do what you think will result in positive outcomes and avoid doing what you think will result in negative outcomes. To do this successfully, however, you will have to learn as much as you can about the other person's system of communication signals. This will help you predict the outcomes of your behavior more accurately.

Culture Shock

Culture shock refers to the psychological reaction you experience when you're in a culture very different from your own (Furnham and Bochner 1986). Culture shock is normal; most people experience it when entering a new and different culture. Nevertheless, it can be unpleasant and frustrating. Part of this results

According to recent research, the most important skill to ward off depression is the ability to recognize and tolerate ambiguity (Yapko 1997, p.75). Would it follow that members of those cultures that foster a tolerance for ambiguity are less likely to experience depression? What might this mean for interpersonal communication?

from the feelings of alienation, conspicuousness, and difference from everyone else. When you lack knowledge of the rules and customs of the new society, you cannot communicate effectively. You are apt to blunder frequently and seriously. In your culture shock you may not know basic things:

- how to ask someone for a favor or pay someone a compliment;
- how to extend or accept an invitation for dinner;
- how early or how late to arrive for an appointment or how long to stay;
- how to distinguish seriousness from playfulness and politeness from indifference;
- how to dress for an informal, formal, or business function;
- how to order a meal in a restaurant or how to summon a waiter.

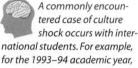

A commonly encountered case of culture shock occurs with international students. For example, for the 1993–94 academic year, there were 449,749 international students (New York Times January 4, 1995, A17). The ten countries sending the most students to the United States are China (44,381 students), Japan (43,770), Taiwan (37,581), India (34,796), South Korea (31,076), Canada (22,655), Hong Kong (13,752), Malaysia (13,718), Indonesia (11,744), and Thailand (9,537). If you are an international student, can you describe your culture shock experiences? If you are not an international student, can you visualize the culture shock you might experience if you were to study in another culture?

Anthropologist Kalervo Oberg (1960), who first used the term culture shock, notes that it occurs in stages. These stages are useful for examining many encounters with the new and the different. Going away to college, moving in together, or joining the military, for example, can also result in culture shock.

Stage One: The Honeymoon   At first you experience fascination, even enchantment, with the new culture and its people. You finally have your own apartment. You're your own boss. Finally, on your own! When in groups of people who are culturally different, this stage is characterized by cordiality and friendship among these early and superficial relationships. Many tourists remain at this stage because their stay in foreign countries is so brief.

Stage Two: The Crisis   Here, the differences between your own culture and the new one create problems. No longer do you find dinner ready for you unless you do it yourself. Your clothes are not washed or ironed unless you do them yourself. Feelings of frustration and inadequacy come to the fore. This is the stage at which you experience the actual shock of the new culture. In one study of foreign students coming from over 100 countries and studying in eleven countries, it was found that 25 percent of the students experienced depression (Klineberg and Hull 1979).

Stage Three: The Recovery   During this period you gain the skills necessary to function effectively. You learn how to shop, cook, and plan a meal. You find a local laundry and figure you'll learn how to iron later. You learn the language and ways of the new culture. Your feelings of inadequacy subside.

Which of these four theories—language relativity, uncertainty reduction, maximizing outcomes, or culture shock—do you feel offers the greatest insight into the role of culture in communication?

Stage Four: The Adjustment   At this final stage, you adjust to and come to enjoy the new culture and the new experiences. You may still experience periodic difficulties and strains, but on a whole, the experience is pleasant. Actually, you're now a pretty decent cook. You're even coming to enjoy it. You're making a good salary so why learn to iron?

People may also experience culture shock when they return to their original culture after living in a foreign culture, a kind of reverse culture shock (Jandt 1995). Consider, for example, the Peace Corps volunteers who work in a rural and economically deprived area. Upon returning to Las Vegas or Beverly Hills they may experience culture shock. Sailors who served long periods aboard ship and then return to an isolated farming community might also experience culture shock. In these cases, however, the recovery period is shorter and the sense of inadequacy and frustration is less.

Intercultural Communication

Understanding the role of culture in communication is an essential foundation for understanding intercultural communication as it occurs interpersonally, in small groups, in public speaking, or in the media and for appreciating the principles for effective intercultural communication.

The Nature of Intercultural Communication

Intercultural communication refers to communication between persons who have different cultural beliefs, values, or ways of behaving. The model in Figure 3.1 illustrates this concept. The larger circles represent the culture of the individual communicator. The inner circles identify the communicators (the sources/receivers). In this model each communicator is a member of a different culture. In some instances the cultural differences are relatively slight—say, between persons from Toronto and New York. In other instances the cultural differences are great—say, between persons from Borneo and Germany, or between persons from rural Nigeria and industrialized England.

What role or part does intercultural communication play in your personal, social, and professional life? Has this changed in the last ten years? Is it likely to change in the next ten years? What factors have contributed to make your own social environment—school, neighborhood, workplace—more interculturally conscious?

All messages originate from a specific and unique cultural context, and that context influences their content and form. You communicate as you do largely as a result of your culture. Culture (along with the processes of enculturation and acculturation) influences every aspect of your communication experience.

You receive messages through the filters imposed by your cultural context. That context influences what you receive and how you receive it. For example, some cultures rely heavily on television or newspapers and trust them implicitly. Others rely on face-to-face interpersonal interactions, distrusting many of the mass communication systems.

Principles of Intercultural Communication

Murphy's law ("If anything can go wrong, it will") is especially applicable to intercultural communication. Intercultural communication is, of course, subject to all the same barriers and problems as are the other forms of communication that we discuss throughout this text. Drawing on a number of intercultural researchers, we cover here the principles designed to counteract the barriers that

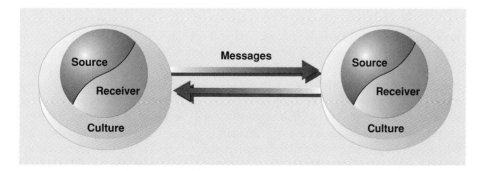

Figure 3.1   A Model of Intercultural Communication.
This basic model of intercultural communication is designed to illustrate that culture is a part of every communication transaction. Can you visualize a different type of model? How would you diagram the intercultural communication process?

are unique to intercultural communication (Barna 1991, Ruben 1985, Spitzberg 1991).

Prepare Yourself   There is no better preparation for intercultural communication than learning about the other culture. Fortunately, there are numerous sources to draw on. View a video or film that presents a realistic view of the culture. Read about the culture by persons from that culture as well as by outsiders. Scan magazines from that culture. Talk with members of that culture. And of course read those works addressed to people who need to communicate with those from other cultures. For example, recent titles include: *Do's and Taboos of Hosting International Visitors* (Axtell 1990), *When In Rome. . . A Business Guide to Cultures and Customs in 12 European Nations* (Mole 1990). *Do's and Taboos around the World* (Axtell 1993), *The Executive Guide to Asia-Pacific Communications* (James 1995), *How to Negotiate Anything With Anyone Anywhere Around the World* (Acuff 1993), and *Internationally Yours: Writing and Communication Successfully in Today's Global Marketplace* (DeVries 1994).

Recognize and Face Fears   A major factor that stands in the way of effective intercultural communication is fear (Gudykunst, 1990; Stephan and Stephan, 1985). For example, you may fear for your self-esteem. You may become anxious about your ability to control the intercultural situation or you may worry about your own level of discomfort. You may fear saying something that will be considered politically incorrect or culturally insensitive and thereby losing face.

You may fear that you will be taken advantage of by the member of this other culture. Depending upon your own stereotypes you may fear being lied to, financially duped, or made fun of.

You may fear that members of this other group will react to you negatively. You may fear, for example, that they will not like you or may disapprove of your attitudes or beliefs or perhaps even reject you as a person. Conversely, you may fear negative reactions from members of your own group. They might, for example, disapprove of your socializing with the culturally different.

These fears—coupled with the greater effort that intercultural communication takes and the ease with which you communicate with those who are culturally similar—can easily lead some people to give up. Some fears are reasonable. In many cases, however, they are groundless. Either way, they need to be assessed logically and their consequences weighed carefully. Then you'll be able to make informed choices about your communications.

Can you identify any fears you have about interacting in intercultural situations? Can you identify the origin of your fears?

Recognize Differences Between Yourself and the Culturally Different   Perhaps the most prevalent barrier to intercultural communication occurs when you assume that similarities exist and that differences do not. This is especially true in the area of values, attitudes, and beliefs. You might easily accept different hairstyles, clothing, and foods. In basic values and beliefs, however, you may assume that deep down everyone is really alike. They aren't. When you assume similarities and ignore differences, you will fail to notice important distinctions and when communicating will convey to others that your ways are the right ways and that their ways are not important to you. Consider this example. An American invites a Filipino coworker to dinner. The Filipino politely refuses. The American is hurt and feels that the Filipino does not want to be friendly. The Filipino is hurt and concludes that the invitation was not extended sincerely. Here, it seems, both the American and the Filipino assume that their customs for inviting people to dinner are the same when, in fact, they are not. A Filipino expects to be invited several times before accepting a dinner invitation. When an invitation is given only once it is viewed as insincere.

Here's another example. An American college student hears the news that her favorite uncle has died. She bites her lip, pulls herself up, and politely excuses herself from the group of foreign students with whom she is having dinner. The Russian thinks: "How unfriendly." The Italian thinks: "How insincere." The Brazilian thinks: "How unconcerned." To many Americans, it is a sign of bravery to endure pain (physical or emotional) in silence and without any outward show of emotion. To members of other groups, such silence is often interpreted negatively to mean that the individual does not consider them friends who can share such sorrow. To members of other cultures, people are expected to reveal to friends how they feel.

Can you conceive of situations where a too-focused concern on differences could create intercultural communication problems?

Recognize Differences Among the Culturally Different Group   Within every cultural group there are wide and important differences. As all Americans are not alike, neither are all Indonesians, Greeks, Mexicans, and so on. When we ignore these differences we are guilty of stereotyping. We assume that all persons covered by the same label (in this case a national or racial label) are the same. A good example of this is seen in the use of the term "African American." The term stresses the unity of Africa and those who are of African descent and is analogous to "Asian American" or "European American." At the same time, it ignores the great diversity within this continent when, for example, it is used as analogous to "German American" or "Japanese American." "Nigerian American" or "Ethiopian American," on the other hand, would be analogous to, say, "German American." Within each culture there are smaller cultures that differ greatly from each other and from the larger culture.

Recognize Differences in Meaning   Be especially sensitive to this simple principle in intercultural communication: meaning exists not in words but in people (a principle we return to in Unit 7). Consider, for example, the differences in meaning for such words as *woman* to an American and a Muslim, *religion* to a born-again Christian and an atheist, and *lunch* to a Chinese rice farmer and a Madison Avenue advertising executive. Even though the same word is used, its meanings will vary greatly depending on the listeners' cultural definitions.

A left-handed American who eats with the left hand may be seen by a Muslim as obscene. To the Muslim, the left hand is not used for eating or for shaking hands but to clean oneself after excretory functions. So, using the left hand to eat or to shake hands is considered insulting and obscene.

Follow Cultural Rules and Customs   Each culture has its own rules for communicating (Barna 1991; Ruben 1985; Spitzberg 1991). These rules identify what is appropriate and what is inappropriate. Thus, in American culture you would call a person you wish to date three or four days in advance. In certain Asian cultures, you might call the person's parents weeks or even months in advance. In

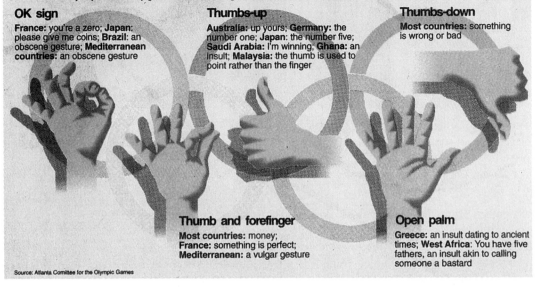

The Olympic don'ts of gestures

Olympic volunteers who will be working with international visitors are being trained to be careful what they say or what they gesture. Here's what gestures mean in other countries:

OK sign
France: you're a zero; **Japan:** please give me coins; **Brazil:** an obscene gesture; **Mediterranean countries:** an obscene gesture

Thumbs-up
Australia: up yours; **Germany:** the number one; **Japan:** the number five; **Saudi Arabia:** I'm winning; **Ghana:** an insult; **Malaysia:** the thumb is used to point rather than the finger

Thumbs-down
Most countries: something is wrong or bad

Thumb and forefinger
Most countries: money; **France:** something is perfect; **Mediterranean:** a vulgar gesture

Open palm
Greece: an insult dating to ancient times; **West Africa:** You have five fathers, an insult akin to calling someone a bastard

Source: Atlanta Comittee for the Olympic Games

With nonverbal messages, the potential differences seem even greater. Thus, the over-the-head clasped hands that signifies victory to an American may signify friendship to a Russian. To an American, holding up two fingers to make a V signifies victory. To certain South Americans, however, it is an obscene gesture that corresponds to the American's extended middle finger. This figure highlights some of these differences. Can you identify others?

Can you identify two communication rules followed by most members of your culture?

Consider how cultural differences underlie answers to such questions as:
- *Should abortion be declared illegal?*
- *Should those who commit hate or bias crimes be given harsher sentences?*
- *Should assisted suicides be legalized?*

American culture you say, as a general friendly gesture and not as a specific invitation, "come over and pay us a visit." To members of other cultures, this comment is sufficient for the listeners actually to come to visit at their convenience. In some cultures, people show respect by avoiding direct eye contact with the person to whom they are speaking. In other cultures this same eye avoidance would signal disinterest. If a young American girl is talking with an older Indonesian man, for example, she is expected to avoid direct eye contact. To an Indonesian, direct eye contact in this situation would be considered disrespectful. In some southern European cultures men walk arm in arm. Other cultures (the United States, for example) consider this inappropriate.

A good example of a series of rules for an extremely large and important culture that many people do not know appears in Table 3.4. "Ten Commandments for Communicating with People with Disabilities." The suggestions offered here are considered appropriate in the United States but not necessarily in other cultures. For example, although the phrase "person with mental retardation" is accepted in most of the United States, it was considered offensive to many in the United Kingdom (Fernald 1995).

Think about your own ability to deal with intercultural communication situations by considering how you would deal with each of the following obstacles to

Table 3.4	Ten Commandments for Communicating with People with Disabilities

Some research has suggested that able-bodied instructors communicate differently with students who have and students who don't have disabilities (Hart and Williams 1995). Do you communicate differently? Note also that these suggestions are directed at the non-disabled person communicating with the person with disabilities. How would you write "the ten commandments for persons with disabilities communicating with persons without disabilities?" Put differently, what can the person with disabilities do to make communication with those without disabilities easier and more effective?

1. Speak directly rather than through a companion or sign language interpreter who may be present.
2. Offer to shake hands when introduced. People with limited hand use or an artificial limb can usually shake hands and offering the left hand is an acceptable greeting.
3. Always identify yourself and others who may be with you when meeting someone with a visual impairment. When conversing in a group, remember to identify the person to whom you are speaking.
4. If you offer assistance, wait until the offer is accepted. Then listen or ask for instructions.
5. Treat adults as adults. Address people who have disabilities by their first names only when extending that same familiarity to all others. Never patronize people in wheelchairs by patting them on the head or shoulder.
6. Do not lean against or hang on someone's wheelchair. Bear in mind that disabled people treat their chairs as extensions of their bodies.
7. Listen attentively when talking with people who have difficulty speaking and wait for them to finish. If necessary, ask short questions that require short answers, a nod, or shake of the head. Never pretend to understand if you are having difficulty doing so. Instead repeat what you have understood and allow the person to respond.
8. Place yourself at eye level when speaking with someone in a wheelchair or on crutches.
9. Tap a hearing-impaired person on the shoulder or wave your hand to get his or her attention. Look directly at the person and speak clearly, slowly, and expressively to establish if the person can read your lips. If so, try to face the light source and keep hands, cigarettes, and food away from your mouth when speaking.
10. Relax. Don't be embarrassed if you happen to use common expressions such as "See you later," or "Did you hear about this?" that seem to relate to a person's disability.

Source: United Cerebral Palsy Associations, Inc.

"Ten Commandments for Communicating with People with Disabilities," *The New York Times.* June 7, 1992. Copyright © 1992 by the New York Times. Reprinted by permission.

intercultural understanding and communication. Make a note to return to these examples after you have finished the first part of this text, especially Unit 9, and see if your answers remain the same or change as a result of your reading.

1. Your friend makes fun of Radha, who comes to class in her native African dress. You feel you want to object to this.
2. Craig and Louise are an interracial couple. Craig's family treat him fairly but virtually ignore Louise. They never invite Craig and Louise as a couple to dinner or to partake in any of the family affairs. The couple decide that they should confront Craig's family and ask your advice.

3. Malcolm is a close friend and is really an open-minded person. But he has the habit of referring to members of other racial and ethnic groups with derogatory language. You decide to tell him that you object to this way of talking.

4. Tom, a good friend of yours, wants to ask Pat out for a date. Both you and Tom know that Pat is a lesbian and will refuse the date and yet Tom says he's going to have some fun and ask her anyway—just to give her a hard time. You think this is wrong and want to tell Tom you think so.

5. Your parents persist in holding stereotypes about other religious, racial and ethnic groups. These stereotypes come up in all sorts of conversations. You are embarrassed by these attitudes and feel you must tell your parents how incorrect you think these stereotypes are.

6. Lenny, a colleague at work, recently underwent a religious conversion. He now persists in trying to get everyone else—yourself included—to undergo this same religious conversion. Every day he tells you why you should convert, gives you literature to read, and otherwise persists in trying to convert you. You decide to tell him that you find this behavior offensive.

Summary	U N I T I N B R I E F

A RETURN TO OBJECTIVES:

In this unit we explored the nature of culture and identified some key principles: Specifically, we attempted to answer four basic questions: (1) What is culture and how is it transmitted? And how do the related processes of enculturation and acculturation fit into the picture? (2) How do cultures differ from each other in terms of collectivist and individualistic, low and high context, and high and low power distance? How do these differences impact on interpersonal communication? (3) What general principles or theories might help us explain the role of culture in interpersonal communication? (4) What is intercultural communication and what are its central principles?

The Nature of Culture	How Cultures Differ	Theories of Culture and Communication	Intercultural Communication
Culture: The relatively specialized life-style of a group of people (values, beliefs, artifacts, ways of behaving) that are passed from one generation to the next by means of communication (not genes).	**Collectivist cultures** emphasize the group and subordinate the individual's goals to those of the group. Individualistic cultures emphasize the individual and subordinate the group's goals to the individuals.	**Language relativity** concerns the role of language in influencing what you see and how you see it and assumes those speaking widely differing languages will see the world differently.	**Intercultural communication** refers to communication between people who have different cultures, beliefs, values, or ways of behaving.
Enculturation: The process through which you learn the culture into which you are born.	In **high-context cultures** much of the information is in the context; in **low context cultures** the information is explicitly stated in the verbal message.	**Uncertainty avoidance theory** holds that the greater the uncertainty and ambiguity the greater the communication difficulty.	Some intercultural communication principles include: Prepare yourself, recognize and face fears, recognize differences between yourself and the culturally different, recognize
Acculturation: The process by which you learn the rules and norms of a culture different from your native culture and which modifies your original or native culture.	In high **power distance** cultures power is concentrated in the hands of a few and there is great difference between those with and those without power. In low power distance cultures, the power is more equally shared throughout the citizenry.	**Maximizing outcomes** holds that intercultural communication (or any communication) will be guided by the goal of maximizing positive outcomes.	differences among the culturally different, recognize meaning differences in verbal and nonverbal messages, and follow cultural rules and customs.
		Culture shock refers to the psychological reaction to being in a culture different from one's own, often with feelings of alienation and conspicuousness.	

UNIT
4
The Self in Interpersonal Communication

Unit Topics	Unit Objectives
	After completing this unit, you should be able to:
Self-Concept Others' Images of You Social Comparisons Your Own Interpretations and Evaluations	1. Define *self-concept* and explain how it develops
Self-Awareness The Four Selves Increasing Self-Awareness	2. Explain the Johari window and define the *open, blind, hidden,* and *unknown selves* 3. Explain how self-awareness can be increased
Self-Esteem Attack Your Self-Destructive Beliefs Engage in Self-Affirmation Seek Out Nourishing People Work on Projects That Will Result in Success	4. Define *self-esteem* and explain how it might be raised
Self-Disclosure Factors Influencing Self-Disclosure Rewards of Self-Disclosure Dangers of Self-Disclosure: Risks Ahead Self-Disclosure Guidelines	5. Define *self-disclosure* 6. Explain the factors that influence self-disclosure 7. Identify the major rewards and dangers involved in self-disclosure 8. Explain the guidelines for making and for responding to self-disclosures

---

EXPERIENTIAL LEARNING VEHICLES

No. 3, "I'd Prefer to Be," pp. 442–443 offers a means for exploring the self and communication. No. 5, "Time for Self-Disclosure," pp. 444–445, allows for the exploration of self-disclosure. No. 7, "Perceiving My Selves," pp. 446–448, stimulates discussion of self concept, self-awareness, and self-esteem.

Who you are and how you see yourself influence the way you communicate with others and the way others communicate with you. Your self-concept, self-awareness, and self-esteem all play a significant role in your interpersonal interactions.

Self-Concept

You no doubt have an image of who you are; this is your self-concept. It consists of your feelings and thoughts about your strengths and weaknesses, your abilities and limitations. Your self-concept develops from at least three sources: (1) the image of you that others have and that they reveal to you, (2) the comparisons you make between yourself and others, and (3) the way you interpret and evaluate your own thoughts and behaviors (Figure 4.1).

Others' Images of You

If you wished to see the way your hair looked, you would likely look in a mirror. But what would you do if you wanted to see how friendly or how assertive you are? According to Charles Horton Cooley's (1922) concept of the *looking-glass self,* you would look at the image of yourself that others reveal to you through the way they treat you and react to you.

You would look especially to those who are most significant in your life—to your *significant others.* As a child, you would look to your parents and then to your teachers. As an adult, you might look to your friends, romantic partners, and colleagues at work. If these significant others think highly of you, you will see this positive image of yourself reflected in their behaviors; if they think little

Figure 4.1   The Sources of Self-Concept.
This diagram illustrates the three sources that form our self-concepts: others' images of you, the social comparisons you make with others, especially your peers, and your own interpretations and evaluations of your own feelings and behaviors. Of course, these three sources will all exert different degrees of influence depending on the specific aspect of self-concept on which you focus. Consider, for example, which source is most influential on your physical appearance self-concept? On your athletic ability self-concept? On your future success self-concept?

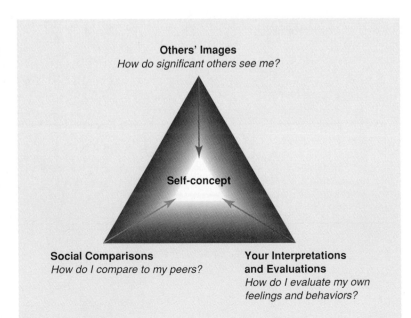

of you, you will see a more negative image. These reflections that you see in others help you define your self-concept.

Social Comparisons

Another way you develop your self-concept is by comparing yourself with others. When you want to gain insight into who you are and how effective or competent you are, you probably look to your peers. For example, after an examination you probably want to know how you performed relative to the other students in your class. If you play on a baseball team, it's important to know your batting average in comparison with others on the team. You gain an additional perspective when you see your score in comparison with the scores of your peers.

Your Own Interpretations and Evaluations

Much in the way others form images of you based on what you do, you also react to your own behavior; you interpret and evaluate it. These interpretations and evaluations help to form your self-concept. For example, let us say you believe that lying is wrong. If you lie, you will evaluate this behavior in terms of your internalized beliefs about lying. You will thus react negatively to your own behavior. You may, for example, experience guilt if your behavior contradicts your beliefs. In contrast, let's say you pulled someone out of a burning building at great personal risk. You would probably evaluate this behavior positively; you would feel good about this behavior and, as a result, about yourself.

Self-Awareness

Your self-awareness represents the extent to which you know yourself. Understanding how your self-concept develops is one way to increase your self-awareness: the more you understand about the reasons you view yourself as you do, the more you will understand who you are. Additional insight is gained by looking at self-awareness through the Johari model of the self.

The Four Selves

Self-awareness is neatly explained by the model of the four selves (the Johari window). This model, presented in Figure 4.2, has four basic areas, or quadrants, each of which represents a somewhat different self.

The Johari model emphasizes that the several aspects of the self are not separate pieces but are interactive parts of a whole. Each part is dependent on each other part. Like that of interpersonal communication, this model of the self is a transactional one.

The Open Self   The **open self** represents all the information, behaviors, attitudes, feelings, desires, motivations, and ideas that both you and others know. The type of information included here might range from your name, skin color, and sex to your age, political and religious affiliations, and financial situation. Your open self will vary in size, depending on the situation you are in and the person with whom you are interacting. Some people, for example, make you feel

 What is your self-concept? How satisfied are you with it? Are you convinced that you can develop a more positive self-concept? What do you intend to do about it?

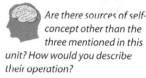 *Are there sources of self-concept other than the three mentioned in this unit? How would you describe their operation?*

Figure 4.2   The Johari Window. *Visualize this model as representing your self. The entire model is of constant size, but each section can vary, from very small to very large. As one section becomes smaller, one or more of the others grow larger. Similarly, as one section grows, one or more of the others must get smaller. For example, if you reveal a secret and thereby enlarge your open self, your hidden self shrinks. Further, this disclosure may in turn lead to a decrease in the size of your blind self (if your disclosure influences other people to reveal what they know about you but that you have not known). The name Johari, by the way, comes from the first names of the two people who developed the model, Joseph Luft and Harry Ingham.* (*Source:* From *Group Processes: An Introduction to Group Dynamics* by Joseph Luft, 1984, p. 60. Reprinted by permission Mayfield Publishing Company, Mountain View, CA.)

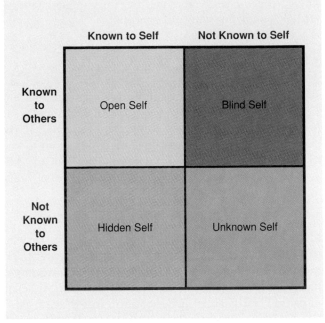

How well do you feel you know yourself? Poll a few people and see how well they feel they know themselves. If the people you poll are like some students, you will find very few people who say they have low self-awareness. How do you explain this? Is everyone exceptionally self-aware?

How would you draw your Johari window to show yourself when interacting with your parents? With your friends? With your college instructors?

comfortable and supported; to them, you open yourself wide, but to others you may prefer to leave most of yourself closed.

Communication depends on the degree to which you open yourself to others and to yourself (Luft 1970). If you do not allow other people to know you (thus keeping your open self small), communication between you and others becomes difficult, if not impossible. You can communicate meaningfully only to the extent that you know others and yourself. To improve communication, work first on enlarging the open self.

The Blind Self   The **blind self** represents all the things about yourself that others know but of which you are ignorant. These may vary from the relatively insignificant habit of saying "You know," rubbing your nose when you get angry, or having a peculiar body odor, to things as significant as defense mechanisms, fight strategies, or repressed experiences.

Some people have a very large blind self and seem totally oblivious of their faults and sometimes (though not as often) of their virtues. Others seem overly eager to have a small blind self. They seek therapy at every turn and join every self-help group. Some feel they know everything there is to know about themselves, that they have reduced the blind self to zero. Most of us lie between these extremes.

Communication and interpersonal relations are generally enhanced as the blind self becomes smaller. But, do not assume from this that people should therefore be forced to see themselves as you see them. This could cause serious problems. Such a revelation might trigger a breakdown in defenses; it might force people to admit their own jealousy or prejudice when they are not psychologically ready to deal with such information. Such revelations are best dealt with cautiously or under the guidance of trained professionals.

The Hidden Self   The **hidden self** contains all that you know of yourself and of others that you keep secret. In any interaction, this area includes everything you do not want to reveal, whether it is relevant or irrelevant to the conversation.

At the extremes, we have the overdisclosers and the underdisclosers. The overdisclosers tell all. They keep nothing hidden about themselves or others. They tell you their marital difficulties, their children's problems, their financial status, and just about everything else. The underdisclosers tell nothing. They talk about you but not about themselves.

The problem with these extremes is that individuals do not distinguish between those who should and those who shouldn't be privy to such information. They also do not distinguish among the types of information they should or should not disclose. The vast majority of people, however, keep certain things hidden and disclose others; they make disclosures to some people and not to others. They are *selective* disclosers.

The Unknown Self   The **unknown self** represents truths about yourself that neither you nor others know. The existence of this self is inferred from a number of sources. Sometimes it is revealed through temporary changes brought about by drugs or through special experimental conditions, such as hypnosis or sensory deprivation. Sometimes this area is revealed by certain projective tests or dreams. Mostly, however, it is revealed by the fact that you are constantly learning things about yourself that you did not know before (things that were previously in the unknown self).

Although you cannot easily manipulate this area, recognize that it does exist and that there are things about yourself and about others that you do not know and may never know.

Increasing Self-Awareness

You can increase your self-awareness in a number of ways: ask yourself about yourself, listen to others, actively seek information about yourself, see your different selves, and increase your open self.

Ask Yourself About Yourself   One way to ask yourself about yourself is to take an informal "Who Am I?" test (Bugental and Zelen 1950). Head a piece of paper "Who Am I?" and write 10, 15, or 20 times "I am . . ." Then complete each of the sentences. Try not to give only positive or socially acceptable responses; just respond with what comes to mind first. Second, take another piece of paper and divide it into two columns. Head one column "Strengths" and the other column "Weaknesses." Fill in each column as quickly as possible. Third, using these first two "tests" as a base, take a third piece of paper, head it "Self-Improvement Goals," and complete the statement "I want to improve my . . ." as many times as you can in, say, five minutes. Since you are constantly changing, these self-perceptions and goals also change and so must be updated frequently. Try taking this self-test before reading the next paragraph.

Your cultural background, of course, will significantly influence your responses to this simple "Who Am I?" test. In one study, for example, participants from Malaysia (a collectivist culture) and from Australia and Great Britain (both individualistic cultures) completed this test. Malaysians produced significantly

What general classes or types of information do you normally keep hidden? What types of information are you least likely to keep hidden?

more group self-descriptions and fewer idiocentric self-descriptions than did the Australian or British members (Bochner 1994; also see Radford, Mann, Ohta, and Nakane 1993). If you completed the "Who Am I?" test, can you identify responses that were influenced by, say, your individualistic or collectivist orientation? Did other cultural factors influence your statements?

Listen to Others   You can learn a lot about yourself by seeing yourself as others do. Conveniently, others are constantly giving you the very feedback you need to increase self-awareness. In every interpersonal interaction, people comment on you in some way—on what you do, what you say, how you look. Sometimes these comments are explicit; most often they are "hidden" in the way in which others look at you, in what they talk about, in their interest in what you say. Pay close attention to this kind of information (both verbal and nonverbal) and use it to increase your own self-awareness.

Actively Seek Information About Yourself   Actively seek out information to reduce your blind self. You need not be so obvious as to say, "Tell me about myself" or "What do you think of me?" But you can use everyday situations to gain self-information: "Do you think I was assertive enough when asking for the raise?" Or "Do you think I'd be thought too forward if I invited myself for dinner?" Do not, of course, seek this information constantly; your friends would surely and quickly find others with whom to interact. But you can make use of some situations—perhaps those in which you are particularly unsure of what to do or how you appear—to reduce your blind self and increase self-awareness.

See Your Different Selves   Each of your friends and relatives views you differently; to each you are a somewhat different person. Yet you are really *all* of these. Practice seeing yourself as do the people with whom you interact. For starters, visualize how you are seen by your mother, your father, your teachers, your best friend, the stranger you sat next to on the bus, your employer, your neighbor's child. Because you are a composite of all these views, it is important that you periodically see yourself through the eyes of others. The experience will give you new and valuable perspectives on yourself.

These suggestions only seem simple; they are actually quite difficult to do. What obstacles can you envision that might prevent you from using these suggestions?

Increase Your Open Self   When you increase your open self and reveal yourself to others, you also reveal yourself to yourself. At the very least, you bring into clearer focus what you may have buried within. As you discuss yourself, you may see connections that you had previously missed, and with the aid of feedback from others you may gain still more insight. Also, by increasing the open self, you increase the likelihood that a meaningful and intimate dialogue will develop; through such interactions you best get to know yourself. Do, however, consider the risks involved in such self-disclosures (discussed in Unit 8).

Self-Esteem

How much do you like yourself? How valuable a person do you think you are? How competent do you think you are? The answers to these questions reflect your self-esteem, the value you place on yourself. People who have high self-esteem, for example, are going to communicate this throughout their verbal and nonverbal messages. The ways they phrase their ideas and questions or the way they hold their head and maintain eye contact are likely to differ greatly from the way the person with low self-esteem would communicate. Similarly, people with different views of themselves will develop and maintain relationships with friends, lovers, and family differently. As you read this unit, think about your own relationships and how the way you see yourself influences them.

Self-esteem is very important because success breeds success. When you feel good about yourself—about who you are and what you are capable of doing— you will perform better. When you think like a success, you are more likely to act like a success. When you think you're a failure, you're more likely to act like a failure. Increasing self-esteem will, therefore, help you to function more effectively in school, in interpersonal relationships, and in careers. Here are a few suggestions for increasing self-esteem.

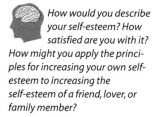

How would you describe your self-esteem? How satisfied are you with it? How might you apply the principles for increasing your own self-esteem to increasing the self-esteem of a friend, lover, or family member?

Attack Your Self-Destructive Beliefs

Self-destructive beliefs are those that damage your self-esteem and prevent you from building meaningful and productive relationships. They may be about yourself ("I'm not creative"; "I'm boring"), your world ("The world is an unhappy place"; "People are out to get me"), and your relationships ("All the good people are already in relationships"; "If I ever fall in love, I know I'll be hurt"). Identifying these beliefs will help you to examine them critically and to see that they are both illogical and self-defeating.

Another way of looking at self-destructive beliefs is to identify what Pamela Butler (1981) calls "drivers"—unrealistic beliefs that may motivate you to act in ways that are self-defeating. For example, the drive to be perfect impels you to try to perform at unrealistically high levels in just about everything you do. Whether it is directed toward work, school, athletics, or appearance, this drive tells you that anything short of perfection is unacceptable and that you are to blame for any imperfections. The drive to be strong tells you that weakness and any of the more vulnerable emotions, such as sadness, compassion, or loneliness, are wrong. Instead of helping you because successful, these drivers almost ensure your failure. Are you motivated by these unrealistic drivers?

Recognizing that you may have internalized self-destructive beliefs is a first step toward eliminating them. A second step involves recognizing that these beliefs are unrealistic and self-defeating. Psychotherapist Albert Ellis (1988; Ellis and Harper 1975) and other cognitive therapists (for example, Beck 1988) would argue that you can accomplish this by understanding why these beliefs are unrealistic and substituting more realistic ones. For example, following Ellis, you might try replacing an unrealistic desire to please everyone in everything you do with a more realistic belief that it would be nice if others were pleased with you but it certainly is not essential. A third step is giving yourself permission to fail, to be less than perfect, to be normal.

Do recognize that it is the *unrealistic* nature of these drivers that creates problems. Certainly, trying hard and being strong are not unhealthy when they are realistic. It is only when they become absolute—when you try to be everything to everyone—that they become impossible to achieve, and create problems.

Engage in Self-Affirmation

Remind yourself of your successes. There are enough people around who will remind you of your failures. Focus, too, on your good acts, your good deeds. Focus on your positive qualities, your strengths, your virtues. Focus on the good relationships you have with friends and relatives.

The way you talk to yourself about yourself influences what you think of yourself. If you talk positively about yourself, you will come to feel more positive about yourself. If you tell yourself that you are a success, that others like you, that you will succeed on the next test, and that you will be welcomed when asking for a date, you will soon come to feel positive about yourself. Table 4.1 presents a useful list of self-affirming phrases. Reading over the list is sure to stimulate your own self-affirmations.

Seek Out Nourishing People

Psychologist Carl Rogers drew a distinction between noxious and nourishing people. Noxious people criticize and find fault with just about everything. Nourishing people, on the other hand, are positive. They are optimists. They reward you, they stroke you, they make you feel good about yourself. Seek out these people.

Work on Projects That Will Result in Success

Some people want to fail, or so it seems. Often, they select projects that will result in failure. Perhaps the projects are too large or too difficult. In any event, they are impossible. Instead, select projects that will result in success. Each success helps build self-esteem. Each success makes the next success a little easier.

When a project does fail, recognize that this does not mean that you are a failure. Everyone fails somewhere along the line. Failure is something that happens; it is not something inside you. Further, your failing once does not mean

Table 4.1	Self-Affirming Phrases

These phrases are general ones that you may wish to make more specific so that they apply more directly to you. What other affirmations would you add? These affirmations are reprinted from Gathering Power Through Insight and Love *by Ken Keyes, Jr., and Penny Keyes. Copyright © 1987 by Living Love Publications.*

I am a lovable and worthy person.

I appreciate and love myself!

The love I give to others I also can offer to myself.

I can live a nurturing, exciting, and creative life.

I am creating the experience of love in my life.

My love comes from me.

I can forgive myself.

I am capable and willing to handle my fears as they come up one at a time.

I can accept imperfection.

I can accept the past and welcome the future.

I deserve to feel good.

I am a worthwhile person and there is a place for me.

I am lovable because I'm here.

I am creative, loving, and nurturing.

I can feel good doing the things I'm skilled at.

I can learn to accept and love everyone unconditionally—including myself.

I am learning to support myself with love.

I release the past and now choose a life of love and fulfillment.

I can ask for what I want with love in my heart.

I am the source of my security and self-esteem.

I don't have to be sick to get nurtured.

I am worthy of a loving relationship.

My world is safe and friendly.

I can be gentle with myself.

I can feel supported even when I don't meet my models of perfection.

There is nothing I have to do to feel loved.

My guilt doesn't help anyone.

I am open to new forms of being acknowledged.

I deserve to be healthy.

I can accept praise and attention at any time.

that you will fail the next time. So put failure in perspective. Do not make it an excuse for not trying again.

Self-Disclosure

One of the most important forms of interpersonal communication that you could engage in is talking about yourself, or self-disclosure. **Self-disclosure** refers to your communicating information about yourself to another person. It may involve information about (1) your values, beliefs, and desires ("I believe in reincarnation"), (2) your behavior ("I committed grand larceny but was never caught"), or (3) your self-qualities or characteristics ("I'm dyslexic"). Because self-disclosure is a type of communication, overt statements about yourself as well as slips of the tongue, and written or public confessions would all be classified as self-disclosing communications. Similarly, you could self-disclose nonverbally by, for example, wearing gang colors, wedding rings, or shirts with slogans that reveal your political or social concerns. Self-disclosure may also involve your

Before reading any further, how would you describe your tendency to self-disclose (a) your feelings of sadness or loneliness, (b) your past indiscretions, (c) your fantasies and dreams, and (d) your weaknesses?

reactions to the feelings of others: for example, when you tell your friend that you are sorry she was fired.

You probably self-disclose for a variety of reasons. Perhaps you feel the need for catharsis, to get rid of guilt feelings, or to confess some wrongdoing. Or you might wish to make yourself look good and so you might self-disclose your good qualities by giving examples of your bravery or compassion or determination. You might also disclose to help the listener, to show the listener, for example, how you dealt with an addiction or succeeded in getting a promotion. And of course you may self-disclose to encourage relationship growth, or to maintain or repair a relationship, or even as a strategy for ending a relationship.

Although self-disclosure may occur as a single message—for example, you tell a stranger on a train that you are thinking about getting a divorce—it is best viewed as a *developing* process in which information is exchanged between people in a relationship over the period of their relationship (Spencer 1993, 1994). Seen as a developing process, we can then appreciate how it changes as the relationship changes, for example, from initial contact through involvement to intimacy and then perhaps to deterioration or dissolution. We can also appreciate how self-disclosure will differ depending on the type of relationship you have with another person, for example, whether the other person is your friend, parent, child, or counselor. Self-disclosure may involve information that you communicate to others freely or that you normally keep hidden. It may supply information ("I earn $45,000) or reveal feelings ("I'm feeling very depressed").

Self-disclosure involves at least one other individual; it cannot be an *intra*personal communication act. To qualify as self-disclosure, the information must be received and understood by another individual. As you can appreciate, self-disclosure can vary from the relatively insignificant ("I'm a Sagittarius") to the highly revealing and deeply personal ("I'm currently in an abusive relationship" or "I'm almost always depressed"). The remaining discussion of this important concept will be more meaningful if you first take the self-disclosure test on page 80.

Factors Influencing Self-Disclosure

Self-disclosure occurs more readily under certain circumstances than others. A few of the more significant factors influencing self-disclosure are identified here.

The Disclosures of Others   Generally, self-disclosure is reciprocal. In any interaction, it is more likely to occur if the other person has previously self-disclosed. This is the **dyadic effect**—what one person in a dyad does, the other does in response. The dyadic effect in self-disclosure takes a kind of spiral form, with each self-disclosure prompting an additional self-disclosure by the other person, which in turn prompts still more self-disclosure, and so on. It's interesting to note that disclosures made in response to the disclosures of others are generally more intimate than those that are not the result of the dyadic effect (Berg and Archer 1983). In some cases, however, we observe a complementary pattern in which one person discloses and the other person listens—a pattern observed, for example, between parents (Berg-Cross, Kidd, and Carr 1990).

This dyadic effect is not universal across cultures. For example, while Americans are likely to follow the dyadic effect and reciprocate with explicit, verbal self-disclosure, Koreans do not (Won-Doornink 1985).

MEDIA & TECHNOLOGY

OUTING

Self-disclosure, as already noted, is a process by which you reveal to other people information about yourself. Although at times you may be forced to self-disclose, we normally think of it as a voluntary process in which you control the amount of information you reveal to others about yourself. There is, however, another side to self-disclosure and that occurs when someone else reveals your hidden self, when someone else takes information from your hidden self and makes it public. Although this third-party disclosure can concern any aspect of one's hidden self, the media have made a special case out of revealing a person's affectional orientation; the process is called "outing" (Gross 1991, 1993).

Outing as a media process began in a relatively obscure gay magazine (*Outweek*). An article, "The Secret Gay Life of Malcolm Forbes," made public Forbes' homosexuality; it "outed" him. On March 3, 1995, the *Wall Street Journal* ran a front page story of Jann Wenner, the multimillionaire owner and publisher of *Rolling Stone, Us, Men's Journal,* and *Family Life.* The story was basically a financial one and focused on the possible effects Wenner's marital breakup would have on his media empire. The headline read: "Jann Wenner's Rift with Wife Shakes Up His Publishing Empire." Somewhat casually noted in the article—without Wenner's permission and against his wishes (Rotello 1995)—was the fact that the new person in Wenner's life was a man. This article, although not the first to discuss Wenner's gay relationship—the *New York Post, Advertising Age,* and *Newsweek* (*Newsweek,* March 20, 1995, p. 58) had run similar stories—it has been singled out because of the prestige of the *Wall Street Journal* and because of the many issues this type of forced disclosure raises.

Many saw this as an invasion of privacy; Wenner's private life is his own and it is up to him whether he wishes to reveal details of his private life. Others saw this as not only appropriate but the only way to deal fairly with gay relationships.

A few weeks later and across the Atlantic the Church of England's third highest ranking cleric, the Bishop of London, David Hope, was pressured by gay and lesbian groups to announce his homosexuality (*New York Times,* March 19, 1995, p. 10). The Bishop called a news conference and condemned the tactics as "seriously intimidatory or worse."

These two cases are especially interesting in terms of self-disclosure and raise the issue of the legitimacy of outing (Gross 1991, 1993; Signorile 1993). In the first case, if Wenner were dating a woman, the media would have mentioned it, but few would have raised the privacy issue. He is a public figure and his divorce is a relevant issue that will likely impact on his financial empire. If the media report on only extramarital heterosexual relationships, is it not at the same time saying that homosexual relationships are illegitimate and that they are not to be spoken of openly?

The David Hope case is different. Here, the Bishop wishes not to discuss his sexuality; he says that it is "ambiguous" and that he is celibate (*New York Times* March 19, 1995, p. 10). Gay organizations in England, however, contend that he is a policy maker in the Church of England. By "outing" him they are preventing him from taking a negative stand against homosexuality as the Church of England has done in the past. The outing serves the purpose of silencing or weakening any potential anti-homosexual stand. It's of interest to note that at a subsequent meeting, the bishops of the Church of England, who represent 70 million members, issued a condemnation of homophobia. They also asked that the church reconsider its generally negative position on lesbian and gay relationships (Morales 1995). For a similar purpose, gay men and lesbians outed Arizona Republican Representative Jim Kolbe after he voted in support of the Defense of Marriage Act. In a sign of things to come, the outing took place largely through the Internet and began within days of his vote (*New York Times* August 3, 1996, p. 6).

When are you most likely to self-disclose? Least likely to self-disclose?

Outing raises an interesting perspective on self-disclosure and the issues discussed here are just a small part of the subject. Further, the concept of outing might legitimately be extended to refer to reveal other hidden information—for example, an athlete's prison record or drug habit, a movie star's ill health or alcoholism, or a politician's friends or financial dealings.

How do you feel about outing? Do you see outing as an invasion of another's privacy? Do you agree or disagree with the British actor, Sir Ian McKellen—an actor who came out on his own—who has argued that the most powerful argument against outing is that it "robs the individual of the joy of taking charge of his or her own life" (McKellen 1996, p. 43)? Do you see it as a legitimate political weapon? If you were the editor of a newspaper, what would be your policy on outing? What guidelines should the media follow in dealing with issues that individuals wish to keep private? At what point does a person lose the right to be considered a private citizen and to privacy?

p. 113

Self Test   *How Willing to Self-Disclose Are You?*

Respond to each of the following questions by indicating the likelihood that you would answer them (and thus disclose such items of information) to other members of this class. Use the following scale:

1 = would definitely self-disclose
2 = would probably self-disclose
3 = don't know
4 = would probably not self-disclose
5 = would definitely not self-disclose

_____ 1. What are your hobbies?
_____ 2. What are your favorite foods?
_____ 3. What is your educational background and how do you feel about it?
_____ 4. What are some of your personal characteristics that you are proud of and that give satisfaction?
_____ 5. What was the happiest moment of your life?
_____ 6. What did your parents do in raising you that you would consider mistakes?
_____ 7. Why do some people dislike you?
_____ 8. What aspects of your personality do you dislike?
_____ 9. With whom have you been sexually intimate?
_____10. With whom would you most like to have a romantic affair?

Thinking Critically About Self-Disclosure

Obviously there are no right or wrong answers to these statements. The major purpose of this test is to stimulate you to think about what you would and would not disclose. These questions were drawn from Jourard's (1971a) list of self-disclosure topics and, according to Jourard, illustrate three levels of disclosure; questions 1–3 illustrate low level intimacy, questions 4–6 moderate levels of intimacy, and questions 7–10 high levels of intimacy. Does your own willingness to self-disclose depend on the intimacy of the topic? For example, would you be most willing to answer questions 1–3 and least willing to answer questions 7–10?

Audience Size   Perhaps because of the many fears about revealing oneself, self-disclosure is more likely to occur in small groups than in large ones. Dyads are perhaps the most common settings. A dyad seems more suitable to self-disclosure because it is easier to deal with one person's reactions and responses than with those of several people. In a dyad, you can attend quite carefully to the responses and, on the basis of support or lack of support, monitor further disclosures, continuing if the situation is supportive and stopping if it is not.

Topic   Certain topics are more likely to be disclosed than others. For example, you would more likely disclose information about your job or hobbies than information about your sex life or financial situation. Self-disclosures about money (for example, the amount of money you owe), personality (for example, the things you feel guilty about), and body (for example, your feelings of sexual adequacy) are less common than self-disclosures about tastes and interests, attitudes and opinions, and work (Jourard 1968, 1971a). Clearly, the topics of money, personality, and body are closely related to your self-concept, and such disclosures are therefore potentially more threatening than are disclosures about tastes in clothing, views on religion, or pressures at work.

Valence   The valence, or positive or negative quality, of a self-disclosure is also significant. Positive self-disclosures are more common than negative self-disclosures and are often made to nonintimates as well as to intimates. You develop a greater attraction for those who engage in positive self-disclosure than for those who engage in negative self-disclosure. This is particularly significant in the early stages of a relationship. Negative self-disclosures to a stranger or even a casual acquaintance are perceived as inappropriate, no doubt because they violate the culture's norms for such communications. This suggests a warning: If your aim is to be perceived as attractive, consider curtailing negative self-disclosures, at least in the early stages of a relationship.

Culture   Culture exerts powerful influence on self-disclosures. For example, people in the United States disclose more than those in Great Britain, Germany, Japan, or Puerto Rico (Gudykunst 1991). American students also disclose more than students from nine different Middle East countries (Jourard 1971a). Singaporean-Chinese students consider more topics to be taboo and inappropriate for self-disclosure than their British colleagues (Goodwin and Lee 1994).

Some cultures view the disclosing of one's inner feelings as a weakness. Some cultures, the United States for example, consider it "out of place" for a man to cry at a happy occasion like a wedding while that same crying would go unnoticed in some Latin cultures. Similarly, in Japan it is considered undesirable to reveal personal information whereas in much of the United States it is not only considered desirable, it is expected (Hall and Hall 1987).

In some cultures—for example, Mexican—there is a strong emphasis on discussing all matters in a positive mode, and this undoubtedly influences the way Mexicans approach self-disclosure as well. Negative self-disclosures, in contrast, are usually made to close intimates and then only after considerable time has elapsed in a relationship. This pattern is consistent with evidence showing that

What factors encourage you to self-disclose? What factors discourage your self-disclosing?

self-disclosure and trust are positively related (Wheeless and Grotz 1977). Additional research finds that the Hispanic reluctance to disclose negative issues (for example, one's positive HIV status) is creating serious problems in preventing and in treating HIV infection (Szapocznik 1995).

There are also important similarities across cultures. For example, people from Great Britain, Germany, the United States, and Puerto Rico are alike in that they are all more apt to disclose personal information such as hobbies and interests, attitudes, and opinions on politics and religion than they are to disclose information on finances, sex, personality, and interpersonal relationships (Jourard 1971a).

The potential rewards and dangers of self-disclosure, then, must be examined in terms of the particular cultural rules. As with all cultural rules, following them brings approval and violating them brings disapproval.

Gender   Most research shows that women disclose more than men but that men and women make negative disclosures about equally (Naifeh and Smith 1984). More specifically, women disclose more than men about their previous romantic relationships, their feelings about their closest same-sex friends, their greatest fears, and what they do not like about their partners (Sprecher 1987). Women also seem to increase the depth of their self-disclosures as the relationship becomes more intimate, while men seem not to change their self-disclosure levels. Men, for example, have more taboo topics that they will not disclose to their friends than do women (Goodwin and Lee 1994). Another difference is that women self-disclose more to members of the extended family than do men (Komarovsky 1964; Argyle and Henderson 1985; Moghaddam, Taylor, and Wright 1993).

Men and women give different reasons for avoiding self-disclosure (Rosenfeld 1979), but they hold the main reason in common: "if I disclose, I might project an image I do not want to project." In a society in which image is so important—in which one's image is often the basis for success or failure—this reason is expected. Other reasons for avoiding self-disclosure, however, are unique to men or women. Lawrence Rosenfeld (1979) sums up males' reasons for self-disclosure avoidance: "If I disclose to you, I might project an image I do not want to project, which could make me look bad and cause me to lose control over you. This might go so far as to affect relationships I have with people other than you." The men's principal objective in avoiding self-disclosure is to maintain control. The general reason women avoid self-disclosure, says Rosenfeld, is that "If I disclose to you, I might project an image I do not want to project, such as my being emotionally ill, which you might use against me and which might hurt our relationship." The women's principal objective for avoiding self-disclosure is "to avoid personal hurt and problems with the relationship."

Receiver Relationship   Your relationship with the person to whom you self-disclose influences the frequency and the likelihood of your self-disclosure (Derlega and Berg 1987). Most studies find that you disclose more often to people who are close to you—your spouse, family, and close friends. In many Latin cultures, for example, in which the extended family is especially close, this tendency may be heightened. Some studies find that you disclose most to persons you like and least to persons you dislike, regardless of how close they are to you. Thus, you

What differences do you find between the self-disclosures of men and women? What cultural differences do you find?

may disclose to a well-liked teacher who is not particularly close and yet not disclose to a brother or sister whom you dislike.

What kinds of self-disclosures are you likely to see on television talk shows? Why do these so engage audiences?

You are more apt to disclose to people you see as accepting, understanding, warm, and supportive. Generally, of course, these are people you are close to and like. Some studies claim that a lasting relationship increases the likelihood of self-disclosure, whereas others find that self-disclosure is heightened in temporary relationships—for example, between "strangers on a train" (Thibaut and Kelley 1959).

As might be expected, husbands and wives self-disclose to each other more than they do to any other person or group of persons. Marital status, at least for men, even affects self-disclosure to friends. Married men disclose significantly less to friends than do unmarried men. The marital status of women, however, does not affect the amount of their self-disclosure to friends. One possible reason for this gender difference, as Jeanne Tschann (1988) observes, may be that women "place a higher value on personal relationships than men do, with the result that women continue friendships even when basic intimacy needs are being met by a spouse, while married men allow friendships to atrophy."

Rewards of Self-Disclosure

The obvious question when the topic of self-disclosure arises is "Why?" Why should anyone self-disclose to anyone else? What is it about this type of communication that merits its being singled out and discussed at length? Research shows

What is the relationship between self-esteem and self-disclosure? For example, are high-self-esteem individuals likely to engage in more- or less-than-average self-disclosure? Are high-self-esteem individuals likely to engage in more positive or more negative disclosures than low-self-esteem individuals? How would you go about answering one or both of these questions?

clearly that the benefits are many. Self-disclosure influences how many friends you have and whether people think you are psychologically stable or maladjusted. It affects your general level of happiness and satisfaction, your level of self-awareness, your psychological and physiological health, and your general effectiveness in interpersonal relationships (Chaikin and Derlega 1974; Derlega, Margulis, and Winstead 1987), as well as the extent to which counselors are liked by their clients (VandeCreek and Angstadt 1985). Let's look at a few of these benefits in more detail.

Knowledge of Self   By self-disclosing, you gain a new perspective on yourself, a deeper understanding of your own behavior. After a thorough review of the self-disclosure and mental-adjustment literature, Paul Cozby (1973), concluded that "persons with positive mental health . . . are characterized by high disclosure to a few significant others and medium disclosure to others in the social environment. Individuals who are poorly adjusted . . . are characterized by either high or low self-disclosure to virtually everyone in the social environment." It is selective self-disclosure, or self-disclosure in moderation, then, that seems to characterize the well-adjusted personality (Bochner 1984).

Ability to Cope   An improved ability to deal with your problems, especially guilt, frequently comes through self-disclosure (Cherry 1991). One of the great fears many people have is that they will not be accepted because of some dark secret, because of something they have done, or because of some feeling or attitude they may have. We feel that these things might be the basis for rejection, so we develop guilt. By self-disclosing such feelings and being supported rather than rejected, we are better prepared to deal with the guilt and perhaps reduce or even eliminate it. Even self-acceptance is difficult without self-disclosure. We accept ourselves largely through the eyes of others. If we feel that others will reject us, we are apt to reject ourselves as well.

Communication Effectiveness   Self-disclosure can improve communication effectiveness. Because you understand another's messages largely to the extent that you understand the person, you can better understand what a person means if you know that person well. You can tell what certain nuances mean, know when that person is joking, recognize when sarcasm is prompted by fear and when by resentment, and so on. Self-disclosure seems an essential condition for getting to know and for feeling comfortable with another individual.

Can you think of any relationship problems that might arise when self-disclosure is extremely high? Extremely low? How would you describe the relationship between self-disclosure and meaningfulness for one of your friendships or romantic relationships?

Meaningfulness of Relationships   Self-disclosure may help you achieve a closer relationship with the person to whom you self-disclose (Schmidt and Cornelius 1987). Couples who engage in significant self-disclosure are found to remain together longer than couples who do not (Sprecher 1987) and couples who self-disclose honestly have higher marital satisfaction (Dickson-Markman 1984). Progressive self-disclosure among couples, along with appropriate responding to the disclosures of the other person, significantly increases the chances of relationship development (Falk and Wagner 1985). There is some evidence, however, that shows that relationship satisfaction is greatest when self-disclosure is moderate and that satisfaction is significantly less with low levels and high levels of disclosure (Gilbert 1975).

Interestingly enough, your affection for your partner increases when you self-disclose. Men, but not women, also increase their affection for their partner when the partner self-discloses. This finding seems to reinforce the notion that women, at least in some cases, do not respond positively to the disclosures of men (Sprecher 1987).

Physiological Health   People who self-disclose are less vulnerable to illness (Pennebacker 1991). Self-disclosure seems to protect the body from the damaging stresses that accompany nondisclosure. For example, bereavement over the death of someone very close is linked to physical illness for those who bear it alone and in silence but is unrelated to any physical problems for those who share their grief with others. Similarly, women who have suffered sexual trauma experience a variety of illnesses (among them headaches and stomach problems). Women who keep these experiences to themselves, however, suffer much more than those who talk with others about these traumas.

Dangers of Self-Disclosure: Risks Ahead

As is usually the case, when the potential rewards are great so are the risks. Self-disclosure is no exception; the risks can be personal, relational, and professional and can be considerable. Weigh these potential risks carefully before engaging in significant self-disclosure.

Personal Risks   If you self-disclose aspects of your life that are greatly at variance with the values of those to whom you disclose, you may be met by rejection from even the closest friends and family members. Men and women who disclose that they have AIDS, for example, may find their friends and family no longer wanting to be quite as close as before.

Relational Risks   Even in close and long-lasting relationships, self-disclosure can cause problems. "Uncensored candor," notes interpersonal researcher Arthur Bochner (1984), "is a bad idea." Total self-disclosure may prove threatening to a relationship by causing a decrease in mutual attraction, trust, or any of the bonds holding the individuals together. Self-disclosures concerning infidelity, romantic fantasies, past indiscretions or crimes, lies, or hidden weaknesses and fears could easily have such negative effects.

What specific risks might the disclosure of HIV+ status entail in your community? At your school? At your place of employment? How would the benefits of disclosure compare with the risks?

Professional Risks   The extensive media coverage of the gays and lesbians in the military who are coming out in protest of the "don't ask, don't tell" policy amply illustrates the professional dangers that self-disclosure may entail. Openly gay and lesbian military personnel, as well as those in education, fire departments, law enforcement, or health care agencies—to cite just a few examples—may find themselves confined to desk jobs, prevented from further advancement, or even charged with criminal behavior and fired. Similarly, politicians who disclose that they have been seeing a psychiatrist may later face loss of party and voter support. Teachers who disclose former or current drug use or cohabitation with students may find themselves denied tenure, teaching at undesirable hours, and eventually falling victim to "budget cuts." Further, teachers or students who, in the supportive atmosphere of their interpersonal communication course, disclose details about their sex life or financial condition or reveal self-doubts, anxieties, and fantasies may find some less-than-sympathetic listeners later using that information against them.

In making your choice between disclosing and not disclosing, keep in mind—in addition to the advantages and dangers already noted—the irreversible nature of communication, discussed in Unit 2. Regardless of how many times you may try to qualify something or take it back, once you have said something you cannot withdraw it. You cannot erase the conclusions and inferences listeners have made on the basis of your disclosures. This is not to suggest that you therefore refrain from self-disclosing, but only that it is important to remember that communication is irreversible.

Self-Disclosure Guidelines

Because self-disclosure is so important and so delicate a matter, guidelines are offered here for (1) deciding whether and how to self-disclose and (2) responding to the disclosures of others.

Guidelines for Making Self-Disclosures   In addition to weighing the potential rewards and dangers of self-disclosure already discussed, consider the following guidelines; they will help raise the right questions before you make what must be *your* decision.

Consider the Motivation for the Self-Disclosure   Self-disclosure should be motivated by a concern for the relationship, for the others involved, and for oneself. Some people self-disclose out of a desire to hurt the listener. Persons who tell their parents that they never loved them or that the parents hindered rather than helped their emotional development may be disclosing out of a desire to hurt and perhaps punish rather than to improve the relationship. Neither, of course, should self-disclosure be used to punish oneself, perhaps because of some guilt feeling or unresolved conflict. Self-disclosure should serve a useful and productive function for all persons involved.

Consider the Appropriateness of the Self-Disclosure   Self-disclosure should be appropriate to the context and to the relationship between you and your listener. Before making any significant self-disclosure, ask whether this is the right time and place. Could a better time and place be arranged? Ask, too, whether this self-disclosure is appropriate to the relationship. Generally, the more intimate the disclosures, the closer the relationship should be. It is probably best to resist intimate disclosures (especially negative ones) with nonintimates or casual acquaintances, or in the early stages of a relationship.

Consider the Disclosures of the Other Person   During your disclosures, give the other person a chance to reciprocate with his or her own disclosures. If reciprocal disclosures are not made, reassess your own self-disclosures. It may be a signal that for this person at this time and in this context, your disclosures are not welcome or appropriate. So it is generally best to disclose gradually and in small increments. When you disclose too rapidly and all at once, you can't monitor your listener's responses and retreat if they are not positive enough. Further, you prevent the listener from responding with his or her own disclosures and thereby upset the natural balance that is so helpful in this kind of communication exchange.

Consider the Possible Burdens Self-Disclosure Might Entail   Carefully weigh the potential problems that you may incur as a result of your disclosure. Can you afford to lose your job if you disclose your prison record? Are you willing to risk relational difficulties if you disclose your infidelities? Also, ask yourself whether you are making unreasonable demands on the listener. For example, consider the person who swears his or her mother-in-law to secrecy and then self-discloses having an affair with a neighbor. This disclosure places an unfair burden on the mother-in-law, who is now torn between breaking her promise of secrecy or allowing her child to believe a lie. Parents often place unreasonable burdens on their children by self-disclosing relationship problems, financial difficulties, or self-doubts without realizing that the children may be too young or too emotionally involved to deal effectively with this information.

What other guidelines would you suggest be followed in deciding whether or not to self-disclose?

Guidelines for Responding to Self-Disclosures   When someone discloses to you, it is usually a sign of trust and affection. In serving this most important receiver function, keep the following guidelines in mind. These guidelines will help you facilitate the disclosures of another person.

Practice the Skills of Effective and Active Listening   The skills of effective listening (Unit 7) are especially important when listening to self-disclosures: listen actively, listen for different levels of meaning, listen with empathy, and listen with an open mind. Paraphrase the speaker so that you can be sure you understand both the thoughts and the feelings communicated. Express an understanding of the speaker's feelings to allow the speaker the opportunity to see them more objectively and through the eyes of another. Ask questions to ensure your own understanding and to signal your interest and attention.

Support and Reinforce the Discloser   Express support for the person during and after the disclosures. Try refraining from evaluation. Concentrate on understanding and empathizing with the discloser. Allow the discloser to choose the pace; don't rush the discloser with the too-frequent "So how did it all end?" response. Make your supportiveness clear to the discloser through your verbal and nonverbal responses: Maintain eye contact, lean toward the speaker, ask relevant questions, and echo the speaker's thoughts and feelings.

Under what circumstances is it appropriate to tell a person that you really don't want to hear these disclosures? How could you do this diplomatically?

Keep the Disclosures Confidential   When a person discloses to you, it is because she or he wants you to know the feelings and thoughts that are communicated. If you reveal these disclosures to others, negative effects are inevitable. Revealing what was said will probably inhibit future disclosures by this individual in general and to you in particular, and it is likely that your relationship will suffer considerably. But most important, betraying a confidence is unfair; it debases what could be and should be a meaningful interpersonal experience.

Don't Use the Disclosures Against the Person   Many self-disclosures expose some kind of vulnerability or weakness. If you later turn around and use disclosures against the person, you betray the confidence and trust invested in you. Regardless of how angry you might get, resist the temptation to use the disclosures of others as weapons—the relationship is sure to suffer and may never fully recover.

You may wish to try weighing the rewards and dangers of the self-disclosure suggestions offered here and respond to the following brief cases. In making your decision, consider such questions as these: Will the self-disclosure help accomplish what the person wishes to accomplish? Is the self-disclosure appropriate? To the listener? To the speaker-listener relationship? (For example, in situation B, Tom wants to disclose on the telephone. Is this appropriate?)

Mary and Jim have been married for 12 years. Mary has been honest about most things and has self-disclosed a great deal to Jim—about her past romantic encounters, her fears, her insecurities, her ambitions, and so on. Yet Jim doesn't reciprocate. He almost never shares his feelings and has told Mary almost nothing about his life before they met. Mary wonders whether she should continue to self-disclose or whether she should begin to limit her disclosures.

Sara has been living in a romantic relationship with another woman for the past several years. Sara wants to tell her parents, with whom she has been very close throughout her life, but can't seem to get up the courage to do so. She decides to tell them in a long letter.

A mother of two teenage children (one boy, one girl) has been feeling guilty for the past year over a romantic affair she had with her brother-in-law while her husband was in prison. She and her husband have been divorced for the last few months. She wants to self-disclose this affair and her guilt to her children.

Martin, a college student, recently found out he is HIV positive. Although he has sought the support of various groups, he wonders if he should tell his parents. His parents are in their 70s and relatively uneducated; they know little about the problems associated with HIV infection. He wants to tell them, but he fears that they will be unable to deal effectively with the news. He also fears that they will reject him, perhaps out of fear, perhaps out of their belief that AIDS is a disease that "good people" don't get.

Summary	U N I T I N B R I E F

A RETURN TO OBJECTIVES:

In this unit we explored the self in interpersonal communication, focusing on four basic questions: (1) What is self-concept and how does it develop? (2) What is self-awareness and how might it be increased? (3) What is self-esteem and how might it be increased? (4) What is self-disclosure? What factors influence self-disclosure? What are its potential rewards and dangers? And what guidelines are useful in making decisions to self-disclose and in listening to the disclosures of others?

Self-concept	Self-awareness	Self-esteem	Self-disclosure
Self-concept is the image you have of who you are. **Sources of self-concept:** ◆ Others' images of you. ◆ Social comparisons. ◆ Your own interpretations and evaluations.	**Self-awareness** is your knowledge of yourself; the extent to which you know who you are. **The four selves:** ◆ *Open self:* Information known to self and others. ◆ *Blind self:* Information known only to others. ◆ *Hidden self:* Information known only to self. ◆ *Unknown self:* Information known to neither self nor others. **Increasing self-awareness:** ◆ Ask yourself about yourself. ◆ Listen to others. ◆ Actively seek information about yourself. ◆ See your different selves. ◆ Increase your open self.	**Self-esteem** is the value you place on yourself; your perceived self-worth. **Increasing self-esteem:** ◆ Attack your self-destructive beliefs. ◆ Engage in self-affirmation. ◆ Seek out nourishing people. ◆ Work on projects that will result in success.	**Definition:** Revealing information about yourself to others, usually information normally hidden. **Influencing factors:** Disclosures of others, audience size, topic, valence, culture, gender, receiver relationship. **Rewards:** Self-knowledge, ability to cope, communication effectiveness, meaningfulness of relationships, physiological health. **Dangers:** Personal risks, relational risks, professional risks, irreversibility. **Guidelines:** ◆ Self-Disclosing: Consider motivation, appropriateness, the disclosures of others, and the possible burdens imposed. ◆ Responding to disclosures of others: Listen effectively, support and reinforce the discloser, keep disclosures confidential, do not use disclosures as weapons.

UNIT

5

Apprehension and Assertiveness

Unit Topics	Unit Objectives
	After completing this unit, you should be able to:
Speaker Apprehension The Nature of Speaker Apprehension Theories of Speaker Apprehension and Its Management Empowering Apprehensives	1. Define *communication apprehension* 2. Explain the major theories of speaker apprehension and the management strategies suggested by them 3. Explain the suggestions for empowering apprehensives
Assertiveness Principles for Increasing Assertiveness	4. Define and distinguish among *assertiveness*, *non-assertiveness*, and *aggressiveness* 5. Explain the principles for increasing assertiveness

---

EXPERIENTIAL LEARNING VEHICLE

Vehicle No. 6, "Analyzing Assertiveness," pp. 445–446, will prove useful for discussion on and for role-playing assertiveness.

Among the most important interpersonal communication skills are those of reducing communication apprehension and increasing assertiveness. Many of us are apprehensive (or shy or reticent) in different communication situations and to different degrees. Similarly, many of us are reluctant to assert ourselves, to speak up for our rights. In this unit, the related issues of apprehension and assertiveness are addressed with a view to increasing our understanding of these qualities and to enabling us to manage our own apprehension and assertiveness more effectively.

Speaker Apprehension

Speaker apprehension is one of the most extensively researched variables in the entire field of interpersonal communication and so we know a great deal about this major problem that many people experience. First, we look at the nature of speaker apprehension and define it and look at the factors that influence our level of apprehension. Second, we look at some of the theories of apprehension and how, on the basis of these theories, we can more effectively manage or control it.

This discussion will prove more valuable to you if you first take the brief self-test titled "How Apprehensive Are You?"

The Nature of Speaker Apprehension

Now that you have a general idea of your own communication apprehension, it might be of interest to note that "communication apprehension is probably the most common handicap . . . suffered by people in contemporary American society" (McCroskey and Wheeless 1976). According to surveys of college students, between 10 percent and 20 percent suffer "severe, debilitating communication apprehension," while another 20 percent suffer from "communication apprehension to a degree substantial enough to interfere to some extent with their normal functioning."

How would you characterize your own apprehension in terms of trait and state?

Definitions   The term **communication apprehension** (and shyness, unwillingness to communicate, stage fright, reticence) refers to a state of fear or anxiety about communication interaction. People develop negative feelings and predict negative results as a function of engaging in communication interactions. They feel that whatever gain would accrue from engaging in communication would be outweighed by the fear. To those with high communication apprehension, the communication interaction isn't worth the fear it engenders.

Trait apprehension refers to fear of communication generally, regardless of the specific situation. It appears in dyadic, small-group, public speaking, and mass communication situations. **State apprehension**, in contrast, is specific to a given communication situation. For example, a speaker may fear public speaking but have no difficulty with dyadic communication, or a speaker may fear job interviews but have no fear of public speaking. State apprehension is extremely common; it is experienced by most people in some situations.

Speaker apprehension exists on a continuum. People are not either apprehensive or unapprehensive. We all experience some degree of apprehension. Some people are extremely apprehensive and become incapacitated in a communication situation. They suffer a great deal in a society oriented, as ours is, around

How Apprehensive Are You?

Self Test

This questionnaire is composed of 6 statements concerning your feelings about communicating in interpersonal conversations. Please indicate in the space provided the degree to which each statement applies to you by marking whether you

1 = strongly agree
2 = agree
3 = are undecided
4 = disagree
5 = strongly disagree

There are no right or wrong answers. Many of the statements are similar to other statements; do not be concerned about this. Work quickly; record your first impression.

_____1. While participating in a conversation with a new acquaintance, I feel very nervous.
_____2. I have no fear of speaking up in conversations.
_____3. Ordinarily I am very tense and nervous in conversations.
_____4. Ordinarily I am very calm and relaxed in conversations.
_____5. While conversing with a new acquaintance, I feel very relaxed.
_____6. I'm afraid to speak up in conversations.

Thinking Critically About Interpersonal Apprehension

To compute your score, merely add or subtract your scores for each item as indicated below. (Note that a base of 18 is used in the formulas; this is done so that all scores come out as positive numbers.)

18 plus scores for items 2, 4, and 5
minus scores for items 1, 3, and 6

A score above 18 shows some degree of apprehension. Of course, conversations vary widely in the degree to which they may lead to apprehension. For which types do you experience the greatest fear? The least fear? Do others experience apprehension when talking to you?

Source: James C. McCroskey, *Introduction to Rhetorical Communication,* 6th ed. (Englewood Cliffs, NJ: Prentice-Hall, 1993).

communication and in which one's success depends on the ability to communicate effectively. Others are so mildly apprehensive that they appear to experience no fear at all when confronted by communication situations; they actively seek out communication experiences and rarely feel any significant apprehension. Most of us fall between these two extremes.

In what communication situations (interpersonal, group, or public) are you most apprehensive? Why do you suppose this is so?

Culture and Speaker Apprehension   Apprehension, shyness, and the willingness to communicate generally varies from one culture to another (Breidenstein-Cutspec and Goering 1989). For example, in one study of shyness Israelis were found to be the least shy (only 24% reported they were currently experiencing shyness, compared to, for example, Mexicans (39%), Americans (42%), Germans (50%), Taiwanese (55%), and Japanese (60%) (Carducci and Zimbardo 1995). In a study of the willingness to communicate, American college students indicated the highest willingness to communicate, whereas students from Micronesia indicated the lowest. Micronesian students also indicated the highest degree of shyness while, in this study, Puerto Ricans reported the lowest (McCroskey and Richmond 1990).

When the interpersonal communication is intercultural communication additional uncertainty, fear, and anxiety, all of which are intimately related to speaker apprehension (Stephan and Stephan 1985), may be experienced. When you are in an intercultural situation—say your coworkers are largely people of cultures very different from your own—you are more uncertain about the situation and about their possible responses and you are more likely to experience heightened speaker apprehension. Not surprisingly, most people react negatively to high uncertainty and develop a decreased attraction for these other people (Gudykunst and Nishida 1984; Gudykunst, Yang, and Nishida 1985). When you are sure of the situation and can predict what will happen, you are more likely to feel comfortable and at ease. But when the situation is uncertain and you cannot predict what will happen, you become more apprehensive (Gudykunst and Kim 1992).

Intercultural situations can also engender fear. You might, for example, fear saying something that will prove offensive or revealing your own prejudices or ethnocentrism. The fear easily translates into apprehension.

Intercultural situations can also create anxiety, a feeling very similar to apprehension. Anxiety may be felt for a number of reasons (Stephan and Stephan 1985). For example, your prior relationships with members of a culturally different group will influence your apprehension. If your prior relationships were few or if they were unpleasant, then you are likely to experience greater apprehension when dealing with these members than if these prior experiences were numerous and positive.

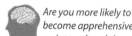 *Are you more likely to become apprehensive in an intercultural situation than in a situation in which everyone is culturally similar to you? How would you describe the reasons for your specific intercultural apprehension?*

Your thoughts and feelings about the group will also influence your apprehension. For example, if you have little knowledge of the other culture, hold stereotypes and prejudices, are high in ethnocentrism, or if you feel that you are very different from these others, then you are likely to experience more apprehension than if you saw these people as similar to you.

The situation you are in can also exert influence. If, for example, you feel that members of another group are competing with you or evaluating you, then you are likely to experience more apprehension than if the situation were more cooperative and equal. Similarly, unstructured and ambiguous situations create more anxiety because you aren't quite sure what is expected of you. Also, your status relative to the others in the group will influence your anxiety; if you are lower in status, you are likely to experience greater anxiety than if you were higher in status.

Apprehensive Behaviors   Generally, apprehension leads to a decrease in the frequency, strength, and likelihood of engaging in communication transactions. High apprehensives avoid communication situations and, when forced to participate, do so as little as possible. This reluctance to communicate shows itself in a variety of forms. For example, those with high apprehension are found to be less willing to communicate, to volunteer, and to work with the terminally ill than were those who were low in apprehension (Ayres and Hopf 1995). In small group situations, apprehensives not only talk less but also avoid the seats of influence—for example, those in the group leader's direct line of sight. High apprehensives are less likely to be seen as leaders in small group situations regardless of their actual behaviors. Even in classrooms, they avoid seats where they can be easily called on, and they maintain little direct eye contact with the instructor, especially when a question is likely to be asked. Related to this is that apprehensives

How might apprehension play a role in your professional life? To what extent might apprehension affect you adversely? Might it help you?

have more negative attitudes toward school, earn poorer grades, and are more likely to drop out of college (McCroskey, Booth-Butterfield, and Payne 1989).

Both teachers and students also consider apprehensives to be less desirable social choices. Apprehensives disclose little and avoid occupations with heavy communication demands (for example, teaching or public relations). Within their occupation, they are less desirous of advancement, largely because of the associated increase in communication. High apprehensives feel less satisfied with their jobs, probably because they are less successful in advancing and in developing interpersonal relationships. High apprehensives are even less likely to get job interviews. In the United States we value "rugged individualism and the conquering of new environments, whether in outer space or in overseas markets. Personal attributes held high in our social esteem are leadership, assertiveness, dominance, independence, and risk taking. Hence a stigma surrounding shyness" (Carducci and Zimbardo 1995, p. 66).

Apprehensives also engage more in steady dating, a finding that is not unexpected. One of the most difficult communication situations is asking for a first date. Consequently, once a dating relationship has been established, the apprehensive is reluctant to give it up and go through the anxiety of another first date and another get-acquainted period.

All this does not mean that apprehensives are ineffective or unhappy people. Most apprehensives have learned or can learn to deal with their communication anxiety.

Influences on Communication Apprehension   Research has identified several factors that increase communication apprehension (McCroskey and Daly 1987; Beatty 1988; Richmond and McCroskey 1989). A knowledge of these factors will help you to increase your understanding and control of your own apprehension.

◆ Degree of evaluation. The more you perceive the situation as one in which you will be evaluated, the greater your apprehension is likely to be.

Shyness researchers Carducci and Zimbardo (1996, p. 66) have observed: "The people given the most attention in our society are expressive, active, and sociable. We single out as heroes, actors, athletes, politicians, television personalities, and rock stars—people expert at calling attention to themselves: Madonna, Rosanne, Howard Stern. People who are most likely to be successful are those who are able to obtain attention and feel comfortable with it." What do you think of this observation? What evidence in support or in contradiction can you adduce?

Employment interviews, for example, provoke anxiety largely because they are highly evaluative.

♦ Subordinate status. When you feel that others are better communicators than you are or that they know more than you do, your apprehension increases. For example, shy students report particular difficulty in speaking with authorities (Zimbardo 1977).

♦ Degree of conspicuousness. The more conspicuous you are, the more likely you are to feel apprehensive. This is why delivering a speech to a large audience is more anxiety provoking than speaking in a small group; you are more conspicuous before the large group—you stand out, and all attention is on you.

♦ Degree of unpredictability. The more unpredictable the situation, the greater your apprehension is likely to be. Ambiguous and new situations are unpredictable; you cannot know beforehand what they will be like, hence you become anxious. A similar condition seems to increase your shyness when interacting with strangers; 70 percent of shy students surveyed said they were especially shy with strangers (Zimbardo 1977).

♦ Degree of dissimilarity. When you feel you have little in common with your listeners, you are likely to feel anxious.

♦ Prior successes and failures. Your experience in similar situations greatly influences the way you respond to new ones. Prior success generally (though not always) reduces apprehension, whereas prior failure generally (though not always) increases apprehension. There is no mystery here: Prior success says that you can succeed this time as well; prior failure warns that you may fail again.

♦ Lack of communication skills and experience. If you lack skills in typing, you can hardly expect to type very well. If you have never asked for a raise and have no idea how to go about doing it, for example, it is perfectly reasonable that you will feel apprehension.

What do you think has contributed to your current level of communication apprehension? For example, can you identify early childhood influences?

Theories of Speaker Apprehension and Its Management

What causes speaker apprehension? Can it be controlled or managed effectively? Following communication researchers Virginia Richmond and James McCroskey (1996) we can distinguish three theoretical (and eminently practical) approaches to understanding speaker apprehension and how it may be managed or controlled: cognitive restructuring, systematic desensitization, and skill acquisition.

Cognitive Restructuring   This theory holds that your own unrealistic beliefs generate a fear of failure. Because you set yourself unachievable goals (Everyone must love me, I have to be thoroughly competent, I have to be the best in everything), you logically fear failure. This fear of failure (and the irrational beliefs behind it) are at the foundation of your apprehension (for example, Markway, Carmin, Pollard, and Flynn 1992). Cognitive restructuring, then, advises you to change your irrational beliefs and substitute more rational ones (It would be nice if everyone loved me but I don't need that to survive. I can fail. Although it would be nice, I don't have to be the best in everything.) Your last step is to practice your new more rational beliefs (Ellis and Harper 1975; Ellis 1988).

The process may go something like this: Unrealistic beliefs give rise to anxiety because you know you can never achieve these unrealistically high goals and that you'll fail at some point. There's not a speaker in the world who wouldn't fail given these unrealistic beliefs. You then focus on the inevitable failure; you can almost see yourself failing. This image leads to a loss of confidence and further visions of failure.

A special type of cognitive restructuring is **performance visualization,** designed specifically to reduce the outward manifestations of speaker apprehension and also to reduce negative thinking (Ayres and Hopf 1993; Ayres, Ayres, Grudzinskas, Hopf, Kelly, and Wilcox 1995). This technique, not surprisingly, has been shown to be significantly more effective with those who can create vivid mental images (Ayres, Hopf, and Ayres 1994). The first part of performance visualization is to develop a positive attitude and a positive self-perception. This involves visualizing yourself in the role of the effective public speaker. Visualize yourself walking to the front of the room—fully and totally confident. You scan the audience and slowly begin your speech. Throughout the speech you are fully in control of the situation. The audience is in rapt attention and as you finish, bursts into wild applause. Throughout this visualization, avoid all negative thoughts.

As you visualize yourself giving an effective public speech, take special note of how you walk, look at your listeners, handle your notes, respond to questions, and especially how you feel about the whole experience.

The second part of performance visualization is designed to help you model your performance on that of an especially effective speaker. Here you would view a particularly competent public speaker on video and make a mental movie of it. As you review the actual and the mental movie, you begin to shift yourself into the role of the speaker. You, in effect, become this effective speaker.

Systematic Desensitization   Systematic desensitization is a technique for dealing with a variety of fears including those involved in public communication (Wolpe 1957). The general assumption of systematic desensitization is that apprehension was learned, and because it was learned, it can be unlearned. The procedure involves creating a hierarchy of behaviors leading up to the desired but feared behavior (say, speaking before an audience). One specific hierarchy might look like this:

- ◆ Giving a speech in class;
- ◆ Introducing another speaker to the class;
- ◆ Speaking in a group in front of the class;
- ◆ Answering a question in class;
- ◆ Asking a question in class.

You would begin at the bottom of this hierarchy and rehearse this behavior mentally over a period of days until you can clearly visualize asking a question in class without any uncomfortable anxiety. Once you can accomplish this, you can move to the second level. Here you would visualize the somewhat more threatening, answering a question. Once you can do this, you can move to the third level, and so on until you get to the desired behavior.

Skill Acquisition   The third general approach to speaker apprehension holds that you develop apprehension largely because you see yourself as having inadequate skills. So, you logically fear failing. The strategy for managing apprehension, therefore, is to acquire the specific skills involved in any given behavior. For example, the skills for business communication would involve a number of more specific skills. These more specific skills would be mastered

Can you identify unrealistic beliefs that you have about your own interpersonal behaviors? Your interpersonal relationships? What problems do these cause?

Can you create a hierarchy of at least ten behaviors that vary in terms of your level of apprehension? Begin with behavior 1, identifying a situation in which you have little to no apprehension, and then work up to behavior 10, identifying a situation in which you have great apprehension. What distinguishes the situations with low numbers from situations with high numbers?

individually and then put together into the process of, say, talking with subordinates and supervisors. For example, some such skills would include presenting a positive self-image, complimenting the work of others, criticizing tactfully another's performance, and so on. Other types of skills might be using deep breathing to relax yourself, creative visualization so that you can see yourself as successful, or self-affirmation to help you feel more positively about yourself.

With mastery, the task—in this case business communication, but it could just as logically be any task—becomes less forbidding and hence less anxiety provoking. With mastery also come successful experiences. These successes help build your confidence and further lessen anxiety. It is probably impossible to eliminate communication apprehension. However, we can manage apprehension effectively so that it does not debilitate us or prevent us from achieving goals that require us to communicate in a variety of situations. Here are some additional suggestions for building skills:

◆ Prepare and practice. The more preparation and practice you put into something, the more comfortable you feel with it and, consequently, the less apprehension you feel. If you are apprehensive telling jokes, then practice the joke you wish to tell. Rehearse it mentally and perhaps aloud until you are comfortable with it.

◆ Focus on success. Think positively. Concentrate your energies on doing the very best job you can in whatever situation you are in. Visualize yourself succeeding, and you stand a good chance of doing just that. Remember that having failed in the past does not mean that you must fail again in the future. You now have new skills and new experiences, and they increase your chances for success.

◆ Familiarize yourself with the situation. The more familiar you are with the situation, the better. The reason is simple: When you are familiar with the situation and with what will be expected of you, you are better able to predict what will happen. This will reduce ambiguity and make you feel more comfortable.

How will apprehension affect your professional life? Your relational life?

◆ Put communication apprehension in perspective. The world will not cave in if you do not succeed in any communication situation.

◆ Try to relax. Apprehension is reduced when you are physically and mentally relaxed. For example, knowing that you have acquired new communication skills and that you have prepared yourself for the task of asking for a raise should help alleviate your normal anxiety.

◆ Acquire communication skills and experience. Acquire whatever experience will help you master the tasks at which you want to be effective.

Empowering Apprehensives

At the same time that you want to manage and perhaps lessen your own apprehension, consider the values and means of empowering others to manage and better control their apprehension or shyness. Here are some suggestions based largely on the insights of shyness researchers Carducci and Zimbardo (1996):

◆ Don't overprotect the shy person, especially the shy child. If you constantly rush to the child's aid every time he or she experiences social anxiety, the child will never learn how to cope with it. Instead, be supportive (indirectly). Nudge, instead of push, the child (or the adult) to try out new communication situations.

◆ Demonstrate your understanding and empathy for the other person's shyness. Don't minimize their fear of communication situations, something those with little apprehension often do. Practice active listening, should you sense they wish to discuss their anxiety and shyness.

◆ Help the shy person to develop self-esteem. Often apprehensives lack self-esteem and may feel inadequate in social situations. Expressing positiveness toward them may help.

◆ In social gatherings with shy people make sure you don't monopolize the conversation and that you give the shy person opportunities to speak; ask their opinions.

◆ When appropriate, try to steer the conversation in the direction of the shy person's expertise and area of competence.

◆ Avoid making the shy person the center of attention. That is exactly what they do not want.

◆ And never make their shyness the topic of a group conversation. Saying, "Oh Jane; she's so bright but she's so shy" only makes it more difficult for Jane to even open her mouth.

Read the following "Dear Abby" letter. Do the sentiments in this letter suggest any changes in your behaviors in dealing with shy people?

D E A R   A B B Y

Thank you for printing the letter from the teenage girl who was struggling with shyness.

I, too, am a very shy and quiet person. I've been this way all my life. I can't tell you how many people have said, "You sure are quiet." I can't imagine anyone going up to a person and saying, "You sure have a big mouth!"

I would like to reassure everyone that I know I am quiet, but I am a very well-adjusted, happy person who enjoys being quiet. I am quiet because I have nothing to say, and I don't want to fill the quietness with empty chatter. I would find it quite exhausting to make small talk, or worse yet, try to be the life of the party, or the center of attention.

In the past, I have tried to talk more and be more outgoing so people would like me better, but it did not become me . . . it was not natural.

It has taken me years to like myself just the way I am. I have many friends who like me just the way I am, so to the others who are disturbed by my quietness and shy personality, please leave me alone. Please don't try to make me feel that there is something wrong with me because I am different from you who feel compelled to talk all the time.

Abby, if you print this—and I hope you do—you will be doing an enormous favor to all the shy, quiet people who read your column. There are more of us than you could possibly imagine.

—Quiet in Atlanta

Dear Quiet:
Here's your letter, which should make a highly audible statement, and will put an end to that question—"Why are you so quiet?"

"Small Talk a Big Problem for Shy People" taken from a *Dear Abby* column by Abigail Van Buren. Dist. by Universal Press Syndicate. Reprinted with permission. All rights reserved.

Assertiveness is often thought of as being especially useful in business or professional communication, and yet it is equally important among friends, lovers, and family members. How assertive are you with those close to you? How assertive are you with casual associates?

Assertiveness

A number of interesting experiments illustrate just how passive many people have become (Moriarty 1975). In one experiment, subjects taking a psychological test were placed near a confederate of the experimenter's who played loud rock-and-roll music during the test. Of the 20 subjects, 16 made no comment at all. Even when the students were told they would receive mild electric shocks for wrong answers, 16 of the 20 subjects still said nothing to the music player. In one variation, experimenters approached people after they had left a phone booth; the experimenters claimed they had lost a ring and asked the people leaving the phone booth whether they would mind emptying their pockets to see if they had perhaps picked it up. Of the 20 adult males who were approached, 16 emptied their pockets (80 percent). When the experiment was repeated using graduate students, 20 of 24 men (83 percent) emptied their pockets. "I believe," concludes Moriarty, "that many of us have accepted the idea that few things are worth getting into a hassle about, especially with strangers. And I believe this is particularly true of younger people."

Do you see cultural differences in attitudes toward assertiveness or in actual assertive behaviors?

Do realize that as with speaker apprehension, there will be wide cultural differences when it comes to assertiveness. For example, the values of assertiveness are more likely to be extolled in individualistic cultures than in collectivist cultures. Assertiveness will be valued more by those cultures which stress competition, individual success, and independence. It will be valued much less by those cultures which stress cooperation, group success, and interdependence of all members on each other. American students, for example, are found to be significantly more assertive than Japanese or Korean students (Thompson, Klopf, and Ishii 1991; Thompson and Klopf 1991, 1995). Thus, situations that may call for assertiveness in one culture and may prove an effective strategy, may, in another culture, create problems. Assertiveness with an elder in many Asian and Hispanic cultures may be seen as insulting and disrespectful.

Assertiveness in interpersonal communication may be further explained by examining the distinctions among nonassertiveness, aggressiveness, and assertive communication.

Nonassertiveness Nonassertiveness comes in two forms: situational and generalized. **Situational nonassertiveness** refers to a lack of assertiveness only in certain kinds of situations—for example, those that create a great deal of anxiety or those in which authority must be exercised.

Generalized nonassertiveness, as the term implies, is nonassertive behavior that is typically demonstrated. People who exhibit this behavior are timid and reserved and are unable to assert their rights regardless of the situation. These people do what others tell them to do—parents, employers, and the like—without questioning and without concern for what is best for them. When these persons' rights are infringed upon, they do nothing about it and sometimes accuse themselves of being nonaccepting. Generalized nonassertive persons often ask permission from others to do what it is their perfect right to do.

In what situations are you nonassertive? Aggressive? Assertive? What is it about these situations that leads you to behave differently?

Aggressiveness Aggressiveness also comes in two forms. **Situationally aggressive** people are aggressive only under certain conditions or in certain situations. For example, they may become aggressive after being taken advantage of over a long period or by someone for whom they have done a great deal. These people are normally not aggressive; only in certain situations do they behave aggressively.

Generally aggressive people, however, meet all or at least most situations with aggressive behavior. These people seem in charge of almost all situations; regardless of what is going on, they take over. They appear to think little of the opinions, values, or beliefs of others, and yet they are extremely sensitive to criticisms of their own behavior. Consequently, they frequently get into arguments with others and find that they have few friends. They think little of others, and others think little of them.

What's your initial impression of nonassertive people? Of aggressive people? How do these people act to communicate their lack of assertiveness or their aggressiveness?

Assertive Communication Assertive communication—communication that enables you to act in your own best interests without denying or infringing upon the rights of others—is the desired alternative. Assertive individuals are willing to assert their own rights, but unlike their aggressive counterparts, they do not hurt others in the process. Assertive individuals speak their minds and welcome others doing likewise. In *Your Perfect Right* (1970), the first book on assertiveness training, Robert Alberti and Michael Emmons note that "behavior which enables a person to act in his own best interest, to stand up for himself without undue anxiety, to express his honest feelings comfortably, or to exercise his own rights without denying the rights of others we call *assertive behavior.*" Furthermore, "the assertive individual is fully in charge of himself in interpersonal relationships, feels confident and capable without cockiness or hostility, is basically spontaneous in the expression of feelings and emotions, and is generally looked up to and admired by others." Surely, this is the picture of an effective individual. Not surprisingly, it is the picture of the person who experiences high job satisfaction (Rabin and Zelner 1992) and possesses greater dating skills (Prisbell 1986).

Four characteristics define assertiveness in interpersonal communication (Norton and Warnick 1976). Assertive individuals are:

◆ **Open:** They engage in frank expressions of their feelings.
◆ **Not Anxious:** They readily volunteer opinions and beliefs, deal directly with stressful interpersonal communication situations, and question others without fear.
◆ **Contentious:** They stand up and argue for their rights, even if this entails unpleasantness with others.
◆ **Not Intimidated:** They hold fast to their beliefs and are not easily persuaded.

How would you classify yourself in terms of these four characteristics?

Assertive people are assertive when they want to be, but they can be nonassertive if the situation seems to call for it. For example, we might wish to be nonassertive in a situation in which assertiveness might emotionally hurt the other person. Let us say that an older relative wishes us to do something for her or him. We could assert our rights and say no, but in doing so we would probably hurt this person; it might be better simply to do as asked. Of course, there are limits that should be observed. We should be careful, in such a situation, that we are not hurt instead. For example, the parents who want their child to continue to live at home until marriage may be hurt by the child's assertive behavior in refusing, yet the alternative is to hurt oneself.

Principles for Increasing Assertiveness

Most assertiveness trainers generally assume that most people are situationally nonassertive. Most people are able to modify their behavior, with a resulting increase in general interpersonal effectiveness and self-esteem. Those who are generally nonassertive, however, probably need extensive training with a therapist. Those who are only moderately nonassertive and wish to understand their lack of assertiveness—and perhaps behave differently in certain situations—should find the following principles of value.

Analyze the Assertive Communications of Others   The first step in increasing assertiveness is to understand the nature of assertive behaviors. This understanding should already have been achieved on an intellectual level. What is necessary and more important is to understand actual assertive behaviors, and the best way to start is to observe and analyze the behavior of others. Learn to distinguish the differences among assertive, aggressive, and nonassertive behaviors. Focus on what makes one behavior assertive and another behavior aggressive or nonassertive. Listen to what is said and how it is said.

What media personality do you feel is an especially effective assertive communicator?

Analyze Your Own Communications   After you have acquired some skills in observing the behaviors of others, turn your analysis to yourself. Analyze situations in which you are normally assertive, nonassertive, and aggressive. What characterizes these situations? What do the situations in which you are normally aggressive have in common? How do these situations differ from the ones in which you are normally nonassertive?

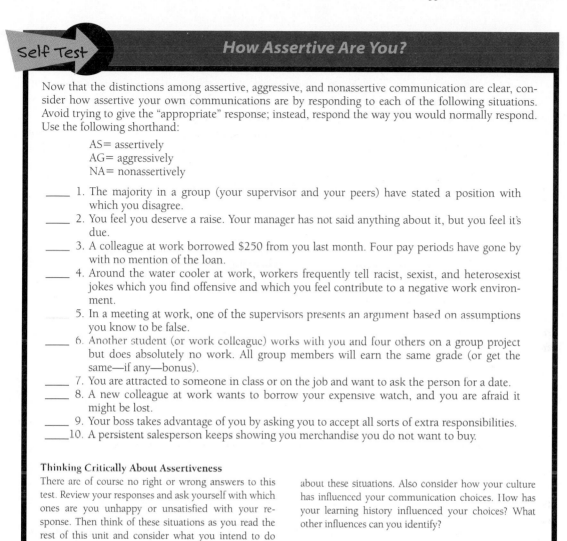

Self Test

How Assertive Are You?

Now that the distinctions among assertive, aggressive, and nonassertive communication are clear, consider how assertive your own communications are by responding to each of the following situations. Avoid trying to give the "appropriate" response; instead, respond the way you would normally respond. Use the following shorthand:

AS= assertively
AG= aggressively
NA= nonassertively

_____ 1. The majority in a group (your supervisor and your peers) have stated a position with which you disagree.

_____ 2. You feel you deserve a raise. Your manager has not said anything about it, but you feel it's due.

_____ 3. A colleague at work borrowed $250 from you last month. Four pay periods have gone by with no mention of the loan.

_____ 4. Around the water cooler at work, workers frequently tell racist, sexist, and heterosexist jokes which you find offensive and which you feel contribute to a negative work environment.

_____ 5. In a meeting at work, one of the supervisors presents an argument based on assumptions you know to be false.

_____ 6. Another student (or work colleague) works with you and four others on a group project but does absolutely no work. All group members will earn the same grade (or get the same—if any—bonus).

_____ 7. You are attracted to someone in class or on the job and want to ask the person for a date.

_____ 8. A new colleague at work wants to borrow your expensive watch, and you are afraid it might be lost.

_____ 9. Your boss takes advantage of you by asking you to accept all sorts of extra responsibilities.

_____10. A persistent salesperson keeps showing you merchandise you do not want to buy.

Thinking Critically About Assertiveness

There are of course no right or wrong answers to this test. Review your responses and ask yourself with which ones are you unhappy or unsatisfied with your response. Then think of these situations as you read the rest of this unit and consider what you intend to do about these situations. Also consider how your culture has influenced your communication choices. How has your learning history influenced your choices? What other influences can you identify?

Analyze your own nonverbal behaviors. How do you stand when you are assertive? Aggressive? Nonassertive? What tone of voice do you use? What kind of eye contact do you maintain? What do you do with your hands? Your nonverbal behaviors are probably different for each type of behavior.

Rehearse Assertive Communications   Several systems are available for effective rehearsal of assertive behaviors. One of the most popular is to select a situation in which you are normally nonassertive and build a hierarchy that begins with a relatively nonthreatening behavior and ends with the desired behavior. For example, let us say that you have difficulty speaking in class and that the desired behavior is to speak your mind in class. You might construct a hierarchy of situations that lead up to speaking in class. It could begin with simply visualizing yourself sitting in class. You might then visualize yourself sitting in class in a state of relaxation. Once you have mastered this visualization, proceed to the next step, visualizing the instructor asking a question. Once you are able to visualize this situation and remain relaxed throughout, visualize the instructor asking you the question. Visualize this situation until you can do so while relaxed. Then try visualizing yourself answering the question. Again, repeat this until you can do it while fully relaxed. Next visualize volunteering your opinion in class—the desired behavior. Visualize this until you can do so while totally relaxed.

You might add the vocal dimension by answering out loud the question you imagine the teacher asking you. Again, do this until you have no difficulty. Next try doing this in front of a supportive friend or group of friends. After this rehearsal, you are probably ready for the next step.

Communicate Assertively   This step is naturally the most difficult but obviously the most important. You can increase assertiveness only by acting out assertive communications; you cannot become assertive by communicating nonassertively.

Again, do this in small steps. In keeping with the previous example, try to answer a question you are sure of before volunteering an opinion or arguing with the instructor.

Throughout this book, the specific skills that contribute to assertive communication are considered. Here is just a brief sampling that you may find useful to keep in mind as you make your way through the remainder of this text:

Can you identify at least ten situations in which assertiveness would probably be the wrong mode of response?

- ◆ Use the characteristics of effective interpersonal interaction, especially those of confidence, interaction management, and expressiveness (Unit 8).
- ◆ Communicate directly, using, for example, I-messages in which you state what you want and what you expect (Unit 9).
- ◆ Speak, gesture, and listen with power; in speaking, avoid, for example, hesitations, disqualifiers, self-critical statements, and statements that ask for approval and agreement; nonverbally, avoid excessive movements and especially self-touching movements which communicate discomfort; and listen attentively, respond visibly but in moderation, and maintain eye contact (Unit 19).
- ◆ Confront power plays with an effective management strategy rather than ignoring them or treating them as isolated instances (Unit 19).
- ◆ Use compliance-gaining and compliance-resisting strategies as appropriate (Unit 20).
- ◆ Employ the skills of argumentativeness; for example, treat disagreements objectively, avoid interrupting (it often communicates anxiety), and avoid excessive emotionalism (Unit 20).
- ◆ Use appropriate conflict resolution strategies, for example, avoiding blaming the other person, argue actively, and focus on the present (Unit 20).

Are these assertive behaviors equally effective for men and women? How would you go about learning which behaviors work best for women and which behaviors work best for men?

Once you have communicated assertively, *reward yourself.* Give yourself something you want—an ice-cream cone, a CD, a new jacket. The desired behavior will be more easily and permanently learned if you reward yourself immediately after engaging in the behavior. Try not to delay the reward too long: Rewards work best when they are immediate.

After communicating, get feedback from others. Start with people who are generally supportive. They should provide you with the social reinforcement so helpful in learning new behavioral patterns. This feedback is particularly important because your intention and the perception of your behavior by an observer may be totally different. For example, you may behave in certain ways with the intention of communicating confidence, but the observer may perceive arrogance. Thus, another person's perception of your behavior can often help you to see yourself as others do.

In all behaviors, but especially with new behaviors, recognize that you may at first fail. You might, for example, try to answer the teacher's question and find that not only do you have the wrong answer but you also do not even understand the question. You might raise your hand and find yourself at a loss for words when you are recognized. Such incidents should not discourage you; realize that in all attempts to change behaviors, you will experience both failure and success.

A note of caution should be added to this discussion. It is easy to visualize a situation in which people are talking behind you in a movie and, with your newfound enthusiasm for assertiveness, you tell these people to be quiet. It is also easy to visualize your getting into a fight you really don't want. It is equally easy to visualize asserting yourself with someone you care for, only to find that as a result this person bursts into tears, unable to handle your new behavior. In applying these principles, then, be careful. In making the choice as to whether or not to act assertively—and, in fact, with any interpersonal choice you make—weigh the potential consequences.

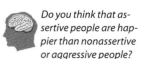

Do you think that assertive people are happier than nonassertive or aggressive people? How would you go about collecting evidence bearing on this question?

Summary   UNIT IN BRIEF

A RETURN TO OBJECTIVES:

In this unit we focused on two basic questions: (1) What is speaker apprehension, how does it develop, and how can you better manage or control it? (2) What is assertive communication and how can you more effectively manage situations calling for assertive responses?

Definitions	Management Principles
Apprehension: A state of fear or anxiety about communication situations.	**Theories and management of communication apprehension:**
Trait apprehension: A fear of communication generally.	◆ **Cognitive restructuring** focuses on unrealistic beliefs and seeks to substitute more realistic ones.
State apprehension: A fear of communication that is specific to a situation (for example, an interview or public speaking situation).	◆ **Systematic desensitization** attempts to train you to respond without apprehension to increasingly more anxiety provoking situations.
	◆ **Skill acquisition** focuses on training you to master the skills involved in situations that normally provoke apprehension. Among the general skills are: Acquire communication skills and experience, prepare and practice, focus on success, familiarize yourself with the situation, be aware that physical relaxation helps, and put communication apprehension in perspective.
Nonassertiveness: An inability to assert oneself or to stand up to defend one's rights in most or all situations (generalized nonassertiveness) or in certain situations (situational nonassertiveness).	**Increasing assertiveness:**
	◆ Analyze the assertive communications of others.
Aggressiveness: Behavior that serves self-interests without any consideration for the rights of others.	◆ Analyze your own communications.
	◆ Rehearse assertive communications.
Assertive communication: Communication that enables a person to act in his or her own best interests without denying the rights of others.	◆ Communicate assertively.

UNIT

6

Perception in Interpersonal Communication

Unit Topics	Unit Objectives
	After completing this unit, you should be able to:
The Perception Process Sensory Stimulation Occurs Sensory Stimulation Is Organized Sensory Stimulation Is Interpreted-Evaluated	1. Define *interpersonal perception* and explain its major stage
Attribution Attribution Processes Attribution Errors	2. Explain the process of *attribution* and the criteria used in making causal judgments 3. Explain the *self-serving bias* and the *fundamental attribution error*
Perceptual Processes Implicit Personality Theory The Self-Fulfilling Prophecy Perceptual Accentuation Primacy-Recency Consistency Stereotyping	4. Define and explain the relevance in interpersonal perception of the following: *implicit personality theory, self-fulfilling prophecy, perceptual accentuation, primacy-recency, consistency,* and *stereotype*
Increasing Accuracy in Interpersonal Perception Reducing Uncertainty Checking Perceptions Perceiving Critically	5. Identify the guidelines for increasing accuracy in interpersonal perception

---

EXPERIENTIAL LEARNING VEHICLES

Vehicles No. 3, "I'd Prefer to Be," pp. 442–443, No. 7, "Perceiving My Selves," pp. 446-447, and No. 12, "Who?" pp. 452–453, illustrate a wide variety of principles and problems of perception.

Perception is the process by which you become aware of objects, events, and, especially, people through your senses: sight, smell, taste, touch, and hearing. Perception is an active, not a passive process. Your perceptions result from what exists in the outside world *and* from your own experiences, desires, needs and wants, loves and hatreds. Among the reasons perception is so important in interpersonal communication is that it influences your communication choices. The messages you send and listen to will depend on how you see the world, on how you size up specific situations, on what you think of the people with whom you interact. Understanding perception will also help clarify why two people can see the same situation very differently—a frequent cause of interpersonal misunderstanding and conflict. Further, your accuracy in perception can be improved. Perception of a distorted world can only distort communication.

The Perception Process

Perception occurs in three stages, which are continuous and blend into one another: (1) Your senses pick up some kind of stimulation, (2) you organize the stimuli in some way, and (3) you interpret and evaluate what you perceive (Figure 6.1).

Sensory Stimulation Occurs

At this first stage, your sense organs are stimulated—you hear the Rolling Stones' new recording, you see a friend, you smell someone's perfume, you taste a juicy orange, you feel another's sweaty palm.

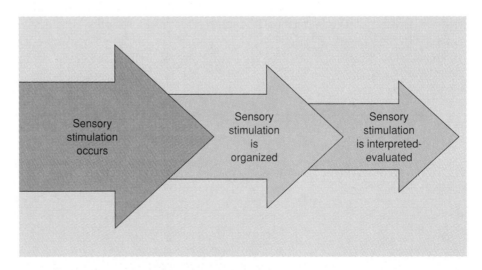

Figure 6.1   The Three Stages of the Perception Process.
The three triangles are designed to illustrate that the stages of perception overlap one another. Also, as the process goes from sensory stimulation to interpretation and evaluation, the focus narrows; for example, you organize part of what you sensed and you interpret and evaluate part of what you organized. After you read this unit, try drawing an alternative visualization of the process of perception.

Naturally, you do not perceive everything; rather, you engage in **selective perception**, a general term that includes selective attention and selective exposure. In **selective attention**, you attend to those things that you anticipate will fulfill your needs or will prove enjoyable. For example, when daydreaming in class, you do not hear what the teacher is saying until your name is called. Your selective attention mechanism focuses your senses on your name.

In **selective exposure**, you expose yourself to people or messages that will confirm your existing beliefs, that will contribute to your objectives, or that will prove satisfying in some way. For example, after you buy a car, you are more apt to read and listen to advertisements for the car you just bought because these messages tell you that you made the right decision. At the same time, you would avoid advertisements for the cars that you considered but eventually rejected because these messages would tell you that you made the wrong decision.

Can you recall a recent example of selective attention or selective exposure? How did it happen? What purposes did it serve?

You are also more likely to perceive stimuli that are greater in **intensity** than surrounding stimuli and those that have **novelty** value (Lahey 1989). For example, television commercials normally play at a greater intensity than regular programming to ensure that you take special notice. You are also more likely to notice the coworker who dresses in a novel way than you are to notice the one who dresses like everyone else. You will quickly perceive someone who shows up in class wearing a tuxedo or at a formal party in shorts.

An obvious implication here is that you perceive only a very small portion of what you could perceive. Just as there are limits on how far you can see, there are also limits on the quantity of stimulation you can take in at any given time.

Sensory Stimulation Is Organized

At the second stage, you organize the sensory stimulations according to certain principles. For example, according to the principle of **proximity**, you perceive as a group persons who are physically close together. You see them as having something in common. You probably perceive family members or members of a club as having similar attitudes, values, and beliefs. According to the principle of **resemblance**, you group people who are similar in appearance and distinguish them from those who are dissimilar. For example, you might perceive members of the same race to have similar values and opinions. You might perceive people who dress similarly (for example, business executives in their gray suits) to be similar in attitudes or behaviors.

Be aware, of course, that neither of these principles will necessarily yield accurate information. Such information should serve only as hypotheses or possibilities that need to be investigated further, not as true conclusions that should be acted upon.

Sensory Stimulation Is Interpreted-Evaluated

The third step in the perceptual process is interpretation-evaluation (hyphenated because the two processes cannot be separated). This step is inevitably subjective; your interpretations-evaluations are greatly influenced by your experiences, needs, wants, values, beliefs about the way things are or should be, expectations, physical and emotional state, and so on. When your child is being particularly difficult, your interpretation and evaluation of that behavior will vary, depending on, for example, whether you just got home from a hard day at work and are trying to get your term paper done or whether you are on the phone and eager for an excuse to get off.

Obviously, there is much room at this stage for disagreement. Although we may all be exposed to the same external stimulus, the way we interpret-evaluate (and organize) it will differ from person to person and from one time to another for the same person. A good way to appreciate this principle is to visualize specific situations as perceived by different people. Consider, for example, the following situations. How might each of the people named perceive the situation. If possible, share your perceptions in a group or with the entire class.

> *Pat, a single parent, has two small children (ages 7 and 12) who often lack some of the important things children their age should have, e.g., school supplies, sneakers, and toys because Pat can't afford them. Yet, Pat smokes 2 packs of cigarettes a day.*
>
> > *Pat sees . . .*
> > *The 12-year-old daughter sees . . .*
> > *Pat's parents (who also smoke 2 packs a day) see . . .*
> > *The children's teacher sees . . .*
>
> *Pat has extremely high standards and feels that getting all As in college is an absolute necessity and would be devastated with even one B. In fear of earning that first B (after three and a half years of college), Pat cheats on an examination in a Family Communication course and gets caught by the instructor.*
>
> > *Pat sees . . .*
> > *The instructor sees . . .*
> > *The average B- student sees . . .*
>
> *Pat, a supervisor in an automobile factory, has been ordered to increase production or be fired. In desperation Pat gave a really tough message to the workers—many of whom were greatly insulted and as a result slowed down rather than increased their efforts.*
>
> > *Pat sees . . .*
> > *The average worker sees . . .*
> > *Pat's supervisor sees . . .*
> > *The average stockholder sees . . .*

Before reading about the specific processes that you use in perceiving other people, examine your own perception strategies by taking the self-test on page 112, "How Accurate Are You at People Perception?"

Attribution

Think about each of the following situations:

1. A woman is begging in the street.
2. A store owner kills a thief.
3. A father leaves his children.

In making an evaluation of another person, you probably assume that you first think about the person and then make the evaluation. Some research claims, however, that you really don't think before assigning any perception to a positive or negative value. This research argues that all perceptions have a positive or negative value attached to them and that these evaluations are most often automatic and involve no conscious thought. Immediately upon perceiving a person, idea, or thing, a positive or negative value is attached (New York Times, August 8, 1995, C1, C10). What do you think of this? One bit of evidence against this position would be to identify three or four or five things, ideas, or people about which you feel completely neutral. Can you do it?

To what do you attribute the causes of these situations? Did the begging, killing, and abandonment result from something within the person or from within the situation? The way you would answer these questions is neatly explained in **attribution theory**. Attribution theory explains the process you go through in trying to understand your own and others' behaviors, particularly the reasons or motivations for these behaviors.

Attribution helps you to make sense of what you perceive, of what is going on in your world (Zanden 1984). It helps you to impose order and logic and to better understand the possible causes of the behaviors you observe.

Attribution also helps you to make predictions about what will happen, what others are likely or unlikely to do. If you can be reasonably sure that Pat gave money out of a desire to help the poor (that is, you can attribute the behavior to a desire to help), then you can make predictions about Pat's future behaviors that are more likely to be correct than predictions made without this initial attribution to guide you.

Attribution Processes

In trying to discover the causes of another's behavior, your first step is to determine whether the individual or some outside factor is responsible. That is, you must first determine whether the cause is **internal** (for example, due to some personality trait) or **external** (for example, due to some situational factor). Internal

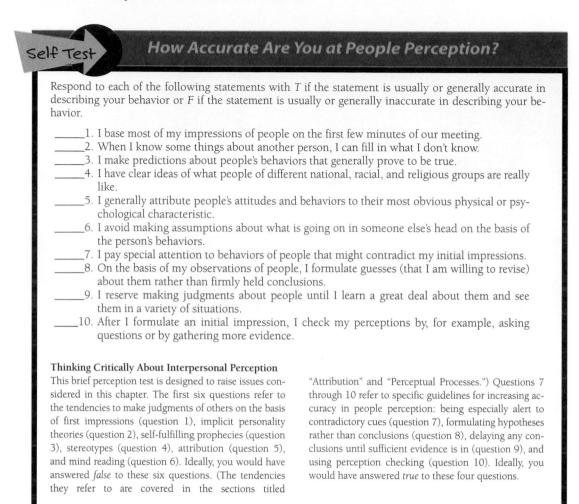

How Accurate Are You at People Perception?

Respond to each of the following statements with *T* if the statement is usually or generally accurate in describing your behavior or *F* if the statement is usually or generally inaccurate in describing your behavior.

_____1. I base most of my impressions of people on the first few minutes of our meeting.
_____2. When I know some things about another person, I can fill in what I don't know.
_____3. I make predictions about people's behaviors that generally prove to be true.
_____4. I have clear ideas of what people of different national, racial, and religious groups are really like.
_____5. I generally attribute people's attitudes and behaviors to their most obvious physical or psychological characteristic.
_____6. I avoid making assumptions about what is going on in someone else's head on the basis of the person's behaviors.
_____7. I pay special attention to behaviors of people that might contradict my initial impressions.
_____8. On the basis of my observations of people, I formulate guesses (that I am willing to revise) about them rather than firmly held conclusions.
_____9. I reserve making judgments about people until I learn a great deal about them and see them in a variety of situations.
_____10. After I formulate an initial impression, I check my perceptions by, for example, asking questions or by gathering more evidence.

Thinking Critically About Interpersonal Perception

This brief perception test is designed to raise issues considered in this chapter. The first six questions refer to the tendencies to make judgments of others on the basis of first impressions (question 1), implicit personality theories (question 2), self-fulfilling prophecies (question 3), stereotypes (question 4), attribution (question 5), and mind reading (question 6). Ideally, you would have answered *false* to these six questions. (The tendencies they refer to are covered in the sections titled "Attribution" and "Perceptual Processes.") Questions 7 through 10 refer to specific guidelines for increasing accuracy in people perception: being especially alert to contradictory cues (question 7), formulating hypotheses rather than conclusions (question 8), delaying any conclusions until sufficient evidence is in (question 9), and using perception checking (question 10). Ideally, you would have answered *true* to these four questions.

Can you identify an example from your own experience in which you attributed someone's behavior to internal or external causes? What evidence did you use in reaching your conclusion?

and external are the two kinds of causality with which attribution theory is concerned. Note that your assessment of someone's behavior as internally or externally motivated will greatly influence your evaluation of that person. If you judge people's cooperative behavior as internally caused (that is, as motivated by their personality), you are more apt to form a positive evaluation of them and, eventually, to like them. In contrast, if you judge that same behavior to be externally caused (the watchful eye of the boss is forcing someone to behave cooperatively, for example), you are more apt to form a negative evaluation and, eventually, to dislike the person (because he or she is not "really" or "genuinely" cooperative).

Consider another example. You look at a teacher's grade book and observe that ten Fs were assigned in cultural anthropology. In an attempt to discover what this reveals about the teacher, you first have to discover whether the teacher was in fact responsible for the assignment of the ten Fs or whether the grading could be attributed to external factors. Let's say you discover that the examinations on which the grades were based had been made up by a faculty committee, which also set the standards for passing or failing. In this case, you could not attribute any particular motives to this teacher because the behavior was not internally caused.

MEDIA & TECHNOLOGY

CENSORSHIP IN CYBERSPACE

Currently, there is great debate on whether or not cyberspace, particularly the Internet, should be subject to censorship (cf. Smith 1994; *New York Times,* June 13, 1996, A1, B10–11). The issues raised are interesting ones but are extremely difficult to resolve. Germany, for example, has recently put pressure on certain Internet vendors to censor messages that may be considered pornographic. Other countries are likewise exerting pressure to have the Internet conform to their own system of morality. And, of course, within the United States, many are calling for censorship for different reasons.

One problem in reaching a decision is deciding what (if anything) should or should not be subject to censorship. For example, will books that are banned by certain school districts be removed from the Internet? Will philosophical, religious, and social viewpoints be subject to censorship? Where should the line be drawn to protect free speech on the one hand and prevent harassment and hate speech on the other? Or, even more basically, should any speech be censored?

Arguments over censorship on the Internet that have been given the most media coverage focus on children. Arguments in favor of censorship, for example, focus on the ready access that children have to the Internet. While magazines, movies, and videos, for example, can be restricted to "adults only," the Internet is open to anyone with computer access. And because such access is getting easier and less expensive, this increases the opportunities for children to not only view pornographic materials but also to communicate with others about sex. One of the major arguments made in favor of censorship is that adults can easily lure children into sexual discussions and even meetings through Internet communications.

Arguments against censorship stress that the laws are simply unworkable. For example, one of the proposals in New York State would make it a crime for an adult to communicate with a minor about sex. But, how is the adult to know that the person he or she is talking to is really a minor? If children want to communicate with adults about sex, they can simply present themselves as adults. How is the adult at the other end to know whether he or she is speaking with a 16-year-old or a 30-year-old? Yet, if discovered, the adult could face criminal prosecution. Also, much as a movie house or bar that admits or serves minors can be held responsible and face criminal charges, so could Internet carriers. And if so, doesn't this put the carrier in the position of having to censor its messages and thereby violate rights to free speech?

Another censorship issue is what is called "hate speech"—speech directed against a particular cultural group. And the issue here is simply whether people should be able to say anything they wish or should they be prevented from using, for example, hate speech? Should hate speech be added to such restrictions on free speech as libel (a written statement that defames or causes some damage to an individual's reputation) or slander (verbal defamation)?

Internet censorship has given new dimensions to the concept of the gatekeeper. Gatekeepers are individuals or groups through which a message passes in going from sender to receiver. The gatekeeper filters the messages you receive. Teachers are perfect examples of gatekeepers. Teachers read the various books and journal articles in an area of study. They listen to convention papers, share information among themselves, and conduct their own research. From all this information, they pass *some* of it on to you. Textbook authors, editors of newspapers, magazines, and publishing houses are also gatekeepers. They allow only certain information to get through.

On the Internet, certain mailing lists are "moderated." When you wish to post a message on a moderated list, a moderator (that is, gatekeeper) will first read your message and then decide if it is suitable to be posted. If he or she feels that it is not suitable it may simply be rejected or may be returned to you for editing or refocusing (LeBlanc and LeBlanc 1995). For example, in a scientific or instructional mailing list, postings may be rejected because they do not focus sufficiently on the topic with which the group is concerned. Mailing lists dealing with controversial topics may be moderated to keep out personal attacks and to let in serious discussions of opposing views. Lists devoted to offering support for its members may be moderated to keep the postings supportive so that members feel safe.

The gatekeeper, then, limits and focuses the messages you receive and can have both positive and negative consequences. The teacher or Internet moderator, for example, enable others to learn a great deal more by keeping the information focused on a topic and excluding that which would confuse users or distort the purposes of the class or group. At the same time, however, gatekeeping or moderating can be seriously abused. Thus, for example, in a history class an instructor may unfairly emphasize the contributions of one cultural group and de-emphasize the contributions of another, may focus on the positive qualities of one group and on the negative qualities of another group. In an Internet mailing list dealing with controversial topics, the moderator may exclude postings which do not agree with his or her position instead of those that are simply insulting or not clearly focused on the topic.

You may find it interesting to further personalize this discussion by asking yourself how the following people function as gatekeepers: your college librarian, your romantic partner (past or present), your best friend, your parents or children.

Try drafting a law governing censorship of the Internet. What material, if any, would you censor? To what material would you be sure to protect free access? What arguments could you advance for or against censorship?

p. 147

On the other hand, let's assume the following: This teacher made up the examination without any assistance, no departmental or university standards were used, and the teacher made up a personal set of standards for passing and failing. Now you would be more apt (though perhaps not fully justified) to attribute the ten Fs to internal causes. You would be strengthened in your beliefs that there was something within this teacher, some personality characteristic, for example, that led to this behavior if you discovered that (1) no other teacher in anthropology gave nearly as many Fs, (2) this particular teacher frequently gives Fs in cultural anthropology, (3) this teacher frequently gives Fs in other courses as well, and (4) this teacher is the only one responsible for assigning grades and could have assigned grades other than F. These four bits of added information would lead you to conclude that there was something within this teacher that motivated the behavior. In forming such causal judgments, which you make every day, you use four principles: (1) consensus, (2) consistency, (3) distinctiveness, and (4) controllability.

Consensus: Similarity to Others   When you focus on the principle of **consensus**, you ask essentially, "Do other people react or behave in the same way as the person on whom I am focusing?" That is, is the person acting in accordance with the consensus? If the answer is no, you are more likely to attribute the behavior to some internal cause. In the previous example, you were strengthened in your belief that something internal caused the Fs to be given when you learned that other teachers did not do this; that is, there was low consensus. When only one person acts contrary to the norm, you are more likely to attribute that person's behavior to internal motivation. If all teachers gave many Fs (that is, if there was high consensus), you would be more likely to look for causality outside the individual teacher; you might conclude that the anthropology department uses a particular curve in determining grades or that the students were not very bright—or any other reason external to the specific teacher.

Do men and women attribute behavior to internal or external causes with the same frequency? How would you go about researching this question?

Consistency: Similarity over Time   When you focus on the principle of **consistency**, you ask if this person repeatedly behaves in the same way in similar situations. If the answer is yes, there is high consistency, and you are likely to attribute the behavior to internal motivation. The fact that this teacher frequently gives Fs in cultural anthropology leads you to attribute the cause to the teacher rather than to outside sources. If, on the other hand, there was low consistency—that is, if this teacher rarely gives Fs—you would be more likely to look for reasons external to the teacher. You might consider, for example, the possibility that this specific class was not very bright or that the department required the teacher to start giving out Fs, and so on. That is, you would look for causes external to the teacher.

Distinctiveness: Similarity in Different Situations   When you focus on the principle of **distinctiveness**, you ask if this person reacts in similar ways in different situations. If the answer is yes, there is low distinctiveness, and you are likely to conclude that the behavior has an internal cause. The fact that the teacher reacted the same way (gave lots of Fs) in different situations (other courses) led you to conclude that this particular class was not distinctive and that the motivation for the behavior could not be found in a unique situation. You further concluded that this behavior must be due to the teacher's inner motivation. Consider the alternative: if this teacher gave all high grades and no Fs in other courses (that is, if the cultural anthropology class situation was highly distinctive), you would conclude that the motivation for the failures was to be found in sources outside the teacher and for reasons unique to this class.

Controllability: Was the Person in Control of the Behavior?   Let's say your friend is an hour late for a dinner appointment (cf. Weiner, Amirkhan, Folkes, and Verette 1987). How would you feel about the following two possible excuses?

> EXCUSE 1: I was reading this book, and I just couldn't put it down. I had to find out who the killer was.
>
> EXCUSE 2: I was stuck on the subway for two hours; a water main broke, killing all the electricity.

It's very likely you would resent the first and accept the second excuse. The first excuse says that the reason for the lateness was controllable: your friend

One of the great tragedies of our time is homelessness. Part of the difficulty that homeless people must face is how they are seen by others. What are your perceptions of homeless people? What are they based on? In terms of attribution theory, do your perceptions attribute homelessness to internal or external factors? To controllable or uncontrollable factors? How might these attributions influence the way you treat and respond to homeless people on a day-to-day basis?

chose to be late by completing the novel. You therefore hold your friend responsible for wasting your time and for a lack of consideration. The second excuse says that the reason was uncontrollable: You cannot hold your friend responsible for the subway breakdown or for the lateness. Generally, excuses involving uncontrollable factors are more effective than those involving controllable factors. You may wish to test this observation against your own experience in making or receiving excuses.

Think about your own tendency to make similar judgments based on controllability. For example, how you would respond to such situations as the following:

◆ Doris fails her midterm history exam.
◆ Sidney's car is repossessed because he failed to make the payments.
◆ Margie is 150 pounds overweight and is complaining that she feels awful.
◆ Thomas's wife has just filed for divorce and he is feeling depressed.

Very probably you would be sympathetic to each of these people if you felt they were not in control of what happened—for example, if the examination was unfair, if Sidney lost his job because of employee discrimination, if Margie has a glandular problem, and if Thomas's wife is leaving him for a wealthy drug dealer. On the other hand, you might blame these people for their problems if you felt that they were in control of the situation—for example, if Doris partied instead of studied, if Sidney gambled his payments away, if Margie ate nothing but junk food and refused to exercise, and if Thomas had been repeatedly unfaithful and his wife finally gave up trying to change him.

In perceiving other people and especially in evaluating their behavior, you frequently ask if the person was in control of the behavior. Generally, research shows that if you feel people are in control of negative behaviors, you will come to dislike them. But you feel sorry for someone who you feel is not in control of negative behaviors, and you will not blame the person for his or her negative circumstances.

Low consensus, high consistency, low distinctiveness, and high controllability lead to an attribution of internal causes. As a result you praise or blame the person for his or her behaviors. High consensus, low consistency, high distinctiveness, and low controllability lead to an attribution of external causes. As a result you might consider this person lucky or unlucky. Table 6.1 summarizes these four principles of attribution.

Attribution Errors

Attribution of causality can lead to several major barriers. Your tendency to make judgments of others' behaviors can lead you to mind read the motives of another person and confuse guesses with valid conclusions. This tendency is common in a wide variety of situations (attempts to mind read are shown in italics): You forgot my birthday; *you don't love me.* You don't want to go to my parents' house for dinner; *you've never liked my parents.* You don't want to go to that interview; *you lack self-confidence.*

The Self-Serving Bias   The **self-serving bias** is a barrier designed to preserve your self-esteem. When you evaluate your own behaviors by taking credit for the positive and denying responsibility for the negative, you are committing the self-serving bias. You are more likely to attribute your own negative behaviors to uncontrollable factors. For example, you are more likely to attribute getting a D on an exam to the difficulty of the test rather than to your failure to prepare adequately for it. And you are more likely to attribute your positive behaviors to controllable factors, to your own strength or intelligence or personality. For example,

Can you explain, with the concepts of attribution—especially controllability but also consensus, consistency, and distinctiveness— the attitudes that many people have about the homeless? About drug addicts or alcoholics? About successful politicians, scientists, or millionaires? Can you describe the way in which you would use consensus, consistency, distinctiveness, and controllability in explaining why your best friend is being charged with armed robbery? In explaining why you feel depressed today?

Table 6.1 A Summary of Causal Attribution	
Situation: John was fired from a job he began a few months ago. On what basis will you decide whether this behavior is internally caused (and John is, therefore, responsible) or externally caused (and John is not responsible)?	
Internal If	**External If**
No one else was fired. (low consensus)	Lots of others were fired. (high consensus)
John was fired from lots of other jobs. (high consistency)	John was never fired from any other job. (low consistency)
John has failed at lots of other things. (low distinctiveness)	John has always been successful. (high distinctiveness)
John could have been retained if he agreed to move to another shop. (high controllability)	John was not given any alternatives. (low controllability)

Can you identify examples of the self-serving bias in any of your own recent perceptual judgments? What purposes did this serve? Would you make the same judgment today?

after getting an A on an exam, you are more likely to attribute it to your ability or hard work (Bernstein, Stephan, and Davis 1979).

There is some evidence (though it is not overwhelming) that we explain the behaviors of in-group and out-group members differently (Taylor and Jaggi 1974; Berry, Poortinga, Segall, and Dasen 1992). For example, there seems to be a tendency to explain the negative behavior of members of one's own culture as externally or situationally caused but to explain the very same behavior of members of other cultures as internally motivated. Thus, for example, you would be more apt to attribute a high school dropout rate (a negatively evaluated behavior) to external sources (teachers who were not motivating or irrelevant educational programs) if this was shown to be true of your own cultural group. If, on the other hand, it were shown to be true of another culture then you would be more apt to attribute it to internal sources (the students aren't interested in education; they lack motivation).

Alternatively, we seem to explain members' positive behavior as internally motivated and non-members' positive behaviors as externally motivated. Thus, you would be more apt to explain a high record of charitable contributions for members of your own culture with something like "we're a charitable people; we believe in helping others." If this is shown to be true for members of another culture, you would be more apt to say something like "they're rich; they need tax deductions."

Sometimes we construct defensive attributions where we try to explain behavior in ways that make us seem less vulnerable. One way we do this is with unrealistic optimism, the belief that good things are more likely to happen to us than to others. For example, most people think that they will ultimately experience more good things and less bad things than their peers (Aronson 1994). A similar belief is the just world hypothesis, the belief that bad things will happen only to bad people. Since we are good people, good things will happen to us. Of course, in our mindful state we know that good things often happen to bad people and that bad things often happen to good people.

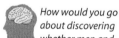

How would you go about discovering whether men and women use the self-serving bias differently when perceiving others? What would you predict?

The Fundamental Attribution Error   Perhaps the major difficulty in making accurate attributions is the fundamental attribution error: the tendency to conclude that people do what they do because that's the kind of people they are, not because of the situation they are in. When Pat is late for an appointment, we are more likely to conclude that Pat is inconsiderate or irresponsible rather than attribute the lateness to the bus breaking down or to a traffic accident. When we commit the fundamental attribution error we overvalue the contribution of internal factors and undervalue the influence of external factors.

When you explain your own behavior you also favor internal explanations although not to as great an extent as when explaining the behaviors of others. In one study, managers who evaluated their own and the performance of their subordinates, used more internal explanations when evaluating the behavior of their subordinates than they did in evaluating their own (Martin and Klimoski 1990). One reason for giving less weight to internal factors in explaining our own behavior than we do in explaining the behavior of others is that we know the situation surrounding our own behavior. We know, for example, what's going on in our love life and we know our financial condition, so we naturally see the influence of these factors. But we rarely know as much about others, so we are more likely to give less weight to these external (and unknown) factors in their cases.

This fundamental attribution error is at least in part culturally influenced. For example, in the United States people are more likely to explain behavior by saying that people did what they did because of who they are. But when Hindus in India were asked to explain why their friends behaved as they did, they gave greater weight to external factors than did Americans in the United States (Miller 1984; Aronson 1994). Further, Americans have little hesitation in offering causal explanations of a person's behavior ("Pat did this because. . . "). Hindus, on the other hand, are generally reluctant to explain a person's behavior in causal terms (Matsumoto 1994).

Can you describe examples of the fundamental attribution error from your own recent perceptual judgments? Have others made this error in judging your motivations?

Let's return to the three examples with which we opened this discussion of attribution as a way of summarizing the principles of consensus, consistency, distinctiveness, and controllability. Generally, you would consider the three actions—begging, killing, and abandonment—to result from something inherent in the begging woman, the store owner, and the father if other people behaved differently in situations similar to these (low consensus), if these people had engaged in these behaviors in the past (high consistency), if these people behaved similarly in other situations (low distinctiveness), and if these people were in control of their own behaviors (high controllability). Under these conditions, you would conclude that the persons bear the responsibility for their behaviors.

Alternatively, you would consider these actions to have resulted from something external to the persons if many other people reacted the same way in similar situations (high consensus), if these people had never behaved in this way before (low consistency), if these people never engaged in these behaviors in different situations (high distinctiveness), and if these people were not in control of their own behavior (low controllability). Under these conditions, you could conclude that these actions resulted from external factors, that these people had little or no control and that, therefore, they may not be personally responsible.

Think about how you would explain such cases as the following in terms of attribution theory. For example, do you think the individual's behavior was due to internal causes—for example, personality characteristics, and traits or personal motives—or external causes—for example, the particular situation, the demands of others who might be in positions of authority, or the behaviors of others? The behavior in question appears in italics.

1. *Mita's performance in the race was disappointing.* For the last few days she had to tend to her sick grandfather and got too little sleep.
2. *Peter just quit his job.* No one else that you know has quit this same job once before.
3. *Karla just failed her chemistry test.* A number of other students (in fact, some 40 percent of the class) also failed the test. Karla has never failed a chemistry test before and, in fact, has never failed any other test in her life.

4. *Juan earned a substantial income from real estate.* His brother made the investment decisions for both of them.

5. *Liz tasted the wine, rejected it, and complained to the waiter.* No one else in the place complained about the wine. Liz has complained about the wine before and has frequently complained that her food was seasoned incorrectly, that the coffee was cold, and so on.

6. *Russell took the schoolchildren to the zoo.* Russell works for the board of education in a small town, and taking the students on trips is one of his major functions. All people previously on the job have taken the students to the zoo. Russell has never taken any other children to the zoo.

7. *John ran from the dog.* A number of other people also ran from this dog. I was surprised to see John do this because he has never run from other animals before and never from this particular dog.

8. *Donna received A's on all her speeches.* In fact, everyone in the class got A's. This was the first A that Donna has ever received in public speaking and the first A she has ever received in any course.

What information contained in the brief behavior descriptions enabled you to make judgments concerning (1) consensus, (2) consistency, (3) distinctiveness, and (4) controllability? What combination of these principles would lead you to conclude that the behavior was internally motivated? What combination would lead you to conclude that the behavior was externally motivated?

Perceptual Processes

Several processes influence what you perceive and what you fail to perceive. These processes help to explain why you make some predictions and not others and also help you impose order on the enormous amount of data that impinges on your senses. They enable you to simplify and categorize the vast amount of information around you. Note, however, that each of these six processes presents potential barriers to accurate perception. In some cases, they lead to oversimplification or distortion of information.

Implicit Personality Theory

Each person has a subconscious or implicit system of rules that says which characteristics of an individual go with other characteristics. Consider, for example, the following brief statements. Note the word in parentheses that you think best completes each sentence:

> *Carlo is energetic, eager, and (intelligent, stupid).*
> *Kim is bold, defiant, and (extroverted, introverted).*
> *Joe is bright, lively, and (thin, heavy).*
> *Ava is attractive, intelligent, and (likable, unlikable).*

Susan is cheerful, positive, and (outgoing, shy).
Angel is handsome, tall, and (friendly, unfriendly).

Certain of these choices seem right and others seem wrong. What makes some seem right is your **implicit personality theory**, the system of rules that tells you which characteristics go with which other characteristics. Your theory may, for example, have told you that a person who is energetic and eager is also intelligent, not stupid, although there is no logical reason why a stupid person could not be energetic and eager.

The widely documented **halo effect** is a function of the implicit personality theory (Dion, Berscheid, and Walster 1972; Riggio 1987). If you believe a person has some positive qualities, you are likely to infer that she or he also possesses other positive qualities. There is also a **reverse halo effect**: if you know a person possesses several negative qualities, you are more likely to infer that the person also has other negative qualities.

What is your implicit personality theory for
- *the bright, dedicated, and aggressive college professor?*
- *the out-of-work, dirty, and homeless man on the street?*
- *the stylish, wealthy, and sophisticated penthouse owner?*

Cultural Variation in Implicit Personality Theories As might be expected the implicit personality theories that people hold differ from culture to culture, group to group, and even person to person. For example, the Chinese have a concept *shi gu* which refers to "someone who is worldly, devoted to his or her family, socially skillful, and somewhat reserved" (Aronson 1994, p. 190). This concept is not easily encoded in English as you can tell by trying to find a general concept that covers this type of person. In English, on the other hand, we have a concept of the "artistic type," a generalization which seems absent in Chinese. Thus, although it is easy for speakers of English or Chinese to refer to specific concepts—such as socially skilled or creative—each language creates its own generalized categories. Thus, in Chinese the qualities that make up *shi gu* are more easily seen as going together than they might be for an English speaker; they are part of the implicit personality theory of more Chinese speakers than English speakers.

Similarly, consider the different personality theories that "graduate students" and "blue collar high school dropouts" might have for "college students." Likewise, an individual may have had great experiences with doctors and so may have a very positive personality theory of doctors whereas another person may have had negative experiences with doctors and might thus have developed a very negative personality theory.

Thinking Critically About Implicit Personality Theories Apply implicit personality theories carefully and critically so as to avoid:

- perceiving qualities in an individual that your theory tells you should be present when they actually are not. For example, you see "goodwill" in a friend's "charitable" acts when a tax deduction may have been the "real" motive.
- ignoring or distorting qualities that do not conform to your theory but that are actually present in the individual. For example, you may ignore negative qualities in your friends that you would easily perceive in your enemies.

The Self-Fulfilling Prophecy

A **self-fulfilling prophecy** occurs when you make a prediction that comes true because you act on it as if it were true (Merton 1957). There are four basic steps in the self-fulfilling prophecy:

1. You make a prediction or formulate a belief about a person or a situation. For example, you predict that Pat is awkward in interpersonal encounters.
2. You act toward that person or situation as if that prediction or belief were true. For example, you act as if Pat were awkward.
3. Because you act as if the belief were true, it becomes true. For example, because of the way you act toward Pat, Pat becomes tense and awkward.
4. You observe *your* effect on the person or the resulting situation, and what you see strengthens your beliefs. For example, you observe Pat's awkwardness, and this reinforces your belief that Pat is in fact awkward.

If you expect people to act in a certain way or if you make a prediction about a situation, your predictions will frequently come true because of self-fulfilling prophecy. Consider, for example, people who enter a group situation convinced that the other members will dislike them. Almost invariably they are proved right; the other members do dislike them. What they may be doing is acting in a way that encourages a negative response. Such people fulfill their own prophecies.

A widely known example of the self-fulfilling prophecy is the **Pygmalion effect.** In one study, teachers were told that certain pupils were expected to do exceptionally well, that they were late bloomers. The names of these students were actually selected at random by the experimenters. The results, however, were not random. The students whose names were given to the teachers actually performed at a higher level than the others. In fact, these students' IQ scores even improved more than did the other students'. The teachers' expectations probably prompted them to give extra attention to the selected students, thereby positively affecting their performance (Rosenthal and Jacobson 1968; Insel and Jacobson 1975).

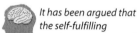

It has been argued that the self-fulfilling prophecy may be used in organizations to stimulate higher performance (Eden 1992; Field 1989). For example, managers could be given the belief that workers can perform at extremely high levels; managers would then act as if this were true and thus create this high level behavior in the workers. How might it be used in the college classroom? How might it be used in parenting?

Thinking Critically About Self-Fulfilling Prophecies   Self-fulfilling prophecies can short-circuit critical thinking and:

- influence another's behavior so that it conforms to your prophecy.
- lead you to see what you predicted rather than what is really there (for example, to perceive yourself as a failure because you have predicted it rather than because of any actual failures).

Perceptual Accentuation

When poor and rich children were shown pictures of coins and later asked to estimate their size, the poor children's size estimates were much greater than the rich children's. Similarly, hungry people perceive food objects and food terms at lower recognition thresholds (needing fewer physical cues) than do people who are not hungry.

This process, called **perceptual accentuation,** leads you to see what you expect and want to see. You see people you like as better looking than those you do

Can you identify situations in which perceptual accentuation played a part in your own perceptions?

not like. You see people you like as smarter than those you do not like. You magnify or accentuate that which will satisfy your needs and wants: The thirsty person sees a mirage of water; the sexually deprived person sees a mirage of sexual satisfaction.

Thinking Critically About Perceptual Accentuation   The tendency to perceive what you want or need can lead you to:

◆ distort your perceptions of reality, perceive what you need or want to perceive rather than what is really there, and fail to perceive what you do not want to perceive. For example, you may not perceive signs of impending problems because you focus on what you want to perceive.

◆ perceive and remember positive qualities more than negative ones (a phenomenon referred to as the **Pollyanna effect**) and thus distort your perceptions of others.

◆ perceive certain behaviors as indicative that someone likes you simply because you want to be liked. For example, general politeness and friendly behavior used as a persuasive strategy (say, by a salesperson) are frequently seen as indicating a genuine personal liking.

Primacy-Recency

Assume for a moment that you are enrolled in a course in which half the classes are extremely dull and half extremely exciting. At the end of the semester, you evaluate the course and the instructor. Would your evaluation be more favorable if the dull classes occurred in the first half of the semester and the exciting classes in the second? Would it be more favorable if the order were reversed? If what comes first exerts the most influence, this is a **primacy effect**. If what comes last (or most recently) exerts the most influence, this is a **recency effect**.

In the classic study on the effects of primacy-recency in interpersonal perception, Solomon Asch (1946) read a list of descriptive adjectives to a group of students and found that the effects of order were significant. A person described as "intelligent, industrious, impulsive, critical, stubborn, and envious" was evaluated more positively than a person described as "envious, stubborn, critical, impulsive, industrious, and intelligent." There is a tendency to use early information to get a general idea about a person and to use later information to make this impression more specific. The obvious practical implication of primacy-recency is this: The first impression you make is likely to be the most important. It is through this that others will filter additional information in formulating a picture of how they perceive you.

What role do your first impressions play in perceiving people? Have you ever been wrong? Do others form impressions of you based on an initial interaction? Have these people ever been wrong? What might you do to make your first impressions more accurate?

Thinking Critically About Primacy and Recency   The tendency to give greater weight to early information and to interpret later information in light of early impressions can distort your critical thinking and lead you to:

◆ formulate a total picture of an individual on the basis of initial impressions that may not be typical or accurate (for example, judging a job applicant as generally nervous when he or she may simply be showing normal nervousness at being interviewed for a much-needed job).

How would you go about testing the following hypothesis: A primacy effect operates in college students' perceptions of instructors, but a recency effect operates in college instructors' perceptions of students?

♦ discount or distort subsequent perceptions so as not to disrupt your initial impression. For example, you may fail to see signs of deceit in someone you like because of your early impressions.

Consistency

The tendency to maintain balance among perceptions or attitudes is called **consistency** (McBroom and Reed 1992). You expect certain things to go together and other things not to go together. On a purely intuitive basis, for example, respond to the following sentences by noting your *expected* response:

1. I expect a person I like to (like, dislike) me.
2. I expect a person I dislike to (like, dislike) me.
3. I expect my friend to (like, dislike) my friend.
4. I expect my friend to (like, dislike) my enemy.
5. I expect my enemy to (like, dislike) my friend.
6. I expect my enemy to (like, dislike) my enemy.

According to most consistency theories, your expectations would be as follows: You would expect a person you liked to like you (1) and one you disliked to dislike you (2). You would expect a friend to like a friend (3) and to dislike an enemy (4). You would expect your enemy to dislike your friend (5) and to like your other enemy (6). All these expectations are intuitively satisfying.

Further, you would expect someone you liked to possess characteristics you like or admire. And you would expect your enemies not to possess characteristics you like or admire. Conversely, you would expect people you liked to lack unpleasant characteristics and those you disliked to possess unpleasant characteristics.

 Using consistency theory, how would you explain what goes on in your head when one of your favorite people does something you evaluate negatively? How would you explain what happens when someone you dislike says good things about you?

Thinking Critically About Consistency   Uncritically assuming that an individual is consistent can lead you to:

♦ ignore or distort your perceptions of behaviors that are inconsistent with your picture of the whole person. For example, you may misinterpret Karla's unhappiness because your image of Karla is "happy, controlled, and contented."
♦ see certain behaviors as positive if you interpreted other behaviors positively (the halo effect) or as negative if you interpreted other behaviors negatively (the reverse halo effect).

Stereotyping

What kinds of stereotypes do others apply to you? How accurate are they? On what are they based?

One of the most common shortcuts in interpersonal perception is stereotyping. A sociological or psychological **stereotype** is a fixed impression of a group of people. We all have attitudinal stereotypes—of national, religious, sexual, or racial groups, or perhaps of criminals, prostitutes, teachers, or plumbers. If you have these fixed impressions, you will, upon meeting a member of a particular group, often see that person primarily as a member of that group and apply to him or her all the characteristics you assign to that group. If you meet someone who is a prostitute, for example, there is a host of characteristics for prostitutes that you may apply to this one person. To complicate matters further, you will often see in this person's behavior the manifestation of characteristics that you would not see if you did not know that this person was a prostitute. Stereotypes distort accurate perception. They prevent you from seeing an individual as an individual rather than as a member of a group.

Thinking Critically About Stereotyping   The tendency to group people and to respond to individuals primarily as members of groups can lead you to:

- perceive an individual as possessing those qualities (usually negative) that you believe characterize his or her group (for example, all Mexicans are . . . or all Baptists are . . .) and, therefore, fail to appreciate the multifaceted nature of all individuals and groups.
- ignore each person's unique characteristics and, therefore, fail to benefit from the special contributions each individual can bring to an encounter.

The following brief dialogue illustrates each of the processes of perception discussed. It is designed to reinforce an understanding of the processes of perception. Read the following dialogue and identify the operation of each of the six processes of perception.

PAT: All I had to do was to spend two seconds with him to know he's an idiot. I said I went to Graceland, and he asked what that was. Can you believe it? Graceland! The more I got to know him, the more I realized how stupid he was. A real loser; I mean, really.

CHRIS: Yeah, I know what you mean. Well, he is a jock, you know.

PAT: Jocks! The worst. And I bet I can guess who he goes out with. I'll bet it's Lucy.

CHRIS: Why do you say that?

PAT: Well, I figure that the two people I dislike would like each other. And I figure you must dislike them, too.

CHRIS: For sure.

PAT: By the way, have you ever met Marie? She's a computer science major, so you know she's bright. And attractive—really attractive.

CHRIS: Yes, I went out of my way to meet her, because she sounded like she'd be a nice person to know.

PAT: You're right. I knew she'd be nice as soon as I saw her.

CHRIS: We talked at yesterday's meeting. She's really complex, you know. I mean really complex. Really.

PAT: Whenever I think of Marie, I think of the time she helped that homeless man. There was this homeless guy—real dirty—and he fell, running across the street. Well, Marie ran right into the street and picked this guy up and practically carried him to the other side.

CHRIS: And you know what I think of when I think of Lucy? The time she refused to visit her grandmother in the hospital. Remember? She said she had too many other things to do.

PAT: I remember that—a real selfish egomaniac. I mean really.

In a study of stereotypes on British television it was found that gender stereotypes hadn't changed much over the last ten years and that these were comparable to those found on North American television (Furnham and Bitar 1993). Other research suggests that these stereotypes have changed and that television depictions of men and women are erasing the stereotypes (Vernon, Williams, Phillips, and Wilson 1990). Do you find gender stereotypes on television? How many can you identify? Do you find evidence to suggest that gender stereotyping is lessening? Does the media perpetuate stereotypes on the basis of race, age, class, or affectional orientation? Can you give specific examples? In terms of stereotypes, how does what's on television compare to what's in a newspaper?

Increasing Accuracy in Interpersonal Perception

Successful interpersonal communication depends largely on the accuracy of your interpersonal perception. As a preface, do realize that in addition to your perception of another's behaviors (verbal or nonverbal), you can also perceive what you think another person is feeling or thinking (Laing, Phillipson, and Lee 1966; Littlejohn 1992). You can, for example, perceive Pat kissing Chris. This is a simple, relatively direct perception of some behavior. But you can also sense (or perceive)—on the basis of the kiss—that Pat loves Chris. Notice the difference: you have observed the kiss but have not observed the love. (Of course, you could continue in this vein and, from your conclusion that Pat loves Chris, conclude that Pat no longer loves Terry. That is, you can always formulate a conclusion on the basis of a previous conclusion. The process is unending.)

The important point to see here is that when your perceptions are based on something observable (here, the kiss), you have a greater chance of being accurate when you describe this kiss or even when you interpret and evaluate it. As you move further away from your actual observation, however, your chances of being accurate decrease—when, for example, you try to describe or evaluate the love. Generally, when you draw conclusions on the basis of what you think someone is thinking as a result of the behavior, you have a greater chance of making errors than when you stick to conclusions about what you observe yourself.

We have already identified lots of pitfalls to avoid in using the various processes, for example, the self-serving bias, the fundamental error in attribution, and the numerous potential problems in each of the six perceptual processes. There are, however, two major additional suggestions and a few brief cautions that may be offered.

Reducing Uncertainty

All communication interactions involve uncertainty and ambiguity. Communicating in new situations or with people from other cultures is likely to involve higher uncertainty than communicating in familiar settings with people much like yourself (Berger and Bradac 1982; Gudykunst 1989, 1993). So, if you are from a culture that has strong uncertainty avoidance tendencies (Unit 3), you might find communication with strangers or intercultural communications more stressful than someone from a weak uncertainty avoidance culture.

Although your culture will influence how important uncertainty is, all people use communication to reduce uncertainty so they can better describe, predict, and explain the behaviors of others. Some cultures may do so indirectly and others directly, some may do it very quickly and others will take more time; but, reducing uncertainty in some way seems a universal tendency. Reducing your uncertainty about another person will not only make your communication more effective, but will also increase your liking for the person (Douglas 1994).

A variety of strategies can help reduce uncertainty. Observing another person while he or she is engaged in an active task, preferably interacting with others in social (and informal) situations, will often tell you a great deal about the person, since people are less apt to monitor their behaviors and are more likely to reveal their true selves in informal situations.

Another way is to ask others about the person. For example, you might ask a colleague if a third person finds you interesting and might like to have dinner with you. You can also manipulate the situation in such a way that you observe the person in more specific and more revealing contexts. Employment interviews, theatrical auditions, and student teaching are some of the ways in which the situation can be manipulated to observe how the person might act and react and hence to reduce uncertainty about the person.

Of course, you can interact with the individual. You can ask questions: "Do you enjoy sports?" "What did you think of that computer science course?" "What would you do if you got fired?" You also gain knowledge of another by disclosing information about yourself. Your self-disclosure creates a relaxed environment that encourages subsequent disclosures from the person about whom you wish to learn more.

In situations of great uncertainty the techniques of effective communication (for example, active listening, perception checking, being specific, and seeking feedback) take on special importance. Active listening (Unit 7) and perception checking techniques (later in Unit 6), for example, help you to check on the accuracy of your perceptions and allow you the opportunity to revise and amend any incorrect perceptions. Being specific reduces ambiguity and the chances of misunderstandings. Misunderstanding is a lot more likely when talking about "neglect" (a highly abstract concept) than when talking about "forgetting your last birthday" (a specific event).

What strategies do you use for reducing uncertainty when meeting someone for the first time? Is this more complicated in opposite sex or same sex relationships? In culturally similar or culturally different groups?

Seeking feedback helps you to correct any possible misconceptions almost immediately. Seek feedback on whether you are making yourself clear ("Does that make sense?" "Do you see where to put the widget?") as well as on whether you understand what the other person is saying ("Do you mean that you will never speak with them again? Do you mean that literally?")

Although you are always in danger of misperceiving and misevaluating another person, you are in special danger in intercultural situations. So, try to resist the natural tendency to judge others quickly and permanently. Prejudices and biases complicate such communication further; when combined with high uncertainty they are sure to produce judgments you'll want to revise. A judgment made early is likely to be based on too little information. Because of this, flexibility and a willingness to revise opinions are essential intercultural skills.

Checking Perceptions

Perception checking is one of the most valuable techniques for making your perceptions more accurate. In its most basic form, perception checking consists of two steps:

1. Describe (in tentative terms) what you think is happening. Try to do this as descriptively (not evaluatively) as you can.

   ◆ You seem depressed. You say you feel fine about the breakup, but you don't seem happy.
   ◆ You don't seem to want to go out this evening.

How would you use perception checking in such situations as these: (a) your friend says he wants to drop out of college, (b) your cousin hasn't called you in several months though you have called her at least six times, (c) another student seems totally detached from everything that happens in class?

- ◆ You seemed disturbed when he said . . .
- ◆ You sound upset with my plans.

2. Ask the other person for confirmation. Do be careful that your request for confirmation does not sound as though you already know the answer. So avoid phrasing your questions defensively. Avoid saying, for example, "You really don't want to go out, do you; I knew you didn't when you turned on that lousy television." Instead, ask for confirmation in as supportive a way as possible: "Would you rather watch TV?"

- ◆ Are you really okay about the breakup?
- ◆ Do you feel like going out, or would you rather stay home?
- ◆ Are you disturbed?
- ◆ Did my plans upset you?

As these examples illustrate, the goal of perception checking is not to prove that your initial perception is correct but to explore further the thoughts and feelings of the other person. With this simple technique, you lessen your chances of misinterpreting another's feelings. At the same time, you give the other person an opportunity to elaborate on his or her thoughts and feelings.

Perceiving Critically

In addition to reducing uncertainty and checking your perceptions, exercise appropriate critical thinking guidelines.

Recognize your own role in perception. Your emotional and physiological state will influence the meaning you give to your perceptions. The sight of raw clams may be physically upsetting when you have a stomachache but mouthwatering when you are hungry.

Avoid early conclusions. On the basis of your observations of behaviors, formulate hypotheses to test against additional information and evidence rather than drawing conclusions you then look to confirm. Delay formulating conclusions until you have had a chance to process a wide variety of cues.

Avoid the one-cue conclusion. Look for a variety of cues pointing in the same direction. The more cues pointing to the same conclusion, the more likely it is that your conclusion will be correct. Be especially alert to contradictory cues, cues that refute your initial hypotheses. It is relatively easy to perceive cues that confirm your hypotheses but more difficult to acknowledge contradictory evidence. At the same time, seek validation from others. Do others see things in the same way you do? If not, ask yourself if your perceptions may be in some way distorted.

Has the failure to follow any of these suggestions ever resulted in perceptual mistakes?

Avoid mind reading. Regardless of how many behaviors you observe and how carefully you examine them, you can only *guess* what is going on in someone's mind. A person's motives are not open to outside inspection; you can only make assumptions based on overt behaviors. Substitute perception checking ("Did you realize that my birthday was Thursday?") for mind reading ("You forgot my birthday because you don't really love me").

Beware of your own biases. Know when your perceptual evaluations are unduly influenced by your own biases: for example, perceiving only the positive in people you like and only the negative in people you do not like.

Summary	U N I T I N B R I E F

A RETURN TO OBJECTIVES:

In this unit we examined perception, a fundamental process in all interpersonal communication encounters. We focused on four questions: (1) What is perception and what are its principal stages? (2) What is attribution and what information do you use when you attribute motives to others and to yourself? What are the major errors of attributions? (3) What are the basic processes involved in interpersonal perception? (4) How might you increase your accuracy in perception?

Definitions	Processes	Accuracy
Perception: The process by which you become aware of objects and events in the external world. Perception occurs in three stages: (1) occurrence of sensory stimulation, (2) organization of sensory stimulation, and (3) interpretation-evaluation of sensory stimulation.	**Implicit personality theory:** Certain characteristics go with certain other characteristics. **Self-fulfilling prophecy:** Predictions influence behaviors. **Perceptual accentuation:** Tendency to perceive what you expect to perceive. **Primacy-recency:** First impressions often serve as filters for more recent information. **Consistency:** Perception is influenced by your expectation of consistent or balanced behaviors. **Stereotyping:** Fixed impressions about a group influence your perceptions of individual members	**Reduce uncertainty.** **Perception check.** **Perceive critically,** for example, recognize your role in perception, formulate hypotheses rather than conclusions, look for a variety of cues (especially contradictory ones), avoid mind reading, beware of your own biases.
Attribution: The process through which you try to understand the behaviors of others (and your own, in **self-attribution**), particularly the reasons or motivations for these behaviors.	**Consensus:** The degree to which a person's behavior conforms to the norm. **Consistency:** The degree to which the same behavior occurs in other, similar situations. **Distinctiveness:** The degree to which the same behavior occurs in different situations. **Controllability:** The extent to which the person is in control of his or her behavior.	The **self-serving bias** may lead you to attribute positive motives to your own and negative motives to the behaviors of others. The **fundamental attribution error** may lead you to attribute too much influence to the belief that people do what they do because that's the kind of people they are and not enough weight to the influence of the specific situation they are in.

UNIT
7

Listening in Interpersonal Communication

Unit Topics	Unit Objectives
	After completing this unit, you should be able to:
The Listening Process Receiving Understanding Remembering Evaluating Responding	1. Define *listening* and its five stages
Listening, Culture, and Gender Culture and Listening Gender and Listening	2. Explain the role of culture and gender and how they may influence listening
Effective Listening Participatory and Passive Listening Empathic and Objective Listening Nonjudgmental and Critical Listening Surface and Depth Listening	3. Define and distinguish among *participatory* and *passive listening, empathic* and *objective listening, nonjudgmental* and *critical listening,* and *surface* and *depth listening*
Active Listening Purposes of Active Listening Techniques of Active Listening	4. Define *active listening* and identify its major functions and techniques

---

EXPERIENTIAL LEARNING VEHICLE

Vehicle No. 8, "Sequential Communication," pp. 448–449, illustrates the difficulties involved in listening and some of the types of errors that occur. No. 15, "Giving and Taking Directions," pp. 456–458, will further illustrate the difficulties in listening.

If you were to measure importance in terms of time spent, listening would be your most important communication activity because it engages most of your communication time (see Figure 7.1). Another way to gauge the importance of listening is to look at the purposes that listening serves and the many benefits that you can derive from listening more effectively. Listening serves the same purposes already noted for interpersonal communication: to learn, to relate, to influence, to play, and to help. Table 7.1 summarizes some of the benefits of effective listening.

There's no denying that you listen a great deal. Whether you listen effectively and efficiently, however, is another matter. In actual practice, most people are relatively poor listeners; their listening behavior could be much improved. Training in listening does increase listening effectiveness (Barker et al. 1992). Given the amount of time spent listening, such improvement seems well worth the required effort. And it does take effort.

Before reading about the principles and techniques of listening, examine your own listening habits by taking the self-test "How Good a Listener Are You?"

Listening Process

Listening is not the same as hearing. Hearing is a physiological process that occurs when you are in the vicinity of vibrations in the air and these vibrations impinge on your eardrum. Hearing is basically a passive process that occurs without any attention or effort on your part. Listening is different.

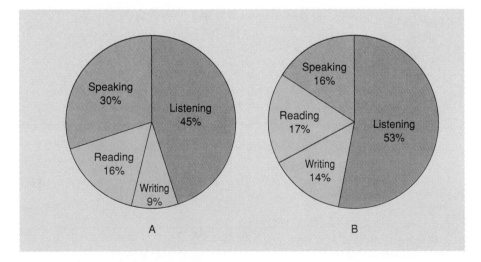

Figure 7.1   The Time Spent in Listening.
This figure diagrams the results of two studies and confirms the point that listening occupies an enormous part of our communication life. Note that in both studies, one (Rankin 1929) using adults as subjects (A) and one (Barker, Edwards, Gaines, Gladney, and Holley 1980) using college students (B), listening occupied more time than any other communication activity. The results of other studies, using people in business, for example, further confirm the importance of listening. What would a pie chart of your communication activities look like? Would listening be the largest area?

Table 7.1	**Purposes and Benefits of Effective Listening**

This table identifies the major purposes and benefits of effective listening. Can you identify other purposes and benefits? Under what headings would you explain the purposes and benefits of listening?

Purposes and Benefits	**Examples**
Learn: Acquire knowledge of others, the world, and yourself and profit from the insights of others who have learned or seen what you have not.	Listening to Peter about his travels to Cuba will help you understand more about Peter as well as about life in a communist country.
Avoid difficulties by hearing and being able to respond to warnings before problems develop or escalate and become impossible to control.	Listening to student reactions (instead of responding with "Students just don't want to work hard") will help the teacher plan more effective and relevant classes and be better able to respond to students' real needs and concerns.
Make reasoned and reasonable choices by acquiring information relevant to decisions you'll make in business or professional life.	Listening to the difficulties your sales staff has (instead of responding with "You're just not trying hard enough") may help you design a more effective advertising campaign or offer more pertinent sales training.
Relate: Form and maintain friendships and love relationships on the basis of social acceptance and popularity because people come to like those who are attentive and supportive.	Others will increase their liking for you once they feel you have genuine concern for them.
Influence: Have an effect on the attitudes and behaviors of others because people are more likely to respect and follow those whom they feel have listened to and understood them.	Workers are more likely to follow your advice once they feel you have truly listened to and heard their points of view, concerns, and insights.
Play: Know when to suspend critical and evaluative thinking and when simply to engage in passive and accepting listening.	Listening to the stories and anecdotes of coworkers will allow you to gain a more comfortable balance between the world of work and the world of play and perhaps to see humor in a world of seriousness.
Help: Be able to assist other people because you hear more, empathize more, and come to understand others more deeply.	Listening to your child's complaints about her teacher (instead of responding with "Now what did you do wrong?") will put you in a better position to help your child cope with school and with her teacher.

Listening involves a series of five steps: receiving, understanding, remembering, evaluating, and responding (Figure 7.2). Note that the listening process is a circular one. The responses of one person serve as the stimuli for the other person, whose responses in turn serve as the stimuli for the first person, and so on.

Receiving

Listening begins with receiving the messages the speaker sends. The messages are both verbal and nonverbal; they consist of words as well as gestures, facial expressions, and variations in volume and rate.

What purpose does your listening serve most of the time? Do you listen for a reason in addition to the five noted here? In what types of listening situations are you at your best? At your worst?

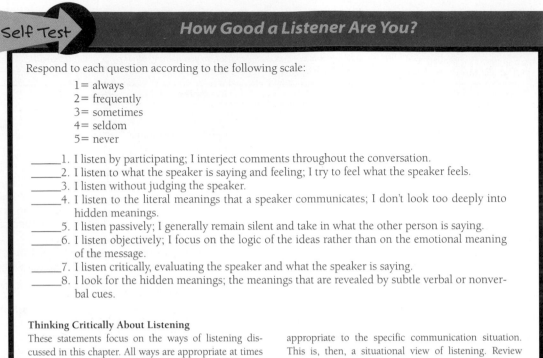

Self Test

How Good a Listener Are You?

Respond to each question according to the following scale:

1 = always
2 = frequently
3 = sometimes
4 = seldom
5 = never

_____1. I listen by participating; I interject comments throughout the conversation.
_____2. I listen to what the speaker is saying and feeling; I try to feel what the speaker feels.
_____3. I listen without judging the speaker.
_____4. I listen to the literal meanings that a speaker communicates; I don't look too deeply into hidden meanings.
_____5. I listen passively; I generally remain silent and take in what the other person is saying.
_____6. I listen objectively; I focus on the logic of the ideas rather than on the emotional meaning of the message.
_____7. I listen critically, evaluating the speaker and what the speaker is saying.
_____8. I look for the hidden meanings; the meanings that are revealed by subtle verbal or nonverbal cues.

Thinking Critically About Listening

These statements focus on the ways of listening discussed in this chapter. All ways are appropriate at times and all ways are inappropriate at times. It depends. So, the only responses that are really inappropriate are "always" and "never." Effective listening is listening that is appropriate to the specific communication situation. This is, then, a situational view of listening. Review these statements and try to identify situations in which each statement would be appropriate and situations in which each statement would be inappropriate.

Are you satisfied with the level of listening that others give you? How might you go about increasing their level?

At this stage, you note not only what is said (verbally and nonverbally) but also what is omitted. You receive, for example, your friend's summary of good deeds as well as the omission of all the broken promises. In receiving, try to:

◆ focus your attention on the speaker's verbal and nonverbal messages, on what is said and on what is not said.
◆ avoid distractions in the environment.
◆ focus your attention on the speaker rather than on what you will say next.
◆ maintain your role as listener and avoid interrupting.

Understanding

Understanding is the stage at which you learn what the speaker means—the thoughts and emotional tone. In understanding, try to:

◆ relate the new information the speaker is giving to what you already know.
◆ see the speaker's messages from the speaker's point of view; avoid judging the message until you fully understand it as the speaker intended it.
◆ ask questions for clarification, if necessary; ask for additional details or examples if they are needed.
◆ rephrase (paraphrase) the speaker's ideas in your own words.

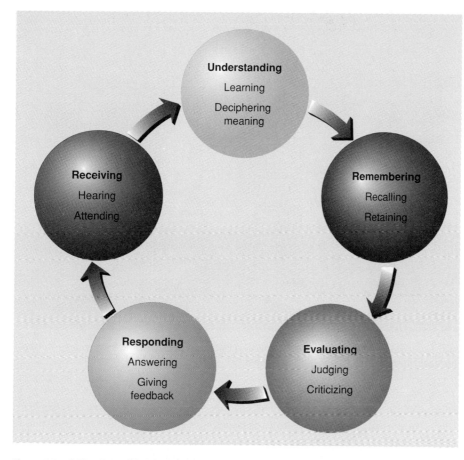

Figure 7.2 A Five-Stage Model of Listening.
Do recognize that at each stage there will be lapses. For example, at the receiving stage a listener receives part of the message but because of noise and perhaps other reasons fails to receive other parts. Similarly, at the stage of understanding, a listener understands part of the message but because of the inability to share another's meanings fully fails to understand other parts. The same is true for remembering, evaluating, and responding. This model draws on a variety of previous models that listening researchers have developed (for example, Alessandra 1986; Barker and Gaut 1996; Brownell 1987; Steil, Barker, and Watson 1983).

Remembering

For listening to take place, you need to remember the messages. In some small-group and public speaking situations, you can augment your memory by taking notes or by taping the messages. In most interpersonal communication situations, however, note taking is inappropriate, although you often do write down a telephone number, an appointment, or directions.

For example, when Susan says she is planning to buy a new car, the effective listener remembers this and at later meetings asks about the car. When Joe says his mother is ill, the effective listener remembers this and inquires about her health later in the week.

What you remember is actually not what was said but what you think (or remember) was said. Memory for speech is not reproductive; you don't simply

How effective a listener are you? Are you satisfied with this? How might you improve your listening effectiveness?

With which stage of listening do you think people have the most trouble? With which stage do you have the most trouble? What might you do about it?

reproduce in your memory what the speaker said. Rather, memory is *reconstructive*; you actually reconstruct the messages you hear into a system that makes sense to you.

To illustrate this important concept, try to memorize the list of 12 words presented below (Glucksberg and Danks 1975). Don't worry about the order of the words. Only the number remembered counts. Take about 20 seconds to memorize as many words as possible. Don't read any further until you have tried to memorize the list of words.

BED	DREAM	COMFORT
REST	WAKE	SOUND
AWAKE	NIGHT	SLUMBER
TIRED	EAT	SNORE

Now close the book and write down as many of the words from this list as you can remember. Don't read any further until you have tested your own memory.

If you are like my own students, you not only remembered a good number of the words on the list, but you also "remembered" at least one word that was not on the list: "sleep." You did not simply reproduce the list; you reconstructed it. In this case, you gave the list meaning, and part of that meaning included the word "sleep." You frequently reconstruct messages so they make sense to you. In the process, however, the messages often get distorted. In remembering, try to:

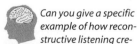
Can you give a specific example of how reconstructive listening created communication difficulties?

- ◆ identify the central ideas and the major support advanced.
- ◆ summarize the message in a more easily retained form, but be careful not to ignore crucial details or qualifications.
- ◆ repeat names and key concepts to yourself or, if appropriate, aloud.

Evaluating

Evaluating consists of judging the messages in some way. At times, you may try to evaluate the speaker's underlying intentions or motives. Often this evaluation process goes on without much conscious awareness. For example, Elaine tells you that she is up for a promotion and is really excited about it. You may then try to judge her intention: She wants you to use your influence with the company president or she's preoccupied with the promotion and so tells everyone or she's looking for a compliment.

In other situations, your evaluation is more in the nature of critical analysis. For example, in listening to proposals advanced in a business meeting, you might ask: Are they practical? Will they increase productivity? What's the evidence? Is there contradictory evidence? In evaluating, try to:

◆ resist evaluation until you fully understand the speaker's point of view.
◆ assume that the speaker is a person of goodwill, and give the speaker the benefit of any doubt by asking for clarification on positions to which you feel you might object.
◆ distinguish facts from inferences (see Unit 12), opinions, and personal interpretations by the speaker.
◆ identify any biases, self-interests, or prejudices that may lead the speaker to slant unfairly what is presented.

Responding

Responding occurs in two phases: (1) responses you make while the speaker is talking and (2) responses you make after the speaker has stopped talking. These responses are feedback—information that you send back to the speaker; this information tells the speaker how you feel and what you think about his or her messages (Unit 15). Responses made while the speaker is talking should be supportive and should acknowledge that you are listening to the speaker. These responses include what nonverbal researchers call **back-channeling cues**, such as "I see," "yes," "uh-huh," and similar signals that let the speaker know you are listening.

Responses made after the speaker has stopped talking are generally more elaborate and might include expressing empathy ("I know how you must feel"), asking for clarification ("Do you mean that this new health plan is to replace the old one?"), challenging ("I think your evidence is weak here"), and agreeing ("You're absolutely right on this; I'll support your proposal"). In responding, try to:

◆ be supportive of the speaker throughout the speaker's talk by using and varying your back-channeling cues; using only one back-channeling cue—for example, saying "uh-huh" throughout—will make it appear that you are not listening but are on automatic pilot.
◆ express support for the speaker in your final responses (especially).
◆ be honest; the speaker has a right to expect honest responses, even if they express disagreement.
◆ own your responses; state your thoughts and feelings as your own, and use I-messages (for example, say "I think the new proposal will entail greater expense than you outlined" rather than "Everyone will object to the plan for costing too much").

With which of the five stages of the listening process do you have the most difficulty? The least difficulty?

Table 7.2	Some Problem-Causing Ways of Responding in Listening	
Listener Type	**Listening (Responding) Behavior**	**(Mis)interpreting Thoughts**
The static listener	Gives no feedback, remains relatively motionless, reveals no expression.	Why isn't she reacting? Am I not producing sound?
The monotonous feedback giver	Seems responsive but the responses never vary; regardless of what you say, the response is the same.	Am I making sense? Why is he still smiling? I'm being dead serious.
The overly expressive listener	Reacts to just about everything with extreme responses.	Why is she so expressive? I didn't say anything that provocative. She'll have a heart attack when I get to the punchline.
The reader/writer	Reads or writes while "listening" and only occasionally glances up.	Am I that boring? Is last week's student newspaper more interesting than me?
The eye avoider	Looks all around the room and at others but never at you.	Why isn't he looking at me? Do I have spinach on my teeth?
The preoccupied listener	Listens to other things at the same time, often with headphones with the sound so loud that it interferes with your own thinking.	When is she going to shut that music off and really listen? Am I so boring that my talk needs background music?
The waiting listener	Listens for a cue to take over the speaking turn.	Is he listening to me or rehearsing his next interruption?
The thought-completing listener	Listens a little and then finishes your thought.	Am I that predictable? Why do I bother saying anything? He already knows what I'm going to say.

 What other difficult listeners might you add to this table?

Table 7.2 identifies some types of difficult listeners and their problem-causing ways of responding. Review this table and try to see if it includes some of your own listening behaviors.

Listening, Culture, and Gender

Listening is difficult, in part, because of the inevitable differences in the communication systems between speaker and listener. Because each person has had a unique set of experiences, each person's meaning system is going to be different from each other person's. When speaker and listener come from different cultures or are of different genders the differences and their effects are naturally much greater. Consider culture first.

Culture and Listening

Among the cultural differences we may consider are those concerning language, nonverbal communication, style, story versus evidence, credibility, and feedback. These will give you an idea of some of the many cultural factors that can influence listening.

Speech and Language   Even when speaker and listener speak the same language, they speak it with different meanings and different accents. No two speakers speak exactly the same language. Every speaker speaks an idiolect, a unique variation of the language (King and DiMichael 1992). Speakers of the same language will, at the very least, have different meanings for the same terms because they have had different experiences.

Speakers and listeners who have different native languages and who may have learned English as a second language will have even greater differences in meaning. Translations are never precise and never fully capture the meaning in the other language. Your meaning for "house"—if learned in a culture with family homes surrounded by lots of land around them—is going to be very different from someone who learned the word living in a neighborhood of high-rise tenements. Although you will each hear the same word, the meanings you'll each create will be drastically different. In adjusting your listening—especially when in an intercultural setting—understand that the speaker's meanings may be very different from yours even though you are each speaking the same language.

In many classrooms throughout the country, there will be a wide range of accents. Those whose native language is a tonal one such as Chinese (where differences in pitch signal important meaning differences) may speak English with variations in pitch that may seem puzzling to others. Those whose native language is Japanese may have trouble distinguishing "L" from "R" since Japanese does not make this distinction. The native language acts as a filter and influences the accent given to the second language.

Do you stereotype others on the basis of their speech and language? Do others stereotype you because of the way you speak?

Nonverbal Behavioral Differences   Speakers from different cultures have different display rules, cultural rules that govern what nonverbal behaviors are appropriate and which are inappropriate in a public setting. As you listen to another person, you also "listen" to their nonverbals (Units 9, 12, and 13 cover this area). If these are drastically different from what you expect on the basis of the verbal message, you may see them as a kind of interference or perhaps as contradictory messages. Also, different cultures may give very different meanings to the same nonverbal gesture, a point well made in the illustration of the Olympic hand signals in Unit 3.

Direct and Indirect Styles   Some cultures—Western Europe and the United States, for example—favor a direct style in communication; they advise us to "say what you mean and mean what you say." Many Asian cultures, on the other hand, favor an indirect style; they emphasize politeness and maintaining a positive public image rather than absolute truth. Listen carefully to persons with different styles of directness. Consider the possibility that the meanings the speaker wishes to communicate with, say, indirectness, may be very different from the meanings you would communicate with indirectness.

Can you think of a media personality who is evaluated very differently by members of different cultures?

Credibility   What makes a speaker credible or believable will vary from one culture to another. In some cultures, people would claim that competence is the most important factor in, say, choosing a teacher for their preschool children. In other cultures, the most important factor might be the goodness or morality of the teacher. Similarly, members of different cultures may perceive the credibility of the various media very differently. For example, members of a repressive society in which the government controls television news may come to attribute little credibility to such broadcasts. After all, this person might reason, television news is simply what the government wants you to know. This may be hard to understand or even recognize by someone raised in the United States, for example, where the media are free of such political control.

Have you ever been a party to or a witness of listening problems caused by the failure to recognize cultural differences? What could have been done to prevent such listening failures?

Feedback   Members of some cultures give very direct and very honest feedback. Speakers from these cultures—the United States is a good example—expect the feedback to be an honest reflection of what their listeners are feeling. In other cultures—Japan and Korea are good examples—it's more important to be positive, so they may respond with compliments (say, in commenting on a business colleague's proposal) even though they don't feel it. Listen to feedback, as you would all messages, with the recognition that cultures view feedback differently.

Gender and Listening

Men and women learn different styles of listening just as they learn different styles of using verbal and nonverbal messages. Not surprisingly, these different styles can create major difficulties in opposite sex interpersonal communication. According to Deborah Tannen (1990) in her best-selling *You Just Don't Understand: Women and Men in Conversation*, women seek to build rapport and establish a closer relationship and use listening to achieve these ends. Men, on the other hand, will play up their expertise, emphasize it, and use it in dominating the interaction. Women play down their expertise and are more interested in communicating supportiveness. Tannen argues that the goal of a man in conversation is to be given respect and so he seeks to show his knowledge and expertise. A woman, on the other hand, seeks to be liked and so she expresses agreement.

Men and women also show that they are listening in different ways. In conversation, a woman is more apt to give lots of listening cues such as interjecting "yeah, uh-uh," nodding in agreement, and smiling. A man is more likely to listen quietly, without giving lots of listening cues as feedback. Subsequent research seems to confirm Tannen's position. For example, an analysis of calls to a crisis center in Finland revealed that calls received by a female counselor were significantly longer for both men and women callers (Salminen and Glad 1992). It is likely that the greater number of listening cues given by the women encouraged the callers to keep talking. This same study also found that male callers were helped by "just listening" whereas women callers were helped by "empathic understanding."

Tannen argues, however, that men do listen less to women than women listen to men. The reason, says Tannen, is that listening places the person in an inferior position whereas speaking places the person in a superior position. Men may seem to assume a more argumentative posture while listening, as if getting ready to argue. They may also appear to ask questions that are more argumentative or that seek to puncture holes in your position as a way to play up their own expertise. Women are more likely to ask supportive questions and perhaps offer criticism that is more positive than men. Women let the speaker see that they are listening. Men, on the other hand, use fewer listening cues in conversation. Men and women act this way to both men and women; their customary ways of talking do not seem to change depending on whether the listener is male or female.

There is no evidence to show that these differences represent any negative motives on the part of men to prove themselves superior or of women to ingratiate themselves. Rather, these differences in listening seem largely the result of the way in which men and women have been socialized.

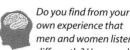

Do you find from your own experience that men and women listen differently? How would you go about testing one of these assumptions about the differences in the listening of men and women?

Effective Listening

Because you listen for different purposes, the principles of effective listening should vary from one situation to another. The following four dimensions of listening illustrate the appropriateness of different listening modes for different communication situations.

Participatory and Passive Listening

The general key to effective listening in interpersonal situations is active participation. Perhaps the best preparation for participatory listening is to *act* (physically and mentally) like a participant. For many people, this may be the most abused rule of effective listening. Recall, for example, how your body almost automatically reacts to important news: Almost immediately, you assume an upright posture, cock your head to the speaker, and remain relatively still and quiet. You do this almost reflexively because this is the way you listen most effectively. Even more important than this physical alertness is mental alertness. As a listener, participate in the communication interaction as an equal partner with the speaker, as one who is emotionally and intellectually ready to engage in the sharing of meaning.

Effective participatory listening is expressive. Let the listener know that you are participating in the communication interaction. Nonverbally, maintain eye contact, focus your concentration on the speaker rather than on others present, and express your feelings facially. Verbally, ask appropriate questions, signal understanding with "I see" or "yes," and express agreement or disagreement as appropriate.

Passive listening is, however, not without merit and some recognition of its value is warranted. Passive listening—listening without talking or directing the speaker in any obvious way—is a powerful means of communicating acceptance. This is the kind of listening that people ask for when they say, "Just listen to me." They are essentially asking you to suspend your judgment and "just listen". Passive listening allows the speaker to develop his or her thoughts and ideas in the presence of another person who accepts but does not evaluate, who supports but does not intrude. By listening passively, you provide a supportive and receptive environment. Once that has been established, you may wish to participate in a more active way, verbally and nonverbally.

Some people would argue that "passive listening" is not a type of listening but rather just hearing. Do you see any value in the concept of "passive listening?"

In regulating participatory and passive listening, keep the following in mind:

◆ All listening is hard work. Unaided, people are likely to follow the law of least effort and do whatever is easiest. Combat this tendency. Avoid, too, "the entertainment syndrome," the expectation to be amused by a speaker (Floyd 1985).

◆ Whether participatory or passive, listening will be aided if you combat noise. Remove distractions or other interference (newspapers, magazines, stereos) so that your listening task will have less competition.

◆ Avoid preoccupation with yourself or with external issues. Avoid focusing on your own performance in the interaction or on rehearsing your responses. Avoid, too, focusing on matters that are irrelevant to the interaction—for example, what you did Saturday night or your plans for this evening.

◆ Use the thought-speech time differential effectively. Because you can process information faster than the average rate of speech, there is often a time lag. Use this time to summarize the speaker's thoughts, formulate questions, and draw connections between what the speaker says and what you already know.

◆ Assume there is value in what the speaker is saying. Resist assuming that what you have to say is more valuable than the speaker's remarks.

Empathic and Objective Listening

If you want to understand what a person means and what a person is feeling, you need to listen empathically: Feel with them, see the world as they see it, feel what they feel.

Although empathy is preferred in most situations, there are times when you need to go beyond empathy and look at the situation more objectively. It is important to listen to a friend tell you how the entire world hates him or her and to understand how your friend feels and why. But at times you may need to look a bit more objectively at the situation and perhaps see beyond what your friend sees. Sometimes you have to put your empathic responses aside and listen with objectivity and detachment.

In adjusting your empathic and objective listening focus, keep the following recommendations in mind:

 What types of communication situations call for the most empathy? Are there types of communication situations where empathy can actually create interpersonal problems?

◆ See the sequence of events as punctuated from the speaker's point of view, and see how this can influence what the speaker says and does (Unit 2).

◆ View the speaker as an equal. To encourage openness and empathy, try to eliminate any physical or psychological barriers to equality; for example, step from behind the large desk separating you from your employees. Avoid interrupting, a sign that you feel what you have to say is more important.

◆ Seek to understand both thoughts and feelings. Do not consider your listening task finished until you have understood what the speaker is feeling as well as thinking.

◆ Avoid "offensive listening," the tendency to listen to bits and pieces of information that will help you attack the speaker or find fault with something the speaker has said.

◆ Beware of the "friend-or-foe" factor that may lead you to distort messages because of your attitudes toward another person. For example, if you think

Freddy is stupid, then it will take added effort to listen objectively to Freddy's messages and to hear anything that is clear or insightful.

Nonjudgmental and Critical Listening

Effective listening involves listening nonjudgmentally to help you understand, and listening critically to help you make an evaluation or judgment. Clearly, you should first listen for understanding while suspending judgment. Only after you have fully understood the messages should you evaluate or judge. Listening with an open mind is extremely difficult. It is not easy, for example, to listen to arguments against some deeply held belief or to criticisms of something you value highly.

Supplement open-minded listening with critical listening. Listening with an open mind will help you better understand the messages; listening with a critical mind will help you better analyze and evaluate the messages. To listen effectively, exercise both levels.

In adjusting your nonjudgmental and critical listening, consider the following:

◆ Keep an open mind. Delay evaluation until you have fully understood the intent and the content of the message being communicated.

◆ Avoid distorting messages through oversimplification or leveling—the tendency to eliminate details and to simplify complex messages so they are easier to remember. Also avoid filtering out unpleasant or undesirable messages; you may miss the very information you need to change your assumptions or your behaviors.

◆ Recognize your own biases; everyone has them. They may interfere with accurate listening and cause you to distort the messages you hear. They may lead you to "hear" according to your own biases, prejudices, and expectations. For example, are your ethnic, national, or religious biases preventing you from appreciating a speaker's point of view? Biases may also lead you to give increased importance to something because it confirms your prejudices or to minimize it because it contradicts them.

◆ Avoid uncritical listening when you need to make evaluations and judgments.

In which situations or with which people do you have the greatest difficulty listening nonjudgmentally? The greatest difficulty listening empathically? Why?

Table 7.3 identifies additional pitfalls to avoid as you strengthen your abilities to listening critically.

Surface and Depth Listening

In Shakespeare's *Julius Caesar,* Marc Antony, delivering Caesar's funeral oration, says: "I come to bury Caesar, not to praise him. . . . The evil that men do lives after them. . . . The good is oft interred with their bones." And later: "For Brutus is an honorable man. . . . So are they all, all honorable men." But Antony did come to praise Caesar and to convince the crowd that Brutus was not an honorable man. He came to incite the crowd to avenge the death of Caesar.

In most messages, there is an obvious meaning that a literal reading of the words and sentences reveals. But there is often another level of meaning. Sometimes, as in *Julius Caesar,* it is the opposite of the expressed literal meaning;

Table 7.3   Critical Listening Pitfalls

The first three distortions were first introduced in The Fine Art of Propaganda, *prepared for the Institute for Propaganda Analysis in the 1940s (Lee and Lee 1972, 1995). The last three come from a more contemporary study of persuasive techniques (Pratkanis and Aronson 1991). The unethical individual (one who distorts the truth) uses these techniques to gain your compliance without logic or evidence; it is up to the critical listener to identify these and not be fooled by them. Can you identify any additional pitfalls that you should be on the lookout for?*

Technique	Listening Strategy
Name-calling involves giving an idea, a group of people, or a political philosophy a bad name ("atheist," "Neo-Nazi," "cult"). In the opposite of name-calling the speaker tries to make you accept some idea by associating it with things you value highly ("democracy," "free speech," "academic freedom").	Remember that labels are useful most of the time but they can often obscure the actual person or idea. Listen first to evidence and argument; never take labels as evidence or reasons for judgment.
Testimonial involves using the image associated with some person to gain your approval (if you respect the person) or your rejection (if you do not respect the person). This is the technique of advertisers who use people dressed up to look like doctors or plumbers or chefs to sell their products.	Listen carefully to the person's credentials; be suspicious when you hear such phrases as "experts agree," "scientists say," "good cooks know," or "dentists advise." Ask yourself exactly who these experts are and what the source of their expertise is.
Bandwagon is a technique that tries to persuade you to accept or reject an idea or proposal because "everybody is doing it," so "jump on the bandwagon."	You'll hear this technique used frequently during election time where results of polls are used to get you to join the group and vote for one person or another. Again, listen to the evidence; 50,000 Frenchmen—as the saying goes—can be wrong.
Granfallon—a term taken from a novel by Kurt Vonnegut—refers to the tendency of people to see themselves as constituting a cohesive and like-minded group because they are given a label. The name might be religious: "As Christians (Jews, Muslims, Hindus) we know that …" Or, it might be a cultural label: "As Native Americans (African Americans, Hispanics, Arabs) we should …" or an occupational one: "As teachers (blue collar workers, artists, journalists, athletes) we agree that …"	The problem with this "reasoning" is that it divides the word into "we" and "they" and this inevitably simplifies the situation and ignores the vast individual differences in any group covered by such broad labels. Listen to such comments as gross and oversimplified generalizations; generalizations ignore too many important individual differences.
Agenda-setting involves claiming that a particular issue is crucial and all others are unimportant and insignificant. This technique is used frequently in interpersonal conflict situations where each person may claim that his or her objection or need is the important one and that the other person's are unimportant.	In almost all situations, and especially in interpersonal conflict situations, there are many issues and many sides to each issue. Often the person proclaiming "X is the issue" really means "I'll be able to get my way if you focus solely on X and ignore the other issues."
Attack involves accusing another person (usually an opponent) of some serious wrongdoing so that the issue under discussion never gets examined. "Arguments" such as "How can I ever believe you after you lied."	Although a person's personal reputation and past behavior are often relevant, listen most carefully to the issue at hand. When personal attack draws attention away from other issues, then it becomes fallacious.

Thumb through a recent magazine with these critical listening pitfalls in mind. Can you identify any of these in current advertisements? Which pitfalls seem to be used most often? Which are effective in persuading you?

sometimes it seems totally unrelated. In reality, few messages have only one level of meaning. Most function on two or three levels at the same time. Consider some of these frequently heard messages: A friend asks you how you like his new haircut. Another friend asks you how you like her painting. On one level, the meaning is clear: Do you like the haircut? Do you like the painting? It is reasonable to assume, however, that on another level your friends are asking you to say something positive—about his appearance, about her artistic ability. The parent who seems at first to be complaining about working hard at the office or in the home may be asking for appreciation. The child who talks about the unfairness of the other children in the playground may be asking for some expression of caring. To appreciate these other meanings, you need to engage in depth listening.

When listening interpersonally, be particularly sensitive to different levels of meaning. If you respond only to the surface-level communication (the literal meaning), you will miss the opportunity to make meaningful contact with the other person's feelings and real needs. Suppose you say to your parent, "You're always complaining. I bet you really love working so hard." You may be failing to answer a very real call for understanding and appreciation.

In regulating your surface and depth listening, consider the following:

Might listening "in depth" get you into trouble? What principle or suggestion would you offer to combat this possibility?

◆ Focus on both verbal and nonverbal messages. Recognize both consistent and inconsistent "packages" of messages and take these cues as guides to the meaning the speaker is trying to communicate. Ask questions when in doubt. Listen also to what is omitted.

◆ Listen for both content and relational messages. The student who constantly challenges the teacher is on one level communicating disagreement over content; the student is debating the issues. However, on another level—the relationship level—the student may be voicing objections to the instructor's authority or authoritarianism. If the instructor is to deal effectively with the student, he or she must listen and respond to both types of messages.

◆ Make special note of statements that refer to the speaker. Remember that people inevitably talk about themselves from their own point of view, colored by their needs and desires, and influenced by their own experiences.

◆ Do not disregard the literal (surface) meaning of interpersonal messages in your attempt to uncover the more hidden (deep) meanings. If you do, you will quickly find that your listening problems disappear: No one will talk to you anymore. Balance your attention between the surface and the underlying meanings. Respond to the various levels of meaning in the messages of others as you would like others to respond to yours—sensitively but not obsessively, readily but not overambitiously.

As stressed throughout this discussion, listening is situational; the type of listening that is appropriate varies with the situation. You can visualize a listening situation as one in which you have to make choices among at least the four dimensions of listening just discussed (Figure 7.3). Each listening situation should call for a somewhat different configuration of listening responses; the art of effective listening is largely one of making appropriate choices along these four dimensions.

Participatory	___:___:___:___:___:___	Passive
Empathic	___:___:___:___:___:___	Objective
Nonjudgmental	___:___:___:___:___:___	Critical
Surface	___:___:___:___:___:___	Deep

Figure 7.3   Listening Choices.
Effective listening is largely a matter of adjusting your behavior along such dimensions as these. Some situations will call for listening that is highly participatory, empathic, nonjudgmental, and surface focused. Other situations will call for listening that is more passive, objective, critical, and depth focused. What type of listening do you think would be most appropriate for such situations as these (mark each of the scales above to represent the type of listening you would use)? (1) Your steady dating partner for the last five years tells you that spells of depression are becoming more frequent and more long lasting; (2) Your history instructor gives a lecture on the contribution of the ancient Greeks to modern civilization; (3) A physician delivers an analysis of recent physical tests and recommendations; (4) A best friend talks about family problems.

Active Listening

Active listening is one of the most important communication skills you can learn (Gordon 1975). Consider the following brief comment and some possible responses:

APHRODITE: That creep gave me a C on the paper. I really worked on that project, and all I get is a lousy C.

APOLLO: That's not so bad; most people got around the same grade. I got a C, too.

ATHENA: So what? This is your last semester. Who cares about grades anyway?

ACHILLES: You should be pleased with a C. Peggy and Michael both failed, and John and Judy got Ds.

DIANA: You got a C on that paper you were working on for the last three weeks? You sound really angry and hurt.

Which of the four responses given to Aphrodite would you be most likely to give? Why? In what types of situations do you engage in active listening? Does it serve useful functions? In what situations might active listening be counterproductive?

All four listeners are probably eager to make Aphrodite feel better, but they go about it in very different ways and, you can be sure, with very different outcomes. The first three listeners give fairly typical responses. Apollo and Athena both try to minimize the significance of a C grade, a common response to someone who has expressed displeasure or disappointment. Usually, it is also inappropriate. Although well-intentioned, this response does little to promote meaningful communication and understanding. Achilles tries to give the C grade a more positive meaning. Note, however, that all three listeners also say a great deal more: that Aphrodite should not be feeling unhappy, that these feelings are not legitimate. These responses deny the validity of these feelings and put Aphrodite in the position of having to defend them.

Diana, however, is different. Diana uses **active listening**, a process of sending back to the speaker what the listener thinks the speaker meant, both literally and emotionally. Active listening does not mean simply repeating the speaker's exact words. It is rather a process of putting into some meaningful whole your understanding of the speaker's total message—the verbal and the nonverbal, the content and the feelings.

MEDIA & TECHNOLOGY

TALK RADIO

One of the most popular television shows today is *Frazier,* a situation comedy based on the life of a talk radio show psychologist. And we all remember that it was through talk radio that Tom Hanks and Meg Ryan got together in *Sleepless in Seattle.* Media researchers Cameron Armstrong and Alan Rubin (1989, p. 84) note that talk radio enables listeners to "communicate with the outside world, get quick answers to questions, express opinions, and simply talk to other people. In short, talk radio allows for interpersonal communication." By placing a call, anxiety and loneliness are lessened and psychological and physical security are increased (Armstrong and Rubin 1989). Not only does talk radio allow for interpersonal communication, it also deals with it as a major subject. In fact, one of the newest developments in talk radio is the focus on interpersonal communication and relationships with popular communication authors like John Gray, Zig Ziglar, and Wayne Dyer offering insight and advice (*New York Times,* July 1, 1996, p. D7).

Armstrong and Rubin find seven motives for listening to talk radio. Generally, they find that people listen for relaxation, exciting entertainment, convenience, voyeurism or escape, useful information, passing the time, and companionship. These motives are not unlike those found for face-to-face interpersonal communication (Rubin, Perse, and Barbato 1988, see Unit 1, Figure 1.3).

Talk radio is a kind of substitute for interpersonal, face-to-face interaction and is similar to communicating via computer. In both talk radio and computer communication, there is significantly less ego involvement and much less potential threat to self-esteem. Both systems allow for a greater amount of anonymity (and hence psychological security and protection) than does face-to-face interaction. And yet, they provide many of the same rewards as does interpersonal face-to-face communication.

Talk radio may also be an extremely persuasive medium. After the bombing of a federal building in Oklahoma City in April 1995, much criticism and defense was heard about talk radio. President Clinton criticized the extremists on talk radio for inciting and nourishing an antigovernment sentiment and connected the bombing to "right-wing hate radio" (*Newsweek,* May 8, 1995, p. 44). Talk radio hosts such as Rush Limbaugh and G. Gordon Liddy rushed to the defense of talk radio and the right to criticize the government, arguing that the bombing had nothing to do with talk radio (*Newsweek* May 8, 1995, p. 39). Howard Halpern, president of the American Academy of Psychotherapists, writing to the *New York Times* (May 5, 1995, p. A30), argued that extremist talk is dangerous because it cuts the empathic bond of the listener with those who are attacked; it shows the members of the attacked group to be different and deserving of hate. By doing so, it allows and may even encourage physical attacks and mass violence, argues Halpern.

Talk radio provides avenues for minority points of view in a similar way as cable television. Some would argue that this is essential because the large media—the networks, national magazines, and major newspapers—will not cover such perspectives because they are focused on echoing the majority point of view.

Do you listen to talk radio? If so, what purposes does it serve for you? Are you influenced by the points of view you hear expressed on talk radio? How persuasive is talk radio compared with, say, interpersonal interaction with college friends? Compared with network reporting? What type of person listens to talk radio? Is the typical listener male or female? How popular is talk radio among college students? For example, how much time do college students spend listening to talk radio? How often is talk radio a topic of conversation among college students?

p. 159

Purposes of Active Listening

Active listening serves a number of important purposes. First, **it shows that you are listening** and often that is the only thing the speaker really wants—to know that someone cares enough to listen.

Second, it helps you **check how accurately you have understood what the speaker said and meant.** By reflecting back what you perceive to be the speaker's meaning, you give the speaker an opportunity to confirm, clarify, or amend your perceptions. In this way, future messages have a better chance of being relevant and purposeful.

Third, through active listening, you **express acceptance of the speaker's feelings.** Note that in the sample responses given, the first three listeners challenge the speaker; they refuse to give the expressed feelings legitimacy. The active listener accepts the speaker. The speaker's feelings are not challenged; rather, they are echoed in a sympathetic and empathic manner. Note, too, that in the first three responses, the feelings of the speaker are denied without ever actually being identified. Diana, however, not only accepts these feelings but also identifies them explicitly, again allowing the opportunity for correction.

Interestingly enough, when confronted by a person in distress, those listeners who try to solve the person's problem or who veer off the issue by engaging in "chitchat" come away significantly more depressed than those listeners who show acceptance of the distressed person's problems or who use supportive listening techniques (Notarius and Herrick 1988).

Would you find it difficult to listen actively to friends complaining that insurance premiums on their jaguars were going up? Would you find it difficult to listen actively to friends complain that their rent was going up and they feared becoming homeless?

Fourth, in active listening you **prompt the speaker to further explore his or her feelings and thoughts.** The active listening response gives the speaker the opportunity to elaborate on these feelings without having to defend them. Active listening sets the stage for meaningful dialogue, a dialogue of mutual understanding. In stimulating this further exploration, active listening also encourages the speaker to resolve his or her own conflicts.

Techniques of Active Listening

Three techniques will help you master active listening. At first, these principles may seem awkward and unnatural. With practice, however, they will flow and blend into a meaningful and effective dialogue.

Paraphrase the Speaker's Meaning

State in your own words what you think the speaker meant. This paraphrase helps to ensure understanding because the speaker can correct or modify your restatement. It also communicates your interest and your attention. Everyone wants to feel attended to, especially when angry or depressed. The active listening paraphrase confirms this.

When you paraphrase the speaker's meanings, you give the speaker a kind of green light to go into more detail, to elaborate. Thus, when you echo the thought about the C grade, the speaker can elaborate on why that grade was important. Make your paraphrases objective; be careful not to lead the speaker in the direction you think best. Also, be careful that you do not maximize or minimize the speaker's emotions; try to echo these feelings as accurately as you can.

When was the last time you needed someone to be an active listener? What happened? When was the last time you served as an active listener for someone? Might either of these interactions have been improved by the three principles discussed here?

Express Understanding of the Speaker's Feelings In addition to paraphrasing the content, echo the feelings you believe the speaker expressed or implied. This enables you to check your perception of the speaker's feelings and provides the speaker with the opportunity to see his or her feelings more objectively.

Expressing understanding is especially helpful when someone is angry, hurt, or depressed. Hearing these feelings objectively and seeing them from a less impassioned perspective will help in dealing effectively with them.

Most of us hold back our feelings until we are certain that others will be accepting. We need to hear statements such as "I understand" and "I see how you feel." When we feel that our emotions are accepted, we then feel free to go into more detail. Active listening provides the speaker with this important opportunity.

Ask Questions Ask questions to make sure that you understand the speaker's thoughts and feelings and to secure additional helpful information. Design your questions to provide just enough stimulation and support for the speaker to express the thoughts and feelings he or she wants to express. Avoid questions that pry into irrelevant areas or that challenge the speaker in any way.

Consider this dialogue and note the active listening techniques used throughout:

> PAT: That creep demoted me. He told me I wasn't an effective manager. I can't believe he did that, after all I've done for this company.

CHRIS: I can understand your anger. You've been manager for three or four months now, haven't you?

PAT: A little over three months. I know I was on trial, but I thought I was doing a good job.

CHRIS: Can you get another trial?

PAT: Yes, he said I could try again in a few months. But I feel like a failure.

CHRIS: I know what you mean. It's not a pleasant feeling. What else did he say?

PAT: He said I had trouble getting the paperwork done on time.

CHRIS: You've been late filing the reports?

PAT: A few times.

CHRIS: Is there a way to delegate the paperwork?

PAT: No, but I think I know now what needs to be done.

CHRIS: You sound as though you're ready to give that manager's position another try.

PAT: Yes, I think I am, and I'm going to let him know that I intend to apply in the next few months.

In what situations would active listening be inappropriate?

Even in this brief interaction, Pat has moved from unproductive anger with the supervisor as well as a feeling of failure to a determination to correct an unpleasant situation. Note, too, that Chris did not offer solutions but "simply" listened actively.

Here are several situations in which active listening responses seem appropriate. How would you respond to these situations?

1. Your friend Karla has been married for the last three years and has two small children, one two years old and one six months. Karla has been having an affair with a colleague at work. Her husband discovered this and is now suing for divorce. She confides this to you and says, "I really don't know what I'm going to do. I may lose the kids. I could never support myself and live the way we do now. I sure love that BMW. I wish these last two months had never happened and that I had never started up with Taylor."

2. Your boss, Ruth, has been an especially hard supervisor to work for. On several occasions, she filed negative evaluation reports on you and other members of your department. This has prevented you and others from getting merit raises in at least three instances. She is a perfectionist who doesn't understand that people make mistakes. During lunch, she comes over to your table and tells you that she has been fired and has to clean out her desk by 3 p.m. She says, "I can't believe they did this to me; I was the best supervisor they had. Our production level was always the highest in the company. They're idiots. Now I don't know what I'm going to do. Where will I get another job?"

3. Your mother has been having a difficult time at work. She was recently passed up for promotion and has received one of the lowest merit raises given in the company. She says, "I'm not sure what I did wrong. I do my work, mind my own business, don't take my sick days like everyone else. How could they give that promotion to Manuela, who's only been with the company for two years? I've given them seven years. Maybe I should just quit and try to find something else."

Summary	U N I T I N B R I E F

A RETURN TO OBJECTIVES:

In this unit we examined perception, a fundamental process in all interpersonal communication encounters. We focused on three questions(1) What is perception and what are its principal stages? (2) What is attribution and what information do you use when you attribute motives to others and to yourself? What are the major errors of attributions? (3) What are the basic processes involved in interpersonal perception? (4) How might you increase your accuracy in perception?

Definitions	Functions and Purposes	Techniques and Guidelines
Listening: An active process of receiving, understanding, remembering, evaluating, and responding to communications.	To **learn,** to acquire information To **relate,** to help form and maintain relationships To **influence,** to have an effect on the attitudes and behaviors of others To **play,** to enjoy oneself To **help,** to assist others	**Participatory-passive:** The extent to which you participate actively in the interaction. **Empathic-objective:** The extent to which you focus on feeling what the speaker is feeling. **Nonjudgmental-critical:** The extent to which you accept and support the speaker. **Surface-depth:** The extent to which you focus on the obvious surface meanings.
Active listening: A process of sending back to the speaker what you think the speaker meant in content and in feeling.	To show that you are listening To help you check on the accuracy of your understanding To express acceptance of the speaker's feelings To stimulate the speaker to explore further feelings and thoughts	Paraphrase by repeating in your own words the speakers' thoughts and feelings (as you understand them). Express understanding for the speaker. Ask questions to clarify what the speaker means and to stimulate the speaker to continue.

UNIT
8
Effectiveness in Interpersonal Communication

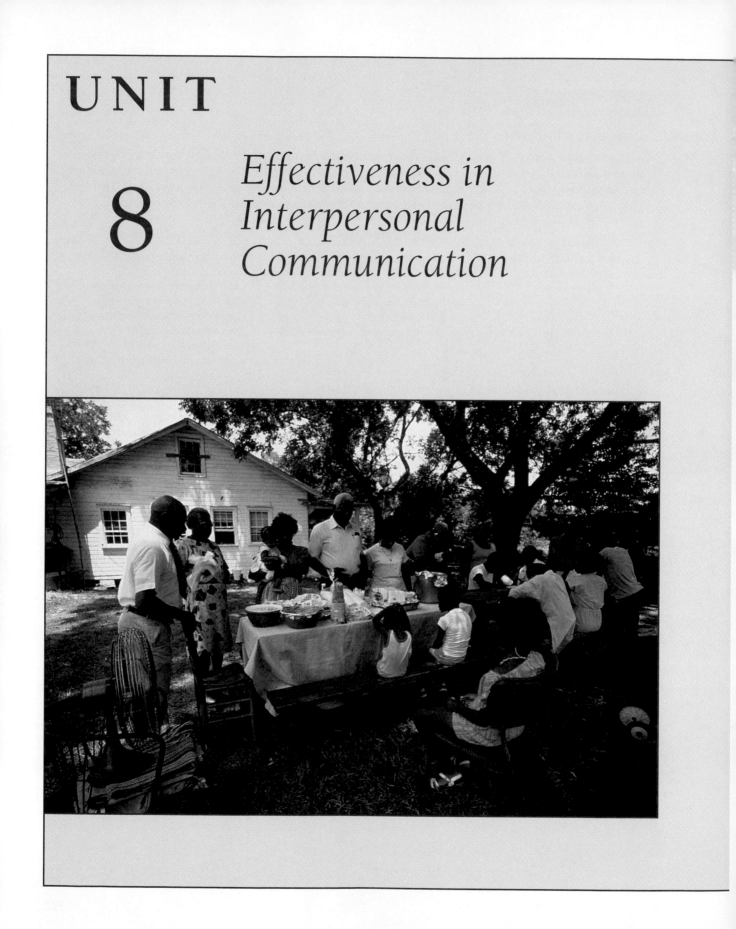

Unit Topics	Unit Objectives
	After completing this unit, you should be able to:
Skills About Skills Mindfulness Flexibility Cultural Sensitivity Metacommunicational Ability	1. Explain the concept of effectiveness in interpersonal communication 2. Explain *mindfulness, flexibility, cultural sensitivity,* and *metacommunicational ability* as they apply to interpersonal effectiveness
A Humanistic Model of Interpersonal Effectiveness Openness Empathy Supportiveness Positiveness Equality	3. Define *openness, empathy, supportiveness, positiveness,* and *equality* as they relate to interpersonal communication effectiveness
A Pragmatic Model of Interpersonal Effectiveness Confidence Immediacy Interaction Management Expressiveness Other-Orientation	4. Define *confidence, immediacy, interaction management, expressiveness,* and *other-orientation* as they relate to interpersonal communication effectiveness

---

EXPERIENTIAL LEARNING VEHICLES

Vehicles No. 15, "Giving and Taking Directions," pp. 456–458, No. 22, "Analyzing a Conflict Episode," pp. 464–466, and No. 24, "The Television Relationship," pp. 467–468, highlight the principles of interpersonal communication effectiveness.

Your interpersonal communication, like any of your behaviors, can vary from extremely effective to extremely ineffective. Still, no interpersonal encounter is ever a total failure or a total success; each could have been worse and each could have been better.

Interpersonal skills exist on two levels. On the specific level, there are the skills of being open or empathic, for example. These skills help you express your openness and empathy when you wish. On a higher level—a metaskill level—there are skills for regulating the specific skills. These metaskills—for example, flexibility and cultural sensitivity—help you regulate your openness and empathy as the specific situation warrants. In being open or empathic, for instance, you need to do so with flexibility and with sensitivity to the specific cultural context. Both types of skills are essential to interpersonal effectiveness.

The skills identified here come from research conducted primarily over the last 25 years by a large number of interpersonal communication researchers (Gibb 1961; Hart and Burks 1972; Hart, Carlson, and Eadie 1980; Bochner and Kelly 1974; Wiemann 1971; Spitzberg and Hecht 1984; Rubin and Nevins 1988; Spitzberg and Cupach 1984, 1989; Watzlawick, Beavin, and Jackson 1967; Watzlawick 1977; Lederer 1984; Lederer and Jackson 1968; Kim 1991). What follows is a synthesis.

Skills About Skills

Four metaskills will help you regulate your use of the more specific skills: mindfulness, flexibility, cultural sensitivity, and metacommunication.

Mindfulness

After you have learned a skill or rule, you may have a tendency to apply it without thinking, or "mindlessly"—without, for example, considering the novel aspects of a situation. For instance, after learning the skills of active listening, many will use them in response to all situations. Some of these responses will be appropriate, but others will prove inappropriate and ineffective. In interpersonal and even in small-group communication (Elmes and Gemmill 1990), apply the skills **mindfully** (Langer 1989).

Langer (1989) offers several suggestions for increasing mindfulness that will prove useful in most interpersonal situations. As you read through these suggestions, try to provide a specific example or application for each of these suggestions.

How mindful are you of your own communication behavior? Are you equally mindful of the communications of others, for example, your close friends?

♦ Create and recreate categories. See an object, event, or person as belonging to a wide variety of categories. Avoid storing in memory an image of a person, for example, with only one specific label; it will be difficult to recategorize the image later.

♦ Be open to new information, even if it contradicts your most firmly held stereotypes.

♦ Be open to different points of view. This will help you avoid the tendency to blame outside forces for your negative behaviors ("that test was unfair") and internal forces for the negative behaviors of others ("Pat didn't study," "Pat isn't very bright"). Be willing to see your own and others' behaviors from a variety of perspectives.

◆ Beware of relying too heavily on first impressions (Chanowitz and Langer 1981; Langer 1989). Treat your first impressions as tentative, as hypotheses.

Flexibility

Before reading about flexibility, try taking the self-test on pages 156 and 157, "How Flexible In Communication Are You?"

Another popular test of flexibility includes statements such as "People should be frank and spontaneous in conversation," "When angry, a person should say nothing rather than say something he or she will be sorry for later," and "It is better to speak your gut feelings than to beat around the bush." The test asks you to indicate how true you believe these statements to be. The "preferred" answer to all such questions "sometimes true," underscores the importance of flexibility in all interpersonal encounters (Hart and Burks 1972; Hart, Carlson, and Eadie 1980). Although we provide general principles for effective interpersonal communication, be flexible when applying them and be sensitive to the unique factors of every situation. Thus, you may need to be frank and spontaneous when talking with a close friend about your feelings, but you may not want to be so open when talking with your grandmother about the dinner she prepared that you disliked.

Cultural Sensitivity

In applying the skills for interpersonal effectiveness, be sensitive to the cultural differences among people. What may prove effective for upper-income people working in the IBM subculture of Boston or New York may prove ineffective for lower-income people working as fruit pickers in Florida or California. What works in Japan may not work in Mexico. The close physical distance that is normal in Arab cultures may prove too familiar or too intrusive in much of the United States and Northern Europe. The empathy that most Americans welcome may be uncomfortable for the average Korean (Yun 1976). The specific skills discussed below are considered generally effective in the United States and among most people living in the United States. In Unit 3 we identified several guidelines for more effective intercultural communication; they are the same principles to follow in achieving cultural sensitivity.

◆ Prepare yourself. Read. Listen. Watch.
◆ Recognize and face fears.
◆ Recognize differences between yourself and the culturally different.
◆ Be careful not to ignore differences among the culturally different group.
◆ Recognize differences in meaning.
◆ Avoid violating cultural rules and customs.

 What other suggestions would you offer for increasing cultural sensitivity?

Metacommunicational Ability

Much of our talk concerns people, objects, and events in the world. But we also talk about our talk. We **metacommunicate**; that is, we communicate about our communication. Our interpersonal effectiveness often hinges on this ability to

How Flexible In Communication Are You?

Here are some situations that illustrate how people sometimes act when communicating with others. The first part of each situation asks you to imagine that you are in the situation. Then, a course of action is identified and you are asked to determine how much your own behavior would be like the action described in the scenario. Respond to each statement according to the following scale:

1=NOT AT ALL like you
2=NOT MUCH like you
3=SOMEWHAT like you
4=A LOT like you
5=EXACTLY like you

IMAGINE:

_____ 1. Last week, as you were discussing your strained finances with your family, family members came up with several possible solutions. Even though you already decided on one solution, you decided to spend more time considering all the possibilities before making a final decision.

_____ 2. You were invited to a Halloween party and assuming it was a costume party, you dressed as a pumpkin. When you arrived at the party and found everyone else dressed in formal attire, you laughed and joked about the misunderstanding, and decided to stay and enjoy the party.

_____ 3. You have always enjoyed being with your friend Chris, but do not enjoy Chris's habit of always interrupting you. The last time you met, every time Chris interrupted you, you then interrupted Chris to teach Chris a lesson.

_____ 4. Your daily schedule is very structured and your calendar is full of appointments and commitments. When asked to make a change in your schedule, you replied that changes are impossible before even considering the change.

_____ 5. You went to a party where over 50 people attended. You have a good time, but spent most of the evening talking to one close friend rather than meeting new people.

_____ 6. When discussing a personal problem with a group of friends, you notice that many different solutions were offered. Although several of the solutions seemed feasible, you already had your opinion and did not listen to any of the alternative solutions.

_____ 7. You and a friend are planning a fun evening and you're dressed and ready ahead of time. You find that you are unable to do anything else until your friend arrives.

_____ 8. When you found your seat at the ball game, you realized you did not know anyone sitting nearby. However, you introduced yourself to the people sitting next to you and attempted to strike up a conversation.

_____ 9. You had lunch with your friend Chris, and Chris told you about a too-personal family problem. You quickly finished your lunch and stated that you had to leave because you had a lot to do that afternoon.

_____10. You were involved in a discussion about international politics with a group of acquaintances and you assumed that the members of the group were as knowledgeable as you on the topic; but, as the discussion progressed, you learned that most of the group knew little about the subject. Instead of explaining your point of view, you decided to withdraw from the discussion.

_____11. You and a group of friends got into a discussion about gun control and, after a while, it became obvious that your opinions differed greatly from the rest of the group. You explained your position once again, but you agreed to respect the group's opinion also.

_____12. You were asked to speak to a group you belong to, so you worked hard preparing a 30-minute presentation; but at the meeting, the organizer asked you to lead a question and answer session instead of giving your presentation. You agreed, and answered the group's questions as candidly and fully as possible.

_____13. You were offered a managerial position where every day you would face new tasks and challenges and a changing day-to-day routine. You decided to accept this position instead of one that has a stable daily routine.

_____14. You were asked to give a speech at a Chamber of Commerce breakfast. Because you did not know anyone at the breakfast and would feel uncomfortable not knowing anyone in the audience, you declined the invitation.

Thinking Critically About Flexibility

To compute your score:

1. Reverse the scoring for items 4, 5, 6, 7, 9, 10, and 14. That is, for each of these questions, substitute as follows:

   If you answered 5, reverse it to 1
   If you answered 4, reverse it to 2
   If you answered 3, it remains 3
   If you answered 2, reverse it to 4
   If you answered 1, reverse it to 5

2. Add the scores for all 14 items. Be sure that you use the reversed scores for items 4, 5, 6, 7, 9, 10, and 14 instead of your original responses. Use your original scores for items 1, 2, 3, 8, 11, 12, and 13.

In general, you can interpret your score as follows:

65–70=much more flexible than average
57–64=more flexible than average
44–56=about average
37–43=less flexible than average
14–36=much less flexible than average.

Do you agree with the assumption made that flexibility is an essential ingredient in communication effectiveness? Are you satisfied with your level of flexibility? What might you do to cultivate greater communication flexibility?

Source: This scale was developed by Matthew M. Martin and Rebecca B. Rubin, "Development of a Communication Flexibility Measure," *The Southern Communication Journal* 59 (Winter 1994):171–178 and is reprinted by permission.

metacommunicate. Let's say that someone says something positive but in a negative way; for example, the person says, "Yes, I think you did . . . a good job," but shows no enthusiasm and avoids eye contact. You are faced with several alternatives. You may respond to the message as positive or as negative. Another alternative, however, is to talk about the message and say something like, "I'm not sure I understand whether you're pleased or displeased with what I did. You said you were pleased, but I detect dissatisfaction in your voice. Am I wrong?" In this way, you may avoid lots of misunderstandings.

Here are a few suggestions for increasing your metacommunicational effectiveness:

◆ Give clear feedforward. This will help the other person get a general picture of the message that will follow; feedforward provides a kind of schema that makes information processing and learning easier.

◆ Confront contradictory or inconsistent messages. At the same time, explain messages of your own that may appear inconsistent to your listener.

◆ Explain the feelings that go with the thoughts. Often people communicate only the thinking part of their message, with the result that listeners are not able to appreciate the other parts of the meaning.

What part does cultural sensitivity plan in your everyday inter-personal encounters? Can you give an example of a recent in-teraction in which cultural sensitivity played an important role? Can you give an example where cultural sensitivity was noticeably absent?

◆ Paraphrase your own complex messages. Similarly, to check on your under-standing of another's message, paraphrase what you think the other person means and ask whether you are accurate.

◆ "Negotiate meanings." If you have doubts about another's meaning, don't as-sume; instead, ask even in the middle of a conversation (Varonis and Gass 1985, Gudykunst 1991). In intercultural situations, the request for clarifica-tion usually comes from the person whose native language is the language being used (Gudykunst 1991).

◆ Talk about your talk only to gain an understanding of the other person's thoughts and feelings. Avoid substituting talk about talk for talk about a specific problem.

As the characteristics of interpersonal effectiveness are reviewed, be mindful, flexible, and culturally sensitive, and remember that you can talk about your talk to further clarify meaning.

A Humanistic Model of Interpersonal Effectiveness

In the humanistic (sometimes referred to metaphorically as "soft") approach to interpersonal effectiveness presented here, five general qualities are considered: openness, empathy, supportiveness, positiveness, and equality. In general, these qualities foster meaningful, honest, and satisfying interactions. This approach be-gins with the qualities that philosophers and humanists feel define superior hu-

MEDIA & TECHNOLOGY

EFFECTIVE COMPUTER COMMUNICATION

In an early study of mediated versus face-to-face communication it was found that telephone group conferences allowed for easy access to the floor and promoted good attention and eager participation (Remp 1974). Telephone groups also felt less pressure to conform to group opinion and were more comfortable changing their positions. There was productive conflict but no hostility.

More recent research has focused on computer groups and has compared them with face-to-face groups (Olaniran 1994; Kiesler and Sproull 1992; Harris 1995). Compared with face-to-face groups, computer groups:

◆ generated a greater number of unique ideas;
◆ proposed more unconventional or risky decisions;
◆ took longer to reach agreement;
◆ engaged in more explicit and outspoken advocacy;
◆ had more equal participation among members.

One researcher has proposed that the student preference for computer mediated over face-to-face communication was because in mediated communication the students didn't have to worry about the rules for interpersonal communication, such as those for eye contact and body communication, and this reduced concerns about shyness (Mendoza 1995). Research is just beginning to identify the differences between the various forms of communication and their computer counterparts. Similarly, the insights from these studies are just beginning to be incorporated into interpersonal communication courses and textbooks (cf. Harris 1995).

Here are some guidelines for making your own online communication more effective:

◆ Watch your spelling. If you have a spell check use it.
◆ Remember that what you write can easily be made public. So—to quote Sidney Biddle Barrows—"Never say anything on the [Internet] that you wouldn't want your mother to hear at your trial."
◆ Follow the rules of netiquette, for example, don't spam or flame (see Media and Technology boxes in Unit 14).
◆ Clean up your writing—consider your choices for communicating mindfully.
◆ Follow the suggestions and guidelines for interpersonal communication generally; after all, they aren't that different.
◆ Be explicit of your good intentions; avoid the possibility of being misunderstood. If, for example, you think your sarcasm may not be interpreted as humor, then use an emoticon that shows you smiling:-).

p. 179

man relationships, and from these generalizations it derives specific behaviors that should characterize effective interpersonal communication.

Openness

Openness refers to at least three aspects of interpersonal communication. First, it refers to your willingness to self-disclose—to reveal information about yourself that might normally be kept hidden—provided that such disclosure is appropriate (see Unit 4). Openness shown by only one person is usually insufficient. For interpersonal communication to be effective, it must be **bilateral**: "the exchange of personal, private information must be reciprocal" (Montgomery 1981).

Second, openness refers to a willingness to react honestly to the messages of others. Silent, uncritical, and immovable psychiatrists may be of some help in a clinical situation, but they are generally boring conversationalists. Usually we want people to react openly to what we say, and we feel we have a right to expect this. We demonstrate openness by responding spontaneously and without subterfuge to the communications and the feedback of others.

Third, openness refers to the "owning" of feelings and thoughts. To be open in this sense is to acknowledge that the feelings and thoughts we express are ours and that we bear the responsibility for them; we do not try to shift the responsibility for our feelings to others. For example, consider these comments:

1. Your behavior was grossly inconsiderate.
2. Everyone thought your behavior was grossly inconsiderate.
3. I was really disturbed when you told my father he was an old man.

Comments 1 and 2 do not demonstrate ownership of feelings. In comment 1, the speaker accuses the listener of being inconsiderate without assuming any responsibility for the judgment. In comment 2, the speaker assigns responsibility to the convenient but vague "everyone" and again assumes none of the responsibility. In comment 3, however, we see a drastic difference. Note that here the speaker is taking responsibility for his or her own feelings ("*I* was really disturbed").

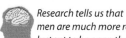 *Research tells us that men are much more reluctant to be open than women. Why do you think this is so? Is this changing? Is this true in all cultures?*

When you own your messages, you use I-messages instead of you-messages. Instead of saying, "You make me feel so stupid when you ask what everyone else thinks but don't ask my opinion," you would own your feelings and say, for example, "I feel stupid when you ask everyone else what they think but don't ask me." When you own your feelings and thoughts—when you use I-messages—you say, in effect, "This is how *I* feel," "This is how *I* see the situation," and "This is what *I* think," with the *I* always emphasized. Instead of saying, "This discussion is useless," you would say, "*I'm* bored by this discussion," "*I* want to talk more about myself," or any other such statement that includes a reference to the fact that you are making an evaluation and not describing objective reality. By doing so, you make it explicit that your feelings result from the interaction between what is going on outside your skin (what others say, for example) and what is going on inside your skin (your preconceptions, attitudes, and prejudices).

Empathy

Perhaps the most difficult communication quality to achieve is the ability to empathize with another person. The term **empathy** was derived from Greek to translate the German word *Einfuhlung,* meaning "feeling with." To **empathize** with someone is to feel as that person feels, to experience what the other is experiencing from that person's point of view without losing your own identity. To **sympathize**, in contrast, is to feel *for* the person—to feel sorry for the person, for example. To empathize is to feel *as* the person feels, to walk in the same shoes, to feel the same feelings in the same way. Empathy, then, enables you to understand, emotionally as well as intellectually, what another person is experiencing.

Animal researchers have argued that some animals show empathy. For example, consider the male gorilla who watched a female try in vain to get water that collected in an automobile tire and who then secured the tire and brought it to the female. This gorilla, it has been argued, demonstrated empathy; he felt the other gorilla's thirst (Angier 1995). Similarly, the animal who cringes when another of its species gets hurt seems also to be showing empathy.

To achieve empathy it is first necessary to be relatively calm and to free yourself from your own intense emotions (Goleman 1995). If, for example, you are angry, you'll be so caught up in your own anger that you'll be unable to feel or even hear the other person's perhaps equally justified anger or sadness or fear.

Should you wish to achieve empathy, your first step is to avoid evaluating the other person's behaviors. If you evaluate them as right or wrong, good or bad, you will see the behaviors through these labels and will fail to see a great deal more that might not be consistent with them. Therefore, resist the temptation to evaluate, to judge, to interpret, to criticize. Focus, instead, on understanding.

Second, learn as much as you can about the other person's desires, experiences, abilities, fears, and so on. The more you know about a person, the more you will be able to see what that person sees and feel what that person feels. Try to understand the reasons and the motivations for the person's feelings.

Third, try to experience emotionally what the other person is feeling from his or her point of view. Playing the role of the other person in your mind (or even out loud) can help you see the world a little more as the other person does.

Most people find it easier to communicate empathy in response to a person's positive statements (Heiskell and Rychlak 1986). So perhaps we have to exert special effort to communicate empathy for negative statements. We can do so both nonverbally and verbally. Here are a few suggestions for communicating empathy nonverbally and verbally (Authier and Gustafson 1982):

◆ Express your active involvement with the other person through appropriate facial expressions and gestures.

◆ Focus your concentration; maintain eye contact, an attentive body posture, and physical closeness.

◆ Reflect back to the speaker the feelings (and their intensity) that you think are being experienced to help you to check on the accuracy of your perceptions and to show your desire to understand the speaker's feelings.

◆ Make tentative statements about what you think the person is feeling: for example, "I get the impression you're angry with your father" or "I hear anger in your voice."

◆ Use your own relevant self-disclosures to communicate your understanding of and involvement in what the other is experiencing.

◆ Address mixed messages in order to foster more open and honest communication. When your friend verbally expresses contentment but shows nonverbal signs of depression it may be prudent to question the apparent discrepancy.

Although empathy is almost universally considered positive, there is some evidence to show that even it has a negative side. For example, people are most empathic with those who are similar—racially and ethnically as well as in appearance and social status. The more empathy one feels towards one's own group, the less empathy—possibly even hostility—one feels toward other groups. The same

Does this example convince you that animals can experience empathy? What other evidence would you want before accepting the idea that animals can and do experience empathy? How would you go about proving this?

After reviewing the research on the empathic and listening abilities of men and women, Pearson, West, and Turner (1994) conclude: "Men and women do not differ as much as conventional wisdom would have us believe. In many instances, she thinks like a man, and he thinks like a woman because they both think alike." Does your experience support or contradict this observation?

In what types of interpersonal situations do you feel most in need of supportiveness? How do you signal this need to other people?

 In what situations do you think empathic responses would be inappropriate?

empathy that increases your understanding of your own group decreases your understanding of other groups. So, while empathy may encourage group cohesiveness and identification, it can also create dividing lines between one's own group and "them" (Angier 1995).

Supportiveness

Supportiveness, a concept that owes much to the work of Jack Gibb (1961), is fostered by your being (1) descriptive rather than evaluative and (2) provisional rather than certain.

Descriptiveness   Consider the following sentence sets.

1A.   I can't wait to meet him.
1B.   He sure is great looking.
1C.   His hair is black and his eyes are green.

2A.   I'm sure glad we went on strike for this contract.
2B.   That contract was ideal for labor but will cripple management.
2C.   Workers got a 12 percent raise, more than at any other plant.

Note that the A and C sentences are descriptive. The A sentences describe one's own feelings; the C sentences describe the situation, the "reality." The B sentences, however—which are similar in form to the others—are evaluative. These sentences express the speaker's judgment or evaluation of a person or situation.

   An atmosphere that is descriptive rather than evaluative leads to supportiveness. When we perceive a communication as being a request for information or a description of some event, we generally do not perceive it as threatening. We are not being challenged and have no need to defend ourselves. However, a communication that is judgmental or evaluative often leads us to become defensive, to back off, to erect some kind of barrier between ourselves and the evaluator.

This does not mean that all evaluative communications elicit a defensive response. People often respond to positive evaluations without defensiveness. Even here, however, note that if someone has the power, the knowledge, or the "right" to evaluate us in any way (even positively), it may lead us to feel uneasy and possibly defensive, perhaps anticipating that the next evaluation may not be as favorable.

In a similar way, negative evaluations do not always elicit a defensive response. The would-be actor who wants to improve technique often welcomes negative evaluations. Similarly, many students welcome negative evaluations when they feel they are constructive and lead to improvement in their ability, for example, to communicate or to operate a computer program. Generally, however, an evaluative atmosphere leads people to become more defensive than would a descriptive atmosphere.

In being descriptive (Brougher 1982):

◆ Describe what happened ("I lost the promotion").
◆ Describe how you feel ("I feel miserable," "I feel I've failed").
◆ Explain how this relates to the other person ("Would you mind if we went into the city tonight? I need to forget the job and everything about it").
◆ Avoid accusations or blame ("I should have stayed with my old job and not listened to your brother's lousy advice").
◆ Avoid negative evaluative terms ("Didn't your sister look *horrible* in that red dress?")
◆ Avoid "preaching" ("Why don't you learn something about word processing before you open your mouth?").

Provisionalism   Being **provisional** means having a tentative, open-minded attitude and a willingness both to hear opposing points of view and to change one's position if warranted. Such provisionalism, rather than unwavering certainty, helps to create a supportive atmosphere. Compare these two observations.

1. It's obvious. She just doesn't know the first thing about caring for a relationship. She's so egocentric.
2. It seems to me that she is having trouble in her relationship. Maybe she's too caught up in herself.

Note that sentence 1 claims certainty; it is definite and provides for no other possibility. Sentence 2 expresses essentially the same thought but with a tentativeness, a provisionalism. It is relatively difficult to say anything in response to sentence 1; it appears that everything that needs to be said has already been said. Sentence 2, however, invites comment, involvement, further discussion.

People who "know everything" and who always have a definite answer to any question are rarely appreciated. Such people are set in their ways and seem to tolerate no differences. They have arguments ready for any possible alternative attitude or belief. After a very short time, we become defensive with such people, and we hold back our own opinions rather than subject them to attack. But we open up with people who take a more provisional position, who are willing to change

In what other ways might you show supportiveness?

their minds when reasonable arguments are presented. With such people we feel equal.

Positiveness

You can communicate positiveness in interpersonal communication in at least two ways: (1) stating positive attitudes and (2) complimenting the person with whom you interact.

Attitudes   **Attitudinal positiveness** in interpersonal communication refers to a positive regard for oneself, for the other person, and for the general communication situation. Your feelings (whether positive or negative) become clear during conversation and greatly influence the satisfaction (or dissatisfaction) you derive from the interaction. Negative feelings usually make communication more difficult and can contribute to its eventual breakdown.

Positiveness is seen most clearly in the way you phrase statements. Consider these two sets of sentences.

1A. I wish you wouldn't handle me so roughly.
1B. I really enjoy it when you're especially gentle.

2A. You look horrible in stripes.
2B. You look your best, I think, in solid colors.

The A sentences are negative; they are critical and will almost surely encourage an argument. The B sentences, in contrast, express the speaker's thought clearly but are phrased positively and should encourage cooperative responses.

Compliments   Another aspect of positiveness is **complimenting**, behavior that acknowledges the existence of some positive quality in another person or some action that you evaluate positively. Many people, in fact, structure interpersonal encounters almost solely for the purpose of getting complimented. People may buy new clothes to get complimented, compliment associates so that the associates compliment back, do favors for people to receive thanks, associate with certain people because they are generous with their compliments, and so on. Some people even enter relationships because they hold the promise of frequent compliments.

What constitutes an appropriate compliment will naturally vary with the culture (Dresser 1996). For example, in the United States it would be considered appropriate for a teacher to publicly compliment a student on getting the highest grade in an examination or for a supervisor to compliment a worker for doing an exceptional job on some project. But, in other cultures (collectivist cultures, for example) this would be considered inappropriate because it singles out the individual and separates that person from the group. Similarly, the responses to compliments will vary from one culture to another (Chen 1993). In the United States, a compliment is generally supposed to be accepted graciously; you did a good job and have a right to have that acknowledged. In more collectivist cultures, however, you are expected to deny your right to the compliment and to instead credit the group or the situation—"It was a very easy thing to do," "I didn't do it by myself," "Others deserve the credit," and so on.

What do you do to get others to compliment you? Is it effective?

Equality

Equality is a peculiar characteristic. In any situation, there is probably some inequality. One person will be smarter, richer, better looking, or more athletic. No two people are absolutely equal in all respects. Despite this inequality, interpersonal communication is generally considered more effective when the atmosphere is one of equality, at least in the United States. (In other cultures—in Japan, for example—where status differences greatly influence interpersonal interactions, this presumption of equality would not hold.)

Compare these examples.

1A. When will you learn to phone for reservations? Must I do everything?
1B. One of us should phone for reservations. Do you want me to do it, or do you want to do it?

2A. When the hell are you going to fix this wallpaper? It's coming down on my head!
2B. This wallpaper is coming down on my head. How about we stay home tonight and try to fix it together?

The A sentences lack equality; one person demands compliance and the other is ordered to do something. Questions such as these encourage defensiveness, resentment, and hostility. They provoke arguments rather than solve problems. The B sentences express equality—an explicitly stated desire to work together to address a specific problem. As a general rule, requests (especially courteous ones) communicate equality; demands (especially discourteous ones) communicate superiority.

In an equal interpersonal relationship, disagreement and conflict are seen as attempts to understand differences rather than as opportunities to put down the other person. Disagreements are viewed as ways of solving problems rather than of winning points, getting one's way, or proving oneself superior to the other. Equality does not require that you accept and approve of all the other person's behaviors. Some behaviors are self-destructive or have negative consequences for others, and these may, of course, be challenged—again, out of concern for the other person and for the relationship.

In communicating equality, consider the following.

- Avoid "should" and "ought" statements that signal an unequal relationship (for example, "You really should call your mother more often" or "You should learn to speak up"). These statements put the listener in a one-down position (see Unit 2).
- Avoid interrupting; it signals that what you have to say is more important than what the other person is saying.
- Acknowledge the other person's contributions before expressing your own. Saying "I see," "I understand," or "That's right" lets the other person know you are listening and understanding.
- Avoid correcting another's messages when the original error is of little consequence. Corrections signal an unequal relationship and often embarrass the other person.

Can you think of instances in which a speaker with a superior attitude would be more effective than one with an equality attitude?

A Pragmatic Model of Interpersonal Effectiveness

A pragmatic or behavioral (sometimes referred to metaphorically as "hard") approach to interpersonal effectiveness focuses on specific behaviors that a speaker or listener should use to gain his or her desired outcome. This model, too, offers five qualities of effectiveness: confidence, immediacy, interaction management, expressiveness, and other-orientation. This approach starts from specific skills that research finds to be effective in interpersonal communication, then groups these specific skills into general classes of behavior (for example, interaction management skills, other-orientation skills).

Confidence

The effective communicator has social **confidence**; any anxiety that is present is not readily perceived by others. There is instead an ease with the other person and with the communication situation generally. Everyone has some communication apprehension or shyness (see Unit 9), but the effective interpersonal communicator controls it so that it is not a source of discomfort and does not interfere with communication.

The socially confident communicator is relaxed (not rigid), flexible (not locked into one or two vocal ranges or body movements), and controlled (not shaky or awkward). Researchers find that a relaxed posture communicates a sense of control, superior status, and power (Spitzberg and Cupach 1984, 1989). Tenseness, rigidity, and discomfort, on the other hand, signal a lack of self-control, which in turn signals an inability to control one's environment or other people and gives an impression of being under the power and control of an outside force or another person.

After analyzing the results of a series of five studies, Amerigo Farina concluded (Jones et al. 1984, p. 48): "Whether male or female, ex-mental patient, or average person, a nervous and tense individual was disliked and unequivocally rejected by the workers. The consistency and strength of these findings are noteworthy, and we believe they are in keeping with most people's intuition."

Here are a few additional suggestions for communicating confidence.

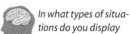 *In what types of situations do you display confidence? In what situations are you lacking in confidence? What distinguishes the two types of situations?*

◆ Take the initiative in introducing yourself to others and in introducing topics of conversation. Taking the initiative will help you communicate confidence and control over the situation.

◆ Use open-ended questions to involve the other person in the interaction (as opposed to questions that merely ask for a yes or no answer).

◆ Use "you-statements"—statements that refer directly to the other person, such as "Do you agree?" or "How do you feel about that?"—to signal your personal attention to the speaker.

◆ Control your emotions. Once your emotions get the best of you, you will appear to have lost confidence.

◆ Admit your mistakes. Only a confident person can openly admit mistakes and not worry about what others will think.

◆ Avoid turning normally declarative sentences into questions by a rising intonation, for example, "I'll arrive at nine?" Asking for agreement generally communicates a lack of confidence.

Immediacy

Immediacy refers to the joining of the speaker and listener, the creation of a sense of togetherness, of oneness. The communicator demonstrating immediacy conveys a sense of interest and attention, a liking for and an attraction to the other person. People respond to language that is immediate more favorably than to language that is not. Immediacy joins speaker and listener; nonimmediacy separates them.

You can communicate immediacy nonverbally and verbally.

- Maintain appropriate eye contact and limit looking around at others.
- Express psychological closeness and openness by, for example, maintaining physical closeness and arranging your body to keep others further away.
- Smile and otherwise express your interest in and concern about the other person.
- Use the other person's name: for example, say, "Joe, what do you think?" instead of "What do you think?" Say "I like that, Mary" instead of "I like that."
- Focus on the other person's remarks. Make the speaker know that you heard and understood what was said, and give the speaker feedback. For example, use questions that ask for clarification or elaboration ("Do you think the same thing is true of baseball?"). Also, refer to the speaker's previous remarks ("Vermont does sound like a great vacation spot").
- Reinforce, reward, or compliment the other person. Make use of such expressions as "I like your new outfit" or "Your comments were really to the point."
- Use self-references in your evaluative statements rather than depersonalizing them. Say, for example, "I think your report is great" rather than "Your report is great" or "Everyone likes your report."

In the United States these immediacy behaviors are generally seen as friendly and appropriate. In other cultures, however, the same immediacy behaviors may be viewed as overly familiar, as presuming that a close relationship exists when it is only one of acquaintanceship. In the United States, we move quickly from Mr. LastName and Ms. LastName to Fred and Ginger, which signals greater immediacy. In more formal countries (Japan and Germany are two examples) a much longer period of acquaintanceship would be necessary before first names would be considered appropriate (Axtell 1993).

How important is immediacy in health communication (communication between health care providers and patients)? Are health care professionals who are more immediate in their communication more effective in gaining a patient's cooperation? How would you go about securing evidence bearing on this question?

Interaction Management

The effective communicator controls the interaction to the satisfaction of both parties. In effective **interaction management**, neither person feels ignored or on stage; each contributes to the total communication exchange. Maintaining your role as speaker or listener and passing the opportunity to speak back and forth—through appropriate eye movements, vocal expressions, and body and facial gestures—are interaction management skills. Similarly, keeping the conversation fluent without long and awkward pauses is a sign of effective interaction management. For example, it has been found that patients are less satisfied with their interaction with their doctor when the silence between their comments and the doctor's response is overly long (Rowland-Morin and Carroll 1990).

The effective interaction manager presents verbal and nonverbal messages that are consistent and reinforce one another. Contradictory signals—a nonverbal message that contradicts the verbal message—are rarely in evidence. It is relevant to note here that women generally use more positive or pleasant nonverbal expressions than men. For example, they smile more, nod in agreement more, and more openly verbalize positive feelings. When expressing anger or power, however, many (though surely not all) women continue using these positive nonverbal signals, which dilute the verbally expressed anger or power. The net result is that we may see such women as being uncomfortable with strong negative emotions and expressions of power, and may therefore be less likely to believe them or to feel threatened by them (Shannon 1987).

Self-Monitoring   Integrally related to interpersonal interaction management is **self-monitoring**, the manipulation of the image you present to others in your interpersonal interactions (Snyder 1987). High self-monitors carefully adjust their behaviors according to the feedback they get from others. They manipulate their interpersonal interactions to give the most effective impression and to produce the desired effect. Low self-monitors, in contrast, are not concerned with the image they present. Rather, they communicate their thoughts and feelings openly, without trying to manipulate the impressions they create. Although there seem to be two clear-cut types of persons—high and low self-monitors—we all engage more or less in selective monitoring, depending on the situation. If you go to a job interview, you are likely to monitor your behaviors very carefully. On the other hand, you are less likely to monitor your performance with a group of friends. You may wish to reflect on the situations and the people with whom are you most likely to self-monitor as you take the self test "Are You A High Self-Monitor?"

What type of self-monitor are you? In what situations are you most likely to self-monitor your behaviors? In what situations are you least likely to self-monitor?

When high and low self-monitors are compared, several interesting differences emerge. For example, high self-monitors are more apt to take charge of a situation, more sensitive to the deceptive techniques of others, and better able to detect self-monitoring or impression management techniques being used by others. High self-monitors prefer to interact with low self-monitors. By interacting with low self-monitors, high self-monitors are better able to assume positions of influence and power. They also seem better able to present their true selves than are low self-monitors. For example, if an innocent person is charged with a crime, to use the example cited by Snyder (1987), a high self-monitor would be able to present his or her innocence more effectively than would a low self-monitor.

A careful reading of the research and theory on self-monitoring, openness, and self-disclosure (a topic reviewed in detail in Unit 4) supports the conclusion that we increase our effectiveness if we are selectively self-disclosing, selectively open, and selectively self-monitoring. To be totally open, to disclose everything to everyone, to ignore the feedback of others, and to refuse to engage in any self-monitoring seem ineffective. The opposite extreme is equally ineffective and should likewise be avoided.

Expressiveness

Expressiveness refers to the skill of communicating genuine involvement in the interpersonal interaction. Similar to openness in its emphasis on involvement, expressiveness includes, for example, taking responsibility for your thoughts and feelings, encouraging expressiveness or openness in others, and providing appropriate feedback.

Some cultures (Italian, for example) encourage expressiveness and teach children to be expressive. Other cultures (Japanese and Thai, for example) encourage a more reserved response style (Matsumoto 1996).

Are You a High Self-Monitor?

The following statements concern personal reactions to a number of different situations. No two statements are exactly alike, so consider each statement carefully before answering. If a statement is true or mostly true as applied to you, write T. If a statement is false or not usually true as applied to you, write F.

_____ 1. I find it hard to imitate the behavior of other people.

_____ 2. At parties and social gatherings, I do not attempt to do or say things that others will like.

_____ 3. I can only argue for ideas which I already believe.

_____ 4. I can make impromptu speeches even on topics about which I have almost no information.

_____ 5. I guess I put on a show to impress or entertain people.

_____ 6. I would probably make a good actor.

_____ 7. In a group of people I am rarely the center of attention.

_____ 8. In different situations and with different people, I often act like very different persons.

_____ 9. I am not particularly good at making other people like me.

_____10. I'm not always the person I appear to be.

_____11. I would not change my opinions (or the way I do things) in order to please someone or win their favor.

_____12. I have considered being an entertainer.

_____13. I have never been good at games like charades or improvisational acting.

_____14. I have trouble changing my behavior to suit different people and different situations.

_____15. At a party I let others keep the jokes and stories going.

_____16. I feel a bit awkward in company and do not show up quite as well as I should.

_____17. I can look anyone in the eye and tell a lie with a straight face (if for a right end).

_____18. I may deceive people by being friendly when I really dislike them.

Thinking Critically About Self-Monitoring

Give yourself one point for each true (T) response you gave to questions 4, 5, 6, 8, 10, 12, 17, and 18, and give yourself one point for each false (F) response you gave to questions 1, 2, 3, 7, 9, 11, 13, 14, 15, and 16. According to research (Gangestad and Snyder 1985; Snyder 1987), scores may be interpreted roughly as follows: 13 or higher = very high self-monitoring, 11–12 = high self-monitoring, 8–10 = low self-monitoring, and 0–7 = very low self-monitoring

Does your score correspond to the image you have of yourself in regard to self-monitoring? Do other people see you as a high or a low self-monitor? Does it make a difference to your interpersonal effectiveness? Do you agree with the findings reported in the text about the differences between high and low self-monitors?

From *Public Appearances, Private Realities* by Mark Snyder. Copyright © 1987 by W. H. Freeman and Company. Reprinted by permission.

In the United States women are expected to participate fully in business discussions, to smile, laugh, and initiate interactions. These behaviors are so expected and seemingly so natural that it seems strange even mentioning them. In many other countries (Arab countries and many Asian countries), however, this expressiveness would be considered inappropriate (Lustig and Koester 1993; Axtell 1993; Hall and Hall 1987).

Expressiveness may be communicated in a wide variety of ways.

◆ Practice active listening by paraphrasing, expressing understanding of the thoughts and feelings of the other person, and asking relevant questions (as explained in Unit 7).

◆ Avoid clichés and trite expressions that signal a lack of personal involvement and originality.

◆ Address mixed messages—messages (verbal or nonverbal) that are communicated simultaneously but that contradict each other. Similarly, address messages that seem somehow unrealistic to you (for example, statements claiming that failing a course doesn't mean anything).

♦ Use I-messages to signal personal involvement and a willingness to share your feelings. Instead of saying, "You never give me a chance to make any decisions," say, "I want to contribute to the decisions that affect both of us."

♦ Use appropriate variations in vocal rate, pitch, volume, and rhythm to convey involvement and interest. Allow your facial muscles to reflect this inner involvement.

♦ Use appropriate gestures. Too few gestures may signal uninterest, while too many may communicate discomfort, uneasiness, and awkwardness.

Although we emphasize the general advantages of expressiveness, can you think of instances when too much expressiveness will create communication problems? In what situations might it be best to use little expressiveness?

Other-Orientation

Some people are self-oriented; they focus almost exclusively on themselves. In interpersonal interaction, this takes the form of doing most of the talking, talking about themselves, and paying no attention to the feedback from others. **Other-orientation** is the opposite; it is the ability to adapt to the other person during the interpersonal encounter. It involves communicating attentiveness and interest in the other person and in what is being said. As you might expect, other-orientation is especially important (and especially difficult) when you are interacting with people who are very different from you as in, for example, talking with people from other cultures.

Other-orientation demonstrates consideration and respect—for example, asking if it's all right to dump your troubles on someone before doing so, or asking if your phone call comes at a good time before launching into your conversation. Other-orientation involves acknowledging others' feelings as legitimate: "I can understand why you're so angry; I would be, too."

You can communicate other-orientation nonverbally and verbally.

What role does other-orientation play in first dates and the impressions that people form of their first dates?

♦ Use focused eye contact, and appropriate facial expressions.

♦ Smile, nod, and lean toward the other person.

♦ Ask the other person for suggestions and opinions. Statements such as "How do you feel about it?" or "What do you think?" go a long way toward focusing the communication on the other person.

♦ Acknowledge the presence and the importance of the other person.

♦ Ask the other person for clarification as appropriate. This will ensure that you understand what the other person is saying from that person's point of view.

♦ Express agreement when appropriate. Comments such as "You're right" or "That's interesting" help to focus the interaction on the other person.

♦ Grant the other person permission to express feelings. You can do this by talking about your own feelings or perhaps by noting how difficult it is to talk about feelings. Statements such as "I feel especially depressed when I'm alone" or "I know how difficult it is to talk openly about feelings for our parents" open up the topic of feelings and give the necessary permission for such a discussion.

Can you identify a specific instance in which one of the qualities identified here figured prominently? Which of the qualities of effectiveness do you consider the most important?

These qualities of interpersonal effectiveness (both the specific skills and the more general skills about skills) are mentioned throughout the text. These qualities should serve as general headings under which the additional and more detailed discussions that follow may be subsumed.

Before leaving these qualities, try identifying which of the qualities would be most significant in each of the following situations. No one answer is correct or incorrect; it is the logic and reasoning that goes into the choice that matters.

1. A college teacher lecturing to a class of 300 students in interpersonal communication.
2. Parents talking with their fifth grader after being told by the teacher that their child doesn't get along well with other students and frequently gets into fights with them.
3. A recent college graduate applying for a job with a conservative banking company.
4. A real estate agent trying to sell a house to a young couple.
5. A young couple experiencing their first major argument.
6. A lawyer—defending an accused murderer—presenting opening remarks to the jury.
7. A doctor telling a patient who recently suffered a heart attack that drastic changes in lifestyle must be made.
8. A single mother answering her young son's questions about why he doesn't have a father as his friends do.
9. A manager explaining to workers why there will be no raises this year.
10. A political candidate explaining to voters that no illegal campaign contributions were received and that the opposing candidate's charges are groundless.

 *Can you identify other qualities that you would add to the list given in this unit? What specific behaviors would help you communicate these qualities?*

Summary   U N I T   I N   B R I E F

A RETURN TO OBJECTIVES:

In this unit we explored interpersonal effectiveness and considered the following: (1) What are the general skills of interpersonal communication? (2) What are the skills that contribute most to a satisfying and supportive interaction? (3) What are the pragmatic qualities of interpersonal effectiveness?

Skills About Skills	Humanistic Model of Effectiveness	Pragmatic Model of Effectiveness
Mindfulness: Be mindful in applying these principles of effectiveness.	**Openness:** Self-disclosure regulation; honest reactions to others; owning one's thoughts and feelings.	**Confidence:** Comfortable, at-ease feeling; control of shyness.
Flexibility: Be flexible in applying the principles; each situation requires a slightly different set of interpersonal behaviors.	**Empathy:** Feeling as the other feels.	**Immediacy:** A sense of contact and togetherness; a feeling of interest and liking.
Cultural Sensitivity: Be careful not to ignore differences between self and other, within the group, or in meaning.	**Supportiveness:** Descriptions and provisionalism encourage a supportive atmosphere.	**Interaction management:** Control of interaction to the satisfaction of both parties; managing conversational turns; self-monitoring as appropriate.
Metacommunication: Metacommunicate to ensure understanding of the other person's thoughts and feelings.	**Positiveness:** Expression of positive attitudes toward self, other, and situation; stroking to acknowledge and reinforce the other person.	**Expressiveness:** Genuine involvement in speaking and listening, expressed verbally and nonverbally.
	Equality: Recognition that both parties are important; an equal sharing of the several communication functions.	**Other-orientation:** Attentiveness, interest, and concern for the other.

PART

2

Messages: Verbal and Nonverbal

PART CONTENTS

9. UNIVERSALS OF VERBAL AND NONVERBAL MESSAGES

10. VERBAL MESSAGES: PRINCIPLES AND PITFALLS

11. VERBAL MESSAGES: BARRIERS TO INTERACTION

12. NONVERBAL MESSAGES: BODY AND SOUND

13. NONVERBAL MESSAGES: SPACE AND TIME

14. MESSAGES AND CONVERSATION

APPROACHING VERBAL AND NONVERBAL MESSAGES

In approaching your study of messages, keep the following in mind:

◆ In normal communication, words are accompanied by nonverbal messages. See messages, therefore, as combinations, as packages, of verbal and nonverbal signals.

◆ Messages systems, both verbal and nonverbal, are social and cultural institutions. They are part of the culture and reflect that culture. The rules of communication will differ from one culture to another; intercultural violations are created easily.

◆ Connect and relate the various aspects of nonverbal communication. Although each nonverbal code is discussed separately (for example, body, space, and time are considered separately), you communicate with different codes simultaneously. Therefore, remember that each code functions together with the other codes in actual interpersonal communication.

◆ Resist the temptation to draw conclusions about people on the basis of isolated bits of message behavior.

◆ Observe. Look at your own communications and interactions and notice the verbal and nonverbal messages discussed here and in class. See in practice what you read about in theory.

UNIT 9

Universals of Verbal and Nonverbal Messages

Unit Topics	Unit Objectives
	After completing this unit, you should be able to:
The Interaction of Verbal and Nonverbal Messages	1. Explain the major ways in which nonverbal and verbal messages interact
Meanings and Messages Meanings Are in People Meanings Are More Than Words and Gestures Meanings Are Unique Meanings Are Both Denotative and Connotative Meanings Are Context-Based	2. Explain these principles of meaning: meanings are in people, meanings are more than words, meanings are unique, meanings are denotative and connotative, and meanings are context-based
Message Characteristics Messages Are Packaged Messages Are Rule-Governed Messages Vary in Directness Messages Vary in Believability Messages and Metacommunication	3. Explain these principles of messages: messages are packaged, messages are rule-governed, messages vary in directness, messages vary in believability, and messages may metacommunicate

EXPERIENTIAL LEARNING VEHICLES

Experiential Learning Vehicle Numbers 9, "Facial Expressions," pp. 449–450, 10, "Eye Contact," p. 450, and 11, "Interpersonal Interactions and Space," pp. 450–451, will help introduce the areas of verbal and nonverbal messages.

You make yourself, your feelings, and your thoughts known to others by encoding your ideas and meanings into a code of verbal and nonverbal signals. The verbal portion is language—the words, phrases, and sentences you use. The nonverbal portion consists of a wide variety of elements—spatial relationships, time orientation, gestures, facial expressions, eye movements, touch, and variations in the rate, volume, and pitch of your speech.

The Interaction of Verbal and Nonverbal Messages

In face-to-face communication, you blend verbal and nonverbal messages to best convey your meanings. Enumerating the six major ways in which nonverbal messages are used with verbal messages helps to highlight this important verbal-nonverbal interaction.

Nonverbal communication is often used to **accent**, to emphasize some part of the verbal message. You might, for example, raise your voice to underscore a particular word or phrase, bang your fist on the desk to stress your commitment, or look longingly into someone's eyes when saying "I love you."

Nonverbal communication may be used to **complement**, to add nuances of meaning not communicated by your verbal message. Thus, you might smile when telling a story (to suggest that you find it humorous) or frown and shake your head when recounting someone's deceit (to suggest your disapproval).

You may deliberately **contradict** your verbal messages with nonverbal movements, for example, by crossing your fingers or winking to indicate that you are lying.

Nonverbal movements may be used to **control**, or to indicate your desire to control, the flow of verbal messages, as when you purse your lips, lean forward, or make hand movements to indicate that you want to speak. You might also put up your hand or vocalize your pauses (for example, with "um") to indicate that you have not finished and are not ready to relinquish the floor to the next speaker.

You can **repeat** or restate the verbal message nonverbally. You can, for example, follow your verbal "Is that all right?" with raised eyebrows and a questioning look, or you can motion with your head or hand to repeat your verbal "Let's go."

You may also use nonverbal communication to take the place of or **substitute** for verbal messages. You can, for example, signal "OK" with a hand gesture. You can nod your head to indicate yes or shake your head to indicate no.

Think about how you integrate verbal and nonverbal messages in your own everyday communications. Try reading each of the following statements and describing (rather than acting out) the nonverbal messages that you would use in making these statements in normal conversation.

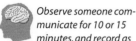
Observe someone communicate for 10 or 15 minutes, and record as many examples as you can find of the six ways in which verbal and nonverbal messages interact. What functions occur most often?

- I couldn't agree with you more.
- Absolutely not, I don't agree.
- Hurry up; we're an hour late already.
- Life is great, isn't it. I just got the job of a lifetime.
- You look fantastic; what did you do to yourself?

Meanings and Messages

Meaning is an active process created by cooperation between source and receiver, speaker and listener, writer and reader. Understanding what meanings are and how they are passed from one person to another is crucial to controlling the verbal and nonverbal message system.

Meanings Are in People

Meaning depends not only on messages (whether verbal, nonverbal, or both) but also on the interaction of these messages and the receiver's own thoughts and feelings. You do not "receive" meaning; you create meaning. You construct meaning out of the messages you receive combined with your own social and cultural perspectives (beliefs, attitudes, and values, for example) (Berger and Luckmann 1980; Delia 1977; and Delia, O'Keefe, and O'Keefe 1982). Words do not mean; people mean. Consequently, to discover meaning, you need to look into people and not merely into words.

To illustrate the implications of the principle that meanings are in people, record your meanings for the terms listed below on the seven-point scales. Write each term's first letter in the appropriate space for the various dimensions of meaning provided, depending on how close you feel the term's meaning is to the adjectives in the scale. Thus, if you feel that a concept is extremely good or extremely bad, place the term's first letter on the space closest to good or bad. If you feel that the concept is quite good or quite bad, then place the first letter in the second or the seventh position. If you feel that the concept is fairly good or fairly bad, then place the first letter in the third or the fifth position. If you feel that the concept is neither good nor bad, then place the first letter in the middle position. Do likewise for all six scales and for all five terms.

Terms: abortion, college, gun control, love, religion

Good	___:___:___:___:___:___:___	Bad
Ugly	___:___:___:___:___:___:___	Beautiful
Weak	___:___:___:___:___:___:___	Strong
Active	___:___:___:___:___:___:___	Passive
Large	___:___:___:___:___:___:___	Small
Hot	___:___:___:___:___:___:___	Cold

Have your meanings changed for such terms as "happiness," "success," and "friendship" over the last several years? In what ways?

If you have the opportunity, compare your meanings with those of others in small groups or in the class as a whole. Are there large differences between your meanings and those of others? How would you describe these differences in terms of connotation and denotation? What accounts for the differences in meanings? That is, what factors contribute to your meanings for these terms? Put differently, how did you acquire the meanings you indicated on these scales? What does this experience illustrate about the principle that meanings are in people?

Meanings Are More than Words and Gestures

When you want to communicate a thought or feeling to another person, you do so with relatively few symbols. These symbols represent just a small part of what you are thinking or feeling, much of which remains unspoken. If you were to try to describe every feeling in detail, you would never get on with the job of living. The meanings you seek to communicate are much more than the sum of the words and nonverbal behaviors you use to represent them.

Because of this, you can never fully know what another person is thinking or feeling. You can only approximate it on the basis of the meanings you receive, which, as already noted, are greatly influenced by who *you* are and what *you* are feeling. Conversely, others can never fully know you; they, too, can only approximate what you are feeling. Failure to understand another person or to

In what ways does this photo illustrate the idea that meanings are more than words and gestures?

be understood is not an abnormal situation. Although it's inevitable, do realize that we can always understand each other a little better than we do now.

Meanings Are Unique

Because meanings are derived from both the messages communicated and the receiver's own thoughts and feelings, no two people ever derive the same meanings. Similarly, because people change constantly, no one person can derive the same meanings on two separate occasions. Who you are can never be separated from the meanings you create. As a result, check your perceptions of another's meanings by asking questions, echoing what you perceive to be the other person's feelings or thoughts, seeking elaboration and clarification, and, in general, practicing the skills identified in the discussion on effective interpersonal perception and listening.

Recognize that as you change, you also change the meanings you create out of past messages. Thus, although the message sent may not have changed, the meanings you created from it yesterday and the meanings you create today may be quite different. Yesterday, when a special someone said, "I love you," you created certain meanings. But today, when you learn that the same "I love you" was said to three other people or when you fall in love with someone else, you drastically change the meanings you perceive from these words.

Meanings Are Both Denotative and Connotative

Consider a word such as "death." To a doctor, this word might mean, or denote, the point at which the heart stops beating, a rather objective description of an event. To a mother whose son has just died, however, the word means much more. It recalls the son's youth, his ambitions, his family, his illness, and so on. To

MEDIA & TECHNOLOGY

EMOTICONS

The recently developed emoticon would be classified as an emblem. The emoticon (sometimes called a "smiley" after the ever-present ☺) is a collection of typed symbols that are given a special meaning in computer communication so that the nuances of the verbal message can be more clearly communicated. The absence of the nonverbal channel where you can clarify your message—smiling or winking to communicate sarcasm or humor, for example—make such typed symbols extremely helpful. In addition to these emoticons a variety of abbreviations have become widely used and have achieved wide agreement as to their meanings. Here are some of the more popular emoticons and abbreviations currently used in computer talk (James and Weingarten 1995; LeBlanc and LeBlanc 1995). Research is just beginning to look into the factors influencing the use of emoticons and the effects they have (Rezabeck and Cochenour 1995).

:-)	= smile; I'm only kidding
:-(	= frown; I'm feeling sad; this saddens me
*	= kiss
:-	= male
>-	= female
{}	= hug
{{{***}}}	= hugs and kisses
;-)	= sly smile
this is important	= underlining, adds emphasis
this is important	= asterisks, adds emphasis
ALL CAPS	= shouting, emphasizing
BTW	= by the way
AFAIK	= as far as I know
IMHO	= in my humble opinion
OTOH	= on the other hand
<G> or <grin>	= grin
IOW	= in other words
IRL	= in real life
ROTFL	= rolling on the floor laughing
TTYL	= talk to you later

Not surprisingly, these symbols are not used universally (Pollack 1996). For example, because it is considered impolite for a Japanese woman to show her teeth when she smiles, the Japanese emoticon for a woman's smile is (^.^) where the dot signifies a closed mouth. A man's smile is written (^_^). Other emoticons popular in Japan but not used in Europe or the United States are (^^) for "cold sweat," (^o^;.) for "excuse me," and (^o^) for "happy."

p. 204

What other emoticons do you use?

her, the word is emotional, subjective, and highly personal. These emotional, subjective, and personal associations are the word's connotative meaning. The **denotation** of a word is its objective definition; the **connotation** is its subjective or emotional meaning.

Now consider a simple nod of the head in answer to the question, "Do you agree?" This gesture is largely denotative and simply says yes. What about a wink, a smile, or an overly rapid speech rate? These nonverbal expressions are more connotative; they express your feelings rather than objective information.

The denotative meaning of a message is general or universal; most people would agree with the denotative meanings and would give similar definitions. Connotative meanings, however, are extremely personal, and few people would agree on the precise connotative meaning of a word or nonverbal behavior.

Meanings Are Context-Based

The same words or behaviors may have totally different meanings when they occur in different contexts. For example, the greeting "How are you?" means "Hello" to someone you pass regularly on the street but means "Is your health improving?" when said to a friend who is hospitalized. A wink to an attractive person on a bus means something completely different from a wink that signifies a put-on or a lie. Similarly, the meaning of a given signal depends on the other behavior it accompanies or is close to in time. Pounding a fist on the table during a speech in support of a politician means something quite different from that same gesture in response to news of a friend's death. Thus, the context in which a message occurs must always be taken into account when you assess meaning.

Message Characteristics

You'll be in a better position to control the message process once the way in which messages work—the principles they follow—is understood. Interpersonal communication messages occur in packages, are governed by rules, vary in directness, vary in believability, and may refer to objects and events in the real world as well as to other messages. Reviewing these five message characteristics enables us to understand better how interpersonal messages are transferred and how we can better control our own.

Messages Are Packaged

The sounds you make with your mouth or the gestures you make with your hands or eyes usually occur in "packages" in which the various verbal and nonverbal behaviors reinforce one another. All parts of the message system usually work together to communicate a unified meaning. When you express anger verbally, your body and face also show anger by tensing, scowling, and perhaps assuming a fighting posture. You often fail to notice this because it seems so natural, so expected. But when the nonverbal messages of someone's posture or face contradict what is said verbally, you take special notice. For example, the person who says, "I'm so glad to see you," but avoids direct eye contact and looks around to see who else is present is sending contradictory messages. You see contradictory messages (also called "mixed messages" by some writers) when couples, whether newly dating or long married, say they love each other but seem to go out of their way to hurt each other nonverbally—for example, by being late for important dates, by flirting with others, or by not touching each other.

In the packaged nature of communication, then, is a warning against the too-easy interpretation of another's meaning, especially as revealed in nonverbal behaviors. Before you identify or guess the meaning of any bit of behavior, look at the entire package or cluster of which it is a part, the way in which the cluster is a

The National Easter Seal Society offers a number of suggestions for communicating with people with disabilities. (Also see "Ten Commandments for Communicating with People with Disabilities," in Unit 3 and "What do you do when you meet a blind person?" on page 182.) Among their recommendations are:

- *Don't use the word* handicapped; *instead, use the word* disability.
- *Don't emphasize the disability; emphasize the person. For example, don't label a person as an epileptic; instead, refer to someone who has epilepsy.*

How would you explain these suggestions in terms of denotation and connotation?

In the classic film The Graduate, *there is a particularly good example of contradictory messages. Benjamin Braddock, the graduate (played by Dustin Hoffman), and Mrs. Robinson (Anne Bancroft) are having an affair, which under normal circumstances would indicate a high degree of intimacy. But Benjamin repeatedly and consistently calls his partner "Mrs. Robinson," which shows that he is uncomfortable with the relationship and that he feels unequal in this partnership with a mature woman. Can you give a similar example of contradictory messages from film, television, or literature?*

response to its context, and the role of the specific nonverbal behavior within that cluster. That attractive person winking in your direction may be giving you the come-on; however, do not rule out the possibility of ill-fitting contact lenses.

Generally, you do not pay much attention to the packaged nature of communication unless there is an incongruity. When you spot a contradiction between the verbal and the nonverbal message, you begin to question the credibility and sincerity of the person.

Are most of your messages packaged consistently or do you communicate different meanings at the same time? Do you know people who frequently communicate different and inconsistent meanings at the same time?

Messages Are Rule-Governed

The rule-governed nature of verbal communication is well-known. These are the rules of a language (the rules of grammar) that native speakers follow in producing and in understanding sentences, although they may be unable to state such rules explicitly.

You learned these rules from observing the behaviors of the adult community. For example, you learned how to express sympathy along with the rules that your culture has established for expressing it appropriately. You learned that touch is permissible under certain circumstances but not under others and which types of touching are permissible and which are not. You learned that women may touch each other in public; for example, they may hold hands, walk arm in arm, engage in prolonged hugging, and even dance together. You also learned that men may not do these things, at least not without inviting social criticism. Further, perhaps most obvious, you learned that certain parts of the body may not be touched and others may. As a relationship changes, so do the rules for touching. As you become more intimate, the rules for touching become less restrictive.

Nonverbal communication is also regulated by a system of rules or norms that state what is and what is not appropriate, expected, and permissible in

How would you state the rules for such common nonverbal messages as (a) smiling, (b) winking, and (c) sitting? In your statement of rules, include answers to the following:
- *What meanings should they be used to communicate?*
- *To whom should these messages be sent? In what situations?*
- *Are there differences in the way women and men should use these messages?*
- *Are there cultural differences that need to be taken into account?*

specific social situations. Of course, these rules vary greatly from one culture to another. Rules are cultural (and relative) institutions; they are not universal laws. In the United States, for example, direct eye contact signals openness and honesty. Among some Latin Americans and Native Americans, however, direct eye contact between, say, a teacher and a student is considered inappropriate, perhaps aggressive; appropriate student behavior is to avoid eye contact with the teacher. From even this simple example it is easy to see how miscommunication can take place. To a teacher in the United States, avoidance of eye contact by a Latin American or Native American could signify guilt, lack of interest, or disrespect, when in fact the child was following her or his own culturally established rules. Table 9.1, drawn from Axtell (1993), gives you an idea of the problems that can arise when you assume that the rules governing message behavior in one culture are the same rules used in other cultures.

A somewhat different system of rules governs communication between sighted and blind or visually impaired persons. The Lighthouse, an organization devoted to enabling blind and partially sighted people to lead independent lives, offers suggestions in the accompanying guidelines, "What Do You Do When You Meet a Blind Person?" Notice as you read the suggestions that they resemble rules for both verbal and nonverbal behavior.

Have you violated any of these suggestions or seen any of them violated? Were you explicitly taught any of these principles?

What Do You Do When You Meet a Blind Person?

On the Street—Ask if assistance would be helpful. Sometimes a blind person prefers to proceed unaided. If the person wants your help, offer your elbow. You should walk a half-step ahead so that your body movements will indicate when to change direction, stop and start, and step up or down at curbside.

Giving Directions—Verbal directions should have the blind person as the reference point. Example: "You are facing Lexington Avenue and you will have to cross it as you continue east on 59th Street."

Handling Money—When giving out bills, indicate the denomination of each so that the blind person can identify it and put it away. Coins are identified by touch.

Safety—Half-open doors are a hazard to everyone, particularly to a blind person. Keep doors closed or wide open.

Dining Out—Guide blind people to the table by offering your arm. Then place their hand on the chair back so they can seat themselves. Read the menu aloud and encourage the waiter to speak directly to the blind person rather than to you. Describe placement of food, using an imaginary clock face (e.g., vegetables are at 2 o'clock, salad plate is at 11 o'clock).

Traveling—Just as a sighted person enjoys hearing a tour guide describe unfamiliar scenery, a blind person likes to hear about indoor and outdoor sights.

Guide Dogs—These are working animals, not pets. Do not distract a guide dog by petting it or by seeking its attention.

Remember—Talk with a blind person as you would with a sighted one, in a normal tone. You may use such expressions as "See you later" and "Did you see that?"

If you enter a room in which a blind person is alone, announce your presence by speaking or introducing yourself. In a group, address blind people by name if they are expected to reply. Excuse yourself when you are leaving.

Always ask before trying to help. Grabbing an arm or pushing is dangerous and discourteous. When you accompany blind people, offer to describe the surroundings.

Source: "What Do You Do When You Meet a Blind Person?" published by The Lighthouse, Inc. Reprinted by permission of The Lighthouse, Inc.

Table 9.1	Some Nonverbal Taboos

These, of course, are only a small number of the nonverbal taboos that exist throughout the world. Can you add any nonverbal taboos to this list?

Nonverbal Behavior	Taboo
Blinking your eyes	Considered impolite in Taiwan
Folding your arms over your chest	Considered disrespectful in Fiji
Waving your hand	Insulting in Nigeria and Greece
Gesturing with the thumb up	Considered rude in Australia
Tapping your two index fingers together	Means that a couple is sleeping together or the request that we sleep together in Egypt
Pointing with the index finger	Considered impolite in many Middle Eastern countries
Bowing to a lesser degree than your host	Implies that you are superior in Japan
With a clenched fist, inserting your thumb between your index and middle finger (called the *fig*)	Considered obscene in some southern European countries
Pointing at someone with your index and third fingers	Means you are wishing evil on the person in some African countries
Resting your feet on a table or chair	Insulting in some Middle Eastern countries

Messages Vary in Directness

Think about how you would respond to someone saying the following sentences.

1A.   I'm so bored; I have nothing to do tonight.
2A.   I'd like to go to the movies. Would you like to come?
1B.   Do you feel like hamburgers tonight?
2B.   I'd like hamburgers tonight. How about you?

The statements numbered 1 are relatively indirect; they are attempts to get the listener to say or do something without committing the speaker. The statements numbered 2 are more direct—they state more clearly the speaker's preferences and then ask the listeners if they agree. A more obvious example of an indirect message occurs when you glance at your watch to communicate that it is late and that you had better be going. Indirect messages have both advantages and disadvantages.

How would you go about discovering if there are gender differences in directness?

Advantages of Indirect Messages   Indirect messages allow you to express a desire without insulting or offending anyone; they allow you to observe the rules of polite interaction. So instead of saying, "I'm bored with this group," you say, "It's getting late and I have to get up early tomorrow," or you look at your watch and pretend to be surprised by the time. Instead of saying, "This food tastes like cardboard," you say, "I just started my diet" or "I just ate." In each instance you are stating a preference but are saying it indirectly so as to avoid offending someone. Not all direct requests, however, should be considered impolite. In one study of

Spanish and English speakers, for example, no evidence was found to support the assumption that politeness and directness were incompatible (Mir 1993).

Sometimes indirect messages allow you to ask for compliments in a socially acceptable manner, such as saying, "I was thinking of getting a nose job." You hope to get the desired compliment: "A nose job? You? Your nose is perfect."

Disadvantages of Indirect Messages   Indirect messages, however, can also create problems. Consider the following dialogue in which an indirect request is made:

PAT: You wouldn't like to have my parents over for dinner this weekend, would you?

CHRIS: I really wanted to go to the shore and just relax.

PAT: Well, if you feel you have to go to the shore, I'll make the dinner myself. You go to the shore. I really hate having them over and doing all the work myself. It's such a drag shopping, cooking, and cleaning all by myself.

Given this situation, Chris has two basic alternatives. One is to stick with the plans to go to the shore and relax. In this case Pat is going to be upset and Chris is going to be made to feel guilty for not helping with the dinner. A second alternative is to give in to Pat, help with the dinner, and not go to the shore. In this case Chris is going to have to give up a much-desired plan and is likely to resent Pat's "manipulative" tactics. Regardless of which decision is made, one person wins and one person loses. This win-lose situation creates resentment, competition, and often an "I'll get even" attitude. With direct requests, this type of situation is much less likely to develop. Consider:

PAT: I'd like to have my parents over for dinner this weekend. What do you think?

CHRIS: Well, I really wanted to go to the shore and just relax.

Many people who communicate directly see those who communicate indirectly as being manipulative. According to Tannen (1994b, p. 92), however, "'manipulative' is often just a way of blaming others for our discomfort with their styles." Do you agree with Tannen? Or, do you think that indirectness is very often intended to be manipulative?

Regardless of what develops next, both individuals are starting out on relatively equal footing. Each has clearly and directly stated a preference. Although at first these preferences seem mutually exclusive, it might be possible to meet both persons' needs. For example, Chris might say, "How about going to the shore this weekend and having your parents over next weekend? I'm really exhausted; I could use the rest." Here is a direct response to a direct request. Unless there is some pressing need to have Pat's parents over for dinner this weekend, this response may enable each to meet the other's needs.

Gender and Cultural Differences in Directness   The popular stereotype in much of the United States holds that women are indirect in making requests and in giving orders. This indirectness communicates powerlessness, discomfort with their own authority. Men, the stereotype continues, are direct, sometimes to the point of being blunt or rude. This directness communicates power and comfort with one's own authority.

Deborah Tannen (1994) provides an interesting perspective on these stereotypes. Women are, it seems, more indirect in giving orders and are more likely to say, for example, "It would be great if these letters could go out today" than "Have these letters out by 3." But, Tannen (1994b, p. 84) argues that "issuing orders indirectly can be the prerogative of those in power" and does in no way show powerlessness. Power, to Tannen, is the ability to chose your own style of communication.

Men, however, are also indirect but in different situations (Rundquist 1992). According to Tannen men are more likely to use indirectness when they express weakness, reveal a problem, or admit an error. Men are more likely to speak indirectly in expressing emotions other than anger. Men are also more indirect when they refuse expressions of increased romantic intimacy. Men are thus indirect, the theory goes, when they are saying something that goes against the masculine stereotype.

Many Asian and Latin American cultures stress the values of indirectness largely because it enables a person to avoid appearing criticized or contradicted and thereby losing face. A somewhat different kind of indirectness is seen in the greater use of intermediaries to resolve conflict among the Chinese than among North Americans, for example (Ma 1992). In most of the United States, however, we are taught that directness is the preferred style. "Be up front" and "tell it like it is" are commonly heard communication guidelines. Contrast these with the following two principles of indirectness found in the Japanese language (Tannen 1994b).

When asked what they would like to change about the communication of the opposite sex, men said they wanted women to be more direct and women said they wanted men to stop interrupting and offering advice (Noble 1994). What one change would you like to see in the communication style of the opposite sex? Of your own sex? How would you describe your own relational communication in terms of direct versus indirect messages? In what specific ways would you want your present communication patterns to change?

◆ *Omoiyari,* close to empathy, says that listeners need to understand the speaker without the speaker being specific or direct. This style obviously places a much greater demand on the listener than would a direct speaking style.

◆ *Sassuru* advises listeners to anticipate a speaker's meanings and use subtle cues from the speaker to infer his or her total meaning.

In thinking about direct and indirect messages, it is important to realize the ease with which misunderstandings can occur. For example, a person who uses an indirect style of speech may be doing so to be polite and may have been taught this style by his or her culture. If you assume, instead, that the person is using indirectness to be manipulative, because your culture regards it so, then miscommunication is inevitable.

Messages Vary in Believability

Of course, we judge the believability of a message in great part by its plausibility (Kraut 1978; Feeley and deTurck 1995). If the message seems plausible or reasonable we are more likely to believe it than if it appeared implausible or unreasonable. However, when there is doubt, where the message could be either true or false and when verbal and nonverbal messages conflict, research shows you are likely to believe the nonverbal. Nonverbal cues, it has been claimed, are more than four times as effective as verbal cues in their impact on interpersonal impressions and ten times more important in expressing confidence (Leathers 1997). For most messages, a good guess is that approximately 60 percent to 65 percent of meaning is communicated nonverbally (Burgoon, Buller, and Woodall 1989).

"Expert lie detectors" were found to be less accurate when they were suspicious of deception than when they were not suspicious (Burgoon, Buller, Ebesu, and Rockwell 1994). What reasons could you advance to explain this finding?

Why do you believe the nonverbal message rather than the verbal one? It may be that you feel verbal messages are easier to fake. Consequently, when there is a contradiction, you are likely to distrust the verbal and accept the nonverbal. Or it may be that nonverbal messages often function below the level of conscious awareness. You learned and perceive them without conscious awareness. Thus,

INTERPERSONAL ETHICS

LYING

A brief dialogue that might take place at a family's dinner introduces this and the next three ethics boxes as a way of raising the issues in practice before considering them in theory.

FRANK: father
BARBARA: daughter
JEFF: son
ALEX: son
LAURA: mother

Frank, Barbara, Jeff, and Alex are sitting in the living room.

FRANK: Look. I don't want anything said to your mother about this. Do you hear me? Not one word.
ALEX: Pop, I really think she should know.
BARBARA: She has a right to know. She has more of a right to know than anyone else.
JEFF: Yeah. I agree. You can't keep this from her. You have no right.
FRANK: I don't give a damn what you kids think. I want her to continue thinking that everything is the way it was. The first one to open their trap is going to have my foot in it.
ALEX: OK, but I don't like it.
JEFF: OK.
BARBARA: I think it stinks but OK.

Assuming that all remain true to their promise, are all four guilty of lying by omission? Are all four equally guilty? Would your answer be different if Frank had just learned he was going to die in the next six months, Laura was in poor health, and Frank feared that the shock might kill her? If one of the children found Frank with a girlfriend, whom he has been seeing romantically for years? If Frank was plotting to commit suicide because he had an incurable illness? Is the behavior of Barbara, Alex, and Jeff unethical because they agree to act against their conscience? Would your answer to this question depend on the age of the children?

Deception researcher Paul Ekman (1985, p. 28) says lying occurs when "one person intends to mislead another, doing so deliberately, without prior notification of this purpose, and without having been explicitly asked to do so by the target [the person the liar intends to mislead]." As this definition implies, lying may be both overt and covert. Although it usually involves overt statements, lying may also be committed by omission. When you omit something relevant, leading others to draw incorrect inferences, you are lying just as surely as if you had stated an untruth. Most of us can appreciate this by recalling times in our youth when our parents, suspicious of what had gone on the previous night, asked us what had happened. Many of us probably recited all the innocent events and omitted what our parents really wanted to know. We were lying, and we knew it.

Similarly, although most lies are verbal, some are nonverbal; in fact, most lies involve at least some nonverbal elements. The innocent facial expression—despite the commission of some wrong—and the knowing nod instead of the honest expression of ignorance are common examples of nonverbal lying (O'Hair, Cody, and McLaughlin 1981). Lies may range from the "white lie" and truth stretching to lies that form the basis of infidelity in a relationship, libel, and perjury.

Before reading about lying as an ethical issue examine your own beliefs about the ethics of lying by taking the self-test on page 187.

Self Test

[When] Is Lying Unethical?

Each of the situations below presents an occasion for a lie. For purposes of this exercise let's define a lie as *a deliberate attempt to mislead another person without forewarning.* How would you rate each in terms of its ethicality, using the scale presented below? Note that many of the situations will lead you to look for more specific information before making your decision. For example, you may want to know how old the child in No. 7 is before making your decision or you may want to know the kind of lie that will be used to get the person in No. 5 to do something good. Because of this you might want to give more than one response for each statement depending upon the specifics of the situation.

1 = definitely ethical
2 = probably ethical
3 = not sure; need to think more about this one
4 = probably unethical
5 = definitely unethical

_____ 1. To lie to a child to protect a fantasy belief, for example, to protect the child's belief in Santa Claus or the Tooth Fairy.

_____ 2. To lie to achieve some greater good, for example, to lie to someone to prevent her or him from committing suicide or from getting depressed or to lie to prevent a burglary or theft.

_____ 3. To lie to protect the reputation of your family, some specific family member, or some third party.

_____ 4. To lie to enable the other person to save face, for example, to agree with an idea you find foolish or to compliment someone when it is undeserved.

_____ 5. To lie to get someone to do something in his or her own best interests, for example, to diet, to stop smoking, or to study harder.

_____ 6. To lie to get what you deserve but can't get any other way, for example, a well-earned promotion or raise or another chance with your relationship partner.

_____ 7. To lie to protect your child from going to jail or facing charges of theft, drug dealing, or murder (though the child is guilty).

_____ 8. To lie to get out of jury duty or to the Internal Revenue Service so as to pay less taxes in April.

_____ 9. To lie to keep hidden information about yourself that you simply don't want to reveal to anyone, for example, your affectional orientation, your financial situation, or your religious beliefs.

_____ 10. To lie to get yourself out of an unpleasant situation, for example, to get out of an extra office chore, a boring conversation, or a conflict with your partner.

Thinking Critically About Lying and Ethics
Each of these situations will be responded to differently by different people, depending on the culture in which they were raised, their beliefs about lying, and their own ethical codes. Is there universal agreement among people on any one of the situations? What cultural beliefs influence the ways in which lying and ethics are looked at? Can you identify situations for which a lie is always unethical? Are there situations in which truth-telling would be unethical and lying would be ethical?

Lying or otherwise hiding the truth is unethical because it prevents another person from learning about possible alternative choices. Consider the situation in which a patient has six months to live. Is it ethical for the doctor or family members to tell the patient that he or she is doing fine? Applying our notion of choice, we would have to conclude that it is not. In not telling the patient the truth, these people are making choices for him or her.

Are there conditions under which the failure to lie would be unethical? What are your obligations as a listener when, for example, you hear someone lying? Are there certain types of lies that a listener might be obligated to expose?

They are in effect preventing the patient from living these last six months as he or she might want to, given the knowledge of imminent death. Similarly, parents who keep the truth about their child's adoption secret after the child has grown up are denying the child the right to make choices he or she might wish to make. Such choices might, for example, concern finding the biological parents or recognizing a different ethnic or religious heritage.

To lie about your infidelity would be unethical because it prevents your partner from making choices that might otherwise be made. Falsely saying "I love you," misrepresenting your abilities in a job interview, even lying about the cleaning power of a detergent are all examples of preventing people from making choices that they might make if they knew your real feelings, your true abilities, or the real power of the detergent.

People may, of course, give up their right to hear all the information that concerns them. A patient may make it known that he or she does not want to know when death will occur. Relationship partners may make an agreement not to disclose their affairs. When this is the case, there is no lying, no deceit, and hence no unethical behavior in withholding such information.

CAN A "LIE" NOT BE A LIE?

Consider the following situation: Your friend arrives wearing a new outfit, looking pretty awful, and asks you what you think of the new look. If your primary concern is with the person asking the question, consider what is really being sought. If the question asks you to evaluate the new outfit, then your obligation is to focus on this and give your honest opinion in as kind and responsive (but truthful) a manner as possible. Thus, instead of saying, "It makes you look old and sickly," you can more appropriately say, "I think you would look much better in something different, something more colorful." If, however, the question about the outfit is simply a way to get positive stroking, address that need and provide the kind of positive response the person is seeking. Here is one of the many instances in which specific content is not important; the psychological need of the person is the primary concern, and it is this that you want to address. Put in terms of the content-relationship axioms discussed in Unit 2, the question is a relationship one, not a content one; the question really focuses on the person and not on the outfit. You are therefore not lying when you say, for example, "You look good," because the real question asked you to say something positive, and you have done so with your compliment.

Here are a few questions that others might ask you; all the questions request information that you are presumed to have. For each question, there are extenuating circumstances that may militate against your responding fully or even truthfully. Consider each question and the mitigating circumstances (these are noted as the **Thoughts** you are thinking as you consider your possible answer). How do you respond?

QUESTION   [A romantic partner asks] Do you love me?
THOUGHT   *I don't want to commit myself, but I don't want to end the relationship, either. I want to allow the relationship to progress further before making any commitment.*
QUESTION   [An interviewer says] You seem a bit old for this type of job. How old are you?
THOUGHT   *I am old for this job, but I need it anyway. Further, it's really illegal for the interviewer to ask my age. I don't want to turn the interviewer off, because I really need this job. Yet I don't want to reveal my age either.*
QUESTION   [A 15-year-old asks] Was I adopted? Who are my real parents?
THOUGHT   *Yes, you were adopted, but I fear that you will look for your biological parents and will be hurt when you find that they are drug dealers and murderers.*

*[The next ethics box appears in Unit 11, page **221**, and deals with fear and emotional appeals.]*

when a discrepancy between the verbal and the nonverbal messages arises, you may get a "feeling" from the nonverbal messages. Because you may not be able to isolate its source, you may assume that it is somehow correct.

Nonverbal cues help you to guess whether or not a person is lying. You also use them to help you discover the underlying truth a lie is meant to conceal. Interestingly enough, as you become more intimate, your ability to detect the underlying truth that your partner is trying to hide *declines*. Research also shows that women are better than men at discovering the underlying truth (McCornack and Parks 1990).

How would you go about discovering if close relationship partners are better at detecting their partners' lies than are casual acquaintances? For an interesting investigation of this question see Metts (1989).

Table 9.2	The Communication Behavior of Liars

This table is based on the extensive research studies and summaries of Knapp and Hall 1992; deTurck and Miller 1985; Miller and Burgoon in DeVito and Hecht 1990; O'Hair, Cody, Goss, and Krayer 1988; Mehrabian 1978; Leathers 1997; Feeley and deTurck 1995. Note that not all studies find the same behaviors indicative of lying, largely because the conditions under which lying is tested are so different. For example, some situations involved the opportunity to rehearse the lie whereas others did not. This table is intended to provide a broad overview of the cues that distinguish lying from truth-telling behavior and not to identify specific cues that should be used to distinguish a liar from a truth-teller.

Liars' Messages	Truth-tellers' Messages
1. Hesitate more; have a greater response latency (pause longer before responding to another's question or statement); use more and longer pauses.	Hesitate less; respond to questions more quickly; pauses less often and for shorter periods of time.
2. Make more speech errors.	Make fewer speech errors.
3. Smile less and appear less friendly and attentive.	Smile more and appear more friendly and attentive.
4. Respond with shorter answers, often simple "yes" or "no" responses.	Elaborate more in their answers.
5. Use more "allness" terms (*never, always, everyone*), generalizing phrases ("stuff like that," "you know"), and nonspecifics ("hung out," "had fun"); use fewer specifics (references to specific people, places, and things).	Use fewer "allness" terms, generalizing phrases, and nonspecifics; use more specifics and make more references to verifiable incidents.
6. Blink more and dilate their pupils more.	Blink less and dilate pupils less.
7. Use more adaptors (self-touching movements) and appear more nervous.	Use fewer adaptors and appear relaxed rather than nervous.
8. Shift their posture more often and use excessive gestures.	Remain more steady in posture and use fewer gestures.
9. Avert gaze more; spend more time looking away from the listener.	Maintain more focused eye contact.
10. Violate the expected nonverbal behaviors.	Follow nonverbally what is expected.

Do couples who talk about their talk understand each other better than couples who do not metacommunicate? How would you go about investigating this question?

What nonverbal cues do you use in detecting whether someone is lying? Table 9.2 presents the findings from a wide variety of research studies on such cues. In reviewing this table, remember that it is important to interpret communication behaviors (verbal and nonverbal) within the context in which they occur. The examples cited should be used to suggest hypotheses, not firm conclusions, about possible deceit. After reviewing the extensive literature on deception, Paul Ekman in *Telling Lies* (1985) cautions: "Evaluating behavioral clues to deceit is hazardous. . . . The lie catcher must always estimate the *likelihood* that a gesture or expression indicates lying or truthfulness; rarely is it absolutely certain."

Messages and Metacommunication

Metacommunication is communication that refers to other communications; it is communication about communication (Unit 6). All behavior, verbal and nonverbal, can be metacommunicational. Verbally, you can say, for example, "This statement is false" or "Do you understand what I am trying to tell you?" Because these sentences refer to communication, they are called metacommunicational statements.

Nonverbal behavior may also be metacommunicational. Obvious examples include crossing one's fingers behind one's back or winking when telling a lie. But the more subtle instances of metacommunication are more interesting: as you say "I had a really nice time" to your blind date, the nonverbal messages—the lack of a smile, the failure to maintain eye contact, the extra-long pauses—contradict the verbal "really nice time" and tell your date that you did not enjoy the evening.

Nonverbal messages may also metacommunicate about other nonverbal messages. The individual who both smiles and avoids direct eye contact or extends a totally lifeless hand shows how one nonverbal behavior may contradict another. Usually when nonverbal behavior is metacommunicational, it reinforces other verbal or nonverbal behavior. You smile when greeting someone, run to meet the person you say you are eager to see, or arrive early for a party you verbally express pleasure in attending. On the negative—though still consistent—side, you may arrive late for a dental appointment (presumably with a less-than-pleasant facial expression) or frown when telling off your boss.

Summary   U N I T   I N   B R I E F

A RETURN TO OBJECTIVES:

In this unit we introduced the message system and looked at some of the major similarities and differences in verbal and nonverbal messages. We focused on three major issues: (1) How do verbal and nonverbal messages interact? (2) What principles govern the communication of meaning from one person to another? (3) What are the major characteristics of both verbal and nonverbal messages?

Verbal and Nonverbal Interaction	Meanings	Message Characteristics
Uses: ◆ **To accent** or emphasize ◆ **To complement** or add to or supplement ◆ **To contradict** or deny ◆ **To regulate** or control ◆ **To repeat** or restate ◆ **To substitute** or take the place of	**Meaning is:** ◆ an active process created by cooperation between source and receiver; ◆ a function of the interaction of messages and the receiver's previous experiences, expectations, attitudes, and so forth. **Meanings are:** ◆ in people ◆ more than words and gestures ◆ unique ◆ both denotative and connotative ◆ context-based	**Packaged:** Communication behaviors occur in clusters. **Rule-governed:** Both verbal and nonverbal messages follow rules. **Directness:** Messages may be direct or indirect. **Believability:** Messages vary in believability. **Metacommunication:** Messages may refer to events in the outside world (object communication) or to other messages (metacommunication).

UNIT

10

Verbal Messages: Principles and Pitfalls

Unit Topics	Unit Objectives
	After completing this unit, you should be able to:
Disconfirmation and Confirmation Racism Sexism Heterosexism Racist, Sexist, and Heterosexist Listening	1. Define *disconfirmation* and the *principle of confirmation* 2. Explain *racism, sexism,* and *heterosexism* as disconfirmation
Excluding Talk and Inclusion The Principle of Inclusion	3. Define *excluding talk* and the *principle of inclusion* and provide examples of each
Talking About Self or Others and Balance The Principle of Balance	4. Define *self-talk, other-talk,* and the *principle of balance* and provide examples of each
Criticism, Praise, and Honest Appraisal The Principle of Honest Appraisal	5. Explain how criticism and praise can cause difficulties and explain the *principle of honesty*

EXPERIENTIAL LEARNING VEHICLES

Vehicles No. 14, "Conversational Analysis: A Chance Meeting," pp. 454–456, and No. 15, "Giving and Taking Directions," pp. 456–458, are useful for illustrating verbal message principles.

This unit continues exploring interpersonal messages and focuses on four major principles and their corresponding pitfalls—ways in which you may create negative effects. Applying these principles and avoiding the pitfalls should help create a more positive environment for all your communications. As you read this unit, you'll note that these principles deal more with relational than with content messages (Unit 2), further underscoring the importance of this level of interpersonal communication.

Disconfirmation and Confirmation

Before reading about these important concepts, take the self-test "How Confirming Are You?" to examine your own message behavior.

Self Test   *How Confirming Are You?*

In your typical communications, how likely are you to display the following behaviors? Use the accompanying scale in responding to each statement:

    5= always
    4= often
    3= sometimes
    2= rarely
    1= never

_____ 1. I acknowledge the presence of another person both verbally and nonverbally.
_____ 2. I acknowledge the contributions of the other person—for example, by supporting or taking issue with what the person says.
_____ 3. During the conversation, I make nonverbal contact by maintaining direct eye contact, touching, hugging, kissing, and otherwise demonstrating acknowledgment of the other person.
_____ 4. I communicate as both speaker and listener with involvement, and with a concern and respect for the other person.
_____ 5. I signal my understanding of the other person both verbally and nonverbally.
_____ 6. I reflect the other person's feelings as a way of showing that I understand these feelings.
_____ 7. I ask questions when appropriate concerning the other person's thoughts and feelings.
_____ 8. I respond to the other person's requests, for example, by returning phone calls and answering letters within a reasonable time.
_____ 9. I encourage the other person to express his or her thoughts and feelings.
_____10. I respond directly and exclusively to what the other person says.

**Thinking Critically About Confirmation
and Disconfirmation**

All 10 statements express confirming behaviors. Therefore, high scores (above 35) reflect a strong tendency to engage in confirmation. Low scores (below 25) reflect a strong tendency to engage in disconfirmation. Can you provide at least one specific message to illustrate how you might express confirmation in each of the ten situations identified in the self-test? For example, for the first statement, you might say: "Hi, Pat, come over and join us" or simply smile and wave Pat to join your group.

Confirmation and disconfirmation—as illustrated in the self-test—refer to the extent to which you acknowledge another person. Consider this situation. Pat arrives home late one night. Chris is angry and complains about Pat's coming home so late. Consider some responses Pat might make:

1. Stop screaming. I'm not interested in what you're babbling about. I'll do what I want, when I want. I'm going to bed.
2. What are you so angry about? Didn't you get in three hours late last Thursday when you went to that office party? So knock it off.
3. You have a right to be angry. I should have called to tell you I was going to be late, but I got involved in an argument at work, and I couldn't leave until it was resolved.

In response 1, Pat dismisses Chris's anger and even indicates dismissal of Chris as a person. In response 2, Pat rejects the validity of Chris's reasons for being angry but does not dismiss either Chris's feelings of anger or Chris as a person. In response 3, Pat acknowledges Chris's anger and the reasons for being angry. In addition, Pat provides some kind of explanation and, in doing so, shows that both Chris's feelings and Chris as a person are important and that Chris deserves to know what happened. The first response is an example of disconfirmation, the second of rejection, and the third of confirmation.

Psychologist William James once observed that "no more fiendish punishment could be devised, even were such a thing physically possible, than that one should be turned loose in society and remain absolutely unnoticed by all the members thereof." In this often-quoted observation, James identifies the essence of disconfirmation (Watzlawick, Beavin, and Jackson 1967; Veenendall and Feinstein 1995).

Disconfirmation is a communication pattern in which you ignore a person's presence as well as that person's communications. You say, in effect, that the person and what she or he has to say are not worth serious attention. Disconfirming responses often lead to loss of self-esteem.

Note that disconfirmation is not the same as **rejection**. In rejection, you disagree with the person; you indicate your unwillingness to accept something the other person says or does. In disconfirming someone, however, you deny that person's significance; you claim that what this person says or does simply does not count.

Confirmation is the opposite communication pattern. In confirmation, you not only acknowledge the presence of the other person but also indicate your acceptance of this person, of this person's definition of self, and of your relationship as defined or viewed by this other person. Confirming responses often lead to gains in self-esteem. You can communicate confirmation (and disconfirmation) in a wide variety of ways. Table 10.1 shows just a few.

Talking with the Grief-stricken   Talking with the grief-stricken provides an interesting perspective on confirmation. Grief is something everyone experiences at some time. It may be experienced because of illness or death, the loss of a highly valued relationship (for example, a romantic breakup), the loss of certain physical or mental abilities, or the loss of material possessions (your house burning down or stock market losses). Consider the following example of one attempt to talk with a grief-stricken individual.

How would you describe your own behavior in terms of confirmation and disconfirmation? How are you (generally) confirming? Disconfirming? In which specific situations are you most likely to be confirming? Most likely to be disconfirming?

How would you do about investigating the connection between self-esteem and the tendency to be confirming-disconfirming?

Table 10.1	Confirmation and Disconfirmation

This table parallels the self-test presented earlier in this unit so that you can see clearly not only the confirming but also the opposite, disconfirming behaviors. As you review this table, try to imagine a specific illustration for each of the ways of communicating disconfirmation and confirmation (Pearson 1993; Galvin and Brommel 1996).

Confirmation	Disconfirmation
1. Acknowledge the presence of the other verbally or nonverbally.	1. Ignore the presence of the other person.
2. Acknowledge the contributions of the other by either supporting or taking issue with what the other says.	2. Ignore what the other says: Express (nonverbally and verbally) indifference to anything the other says.
3. Make nonverbal contact by maintaining direct eye contact, touching, hugging, kissing, and otherwise demonstrating acknowledgment of the other.	3. Make no nonverbal contact; avoid direct eye contact; avoid touching other person.
4. Engage in dialogue—communication in which both persons are speakers and listeners, both are involved, and both are concerned with and have respect for each other.	4. Engage in monologue—communication in which one person speaks and one person listens, there is no real interaction, and there is no real concern or respect for each other.
5. Demonstrate understanding of what the other says and means.	5. Jump to interpretation or evaluation rather than working at understanding what the other means.
6. Reflect the other's feelings to demonstrate your understanding of these feelings.	6. Express your own feelings, ignore feelings of the other, or give abstract intellectualized responses.
7. Ask questions of the other concerning both thoughts and feelings.	7. Make statements about yourself, ignore any lack of clarity in the other's remarks.
8. Acknowledge the other's requests; answer the other's questions, return phone calls, and answer letters.	8. Ignore the other's requests; fail to answer questions, return phone calls, and answer letters.
9. Encourage the other to express thoughts and feelings.	9. Interrupt or otherwise make it difficult for the other to express himself or herself.
10. Respond directly and exclusively to what the other says.	10. Respond tangentially by acknowledging the other's comment but then shifting the focus of the message in another direction.

I just heard that Harry died—I mean—passed away. I'm so sorry. I know exactly how you feel. But, you know, it's for the best. I mean the man was suffering. I remember seeing him last month; he was so weak he could hardly stand. And he looked so sad. He must have been in constant pain. It's better this way. He's at peace. You'll get over it. You'll see. Time heals all wounds. It was the same way with me, and you know how close we were. I mean we were devoted to each other. Everyone said we were the closest pair they had ever seen. And I got over it. So how about we go to dinner tonight? We'll talk about old times. Come on. Come on. Don't be a spoilsport. I really need to get out. I've been in the house all week. Come on, do it for me. After all, you have to forget; you have to get on with your own life. I won't take no for an answer. I'll pick you up at seven.

Here are a few suggestions for avoiding the kind of communication illustrated above and making this often difficult form of communication easier:

◆ Confirm the other person and the person's feelings. "You must miss him a great deal" confirms the person's feelings, for example. Avoid expressions that are disconfirming: "You'll see, things will be better tomorrow."

◆ Give the grieving person permission to grieve. Let the person know that it is acceptable for him or her to grieve in the ways that feel most comfortable— for example, crying or talking about old times.

◆ Avoid trying to force the grief-stricken individual to focus on the bright side, because he or she may not be ready. Avoid expressions such as "You're so lucky you still have some vision left" or "It is better this way; Pat was suffering so much."

◆ Encourage the grieving person to express feelings and talk about the loss. Most people who experience grief welcome the opportunity to talk about it. However, don't try to force the person to talk about experiences or feelings she or he may not be ready to share.

◆ Empathize with the grief-stricken person and communicate this empathic understanding. Let the person know that you can understand what he or she is feeling. Do not assume, though, that your feelings (however empathic) are the same in depth or in kind. If, having never experienced this tragedy, you say to a parent who has lost a child, "I know exactly what you're feeling," you risk arousing resentment. (See Unit 8 for more on empathy.)

◆ Be especially sensitive to leave-taking cues. Don't try to force your presence on someone who is grief stricken or press the person to stay with you or a group of people. When in doubt, ask.

What other suggestions would you make for talking with those experiencing grief? What one commonly heard expression do you find the most troublesome?

Before moving on to some of the specific ways in which disconfirmation is often expressed, make sure the distinctions among confirmation, rejection, and disconfirmation are clear. Try to provide examples of confirmatory, rejecting, and disconfirmatory responses to these three situations.

Your friend, Pat says: "I haven't had a date in the last four months. I'm getting very depressed over this." You respond (disconfirming, rejecting, and confirming):

Chris says: "I think I'm going to look for another job; again, I was passed over for promotion. There's no sense in working here anymore." You respond (disconfirming, rejecting, and confirming):

Chris confides to you about some recent difficulties with Pat: "Pat wants me to quit trying to get a job acting and take that job in advertising so we'll be able to get a decent apartment and get out of debt. But acting is my whole life. I'm afraid if I give up doing what I really want, I'll come to resent Pat and our entire relationship will deteriorate." You respond (disconfirming, rejecting, and confirming):

These concepts of confirmation and disconfirmation also give unique insight into a wide variety of offensive language practices, language that alienates and separates, language that disconfirms. The three obvious practices are racism, sexism, and heterosexism.

Racism

According to Andrea Rich (1974), "any language that, through a conscious or unconscious attempt by the user, places a particular racial or ethnic group in an inferior position is racist." Racist language expresses racist attitudes. It also contributes to the development of racist attitudes in those who use or hear such language.

Racist terms are used by members of one culture to disparage members of other cultures—their customs or their accomplishments. Racist language emphasizes differences rather than similarities and separates rather than unites members of different cultures. Traditionally, racist language has been used by the dominant group to establish and maintain power over other groups. Today, however, it is used by racists (or the racist-talking) in all groups. The social consequences of racist language in terms of employment, education, housing opportunities, and general community acceptance are well known.

Many people feel that it is permissible for members of a culture to refer to themselves with racist terms. That is, Asians may use the negative terms referring to Asians, Italians may use the negative terms referring to Italians, and so on. This issue is seen clearly in rap music where performers use such racial terms (*New York Times*, January 24, 1993, 1, 31). The reasoning seems to be that groups should be able to laugh at themselves.

It is interesting to note that the terms denoting some of the major movements in art—for example, "impressionism" and "cubism"—were originally applied negatively. The terms were adopted by the artists themselves and eventually became positive. A parallel can be seen in the use of the word "queer" by some lesbian and gay organizations. Their purpose in using the term is to cause it to lose its negative connotation.

One possible problem, though, is that such terms may not lose their negative connotations and may simply reinforce the negative stereotypes that society has already assigned to certain groups. By using these terms, members may come to accept the labels with their negative connotations and thus contribute to their own stereotyping.

It has often been pointed out (Davis 1973; Bosmajian 1974; Purnell 1982) that there are aspects of language that may be inherently racist. For example, Davis's examination of English found 134 synonyms for "white." Of these, 44 have positive connotations (for example, "clean," "chaste," and "unblemished") and only 10 have negative connotations (for example, "whitewash" and "pale"); the remaining synonyms are relatively neutral. Of the 120 synonyms for "black," 60 were found to have unfavorable connotations ("unclean," "foreboding," and "deadly") and none to have positive connotations.

Consider such phrases as the following.

- the Korean doctor
- the Latino prodigy
- the African American mathematician
- the white nurse
- the Eskimo physicist

In some cases, of course, the racial identifier may be relevant, as in, say, "The Korean doctor argued for hours with the French doctor while the Swiss tried to secure a compromise." Here the aim might be to identify the nationality of the doctor as you would if you had forgotten her or his name.

Often, however, such identifiers are used to emphasize that the combination of race and occupation (or talent or accomplishment) is rare and unexpected, that this member of the race is an exception. It also implies that racial factors are

One possible problem with this assumption is that these terms may just reinforce the negative stereotypes that society has already assigned this group. By using these terms, members may come to accept these labels with their negative connotations and thus contribute to their own stereotyping. Others would argue that by using such terms they are making them less negative. The use of the word queer, for example, by militant gay and lesbian groups is designed to give a negatively evaluated term a positive spin. What are your feelings about this issue?

How would you describe male-female relationships in organizations with which you're familiar, for example, your college, supermarket, post office? How do male-female work relationships in the United States differ from those in other cultures with which you're familiar?

somehow important in the context. As noted, there are times when this may be true, but most often race would be irrelevant.

Sexism

Consider some of the language used to refer to women. A woman traditionally loses her maiden name when she marries and, in certain instances, loses her first name as well. She changes from "Ann Smith" to "Mrs. John Jones."

We say that a woman "marries into" a man's family and that a family "dies out" if there are no male children. In the United States, one does not usually speak of a man marrying into a woman's family (unless the family is extremely prestigious or wealthy), and a family can still "die out" even if there are ten female children. In some marriage ceremonies, you can still hear "I now pronounce you man and wife," not "man and woman" or "husband and wife." The man retains his status as man, but the woman changes hers from woman to wife. Barrie Thorne, Cheris Kramarae, and Nancy Henley, in *Language, Gender and Society* (1983), summarize this line of research by noting that "women tend to be defined by their relation to men. . . . The available and 'approved' titles, pronouns, lexicons, and labels," they note, "reflect the fact that women (as well as other subordinates) have been named by others."

Julia Stanley, for example, researched terms indicating sexual promiscuity, finding 220 terms referring to a sexually promiscuous woman but only 22 terms for a sexually promiscuous man (Thorne, Kramarae, and Henley 1983). Surely, there are as many promiscuous men as there are promiscuous women, yet the English language fails to reflect this. If the number of terms indicates the importance of a

In one study seventh-grade science textbooks were found to contain sexist language and failed to integrate the achievements of women scientists and to provide the necessary information on women's health (Potter and Rosser 1992). Do you find this kind of sexism in your college textbooks? Can you identify specific examples? Can you find examples of racism? Examples of heterosexism?

concept to a culture, then promiscuity among women is significant (that is, it is "abnormal" or "beyond the norm") and something to take special notice of, whereas promiscuity among men is not significant (that is, it is "normal"), and therefore no special notice need be taken of it.

The National Council of Teachers of English (NCTE) has proposed guidelines for nonsexist (gender-free, gender-neutral, or sex-fair) language. These guidelines concern the use of generic "man," "he," and "his" as well as sex role stereotyping (Penfield 1987).

Generic "Man"   The word "man" refers most clearly to an adult male. To use the term to refer to both men and women emphasizes "maleness" at the expense of "femaleness." Similarly, the terms "mankind," "the common man," or even "cavemen" imply a primary focus on adult males. Gender-neutral terms can easily be substituted. Instead of "mankind," you can say "humanity," "people," or "human beings." Instead of "the common man," you can say "the average person" or "ordinary people." Instead of "cavemen," you can say "prehistoric people" or "cave dwellers." Similarly, the use of "policeman," "fireman," "salesman," "chairman," "mailman," and other terms that presume maleness as the norm and femaleness as a deviation from this norm are clear and common examples of sexist language. Consider using nonsexist alternatives for these and similar terms; make these alternatives (for example, "police officer," "mail carrier," and "firefighter") part of your active vocabulary.

Generic "He" and "His"   The use of the masculine pronoun to refer to any individual regardless of sex further illustrates the extent of linguistic sexism. There seems to be no legitimate reason why the feminine pronoun could not alternate with the masculine pronoun in referring to hypothetical individuals, or why such terms as "he and she" or "her and him" could not be used instead of just "he" or "him." Alternatively, we can restructure our sentences to eliminate any reference to gender. Here are a few examples from the NCTE Guidelines (Penfield 1987):

Sexist	Gender-Free
The average student is worried about his grades.	The average student is worried about grades.
Ask the student to hand in his work as soon as he has finished.	Ask students to hand in their work as soon as they have finished.
When a teacher asks his students for an evaluation, he is putting himself on the spot.	When you ask your students for an evaluation, you are putting yourself on the spot.

Sex Role Stereotyping   The words we use often reflect a sex role bias, the assumption that certain roles or professions belong to men and others belong to women. In eliminating sex role stereotyping, avoid, for example, making the hypothetical elementary school teacher female and the college professor male. Avoid referring to doctors as male and nurses as female. Avoid noting the sex of a professional with terms such as "female doctor" or "male nurse." When you are referring to a specific doctor or nurse, the person's sex will become clear when you use the appropriate pronoun: "Dr. Smith wrote the prescription for her new patient" or "The nurse recorded the patient's temperature himself."

Heterosexism

A close relative of sexism is heterosexism. The term is a relatively new addition to our list of linguistic prejudices. **Heterosexism** refers to language used to disparage lesbians and gay men (Rothblum and Bond 1996).

As in the case of racist and sexist language, we see heterosexism in the derogatory terms used for lesbians and gay men and in more subtle forms. For example, when we qualify a description of a profession—as in "gay athlete" or "lesbian doctor"—we are in effect stating that athletes and doctors are not normally gay or lesbian. Further, we are highlighting the affectional orientation of the athlete and the doctor in a context in which it may have no relevance. This practice is, of course, the same as qualifying by race or gender, as already noted.

Still another instance of heterosexism—and perhaps the most difficult to deal with—is the presumption of heterosexuality. Usually, people assume that the person they are talking to or about is heterosexual. Usually, they are correct, because the majority of the population is heterosexual. At the same time, however, note that heterosexism denies lesbians and gay males their true identity. The practice of assuming that a person is heterosexual is very similar to the presumption of whiteness and maleness that we have made significant progress toward eliminating. Here are a few additional suggestions for avoiding heterosexist, or what some call "homophobic," language.

◆ Avoid offensive nonverbal mannerisms that parody stereotypes when talking about gays and lesbians.

◆ Avoid "complimenting" gay men and lesbians by saying they "don't look it." To gays and lesbians, that is not a compliment. Similarly, expressing disappointment that a person is gay—for example, saying "What a waste!" and meaning it as a compliment—is not really a compliment.

◆ Avoid the assumption that every gay or lesbian knows what every other gay or lesbian is thinking. To do so is very similar to asking someone from Japan why Sony is investing heavily in the United States or, as one comic put it, asking an African American, "What do you think Jesse Jackson meant by that last speech?"

◆ Avoid denying individual differences. Saying things like "Lesbians are so loyal" or "Gay men are so open with their feelings"—statements that ignore the reality of wide differences within any group—are potentially insulting to all groups.

◆ Avoid "overattribution," the tendency to attribute just about everything a person does, says, and believes to being gay or lesbian. This tendency helps to recall and perpetuate stereotypes.

◆ Remember that relationship milestones are important to all people. Ignoring the anniversaries or birthdays of partners is resented by everyone.

Do you find that men and women differ in their use of racist, sexist, and heterosexist language? More specifically, would this type of language appear equally in all-female, all-male, and mixed groups? How does racist, sexist, and heterosexist language in interpersonal interactions differ from such language in more public situations (for example, in print, on television, or in public speeches)? What is the status of your own language concerning sexist, racist, and heterosexist language? How do you feel about this?

Racist, Sexist, and Heterosexist Listening

Just as racist, sexist, and heterosexist attitudes will influence your language, they also influence your listening. In this type of listening you only hear what the speaker is saying through your stereotypes. You assume that what the speaker is saying is unfairly influenced by the speaker's sex, race, or affectional orientation.

Do you find the position taken on sexist, racist, and heterosexist listening a reasonable one? If not, how would you define sexist, racist, and heterosexist listening? Do you find this a useful concept in understanding effective communication? Do you find these types of listening operating in your classes? In your family? In your community? If you wanted to reduce this type of listening, how would you do it?

Sexist, racist, and heterosexist listening occur in a wide variety of situations. For example, when you dismiss a valid argument or attribute validity to an invalid argument, when you refuse to give someone a fair hearing, or when you give less credibility (or more credibility) to a speaker because the speaker is of a particular sex, race, or affectional orientation, you are practicing sexist, racist, or heterosexist listening. Put differently, sexist, racist, or heterosexist listening occurs when you listen differently to a person because of his or her sex, race, or affectional orientation when these characteristics are irrelevant to the message.

But, there are many instances where these characteristics are relevant and pertinent to your evaluation of the message. For example, the sex of the speaker talking on pregnancy, fathering a child, birth control, or surrogate motherhood or fatherhood is, most would agree, probably relevant to the message. And so it is not sexist listening to take the sex of the speaker into account when listening to such messages. It is sexist listening to assume that only one sex has anything to say that's worth hearing or that what one sex says can be discounted without a fair hearing. The same is true when listening through a person's race or affectional orientation.

Excluding Talk and Inclusion

"Excluding talk" is used here as a general term to refer to communication that excludes certain people, though on the surface it may appear to apply to everyone. You see this in a wide variety of forms. It is seen, for example, in the use of some in-group language in the presence of some out-group member. When doctors get together and discuss medicine, there is no problem. But when they get together with someone who is not a doctor, they often fail to adjust to this new person. Instead, they simply continue with discussions of prescriptions, symptoms, medication, and all the talk that excludes others present.

Excluding talk also occurs when people of the same nationality get together within a larger, more heterogeneous group and use the language of their nationality, sometimes just isolated words, sometimes sentences, and sometimes entire conversations. The use of these terms in the presence of nonmembers emphasizes their status as outsiders and excludes these people from full participation in the communication act.

Another form of excluding talk is the use of the terms of one's own cultural group as universal, as applying to everyone. In using such terms others are excluded. For example, *church* refers to the place of worship for specific religions, not all religions. Similarly, *Bible* refers to the Christian religious scriptures and is not a general term for "religious scriptures". Nor does "Judeo-Christian tradition" include the religious traditions of everyone. Similarly, the use of the terms *marriage, husband,* and *wife* refer to some heterosexual relationships and exclude others; they also exclude gay and lesbian relationships.

The Principle of Inclusion

Instead of trying to emphasize the exclusion of one or more members, consider the principle of inclusion. Regardless of the type of communication situation we are in, everyone needs to be included in the interaction. Even if job-related issues have to be discussed in the presence of a nonmember, that person can be included in a variety of ways, for example, by seeking the nonmember's perspective or drawing an analogy from his or her field.

Another way to practice inclusion is to fill in relevant details discussed by the group for those who may be unaware. For example, when people, places, or events are mentioned in a group discussion, briefly identify them for those to whom they may be unfamiliar. Brief parenthetical identifying phrases are usually sufficient: "Margo—she's Jeff's daughter—loved San Francisco State."

When someone asks a question or makes a comment requiring a response, be sure to respond in some way. Even if you are talking, attending to someone else, or otherwise engaged, respond in some way to indicate your acknowledgment of the comment—verbally, if possible, or nonverbally with a nod or smile, for example. Practicing inclusion is so easy that it is surprising that it is violated so blatantly and so often. When inclusion is practiced, everyone gains a great deal more satisfaction from the interaction.

Also, consider the vast array of alternative terms that are inclusive rather than exclusive. For example, the Association of American University Presses (Schwartz 1995) recommends using *place of worship* instead of *church* when you wish to include the religious houses of worship of all people. Similarly, *committed relationship* is more inclusive than *marriage, couple's therapy* is more inclusive than *marriage counseling,* and *life partner* is more inclusive than *husband* or *wife. Religious scriptures* is more inclusive than *Bible.* Of course, if you are referring to, say, a specific Baptist church or married heterosexual couples then the terms *church* and *marriage* are perfectly appropriate.

On your college campus, which would be considered the most offensive: sexist, racist, or heterosexist language? Least offensive? Are you ever in situations where this language is the approved and expected form of discourse? What is your ethical obligation when it comes to racist, sexist, and heterosexist talk? For example, do you have an obligation to voice disapproval when others use such language?

Talking About Self or Others and Balance

Many people—friends and family members are surely among them—act and talk as if they were the center of the universe. They talk constantly about themselves—about their jobs, their accomplishments, their plans, their families, their love lives, their problems, their successes, and sometimes even their failures. Rarely do they ask how we are, what we think (except perhaps about them), or what our plans are. Other people go to the other extreme and never talk about themselves. They are the underdisclosers we discussed in Unit 4, the people who want to learn everything about you but are not willing to share anything about themselves that might make them vulnerable. As a result, we come away from the interaction with the feeling that they either did not like us very much or did not trust us. Otherwise, we feel, they would have revealed something of themselves.

If you asked your friends how often you talk about yourself versus how often you talk about them, what do you think they would say? Use a ten-point scale for "self-talk" and a ten-point scale for "other-talk." Now ask a few friends. How accurate were you?

The Principle of Balance

Admittedly, it is not easy to steer a comfortable course between too much and too little self-talk. Moreover, there are certainly times when we just cannot stop talking about a new job or new romantic partner. Under most circumstances, however, we should strive for interactions governed by the principle of balance—some self-talk, some other-talk, never all of either one. Communication is a two-way process: Each person needs to function as source and as receiver, and

MEDIA & TECHNOLOGY

LEARNING THE JARGON—20 BASIC TERMS

Here are a few terms that you'll come across as you connect media and technology with face-to-face interpersonal communication. If you are knowledgeable about computer technology, what other terms should be added here? Share a word with others.

Address. A unique name given to every computer connected to the Internet to insure that information is sent to exactly the right person.

BBS. Bulletin board system. A collection of electronic bulletin boards on which members may post messages for others to read.

Chat. Live conversation between or among other computer users.

e-mail/snail mail. E-mail is electronic mail; mail sent from one person to another over a network of computers; opposed to "snail" mail which is mail sent the traditional way by the post office. My e-mail address—also called *userid*—is *jdevito@shiva.hunter.cuny.edu* and is read as jay devito at shiva dot hunter dot cuny dot e-d-u. The president of the United States e-mail address is *president@whitehouse.gov*.

Emoticon. Also called a "smiley" (after the familiar smiling face that accompanies so many messages), an emoticon is a set of typed characters that communicate the emotional tone of your message much like the smiley face communicates "happy" or "cheer up." The Media and Technology box in Unit 9 identifies several popular emoticons.

FAQ. Abbreviation for "frequently asked questions". FAQs are files of frequently asked questions about how to operate a particular computer program or file. Mailing lists and newsgroups maintain lists of FAQs so that new members may get answers to their questions without sending additional help messages. Reading the FAQs is an essential rule of netiquette (discussed more fully in the Media and Technology box in Unit 14).

Finger. A program that enables you to obtain information about a computer user or organization.

Flame/Flame war. A flame is a personal attack on another person; a flame war is an exchange of personal attacks on a large scale. Flaming is generally frowned upon as it hinders the group's normal functioning. Flaming is a good way to start a conflict; see the Media and Technology box in Unit 14.

Hacker/Cracker. A hacker is a computer user who greatly enjoys exploring the ins and outs of computers, sometimes obsessively. A cracker is one who breaks into computer systems to create problems or to steal information.

Handle. In computer communications, the name an individual uses for online identification. The term is also used to refer to the element in an object that enables you to move or resize it.

Hypertext. Elements of text (usually in some display font) that enable you to select it and thereby jump to another part of the document or to another file. In a more limited sense, the boldface terms in this text are hypertext in that they lead you to the glossary.

Internet. A worldwide system of connected computers. The Internet supports, for example, e-mail, gopher, the World Wide Web, and ftp.

Lurking. Observing rather than participating in, say, an online newsgroup. Lurking is recommended until you get to know the system and its peculiar rules. A lurker is a person who lurks.

Netiquette. The rules of etiquette for online communication. See the Media and Technology box in Unit 14 for some of the rules of netiquette.

Newsgroups. Message areas that are organized by subject and which may be read or added to by members.

Posting. Placing a message into a network, for example, onto a bulletin board.

Real time. Communication that is received as it is sent.

Signature. Information that is regularly attached to your e-mail or messages that you post. Signatures usually contain the person's contact address and perhaps a favorite quotation.

Sysop. Abbreviation for *systems operator*, the person who is in charge of a bulletin board service or similar computer system.

Thread. A conversational theme introduced in a particular message and then followed up with replies, along with replies to the replies, and so on.

Web browser. A program that enables you to surf the World Wide Web, for example, Netscape Navigator or Microsoft's Internet Explorer.

p. 244

each person should have a chance to function as subject. Balanced communication interactions are more satisfying and more interesting. We all get bored with too much talk about the other person, and, let's face it, others get bored with too much talk about us. The principle of balance is a guide to protect both us and others.

Criticism, Praise, and Honest Appraisal

Throughout your communication experiences, you are expected to criticize, to evaluate, and otherwise to render some kind of judgment. Especially in helping professions, such as teaching, nursing, or counseling, criticism is an important and frequently used skill. In short, criticism is a most useful and important part of your interactions and your communications generally. The problem arises when criticism is used outside of its helping function, when it is inappropriate or excessive. An important interpersonal skill is to develop a facility for detecting when a person is asking for criticism and when that person is simply asking for a compliment. For example, when a friend asks how you like the new apartment, he or she may be searching for a compliment rather than wanting you to itemize all the things wrong with it.

Sometimes the desire to be liked (or perhaps the need to be appreciated) is so strong that we go to the other extreme and paint everything with praise. The most ordinary jacket, the most common thought, the most average meal are given extraordinary praise, way beyond their merits. The overly critical and the overly

If you could classify your last 100 comments into two categories—those of praise and criticism—how many would be in each? What do you think of these relative emphases? How do you generally respond to praise? To criticism?

What advice would you give this woman giving criticism? What advice would you give the person receiving the criticism?

complimentary soon find that their comments are no longer met with concern or interest.

The Principle of Honest Appraisal

As an alternative to excessive criticism or praise, consider the principle of honest appraisal. Tell the truth, but note that there is an art to truth telling, just as there is an art to all other forms of effective communication. First, distinguish between instances in which an honest appraisal is sought and those in which the individual needs a compliment. Respond to the appropriate level of meaning. Second, if an honest appraisal is desired and if yours is a negative one, give some consideration to how you should phrase your criticism. Here are a few suggestions on giving criticism:.

How would you go about discovering if any one of these suggestions actually has a positive effect and if its opposite has a negative effect?

- ◆ Focus on the event or the behavior rather than on personality; for example, say "This paper has four errors and needs retyping" rather than "You're a lousy typist; do this over."
- ◆ State criticism positively, if possible. Rather than saying "You look terrible in black," say "You look much better in bright colors."
- ◆ Be constructive; explain what could be done to make it better.
- ◆ Own your thoughts and feelings. Instead of saying "Your report was unintelligible," say "I had difficulty following your ideas."
- ◆ State your concern for the other person along with your criticism, if appropriate. Instead of saying "The introduction to your speech is boring," say "I really want your speech to be great; I'd open with some humor to get the audience's attention." Say "I want you to make a good impression. I think the dark suit would work better."
- ◆ Avoid ordering or directing the other person to change; try identifying possible alternatives. Instead of saying "Don't be so forward when you're first introduced to someone," say "I think they might respond better to a less forward approach."
- ◆ Be specific. Instead of saying "This paper is weak," as some English teachers might, say "I think the introduction wasn't clear enough. Perhaps a more specific statement of purpose would have worked better."
- ◆ Avoid mind reading. Instead of saying "Don't you care about the impression you make? This report is terrible," say "I think I would use a stronger introduction and a friendlier writing style."
- ◆ Express criticism face-to-face (rather than by letter, memo, e-mail, or even phone) whenever possible.
- ◆ Express criticism in private. This is especially important when dealing with members from cultures where public criticism could result in a serious loss of face.
- ◆ If you do express criticism that seems to prove destructive, it may be helpful to offer a direct apology or to disclaim any harmful intentions (Baron 1990).
  In expressing praise, keep the following in mind:
- ◆ Use I-messages. Instead of saying "That report was good," say "I thought that report was good" or "I liked your report."

◆ Make sure your affect communicates your positive feelings. Often when people praise others simply because it is the socially correct response, they may betray their lack of conviction with too little or inappropriate affect.

◆ Name the behavior you're praising. Instead of saying "That was good," say "I enjoyed your speech" or "I thought your introduction was great."

◆ Take culture into consideration. Many Asians, for example, feel uncomfortable when praised because it is often taken as a sign of veiled criticism (Dresser 1996).

Summary   U N I T   I N   B R I E F

A RETURN TO OBJECTIVES:

In this unit we covered a variety of principles that will prove generally useful in interpersonal communication; when conscientiously applied, they should go a long way toward both reducing the frequency of some annoying and destructive habits and making verbal interaction more pleasant and productive. We focused on the following questions: (1) What is disconfirmation and confirmation (and the related sexist, racist, and heterosexist communications) and how can these hinder or foster effective interpersonal communication? (2) What is excluding and inclusive talk and how can these be managed more effectively? (3) What is the difference between self- and other-talk and how can you more effectively balance these? (4) How can you more effectively communicate both criticism and praise?

Avoid These Patterns	Practice These Principles
Disconfirmation: Communication that ignores another.	**The principle of confirmation:** Express acknowledgment and acceptance of others; avoid racist, sexist, and heterosexist expressions.
Excluding others, in-group talk: Talk that includes some and excludes others.	**The principle of inclusion:** Include everyone present in the interaction.
Excessive self-talk, excessive other-talk: Communication that is unbalanced in terms of self and other.	**The principle of balance:** Talk about yourself and about the other for balance.
Excessive criticism or praise: Talk that is basically dishonest.	**The principle of honest appraisal:** Say what you feel, but gently.

UNIT

11

Verbal Messages: Barriers to Interaction

Unit Topics	Unit Objectives
	After completing this unit, you should be able to:
Polarization Correcting Polarization	1. Define polarization and identify specific examples
Intensional Orientation Cultural Identifiers Correcting Intensional Orientation	2. Define intensional orientation and extensional orientation and identify specific examples
Fact-Inference Confusion Pragmatic Implication Correcting Fact-Inference Confusion	3. Define *fact-inference confusion* and identify specific examples
Allness Correcting Allness	4. Define *allness* and identify specific examples
Static Evaluation Correcting Static Evaluation	5. Define *static evaluation* and identify specific examples
Indiscrimination Ethnocentrism Correcting Indiscrimination	6. Define *indiscrimination* and identify specific examples 7. Define *ethnocentrism*

EXPERIENTIAL LEARNING VEHICLES

Vehicles No. 14, "Conversational Analysis: A Chance Meeting," pp. 454–456, No. 15, "Giving and Taking Directions," pp. 456–458, and No. 22, "Analyzing a Conflict Episode," pp. 464–466, will provide different perspectives on verbal messages and especially barriers to interaction.

Interpersonal communication is fragile—in part because of its complexity and in part because it is a human process, subject to all the failings and problems of fallible people. Chief among these problems are what are called **barriers**.

The term "barriers" is used not to convey the idea that communicators function as machines or that communication is a mechanical process. Rather it emphasizes that meaningful interpersonal communication may lose some of its effectiveness when communicators think or behave in certain ways. Recognize that these barriers are of human origin and development; it is the communicators who, for one reason or another, create and maintain them.

All seven barriers discussed here—polarization, intensional orientation, bypassing, fact-inference confusion, allness, static evaluation, and indiscrimination—are ways in which your verbal messages describe the world in illogical, distorted, or unscientific ways. Some contemporary writers now refer to these barriers as "cognitive distortions" (Burns 1980; Beck 1988).

Consider an analogy between verbal messages and geographic maps: Maps that accurately portray the world assist you in getting from one place to another. To the extent that such maps inaccurately portray the world, they hinder you. Verbal messages are like maps. When they accurately represent reality, they aid effective and meaningful interpersonal communication; when they distort reality, they hinder effective and meaningful interpersonal communication.

The seven barriers may also be viewed as ways in which language does not reflect reality, ways in which language contradicts the scientifically known world (Table 11.1).

Polarization

Polarization, often referred to as the fallacy of "either-or," is the tendency to look at the world and to describe it in terms of extremes—good or bad, positive or negative, healthy or sick, brilliant or stupid, rich or poor, and so on. Polarized statements come in many forms, for example:

◆ After listening to the evidence, I'm still not clear who the good guys are and who the bad guys are.
◆ Well, are you for us or against us?
◆ College had better get me a good job. Otherwise, this has been a big waste of time.

Most people exist somewhere between the extremes of good and bad, healthy and sick, brilliant and stupid, rich and poor. Yet there seems to be a strong tendency to view only the extremes and to categorize people, objects, and events in terms of these polar opposites. You can easily demonstrate this tendency by filling in the opposites for each of the following words:

Opposite

Tall__:__:__:__:__:__   _____
Heavy__:__:__:__:__:__   _____
Strong__:__:__:__:__:__   _____
Happy__:__:__:__:__:__   _____
Legal__:__:__:__:__:__   _____

Table 11.1	Assumptions about the World and the Use and Misuse of Language	

This table is an attempt to identify some of the assumptions about the world and the way in which these assumptions are violated in illogical language and accurately reflected in logical language. It will serve as an overview of the discussion in this unit.

Assumptions About the World	Illogical Language; Language that Distorts Reality	Logical Language; Language that Accurately Reflects Reality
Most of reality exists between the extremes.	Divides the world into extremes, good-bad, rich-poor, success-failure (polarization).	Uses middle terms, terms that reflect middle ground.
Words and the things they represent are very different; words are not things.	Treats words as if they were things (intensional orientation).	Treats words as abstractions of things, not the things themselves (extensional orientation).
Not all statements are factual.	Treats factual and inferential statements the same (fact-inference confusion).	Distinguishes between factual and inferential statements and treats them differently.
People and events are too complex to ever be known or described completely.	Assumes completeness and finality (allness).	Assumes there is always more to be known, more to be said.
The world and its people are constantly changing.	Holds static and unchanging notions about people and events (static evaluation).	Includes time as a variable in all messages.
Everyone and everything is unique.	Sees individuals through general labels and stereotypes (indiscrimination).	Distinguishes between individuals even when covered by the same general label.

Filling in the opposites should have been relatively easy and quick. The words should also have been fairly short. Further, if a number of people supplied opposites, there should be a high degree of agreement among them.

Now try to fill in the middle positions with words meaning, for example, "midway between tall and short," "midway between heavy and light," and so on. Do this before reading any further.

The midway responses (compared to the opposites) were probably more difficult to think of and took you more time. The responses should also have been either fairly long words or phrases of several words. Further, you would probably find little agreement among different people completing this same task.

Consider the familiar bell-shaped curve. If you selected 100 people at random, you would find that their intelligence, height, weight, income, age, health, and so on would fall into a bell-shaped or "normal" distribution. Few items exist at either of the two extremes, but as you move closer to the center, more and more items are included. This is true of any random sample. Yet many people tend to concentrate on the ends of this curve and ignore the middle, which contains the vast majority of cases.

It is legitimate to phrase certain statements in terms of two values. For example, this thing you are holding is either a book or it is not. Clearly, the classes "book" and "not-book" include all possibilities. There is no problem with this kind of statement. Similarly, you may say that a student will either pass this course or will not, as these two categories include all the possibilities.

Do you accept or reject any of the "assumptions about the world" as identified in Table 11.1? Can you think of other assumptions that might influence the way in which language is used?

One of the advantages of extreme terms is that they call greater attention to your thoughts than do middle terms or qualified phrases. Do the media, for example, give greater attention to ideas phrased in the extreme than to ideas phrased more logically as somewhere between the extremes?

Correcting Polarization

You create problems when you use this either-or form in situations where it is inappropriate: for example, "The politician is either for us or against us." Note that these two choices do not include all possibilities; the politician may be for us in some things and against us in others, or he or she may be neutral. During the Vietnam War, there was a tendency to categorize people as either "hawk" or "dove," but clearly many people were neither and many were probably both—hawks on certain issues and doves on others.

Recognize that the vast majority of cases exist between extremes. Don't allow the ready availability of extreme terms to obscure the reality of what lies in between.

Intensional Orientation

Intensional orientation refers to the tendency to view people, objects, and events in terms of how they are talked about or labeled rather than in terms of how they actually exist. **Extensional orientation** is the opposite, the tendency to look first at the actual people, objects, and events and only then at the labels. It is the tendency to be guided by what you see happening rather than by the way something or someone is talked about or labeled. Intensional orientation is seen in such statements as these.

- ◆ Rabbit! How could anyone eat rabbits? They're so cute and cuddly.

How might the barriers identified here apply to Internet communication? Are these barriers easier or more difficult to resolve than those created in face-to-face communication?

◆ But she's a lesbian (African American, Italian, born-again Christian).

◆ It contains polyoxymorons, so it should work on this cough.

Intensional orientation occurs when you act as if the words and labels are more important than the things they represent—as if the map is more important than the territory. In its extreme form, intensional orientation is seen in the person who is afraid of dogs and who begins to sweat when shown a picture of a dog or when hearing people talk about dogs. Here the person is responding to a label as if it were the actual thing.

Intensional orientation is seen in the numerous studies on credibility (Riggio 1987). These studies demonstrate that you are influenced more when you assume that the message comes from a highly credible source than when you assume it comes from an average individual. Such studies have shown, for example, that you will evaluate a painting highly if you think it was painted by a famous artist, but you will give it a low evaluation if you think it was produced by a little-known artist. In all such credibility studies, the influencing factor was not the message itself—the painting or the speech, for example—but the name attached to it. Advertisers have long known the value of this type of appeal and have capitalized on it by using popular figures from sports or music, for example, to endorse sneakers, soft drinks, and underwear.

 Visualize yourself seated with a packet of photographs before you, each showing a person you have never seen before. You are asked to scratch out the eyes in each photograph. You are further told that this is simply an experiment and that the individuals whose pictures you have will not be aware of anything that has happened here. As you progress through the pictures, scratching out the eyes, you come upon a photograph of your mother. What do you do? Are you able to scratch out the eyes as you have done with the pictures of the strangers? Or have you somehow lost your ability to scratch them out? Are you responding intensionally or extensionally?

Cultural Identifiers

Having said that the word is not the thing, does not mean that words do not have effects. They do. This is seen most clearly in the negative reactions to, for example, racist language (discussed at length in Unit 10). It is also seen in the use of labels that may be perceived as culturally insensitive or culturally unaware. Here, for example, are some of the terms that cause confusion in communicating with and about members of diverse cultural groups. As always, when in doubt, find out. The preferences and many of the specific examples identified here are drawn largely from the findings of the Task Force on Bias-Free Language of the Association of American University Presses (Schwartz 1995).

Generally: Most African Americans prefer *African American* to *black* (Hecht, Ribeau, and Collier 1993) though *black* is often used with *white* and is used in a variety of other contexts (for example, Department of Black and Puerto Rican Studies, the *Journal of Black History,* and Black History Month). The American Psychological Association recommends that both terms be capitalized but the *Chicago Manual of Style* (the manual used by most newspapers and publishing houses) recommends using lower case. The terms *negro* and *colored,* although used in the names of some organizations (for example, the United Negro College Fund and the National Association for the Advancement of Colored People) are not used outside of these contexts.

White is generally used to refer to those whose roots are in European cultures and is usually used to exclude Hispanics. On the analogy of *African American* comes the phrase *European American.* Few *European Americans,* however, would want to be called that; most would prefer their national origins emphasized, for example, *German American* or *Greek American.* This preference may well change as Europe moves into a more cohesive and united entity. *People of color*—a more literary sounding term appropriate perhaps to public speaking but sounding awkward in most conversations—is preferred to *non-white,* which implies that whiteness is the norm and non-whiteness is a deviation from that norm. (The same is true of the term *non-Christian.*)

How would you go about discovering the reasons people have for wanting to be identified by a specific cultural label? What is the single most important factor?

Generally: *Hispanic* is used to refer to anyone who identifies himself or herself as belonging to a Spanish speaking culture. *Latina* (female) and *Latino* (male) refer to those whose roots are in one of the Latin American countries, for example, Haiti, Dominican Republic, Nicaragua, or Guatemala. *Hispanic American* refers to those United States residents whose ancestry is a Spanish culture and includes Mexican, Caribbean, and Central and South Americans. In emphasizing a Spanish heritage the term is really inadequate in referring to those large numbers in the Caribbean and in South America whose origins are French or Portuguese. *Chicana* (female) and *Chicano* (male) refer to those with roots in Mexico, though it often connotes a nationalist attitude (Jandt 1995) and is considered offensive by many Mexican Americans. *Mexican American* is preferred.

Inuk (pl. *Inuit*), also spelled with two "n's" (*Innuk* and *Innuit*), is preferred to *Eskimo* (a term the United States Census Bureau uses) which was applied to the indigenous peoples of Alaska by Europeans and means literally "raw meat eaters."

Indian refers only to someone from India and is incorrectly used when applied to members of other Asian countries or to the indigenous peoples of North America. *American Indian* or *Native American* is preferred, though many Native Americans refer to themselves as *Indians* and *Indian people.* The term *native American* (with a lower case *n*) is most often used to refer to persons born in the United States. Although the term technically could refer to anyone born in North or South America, people outside the United States generally prefer more specific designations such as *Argentinean, Cuban,* or *Canadian.* The term *native* means an indigenous inhabitant; it is not used to mean "someone having a less developed culture".

Muslim is the preferred form (rather than the older *Moslem*) to refer to a person who adheres to the religious teachings of Islam. *Quran* (rather than *Koran*) is the preferred term for the scriptures of Islam.

When history was being written with a European perspective, it was taken as the focal point and the rest of the world was defined in terms of its location from Europe. Thus, Asia became the east or the orient and Asians became *Orientals*—a term that is today considered inappropriate or "Eurocentric." Thus, people from Asia are *Asians* just as people from Africa are *Africans* and people from Europe are *Europeans.*

Generally: *Gay* is the preferred term to refer to a man who has an affectional preference for another man and *lesbian* is the preferred term for a woman who has an affectional preference for other women. (*Lesbian* means "homosexual woman" so the phrase *lesbian woman* is redundant.) This preference for the term *lesbian* is not universal among homosexual women; in one survey, for example, 58% preferred "lesbian"; 34% preferred "gay" (Lever 1995). *Homosexual* refers to both gays and lesbians but more often to a sexual orientation to members of one's own sex. *Gay* and *lesbian* refer to a life style and not just to sexual orientation. *Gay* as a noun, although widely used, may prove offensive in some contexts, for example, "We have two gays on the team." Although used within the gay community in an effort to remove the negative stigma through frequent usage, the term *queer*—as

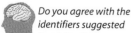

Do you agree with the identifiers suggested here? Are there preferred alternatives that are more current?

in "queer power"—is often resented when used by outsiders. Because most scientific thinking holds that sexuality is not a matter of choice, the term *sexual orientation* rather than *sexual preference* or *sexual status* (which is also vague) is preferred (cf. LeVay 1996; Burr 1996).

Generally: The term *girl* should only be used to refer to very young females and is equivalent to *boy*. Neither term should be used for people older than, say, 13 or 14. *Girl* is never used to refer to a grown woman, nor is *boy* used to refer to persons in blue collar positions, as it once was. *Lady* is negatively evaluated by many because it connotes the stereotype of the prim and proper woman. *Woman* or *young woman* is preferred. *Older person* is preferred to *elder, elderly, senior,* or *senior citizen* (which technically refers to someone older than 65).

Correcting Intensional Orientation

The corrective to intensional orientation is to focus first on the object, person, or event—the territory—and then on the way in which the object, person, or event is talked about—the map or label. Labels are certainly helpful guides, but don't allow them to obscure what they are meant to symbolize.

Fact-Inference Confusion

You can make statements about the world that you observe, and you can make statements about what you have not observed. In form or structure, these statements are similar and cannot be distinguished from each other by any grammatical analysis. For example, you can say, "She is wearing a blue jacket" as well as, "She is harboring an illogical hatred." If you diagrammed these sentences, they would yield identical structures, and yet you know that they are different types of statements. In the first one, you can observe the jacket and the blue color. But how do you observe "illogical hatred"? Obviously, this is not a descriptive statement but an **inferential statement,** a statement that you make not solely on the basis of what you observe but on the basis of what you observe plus your own conclusions.

There is no problem with making inferential statements; you must make them if you are to talk about much that is meaningful. The problem arises when you act as though those inferential statements were **factual statements.** Consider, for example, the following anecdote (Maynard 1963):

> *A woman went for a walk one day and met her friend, whom she had not seen, heard from, or heard of in ten years. After an exchange of greetings, the woman said, "Is this your little boy?" and her friend replied, "Yes. I got married about six years ago." The woman then asked the child, "What is your name?" and the little boy replied, "Same as my father's." "Oh," said the woman, "then it must be Peter."*

The question, of course, is how did the woman know the boy's father's name? The answer is obvious, but only after you recognize that in reading this short passage you have, quite unconsciously, made an inference that is preventing you from arriving at the answer. You have inferred that the woman's friend is a woman. Actually, the friend is a man named Peter.

What cultural identifiers do you prefer? Have these preferences changed over time? How can you let other people know the designations that you want and those that you don't want to be used to refer to you? An interesting exercise—especially in a large and multicultural class—is for each student to write anonymously his or her preferred cultural identification on an index card and have them all read aloud.

Can You Distinguish Facts from Inferences?

Carefully read the following report, modeled on that developed by William Haney (1973), and the observations based on it. Indicate whether you think the observations are true, false, or doubtful on the basis of the information presented in the report. Write T if the observation is definitely true, F if the observation is definitely false, and ? if the observation may be either true or false. Judge each observation in order. Do not reread the observations after you have indicated your judgment, and do not change any of your answers.

A well-liked college teacher had just completed making up the final examinations and had turned off the lights in the office. Just then a tall, broad figure appeared and demanded the examination. The professor opened the drawer. Everything in the drawer was picked up and the individual ran down the corridor. The dean was notified immediately.

_____ 1. The thief was tall and broad.
_____ 2. The professor turned off the lights.
_____ 3. A tall figure demanded the examination.
_____ 4. The examination was picked up by someone.
_____ 5. The examination was picked up by the professor.
_____ 6. A tall figure appeared after the professor turned off the lights in the office.
_____ 7. The man who opened the drawer was the professor.
_____ 8. The professor ran down the corridor.
_____ 9. The drawer was never actually opened.
_____10. Three persons are referred to in this report.

Thinking Critically About Facts and Inferences
This test is designed to trap you into making inferences and treating them as facts. Statement 3 is true (it's in the report), Statement 9 is false (the drawer was opened), but all other statements are inferences and should have been marked ?. Review these 8 statements to see why you cannot be certain that any of them are either true or false.

Watch a few television situation comedies. How many of the plot turns can be attributed to fact-inference confusion?

Perhaps the classic example of this type of fact-inference confusion concerns the case of the "empty" gun that unfortunately proves to be loaded. With amazing frequency, we find in the newspapers examples of people being so sure that the guns are empty that they point them at someone else and fire. Often, of course, they are empty. But, unfortunately, often they are not. Here one draws the *inference* that the gun is empty, but acts as if it were a *fact* and fires the gun.

You may wish to test your ability to distinguish facts from inferences by taking the self-test "Can You Distinguish Facts from Inferences?"

Pragmatic Implication

Do you ever confuse facts with inferences? What creates the confusion? What effects does the confusion have on your own interpersonal communications?

A related communication barrier is raised by what linguist philosophers call **pragmatic implication**. Consider the following: The sales manager has been replaced. You know that this manager was not doing a particularly good job and that many sales representatives complained about poor leadership. On the basis of this knowledge, you draw a pragmatic implication, an inference that is probably but not necessarily true. In this example, you infer that the sales manager was fired. Now, there is nothing wrong with drawing such inferences; we all do it. The problem comes in when we forget or disregard the fact that they are inferences and not facts.

This type of situation occurs every day. You see your supervisor in a romantic restaurant with the new sales manager. You make the pragmatic implications that they are having an affair. You might further infer that the reason the old sales manager was fired was because of the supervisor's affair with the new manager.

When inferences are made on top of inferences, it often becomes difficult to distinguish exactly where the facts stopped and the inferences began.

Correcting Fact-Inference Confusion

Some of the essential differences between factual and inferential statements are summarized in Table 11.2. Distinguishing between these two types of statements does not imply that one type is better than the other. Both types of statements are useful; both are important. The problem arises when you treat an inferential statement as if it were fact. Phrase your inferential statements as tentative. Recognize that such statements may prove to be wrong. Leave open the possibility of other alternatives.

Allness

The world is infinitely complex, and because of this you can never say all there is to say about anything—at least not logically. This is particularly true in dealing with people. You may *think* you know all there is to know about certain individuals or about why they did what they did, yet clearly you do not know all. You can never know all the reasons you yourself do something, so there is no way you

Table 11.2	Differences Between Factual and Inferential Statements

These differences highlight the important distinctions between factual and inferential statements and are based on the discussions of Haney (1973) and Weinberg (1959). As you go through this table consider how you would classify such statements as: "God exists," "Democracy is the best form of government," "This paper is white," "The Internet will grow in size and importance over the next ten years," and "This table is based on Haney and Weinberg."

Factual Statements	Inferential Statements
1. May be made only after observation.	1. May be made at any time.
2. Are limited to what has been observed.	2. Go beyond what has been observed.
3. May be made only by the observer.	3. May be made by anyone.
4. May be about only the past or the present.	4. May be about any time—past, present, or future.
5. Approach certainty.	5. Involve varying degrees of probability.
6. Are subject to verifiable standards.	6. Are not subject to verifiable standards.

can know all the reasons why your parents or your friends or your enemies did something.

You may, for example, be assigned to read a textbook and, because previous texts have been dull and because perhaps the first chapter of this one is dull, you might infer that all the rest of the book will likewise be dull. Of course, the rest of a book is often even worse than its beginning. Yet it could be that the rest of the book would prove exciting were it read with an open mind. The problem here is that you run the risk of judging an entire text in such a way as to preclude any other possibilities. If you tell yourself that the book is dull, it will probably seem dull; if you say a required course will be useless, it will be extremely difficult for the instructor to make the course anything but what you have defined it to be. Only occasionally do people allow themselves to be proven wrong.

The parable of the six blind men and the elephant is an excellent example of an "allness orientation"—the tendency to judge the whole on the basis of experience with only some part of the whole—and its attendant problems. You may recall from elementary school the poem by John Saxe that concerns six blind men of Indostan who came to examine an elephant, an animal they had only heard about. The first blind man touched the elephant's side and concluded that the elephant was like a wall. The second felt the tusk and said the elephant must be like a spear. The third held the trunk and concluded that the elephant was much like a snake. The fourth touched the knee and knew the elephant was like a tree. The fifth felt the ear and said the elephant was like a fan. And the sixth grabbed the tail and concluded that the elephant was like a rope. Each of these learned men reached his own conclusion regarding what the elephant was really like. Each argued that he was correct and that the others were wrong.

Each, of course, was correct; at the same time, however, all were wrong. The point this parable illustrates is that everyone is in the position of the blind men. You can never see all of anything; you can never experience anything fully. You see part of an object, an event, or a person—and on that limited basis conclude what the whole is like. This procedure is universal, and you follow it because you cannot possibly observe everything. Yet recognize that when making judgments of the whole based on only a part, you are actually making inferences that can later be proven wrong. If you assume that you know everything there is to know about something or someone, you fall into the pattern of misevaluation called **allness**.

Famed British prime minister Disraeli once said that "to be conscious that you are ignorant is a great step toward knowledge." This observation is an excellent example of a *nonallness* attitude. If you recognize that there is more to learn, more to see, more to hear, you leave yourself open to this additional information, and you are better prepared to assimilate it.

Correcting Allness

A useful device to help remember to avoid allness is to end each statement, sometimes verbally but always mentally, with an **etc.** (et cetera), a reminder that there is more to learn, more to know, more to say—a reminder that every statement is inevitably incomplete.

 Do you ever commit the fallacy of allness? Do you, for example, group all teachers together? All gay people? All politicians? All born-again Christians? All atheists? All African Americans? All European Americans? All Jews? All Hispanics?

Some people overuse the et cetera. They use it as a substitute for being specific, which really defeats its purpose. Instead, it should be used to mentally remind yourself that there is more to know and more to say.

Static Evaluation

Static evaluation is the tendency to retain evaluations without change, while the reality to which they refer is constantly changing. A verbal statement about an event or person remains static and unchanging, while the object or person to whom it refers may change enormously. Alfred Korzybski (1933) used an interesting illustration in this connection: In a tank there is a large fish and many small fish that are its natural food source. Given freedom in the tank, the large fish will eat the small fish. After some time, the tank is partitioned, with the large fish on one side and the small fish on the other, divided only by glass. For a time, the large fish will try to eat the small fish but will fail; each time it tries, it will knock into the glass partition. After some time, it will "learn" that trying to eat the small fish means difficulty, and it will no longer go after them. Now, however, the partition is removed and the small fish swim all around the big fish. But the big fish does not eat them and in fact will die of starvation while its natural food swims all around. The large fish has learned a pattern of behavior, and even though the actual territory has changed, the map remains static.

While you would probably agree that everything is in a constant state of flux, the relevant question is whether you act as if you know this. Do you act in accordance with the notion of change, instead of just accepting it intellectually? Do you treat your little sister as if she were 10 years old, or do you treat her like the 20-year-old woman she has become? Your evaluations of yourself and others must keep pace with the rapidly changing real world. Otherwise you will be left with attitudes and beliefs about a world that no longer exists—what are called static evaluations.

Correcting Static Evaluation

To guard against static evaluation, date your statements and especially your evaluations. Remember that Gerry Smith—1984— is not Gerry Smith—1995—; academic abilities—1995— are not academic abilities—1996—. T. S. Eliot, in *The Cocktail Party,* said that "what we know of other people is only our memory of the moments during which we knew them. And they have changed since then . . . at every meeting we are meeting a stranger."

Indiscrimination

Nature seems to abhor sameness at least as much as vacuums, for nowhere in the universe can you find identical entities. Everything is unique. Language, however, provides common nouns, such as "teacher," "student," "friend," "enemy," "war," "politician," "liberal," and the like, which may lead you to focus on similarities. Such nouns can lead you to group together all teachers, all students, and all friends and perhaps divert attention from the uniqueness of each individual, object, and event.

Here is a photo of the AIDS quilt on display in Washington, D.C. Each panel contains the name of a person who died of AIDS. In what ways do you see the barriers to verbal interaction covered in this unit operate in discussions of AIDS and of people with AIDS?

 Have people ever committed indiscrimination against you because of your membership in a particular group? For example, have people ever assumed incorrectly that you believed something or behaved in a particular way because of your sex, race, nationality, religion, or affectional orientation?

The misevaluation of **indiscrimination**, then, occurs when you focus on classes of individuals, objects, or events and fail to see that each is unique and needs to be looked at individually. Indiscrimination can be seen in statements such as these.

- He's just like the rest of them: lazy, stupid, and a real slob.
- I really don't want another Martian on the board of directors. One is enough for me.
- Read a romance novel? I read one when I was 16. That was enough to convince me.

Ethnocentrism

An interesting perspective can be gained on indiscrimination by looking briefly at ethnocentrism, the tendency to see others and their behaviors through your own cultural filters. **Ethnocentrism** is the tendency to evaluate the values, beliefs, and behaviors of your own culture as being more positive, logical, and natural than those of other cultures. Ideally, you would see both yourself and others as different but equal, with neither being inferior or superior. In ethnocentric thinking, there is no discrimination among the members of other groups; rather, there is discrimination against members of other groups.

INTERPERSONAL ETHICS

FEAR AND EMOTIONAL APPEALS

FRANK: father
BARBARA: daughter
ALEX: son
LAURA: mother

LAURA: Barbara, I can't believe what you're telling me. Of the three of you kids, you were the last one I would think would want to marry someone of another race and religion. After all I did for you? I can't believe you're going to do this to me. I'll never be able to face the rest of the family. You're destroying everything. You're throwing away everything we tried to do for you. I just want to die. Your father is going to have a heart attack.

FRANK: Listen. You marry that creep and we're through. You'll never be allowed in this house again. Don't ever call; don't ever write. You marry this guy and you have no family. And your kids will have no grandparents. We will never ever ever see you again. To us, you'll be dead.

LAURA: And if I ever see you even reading about his religion, I'll die.

ALEX: And I'm going to get the guys together and knock that guy's teeth out if I ever see him around here.

FRANK: Now, Alex, I don't think that's going to be necessary.

Are these parents and brother ethical in their use of emotional and fear appeals? Is Frank's threat ethical? Is Alex's physical threat (and Frank's implicit agreement with it) any different ethically from the emotional or interpersonal threats? What (if anything) would you have to know to answer this question? For example, would your answer be different if Laura was honestly expressing her feelings? If Laura was using this appeal merely as a persuasive strategy to keep Barbara from marrying outside her race and religion? If Frank thought that this type of appeal was the only one that would keep Barbara from marrying this man and that she would—later in life—be grateful to him? If the issue centered on Barbara's intention to change her own religion and join a religious cult? If Barbara was 18 years old? If Barbara was 55 years old (and never married but always wanted to be)?

One of the most widely discussed ethical issues in communication is the legitimacy of appeals based on fear and emotion. Although this topic is frequently focused on public and mass communication situations, it is even more applicable to interpersonal encounters. It is also appropriate to discuss in this unit since fear and emotion—especially when used unethically—often set up barriers to authentic communication. When fear and emotion are used to prevent communication—when they erect barriers—between you and your right to information bearing on life's choices then they would be considered unethical.

Consider the mother who does not want her teenage son or daughter of 18 or 19 to move out of the house. Depending on her ingenuity, the mother might focus on instilling fear in the teenager for his or her own well-being ("Who'll care for you? You won't eat right. You'll get sick") or, more frequently, for the mother's well-being. The caricature of a mother having a heart attack at the first sign of a child's leaving is probably played out every day, in various forms, throughout the world. But whether a heart attack or some other gross difficulty is invoked, the appeal is built on fear. Obviously, few children want to be the cause of their mother's suffering.

Similar issues are raised when we consider the use of emotional appeals in attempting to change attitudes, beliefs, and behaviors. The case of a real estate broker appealing to your desire for status, a friend who wants a favor appealing to your desire for social approval, and a salesperson appealing to your desire for sexual rewards are all familiar examples. The question they all raise is simply, "Is this type of appeal justified?"

Many arguments can be advanced on both sides of the issue. The "everyone is doing it" argument is perhaps the most familiar, but it does not address the question of whether such appeals are ethical. Another argument is that because people are composites of logic and emotion, effective appeals must be based in part on emotions. Again, however, this does not answer the question of whether emotional appeals are ethical; it merely states that they are effective.

When is it ethical to use fear and emotion to persuade another person? When is it unethical? What ethical guidelines would you propose for the use of fear and emotional appeals?

*[The next ethics box appears in Unit 17, page **324**, and deals with censorship.]*

Ethnocentrism exists on a continuum (see Table 11.3). People are not either ethnocentric or not-ethnocentric; rather, most are somewhere between these polar opposites. Of course, your degree of ethnocentrism varies, depending on the group on which you focus. For example, if you are Greek American, you may have a low degree of ethnocentrism when dealing with Italian Americans but a high degree when dealing with Turkish Americans or Japanese Americans. Most important for our purposes is that your degree of ethnocentrism (and we are all ethnocentric to at least some degree) will influence your interpersonal interactions.

 Would it be possible for a person to follow the principle of indiscrimination and still be ethnocentric? And still have stereotypes?

Ethnocentric thinking is at the heart of the common practice of stereotyping national, sexual, racial, and religious groups. A **stereotype** is a relatively fixed mental picture of some group that is applied to each individual of the group without regard to his or her unique qualities. It is important to note that although stereotypes are usually thought of as negative, they may also be positive. You can, for example, consider certain national groups as lazy or superstitious or mercenary or criminal, but you can also consider them as intelligent, progressive, honest, hardworking, and so on. Regardless of whether such stereotypes are positive or negative, however, the problems they create are the same. They provide shortcuts that are usually inappropriate. For example, when you see someone through a stereotype, you invariably fail to devote sufficient attention to his or her unique characteristics.

Would it be possible to have ethnocentric thinking without indiscrimination? Does prejudice depend on indiscrimination?

There is nothing wrong with classifying. In fact, it is an extremely useful method of dealing with any complex matter; it puts order into thinking. The problem arises not from classification itself but from the application of an evaluative label to that class and the use of that label as an "adequate" map for each and every individual in the group.

Correcting Indiscrimination

A useful antidote to indiscrimination is the **index**, a verbal or mental subscript that identifies each individual in a group as an individual even though all mem-

Table 11.3	The Ethnocentrism Continuum

This table summarizes some of the interconnections between ethnocentrism and communication. In this table, five degrees of ethnocentrism are identified; in reality, of course, there are as many degrees as there are people. The "communication distances" are general terms that highlight the attitude that dominates that level of ethnocentrism. Under "communications" are some of the major ways people might interact given their particular degree of ethnocentrism. Can you identify your own ethnocentrism on this table? For example, are there groups to which you have low ethnocentrism? Middle? High? What accounts for these differences? This table draws on the work of a number of intercultural researchers (Lukens 1978; Gudykunst and Kim 1984; Gudykunst 1991).

Degree of Ethnocentrism	Communication Distance	Communications
Low	Equality	Treats others as equals; views different customs and ways of behaving as equal to one's own.
	Sensitivity	Wants to decrease distance between self and others.
	Indifference	Lacks concern for others; prefers to interact in a world of similar others.
	Avoidance	Avoids and limits communications, especially intimate ones with interculturally different others.
High	Disparagement	Engages in hostile behavior; belittles others; views different cultures and ways of behaving as inferior to one's own.

bers of the group may be covered by the same label: politician$_1$ is not politician$_2$; teacher$_1$ is not teacher$_2$. The index helps us to discriminate *among* without discriminating *against*.

Here is a brief dialogue written to illustrate the various barriers to communication discussed in this unit as they might apply to interpersonal relationships. Try identifying the barriers illustrated. Also think about why these statements establish barriers and how the people in the dialogue might have avoided the barriers.

PAT: Look, do you care about me or don't you? If you do, then you'll go away for the weekend with me as we planned originally.

CHRIS: I know we planned to go, but I got this opportunity to put in some overtime, and I really need the extra money.

PAT: Look, a deal is a deal. You said you'd go, and that's all that really matters.

CHRIS: Pat! You never give me a break, do you? I just can't go; I have to work.
PAT: All right, all right. I'll go alone.
CHRIS: Oh, no you don't. I know what will happen.
PAT: What will happen?
CHRIS: You'll go back to drinking again. I know you will.
PAT: I will not. I don't drink anymore.
CHRIS: Pat, you're an alcoholic and you know it.
PAT: I am not an alcoholic.
CHRIS: You drink, don't you?
PAT: Yes, occasionally.
CHRIS: Occasionally? Yeah, you mean two or three times a week, don't you?
PAT: That's occasionally. That's not being an alcoholic.
CHRIS: Well, I don't care how much you drink or how often you drink. You're still an alcoholic.
PAT: Anyway, what makes you think I'll drink if I go away for the weekend?
CHRIS: All those weekend ski trips are just excuses to drink. I've been on one of them—remember?
PAT: Well, see it your way, my dear. See it your way. I'll be gone right after I shower. [*Thinking: I can't wait to get away for the weekend.*]
CHRIS: [*Thinking: Now what have I done? Our relationship is finished.*]

Summary   UNIT IN BRIEF

A RETURN TO OBJECTIVES:

In this unit we covered some of the barriers to interpersonal communication, for example: (1) What is polarization and what can be done to eliminate it? (2) What is intensional orientation and how can it be combated? (3) How do facts and inferences differ and how can they better be distinguished? (4) What is allness and how can it be corrected? (5) What is static evaluation and how can a more process orientation be integrated into our talk? (6) What are indiscrimination and ethnocentrism and how can they be reduced?

Barrier	Communication Problem	Correctives
Polarization	Tendency to describe the world in terms of extremes or polar opposites.	Use middle terms and qualifiers.
Intensional orientation	Tendency to view the world in the way it is talked about or labeled.	Respond to things first; look for the labels second.
Fact-inference confusion	Tendency to confuse factual and inferential statements and to respond to inferences as if they were facts.	Distinguish facts from inferences and respond to inferences as inferences, not as facts.
Allness	Tendency to describe the world in extreme terms that imply one knows all or is saying all there is to say.	Avoid allness terms; recognize that one can never know all or say all about anything; use *etc.*
Static Evaluation	Tendency to describe the world in static terms, denying constant change.	Recognize the inevitability of change; date statements and especially evaluations.
Indiscrimination	Tendency to group unique individuals or items because they are covered by the same term or phrase.	Recognize that sameness does not exist; index terms and statements.

UNIT

12 *Nonverbal Messages: Body and Sound*

Unit Topics	Unit Objectives
	After completing this unit, you should be able to:
Communication Through Body Movement	1. Define and provide examples of *emblems, illustrators, affect displays, regulators,* and *adaptors*
Facial Communication Facial Management Techniques The Facial Feedback Hypothesis The Influence of Context and Culture	2. Identify the types of information communicated by facial expressions
Eye Communication Eye Contact Functions Eye Avoidance Functions Pupil Dilation	3. Describe the functions of eye contact and eye avoidance 4. Explain the types of information communicated by pupil dilation and constriction
Touch Communication The Meanings of Touch Touch Avoidance Who Touches Whom Where: Gender and Cultural Differences	5. Explain the meanings touch communicates
Smell Communication Attraction Messages Taste Messages Memory Messages Identification Messages	6. Identify the major types of messages that smell communicates
Paralanguage and Silence Paralanguage Silence	7. Define *paralanguage* and *silence* and explain their major functions

---

EXPERIENTIAL LEARNING VEHICLES

Vehicles No. 9, "Facial Expressions," pp. 449–450, No. 10, "Eye Contact," p. 450, and 12, "Who?" pp. 452–453 will all prove useful in illustrating the role of nonverbal messages in interpersonal communication.

Of all the nonverbal communication systems, the body is surely the most important. With the body we communicate a wide variety of messages through gestures, facial expressions, eye movements, and touching behavior. We also communicate through sound and silence. Each of these major areas of nonverbal communication is examined in this unit.

Communication Through Body Movement

Of course, the body communicates even without movement. For example, others may form impressions of you from your general body build, from your height and weight, and from your skin, eye, and hair color. Assessments of your power, your attractiveness, and your suitability as a friend or romantic partner are often made on the basis of your physical body (Sheppard and Strathman 1989).

We also, of course, communicate with body movements (Table 12.1). An especially useful classification of body movement (sometimes called **kinesics**) identifies five types: emblems, illustrators, affect displays, regulators, and adaptors (Ekman and Friesen 1969).

What messages does your general physical appearance communicate about you? Check your theories with those who know you. What general appearance factors do you use to make judgments about others? Can you state these judgments in terms of the principles that you used to make them, using the form, "People who are green are clever"?

Emblems Emblems substitute for words. **Emblems** are body movements that have rather specific verbal translations. Emblems are nonverbal substitutes for specific words or phrases: for example, the nonverbal signs for "OK," "peace," "come here," "go away," "who me?" "be quiet," "I'm warning you," "I'm tired," and "it's cold." Emblems are as arbitrary as any words in any language. Consequently, your present culture's emblems are not necessarily the same as your culture's emblems of 300 years ago or the same as the emblems of other cultures. For example, the sign made by forming a circle with the thumb and index

Table 12.1	The Five Body Movements

Can you identify similar gestures that mean different things in different cultures and that might create interpersonal misunderstandings?

	Name and Function	Examples
	Emblems directly translate words or phrases.	"OK" sign, "come here" wave, hitchhiker's sign
	Illustrators accompany and literally "illustrate" verbal messages.	Circular hand movements when talking of a circle; hands far apart when talking of something large
	Affect displays communicate emotional meaning.	Expressions of happiness, surprise, fear, anger, sadness, disgust/contempt
	Regulators monitor, maintain, or control the speaking of another.	Facial expressions and hand gestures indicating "keep going," "slow down," or "what else happened?"
	Adaptors satisfy some need.	Scratching one's head

finger may mean "nothing" or "zero" in France, "money" in Japan, and something sexual in certain southern European cultures. But just as the English language is spreading throughout the world, so, too, is the English nonverbal language. The American use of this emblem to mean "OK" is spreading just as fast, for example, as English technical and scientific terms.

Illustrators **Illustrators** accompany and literally illustrate the verbal messages. Illustrators make your communications more vivid and help to maintain your listener's attention. They also help to clarify and make more intense your verbal messages. In saying, "Let's go up," for example, you probably move your head and perhaps your finger in an upward direction. In describing a circle or a square, you more than likely make circular or square movements with your hands.

We are aware of illustrators only part of the time; at times, they may have to be brought to our attention. Illustrators are more universal than emblems; they are more common than emblems from one place to another and throughout time.

Affect Displays **Affect displays** are the movements of the face that convey emotional meaning—the expressions that show anger and fear, happiness and surprise, eagerness and fatigue. They are the facial expressions that give you away when you try to present a false image and that lead people to say, "You look angry. What's wrong?" We can, however, consciously control affect displays, as actors do when they play a role. Affect displays may be unintentional (as when they give you away) or intentional (as when you want to show anger, love, or surprise).

Regulators **Regulators** monitor, maintain, or control the speaking of another individual. When you listen to another, you are not passive; you nod your head, purse your lips, adjust your eye focus, and make various paralinguistic sounds such as "mm-mm" or "tsk." Regulators are culture-bound: each culture develops its own rules for the regulation of conversation. Regulators also include such broad movements as shaking your head to show disbelief or leaning forward in your chair to show that you want to hear more.

Regulators communicate what you expect or want speakers to do as they are talking: for example, "Keep going," "Tell me what else happened," "I don't believe that—are you sure?" "Speed up," and "Slow down." Speakers often receive these nonverbal signals without being consciously aware of them. Depending on their degree of sensitivity, they modify their speaking behavior in accordance with these regulators.

Adaptors **Adaptors** satisfy some need and usually occur without conscious awareness; they are unintentional movements that usually go unnoticed. Nonverbal researchers identify three types of adaptors based on their focus, direction, or target: self-adaptors, alter-directed adaptors, and object adaptors (Burgoon, Buller, and Woodall 1995).

Self-adaptors usually satisfy a physical need, especially to make you more comfortable, for example, scratching your head to relieve an itch, moistening your lips because they feel dry, or pushing your hair out of your eyes. When these adaptors occur in private, they occur in their entirety: You scratch until the itch is gone. But in public, these adaptors usually occur in abbreviated form. When people are watching you, for example, you might put your fingers to your head and

Research shows that women smile more than men, even when making negative comments or expressing negative feelings (see Shannon 1987). What implications does this have for male-female communication? What implications might this have for child rearing? For teaching?

move them around a bit but probably not scratch with the same vigor as when in private.

Alter-adaptors are the body movements you make in response to your current interactions. Examples would include crossing your arms over your chest when someone unpleasant approaches or moving closer to someone you like.

Object-adaptors are those that involve your manipulation of some object. Frequently observed examples include punching holes in or drawing on the styrofoam coffee cup, clicking a ball point pen, or chewing on a pencil. Object adaptors are usually signs of negative feelings; for example, you emit more adaptors when feeling hostile than when feeling friendly. Further, as anxiety and uneasiness increase, so does the frequency of adaptors (Burgoon, Buller, and Woodall 1995).

Facial Communication

Throughout your interpersonal interactions, your face communicates, especially your emotions. In fact, facial movements alone seem to communicate the degree of pleasantness, agreement, and sympathy felt; the rest of the body doesn't provide any additional information. For other aspects, however—for example, the intensity with which an emotion is felt—both facial and bodily cues are used (Graham, Bitti, and Argyle 1975; Graham and Argyle 1975).

Some nonverbal communication researchers claim that facial movements may communicate at least the following eight emotions: happiness, surprise, fear, anger, sadness, disgust, contempt, and interest (Ekman, Friesen, and Ellsworth 1972). Others propose that in addition, facial movements may communicate bewilderment and determination (Leathers 1990).

Try to communicate surprise using only facial movements. Do this in front of a mirror, and try to describe in as much detail as possible the specific movements of the face that make up surprise. If you signal surprise as most people do, you probably exhibit raised and curved eyebrows, long horizontal forehead wrinkles, wide-open eyes, dropped-open mouth, and lips parted with no tension. Even if there were differences—and clearly there would be from one person to another—you could probably recognize the movements listed here as indicative of surprise.

Of course, some emotions are easier to communicate and to decode than others. For example, in one study, happiness was judged with an accuracy ranging from 55 percent to 100 percent, surprise from 38 percent to 86 percent, and sadness from 19 percent to 88 percent (Ekman, Friesen, and Ellsworth 1972). Research finds that women and girls are more accurate judges of facial emotional expression than men and boys (Hall 1984; Argyle 1988).

Facial Management Techniques

As you learned the nonverbal system of communication, you also learned certain facial management techniques: for example, to hide certain emotions and to emphasize others. Table 12.2 identifies four types of facial management techniques that you will quickly recognize as being frequently and widely used (Ekman and Friesen 1978; Malandro, Barker, and Barker 1989).

These facial management techniques are learned along with display rules, which tell you what emotions to express when; they are the rules of appropriate-

Table 12.2	Facial Management Techniques

These facial management techniques are learned along with display rules which tell you what emotions to express when; they are the rules of appropriateness. For example, when someone gets bad news in which you may secretly take pleasure, the display rule dictates that you frown and otherwise nonverbally signal your displeasure. Violators of these rules are generally judged very harshly.

Technique	Function	Example
Intensifying	To exaggerate a feeling	Exaggerating surprise when friends throw you a party, to make your friends feel better
Deintensifying	To underplay a feeling	To cover up your own joy in the presence of a friend who didn't receive such good news
Neutralizing	To hide a feeling	To cover up your sadness so as not to depress others
Masking	To replace or substitute the expression of one emotion for another	To express happiness in order to cover up your disappointment at not receiving the gift you had expected

ness. For example, when someone gets bad news in which you may secretly take pleasure, the display rule dictates that you frown and otherwise nonverbally signal your displeasure. If you violate these display rules, you will be judged insensitive.

The Facial Feedback Hypothesis

In one interesting study participants held a pen in their teeth to simulate a sad expression. They then rated photographs. Results showed that mimicking sad expressions actually increased the degree of sadness the subjects reported feeling when viewing the photographs (Larsen, Kasimatis, and Frey 1992). This finding is an example of the facial feedback hypothesis that holds that your facial expression influences physiological arousal (Lanzetta, Cartwright-Smith, and Kleck 1976; Zuckerman, Klorman, Larrance, and Spiegel 1981).

Further support for this hypothesis comes from a study which compared participants who (1) feel emotions such as happiness and anger with those who (2) both feel and express these emotions. In support of the facial feedback hypothesis, subjects who felt and expressed the emotions became emotionally aroused faster than did those who only felt the emotion (Hess, Kappas, McHugo, and Lanzetta 1992). So, not only does your facial expression influence the judgments and impressions that others have of you; they also influence your *level* of emotional arousal (Cappella 1993).

How would you go about discovering if the ability to use facial management techniques is related to a person's social or professional success?

Can you design an experiment to assess the effects of facial feedback?

The Influence of Context and Culture

The same facial expressions are seen differently if people are given different contexts. For example, when a smiling face was presented looking at a glum face, the smiling face was judged to be vicious and taunting. But, when the same smiling face is presented looking at a frowning face, it is judged peaceful and friendly (Cline 1956).

The wide variations in facial communication that we observe in different cultures seem to reflect which reactions are publicly permissible, rather than a difference in the way emotions are facially expressed. For example, Japanese and American students watched a film of an operation (Ekman 1985). The students were videotaped in both an interview situation about the film and alone while watching the film. When alone, the students showed very similar reactions, but in the interview, the American students displayed facial expressions indicating displeasure, whereas the Japanese students did not show any great emotion. Similarly, Japanese women are not supposed to reveal broad smiles and so will hide their smile, sometimes with their hands (cf. Ma 1996). Women in the United States, on the other hand, have no such restrictions and so are more likely to smile openly. Thus, the difference may not be in the way different cultures express emotions but rather in the cultural rules for displaying emotions in public (cf. Matsumoto 1991).

Similarly, cultural differences exist in decoding the meaning of a facial expression. For example, American and Japanese students judged the meaning of a smiling and a neutral facial expression. The Americans rated the smiling face as more attractive, more intelligent, and to display greater sociability than the neutral face. The Japanese, however, rated the smiling face as more sociable but not as more attractive. The Japanese, in fact, rated the neutral face as the more intelligent (Matsumoto and Kudoh 1993).

Researchers have long been interested in whether you can really hide emotions or whether they somehow reveal themselves below the level of conscious awareness. Slow-motion films of therapy patients show that their expressions often change dramatically during the therapy session (Haggard and Isaacs 1966). For example, a frown would change to a smile and then quickly back to a frown. If the film was played at normal speed, the smile would go unnoticed. These expressions, some theorists argue, indicate a person's real emotional state. Is your contempt encoded facially without your being aware of it or even without observers begin aware of it? How would you go about testing this theory?

Eye Communication

The messages communicated by the eyes vary depending on the duration, direction, and quality of the eye behavior. For example, in every culture there are rather strict, though unstated, rules for the proper duration for eye contact. In much of England and the United States, for example, the average length of gaze is 2.95 seconds. The average length of mutual gaze (two persons gazing at each other) is 1.18 seconds (Argyle 1988; Argyle and Ingham 1972). When eye contact falls short of this amount, you may think the person is uninterested, shy, or preoccupied. When the appropriate amount of time is exceeded, you may perceive this as showing high interest.

In much of the United States direct eye contact is considered an expression of honesty and forthrightness. But, the Japanese often view this as a lack of respect. The Japanese will glance at the other person's face rarely and then only for very short periods (Axtell 1990a). In many Hispanic cultures direct eye contact signifies a certain equality and so should be avoided by, say, children when speaking to a person in authority. Try visualizing the potential misunderstandings that eye communication alone could create when people from Tokyo, San Francisco, and San Juan try to communicate.

The direction of the eye also communicates. Generally, in communicating with another person, you would glance alternatively at the other person's face, then away, then again at the face, and so on. When these directional rules are broken, different meanings are communicated—abnormally high or low interest, self-consciousness, nervousness over the interaction, and so on. The quality—how wide or how narrow your eyes get during interaction—also communicates meaning, especially interest level and such emotions as surprise, fear, and disgust.

On average we blink about 15 times a minute, in part to lubricate and protect the eye. You may increase blinking if you're uncomfortable or under lots of stress. For example, you would probably increase your blinking rate if you were being interrogated by the police. As noted in Unit 9 (see Table 9.2) excess blinking is one of the cues people use to detect lying and so it may communicate a kind of nervousness over telling a lie. In actual fact, however, it may be due to dry eyes.

What are some other meanings that eye blinking can communicate? Do these meanings differ depending on the sex of the people communicating?

Eye Contact Functions

You use eye contact to serve several important functions (Knapp and Hall 1992; Malandro, Barker, and Barker 1989; Marshall 1983; Marsh 1988).

To Monitor Feedback   When you talk with someone, you look at the person intently, as if to say, "Well, what do you think?" or "React to what I've just said." You also look at speakers to let them know that you are listening. Studies show that listeners gaze at speakers more than speakers gaze at listeners (Knapp and Hall 1992). The percentage of interaction time spent gazing while listening, for example, ranges from 62 percent to 75 percent; the percentage of time spent gazing while talking, however, ranges from 38 percent and 41 percent. When these percentages are reversed—when a speaker gazes at the listener for longer than "normal" periods or when a listener gazes at the speaker for shorter than "normal" periods—the conversational interaction becomes awkward. You may wish to

Women make eye contact more and maintain it longer (both in speaking and in listening) than do men (Argyle 1988; Mulac, Studley, Wiemann and Bradac 1987). This holds true whether the woman is interacting with other women or with men. This difference in eye behavior may result from women's tendency to display their emotions more than men; eye contact is one of the most effective ways of communicating emotions. Another possible explanation, as Evan Marshall (1983) argues, is that women have been conditioned more than men to seek positive feedback from others. Women may thus use eye contact in trying to seek this visual feedback. Why do you think women make eyes contact more and maintain it longer than men?

try this with a friend. Even with mutual awareness, you will notice the discomfort caused by this seemingly minor communication change.

To Maintain Interest and Attention   When you speak with two or three other people, you maintain eye contact to secure the attention and interest of your listeners. When someone fails to pay the attention you want, you probably increase your eye contact, hoping your focus on this person will increase attention. When making an especially important point, you would look intently at your listeners—assuming what nonverbal researchers call "visual dominance behavior"—almost as a way of preventing them from devoting any attention to anything but what you are saying.

To Regulate the Conversation   Eye communication can also regulate or control the conversation. For example, with eye movements you can inform the other person that the channel of communication is open and that she or he should now speak. A clear example of this occurs in the college classroom, where the instructor asks a question and then locks eyes with a student. Without any verbal message, it is assumed that the student should answer the question. Similarly, when you are nearing the end of what you want to say, you will probably focus eye contact on the person you think wants to speak next and then turn over the conversation to that person.

To Signal the Nature of the Relationship   Eye communication also helps signal the nature of the relationship between two people—for example, one of positive or negative regard. In the United States when you like someone, you increase your eye contact. When eye contact exceeds 60 percent in an interaction, the people are probably more interested in each other than in the verbal messages being exchanged (Argyle 1988).

Eye contact in the higher primates is often used to signal status and aggression. Among many younger people prolonged eye contact from a stranger is taken to signify aggressiveness and has frequently prompted physical violence—just for looking perhaps a little longer than is considered normal in that specific culture (Matsumoto 1996). A less extreme way to assert one's position is with **visual dominance behavior** (Exline, Ellyson, and Long 1975). The average person maintains a higher level of eye contact while listening and a lower level while speaking. When people want to signal dominance, they may reverse this pattern and maintain a high level of eye contact while talking but a much lower level while listening. Another way people try to signal dominance is to lower their eyebrows. Research does support this general interpretation of the behavior. For example, faces with lowered eyebrows, in both cartoons and photographs, were judged to communicate greater dominance than raised eyebrows (Keating, Mazur, and Segall 1977). Eye movements may also signal whether the relationship between two people is amorous, hostile, or indifferent.

Can you describe the specific eye movements you would make if you wanted to signal a friendly interest in someone? If you wanted to signal "stay away from me"?

To Compensate for Physical Distance   Eye movements are often used to compensate for increased physical distance. By making eye contact, we overcome psychologically the physical distance between us. When we catch someone's eye at a party, for example, we become psychologically close even though we may be separated by considerable physical distance. Eye contact and other expressions of psychological closeness, such as self-disclosure and intimacy, have been found to vary in proportion to each other.

Eye Avoidance Functions

The eyes, the sociologist Erving Goffman observed in *Interaction Ritual* (1967), are "great intruders." When you avoid eye contact or avert your glance, you allow others to maintain their privacy. You probably do this when you see a couple arguing, say, in the street or on a bus. You turn your eyes away as if to say, "I don't mean to intrude; I respect your privacy." Goffman refers to this behavior as **civil inattention.**

Eye avoidance can also signal lack of interest—in a person, a conversation, or some visual stimulus. At times, like the ostrich, we hide our eyes to try to cut off unpleasant stimuli. Notice, for example, how quickly people close their eyes in the face of some extreme unpleasantness. Interestingly enough, even if the unpleasantness is auditory, we tend to shut it out by closing our eyes. At other times, we close our eyes to block out visual stimuli and thus heighten our other senses; for example, we often listen to music with our eyes closed. Lovers often close their eyes while kissing, and many prefer to make love in a dark or dimly lit room.

Pupil Dilation

In the fifteenth and sixteenth centuries, Italian women put drops of belladonna (which literally means "beautiful woman") into their eyes to enlarge the pupils so they would look more attractive. Contemporary research supports the intuitive logic of these women: dilated pupils are in fact judged more attractive than constricted ones (Hess 1975; Marshall 1983).

In one study, photographs of women were retouched (Hess 1975). In one set of photographs, the pupils were enlarged, and in the other they were made smaller. Men were then asked to judge the women's personalities from the photographs. The photos of women with small pupils drew responses such as cold, hard, and selfish; those with dilated pupils drew responses such as feminine and soft. However, the male observers could not verbalize the reasons for the different perceptions. Pupil dilation and reactions to changes in the pupil size of others both seem to function below the level of conscious awareness.

Although belladonna is no longer used, the cosmetics industry has made millions selling eye enhancers—eye shadow, eyeliner, false eyelashes, and tinted contact lenses that change eye color. These items function (ideally, at least) to draw attention to these most powerful communicators.

Pupil size also reveals your interest and level of emotional arousal. Your pupils enlarge when you are interested in something or when you are emotionally aroused. When homosexuals and heterosexuals were shown pictures of nude bodies, the homosexuals' pupils dilated more when viewing same-sex bodies, whereas the heterosexuals' pupils dilated more when viewing opposite-sex bodies (Hess, Seltzer, and Schlien 1965). These pupillary responses are unconscious and are even observed in persons with profound mental retardation (Chaney, Givens, Aoki, and Gombiner 1989).

Touch Communication

Touch communication, also referred to as **haptics**, is perhaps the most primitive form of communication. Developmentally, touch is probably the first sense to be used; even in the womb the child is stimulated by touch. Soon after birth, the child is fondled, caressed, patted, and stroked. In turn, the child explores its world through touch. In a very short time, the child learns to communicate a wide variety of meanings through touch.

The Meanings of Touch

Touch may communicate five major meanings (Jones and Yarbrough 1985). *Positive emotions* may be communicated by touch, mainly between intimates or others who have a relatively close relationship. Among the most important of these positive emotions are support, appreciation, inclusion, sexual interest or intent, and affection. It is interesting to note that people in relationships touch each other more during the intermediate stage than in either the beginning or firmly established relationship stages (Guerrero and Andersen 1991). Additional research found that touch communicated such positive feelings as composure, immediacy, affection, trust, similarity and quality, and informality (Burgoon 1991). Touch has also been found to facilitate self-disclosure (Rabinowitz 1991).

Touch often communicates *playfulness,* either affectionately or aggressively. When touch is used in this manner, the playfulness de-emphasizes the emotion and tells the other person that it is not to be taken seriously. Playful touches lighten an interaction.

Touch may also *control* the behaviors, attitudes, or feelings of the other person. Such control may communicate a number of messages. To ask for compliance, for example, we touch the other person to communicate, "Move over," "Hurry," "Stay here," or "Do it." Touching to control may also communicate dominance (Henley 1977). The higher-status and dominant person, for example, initiates touch. In fact, it would be a breach of etiquette for the lower-status person to touch the person of higher status.

Ritualistic touching centers on greetings and departures. Shaking hands to say "hello" or "goodbye" is perhaps the clearest example of ritualistic touching, but we might also hug, kiss, or put an arm around another's shoulder.

Task-related touching is associated with the performance of some function. This ranges from removing a speck of dust from another person's face to helping someone out of a car or checking someone's forehead for fever. Task-related touching seems generally to be regarded positively. For example, book borrowers had a more positive attitude toward the library and the librarian when touched lightly, and customers gave larger tips when lightly touched by the waitress (Marsh 1988). Similarly, diners who were touched on the shoulder or hand when being given their change in a restaurant, tipped more than diners who were not touched (Crusco and Wetzel 1984).

Touch Avoidance

Much as we have a need and desire to touch and be touched by others, we also have a tendency to avoid touch from certain people or in certain circumstances (Andersen and Leibowitz 1978). Before reading about the research findings on touch avoidance, you may wish to take the accompanying touch avoidance self-test.

Among the important findings is the observation that touch avoidance is positively related to communication apprehension. Those who fear oral communication also seem to score high on touch avoidance. (You may wish to compare your scores on this touch avoidance test with your scores on the communication apprehension test presented in Unit 5.) Touch avoidance is also high among those who self-disclose little; both touch and self-disclosure are intimate forms of communication, and people who are reluctant to get close to another person by self-disclosure also seem reluctant to get close through touch. The tendency to avoid communication seems a general one that applies to all forms of communication.

Older people have higher touch avoidance scores for opposite-sex persons than do younger people. Apparently, as we get older we are touched less by members of the opposite sex, and this decreased frequency of touching may lead us to avoid touching. Males score higher than females on same-sex touch avoidance. This accords well with our stereotypes: Men avoid touching other men, but women may and do touch other women. Women, it was also found, have higher touch avoidance scores for opposite-sex touching than do men.

Consider, as Nancy Henley suggests in her Body Politics (1977), who would touch whom—say, by putting an arm on the other person's shoulder or by putting a hand on the other person's back—in the following dyads: teacher and student, doctor and patient, master and servant, manager and worker, minister and parishioner, police officer and accused, business executive and secretary. Most people would say that the first person in each dyad would be more likely to touch the second person than the other way around. It is the higher-status person who is permitted to touch the lower-status person. What implications does this have for your own touching and being touched?

On the basis of your observations for a period of one day (admittedly, much too short a time), what general conclusions can you draw about the following: Whom do you touch the most? Whom do you avoid touching? Who touches you the most? What meanings do you use touch to communicate? What meanings do you derive from being touched by others?

Self Test

Do You Avoid Touch?

This instrument is composed of 18 statements concerning how you feel about touching other people and being touched. Please indicate the degree to which each statement applies to you according to the following scale:

1 = strongly agree
2 = agree
3 = are undecided
4 = disagree
5 = strongly disagree

_____ 1. A hug from a same-sex friend is a true sign of friendship.
_____ 2. Opposite-sex friends enjoy it when I touch them.
_____ 3. I often put my arm around friends of the same sex.
_____ 4. When I see two friends of the same sex hugging, it revolts me.
_____ 5. I like it when members of the opposite sex touch me.
_____ 6. People shouldn't be so uptight about touching persons of the same sex.
_____ 7. I think it is vulgar when members of the opposite sex touch me.
_____ 8. When a member of the opposite sex touches me, I find it unpleasant.
_____ 9. I wish I were free to show emotions by touching members of the same sex.
_____10. I'd enjoy giving a massage to an opposite-sex friend.
_____11. I enjoy kissing a person of the same sex.
_____12. I like to touch friends that are the same sex as I am.
_____13. Touching a friend of the same sex does not make me uncomfortable.
_____14. I find it enjoyable when my date and I embrace.
_____15. I enjoy getting a back rub from a member of the opposite sex.
_____16. I dislike kissing relatives of the same sex.
_____17. Intimate touching with members of the opposite sex is pleasurable.
_____18. I find it difficult to be touched by a member of my own sex.

Thinking Critically About Touch Avoidance

To score this questionaire:

1. Reverse your scores for items 4, 7, 8, 16, and 18. Use these reversed scores in all future calculations.
2. To obtain your same-sex touch avoidance score (the extent to which you avoid touching members of your sex), total the scores for items 1, 3, 4, 6, 9, 11, 12, 13, 16, and 18.
3. To obtain your opposite-sex touch avoidance score (the extent to which you avoid touching members of the opposite sex), total the scores for items 2, 5, 7, 8, 10, 14, 15, and 17.
4. To obtain your total touch avoidance score, add the subtotals from steps 2 and 3.

The higher the score, the higher the touch avoidance—that is, the greater your tendency to avoid touch. In studies by Andersen and Leibowitz (1978), who constructed this test, average opposite-sex touch avoidance scores for males was 12.9 and for females 14.85. Average same-sex touch avoidance scores were 26.43 for males and 21.70 for females. How close are you to these averages? Can you identify the influences that have led you to have the touch avoidance tendencies you now have?

Adapted from "The Development and Nature of the Construct Touch Avoidance," by Peter Andersen and Ken Liebowitz, *Environmental Psychology and Nonverbal Behavior* 3 (1978):89–106. Reprinted by permission of Plenum Publishing Corporation.

Who Touches Whom Where: Gender and Cultural Differences

A great deal of research has been directed at the question of who touches whom where. Most of it has attempted to address two basic questions: (1) Are there gender differences? Do men and women communicate through touch in the same way? Are men and women touched in the same way? (2) Are there cultural differences? Do people in widely different cultures communicate through touch in the same way?

Gender Differences and Touch   Early research reported that touching and being touched differ little between men and women (Jourard 1968). Men touch and are touched as often and in the same places as women. The major exception to this finding is the touching behavior of mothers and fathers. Mothers touch children of both sexes and of all ages more than do fathers. In fact, many fathers go no further than touching the hands of their children. More recent research has found differences.

Contrary to popular stereotype, research shows that females initiate more opposite-sex touching (especially more opposite sex touching designed to control) than do men (Jones 1985). In another study, women were found to initiate touch more in married relationships and less in casual romantic relationships than did men (Guerrero and Andersen 1994).

Opposite-sex friends report more touching than do same-sex friends. Both male and female college students report that they touch and are touched more by their opposite sex friends than by their same-sex friends. No doubt the strong societal bias against same-sex touching accounts for these generalizations.

Cultural Differences and Touch   The several functions and examples of touching discussed here have been based on studies in North America; in other cultures these functions might not be served in the same way. In some cultures, for example, some task-related touching is viewed negatively and is to be avoided. Among Koreans, it is considered disrespectful for a store owner to touch a customer in, say, handing back change; it is considered too intimate a gesture. Members of other cultures, expecting such touching, may consider the Korean's behavior cold and insulting. Muslim children are not supposed to touch members of the opposite sex, which can easily be interpreted as unfriendly by American children who are used to touching each other (Dresser 1996).

For example, in one study on touch, college students in Japan and in the United States were surveyed (Barnlund 1975). Students from the United States reported being touched twice as much as did the Japanese students. In Japan, there is a strong taboo against strangers touching, and the Japanese are therefore especially careful to maintain sufficient distance.

Some cultures are contact cultures and others are noncontact cultures. Members of contact cultures (for example, Southern European) maintain close distances, touch each other in conversation, face each other more directly, and maintain longer and more focused eye contact. Members of noncontact cultures (for example, Northern European or Japan) maintain greater distance in their interactions, touch each other only rarely if at all, avoid facing each other directly, and maintain much less direct eye contact. As a result, Northern Europeans and Japanese may be perceived as cold, distant, and uninvolved by Southern Europeans, who may in turn be perceived as pushy, aggressive, and inappropriately intimate.

Women, it seems, are permitted to touch children more than are men. For example, an elementary school female teacher seems to be granted greater latitude in touching children than would a male teacher. Do you agree that this is generally the case? If so, why do you think this attitudinal difference exists?

Smell Communication

Smell communication, or olfactics, is extremely important in a wide variety of situations. Scientists estimate that you can smell some 10,000 different odors (Angier 1995a). Smell is now big business (Kleinfeld 1992). There is some, though not conclusive, evidence showing, for example, that the smell of lemon contributes to a perception of heath, the smell of lavender and eucalyptus seems to increase alertness, and the smell of rose oil seems to reduce blood pressure. Findings such as these have contributed to the growth of aromatherapy and to a new profession of aromatherapists (Furlow 1996). Because humans possess "denser skin concentrations of scent glands than almost any other mammal" it has been argued that it only remains for us to discover how we use scent to communicate a wide variety of messages (Furlow 1996, p. 41). Here are some of the most important messages scent seems to communicate.

Attraction Messages

Do you use smell to communicate? How important is it for you to smell "right?" How much are you willing to spend—say, per month—on products whose primary function is to make you smell better?

In many animal species the female gives off a scent that draws males, often from far distances, and thus ensures the continuation of the species. Humans too emit sexual attractants, called sex pheromones, body secretions that arouse sexual desire. Humans, of course, supplement that with perfumes, colognes, after-shave lotions, powders, and the like to further enhance attractiveness and sexuality. Not surprisingly, biotechnology companies are busily at work with the aim of bottling human sex pheromones (Bishop 1993).

You also use odors to make yourself feel better; after all, you also smell yourself. When the smells are pleasant, you feel better about yourself; when the smells are unpleasant, you feel less good about yourself and probably shower and perhaps put on some cologne.

Taste Messages

Without smell, taste would be severely impaired. For example, it would be extremely difficult to taste the difference between a raw potato and an apple without the sense of smell. Street vendors selling hot dogs, sausages, and similar foods are aided greatly by the smells that stimulate the appetites of passersby.

Memory Messages

Smell is a powerful memory aid; you can often recall situations from months and even years ago when you happen upon a similar smell. One reason why smell can so effectively recall a previous situation is that it is often associated with significant emotional experiences (Rubin, Groth, and Goldsmith 1984; Malandro, Barker, and Barker 1989).

Identification Messages

Smell is often used to create an image or an identity for a product. Advertisers and manufacturers spend millions of dollars each year creating scents for cleaning products and toothpastes, for example, which have nothing to do with their cleaning power. Instead, they function solely to help create an image for the product. There is also evidence that we can identify specific significant others by smell. For example, infants find their mothers' breasts through smell, mothers can identify their new born solely through smell, and young children were able to identify the t-shirts of their brothers and sisters solely on the basis of smell (Porter and Moore 1981; Angier 1995a). And one researcher goes so far as to advise: "If your man's odor reminds you of Dad or your brother, you may want genetic tests before trying to conceive a child" (Furlow 1996, p. 41).

Paralanguage and Silence

Two aspects of nonverbal communication, often considered together because they involve manipulating sound, are paralanguage and silence. Let's consider paralanguage first.

Paralanguage

An old exercise used to increase a student's ability to express different emotions, feelings, and attitudes was to have the student say the following sentence while accenting or stressing different words: "Is this the face that launched a thousand ships?" Significant differences in meaning are easily communicated, depending on where the stress is placed. Consider, for example, the following variations:

1. *Is* this the face that launched a thousand ships?
2. Is *this* the face that launched a thousand ships?
3. Is this the *face* that launched a thousand ships?
4. Is this the face that *launched* a thousand ships?
5. Is this the face that launched a *thousand ships*?

Each of these five sentences communicates something different. Each, in fact, asks a totally different question, even though the words used are identical. All that distinguishes the sentences is stress, one of the aspects of what is called paralanguage. **Paralanguage** is the vocal (but nonverbal) dimension of speech. It refers to the *manner* in which you say something rather than to what you say.

In addition to stress, paralanguage includes such vocal characteristics as rate, volume, and rhythm. Paralanguage also includes the vocalizations we make when laughing, yelling, moaning, whining, and belching; vocal segregates—sound combinations that are not words—such as "uh-uh" and "shh"; and **pitch**, the highness or lowness of vocal tone (Argyle 1988; Trager 1958, 1961).

A good way to appreciate the workings of paralanguage is to examine your own vocal behavior when communicating different meanings. Try reading each of these sentences first to communicate praise and then to communicate criticism: "Now that looks good on you;" "That was some meal;" "You're an expert;" "You're so sensitive;" "Are you ready?" What changes in your vocal expression communicates the differences in meaning?

Are you a fast talker? A slow talker? Does this average rate of speech serve you well?

People Perception and Paralanguage   It does seem that certain voices are symptomatic of certain personality types or certain problems and, specifically, that the personality orientation gives rise to the vocal qualities. When listening to people—regardless of what they are saying—we form impressions based on their paralanguage as to what kind of people they are. Our impressions from paralanguage cues span a broad range and consist of physical impressions (perhaps about body type and certainly about sex and age), personality impressions (they sound shy, they appear aggressive), and evaluative impressions (they sound like good people, they sound evil and menacing, they have vicious laughs).

One of the most interesting findings on voice and personal characteristics is that listeners can accurately judge the status (high, middle, or low) of speakers after hearing a 60-second voice sample. In fact, many listeners reported that they made their judgments in less than 15 seconds. It has also been found that the speakers judged to be of high status were rated as being of higher credibility than those rated of middle or low status.

It is interesting to note that listeners agree with each other about the personality of the speaker even when their judgments are in error. Listeners seem to have stereotyped ideas about the way vocal characteristics and personality characteristics are related, and they use these stereotypes in their judgments.

Persuasion and Paralanguage   The rate of speech is the aspect of paralanguage that has received the most attention. It is of interest to the advertiser, the politician, and, in fact, anyone who tries to convey information or to influence others orally, especially when time is limited or expensive. The research on rate of speech shows that in one-way communication situations, persons who talk fast are more persuasive and are evaluated more highly than those who talk at or below normal speeds (MacLachlan 1979). This greater persuasiveness and higher regard holds true whether the person talks fast naturally or the speech is sped up electronically (as in time-compressed speech).

In one experiment, subjects were asked to listen to taped messages and then to indicate both the degree to which they agreed with the message and their opinions as to how intelligent and objective they thought the speaker was (MacLachlan 1979). Rates of 111, 140, and 191 words per minute were used. (The average speaking rate is about 130 to 150 words per minute.) Subjects agreed most with the fastest speech and least with the slowest speech. Further, they rated the fastest speaker as the most intelligent and objective and the slowest speaker as the least intelligent and objective. Even in experiments in which the speaker was known to have something to gain personally from persuasion (as would, say, a used-car dealer), the speaker who spoke at the fastest rate was the most persuasive. More recent research finds that faster speech rates increase speaker competence and dominance (Buller, LePoire, Aune, and Eloy 1992).

Rapid speech also has the advantage in comprehension. Subjects who listened to speeches at 201 words per minute (about 140 is average) comprehended 95 percent of the message, and those who listened to speeches at 282 words per minute (that is, double the normal rate) comprehended 90 percent. Even though the rates increased dramatically, the comprehension rates fell only slightly. These 5 percent and 10 percent losses are more than offset by the increased speed and thus make the faster rates much more efficient in communicating information. If the speech speeds are increased more than 100 percent, however, comprehension falls dramatically.

Exercise caution in applying this research to your own interpersonal interactions (MacLachlan 1979). Realize that during the time the speaker is speaking, the listener is generating and framing a reply. If the speaker talks too rapidly, there may not be enough time to compose this reply, and resentment may therefore be generated. Furthermore, the increased rate may seem so unnatural that the listener may come to focus on the speed of speech rather than the thought expressed.

How would you go about discovering if you are more persuaded by fast talk than by normal rate or slow talk?

Silence

"Speech," wrote Thomas Mann, "is civilization itself. The word, even the most contradictory word, preserves contact; it is silence which isolates." Philosopher Karl Jaspers, on the other hand, observed that "the ultimate in thinking as in communication is silence," and philosopher Max Picard noted that "silence is nothing merely negative; it is not the mere absence of speech. It is a positive, a complete world in itself." The one thing on which these contradictory observations agree is that silence communicates. Your silence communicates just as intensely as anything you verbalize (see Jaworski 1993).

Functions of Silence   Like words and gestures, silence, too, serves important communication functions. Silence allows the speaker *time to think,* time to formulate and organize his or her verbal communications. Before messages of intense conflict, as well as those confessing undying love, there is often silence. Again, silence seems to prepare the receiver for the importance of these future messages.

Some people use silence as a weapon *to hurt* others. We often speak of giving someone "the silent treatment." After a conflict, for example, one or both individuals might remain silent as a kind of punishment. Silence used to hurt others may also take the form of refusing to acknowledge the presence of another person, as in disconfirmation (see Unit 10); here silence is a dramatic demonstration of the total indifference one person feels toward the other.

Sometimes silence is used as a *response to personal anxiety,* shyness, or threats. You may feel anxious or shy among new people and prefer to remain silent. By remaining silent you preclude the chance of rejection. Only when the silence is broken and an attempt to communicate with another person is made do you risk rejection.

Silence may be used *to prevent communication* of certain messages. In conflict situations, silence is sometimes used to prevent certain topics from surfacing and to prevent one or both parties from saying things they may later regret. In such situations, silence often allows us time to cool off before expressing hatred, severe criticism, or personal attacks, which we know are irreversible.

Like the eyes, face, or hands, silence can also be used *to communicate emotional responses* (Ehrenhaus 1988). Sometimes silence communicates a determination to be uncooperative or defiant; by refusing to engage in verbal communication, you defy the authority or the legitimacy of the other person's position. Silence is often used to communicate annoyance, usually accompanied by a pouting expression, arms crossed in front of the chest, and nostrils flared. Silence may express affection or love, especially when coupled with long and longing stares into each other's eyes.

Of course, you may also use silence when you simply have *nothing to say,* when nothing occurs to you, or when you do not want to say anything. James Russell Lowell expressed this well: "Blessed are they who have nothing to say, and who cannot be persuaded to say it."

What meanings do you communicate with silence?

Cultural Differences and Silence   The communicative functions of silence in the situations just cited are not universal. In the United States, for example, silence is often taken as negative. At a business meeting or even in informal social groups, silence may often be interpreted negatively—perhaps the silent member wasn't listening, has

MEDIA & TECHNOLOGY

THE SPIRAL OF SILENCE

Consider your own tendency to discuss or remain silent about your attitudes and beliefs when interacting with others. Are you equally likely to voice opinions that agree with others as those that disagree? The spiral of silence theory claims that you are more likely to voice agreement positions than disagreement ones (Noelle-Neumann 1973, 1980, 1991; Becker and Roberts 1992; Windahl, Signitzer, and Olson 1992).

The spiral of silence theory argues that when a controversial issue arises, you estimate the opinions of others; you try to estimate public opinion on the issue. You estimate which views are popular and which are not and you also estimate *how* popular these positions are. At the same time, you also judge the likelihood of being punished for expressing minority opinions and the severity of that punishment. And you do this largely by attending to the media. Once these assumptions about the popularity of an issue are formed, you use these to regulate your willingness to express your own opinions on that issue or remain silent.

When you feel your opinions are in agreement with the majority, you are more likely to voice them than if you feel they are in disagreement. Of course there are many reasons you might be reluctant to voice minority opinions. After all, you probably want to be one of the crowd and so you resist any possible isolation that unpopular opinions might impose on you. Another reason is that disagreement often means confrontation with the possibility of being proven wrong, both unpleasant results. And, you may assume that the majority, because they are a majority, must be right; and you of course want to be right, not wrong.

Not all people seem affected by this spiral equally (Noelle-Neumann 1991). For example, younger people and men are more likely to express minority opinions than are older people and women. Educated people are more likely to express minority opinions than are those who are less educated. This is not surprising since the expression of a minority opinion often requires some defense which the educated feel competent to present but the uneducated do not.

As these people remain silent, the media position gets stronger (because those who agree with it are the only ones who are speaking). As the media's position grows stronger, the silence of the opposition also grows. The silence becomes an ever widening spiral.

One of the problems this situation creates is that the media are likely to express the same general opinions, values, and beliefs and thus present a false picture of the extent to which people are in agreement. Those who take their cues from the media are therefore likely to estimate incorrectly the real degree of agreement and disagreement.

Consider your own part in the spiral of silence. How much, if any, do you contribute to this spiral of silence? How much do your peers contribute? To what degree does your college provide for the presentation of minority values, opinions, and beliefs? How does this theory relate to interpersonal communication generally? How does this theory relate to intercultural communication and to the expression of racist, sexist, and heterosexist opinions and attitudes?

p. 276

nothing interesting to add, doesn't understand the issues, is insensitive, is too self-absorbed to focus on the messages of others, or isn't interested in and isn't paying attention to the conversation. Other cultures, however, view silence more positively. In many situations in Japan, for example, silence is preferred to speech (Haga 1988).

The traditional Apache, for example, regard silence very differently (Basso 1972). Among the Apache, mutual friends do not feel the need to introduce strangers who may be working in the same area or on the same project. The strangers may remain silent for several days. During this time they are looking each other over, trying to determine if the other person is all right. Only after this period do the individuals talk. When courting, especially during the initial stages, the Apache remain silent for hours; if they do talk, they generally talk very little. Only after a couple has been dating for several months will they have lengthy conversations. These periods of silence are generally attributed to shyness or self-consciousness. The use of silence is explicitly taught to Apache women, who are especially discouraged from engaging in long discussions with their dates. Silence during courtship is a sign of modesty to many Apache.

What nonverbal cues would you look for to discover whether someone was interested in you romantically? What nonverbal cues do you emit to show your own romantic interest? What cues do you use to communicate your on-the-job competence?

Summary   U N I T   I N   B R I E F

A RETURN TO OBJECTIVES:

In this unit we introduced seven types or channels of nonverbal communication and focused on these questions: (1) What meanings are communicated with body movements? (2) What meanings do facial movements communicate? Do facial movements influence us physically? Does culture influence facial expressions? (3) What messages do eye contact and eye avoidance communicate? (4) What meanings can you communicate by touching? (5) What messages can be communicated by smell? (6) What meanings do variations in paralanguage and (7) silence communicate?

Body Movements (Types)	Facial Communication Functions	Eye Communications
Emblems: Translate words and phrases rather directly.	**To express emotions:** Happiness, surprise, fear, anger, sadness, disgust/contempt, interest, bewilderment, determination.	**Eye gaze:** Monitor feedback, maintain interest/attention, signal conversational turns, signal nature of relationship, compensate for physical distance.
Illustrators: Accompany and literally illustrate the verbal messages.	**To manage meanings communicated:** Intensifying, deintensifying, neutralizing, masking.	**Eye avoidance:** Give others privacy, signal disinterest, cut off unpleasant stimuli, heighten other senses.
Affect displays: Convey emotional meaning.		
Regulators: Monitor or control the speaking of the other person.		**Pupil dilation:** Indicate interest/arousal, increase attractiveness.
Adaptors: Serve some need and are usually performed only partially in public.		

Touch Communication Functions	Smell Functions	Paralanguage Functions and Silence Functions
Positive affect	Attraction	**Paralanguage:** Provide cues for impression formation, provide cues for identifying emotional states; provide cues for judgments of credibility, intelligence, and objectivity.
Playfulness	Taste	
Control	Memory	
Ritual	Identification	**Silence:** Provide thinking time, inflict hurt, hide anxiety, prevent communication, communication feelings, communicate "nothing."
Task-relatedness		

UNIT

13

Nonverbal Messages: Space and Time

Unit Topics	Unit Objectives
	After completing this unit, you should be able to:
Spatial Messages Theories About Space	1. Define *proxemics* and the four proxemic distances 2. Explain *protection, equilibrium,* and *expectancy violation theories* of space
Territoriality Signaling Ownership Signaling Status	3. Define *territoriality* and explain its role in signaling ownership and status
Artifactual Communication Space Decoration Color Communication Clothing and Body Adornment Artifacts and Culture: The Case of Gifts	4. Explain *artifactual communication* and the meanings that space decoration, color, and clothing can communicate
Temporal Communication Cultural Time Psychological Time Time and Status	5. Explain the cultural and psychological perspectives of time 6. Explain time's relationship to status

---

EXPERIENTIAL LEARNING VEHICLES

Vehicles No. 11, "Interpersonal Interactions and Space," pp. 450–451, No. 12, "Who?" pp. 452–453, and No. 13, "The Meanings of Color," pp. 453–454 will help illustrate and personalize the nature of nonverbal messages.

Like verbal behavior, spatial and temporal behaviors also communicate. In this unit, we explore several dimensions of space and time and the ways in which they communicate a variety of messages.

Spatial Messages

Space is an especially important factor in interpersonal communication, although we seldom think about it. Edward T. Hall (1959, 1963, 1966), who has pioneered the study of spatial communication (sometimes called **proxemics**), distinguishes four distances that correspond closely to the major types of relationships: intimate, personal, social, and public (see Figure 13.1).

Intimate Distance   Within **intimate distance**, ranging from the close phase of actual touching to the far phase of 6 to 18 inches, the presence of the other per-

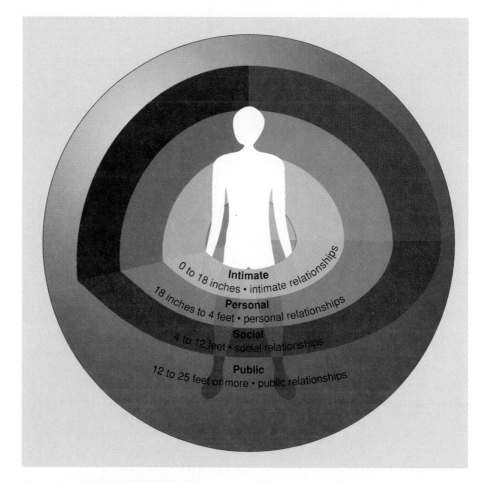

Figure 13.1   The Four Spatial Distances.
Most people would agree that our relationships determine our proxemic distances; intimate relationships create intimate distances and public relationships create public distances, for example. Could you make a case for the reverse assumption, namely that our proxemic distances influence (even determine) our relationships?

son is unmistakable. You experience the sound, smell, and feel of the other's breath. The close phase is used for lovemaking and wrestling, for comforting and protecting. In the close phase, the muscles and the skin communicate, while actual words play a minor role. The far phase allows people to touch each other by extending their hands. The individuals are so close that this distance is not considered proper for strangers in public. Because of the feeling of inappropriateness and discomfort (at least for some Americans) if strangers are this close (say, on a crowded bus), their eyes seldom meet but remain fixed on some remote object.

Personal Distance You carry a protective bubble defining your **personal distance,** which allows you to stay protected and untouched by others and ranges from 18 inches to about 4 feet. In the close phase, people can still hold or grasp each other but only by extending their arms. You can then take into your protective bubble certain individuals—for example, loved ones. In the far phase, you can touch another person only if you both extend your arms. This far phase is the extent to which you can physically get your hands on things; hence, it defines, in one sense, the limits of your physical control over others. At times, you may detect breath odor, but generally at this distance etiquette demands that you direct your breath to some neutral area.

Social Distance At the **social distance,** ranging from 4 to 12 feet, you lose the visual detail you had at the personal distance. The close phase is the distance at which you conduct impersonal business or interact at a social gathering. The far phase is the distance at which you stand when someone says, "Stand away so I can look at you." At this distance, business transactions have a more formal tone than they do when conducted in the close phase. In the offices of high officials, the desks are often positioned so that clients are kept at least this distance away. Unlike the intimate distance, where eye contact is awkward, the far phase of the social distance makes eye contact essential—otherwise, communication is lost. The voice is generally louder than normal at this level. This distance frees you from constant interaction with those with whom you work without seeming rude.

Why do you suppose people who are angry or tense need greater space around them? Do you find this true from your personal experience?

Public Distance **Public distance** ranges from 12 to more than 25 feet. In the close phase, a person seems protected by space. At this distance, you are able to take defensive action should you feel threatened. On a public bus or train, for example, you might keep at least this distance from a drunkard. Although you lose the fine details of the face and eyes, you are still close enough to see what is happening.

At the far phase, you see others not as separate individuals but as part of the whole setting. People automatically sit approximately 30 feet around important public figures, and they seem to do this whether or not there are guards preventing their coming closer. The far phase is the distance by which actors on stage are separated from their audience; consequently, their actions and voices have to be somewhat exaggerated.

The specific distances you would maintain between yourself and another person depend on a wide variety of factors. Some of the factors are presented in Table 13.1.

What factors other than those listed in Table 13.1 might influence the distances you maintain in your conversations?

Table 13.1	Factors Influencing Dyadic Distance
As you read through this table consider your own spatial behavior. For example, do you approach a woman at a different distance than you approach a man? Do you maintain distances different from members of other cultures? Do you stand closer to people you like than to people you don't like? This table is based on the extensive research summary of Burgoon, Buller, and Woodall (1995).	
Influencing Factors	**Sample Research Findings**

Communication Characteristics:
  Gender
  Age
  Race/ethnicity
  Personality
	◆ Women sit and stand closer to each other than do men in same-sex dyads.
	◆ People approach women more closely than they approach men.
	◆ Distance increases with age.
	◆ People maintain closer distances with peers than with persons much older or younger.
	◆ Mexican Americans maintain closer distances than do either blacks or whites.
	◆ Introverts and highly anxious people maintain greater distances than do extroverts.

Relationship Characteristics:
  Familiarity
  Liking
  Status
	◆ Persons familiar with each other maintain shorter distances.
	◆ Persons maintain shorter distances with those they like.
	◆ The greater the status difference, the greater the space.

Context Characteristics:
  Formality
  Purpose of interaction
  Space availability
	◆ The more formal the situation, the greater the space.
	◆ Shorter distances are maintained for cooperative tasks than for competitive tasks.
	◆ The greater the space, the shorter the distance.

Theories About Space

A number of nonverbal communication researchers have offered explanations as to why people maintain the distances they do. Prominent among these explanations are protection theory, equilibrium theory, and expectancy violation theory—rather complex names for simple and interesting concepts.

Protection Theory   **Protection theory** holds that you establish a body buffer zone around yourself as protection against unwanted touching or attack (Dosey and Meisels 1976). When you feel that you may be attacked, your body buffer zone increases; you want more space around you. For example, if you found yourself in a dangerous neighborhood at night, your body buffer zone would probably expand well beyond what it would be if you were in familiar and safe surroundings. If someone entered this buffer zone, you would probably feel threatened and seek to expand that distance by walking faster or crossing the street.

In contrast, when you are feeling secure and protected, your buffer zone becomes much smaller. For example, if you are with a group of close friends and feel secure, your buffer zone shrinks, and you may welcome the close proximity and mutual touching.

Equilibrium Theory **Equilibrium theory** holds that intimacy and distance vary together: the greater the intimacy, the closer the distance; the lower the intimacy, the greater the distance. This theory says that you maintain close distances with those with whom you have close interpersonal relationships and that you maintain greater distances with those with whom you do not have close relationships (Argyle and Dean 1965).

At times, of course, your interpersonal distance does not accurately reflect your level of intimacy. When this happens, you make adjustments. For example, let's say that you have an intimate relationship with someone, but for some reason you are separated—perhaps because you could not get concert seats next to each other or you are at a party and have each been led to different parts of a large banquet hall. When this happens, you probably try to preserve your psychological closeness by maintaining frequent eye contact or perhaps by facing each other.

Can you identify other adjustments you might make if your interpersonal distance does not comfortably reflect the type of relationship you have?

At other times, however, you are forced into close distances with someone with whom you are not intimate (or may even dislike)—for example, on a crowded bus or perhaps in the dentist's chair. In these situations, you also compensate, but in such cases you seek to make the psychological distance greater. Consequently, you might avoid eye contact and turn in an opposite direction. In the dentist's chair, you probably close your eyes to decrease this normally intimate distance. If seated to the right of a stranger, you might cross your legs and turn your torso to the right.

Expectancy Violations Theory **Expectancy violations** theory explains what happens when you increase or decrease the distance between yourself and another in an interpersonal interaction (Burgoon and Hale 1988; Burgoon, Buller, and Woodall 1989). Each culture has certain expectancies for the distance people are to maintain in their conversations. Of course, each person has certain idiosyncrasies. Together, these determine "expected distance." What happens when these expectations are violated?

If you violate the expected distance to a great extent—small violations most often go unnoticed—then the relationship itself comes into focus. The other person begins to turn attention away from the topic of conversation and toward you and your relationship with him or her. It's also interesting to note that those who violate normal expected spatial relationships are judged to be less truthful than those who did not commit such violations (Feeley and deTurck 1995).

Does protection theory explain any of your spatial behaviors? Does equilibrium theory? Expectancy violations theory? Can you give one example to illustrate each theory?

If this other person perceives you positively—for example, you are a high-status person or you are particularly attractive—then you will be perceived even more positively if you violate the norm. If, however, you are perceived negatively and you violate the norm, you will be perceived even more negatively. Thus, the positively evaluated person will be perceived more positively if he or she violates the norm, whereas the negatively evaluated person will be more positively perceived if the distance norm is not violated.

Territoriality

Another type of communication having to do with space is **territoriality**, the possessive reaction to an area or to particular objects. Through territorial behavior, you signal ownership and status. Of course, not all territories are the same (Altman 1975). **Primary territories** are yours and yours alone. **Secondary territories** are associated with you but are not owned by you. **Public territories** belong to or are used by all people. Table 13.2 summarizes these three types.

Signaling Ownership

Can you recall a situation in which your territory was violated? Invaded? Contaminated? How did you respond to these encroachments?

Many male animals stake out a particular territory and signal their ownership to all others. They allow prospective mates to enter but defend the territory against other males of the same species. Among deer, for example, the size of the territory signifies the power of the buck, which in turn determines how many females he will mate with. Less powerful bucks will be able to control only small territories and consequently will mate with only one or two females. This adaptive measure ensures that the strongest members of the species produce most of the offspring.

These same general patterns are believed by many ethologists—scientists who study animal behavior in the animals' natural surroundings—to be integral to human behavior. Some researchers claim that this form of behavior is instinctive and is a symptom of the innate aggressiveness of humans. Others claim that territoriality is learned and is culturally based. Most, however, seem to agree that a great deal of human behavior can be understood and described as territoriality regardless of its possible origin or development (Ardrey 1966).

The Home Field Advantage   When you operate in your own territory, you have an interpersonal advantage. In their own home or office, people take on a kind of leadership role: they initiate conversations, fill in silences, assume relaxed and

Table 13.2	**Three Types of Territory**	

Can you identify specific kinds of primary, secondary, and public territories that you interacted in today? How did the type of territory you were in influence your communications?

Territory	Definition	Example
Primary	Areas you might call your own; your exclusive preserve.	Your room, your desk, your office.
Secondary	Areas that do not belong to you but which you have occupied and with which you are associated.	A table in the cafeteria that you sit at regularly; your neighborhood turf.
Public	Areas that are open to all people.	A movie house, a restaurant, a shopping mall.

comfortable postures, and maintain their positions with greater conviction. Because the territorial owner is dominant, you stand a better chance of getting your raise, your point accepted, and the contract resolved in your favor if you are in your territory (your office, your home) rather than in someone else's (your supervisor's office, for example) (Marsh 1988).

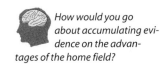

How would you go about accumulating evidence on the advantages of the home field?

Markers   Like animals, humans mark their territory, using three types of markers: central, boundary, and ear markers (Goffman 1971). **Central markers** are items you place in a territory to reserve it for you—for example, a drink at the bar, books on your desk, or a sweater over a library chair.

Boundary markers set boundaries that divide your territory from that of others. In the supermarket checkout line, the bar that is placed between your groceries and those of the person behind you is a boundary marker, as are a fence, the armrests separating your chair from those on either side, and the contours of the molded plastic seats on a bus or train.

Ear markers—a term taken from the practice of branding animals on their ears—are identifying marks that indicate your possession of a territory or object. Trademarks, nameplates, and initials on a shirt or attaché case are all examples of ear markers.

Look around your home and at your belongings. Can you identify examples of central, boundary, and ear markers?

Markers are also important in giving you a feeling of belonging and ownership. For example, students in college dormitories who marked their rooms by displaying personal items stayed in school longer than did those who did not personalize their spaces (Marsh 1988).

Signaling Status

Like animals' territory, the territory of humans communicates status. Clearly, the size and location of the territory indicates something about status. Status is also signaled by the unwritten law granting the right of invasion. Higher-status individuals have a "right" to invade the territory of lower-status persons, but the reverse is not true. The boss of a large company, for example, can barge into the office of a junior executive, but the reverse would be unthinkable. Similarly, a teacher may invade a student's personal space by looking over her or his shoulder as the student writes, but the student cannot do the same to the teacher.

Artifactual Communication

Artifactual communication concerns the messages conveyed by objects that are made by human hands. Thus, aesthetics, color, clothing, jewelry, and even hairstyle are considered artifactual. We look at each of these briefly.

Space Decoration

That the decoration or surroundings of a place exert influence on perceptions should be obvious to anyone who has ever entered a hospital, with its sterile walls and furniture, or a museum, with its imposing columns, glass-encased exhibits, and brass plaques.

Even the way a room is furnished exerts influence on us. In a classic study, researchers attempted to determine if the aesthetic conditions of a room would influence the judgments people made in it (Maslow and Mintz 1956, Mintz 1956). Three rooms were used: One was beautiful, one average, and one ugly. The beautiful room had large windows, beige walls, indirect lighting, and attractive, comfortable furnishings. The average room was a professor's office with mahogany desks and chairs, metal bookcases and filing cabinets, and window shades. The ugly room was painted battleship gray; lighting was provided by an overhead bulb with a dirty, torn shade. The room was furnished to give the impression of a janitor's storeroom in horrible condition. The ashtrays were filled and the window shades torn.

In the three different rooms, students rated art prints in terms of the fatigue/energy and displeasure/well-being depicted in them. As predicted, the students in the beautiful room rated the prints as more energetic and as displaying well-being; the prints judged in the ugly room were rated as displaying fatigue and displeasure, while those judged in the average room were perceived as somewhere between these two extremes.

The way you decorate your private spaces communicates something about who you are. The office with a mahogany desk, bookcases, and oriental rugs communicates importance and status within the organization, just as the metal desk and bare floors communicate a status much further down in the hierarchy. At home, the cost of the furnishings may communicate your status and wealth, and their coordination may communicate your sense of style. The magazines may communicate your interests. The arrangement of chairs around a television set may reveal how important watching television is. Bookcases lining the walls reveal the importance of reading. In fact, there is probably little in your home that would not send messages to others and that others would not use for making inferences about you. Computers, wide-screen televisions, well-equipped kitchens, and oil paintings of great-grandparents, for example, say something about the people who own them. Likewise, the lack of certain items will communicate something about you. Consider, for example, what messages you would get from a home in which there was no television, telephone, or books.

What impressions would someone get seeing your home for the first time? How would you go about discovering if your guesses are correct?

Color Communication

When you are in debt, you speak of being "in the red"; when you make a profit, you are "in the black." When you are sad, you are "blue"; when you are healthy, you are "in the pink"; when you are jealous, you are "green with envy." To be a coward is to be "yellow" and to be inexperienced is to be "green." When you talk a great deal, you talk "a blue streak"; when you are angry, you "see red." As revealed through these time-worn clichés, language abounds in color symbolism.

Colors vary greatly in their meanings from one culture to another. Some of these cultural differences are illustrated in Table 13.3, but before looking at the table think about the meanings your own culture(s) gives to such colors as red, green, black, white, blue, yellow, and purple.

There is some evidence that colors affect us physiologically. For example, respiratory movements increase in the presence of red light and decrease in the presence of blue light. Similarly, eye blinks increase in frequency when eyes are exposed to red light and decrease when exposed to blue. This seems consistent with our intuitive feelings that blue is more soothing and red more provocative. After changing a school's walls from orange and white to blue, the students' blood pressure decreased and their academic performance improved.

fashion –
+
colors –

Table 13.3	Some Cultural Meanings of Color

This table, constructed from the research reported by Henry Dreyfuss (1971), Nancy Hoft (1995), and Norine Dresser (1996), illustrates only some of the different meanings that colors may communicate and especially how they are viewed in different cultures. As you read this table, consider the meanings you give to these colors and where your meanings came from.

Color	Cultural Meanings and Comments
Red	In China red signifies prosperity and rebirth and is used for festive and joyous occasions; in France and the United Kingdom, masculinity; in many African countries, blasphemy or death; and in Japan it signifies anger and danger. Red ink, especially among Korean Buddhists, is used only to write a person's name at the time of death or on the anniversary of the person's death, and creates lots of problems when American teachers use red ink to mark homework.
Green	In the United States green signifies capitalism, go ahead, and envy; in Ireland, patriotism; among some Native Americans, femininity; to the Egyptians, fertility and strength; and to the Japanese, youth and energy.
Black	In Thailand black signifies old age; in parts of Malaysia courage, and in much of Europe death
White	In Thailand white signifies purity; in many Muslim and Hindu cultures, purity and peace; and in Japan and other Asian countries, death and mourning.
Blue	In Iran blue signifies something negative; in Egypt, truth; and in Ghana, joy; among the Cherokee it signifies defeat, and for the Egyptian, virtue and truth
Yellow	In China yellow signifies wealth and authority; in the United States, caution and cowardice; in Egypt, happiness and prosperity; and, in many countries throughout the world, femininity.
Purple	In Latin America purple signifies death; in Europe, royalty; in Egypt, virtue and faith; in Japan, grace and nobility; and in China, barbarism.

Colors surely influence our perceptions and behaviors (Kanner 1989). People's acceptance of a product, for example, is largely determined by its package. For example, the same coffee taken from a yellow can was described as weak; from a dark brown can, too strong; from a red can, rich; and from a blue can, mild. Even our acceptance of a person may depend on the colors worn. Consider, for example, the comments of one color expert (Kanner 1989): "If you have to pick the wardrobe for your defense lawyer heading into court and choose anything but blue, you deserve to lose the case. . . ." Black is so powerful that it can work against the lawyer with the jury. Brown lacks sufficient authority. Green will probably elicit a negative response.

How would you go about discovering if other people think you look better in red or blue? In jeans or dressed more formally?

Clothing and Body Adornment

Clothing serves a variety of functions. It protects you from the weather and, in sports like football, from injury. It helps you conceal parts of your body and so serves a modesty function. Clothing also serves as a **cultural display** (Morris 1977). It communicates your cultural affiliations. In the United States, where

People infer who you are, in part, by the way you dress. Whether these inferences prove to be accurate or inaccurate, they will nevertheless influence what people think of you and how they react to you. Your social class, your seriousness, your attitudes (for example, whether you are conservative or liberal), your concern for convention, your sense of style, and perhaps even your creativity will all be judged—in part at least—from the way you dress. In fact, the very popular New Dress for Success *(1988) and* The New Women's Dress for Success Book *by John Molloy (1996) instructed men and women in how to dress so that they could communicate the image they wanted: for example, efficient, reliable, or authoritative. What impressions do you get from the way the people in the photo are dressed? What impressions might they form about you from the way you are dressed?*

 How do you feel about gang clothing being worn in elementary, high school, or college? Do you think it contributes to violence in the schools? If so, should students be prevented from wearing gang clothing? Or, do you think gang clothing should be covered by the right to freedom of expression? If you were given the authority to make a decision concerning the wearing of gang colors and clothing in the schools in your community, what would you decide? What arguments would you use to defend your decision? How do you feel about school uniforms for elementary school children? For junior and senior high school students?

there are so many ethnic groups, you regularly see examples of dress that tell you from what country the wearers have come.

The very poor and the very rich do not dress in the same way, nor do white- and blue-collar workers or the young and the old (Lurie 1983). People dress, in part at least, to identify with the groups of which they are or want to be members.

Similarly, college students will perceive an instructor dressed informally as friendly, fair, enthusiastic, and flexible, and the same instructor dressed formally as prepared, knowledgeable, and organized (Malandro, Barker, and Barker 1989).

Your jewelry likewise communicates messages about you. Wedding and engagement rings are obvious examples of jewelry that communicate very specific messages. College rings and political buttons also communicate specific messages. If you wear a Rolex watch or large precious stones, others are likely to infer that you are rich. Men with earrings will be judged differently from men without earrings.

The way you wear your hair communicates who you are. Your hair may communicate a concern for being up-to-date, a desire to shock, or perhaps a lack of concern for appearances. Men with long hair will generally be judged as less conservative than men with shorter hair.

In a study on interpersonal attraction, slides of male and female models were shown with and without glasses and were evaluated by both men and women. Results indicated that persons with glasses were rated more negatively than the same persons without glasses (Hasart and Hutchinson 1993).

Clothing also seems to influence your own behavior and the behavior of groups. For example, it has been argued that people who dress casually act more informally (Morland, 1995). Therefore, meetings with such casually dressed people are more likely to involve a freer exchange of thoughts and ideas which stimulates creativity. This casual attire seems to work well in companies that must rely heavily on creative developments such as a computer software company. It's interesting to note in this connection that it was only very recently that IBM relaxed its conservative dress code and allowed some measure of informal dress among its workers (*New York Times,* February 7, 1995, p. B1). But banks and insurance companies, which traditionally have resisted change, prefer a more formal attire that creates distance between workers as well as between employees and customers.

Look carefully at the way you're dressed right now. What messages does your clothing (including your jewelry, hairstyle, makeup, and the colors you're wearing) communicate? Does it communicate different messages to different (types of) people? Are these the messages you want to communicate? What inferences about you would people make on seeing your home?

Artifacts and Culture: The Case of Gifts

An aspect of artifactual communication that is frequently overlooked is the giving of gifts, a practice in which rules and customs vary according to each culture. Here are a few situations where gift giving backfired and created barriers rather than bonds. These examples are designed to heighten your awareness of both the importance of gift giving and of recognizing intercultural differences. What might have gone wrong in each of these situations? These few examples should serve to illustrate the wide variations that exist among cultures in the meaning given to artifacts and in the seemingly simple process of giving gifts (Axtell 1990a, Dresser 1996).

1. You bring chrysanthemums to a Belgian colleague and a clock to a Chinese colleague. Both react negatively.
2. Upon meeting an Arab businessman for the first time—someone with whom you wish to do considerable business—you present him with a gift. He seems to become disturbed. To smooth things over, when you go to visit him and his family in Oman, you bring a bottle of your favorite brandy for after dinner. Your host seems even more disturbed now.
3. Arriving for dinner at the home of a Kenya colleague, you present flowers as a dinner gift. Your host accepts them politely but looks puzzled. The next evening you visit your Swiss colleague and bring 14 red roses. Your host accepts them politely but looks strangely at you. Figuring that the red got you in trouble, on your third evening out you bring yellow roses to your Iranian friend. Again, there was a similar reaction.

4. You give your Chinese friend a set of dinner knives as a gift but she doesn't open it in front of you; you get offended. After she opens it, she gets offended.

5. You bring your Mexican friend a statue of an elephant drinking water from a lake. Your friend says he cannot accept it; his expressions tell you he really doesn't want it.

Possible reasons:

1. Chrysanthemums in Belgium and clocks in China are both reminders of death and that time is running out.
2. Gifts given at the first meeting may be interpreted as a bribe and thus should be avoided. Further, alcohol is prohibited by Islamic law, so should be avoided when selecting gifts for most Arabs.
3. In Kenya, flowers are only brought to express condolence. In Switzerland red roses are a sign of romantic interest. Also, an even number of flowers (or 13) is generally considered bad luck, so should be avoided. Yellow flowers to Iranians signify the enemy and mean that you dislike them.
4. The custom in China is simply not to open gifts in front of the donor. Knives (and scissors) symbolize the severing of a relationship.
5. Among many Latin Americans the elephant's upward trunk symbolizes a holding of good luck; an elephant's downward trunk symbolizes luck slipping away.

 The "Pygmalion gift" is one that is designed to change the person into what the donor wants that person to become. The parent who gives a child books or science equipment may be asking the child to be a scholar. What messages have you recently communicated in your gift-giving behavior? What messages do you think others communicated to you by the gifts they gave you?

Temporal Communication

The study of temporal communication (**chronemics**) focuses on the use of time—how you organize it, how you react to it, and the messages it communicates. Time can be viewed from two major perspectives: cultural and psychological.

Cultural Time

Generally, three types of cultural time are identified (Hall 1959). **Technical time** is precise, scientific time. Milliseconds and atomic years are examples of units of technical or scientific time. This time system is used only in the laboratory, so it seems to have little relevance to our daily lives.

Formal time refers to the manner in which a culture defines time. In the United States, time is divided into seconds, minutes, hours, days, weeks, months, and years. Other cultures use phases of the moon or the seasons to delineate time periods. College courses are divided into 50- or 75-minute periods that meet at various times each week for 10- or 14-week periods called quarters or semesters. A certain number of quarters or semesters equal a college education. Formal time units are arbitrary and have been established by the culture for reasons of convenience.

Informal time refers to a rather loose use of time terms—for example, words such as "forever," "immediately," "soon," "right away," and "as soon as possible." This is the aspect of time that creates the most communication problems because the terms have different meanings for different people.

Displaced and Diffused Time Orientations   Another important distinction can be drawn between displaced and diffused time orientations (Hall 1959). In a **displaced time orientation**, time is viewed exactly. Persons with this orientation will be exactly on time. In a **diffused time orientation**, time is seen as approximate rather than exact. People with this orientation are usually late for appointments because they understand, for example, a scheduled time of 8:00 P.M. as meaning anywhere from 7:45 to 8:15 or 8:30.

Even the accuracy of clocks varies in different cultures and probably reflects each culture's time orientation. In one study (LeVine and Bartlett 1984), clocks in Japan were found to be the most accurate, while clocks in Indonesia were least accurate. Clocks in England, Italy, Taiwan, and the United States fell between these two extremes in accuracy. Not surprisingly, when the speed of pedestrians in these countries was measured, the Japanese were found to walk the fastest and the Indonesians the slowest. Such differences reflect the different ways in which cultures treat time and their general attitude toward the importance of time in everyday life.

Monochronism and Polychronism Another important distinction is that between **monochronic** and **polychronic time orientations** (Hall 1959, 1976, Hall and Hall 1987). Monochronic people or cultures (the United States, Germany, Scandinavia, and Switzerland are good examples) schedule one thing at a time. Time is compartmentalized; there is a time for everything, and everything has its own time. Polychronic people or cultures (Latin Americans, Mediterranean people, and Arabs are good examples), on the other hand, schedule a number of things at the same time. Eating, conducting business with several different people, and taking care of family matters may all be conducted at the same time. No culture is entirely monochronic or polychronic; rather these are general tendencies that are found across a large part of the culture. Some cultures combine both time orientations; Japanese and parts of American culture are examples where both orientations are found. Table 13.4, based on Hall and Hall (1987) identifies some of the distinctions between these two time orientations.

The Social Clock An especially interesting aspect of cultural time is your "social clock" (Neugarten 1979). Your culture and your more specific society maintains a time schedule for the right time to do a variety of important things, for

Table 13.4	Monochronic and Polychronic Time

As you read down this table note the potential for miscommunication that these differences might create when M-time and P-time people interact. Has this difference ever created interpersonal misunderstandings for you?

The Monochronic Person	The Polychronic Person
Does one thing at a time.	Does several things at one time.
Treats time schedules and plans very seriously; they may only be broken for the most serious of reasons.	Treats time schedules and plans as useful (not sacred); they may be broken for a variety of causes.
Considers the job the most important part of one's life, ahead of even family.	Considers the family and interpersonal relationships more important than the job.
Considers privacy extremely important, seldom borrows or lends to others, works independently.	Is actively involved with others, works in the presence of and with lots of people at the same time.

How important is the clock? Is the social clock more important to men or to women?

example, the right time to start dating, to finish college, to buy your own home, to have a child. And you no doubt learned about this clock as you were growing up. On this basis of this social clock you then evaluate your own social and professional development. If you are on time with the rest of your peers—for example, you all started dating at around the same age or you're all finishing college at around the same age—then you will feel well adjusted, competent, and a part of the group. If you are late, you will probably experience feelings of dissatisfaction.

Psychological Time

Psychological time refers to the importance placed on the past, present, or future. In a **past orientation**, you give particular reverence to the past; you might relive old times and regard the old methods as the best. Events are seen as circular and recurring, so that the wisdom of yesterday is applicable also to today and tomorrow. In a **present orientation**, you live in the present for the present. Present activities command your attention; you engage in them not for their future rewards or their past significance but because they are happening now. In its extreme form, this orientation is hedonistic. In a **future orientation**, you give primary attention to the future. You save today, work hard in college, and deny yourself certain enjoyments and luxuries, all because you are preparing for the future.

Researchers have provided some interesting correlations to these different time orientations (Gonzalez and Zimbardo 1985; Rappaport, Enrich, and Wilson 1985). Before reading their conclusions, you may wish to take the self-test "What Time Do You Have?"

One of the findings of this time study is that future income is positively related to future orientation. The more future-oriented a person is, the greater that person's income is likely to be. Present orientation is strongest among lowest-income males.

The time orientation that people develop depends a great deal on their socioeconomic class and personal experiences. Gonzalez and Zimbardo (1985) observe: "A child with parents in unskilled and semi-skilled occupations is usually socialized in a way that promotes a present-oriented fatalism and hedonism. A child of parents who are managers, teachers, or other professionals learns future-oriented values and strategies designed to promote achievement."

Different time perspectives also account for much intercultural misunderstanding, because different cultures often teach their members drastically different time orientations. The future-oriented person who works for tomorrow's goals will frequently look down on the present-oriented person who focuses on enjoying today as being lazy and poorly motivated. In turn, the present-oriented person may see those with strong future orientations as obsessed with accumulating wealth or rising in status.

Another type of time is biological time, which refers to your body clock, the ways your body functions differently at different times. Your intellectual, physical, and emotional lives, according to theories of biorhythms, are lived in cycles. During the up cycle, we function at our best; during the down cycle we function less effectively; and during the changes from an up to a down cycle, we are especially vulnerable to, for example, writer's block, catching cold, or feeling depressed. What do you think of this theory? Detailed explanations and instructions for calculating your biorhythms (your own intellectual, physical, and emotional cycles) can be found in Luce (1971), O'Neil and Phillips (1975), Mallardi (1978), and DeVito (1989).

Time and Status

Time is especially linked to status considerations. For example, the importance of being on time varies with the status of the individual you are visiting. If the person is extremely important, you had better be there on time or even early just in case he or she is able to see you before schedule. As the person's status decreases, so does the importance of being on time. Junior executives, for example, must be on time for conferences with senior executives, but it is even more important to

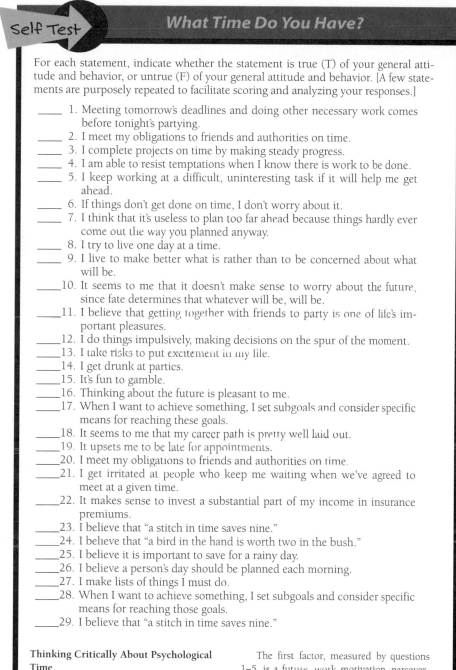

Self Test

What Time Do You Have?

For each statement, indicate whether the statement is true (T) of your general attitude and behavior, or untrue (F) of your general attitude and behavior. [A few statements are purposely repeated to facilitate scoring and analyzing your responses.]

_____ 1. Meeting tomorrow's deadlines and doing other necessary work comes before tonight's partying.

_____ 2. I meet my obligations to friends and authorities on time.

_____ 3. I complete projects on time by making steady progress.

_____ 4. I am able to resist temptations when I know there is work to be done.

_____ 5. I keep working at a difficult, uninteresting task if it will help me get ahead.

_____ 6. If things don't get done on time, I don't worry about it.

_____ 7. I think that it's useless to plan too far ahead because things hardly ever come out the way you planned anyway.

_____ 8. I try to live one day at a time.

_____ 9. I live to make better what is rather than to be concerned about what will be.

_____10. It seems to me that it doesn't make sense to worry about the future, since fate determines that whatever will be, will be.

_____11. I believe that getting together with friends to party is one of life's important pleasures.

_____12. I do things impulsively, making decisions on the spur of the moment.

_____13. I take risks to put excitement in my life.

_____14. I get drunk at parties.

_____15. It's fun to gamble.

_____16. Thinking about the future is pleasant to me.

_____17. When I want to achieve something, I set subgoals and consider specific means for reaching these goals.

_____18. It seems to me that my career path is pretty well laid out.

_____19. It upsets me to be late for appointments.

_____20. I meet my obligations to friends and authorities on time.

_____21. I get irritated at people who keep me waiting when we've agreed to meet at a given time.

_____22. It makes sense to invest a substantial part of my income in insurance premiums.

_____23. I believe that "a stitch in time saves nine."

_____24. I believe that "a bird in the hand is worth two in the bush."

_____25. I believe it is important to save for a rainy day.

_____26. I believe a person's day should be planned each morning.

_____27. I make lists of things I must do.

_____28. When I want to achieve something, I set subgoals and consider specific means for reaching those goals.

_____29. I believe that "a stitch in time saves nine."

Thinking Critically About Psychological Time

This psychological time test measures seven factors. If you scored true for all or most of the questions within any given factor, then you are probably high on that factor. If you scored false for all or most of the questions within any given factor, then you are probably low on that factor.

The first factor, measured by questions 1–5, is a future, work motivation, perseverance orientation. People with this orientation have a strong work ethic and are committed to completing a task despite difficulties and temptations.

The second factor, measured by questions 6–10, is a present, fatalistic, worry-free orientation. People who score high on this factor live one day at a time, not necessarily to enjoy the day but to avoid planning for the next day and to avoid the anxiety about a future that seems determined by fate rather than by anything they can do themselves.

The third factor, measured by questions 11–15, is a present, hedonistic, pleasure-seeking, partying orientation. People with this orientation seek to enjoy the present, take risks, and engage in a variety of impulsive actions. Teenagers score particularly high on this factor.

The fourth factor, measured by questions 16–18, is a future, goal-seeking and planning orientation. People with this orientation derive special pleasure from planning and achieving a variety of goals.

The fifth factor, measured by questions 19–21, is a time sensitivity orientation. People who score high on this factor are especially sensitive to time and its role in social obligations.

The sixth factor, measured by questions 22–25, is a future, pragmatic action orientation. People with this orientation do what they have to do to achieve the future they want. They take practical actions for future gain.

The seventh factor, measured by questions 26–29, is a future, somewhat obsessive daily planning orientation. People who score high on this factor make daily "to do" lists, and devote great attention to specific details and subordinate goals.

Adapted from: "Time in Perspective," by A. Gonzalez and P. Zimbardo, *Psychology Today,* March 1985. Copyright © 1985 by Sussex Publishers, Inc. Reprinted by permission of *Psychology Today.*

be on time for the company president or the CEO. Senior executives, however, may be late for conferences with their juniors but not for conferences with the president. Within any hierarchy, similar unwritten rules are followed with respect to time. This is not to imply that these "rules" are just or fair; they simply exist.

Even the dinner hour and the period between a guest's arrival and the time when dinner is served varies according to status. Among lower-status individuals, dinner is served relatively early. If there are guests, they eat soon after they arrive. For higher-status people, dinner is relatively late, and a longer period elapses between arrival and eating—usually the time it takes to consume two cocktails.

Summary   U N I T   I N   B R I E F

A RETURN TO OBJECTIVES:

In this unit we continued our study of nonverbal communication and considered several additional types of nonverbal messages: (1) How do we communicate with spatial relationships? (2) What messages does territoriality communicate? (3) How do we communicate with artifacts, for example, with space decoration, color, and clothing and body adornment? (4) What messages does time communicate?

Proxemic Distance	Territoriality	Artifactual Communication	Temporal Communication
Types of Distances: Intimate (touching to 18 inches) Personal (18 inches to 4 feet) Social (4 to 12 feet) Public (12 or more feet) **Theories About Space:** Protection Equilibrium Expectancy Violations	**Signaling ownership:** ◆ The home field advantage ◆ Markers (central, boundary, ear) Signaling status	**Space decoration:** Influences perceptions of energy, time, status, and personal characteristics. **Colors:** Communicate different meanings depending on the culture. **Clothing and body adornment:** Serve especially as cultural display. **Artifacts:** Communicate different meanings in different cultures.	**Cultural time:** Technical, formal, and informal. ◆ Displaced and diffused time orientations identify how accurately time is viewed. ◆ Monochronic people do one thing at a time and polychronic people do several things at the same time. **Psychological time:** Past, present, and future orientation.

UNIT

14 Messages and Conversation

Unit Topics	Unit Objectives
	After completing this unit, you should be able to:
The Conversational Process Opening Feedforward Business Feedback Closing Reflections on the Five Stages of Conversation	1. Describe the five-step model of conversation
Conversational Management Initiating Conversations Maintaining Conversations Closing Conversations	2. Explain the processes of initiating, maintaining, and closing conversations
Conversational Problems: Prevention and Repair Preventing Conversational Problems: The Disclaimer Repairing Conversational Problems: The Excuse	3. Define the *disclaimer* and the *excuse* and explain their role in preventing and repairing conversational problems

---

EXPERIENTIAL LEARNING VEHICLES

Experiential Learning Vehicle No. 14, "Conversational Analysis: A Chance Meeting," pp. 454–456 can be used to illustrate the process of conversation and conversational management.

No. 15, "Giving and Taking Directions," pp. 456–458, is useful in illustrating some of the difficulties experienced in conversation.

Interpersonal researcher Margaret McLaughlin (1984) defines conversation as "relatively informal social interaction in which the roles of speaker and hearer are exchanged in a nonautomatic fashion under the collaborative management of all parties." Examining conversation provides an excellent opportunity to look at verbal and nonverbal messages as they are used in day-to-day communications, and thus serves as a useful summary for this second part of the text.

Before reading about the process of conversation, think of your own conversations, the ones that were satisfactory and the ones that were unsatisfactory. Think of a specific recent conversation as you respond to the accompanying self-test, "How Satisfactory Is Your Conversation?" Taking this test now will help highlight the characteristics of conversational behavior and what makes some conversations satisfying and others unsatisfying.

The Conversational Process

Conversation takes place in at least five steps: opening, feedforward, business, feedback, and closing (see Figure 14.1). It is convenient to divide any act—and conversation is no exception—into chunks or stages and view each stage as requiring a choice of what to say and how to say it. In this model the conversation process is divided into five stages, each of which requires that you make a choice as to what you'll do. So, as you read the discussion of these stages visualize a specific encounter that you will have in the near future and consider the choices you would make at each stage.

Opening

The first step is to open the conversation, usually with some kind of greeting: "Hi. How are you?" "Hello, this is Joe." The greeting is a good example of what we earlier called *phatic communication* (Unit 1). It is a message that establishes a connection between two people and opens the channels for more meaningful interaction. Greetings, of course, may be nonverbal as well as verbal. A smile, kiss, or handshake may be as clear an opening as "Hello."

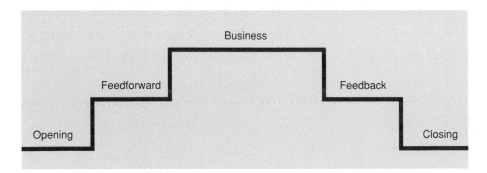

Figure 14.1   A Five-Step Model of Conversation.
This model of the stages of conversation is best seen as a way of talking about conversation and not as the unvarying stages all conversations follow. As you review the model, consider how accurately it depicts conversation as you experience it. Can you develop a more accurate and more revealing model?

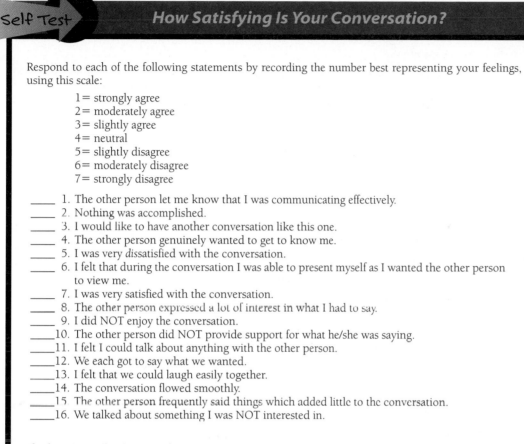

Self Test

How Satisfying Is Your Conversation?

Respond to each of the following statements by recording the number best representing your feelings, using this scale:

1 = strongly agree
2 = moderately agree
3 = slightly agree
4 = neutral
5 = slightly disagree
6 = moderately disagree
7 = strongly disagree

_____ 1. The other person let me know that I was communicating effectively.
_____ 2. Nothing was accomplished.
_____ 3. I would like to have another conversation like this one.
_____ 4. The other person genuinely wanted to get to know me.
_____ 5. I was very *dissatisfied* with the conversation.
_____ 6. I felt that during the conversation I was able to present myself as I wanted the other person to view me.
_____ 7. I was very satisfied with the conversation.
_____ 8. The other person expressed a lot of interest in what I had to say.
_____ 9. I did NOT enjoy the conversation.
_____10. The other person did NOT provide support for what he/she was saying.
_____11. I felt I could talk about anything with the other person.
_____12. We each got to say what we wanted.
_____13. I felt that we could laugh easily together.
_____14. The conversation flowed smoothly.
_____15. The other person frequently said things which added little to the conversation.
_____16. We talked about something I was NOT interested in.

Thinking Critically About Satisfying Conversations

To compute your score, follow these steps:

1. Add the scores for items 1, 3, 4, 6, 7, 8, 11, 12, 13, and 14.
2. Reverse the scores for items 2, 5, 9, 10, 15, and 16 so that 7 becomes 1, 6 becomes 2, 5 becomes 3, 4 remains 4, 3 becomes 5, 2 becomes 6, and 1 becomes 7.
3. Add the reversed scores for items 2, 5, 9, 10, 15, and 16.
4. Add the totals from Steps 1 and 3 to yield your communication satisfaction score.

You may interpret your score along the following scale:

16	32	48	64	80	96	112
Extremely Satisfying	Quite Satisfying	Fairly Satisfying	Average	Fairly Unsatisfying	Quite Unsatisfying	Extremely Unsatisfying

How accurately do you think this scale captures conversational satisfaction? Before reading the remainder of this unit, try to identify those qualities that make a conversation satisfying for you. What interpersonal qualities are most important to making a person a satisfying conversational partner?

This test was developed by Michael Hecht, "The Conceptualization and Measurement of Interpersonal Communication Satisfaction," *Human Communication Research* 4 (1978):253–264 and is reprinted by permission of the author.

In normal conversation, the greeting is reciprocated with a greeting similar in degree of formality and intensity. When it isn't—when the other person turns away or responds coldly to your friendly "Good morning"—you know something is wrong.

Openings are also generally consistent in tone with the main part of the conversation; a cheery "How ya doing today, big guy?" is not normally followed by news of a family death.

Feedforward

At the second step, you usually provide some kind of feedforward, which gives the other person a general idea of the conversation's focus: "I've got to tell you about Jack," "Did you hear what happened in class yesterday?" or "We need to talk about our vacation plans."

Feedforward may also identify the tone of the conversation ("I'm really depressed and need to talk with you") or the time required ("This will just take a minute") (Frentz 1976; Reardon 1987).

Business

At the third step, you talk "business," the substance or focus of the conversation. The term "business" is used to emphasize that most conversations are goal directed; you converse to fulfill one or several of the general purposes of interpersonal communication: to learn, relate, influence, play, or help (see Unit 1). The term is also sufficiently general to incorporate all kinds of interactions. The business is conducted through an exchange of speaker and listener roles. Brief, rather than long, speaking turns characterize most satisfying conversations. Here you talk about Jack, what happened in class, or your vacation plans. This is obviously the longest part of the conversation and the reason for the opening and the feedforward.

Not surprisingly, each culture has its own conversational taboos, topics that should be avoided, especially by visitors from other cultures. Table 14.1 identifies several examples that Roger Axtell in *Do's and Taboos Around the World* (1993) recommends that visitors from the United States avoid.

Feedback

The fourth step is the reverse of the second. Here you reflect back on the conversation to signal that as far as you're concerned the business is completed: "So you want to send Jack a get-well card," "Wasn't that the craziest class you ever heard of ?" or "I'll call for reservations, and you'll shop for what we need."

Of course, the other person may not agree that the business has been completed and may therefore counter with, for example, "But what hospital is he in?" When this happens, you normally go back a step and continue the business.

Closing

The fifth and last step, the opposite of the first step, is the closing, the good-bye, which often reveals how satisfied the persons are with the conversation: "I hope you'll call soon" or "Don't call us, we'll call you." The closing may also be used to

Table 14.1	Conversational Taboos Around the World

Do realize that these examples are not intended to be exhaustive. Rather, they are presented as a reminder that each culture defines what is and what is not an appropriate topic of conversation.

Culture	Conversational Taboos
Belgium	Politics, language differences between French and Flemish, religion
Norway	Salaries, social status
Spain	Family, religion, jobs, negative comments on bullfighting
Egypt	Middle Eastern politics
Nigeria	Religion
Libya	Politics, religion
Iraq	Religion, Middle Eastern politics
Japan	World War II
Pakistan	Politics
Philippines	Politics, religion, corruption, foreign aid
South Korea	Internal politics, criticism of the government, socialism or communism
Bolivia	Politics, religion
Colombia	Politics, criticism of bullfighting
Mexico	Mexican-American War, illegal aliens
Caribbean	Race, local politics, religion

Can you identify additional taboo topics?

schedule future conversations: "Give me a call tomorrow night" or "Let's meet for lunch at twelve."

Reflections on the Five Stages of Conversation

Not all conversations are easily divided into these five steps. Often the opening and the feedforward are combined, as when you see someone on campus, for example, and say, "Hey, listen to this" or when, in a work situation, someone says, "Well, folks, let's get the meeting going." In a similar way, the feedback and the closing might be combined: "Look, I've got to think more about this commitment, OK?"

As already noted, the business is the longest part of the conversation. The opening and the closing are usually about the same length, as are the feedforward and feedback. When these relative lengths are severely distorted, you quickly get the feeling that something is wrong. For example, when someone uses a long feedforward or too short an opening, you suspect that what is to follow is extremely serious.

This model may also help to identify conversation skill deficits and to distinguish effective and satisfying from ineffective and unsatisfying conversations. Think about the following violations and how they can damage an entire conversation. What meanings might each communicate? What impressions of the speaker is the listener likely to develop?

- ◆ Using openings that are insensitive, for example, "Wow, you've gained a few pounds."
- ◆ Using overly long feedforwards that make you wonder whether the other person will ever get to the business.

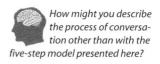

How might you describe the process of conversation other than with the five-step model presented here?

Family meals are in great part conversational experiences. Can you use the five-stage model of conversation presented here to describe the conversations that you have during meals? How do business lunches differ from family meals in terms of the conversation taking place?

- Omitting feedforward before a truly shocking message (for example, the death or illness of a friend or relative), an omission that leads you to see the other person as insensitive or uncaring.
- Doing business without the normally expected greeting, as when you go to a doctor who begins the conversation by saying, "Well, what's wrong?"
- Omitting feedback, which leads you to wonder whether the other person heard what you said or cared about it.
- Omitting an appropriate closing, which makes you wonder whether the other person is disturbed or angry with you.

Of course, each culture will alter these basic steps in different ways. In some cultures, the openings are especially short, whereas in others they are elaborate, lengthy, and sometimes highly ritualized. It is all too easy to violate another culture's conversational rules. Being overly friendly, too formal, or too forward may easily hinder the remainder of the conversation.

Such violations may have significant consequences if people are not mindful (see Unit 8) of these rules and hence do not see violations simply as cultural differences. Rather, we might see the rule violator as aggressive, stuffy, or pushy—and almost immediately dislike the person and put a negative cast on future conversation.

Conversational Management

Speakers and listeners have to work together to make conversation an effective and satisfying experience. They do so by managing conversations in terms of initiating, maintaining, and closing them.

Initiating Conversations

Opening a conversation is especially difficult. Often you may not be sure what to say or how to say it. You may fear being rejected or having someone misunderstand your meaning. Several approaches to opening a conversation can be derived from the elements of the interpersonal communication process discussed in Unit 1:

◆ *Self-references* say something about yourself. Such references may be of the name-rank-and-serial-number type—for example: "My name is Joe. I'm from Omaha." On the first day of class, students might say, "I'm worried about this class" or "I took this instructor last semester; she was excellent."
◆ *Other-references* say something about the other person or ask a question: "I like that sweater." "Didn't we meet at Charlie's?" Of course, there are pitfalls here as well. Generally, it is best not to comment on the person's race ("My uncle married a Korean"), the person's affectional orientation ("Nice to meet you; I have a gay brother"), or physical disability ("It must be awful to be confined to a wheelchair").
◆ *Relational references* say something about the two of you: for example, "May I buy you a drink?" "Would you like to dance?" or simply "May I join you?"
◆ *Context references* say something about the physical, social-psychological, cultural, or temporal context. The familiar "Do you have the time?" is a reference of this type. But you can be more creative and say, for example, "This place seems very friendly" or "That painting is just great."

Keep in mind two general rules. First, be positive. Lead off with something positive rather than something negative. Say, for example, "I really enjoy coming here" instead of "Don't you just hate this place?" Second, do not be too revealing; don't self-disclose too early in an interaction. If you do, you risk making the other person feel uncomfortable.

The Opening Line   Another way of looking at the process of initiating conversations is to examine the infamous "opening line," the opener designed to begin a romantic-type relationship. Interpersonal researcher Chris Kleinke (1986) finds that opening lines are of three basic types:

◆ *Cute-flippant* openers are humorous, indirect, and ambiguous as to whether the one opening the conversation actually wants an extended encounter. Examples include "Is that really your hair?" "Bet I can outdrink you." "I bet the cherry jubilee isn't as sweet as you are."
◆ *Innocuous* openers are highly ambiguous as to whether they are simple comments that might be made to just anyone or whether they are in fact openers designed to initiate an extended encounter. Examples include "What do you think of the band?" "I haven't been here before." "What's good on the menu?" "Could you show me how to work this machine?"
◆ *Direct* openers clearly demonstrate the speaker's interest in meeting the other person. Examples include: "I feel a little embarrassed about this, but I'd like to meet you. Would you like to have a drink after dinner? Since we're both eating alone, would you like to join me?"

What methods other than those described in this unit seem to work for opening a conversation? Which openers do you especially resent? Why? How would your conversational openers differ if you wanted to establish a friendship and if you wanted to establish a romantic relationship?

The opening lines most preferred by both men and women are generally those that are direct or innocuous (Kleinke 1986). The least preferred lines by both men and women are those that are cute-flippant; women dislike these openers even more than men do. Men generally underestimate how much women dislike the cute-flippant openers but probably continue to use them because they are indirect enough to cushion any rejection. Men also underestimate how much women actually like innocuous openers.

Women prefer men to use openers that are relatively modest and to avoid coming on too strong. Women generally underestimate how much men like direct openers. Most men prefer openers that are very clear in meaning, possibly because men are not used to having a woman initiate a meeting. Women also overestimate how much men like innocuous lines.

In Unit 16, initiating an interaction is again considered in the context of relationship development.

Are there cultural differences in the preference for opening lines? How would you go about investigating this question?

Think about how you might open a conversation with the persons described in each of these situations. What general approaches would meet with a favorable response? What general approaches seem frowned on?

1. On the first day of class, you and another student are the first to come into the classroom and are seated in the room alone.
2. You are a guest at a friend's party. You are one of the first guests to arrive and are now there with several other people to whom you have only just been introduced. Your friend, the host, is busy with other matters.
3. You have just started a new job in a large office where you are one of several computer operators. It seems as if most of the other people know each other.
4. You are in the college cafeteria eating alone. You see another student who is also eating alone and who you have seen in your English literature class. You're not sure if this person has noticed you in class.

Maintaining Conversations

In maintaining conversations you follow a variety of principles and rules. Here we give an example of a general principle you follow and its several maxims and the ways in which the speaker and listener turns are exchanged in conversation.

The Principle of Cooperation   During conversation you probably follow the principle of cooperation, agreeing with the other person to cooperate in trying to understand what each is saying (Grice 1975). If you didn't agree to cooperate, then communication would be extremely difficult, if not impossible. You cooperate largely by using four conversational maxims—principles that speakers and listeners in the United States and in many other cultures follow in conversation. Although the names for these maxims may be new, the principles themselves will be easily recognized from your own experiences.

The Maxim of Quantity   You follow the maxim of quantity when you are only as informative as necessary to communicate the intended meaning. Thus, you include information that makes the meaning clear but omit what does not. In following this principle, you give neither too little nor too much information. You see people violate this maxim when they try to relate an incident and digress to give unnecessary information. You find yourself thinking or saying, "Get to the point; so what happened?" This maxim is also violated when necessary information is omitted. In this situation, you find yourself constantly interrupting to ask questions: "Where were they?" "When did this happen?" "Who else was there?"

The Maxim of Quality   You follow the maxim of quality by saying what you know or assume to be true and by not saying what you know to be false. When you are in conversation, you assume that the other person's information is true—at least as far as he or she knows. When you speak with people who frequently violate this principle by lying, exaggerating, or minimizing major problems, you come to distrust what the person is saying and wonder what is true and what is fabricated.

The Maxim of Relation   You follow the maxim of relation when you talk about what is relevant to the conversation. Thus, if you are talking about Pat and Chris and say, for example, "Money causes all sorts of relationship problems," it is assumed by others that your comment is somehow related to Pat and Chris. This principle is frequently violated by speakers who digress widely and frequently interject irrelevant comments.

The Maxim of Manner   You follow the maxim of manner by being clear, by avoiding ambiguities, by being relatively brief, and by organizing your thoughts into a meaningful sequence. Thus, you use terms that the listener understands and omit or clarify terms that you suspect the listener will not understand. You use this maxim when you adjust your speech on the basis of your listener. For example, when talking to a close friend you can refer to mutual acquaintances and to experiences you've shared. When talking to a stranger, however, you either omit such references or explain them. Similarly, when talking with a child, you would simplify your vocabulary so that the child would understand your meaning.

Conversational Maxims and Culture   The four maxims just discussed aptly describe most conversations as they take place in much of the United States. Recognize, however, that these maxims may not apply in all cultures, and other cultures may have other maxims. Some of these maxims may contradict the advice generally given to persons communicating in the United States or in other cultures (Keenan 1976). Here are a few maxims appropriate in cultures other than the United States, but also appropriate to some degree throughout the United States.

Which conversational maxim do you think is the most important? Which do you think is the most frequently violated? Can you identify additional maxims followed by a particular culture?

   In research on Japanese conversations and group discussions, a maxim of preserving peaceful relationships with others may be noted (Midooka 1990). The ways in which such peaceful relationships may be maintained will vary with the person with whom you are interacting. For example, in Japan, your status or position in the hierarchy will influence the amount of self-expression you are expected to engage in. Similarly, there is a great distinction between public and private conversations. This maxim is much more important in public than it is in private conversations, in which the maxim may be and often is violated.

   The maxim of self-denigration, observed in the conversations of Chinese speakers, may require that you avoid taking credit for some accomplishment or make less of some ability or talent you have (Gu 1990). To put yourself down in

In New York City, politeness between cab drivers and riders has never been especially high and has prompted a great deal of criticism. To combat this negative attitude, cab drivers have been give 50 polite phrases and are instructed to use these frequently: "May I open (close) the window for you?" "Madam (Sir), is the temperature O.K. for you?" "I'm sorry, I made a wrong turn. I'll take care of it, and we can deduct it from the fare" (New York Times May 6, 1996, p. B1). What other groups would you like to see get a list of polite phrases to use? Try writing 5 or 10 of these phrases for any specific group.

this way is a form of politeness that seeks to elevate the person to whom you are speaking.

The maxim of politeness is probably universal across all cultures (Brown and Levinson 1988). Cultures differ, however, in how they define politeness and in how important politeness is compared with, say, openness or honesty. Cultures also differ in the rules for expressing politeness or impoliteness and in the punishments for violating the accepted rules of politeness (Mao 1994; Strecker 1993).

Asian cultures, especially Chinese and Japanese, are often singled out because they emphasize politeness more and mete out harsher social punishments for violations than would most people in, say, the United States or Western Europe. This has led some to propose that a maxim of politeness operates in Asian cultures (Fraser 1990). When this maxim operates, it may actually violate other maxims. For example, the maxim of politeness may require that you not tell the truth, a situation that would violate the maxim of quality.

There are also large gender differences (and some similarities) in the expression of politeness (Holmes 1995). Generally, studies from a number of different cultures show that women use more polite forms than men (Brown 1980; Wetzel 1988; Holmes 1995). For example, in informal conversation and in conflict situations women tend to seek areas of agreement more than do men. Young girls are more apt to try to modify disagreements while young boys are more apt to express more "bald disagreements" (Holmes 1995). There are also similarities. For example, both men and women in both the United States and New Zealand seem to pay compliments in similar ways (Manes and Wolfson 1981; Holmes 1986, 1995)

What were you explicitly taught about politeness from your family and teachers? How were you taught these rules (for example, explicitly or by example)?

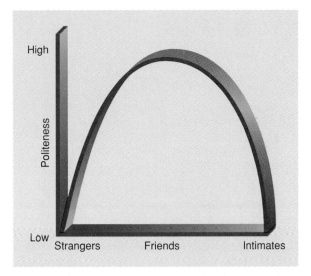

Figure 14.2 Wolfson's Bulge Model of Politeness.
Do you find this model a generally accurate representation of your own level of politeness in different types of relationships? Can you build a case for an inverted U theory (where politeness would be high for both strangers and intimates and low for friends)?

and both men and women use politeness strategies when communicating bad news in an organization (Lee 1993).

Politeness also varies with the type of relationship. One researcher, for example, has proposed that politeness is greatest with friends and considerably less with strangers and intimates and depicts this relationship as in Figure 14.2 (Wolfson 1988; Holmes 1995).

Conversational Turns   The defining feature of conversation is that the speaker and listener exchange roles throughout the interaction. You accomplish this through a wide variety of verbal and nonverbal cues that signal conversational turns—the changing (or maintaining) of the speaker or listener role during the conversation. Combining the insights of a variety of communication researchers (Duncan 1972; Burgoon, Buller, and Woodall 1989; Pearson and Spitzberg 1990), we can look at conversational turns in terms of cues that speakers use and cues that listeners use.

Speaker Cues   You regulate conversation through two major types of cues: turn-maintaining cues and turn-yielding cues. As the term implies, **turn-maintaining cues** are designed to enable you to maintain the speaker role. You can do this with a variety of cues, for example, audibly inhaling to show that you have more to say, continuing a gesture or gestures to show that you have not completed the thought, avoiding eye contact with the listener so there is no indication that you are passing the speaking turn to him or her, sustaining your intonation pattern to indicate that you intend to say more, or vocalizing pauses ("er," "umm") to prevent the listener from speaking and to show that you are still talking (Duncan 1972; Burgoon, Buller, and Woodall 1989).

In most cases, speakers are expected to maintain relatively brief speaking turns and to turn over the speaking role willingly to the listener (when so signaled by the listener). Those who don't are generally perceived as egocentric bores.

With **turn-yielding cues** you tell the listener that you are finished and wish to exchange the role of speaker for that of listener. These cues tell the listener

MEDIA & TECHNOLOGY

THE RULES OF NETIQUETTE

The rules of netiquette are the rules for communicating politely over the Internet. Much as the rules of etiquette provide guidance in communicating in social situations, the rules of netiquette provide guidance for communicating over the Net. These rules, as you'll see, are helpful for making Internet communication more pleasant and easier, for achieving greater personal efficiency, and for putting less strain on the system and on other users. Here are several guidelines suggested by computer researchers (Shea 1994; James and Weingarten 1995; *Time,* special issue, Spring 1995).

◆ Read the FAQs. Before asking questions about the system, read the Frequently Asked Questions; your question has probably been asked before and you'll put less strain on the system.

◆ Don't shout. WRITING IN CAPS IS PERCEIVED AS SHOUTING. It's okay to use caps occasionally to achieve emphasis. If you wish to give emphasis underline, –like this–, or *like this*

◆ Lurk before speaking. Lurking refers to reading the posted notices and reading the conversations without contributing anything; in computer communication, lurking is good, not bad. Lurking will help you learn the rules of the particular group and will help you avoid saying things you'd like to take back.

◆ Don't contribute to traffic jams. Try connecting during off hours, whenever possible. If you are unable to connect, try later, not immediately. It only puts added strain on the system and you're likely to still be unable to connect. In securing information try local information sources before trying more distant sources; it requires fewer connections and less time. Be economical in using files (for example, photographs) that may tie up lines for long periods of time.

◆ Be brief. Follow the maxim of quantity by communicating only the information that is needed; follow the maxim of manner by communicating clearly, briefly, and in an organized way.

◆ Treat newbies (people new to the online world) kindly; you were one once yourself.

◆ Don't send commercial messages to those who didn't request them. Junk mail is junk mail; but on the Internet, the receiver has to pay for the time it takes to read and delete these unwanted messages.

◆ Don't spam. Spamming occurs when you send someone unsolicited mail, repeatedly sending the same mail, or posting the same message on lots of bulletin boards, even when the message is irrelevant to the focus of the group. One of the very practical reasons spamming is frowned upon is that it costs people money. Since you are paying to read your e-mail, for example, you are paying to read something you didn't want in the first place. Another reason, of course, is that it clogs the system, slowing it down for everyone.

◆ Don't flame. Flaming refers to using personal attacks on another user. As in face-to-face conflict, personal attacks are best avoided on the Internet. So, avoid flaming and participating in flame wars.

p. 294

(sometimes a specific listener) to take over the role of speaker. So, for example, at the end of a statement you might add some paralinguistic cue such as "eh?" which asks one of the listeners to assume the role of speaker. You can also indicate that you have finished speaking by dropping your intonation, by a prolonged silence, by making direct eye contact with a listener, by asking some general question, or by nodding in the direction of a particular listener.

In much the same way that you expect a speaker to yield the role of speaker, you also expect the listener to willingly assume the speaking role. Those who don't may be regarded as reticent or unwilling to involve themselves and take equal responsibility for the conversation. For example, in an analysis of turn-taking violations in the conversations of marrieds, the most common violation found was that of no response. Forty-five percent of the 540 violations identified involved a lack of response to an invitation to assume the speaker role (DeFrancisco 1991). Of these "no response" violations, 68 percent were committed by men and 32 percent by women. Other turn-taking violations include interruptions, delayed responses, and inappropriately brief responses. DeFrancisco argues that with these violations, all of which are committed more frequently by men, men silence women in marital interactions.

Listener Cues As a listener, you can regulate the conversation by using a variety of cues. **Turn-requesting cues** let the speaker know that you would like to take a turn as speaker. Sometimes you can do this by simply saying, "I would like to say something," but often you do it more subtly through some vocalized "er" or "um" that tells the mindful speaker that you would now like to speak. This request to speak is also often made with facial and mouth gestures. You can, for example, indicate a desire to speak by opening your eyes and mouth widely as if to say something, by beginning to gesture with your hand, or by leaning forward.

You can also indicate your reluctance to assume the role of speaker by using **turn-denying cues**: for example, intoning a slurred "I don't know" or a brief grunt that signals you have nothing to say. Turn-denying is often accomplished by avoiding eye contact with the speaker who wishes you to take on the role of speaker or by engaging in some behavior that is incompatible with speaking—for example, coughing or blowing your nose.

Back-channeling cues are used to communicate various types of information back to the speaker without your assuming the role of speaker. Some researchers call these "acknowledgment tokens"—brief utterances such as "mm-hm," "uh-huh," and "yeah"—(the three most often used such tokens)—that tell the speaker you are listening (Schegloff 1982; Drummond and Hopper 1993). You can communicate quite a variety of messages with these backchanneling cues; four such types are noted in Table 14.2.

Some backchanneling cues are actually **interruptions**. These interruptions, however, are generally confirming rather than disconfirming. They tell the speaker that we are listening and involved (Kennedy and Camden 1988). Other interruptions are not as confirming and simply take the speaking turn away from the speaker, either temporarily or permanently. Sometimes the interrupter may apologize for breaking in and at other times may not even seem aware of interrupting. Interruptions may serve a variety of specific functions:

- ◆ to change the topic ("I gotta tell you this story before I bust.");
- ◆ to correct the speaker ("You mean four months, not years, don't you?");

How would you describe yourself in terms of giving conversational cues? In receiving them? For example, do you give clear cues or are many ambiguous? Are you quick to understand and respond to the cues of others?

Table 14.2	Functions of Backchanneling Cues

Although we are seldom mindful of using backchanneling cues, we would miss them sorely if our own listeners didn't use them. As you read through this table consider how you communicate the various functions and how responsive you are to the backchanneling cues of others. This table is based on the excellent research summaries of Burgoon, Buller, and Woodall 1995 and Pearson and Spitzberg 1990.

Functions	Examples
To indicate agreement or disagreement	Smiles; nods of approval; brief comments such as "Right" and "Of course"; or a vocalization like "hu-hah" signal agreement. Frowning, shaking your head, or making comments such as "No" or "Never" signal disagreement.
To indicate degree of involvement	An attentive posture, forward leaning, and focused eye contact tell the speaker that you are involved in the conversation. An inattentive posture, backward leaning, and avoidance of eye contact communicate a lack of involvement.
To pace the speaker	Ask the speaker to slow down by raising your hand near your ear and leaning forward or to speed up by continued nodding of your head. Cue the speaker verbally by simply asking the speaker to slow down or to speed up.
To ask for clarification	A puzzled facial expression, perhaps coupled with a forward lean, signals your need for clarification. Or, ask for clarification directly by interjecting Who? When? Where?

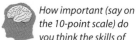

How important (say on the 10-point scale) do you think the skills of giving backchanneling cues are to a satisfying conversation? How sensitive are you to the backchanneling cues of others? How sensitive are others to your backchanneling cues?

- to seek information, to ask a question of clarification ("Do you mean Jeff's cousin?");
- to better or top the speaker with a funnier story or a more extreme example ("If you think that's funny, wait till you hear this. . . .");
- to end the conversation ("I hate to interrupt, but I really have to get back to the office.");
- to introduce essential information ("Your car's on fire.").

One of the most often studied aspects of interruption is gender difference. Do men or women interrupt more? Research here is conflicting. These few research findings will give you an idea of the differing results (Pearson, West, and Turner 1994):

- The more malelike the person's gender identity—regardless of the person's biological sex—the more likely it is that the person will interrupt (Drass 1986).
- Men interrupt more than women do (Zimmerman and West 1975; West and Zimmerman 1977).
- There are no significant differences between boys and girls (ages 2–5) in interrupting behavior (Greif 1980).
- Fathers interrupt their children more than mothers do (Greif 1980).
- Men and women do not differ in their interrupting behavior (Roger and Nesshoever 1983).

Blind and sighted people make use of the same vocal and verbal cues in managing a conversation but the blind make little use of touch cues, postural shifts, and gestures (Sharkey and Stafford 1990). What implications can be drawn from this finding for improving communication between blind and sighted persons?

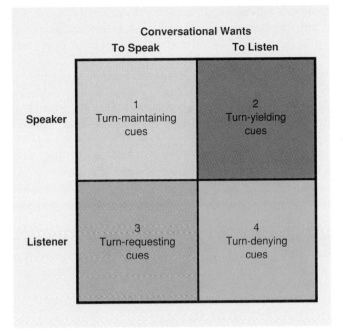

Conversational Wants

	To Speak	**To Listen**
Speaker	1 Turn-maintaining cues	2 Turn-yielding cues
Listener	3 Turn-requesting cues	4 Turn-denying cues

Figure 14.3 Turn-Taking and Conversational Wants.
Quadrant 1 represents the speaker who wishes to speak (continue to speak) and uses turn-maintaining cues; Quadrant 2 the speaker who wishes to listen and uses turn-yielding cues; Quadrant 3 the listener who wishes to speak and uses turn-requesting cues; and Quadrant 4 the listener who wishes to listen (continue listening) and uses turn-denying cues. Backchanneling cues would appear in Quadrant 4, since they are cues that listeners use while they continue to listen. Interruptions would appear in Quadrant 3, though they are not so much cues that request a turn but are actual takeovers of the speaker's position. Does this system allow for the representation of all conversational cues? Are there other types of cues that are not represented here?

The various turn-taking cues and how they correspond to the conversational wants of speaker and listener are summarized in Figure 14.3.

Closing Conversations

Closing a conversation is almost as difficult as opening one. It is frequently an awkward and uncomfortable part of interpersonal interaction. Here are a few suggestions you might consider:

- Reflect back on the conversation and briefly summarize it so as to bring it to a close. For example: "I'm glad I ran into you and found out what happened at that union meeting. I'll probably be seeing you at the meetings next week."
- Directly state the desire to end the conversation and to get on with other things. For example: "I'd like to continue talking, but I really have to run. I'll see you around."
- Refer to future interaction. For example: "Why don't we get together next week sometime and continue this discussion?"
- Ask for closure. For example: "Have I explained what you wanted to know?"
- State that you enjoyed the interaction. For example: "I really enjoyed talking with you."

With any of these closings, it should be clear to the other person that you are attempting to end the conversation. Obviously, you will have to use more direct methods with those who don't take these subtle hints or don't realize that *both* persons are responsible for the interpersonal interaction and for bringing it to a satisfactory close.

Think about how you might go about closing each of the following conversations. What types of closing seem most effective? Which seem least effective?

What ways, in addition to those noted in this unit, have you found for closing conversations? How does closing a telephone conversation differ from closing a face-to-face conversation?

How would you go about discovering if men and women use similar or different conversational closing techniques? What's your initial guess?

1. You and a friend have been talking on the phone for the last hour but not much new is being said. You have a great deal of work to get to and would like to close the conversation. Your friend just doesn't seem to hear your subtle cues.

2. You are at a party and are anxious to meet a person with whom you have exchanged eye contact for the last 10 minutes. The problem is that a friendly, and talkative former teacher of yours is demanding all your attention. You don't want to insult the instructor but at the same time want to make contact with this other person.

3. You have had a conference with a supervisor and have learned what you needed to know. This supervisor, however, doesn't seem to know how to end the conversation, seems very ill at ease, and just continues to go over what has already been said. You have to get back to your desk and must close the conversation.

4. You are at a party and notice a person you would like to get to know. You initiate the conversation but after a few minutes realize that this person is not the kind of person with whom you would care to spend any more time. You want to close this conversation as soon as possible.

Conversational Problems: Prevention and Repair

In conversation, you may anticipate a problem and seek to prevent it. Or you may discover that you said or did something that will lead to disapproval, and you may seek to excuse yourself. Here we give just one example of a device to prevent potential conversational problems (the disclaimer) and one example of a device to repair conversational problems (the excuse). Our purpose is simply to illustrate the complexity of these processes, not to present you with an exhaustive list of the ways conversational problems may be prevented or repaired.

Preventing Conversational Problems: The Disclaimer

Let us say, for example, that you fear your listeners will think your comment is inappropriate in the present context, that they may rush to judge you without hearing your full account, or will think that you are not in full possession of your faculties. In these cases, you may use some form of disclaimer. A **disclaimer** is a statement that aims to ensure that your message will be understood and will not reflect negatively on you.

Think about your own use of disclaimers as you read about the five types discussed here (Hewitt and Stokes 1975; McLaughlin 1984). **Hedging** helps you to separate yourself from the message, so that if your listeners reject your message, they need not reject you (for example, "I may be wrong here, but . . . "). Hedges decrease the attractiveness of both women and men (Wright and Hosman 1983) if they are seen as indicating a lack of certainty or conviction because of some inadequacy. However, if the hedges are seen as indicating a lack of belief in allness (as indicating that no one can know all about any subject), as well as a belief that tentative statements are all one can reasonably make (Hosman 1989; Pearson, Turner, and Todd-Mancillas 1991), they will be more positively received.

Credentialing helps you to establish your special qualifications for saying what you are about to say (for example, "Don't get me wrong, I'm not homophobic"). **Sin licenses** ask listeners for permission to deviate in some way from some normally accepted convention (for example, "I know this may not be the place to discuss business, but . . . "). **Cognitive disclaimers** help you to make the case that you are in full possession of your faculties (for example, "I know you'll think I'm crazy, but let me explain the logic of the case"). **Appeals for the suspension of judgment** ask listeners to hear you out before making a judgment (for example, "Don't hang up on me until you hear my side of the story").

Generally, disclaimers are effective when, for example, you think you might offend listeners in telling a joke (for example, "I don't usually like this type of joke, but . . . "). In one study, for example, 11-year-old children were read a story about someone whose actions created negative effects. Some children heard the story with a disclaimer and others heard the same story without the disclaimer. When the children were asked to indicate how the person should be punished, those who heard the story with the disclaimer recommended significantly lower punishments (Bennett 1990).

But, disclaimers can also get you into trouble. For example, to inappropriately preface remarks with "I'm no liar" may well lead listeners to think that perhaps the speaker *is* a liar. Also, if you use too many disclaimers you may be perceived as someone who doesn't have any strong convictions or as one who wants to avoid responsibility for just about everything. This seems especially true of hedges.

In responding to statements containing disclaimers, it is often necessary to respond to both the disclaimer and to the statement. By doing so, you let the speaker know that you heard the disclaimer and that you aren't going to view this communication negatively. Appropriate responses might be: "I know you're no sexist but I don't agree that . . ." or "Well, perhaps we should discuss the money now even if it doesn't seem right."

Have you heard (or used) any disclaimers over the last few days? How would you explain the functions they were designed to serve? Were they effective?

Repairing Conversational Problems: The Excuse

At times you may say the wrong thing, but because you can't erase the message (communication really is irreversible) you may try to account for it. Perhaps the most common method for doing so is the **excuse.** Excuses pervade all forms of communication and behavior. Although we emphasize their role in conversation, recognize that the excuse is applicable to all human behaviors, not just conversational ones.

You learn early in life that when you do something that others will view negatively, an excuse is in order to justify your performance. The excuse, as C. R. Snyder (1984) notes, "plays a central role in how we get along in life, both with yourself and with other people." Snyder (1984; Snyder, Higgins, and Stucky 1983) defines excuses as "explanations or actions that lessen the negative implications of an actor's performance, thereby maintaining a positive image for oneself and others."

Excuses seem especially in order when we say or are accused of saying something that runs counter to what is expected, sanctioned, or considered "right" by the people involved or by society in general. The excuse, ideally, lessens the negative impact of the message.

Some Motives for Excuse Making   The major motive for excuse making seems to be to maintain our self-esteem, to project a positive image to ourselves and to others. Excuses are also offered to reduce the stress that may be created by a bad performance. We feel that if we can offer an excuse—especially a good one that is accepted by those around us—it will reduce the negative reaction and the subsequent stress that accompanies a poor performance.

Excuses enable you to take risks and engage in behavior that may be unsuccessful; you may offer an anticipatory excuse: "My throat's a bit sore, but I'll give the speech a try." The excuse is designed to lessen the criticism should you fail to deliver an acceptable speech.

Excuses also enable us to maintain effective interpersonal relationships even after some negative behavior. For example, after criticizing a friend's behavior and observing the negative reaction to our criticism, we might offer an excuse such as, "Please forgive me; I'm really exhausted. I'm just not thinking straight." Excuses enable us to place our messages—even our possible failures—in a more favorable light.

Good and Bad Excuses   The most important question to most people is what makes a good excuse and what makes a bad excuse (Snyder 1984; Slade 1995). How can you make good excuses and thus get out of problems, and how can you avoid bad excuses and thus only make matters worse? Good excuse makers use excuses in moderation; bad excuse makers rely on excuses too often. Good excuse makers avoid using excuses in the presence of those who know what really happened; bad excuse makers will make excuses even in these inappropriate situations. Good excuse makers avoid blaming others, especially those they work with; bad excuse makers blame even their work colleagues. In a similar way, good excuse makers do not attribute their failure to others or to the company; bad excuse makers do. Good excuse makers acknowledge their own responsibility for the failure by noting that they did something wrong (not that they lack competence); bad excuse makers refuse to accept any responsibility for their failure.

The best excuses are apologies because they contain three essential elements for a good excuse (Slade 1995):

Have you heard (or used) any excuses lately? How would you explain the functions that these excuses were designed to serve? Were they effective? What was the best excuse you ever heard? What was the worst? What distinguished the best from the worst?

- an acknowledgment of the responsibility;
- a request for forgiveness;
- the suggestion that things will be done better in the future.

The worst excuses are the "I didn't do it" type because they fail to acknowledge responsibility and also because they offer no assurance that this failure will not happen again.

In his introduction to Margaret McLaughlin's insightful *Conversation* (1984), Mark Knapp observes, "While there is something inherently fascinating about discovering the anatomy of behaviors we habitually (and sometimes unthinkingly) perform, the real significance of understanding the structure of conversations is its centrality for understanding human interaction in general." The intention of this unit has been to help you approach this understanding.

Summary   U N I T   I N   B R I E F

A RETURN TO OBJECTIVES:

This unit reviewed the process of conversation and focused on the following questions: (1) What are the major stages in conversation? (2) What is the principle of cooperation and what are its related maxims? How might conversation be more effectively managed? (3) How might conversational problems be prevented and repaired?

Definitions	Processes	Accuracy
Opening: Initiating the conversation. **Feedforward:** Previewing or prefacing the conversation to follow. **Business:** Engaging in the interaction, the reason for the conversation. **Feedback:** Summarizing or reflecting back on the conversation. **Closing:** Bringing the conversation to an end.	**Initiating:** ♦ Self-references ♦ Other-references ♦ Relational references ♦ Context references **Maintaining:** ♦ The principle of cooperation and the maxims of quantity, quality, relation, and manner. ♦ Conversational turn-taking (turn- maintaining, yielding, requesting, denying, and back-channeling cues). **Closing:** ♦ Reflect back on conversation. ♦ Directly state desire to end conversation. ♦ Refer to future interaction. ♦ Ask for closure. ♦ Express pleasure with interaction.	**Prevention:** The **disclaimer,** a statement that helps to ensure that your message will be understood and will not reflect negatively on the speaker. ♦ Hedging ♦ Credentialing ♦ Sin licenses ♦ Cognitive disclaimers ♦ Appeals for the suspension of judgment **Repair:** The **excuse,** an explanation designed to lessen the negative impact of a speaker's messages.

Interpersonal
Relationships

PART CONTENTS

15. UNIVERSALS OF INTERPERSONAL RELATIONSHIPS

16. RELATIONSHIP DEVELOPMENT AND INVOLVEMENT

17. RELATIONSHIP DETERIORATION AND DISSOLUTION

18. RELATIONSHIP MAINTENANCE AND REPAIR

19. POWER IN INTERPERSONAL RELATIONSHIPS

20. CONFLICT IN INTERPERSONAL RELATIONSHIPS

21. FRIENDS AND LOVERS

22. PRIMARY AND FAMILY RELATIONSHIPS

APPROACHING INTERPERSONAL RELATIONSHIPS

In approaching your study of interpersonal relationships, keep the following in mind:

◆ The research results and conclusions presented here are true in a statistical sense. They apply to the average person but not to everyone. Your task is to ask if they apply to you and to your relationships.

◆ Delay your conclusions until you have collected sufficient information. Avoid drawing conclusions about your friends, romantic partners, or, in fact, any of your relationships from isolated bits and pieces of information. Formulate hypotheses to be tested rather than hard-and-fast conclusions.

◆ Look for comparisons and analogies between the situations described here and those in which you find yourself. Ask yourself how your interpersonal life is similar to or different from the situations described here. Which of the skills covered in the following units can you apply to your life at home, at work, at school?

◆ Relationship change, should that be your goal, is not an easy process. And this is doubly true for dysfunctional relationships. Realize that change is often slow and that it may be facilitated with the help of others.

◆ Empowering yourself is one of the goals of this text—to enable you to acquire greater mastery over your own interpersonal life; another goal, however, is the empowering of others, colleagues, friends, lovers, and family, for example. Keep this dual focus in mind as you read the relationship theories and skills.

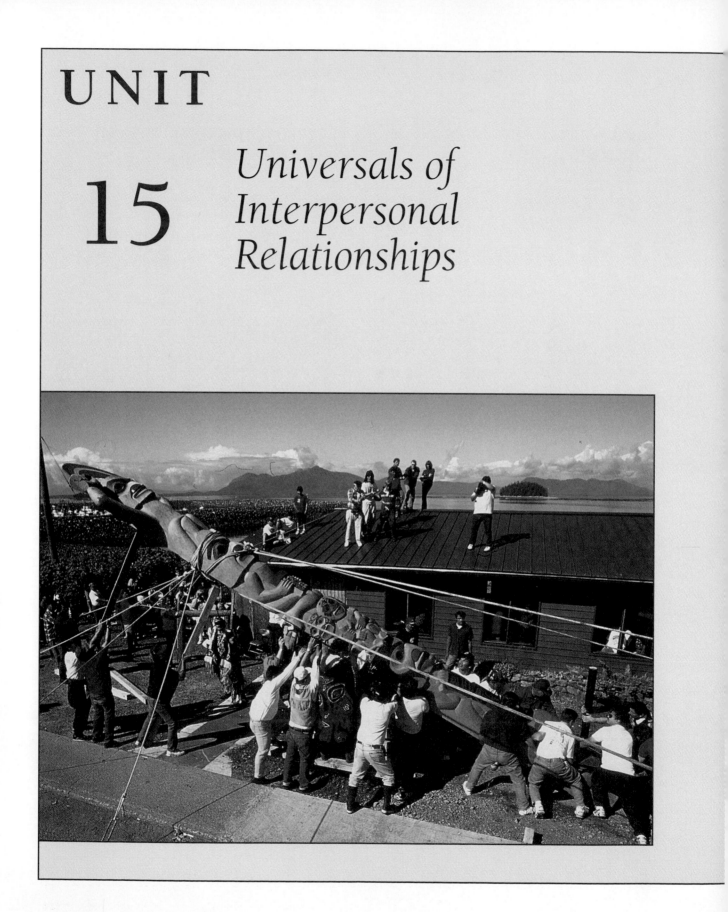

Unit Topics	Unit Objectives
	After completing this unit, you should be able to:
Advantages and Disadvantages of Interpersonal Relationships Advantages of Interpersonal Relationships Disadvantages of Interpersonal Relationships	1. Identify the advantages and disadvantages of interpersonal relationships
Stages in Interpersonal Relationships: Development to Dissolution Contact Involvement Intimacy Deterioration Repair Dissolution Movement Among the Stages	2. Explain the six-stage model of relationships

---

EXPERIENTIAL LEARNING VEHICLES

Vehicle No. 16, "Analyzing Stage Talk," pp. 458–460, is useful for illustrating and analyzing the different messages that are appropriate at each relationship stage. No. 17, "Interpersonal Relationships in Songs and Greeting Cards," pp. 460–461, offers a way to explore the theories and principles of interpersonal relationships as they appear in songs and cards.

Nos. 18, "Mate Preferences," pp. 461–462, 19, "Male and Female," p. 463, 20, "Relationship Repair from Advice Columnists," pp. 463–464, and 24, "The Television Relationship," pp. 467–468, can all be used to gain additional perspectives on interpersonal relationships.

So important is contact with other human beings that when we are deprived of it for long periods, depression sets in, self-doubt surfaces, and we find it difficult to manage even the basics of daily life. Research shows clearly that the most important contributor to happiness—outranking money, job, and sex—is a close relationship with one other person (Freedman 1978). The desire for relationships is universal; they are important to men and to women, to homosexuals and to heterosexuals (Huston and Schwartz 1995).

Advantages and Disadvantages of Interpersonal Relationships

All relationships have the potential of increasing or decreasing your happiness and satisfaction; there are, potentially, both advantages and disadvantages to interpersonal relationships.

Advantages of Interpersonal Relationships

Interpersonal relationships lessen loneliness, help you secure stimulation, enable you to gain in self-knowledge and self-esteem, enhance your physical and emotional well-being, and maximize your pleasures and minimize your pains. Since you anticipate that your relationship will bring advantages, you can look at these advantages as the reasons you develop relationships in the first place.

To Lessen Loneliness   Contact with another human being often lessens loneliness. You want to feel that someone cares, that someone likes you, that someone will protect you, that someone ultimately will love you. Close relationships assure you that someone cares and will be there when needed. Sometimes surrounding yourself with lots of people helps; often, however, a crowd only serves to underscore loneliness. One close relationship usually works a lot better.

When do you experience loneliness most? How long do these feelings usually last? How do your interpersonal relationships help to lessen loneliness?

To Secure Stimulation   Human beings need stimulation; without it, they withdraw—sometimes they die. As plants are heliotropic and orient themselves to light, humans are stimulotropic and orient themselves to sources of stimulation (M. Davis 1973). Human contact is one of the best ways to secure this stimulation—intellectual, physical, and emotional.

To Gain in Self-Knowledge and Self-Esteem   Through contact with others you learn about yourself. Your self-perceptions are greatly influenced by what you think others think of you; if your friends see you as warm and generous, you probably will, too. Contact with others allows you to see yourself from different perspectives and in different roles, as a child or parent, as a coworker, as a manager, as a best friend. You also gain self-knowledge by getting to know others and comparing yourself to them. In fact, social comparison theory holds that you evaluate yourself—your attitudes, talents, values, accomplishments, abilities—primarily by comparing yourself with others.

Healthy interpersonal relationships help enhance self-esteem and self-worth. Simply having a friend or romantic partner (at least most of the time) makes you feel desirable and worthy. When you are fortunate enough to have a supportive partner, the relationship can enhance self-esteem even more.

In recognition of the universal desire for close relationships, many municipalities, universities, and organizations are recognizing domestic partnerships. In some cases, "domestic partnerships" are extended to all unmarried people living together—whether same or opposite sex. In other cases, "domestic partnership" recognition is only available to same-sex couples, on the assumption that opposite-sex couples could get married if they wished to and so need not be included. What do you think of domestic partnerships? What do you think of making the benefits of domestic partnerships (for example, health benefits) available only to same-sex couples?

To Enhance Physical and Emotional Health   Research consistently shows that interpersonal relationships contribute significantly to physical and emotional health (Goleman 1995; Rosengren 1993; Pennebacker 1991). For example, without close interpersonal relationships you are more likely to become depressed; depression, in turn, contributes significantly to physical illness. Isolation, contributes as much to mortality as high blood pressure, high cholesterol, obesity, smoking, or lack of physical exercise (Goleman 1995).

To Maximize Pleasure and Minimize Pain   The most general function served by interpersonal relationships, and one that encompasses all the others, is that of maximizing pleasure and minimizing pain. You have a need to share good fortune as well as your emotional and physical pain. Perhaps this goes back to childhood, when you ran to mother to have your wounds kissed or to be told everything is all right. You now find it difficult to run to mother, so you go to others, generally to friends who will provide the same consolation mother did.

Can you identify the major reasons you developed your three most important relationships? Do you maintain these relationships for the same reasons? If these reasons were no longer present, would you dissolve the relationships?

Disadvantages of Interpersonal Relationships

Although seldom discussed in most presentations of interpersonal relationships, there are potential disadvantages or costs. Four may be mentioned here: pressure for revealing who you really are, increased obligations to share and care for the

Are there other disadvantages that should be mentioned here? Do you normally think of potential disadvantages before entering a relationship or before progressing to a level of greater intimacy?

other person, increased isolation from other generally rewarding relationships, and the difficulties involved in breaking up.

Pressure for Exposure   Close relationships put pressure on you to reveal yourself and to expose your vulnerabilities. While this is generally worthwhile in the context of a supporting and caring relationship, it may backfire if the relationship deteriorates and these weaknesses are used against you. Furthermore, many find no satisfaction in revealing themselves and no advantage in exposing weaknesses.

Increased Obligations   In close relationships one person's behavior influences the other person's, sometimes to great extent. Your time is no longer entirely your own. And although you enter a relationship to spend more time with this special person, you also incur time obligations with which you may not be happy. Similarly, if your money is pooled (as it is in many close relationships), then your financial successes have to be shared, as do your partner's losses. On the positive side, of course, your partner shares your losses and you share in your partner's gains. Perhaps the most difficulties are created by the emotional obligations you incur. To be emotionally responsive and sensitive is not always easy. When one person becomes ill, the pressures of care-taking increase, sometimes to the point of breakdown.

Increased Insulation   Close relationships can result in abandoning other relationships. Sometimes, it involves someone you like but your partner can't stand. So you may give up this person or see him or her less often. More often, however, it's simply a matter of time and energy; relationships take a lot of both. You consequently have less to give to those other and less intimate relationships.

Difficulty in Dissolving   Once entered into, a relationship may prove difficult to get out of. In some cultures, for example, religious pressures may prevent married couples from separating. If children are part of the relationship, it may be emotionally difficult to exit. And, if lots of money is involved, dissolving a relationship can often mean giving up the fortune you have spent your life accumulating.

And, of course, your partner may break your heart. Your partner may leave you—against all your pleading and promises. Your hurt will be in proportion to how much you care and need your partner. The person who cares a lot is hurt a lot, the person who cares little is hurt little; it's one of life's little ironies.

All relationships will bring both advantages and disadvantages; in an imperfect world, that's to be expected. The insights and skills of interpersonal communication and relationships, however, should stack the odds in favor of greater and longer-lived advantages and fewer and shorter-lived disadvantages.

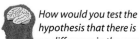

How would you test the hypothesis that there is no difference in the way in which men and women view relationship advantages and disadvantages? In the way in which young and old view such advantages and disadvantages?

Stages in Interpersonal Relationships: Development to Dissolution

You and another person do not become intimate friends immediately upon meeting. Rather, you build an intimate relationship gradually, through a series of steps or stages. The same is true of most relationships. The "love at first sight" phenomenon creates a problem for a stage model of relationships. So, rather than argue that such love cannot occur (my own feeling is that it can and frequently does), it seems wiser to claim that the stage model characterizes *most* relationships for *most* people *most* of the time.

Within each relationship and within each relationship stage, there are dynamic tensions between several opposites. The assumption made by this theory—called **relational dialectics theory**—is that all relationships can be defined by a series of opposites. For example, some research has found three such opposites (Baxter 1988, 1990; Baxter and Simon 1993). The tension between autonomy and connection expresses your desire to remain an individual but also to intimately connect to another person and to a relationship. This theme appears in women's magazines and seems to teach readers to want both autonomy and connection (Prusank, Duran, and DeLillo 1993). The tension between novelty and predictability centers on the dual desires for newness and adventure on the one hand and sameness and comfortableness on the other. The tension between closedness and openness relates to the desires to be in an exclusive relationship and one that is open to different people.

The six-stage model in Figure 15.1 describes the main stages in most relationships. For a particular relationship you might wish to modify the basic model, though as a general description of relationship development the stages seem fairly standard. Do realize, of course, that both partners may not perceive their relationship in the same way; one person, for example, may see the relationship as an intimate one but the other may not.

The six stages of relationships are contact, involvement, intimacy, deterioration, repair, and dissolution. Each stage has an early or initial phase and a late phase. These stages describe relationships as they are; they do not evaluate or prescribe how relationships should be.

Research shows that the closedness-openness tension is more in evidence during the early stages of development and that autonomy-connection and novelty-predictability were more frequent as the relationship progressed (Baxter 1988, 1990; Baxter and Simon 1993). Why do you suppose this is true?

Contact

At the initial phase of the contact stage, there is some kind of **perceptual contact**—you see, hear, and perhaps smell the person. From this you get a physical picture—sex, approximate age, height, and so on. After this perception, there is usually **interactional contact.** Here the contact is superficial and relatively impersonal. This is the stage at which you exchange basic information that is preliminary to any more intense involvement ("Hello, my name is Joe"). Here you initiate interaction ("May I join you?") and engage in invitational communication ("May I buy you a drink?"). According to some researchers, it is at this stage—within the first four minutes of initial interaction—that you decide whether you want to pursue the relationship (Zunin and Zunin 1972).

At the contact stage, physical appearance is especially important because it is the most readily seen. Yet through both verbal and nonverbal behaviors, qualities such as friendliness, warmth, openness, and dynamism are also revealed.

Involvement

At this stage, a sense of mutuality, of being connected develops. Here you experiment and try to learn more about the other person. At the initial phase of involvement, a kind of **testing** goes on. You want to see whether your initial judgment proves reasonable. And so you may ask questions: "Where do you work?" "What

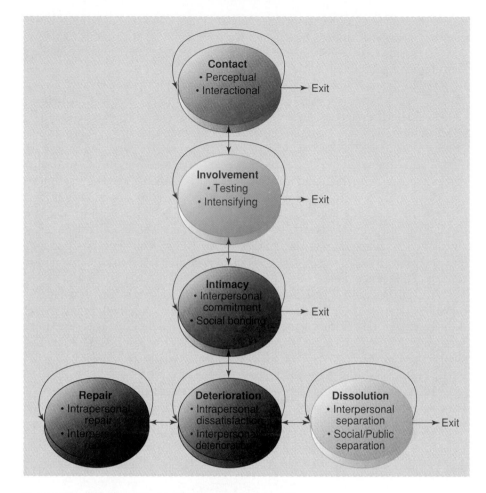

Figure 15.1   A Six-Stage Model of Interpersonal Relationships.
Because relationships differ so widely, it is best to think of any relationship model as a tool for talking about relationships rather than as a specific map that indicates how you move from one relationship position to another. Are there other steps or stages that you can identify that would further explain what goes on in relationship development? What happens when the two people in a relationship experience the stages differently? Can you provide an example from literature or from your own experience?

are you majoring in?" If you want to get to know the person even better, you might continue your involvement by **intensifying** your interaction. Here you not only try to get to know the other person better but also begin to reveal yourself, though in a preliminary way. If in a dating relationship, you might, for example, use such strategies as the following to help you move to the next stage and perhaps to intimacy (Tolhuizen 1989):

◆ increase contact with your partner;
◆ give your partner tokens of affection, for example, gifts, cards, or flowers;
◆ increase your own personal attractiveness;
◆ do things that suggest intensifying the relationship, for example, flirting or making your partner jealous;
◆ become more sexually intimate.

Throughout the relationship process, but especially during the involvement and early intimacy stages, you test your partner; you try to find out how your partner feels about the relationship. Among the strategies you might use are these (Baxter and Wilmot 1984; Bell and Buerkel-Rothfuss 1990):

◆ *Directness.* You ask your partner directly how he or she feels, or you disclose your own feelings on the assumption that your partner will also self-disclose.

◆ *Endurance.* You subject your partner to various negative behaviors (for example, you behave badly or make inconvenient requests) on the assumption that if your partner endures them, he or she is serious about the relationship.

◆ *Indirect suggestion.* For example, you joke about a shared future together, touch more intimately, or hint that you are serious about the relationship. Similar responses from your partner will mean that he or she wishes to increase the intimacy of the relationship.

◆ *Public presentation.* For example, you introduce your partner as your "boyfriend" or "girlfriend" and see how your partner responds.

◆ *Separation.* You separate yourself physically to see how the other person responds. If your partner calls, then you know he or she is interested in the relationship.

◆ *Third party.* You ask mutual friends about your partner's feelings and intentions.

◆ *Triangle.* You set up a triangle and tell your partner that, for example, another person is interested in him or her; then you see how your partner reacts. If your partner shows no interest, it indicates a stronger commitment to you.

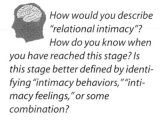

Can you identify any strategies that you have used in testing your friendship or romantic relationships? Can you identify strategies that others have used on you?

Intimacy

At the intimacy stage, you commit yourself still further to the other person and establish a relationship in which this individual becomes your best or closest friend, lover, or companion. You also come to share each other's social networks, a practice followed by members of widely different cultures (Gao and Gudykunst 1995). Not surprisingly, your relationship satisfaction also increases with the move to this stage (Siavelis and Lamke 1992).

The intimacy stage usually divides itself into two phases. In the **interpersonal commitment** phase the two people commit themselves to each other in a private way. In the **social bonding** phase the commitment is made public—perhaps to family and friends, perhaps to the public at large. Here you and your partner become a unit, an identifiable pair.

When the intimacy stage involves a lifetime partnership, you face three main anxieties (Zimmer 1986):

How would you describe "relational intimacy"? How do you know when you have reached this stage? Is this stage better defined by identifying "intimacy behaviors," "intimacy feelings," or some combination?

1. *Security anxiety.* Will my partner leave me for someone else? Will my partner be sexually unfaithful?
2. *Fulfillment anxiety.* Will we be able to achieve a close, warm, and special rapport? Will we be able to have an equal relationship?
3. *Excitement anxiety.* Will boredom and routine set in? Will I lose my freedom and become trapped?

MEDIA & TECHNOLOGY

PARASOCIAL RELATIONSHIPS

A parasocial relationship is one you see yourself as having with a media personality (Rubin and McHugh 1987). At times viewers develop these relationships with real media personalities—O. J. Simpson, Kathy Lee Gifford, or Geraldo Rivera, for example. As a result, they may watch these personalities faithfully and communicate with the individual in their own imaginations. At other times, the relationship is with a fictional character—a doctor on *ER, Roseanne,* or *Walker.* Those who play doctors frequently get mail asking their medical advice. Soap opera stars who are about to be "killed" frequently get warning letters from their parasocial relationship partners. Most people obviously don't go quite this far. Yet, many viewers consider the role real enough to make that actor in that role a bankable spokesperson for a product. For example, actor Susan Sullivan, who played a nurse on television some ten years ago, is still a spokesperson for a particular medication.

CD ROM and Internet videos of our television heroes that we can play over and over provide a natural source for parasocial relationships. The chat sessions that many of these stars hold on the Internet (usually on one of the commercial carriers), where you can talk with them, help create the illusion of a real interpersonal relationship. The screen savers of television stars (those from *Friends, Seinfeld, Home Improvement,* and *Frazier* are currently popular) makes it difficult not to think of them in relationship terms when they face you every time you leave your computer idle for a few minutes.

Parasocial relationships develop from an initial attraction with the character's social and task roles, to a perceived relationship, and finally to a sense that this relationship is an important one (Rubin and McHugh 1987). A viewer's ability to predict the behavior of a character seems to contribute to the development of parasocial relationships (Perse and Rubin 1989). As can be expected, these parasocial relationships are most important to those who spend a great deal of time with the media and who have few interpersonal relationships (Rubin, Perse, and Powell 1985).

Even the relationship between talk show host and guest is a parasocial one, media researcher Janice Peck (1995) argues. The reason is that such relationships are basically one-sided and the roles are not interchangeable. The interaction is not one of dialogue but rather one in which the host controls the interaction and the guests essentially answer the questions the host asks.

In many instances, relationships are not easy to classify into real or parasocial classes. For example, most of us can probably recall at least one real relationship we have had where the talk was basically one-sided, where the roles were not interchangeable, and where the interaction was largely controlled by one person.

Further, in the talk shows where viewers can often write in to meet the guests from the show, the relationships may begin as parasocial but quickly move to real. For example, a *Sally Jesse Raphael* show in early 1995 was devoted to viewers who had crushes on former guests whom the show got together for another episode. Viewers can see the characters on television—and in some ways talk show panelists are very much like dramatic characters in a play—as potential relationship partners. Though such occurrences are infrequent, they happen often enough that people write in with the hope of meeting a guest. On home-shopping programs, you may develop a parasocial relationship with the host (Grant and Guthrie 1991). On some shows you can often talk with the host or with a product's spokesperson. You can, for example, call the number on the screen and talk to Suzanne Sommers or Brian Lamb. As the ability to interact with the television programs increases, the distinction between real and parasocial relationships will become increasingly blurred (cf. Auter and Moore 1993).

Do you see both advantages and disadvantages to parasocial relationships? What are the major advantages? The major disadvantages? Do you maintain parasocial relationships with media personalities? If so, what functions do these relationships serve for you?

p. 310

Of course, not everyone strives for intimacy (Bartholomew 1990). Some are so fearful of the consequences of intimacy that they actively avoid it. Others dismiss intimacy and defensively deny their need for more and deeper interpersonal contact.

Intimacy and Risk   To some people, relational intimacy is extremely risky. To others, it involves only low risk. For example, how true of your attitudes are the following statements?

- It is dangerous to get really close to people.
- I'm afraid to get really close to someone because I might get hurt.
- I find it difficult to trust other people.
- The most important thing to consider in a relationship is whether I might get hurt.

People who agree with these and similar statements see intimacy as involving great risk (Pilkington and Richardson 1988). Such people have fewer close friends, are less likely to have a romantic relationship, have less trust in others, have a low level of dating assertiveness, and are generally less sociable than those who see intimacy as involving little risk.

Intimacy and Social Penetration   As you progress from contact through involvement to intimacy, you can see that the number of topics you talk (**breadth**) about and the degree of "personalness" with which you pursue them (**depth**) increase (Altman and Taylor 1973). Let us represent an individual as a circle and divide that circle into various parts representing the topics of interpersonal communication, or breadth. Visualize the circle and its parts as consisting of concentric inner circles (like an onion) representing the different levels of communication, or depth. Examples are given in Figure 15.2. Each circle contains eight

Security, fulfillment, and excitement anxieties were identified as the major premarital anxieties. Have you experienced these or other anxieties when you considered entering a relationship? What were the circumstances?

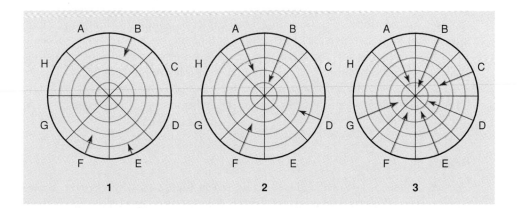

Figure 15.2   Social Penetration with (1) Acquaintance, (2) Friend, and (3) Intimate.
How accurately do the concepts of breadth and depth express your communication in relationships of different intensities? Can you identify other aspects of messages that change as you go from talking to an acquaintance, to a friend, or to an intimate?

topic areas (identified A through H) and five levels of intimacy (represented by the concentric circles). Note that in circle 1, only three topic areas are penetrated. Of these, two are penetrated only to the first level and one to the second. In this type of interaction, three topic areas are discussed, and only at rather superficial levels. This is the type of relationship you might have with an acquaintance. Circle 2 represents a more intense relationship, one that has greater breadth and depth; more topics are discussed and to deeper levels of penetration. This is the type of relationship you might have with a friend. Circle 3 represents a still more intense relationship. Here there is considerable breadth (seven of the eight areas are penetrated) and depth (most of the areas are penetrated to the deepest levels). This is the type of relationship you might have with a lover or a parent.

All relationships—friendships, loves, families—may be described in terms of breadth and depth, concepts that are central to the theory of **social penetration** (Altman and Taylor 1973). In its initial stage, a relationship is normally characterized by narrow breadth (few topics are discussed) and shallow depth (the topics are discussed only superficially). As the relationship grows in intensity and intimacy, both breadth and depth increase. Equally important, these increases are seen as comfortable, normal, and natural progressions.

How would you go about investigating the changes in breadth and depth that take place from contact, to involvement, to intimacy?

Deterioration

This stage—which does not, of course, occur in all relationships—is characterized by a weakening of the bonds between the friends or lovers. The first phase of deterioration is usually **intrapersonal dissatisfaction**: you begin to experience personal dissatisfaction with everyday interactions and begin to view the future with your partner more negatively. If this dissatisfaction grows, you pass to the second phase, **interpersonal deterioration.** You withdraw and grow further and further apart. You share less of your free time. When you are together, there are awkward silences, fewer disclosures, less physical contact, and a lack of psychological closeness. Conflicts become more common and their resolution more difficult.

When a relationship begins to deteriorate, the breadth and depth (which increase as the relationship becomes more intimate) will often reverse themselves—a process of **depenetration**, sometimes referred to as the **reversal hypothesis.** For example, in the process of terminating a relationship, you might eliminate certain topics from your interpersonal interactions and at the same time discuss acceptable topics in less depth. You might reduce the level of your disclosure, revealing less and less of your inner feelings. This reversal does not always occur (Baxter 1983). There is some evidence to show, for example, that, among friends, although depth decreases in the early stages of deterioration, it may later increase (Tolhuizen 1986).

Does your experience support the reversal hypothesis? How would you go about discovering if reversal occurs differently in friendship and romantic relationship deterioration?

Repair

The repair stage is optional and so is indicated in Figure 15.1 by a broken circle. Some relational partners may pause during deterioration and try to repair their relationship. Others, however, may progress—without stopping, without thinking—to dissolution.

At the first phase, **intrapersonal repair,** you analyze what went wrong and consider ways of solving your relational difficulties. You might consider changing your behaviors or perhaps changing your expectations of your partner. You might also evaluate the rewards of your relationship as it is now and the rewards to be gained if your relationship ended.

Should you decide that you want to repair your relationship, you might discuss this with your partner, the **interpersonal repair** phase. You might discuss the problems in the relationship, the corrections you would want to see, and perhaps what you would be willing to do and what you would want the other person to do. This is the stage of negotiating new agreements, new behaviors. You and your partner might try to solve your problems yourselves, seek the advice of friends or family, or perhaps go for professional counseling.

Dissolution

At the dissolution stage the bonds between the individuals are broken. In the beginning, it usually takes the form of **interpersonal separation**, in which you might move into separate apartments and begin to lead lives apart from each other. If this separation proves acceptable and if the original relationship is not repaired, you enter the phase of **social** or **public separation**. If the relationship is a marriage, this phase corresponds to divorce. In some cases, the former partners change the definition of their relationship, and, for example, the "ex-lovers" become "friends" or "business partners". Avoidance of each other and a return to being "single" are among the primary characteristics of dissolution.

Dissolution is also the stage during which the ex-partners begin to look upon themselves as individuals rather than halves of a pair. They try to establish a new and different life, either alone or with another person. Some people, it is true, continue to live psychologically with a relationship that has already been dissolved; they frequent old meeting places, reread old love letters, daydream about all the good times, and fail to extricate themselves from a relationship that has died in every way except in their memory.

In cultures that emphasize continuity from one generation to the next and where being "old-fashioned" is evaluated positively—as in China—interpersonal relationships are likely to be long-lasting and permanent. Those who maintain long-term relationships will be rewarded and those who break relationships will be punished. In cultures where change is seen as positive and being old-fashioned as negative—as in the United States—interpersonal relationships are likely to be more temporary (Moghaddam, Taylor, and Wright 1993). Here the rewards for long-term relationships and the punishments for broken relationships will be significantly less.

Movement Among the Stages

Figure 15.1 contains three types of arrows. The exit arrows indicate that each stage offers the opportunity to exit the relationship. After saying hello, you can say good-bye and exit. The vertical or movement arrows between stages represent the fact that you can move to another stage, either a more intense one (say, from involvement to intimacy) or a less intense one (say, from intimacy to deterioration). You can also go back to a previously established stage. For example, you may have established an intimate relationship with someone but do not want to maintain it at that level. You want it to be less intense. So you may go back to the

How would you distinguish between repair designed to maintain a relationship ("preventive maintenance," to keep the relationship satisfying and functioning smoothly) and repair designed to reverse deterioration ("corrective maintenance," to fix something that is broken or not functioning properly) (M. Davis 1973)? Do these two kinds of repair rely on different strategies?

In what ways does your culture influence the way you view relationship dissolution?

Can you supply personal examples that illustrate the three types of movement among the relationship stages? That is, can you identify a personal relationship that moved from one stage to another? One that has remained at one stage for a relatively long period? One that has resulted in one person's exiting the relationship? Are there other types of movement that should be included in the model?

Table 15.1	Turning Points in Romantic Relationships

Can you identify similar turning points in your own relationships? What turning points were most important to you? If you are in a close relationship now, ask your partner to identify the five most important turning points as he or she sees them and see if these match your own. Don't give any hints or examples (other than those from this study); don't let your partner know what you expect or would like to hear. This table is based on research by Baxter and Bullis (1986).

Turning Point	Examples
Getting-to-know time	The first meeting, the time spent together studying, the first date
Quality time that enables the couple to appreciate one another and their relationship	Meeting the family or getting away together
Physical separation	Separations due to vacations or trips (not to breakups)
External competition	The presence of a new or old rival and demands that compete for relationship time
Reunion	Getting back together after physical separation

involvement stage and reestablish the relationship at that more comfortable level (Masheter and Harris 1986). The self-reflexive arrows—the arrows that loop back to the beginning of the same level or stage—signify that any relationship may become stabilized at any point. You may, for example, maintain a relationship at the intimate level without its deteriorating or returning to the less intense stage of involvement. Or you might remain at the "Hello, how are you?" stage—the contact stage—without ever getting any further involved.

 How would you describe the stages of interpersonal relationships? Is the six-stage model presented here an adequate way to describe most interpersonal relationships as you understand them? Are the concepts of breadth and depth adequate in describing the development and deterioration of interpersonal relationships? What other concepts might prove helpful?

Movement through the various stages is usually a gradual process; you don't jump from contact to involvement to intimacy. Rather, you progress gradually, a few degrees at a time. Yet there are leaps that must and do take place. For example, during the involvement stage of a romantic relationship, the first kiss or the first sexual encounter requires a leap. It requires a change in the kind of communication and in the kind of intimacy experienced by the two people. Before you take these leaps, you probably first test the waters. Before the first kiss, for example, you may hold each other, look longingly into each other's eyes, and perhaps caress each other's face. You might do this (in part) to discover if the leap—the kiss, for example—will be met with a favorable response. No one wants rejection—especially of romantic advances. These major jumps or turning points provide an interesting perspective on how relationships develop. Table 15.1 presents the five most frequently reported turning points in romantic relationships among college students (Baxter and Bullis 1986).

Summary	U N I T I N B R I E F

A RETURN TO OBJECTIVES:

In this unit we introduced interpersonal relationships and focused on two areas: (1) What are the main advantages and disadvantages of interpersonal relationships? (2) What are the stages that a relationship goes through and what kinds of communication take place at each?

Advantages and Disadvantages of Interpersonal Relationships	Stages in Interpersonal Relationships
Advantages of Interpersonal Relationships:	**Contact:**
◆ To alleviate loneliness	◆ Perceptual
◆ To secure stimulation	◆ Interactional
◆ To gain self-knowledge and self-esteem	**Involvement:**
◆ To maximize pleasure and minimize pain	◆ Testing
	◆ Intensification
Disadvantages of Interpersonal Relationships:	**Intimacy:**
◆ Pressure for exposure	◆ Interpersonal commitment
◆ Increased obligations	◆ Social bonding
◆ Increased insulation	**Deterioration:**
◆ Difficulties in dissolving	◆ Intrapersonal dissatisfaction
	◆ Interpersonal deterioration
	Repair:
	◆ Intrapersonal repair
	◆ Interpersonal repair
	Dissolution:
	◆ Interpersonal separation
	◆ Social/public separation

UNIT

16

Relationship Development and Involvement

Unit Topics	Unit Objectives
	After completing this unit, you should be able to:
Theories of Relationship Development Attraction Theory Reinforcement Theory Social Exchange Theory Equity Theory	1. Discuss *attraction, reinforcement, social exchange,* and *equity theories* as explanations of relationship development
Developing Relationships: The First Encounter	2. Explain the steps involved in initiating relationships 3. Indentify the suggestions for communicating in first encounters

EXPERIENTIAL LEARNING VEHICLES

Vehicle Nos. 17, "Interpersonal Relationships in Songs and Greeting Cards," pp. 460–461, 18, "Mate Preferences," pp. 461–463, 19, "Male and Female," p. 463, and 24, "The Television Relationship," pp. 467–468, are useful for discussing and personalizing this material on relationship development and involvement.

Now that we have a general idea of the functions that relationships serve and the various stages of relationships, we can explore relationship development in greater detail. Later units cover relationships as they are maintained in friendship, love, and family situations, and relationships as they deteriorate.

Theories of Relationship Development

A number of theories offer insight into why you develop your relationships. Several theories bearing directly on relationship development have already been discussed.

Uncertainty reduction theory (Unit 6) describes relationship development as a process of reducing uncertainty about one another (Berger and Calabrese 1975). For example, the theory predicts that high uncertainty prevents intimacy, whereas low uncertainty creates intimacy. Similarly, high uncertainty decreases liking for another person, whereas low uncertainty increases liking.

Social penetration theory (Unit 15) describes the progression of a relationship along the communication dimensions of breadth and depth. As a relationship moves to greater intimacy, relationship depth and breadth increase; as a relationship moves away from intimacy, relationship depth and breadth decrease (usually).

Relationship dialectics theory (Unit 15) describes relationships along a series of opposites representing competing desires or motivations, such as the desire for autonomy and the desire to belong to someone, for novelty and predictability, and for closedness and openness.

Rules theory (to be discussed in Unit 18) describes relationships as interactions governed by a series of rules that a couple agrees to follow. When the rules are followed, the relationship is maintained and when they are broken, the relationship experiences difficulty.

In this unit, four additional theories are singled out: attraction theory, reinforcement theory, social exchange theory, and equity theory. The theories offer interesting perspectives on relationships. They help explain what happens in interpersonal relationships (and in interpersonal communication generally) during the stages of development, maintenance, deterioration, and repair. They shed light on important interpersonal processes—for example, power and conflict—and on significant interpersonal relationships, such as friendship, love, and family.

Before reading any further about rules try to identify those rules that operate in one of your important relationships. What is the single most important rule? What would happen if you broke this rule? What would happen if the other person broke this same rule?

Attraction Theory

You are no doubt attracted to some people and not attracted to others. In a similar way, some people are attracted to you and some are not. If you were to examine the people to whom you are attracted and those to whom you are not attracted, you would probably see patterns in your judgments, even though many of them seem unconsciously motivated. Most people are attracted to others on the basis of three major factors: attractiveness (physical appearance and personality), proximity, and similarity.

Attractiveness: Physical Appearance and Personality   When you say, "I find that person attractive," you probably mean either that (1) you find that person physically attractive or that (2) you find that person's personality or behavior attractive. For the most part, you probably like physically attractive rather than physically unattractive people, and you probably like people who possess a pleasant rather than an unpleasant personality. Generally, you attribute positive characteristics to people you find attractive and negative characteristics to people you find unattractive.

Supporting the popular belief, research—in Bulgaria, Nigeria, Indonesia, Germany, and the United States—finds that men consider physical attractiveness in their partner more important than do women (Buss and Schmitt 1993). Similarly, in a study of gay male dating behavior, the physical attractiveness of the partner was the most important factor in influencing how much the person enjoyed his date and how much he wished to date that person again (Sergios and Cody 1985).

Note that the importance of physical attractiveness enters the face-to-face relationship immediately whereas it is only revealed after considerable communication via computer. And then such information often comes gradually: first some general verbal descriptions ("I'm 6 feet tall, brown hair, brown eyes"), then perhaps a photo, and then perhaps a face-to-face meeting (see the Media and Technology box later in this unit). It seems reasonable to assume that physical attractiveness will prove most important when it is immediate and less important when it is revealed after a period of acquaintanceship.

Those who are perceived as attractive are also seen as competent. Interestingly enough, those who are perceived as more competent in communication—as a partner working on a joint task, socially and physically—are also seen as more attractive (Duran and Kelly 1988).

Do you see attractive people as more competent? Do you see competent people as more attractive? What do you think accounts for this connection between competence and attractiveness?

Proximity If you look around at people you find attractive, you will probably notice that they are the ones who live or work close to you. For example, in a study of friendships in a student housing development, researchers found that the closer the students' rooms were to each other, the better the chances that the occupants would become friends (Festinger, Schachter, and Back 1950). The people who became friends were those who had the greatest opportunity to interact.

One reason proximity influences attraction is that it allows you to get to know the other person. You come to like people you know because you can better predict their behavior, and perhaps because of this they seem less frightening than complete strangers do (Berger and Bradac 1982).

Another approach argues that "mere exposure" to others leads you to develop positive feelings for them (Zajonc 1968). In one study (Saegert, Swap, and Zajonc 1973), women who were supposedly participating in a taste experiment were exposed throughout to other people—some ten times, others five times, others two times, others one time, and some not at all. The results showed that the subjects rated highest the persons they had seen ten times, next highest those they had seen five times, and so on down the line. How can you account for these results except by "mere exposure"? Exposure increases attraction when the initial interaction is favorable or neutral. When the initial interaction is negative, repeated exposure may actually decrease attraction.

In what ways can proximity explain your current relationships? Do you find the concept of "mere exposure" useful in explaining them?

Similarity If you could construct your mate, he or she would probably look, act, and think very much like you. By being attracted to people like yourself, you

Research in interpersonal attractiveness shows that you become more attracted to people as a result of being physically close to one another. Can this factor of proximity help to explain the friendships that you have in college? The friendships you have at work? Can it help to explain the romantic relationships you have had?

validate yourself; you tell yourself that you are worthy of being liked. Although there are exceptions, you probably are attracted to your own mirror image, to people who are similar to you in nationality, race, ability, physical characteristics, intelligence, attitudes, and so on.

If you were to ask a group of friends, "To whom are you attracted?" they would probably name very attractive people; in fact, they would probably name the most attractive people they know. But if you were to observe these friends, you would find that they go out with and establish relationships with people who are quite similar to themselves in physical attractiveness. This tendency, known as the **matching hypothesis**, predicts that although you may be attracted to the most physically attractive people, you will date and mate with people who are similar to yourself in physical attractiveness (Walster, Walster, and Berscheid 1978). Intuitively, this seems satisfying. In some cases, however, you notice discrepancies: for example, an attractive person dating someone much less attractive. In cases such as these, you would probably look for compensating factors, for qualities that compensate for the lack of physical attractiveness. Prestige, money, power, intelligence, and various personality characteristics are obvious factors that compensate for a lack of attractiveness.

Similarity in attitudes has been found to be important in attraction in such diverse cultures as the United States, India, Japan, and Mexico (Hatfield and Rapson 1992). Not surprisingly, people who have similar attitudes grow in attraction for each other over time. People who have dissimilar attitudes, on the other hand, grow less attracted to each other (Neimeyer and Mitchell 1988, Honeycutt 1986). You are probably attracted to people who have attitudes similar to your own, who like what you like and who dislike what you dislike. The more significant the attitude, the more important the similarity. Marriages between people with great and salient dissimilarities are more likely to end in divorce than marriages between people who are very much alike (Blumstein and Schwartz 1983).

Attitude similarity is especially significant in initial attraction. It also seems to predict relationship success. People who are similar in attitude become more attracted to each other over time, whereas people who are dissimilar in attitude become less attracted to each other over time (Neimeyer and Mitchell 1988). Also, the more intellectually similar people are, the more they are alike in the way they see the world, the greater their interpersonal attraction to each other (Neimeyer and Neimeyer 1983).

Although many people would argue that "birds of a feather flock together" (the similarity position), others argue that "opposites attract." This latter concept is the principle of **complementarity**. People are attracted to dissimilar others only in certain situations. For example, the submissive student may get along especially well with an assertive teacher but may not get along with an assertive romantic partner. In *A Psychologist Looks at Love* (1944), Theodore Reik argues that you fall in love with people who possess characteristics that you do not possess and actually envy. The introvert, for example, if displeased with being shy, might be attracted to an extrovert.

Affinity-Seeking Strategies   Attractiveness, proximity, and similarity are factors that influence interpersonal attraction apart from anything you may do or say. In addition, however, you can increase your attractiveness by using **affinity-seeking strategies**, which are listed in Table 16.1. These strategies were derived from studies in which people were asked to "produce a list of things people can say or do to get others to like them"; other subjects were asked to identify those things that lead others to dislike them. Thus, the strategies represent what people *think* makes them attractive to others, what people *think* makes people like them, what people *think* makes others feel positive toward them.

Reinforcement Theory

According to **reinforcement theory**, you develop relationships with those who reward you, and you avoid or break up relationships with those who do not reward you or who actually punish you.

Rewards or reinforcements may be social, such as compliments or praise, or they may be material, as in the case of the suitor whose gifts eventually win the hand of the beloved. But rewards can backfire. When overdone, rewards lose their effectiveness and may even lead to negative responses. The people who reward you constantly may become too sweet to tolerate, and you may come to discount whatever they say. Also, the reward must be perceived as genuine and not motivated by selfish concerns if it is to be successful.

You also tend to develop relationships with people *you* reward (Jecker and Landy 1969; Aronson 1980). You come to like people for whom you do favors. You need to justify going out of your way by convincing yourself that the person is worth your effort and is likable.

You may have noticed this phenomenon in your own interactions. You have probably increased your liking for persons after buying them an expensive present or going out of your way to do them a special favor. In these and similar

It has been argued that you don't actually develop an attraction for those who are similar to you but rather develop a repulsion for those who are dissimilar (Rosenbaum 1986). For example, you may be repulsed by those who disagree with you and therefore exclude them from those with whom you might develop a relationship. You are therefore left with a pool of possible partners who are similar to you. What do you think of this repulsion hypothesis?

How does reinforcement theory work in your own relationships? Do you find that you develop relationships with those who reward you and avoid relationships with those who do not reward or who actually punish you? Do you find that you also come to like those you reward?

Recent research shows that the affinity-seeking strategies that teachers use will significantly influence the climate that develops in the classroom. For example, if the teacher is supportive the students are more likely to view the classroom environment as supportive; it appears that the teacher sets the tone and the students follow it by demonstrating supportive behaviors themselves (Cabello and Terrell 1994; Myers 1995). Do you observe this? Can you identify exceptions to this general finding?

Are there ethical implications for the use of affinity-seeking strategies? When is the use of a strategy ethical? When is it unethical? For example, is it ethical for you to use these strategies consciously to get someone to go on a date with you? To get someone to vote for you?

Table 16.1	Affinity-Seeking Strategies: How to Get People to Like Us and Feel Positive Toward Us

Are there any affinity-seeking strategies that you observe regularly that are not included in this table? Are strategies included that you find ineffective? Which strategies work best for you? Which strategies work best on you? In these definitions, the term "Other" is used as shorthand for "other person or persons." This table is based on the research of Bell and Daly (1984).

Altruism. Be of help to Other.
Assumption of control. Appear "in control," as a leader, as one who takes charge.
Assumption of equality. Present yourself as socially equal to Other.
Comfort. Present yourself as comfortable and relaxed when with Other.
Concession of control. Allow Other to assume control over relational activities.
Conversational rule keeping. Follow the cultural rules for polite, cooperative conversation with Other.
Dynamism. Appear active, enthusiastic, and dynamic.
Drawing out Other's disclosures. Stimulate and encourage Other to talk about himself or herself; reinforce disclosures and contributions of Other.
Facilitation of enjoyment. Ensure that activities with Other are enjoyable and positive.
Inclusion of Other. Include Other in your social activities and groupings.
Perceptions of closeness. Create the impression that your relationship with Other is closer than it really is.
Listening. Listen to Other attentively and actively.
Nonverbal immediacy. Communicate interest in Other.
Openness. Engage in self-disclosure with Other.
Optimism. Appear optimistic and positive rather than pessimistic and negative.
Personal autonomy. Appear to Other as an independent and freethinking individual.
Physical attractiveness. Appear to Other as physically attractive as possible.
Presentation of interesting self. Appear to Other as an interesting person to get to know.
Reward association. Appear as one who is able to administer rewards to Other for associating with you.
Self-concept confirmation. Show respect for Other, and help Other to feel positively about himself or herself.
Self-inclusion. Arrange circumstances so that you and Other come into frequent contact.
Sensitivity. Communicate warmth and empathy to Other.
Similarity. Demonstrate that you share significant attitudes and values with Other.

instances, you justify your behavior by believing that the person is worth your efforts. Otherwise, you would have to admit to being a poor judge of character and to spending your money and effort on someone who isn't worth it.

Social Exchange Theory

Social exchange theory, based on an economic model of profits and losses, claims that you develop relationships that enable you to maximize your profits (Chadwick-Jones 1976; Gergen, Greenberg, and Willis 1980; Thibaut and Kelley 1959). The theory begins with the following equation:

Rewards − Costs = Profits

Rewards are anything that you want, that you enjoy, and that you'd be willing to incur costs to obtain. For example, to acquire the reward of financial gain, you might have to work rather than play. To earn an A in an interpersonal communication course, you might have to write a term paper or study more than you want to. To gain a promotion, you might have to do unpleasant tasks or work overtime. Love, affection, status, money, gifts, security, social acceptance, companionship, friendship, and intimacy are just a few examples of rewards for which you would be willing to work (that is, incur costs).

Costs are those things that you normally try to avoid—things you consider unpleasant or difficult. Working overtime, washing dishes and ironing clothes, watching a television show that your partner enjoys but you find boring, dressing in ways that are physically uncomfortable, and doing favors for people you dislike might all be considered costs.

Using this basic economic model, social exchange theory claims that you seek to develop relationships (friendship and romantic) that will give you the greatest profit—relationships in which the rewards are greater than the costs. The preferred relationships, according to this theory, are those that give you the greatest rewards with the least costs.

Comparison Levels   You enter a relationship with a general idea of the kinds of profit you ought to get out of it. This is your **comparison level,** your realistic expectations of what you feel you deserve from a relationship. For example, in a study of couples, it was found that most people expect reasonably high levels of trust, mutual respect, love, and commitment. Their expectations are significantly lower for time spent together, privacy, sexual activity, and communication (Sabatelli and Pearce 1986). When the rewards you get equal or surpass this comparison level, you feel satisfied with your relationship.

You also have a comparison level for alternatives. That is, you probably compare the profits you get from your current relationships with the ones you think you can get from alternative relationships. For example, if you believe you will not be able to find another suitable partner, you are more likely to stay in your relationship, even if it is an abusive one (Berscheid 1985). If you see that the profits from your present relationship are less than the profits you could get from an alternative relationship, you might decide to leave your current relationship and enter this new and potentially more profitable one.

Equity Theory

Equity theory uses the concepts of social exchange but goes a step further. It claims that you develop and maintain relationships in which your ratio of rewards to costs is approximately equal to your partner's (Walster, Walster, and Berscheid 1978; Messick and Cook 1983). An equitable relationship, then, is one in which participants derive rewards that are proportional to their costs. If you work harder for the relationship than your partner does, then equity demands that you should get greater rewards than your partner. If you work equally hard, then equity demands that each of you should get approximately equal rewards. Much research finds that people want equity and feel that relationships should be characterized by equity (Ueleke et al. 1983). The idea behind this is that if you are

Select two friendship or romantic relationships, one that you value highly and one that has deteriorated and dissolved. For each, do a cost-benefit analysis. In one column, identify all the costs, and in the other column identify all the benefits or rewards you derive from the highly valued relationship. Do the same cost-benefit analysis for the relationship that has dissolved. How do the benefits (their number and especially their importance) compare with the costs in both relationships?

Do you compare the rewards and costs of your current relationships with the potential rewards and costs you might derive from alternative relationships? Do you comparison shop in your relationships?

underbenefited (you get less than you put in), you will be angry. If, on the other hand, you are overbenefited (you get more than you put in), you will feel guilty (Walster, Walster, and Traupman 1978). However, some research has questioned this rather neat but intuitively unsatisfying assumption and finds that the overbenefited person is often quite happy and contented; guilt deriving from getting more than you deserve seems easily forgotten (Noller and Fitzpatrick 1993).

Equity theory puts into clear focus the sources of relational dissatisfaction you see every day. For example, in a traditional marriage, both husband and wife may have full-time jobs, but the wife may also do the major share of the household chores. Thus, although both may be deriving equal rewards—they have equally good cars, they live in the same three-bedroom house, and so on—the wife is paying more of the costs. According to equity theory, she will be dissatisfied because of this lack of equity. In a work situation, you see the same dynamic with two management trainees: each does an equal amount of work but one gets a bonus of $2000 and the other a bonus of $5000. Clearly, there is inequity, and there will be dissatisfaction.

Equity and Culture   Equity, of course, is consistent with the capitalistic orientation of Western culture, where each person is paid, for example, according to his or her contributions. The more you contribute to the organization or the relationship, the more rewards you should get out of it. In other cultures, a principle of equality or need might operate. According to the principle of equality, each person would get equal rewards, regardless of their individual contribution. According to the principle of need, each person would get rewards according to their individual need (Moghaddam, Taylor, and Wright 1993). Thus, in the United States equity is found to be highly correlated with relationship satisfaction and with relationship endurance (Schafer and Keith 1980) but, in much of Europe equity seems to be unrelated to satisfaction or endurance (Lujansky and Mikula 1983).

In one study, for example, subjects in the United States and India were asked to read situations in which a bonus was to be distributed between a worker who contributed a great deal but who was economically well-off and a worker who contributed much less but who was economically needy. Their choices were to distribute the bonus equitably (on the basis of contribution), equally, or in terms of need (Berman, Murphy-Erman, and Singh 1985; Moghaddam, Taylor, and Wright 1993). The results are given in Table 16.2.

Try applying the theories just considered to a variety of relationship issues. Read each of the following letters and describe each of the problems in terms of the (1) attraction, (2) reinforcement, (3) social exchange, and (4) equity theories. Do the theories make any predictions about how these situations are likely to be resolved? Do they offer any suggestions as to what the individuals should do?

Love and Age Difference

I'm in love with an older woman. She's 51, and I'm 22 but very mature; in fact, I'm a lot more mature than she is. I want to get married but she doesn't; she says she doesn't love me, but I know she does. She wants to break up our romance and "become friends." How can I win her over?

22 and Determined

 How would you go about discovering who leaves an inequitable relationship first—the one who is getting more profit than deserved or the one getting less profit?

One of the currently debated issues concerning social security payments revolves largely around equity versus need. Some argue that payments should be made on the basis of the person's contributions. That is, the millionaire and the person living at the poverty line should each get out what they put in; payments should be made without regard to need. Others argue that payments should be based on need and that the millionaire, for example, should not receive payments and that the poor person should—regardless of how much they each contributed. How do you feel about equity versus need in social security payments? Applied to relationships, this principle would claim that the partner in a relationship who has the greater need for reward should be given greater rewards and the partner needing fewer rewards should get less. What do you think of this?

Table 16.2	Equity in Cultural Perspective	

How would you distribute the bonus? Do your cultural values and beliefs influence your decision?

Method for Allocating Bonus	Subjects from United States	Subjects from India
Equity (each receives a reward in proportion to the work done)	49%	16%
Equality (each receives the same amount regardless of the amount of work done)	34%	32%
Need (each receives the bonus according to his or her need for the money)	16%	51%

Love and the Best Friend

Chris and I have been living together for the last ten years. Chris is very busy with writing the great American novel. I work two jobs to make ends meet. I also wind up doing the dishes, the cooking, and the cleaning. When I ask Chris to contribute more to running the house, all I get back is complaints about how bad the novel is going and how much work lies ahead. I'm getting fed up. What should I do?

Overworked and Underpaid

Love and Sports

My relationship of the last 20 years has been great—except for one thing: I can't watch sports on television. If I turn on the game, Pat moans and groans until I turn it off. Pat wants to talk; I want to watch the game. I work hard during the week, and on the weekend I want to watch sports, drink beer, and fall asleep on the couch. This problem has gotten so bad that I'm seriously considering separating. What should I do?

Sports Lover

Love and the Dilemma

I'm 29 and have been dating two really great people fairly steadily. Each knows about my relationship with the other, and for a while they went along with it and tolerated what they felt was an unpleasant situation. They now threaten to break up with me if I don't make a decision. To be perfectly honest, I like both of them a great deal; I simply need more time before I can make the decision and ask one to be my life mate. How can I get them to stay with the status quo for maybe another year or so?

Simply Undecided

MEDIA & TECHNOLOGY

Developing Relationships Online

Throughout the units on relationships, we talk about relationships generally based on face-to-face interaction. But many interpersonal relationships are now online and the numbers are growing. The number of Internet users is rapidly increasing and commercial servers are increasing their services for computer relationships. Books such as Phyllis Phlegar's (1995) *Love Online: A Practical Guide to Digital* Dating and Linda K. Fuller's (1996) *Media-Mediated Relationships: Straight and Gay, Mainstream and Alternative Perspectives* attest to the growing importance of online relationships. Even the afternoon television talk shows have focused on computer relationships, getting people together who have established a relationship online but who have never met. Clearly, many are turning to the Internet to find a friend or, more often, a romantic partner. Some are using the Internet as their only means of interaction; others are using it as a way of beginning a relationship and intend to later supplement computer talk with photographs, phone calls, and face-to-face meetings.

There are lots of advantages to establishing relationships online. For example, it is safe in terms of avoiding the potential for physical violence as well as sexually transmitted diseases from someone you really don't know. Unlike relationships established in face-to-face encounters where physical appearance tends to outweigh personality, on the Internet the person's inner qualities are communicated first. Friendship and romantic interaction on the Internet is a natural boon to shut-ins and the extremely shy who find traditional ways of meeting someone difficult. Another obvious advantage is that the number of people you can reach is so vast that it is relatively easy to find someone who matches what you are looking for. Realize that even today there are villages throughout the world where you become friends with and form romantic relationships with others from the village; choice hardly enters into the equation. The situation is analogous to finding a book that covers just what you need from a library of millions of volumes rather than from a local library of several thousands. Still another advantage for many is that the socioeconomic and educational status of people on the Net is significantly higher than you are likely to find in a bar or singles group.

Some researchers have argued that computer talk is more empowering for those with "physical disabilities or disfigurements" where face-to-face interactions are often superficial and often end with withdrawal (Lea and Spears 1995; Bull and Rumsey 1988). By eliminating the physical cues, computer talk equalizes the interaction and does not put the disfigured person, for example, at an immediate disadvantage in a society where physical attractiveness is so highly valued. You are more in control of what you want to reveal of your physical self and of course you may do it gradually.

But, of course, there are also disadvantages. For one thing you can't see what the person looks like. Unless you exchange photos or meet face-to-face you don't know what the person looks like. And even if photos are exchanged, how certain can you be that they are of the person or that they were taken recently? In addition, you cannot hear the person's voice—which, as demonstrated in Unit 11, communicates a great deal of information. Of course, you can always add an occasional phone call to give you this added information.

People can present a false self with little chance of detection. For example, minors may present themselves as adults and adults may present themselves as children for illicit and illegal sexual communications and, perhaps, meetings. Similarly, you can present yourself as rich when you are poor, as mature when you are immature, as serious and committed when you are just enjoying the experience.

Another potential disadvantage—though some might argue it is actually an advantage—is that computer interactions may become all-consuming and may substitute for face-to-face interpersonal relationships.

What do you see as the major advantages and disadvantages of online relationships? Are these the same for men and women? For heterosexuals, homosexuals, and bisexuals? Do you see online relationships being a part of your life in the next ten years? The next 20 years?

p. 341

Developing Relationships: The First Encounter

Perhaps the most difficult and yet most important aspect of relationship development is the beginning—meeting the person, presenting yourself. Here is one description of how the process might work.

Examine the Qualifiers   The first step is to examine the qualifiers, those qualities that make the person you wish to encounter an appropriate choice (Davis 1973). Some qualifiers are open to easy inspection, such as beauty, style of clothes, jewelry, and the like. Other qualifiers are hidden from easy inspection, such as personality, health, wealth, talent, and intelligence. Qualifiers tell you something about who the person is and help you decide whether to pursue this initial encounter.

Determine Clearance   The second step is to discover if this person is available for an encounter (Davis 1973). Is the person wearing a wedding ring? Does the person seem to be waiting for someone else? Does this person seem preoccupied?

Communicating Contact   The last step is making contact. You open the encounter nonverbally and verbally. As a general rule, if you are perceived as being selective—neither hard to get nor easy to get—you will appear more desirable than you would if you appeared at the extremes, that is, as nonselective or as extremely selective (Wright and Contrada 1986).

Nonverbally you might signal this desire for contact in a variety of ways.

What do you find is the single most common mistake that people make in trying to establish nonverbal contact? Do men and women make this mistake equally?

◆ Establish eye contact. The eyes communicate awareness of and interest in the other person. While maintaining eye contact, smile and further signal your interest in and positive response to this other person.

◆ Concentrate your focus. Nonverbally shut off from your awareness the rest of the room. Be careful, however, that you do not focus so directly that you make the person uncomfortable.

◆ Establish physical closeness or at least lessen the physical distance between the two of you. Approach the other person, but not to the point of discomfort, so your interest in making contact is obvious.

◆ Maintain an open posture. Throughout the encounter, maintain a posture that communicates a willingness to enter into interaction with the other person. Hands crossed over the chest or clutched around your stomach communicate a closedness, an unwillingness to let others enter your space.

◆ Reinforce the positive behaviors of the other person to signal continued interest and a further willingness to make contact. Again, nod, smile, or somehow communicate your favorable reaction.

Although nonverbal contact is signaled first, much of your subsequent contact takes place verbally.

◆ Introduce yourself. Try to avoid trite opening lines, such as "Haven't I seen you here before?" It is best simply to say, "Hi, my name is Pat."

◆ Focus the conversation on the other person. Get the other person talking about himself or herself. No one enjoys talking about any topic more than this one. Also, you will gain an opportunity to learn something about the person you want to get to know. For example, the hidden qualifiers or disqualifiers such as intelligence or the lack of it will begin to emerge here.

◆ Give the other person the opportunity to talk and to express his or her own feelings. Asking questions that require a simple yes or no answer are generally ineffective and will prove especially ineffective with Asians, who are reluctant to say no for fear it may offend the other person and feel it creates bad feelings. Instead, use open-ended questions. So, instead of saying "Do you work in the city?" ask "Where do you work?" Instead of saying "Do you come here often?"—a generally poor but popular opener—ask "Where do you usually go on a Saturday night?"

◆ Exchange favors and rewards. Compliment the other person. If you can't find anything to compliment, then you might want to reassess your interest in this person. Stress the positives. Positiveness contributes to a good first impression simply because people are more attracted to positive than to negative people.

◆ Avoid negative or too intimate self-disclosures. Enter a relationship gradually and gracefully. Disclosures should come slowly and should be reciprocal (see Unit 4). Anything too intimate or too negative, when revealed too early in the relationship, will create a negative image. If you cannot resist self-disclosing, try to stick to the positives and to issues that are not overly intimate.

◆ Establish commonalities. Seek to discover in your interaction those things you have in common with the other person—attitudes, interests, personal qualities, third parties, places—anything that will stress your similarities with this other person.

What other suggestions would you offer for making contact with another person? Should these suggestions be different for men and women? For same-sex and opposite-sex relationships?

Summary   U N I T   I N   B R I E F

A RETURN TO OBJECTIVES:

In this unit we focused on relationship development and asked: (1) What are some of the major theories that explain why we develop the relationships we do? (2) What communication behaviors are useful in developing relationships?

Relationship Theories	Steps in Initiating Relationships
Attraction theory: We develop relationships with those we consider attractive (physically and in personality), who are physically close to us, and who are similar to us. **Affinity-seeking strategies:** A wide variety of behaviors designed to get people to like us and to think positively of us, for example: ◆ being altruistic ◆ appearing to be in control ◆ presenting oneself as socially equal ◆ presenting oneself as relaxed and comfortable **Reinforcement theory:** We develop relationships with those who reinforce or reward us. We also come to like those we reward. **Social exchange theory:** We develop relationships that enable us to maximize profits, relationships from which we derive more rewards than costs. **Equity theory:** We develop and maintain relationships in which our ratio of rewards compared to costs is approximately equal to our partner's.	Examine the qualifiers. Determine clearance. Communicate contact: Nonverbally: ◆ Establish eye contact. ◆ Concentrate your focus. ◆ Establish physical closeness. ◆ Maintain an open posture. ◆ Reinforce positive behaviors. Verbally: ◆ Introduce yourself. ◆ Focus conversation on the other person and give the other person the opportunity to express herself or himself. ◆ Exchange favors and rewards. ◆ Avoid negative and too intimate disclosures. ◆ Establish commonalities.

UNIT
17

Relationship Deterioration and Dissolution

Unit Topics	Unit Objectives
	After completing this unit, you should be able to:
The Nature of Relationship Deterioration The Stages of Deterioration The Strategies of Disengagement The Negatives and the Positives	1. Explain the nature of *relationship deterioration*
Some Causes of Relationship Deterioration Unrealistic Beliefs about Relationships Excessive Intimacy Claims Third-Party Relationships Relationship Changes Undefined Expectations Sex-Related Problems Work-Related Problems Financial Difficulties	2. Explain the causes of relationship deterioration
Communication Patterns in Relationship Deterioration Withdrawal Decline in Self-Disclosure Deception Evaluative Behaviors	3. Identify the patterns of communication that characterize relationship deterioration
What the Theories Say About Relationship Deterioration and Dissolution	4. Explain how attraction, reinforcement, social exchange, and equity theories explain relationship deterioration
If the Relationship Ends Break the Loneliness-Depression Cycle Take Time Out Bolster Self-Esteem Remove or Avoid Uncomfortable Symbols Seek Support Avoid Repeating Negative Patterns	5. Explain the suggestions for dealing with the end of a relationship

---

EXPERIENTIAL LEARNING VEHICLES

Vehicle Nos. 19, "Male and Female," p. 463, 20, "Relationship Repair from Advice Columnists," pp. 463–464, and 24, "The Television Relationship," pp. 462–467, will all help illustrate what happens when relationships deteriorate.

Just as a relationship may grow and progress, becoming stronger and more meaningful, it may also wane and regress, becoming weaker and less meaningful. In this unit, we look at relationship deterioration and some of its causes, the communication patterns that characterize relationship deterioration, and some suggestions that may prove useful if the relationship does end.

Even the consideration of dissolution as an important phase of interpersonal relationships implies that this is a viable option. But, in some cultures, relationships—such as marriage—are forever and cannot be dissolved if things go wrong. More important to such cultures are such issues as "How do you maintain a relationship that has problems?" "What can you do to exist within an unpleasant relationship?" "How can you repair a relationship that is troubled?" (Moghaddam, Taylor, and Wright 1993).

Further, the culture will influence the difficulty that a person will go through when relationships break up. For example, married persons whose religion forbids divorce and remarriage will experience religious disapproval and condemnation as well as the same economic and social difficulties everyone else goes through. In the United States, child custody almost invariably goes to the woman and this presents an added emotional burden for the man. In Iran, child custody goes to the man, which presents added emotional burdens for the woman. In India, women experience greater difficulty than men in divorce because of their economic dependence on men, the cultural beliefs about women, and the patriarchal order of the family (Amato 1994).

 What has your culture taught you about relationship deterioration and dissolution? Have these teachings influenced you significantly?

The Nature of Relationship Deterioration

Relationship deterioration refers to the weakening of the bonds that hold people together. The process of deterioration may be gradual or sudden. Gradual deterioration might occur in a situation in which one of the parties in a relationship develops close ties with a new intimate, and this new relationship gradually pushes out the old. Sudden deterioration might occur when a rule that was essential to the relationship (for example, the rule of complete fidelity) is broken and both realize that the relationship cannot be sustained.

The Stages of Deterioration

Interpersonal researcher Steve Duck (1986) proposes that you can best understand the process of deterioration by identifying the phases you might go through in passing from deterioration to dissolution. The process begins at the **breakdown phase**, during which you experience dissatisfaction with the relationship and with each other.

During the **intrapsychic phase**, you brood privately about your dissatisfaction with the relationship and with the other person. Gradually, you may share your feelings, initially with relative strangers and then eventually with close friends.

During the **dyadic phase**, you discuss your problems with your partner and perhaps try to correct the difficulties between you.

If the problems cannot be worked out, and if you decide to exit the relationship, you enter the **social phase**. Here you would share the dissatisfaction and the

At what point would you describe a relationship as "deteriorating"? That is, what has to be going on for you to say that this is happening?

decision to exit the relationship with members of your social group. During this phase, you might try to enlist the support of others. You seek understanding, empathy, and the social support that will help you through the breakup.

The fifth and final phase is the **grave-dressing phase**, during which you create a kind of history of the relationship—its beginnings, its development, and its dissolution. Your intention here is to distance yourself from the relationship and to encourage others to look at you more favorably.

The Strategies of Disengagement

When you wish to exit a relationship, you need some explanation—to yourself as well as to your partner. You develop a strategy for getting out of a relationship that you no longer find satisfying or profitable. Table 17.1 identifies five major disengagement strategies (Cody 1982). As you read down the table, note that the strategies depend on your goal. For example, you are more likely to remain friends if you use de-escalation than if you use justification or avoidance (Banks, Altendorf, Greene, and Cody 1987). You may find it interesting to identify the disengagement strategies you have heard of or used yourself and see how they fit in with these five types.

Table 17.1	**Five Disengagement Strategies**

Think back to your own relationships that you have tried to dissolve or that your partner tried to dissolve. Did you or your partner use any of the strategies listed here? These strategies are taken from research by Michael Cody (1982).

Strategy	Function	Examples
Positive tone	To maintain a positive relationship To express positive feelings for the other person	*I really care for you a great deal but I'm not ready for such an intense relationship.*
Negative identity management	To blame the other person for the breakup To absolve oneself of the blame for the breakup	*I can't stand your jealousy, your constant suspicions, your checking up on me. I need my freedom.*
Justification	To give reasons for the breakup	*I'm going away to college for four years; there's no point in not dating others.*
Behavioral de-escalation	To reduce the intensity of the relationship	*Avoidance; cut down on phone calls; reduce time spent together, especially time alone.*
De-escalation	To reduce the exclusivity and hence the intensity of the relationship	*I'm just not ready for so exclusive a relationship. I think we should see other people.*

Let us say that you were steadily dating someone for the last six months but met someone else with whom you wanted to get serious. What disengagement strategy would you be most likely to use? Why?

The Negatives and the Positives

When relationships deteriorate or break up, a variety of negative outcomes may occur. There is most obviously a loss of all the positives you enjoyed as a result of the relationship. Regardless of how unsatisfying the relationship might ultimately have been, it probably also had many good aspects. These are now lost.

There is also, generally, a loss of self-esteem. You may feel unworthy or perhaps guilty. You may blame yourself for doing the wrong things, not doing the right things, or being responsible for the losses you now confront. And, of course, there are likely to be friends and family members who will give you a hard time, often implying that you are to blame.

There are also practical issues. Most relationship breakups have financial implications, and you may now encounter money. Paying the rent, tuition, or outstanding loans by yourself may prove difficult. If the relationship is a marriage, then there are legal and perhaps religious implications of the breakup. If there are children, the situation becomes even more complicated.

Nevertheless, not all relationships should be sustained. Not all breakups are bad, and few, if any, bad breakups are entirely bad. In the midst of a breakup, this may be difficult to appreciate. In retrospect, it is almost always true.

Some relationships are unproductive for one or both parties, and a breakup is often the best alternative. A breakup may provide an opportunity for the individuals to regain their independence and to become self-reliant again. Some relationships are so absorbing that there is little time for reflection on oneself, on others, and on the relationship itself. Sometimes distance helps. A breakup may also allow you to develop new associations and to explore different types of relationships with different types of people.

So, relational deterioration need not have only negative consequences. For the most part, it is up to you to draw out of any decaying relationship the positive and productive lessons.

 What other advantages and disadvantages of interpersonal relationships can you identify?

Some Causes of Relationship Deterioration

There are as many reasons for relationship deterioration as there are people in relationships. It is, therefore, extremely difficult to identify specific causes for any specific relationship deterioration. Still, some general causes—applicable to a wide variety of breakups—may be identified.

All these "causes" can also be *effects* of relationship deterioration. For example, when things start to go sour, you may remove yourself physically from your partner. This physical separation in turn causes further deterioration by driving you further apart emotionally and psychologically. Similarly, the degree of mutual commitment between you may lessen as other signs of deterioration appear.

Recall that the factors that are important in establishing relationships (discussed in Unit 16) may, when no longer present, contribute to deterioration. For example, when loneliness is no longer reduced by the relationship (when one or both individuals feel lonely frequently or for prolonged periods), the relationship may well be on the road to decay because it is not serving the expected function.

Unrealistic Beliefs about Relationships

The way in which you think about relationships can influence the course of a relationship and is well illustrated in the self-test on the next page, "What Do You Believe About Relationships?"

Excessive Intimacy Claims

In most relationships—especially intense ones—the members make intimacy claims on each other (Blood 1973). Such claims may include expectations that the partner will sympathize and empathize, attend to self-disclosures with total absorption, or share the other's preferences with equal intensity. These intimacy claims often restrict personal freedom and may take the form of possessiveness. To be always responsive, always sympathetic, always loving, always attentive is more than many can manage. In some relationships, the intimacy claims and demands are so great that the partners' individual identities may be in danger of being absorbed or destroyed.

Third-Party Relationships

You establish and maintain relationships to maximize your pleasure and minimize your pain. When this ceases to be the case, the relationship stands little chance of survival. These needs are so great that when they are not met within the existing relationship, their fulfillment will be sought elsewhere. When a new relationship serves these needs better, the old relationship may deteriorate. At times, this may be a romantic interest; at other times, the new relationship may be with a parent or, frequently, a child. When your need for affection or attention, once supplied by the other person, is now supplied by a friend or a child, the primary relationship may be in trouble.

Relationship Changes

The development of incompatible attitudes, vastly different intellectual interests and abilities, and major goal changes may contribute to relationship deterioration. Similarly, changes in behavior may create difficulties. For example, if you once devoted lots of time to your partner and to the relationship and now are totally absorbed with business or school, your relationship is going to face significant repercussions. The person who develops an addiction (to drugs, alcohol, or even stamp collecting) will likewise present the relationship with a serious problem.

Undefined Expectations

Unresolved expectations over who is in charge are a frequent cause of relationship difficulties (Lederer 1984). Often, conflicts over such trivial issues as who does the dishes or who walks the dog mask resentment and hostility concerning some more significant unresolved expectation.

At times, the expectations each person has of the other may be unrealistic, and when reality enters the relationship, difficulties arise. This situation often occurs early in a relationship, when, for example, the individuals think they will want to spend all their time together. When it is discovered that neither one does,

What are (were) your expectations for a primary romantic relationship? Are these expectations realistic? Might these expectations cause problems?

Self Test → *What Do You Believe About Relationships?*

For each of the following statements, select the number (1 to 7) of the category that best fits how much you agree or disagree. Enter that number on the line next to each statement.

        7 = agree completely
        6 = agree a good deal
        5 = agree somewhat
        4 = neither agree nor disagree
        3 = disagree somewhat
        2 = disagree a good deal
        1 = disagree completely

_____ 1. If a person has any questions about the relationship, then it means there is something wrong with it.

_____ 2. If my partner truly loved me, we would not have any quarrels.

_____ 3. If my partner really cared, he or she would always feel affection for me.

_____ 4. If my partner gets angry at me or is critical in public, this indicates he or she doesn't really love me.

_____ 5. My partner should know what is important to me without my having to tell him or her.

_____ 6. If I have to ask for something that I really want, it spoils it.

_____ 7. If my partner really cared, he or she would do what I ask.

_____ 8. A good relationship should not have any problems.

_____ 9. If people really love each other, they should not have to work on their relationship.

_____10. If my partner does something that upsets me, I think it is because he or she deliberately wants to hurt me.

_____11. When my partner disagrees with me in public, I think it is a sign that he or she doesn't care for me very much.

_____12. If my partner contradicts me, I think that he or she doesn't have much respect for me.

_____13. If my partner hurts my feelings, I think that it is because he or she is mean.

_____14. My partner always tries to get his or her own way.

_____15. My partner doesn't listen to what I have to say.

Thinking Critically About Relationship Beliefs
Aaron Beck, one of the leading theorists in cognitive therapy and the author of the popular *Love Is Never Enough,* claims that all of these beliefs are unrealistic and may well create problems in your interpersonal relationships. The test was developed to help people identify potential sources of difficulty for relationship development and maintenance. The more statements that you indicated you believe in, the more unrealistic your expectations are.

Do you agree with Beck that these beliefs are unrealistic and that they will cause problems? Which belief is the most dangerous to the development and maintenance of an interpersonal relationship?

"Beliefs About Your Relationship" from *Love is Never Enough,* by Aaron T. Beck. New York: Harper & Row, 1988, pp. 67–68. Copyright © 1988 by Aaron T. Beck, M.D. Reprinted by permission of HarperCollins Publishers, Inc. and Arthur Pine Associates. Beck notes that this test was adapted in part from the Relationship Belief Inventory of N. Epstein, J.L. Pretzer, and B. Fleming, "The Role of Cognitive Appriasal in Self-Reports of Marital Communications," *Behavior Therapy* 18 (1987):51–69.

each resents this "lessening" of feeling in the other. The resolution of such problems lies in demonstrating that the original expectations are unrealistic and that realistic and satisfying ones can be substituted.

Another kind of undefined expectation may involve the traditional sex-role stereotypes. This finding surely contradicts the move toward equality verbally affirmed by most educated men and women. For example, according to Sara Yogev (1987): "traditional sex-role stereotypes regarding the spouse are closely related to marital satisfaction and . . . deviations from the expected psychological characteristic in which the man is superior to his wife may reduce the level of marital satisfaction for both men and women but more so for women. Thus, while one sees behavioral-social changes (i.e., more women are employed, some even in male-dominated fields), psychological change does not follow immediately on the heels of the behavioral change for either sex."

Consider the research finding of Yogev discussed in this section. Why do you think this was found? Is this changing? What evidence do you have that would support or contradict Yogev's findings?

Sex-Related Problems

Few relationships are free of sexual differences and problems. In fact, sexual problems rank among the top three problems in almost all studies of newlyweds (Blumstein and Schwartz 1983). When these same couples are surveyed later in their relationship, the sexual problems have not gone away; they are just discussed less. Apparently, people resign themselves to living with the problems. In one survey, for example, 80 percent of the respondents identified their marriages as either "very happy" or "happy," but some 90 percent said they had sexual problems (Freedman 1978).

Although sexual frequency is not related to relationship breakdown, sexual satisfaction is. It is the quality, not the quantity, of a sexual relationship that is crucial. When the quality is poor, outside affairs may be sought and these contribute significantly to breakups for all couples, whether married or cohabiting (Blumstein and Schwartz 1983).

Work-Related Problems

Problems associated with either partner's job often lead to difficulties within the relationship. This is true for all types of couples. With heterosexual couples (both marrieds and cohabitants), if the man is disturbed about the woman's job—for example, if she earns a great deal more than he does or devotes a great deal of time to the job—the relationship is in considerable trouble. This is true whether the relationship is in its early stages or is well established (Blumstein and Schwartz 1983). One research study, for example, found that husbands whose wives worked were less satisfied with their own jobs and lives than were men whose wives did not work (Staines, Pottick, and Fudge 1986). This personal dissatisfaction will naturally have negative effects on the relationship.

With homosexual relationships the situation is a bit different (Blumstein and Schwartz 1983; Huston and Schwartz 1995). Gay men, like heterosexual men, are career oriented. Work-related problems may be magnified, since both devote considerable time to work with less time available for the more relational concerns. Lesbians, on the other hand, are less career oriented (than gay men) and are more relationship oriented (than men in general). This may be one reason lesbian relationships seem to last longer than gay male relationships.

A *New York Times* survey (February 24, 1988), based on interviews with 1870 people throughout the United States, found that "even though more women are in the work force and have less time at home, they are still the primary care-givers and the people who pay attention to how, when, what, and where their families eat. . . . The idea of equality at home," the report concludes, "is an illusion." Too often the man expects the woman to work but neither reduces his expectations concerning her household responsibilities nor agrees to assume any of them himself. The man becomes resentful if the woman does not fulfill these expectations, and the woman becomes resentful if she takes on both outside work and full household duties. It is a no-win situation, and the relationship suffers as a result.

Are the attitudes found in this survey similar to the attitudes held by people in your class? If there are differences, what factors might account for them?

Financial Difficulties

In surveys of problems among couples, financial difficulties loom large. Money is a major taboo topic for couples beginning a relationship, yet it proves to be the cause of major problems as people settle into their relationship. One-fourth to one-third of all couples rank money as their primary problem; almost all rank it as one of their major problems (Blumstein and Schwartz 1983).

Money is so important in relationships because of its close connection with power. Money brings power in relationships, as it does in business. The person

Why do you suppose that money is rarely discussed among dating couples? What do you think of prenuptial agreements? Would you enter into one if your partner wanted to? Do you think your partner would enter into one if you wanted him or her to?

bringing in the most money wields the most power. This person has the final say, for example, on the purchase of expensive items as well as on decisions having nothing to do with money. The power that money brings quickly spreads to non-financial issues as well.

Money also creates problems because men and women view it differently (Blumstein and Schwartz 1983). To many men, money is power. To many women, it is security and independence. To men, money is accumulated to exert power and influence. To women, money is accumulated to achieve security and reduce dependence on others. Conflicts over the way the couple's money is to be spent or invested can easily result from such different views. Further, when the wife earns a high income, marital conflict increases and the husband's satisfaction with the relationship decreases (Harrell 1990).

Dissatisfaction with money creates relationship problems for married and co-habiting couples and gay male couples but not for lesbian couples, who seem to care a great deal less about financial matters (Blumstein and Schwartz 1983). This difference has led some researchers to postulate (though without conclusive evidence) that the concern over money and its equation with power and relational satisfaction are largely male attitudes.

How important is money to your relationship decisions and relationship happiness? That is, do you make any relationship decisions on the basis of money? To what extent—if any—does your relationship happiness depend on money?

Communication Patterns in Relationship Deterioration

Relationship deterioration involves special communication patterns. These patterns are in part a response to the deterioration; you communicate the way you do because you feel that your relationship is in trouble. However, these patterns are also causative: The communication patterns you use largely determine the fate of your relationship.

Withdrawal

The easiest communication pattern to see is that of withdrawal (Miller and Parks 1982). Nonverbally, this withdrawal is seen in the greater space you need and the speed with which tempers and other signs of disturbance arise when that space is invaded. Other nonverbal signs of withdrawal include a decrease in eye contact, touching, similarities in clothing, and displays of items associated with the other person, for example, bracelets, photographs, and rings (Knapp and Vangelisti 1992).

Verbally, withdrawal is marked by decreased desire to talk and listen. At times, phatic communication (or something resembling it) is used not as a preliminary to serious conversation but as an alternative, perhaps to avoid confronting the serious issues.

Decline in Self-Disclosure

Self-disclosing communications decline significantly. If the relationship is dying, you may think it not worth the effort. Or you might limit your self-disclosures because you feel that the other person may not accept them or can no longer be trusted to be supportive and empathic.

INTERPERSONAL ETHICS

CENSORING MESSAGES AND INTERACTIONS

Frank: father
Alex: son
Laura: mother

Frank: Listen, Alex. I hear you've been hanging out with the Franklin brothers. I want that stopped. I don't want you hanging around with—hell, I don't want you even seeing—the Franklins. Even from a distance. They're bad news.

Laura: He's right, Alex. Stay away from them from now on.

Frank: Don't act like a know-it-all. You listen to your mother.

Laura: You hear us, Alex? Do you?

Frank: We mean it, Alex. We want you to stay far away from those guys.

Are these parents justified in trying to censor interactions between their son and others they consider undesirable? Would you need additional information about the Franklins to make your decision? How would you answer if:

◆ The Franklin brothers were drug dealers and were trying to persuade Alex to run drugs for them?
◆ The Franklin brothers had AIDS?
◆ The Franklin brothers were of a different race or religion?
◆ Alex was mentally retarded or 11 years old or on parole?

Throughout your life, the messages you receive are censored—a topic that is significant to all stages of relationships and which could have been positioned in any of the relationship units. As you read this box, consider the implications for all the relationship stages.

When you were very young, your parents censored certain television programs, magazines, and movies—perhaps even records—that they thought inappropriate, usually because they were either too sexually explicit or too violent. Currently, the appropriateness or legitimacy of advertising certain products on television, most notably condoms, is being debated. Many would have this material censored.

Similarly, when we were young, our parents may have encouraged us to play with certain children and not to play with others. Sometimes these decisions were based on the character of the other children. Sometimes they were based on the racial, religious, or national background of the would-be friends. Today, the most obvious instances in which interactions are prevented are those involving interracial marriage and homosexual relations. These prohibitions prevent certain people from interacting in the manner in which they choose. If an interracial couple wish to marry, they must be careful in choosing where the ceremony is performed and where they will settle. Interracial couples run into difficulty finding housing, employment, and, most significantly, acceptance into a community. Gay men and lesbians encounter the same difficulty, and consequently many are forced to live "straight" lives—at least on the surface.

If, for example, you run a business, should you have the right to refuse someone a job because he or she is married to an individual of another race or has an affectional orientation different from yours? And if you do have the right to choose your employees on the basis of such preferences, do you still retain the rights to protection by the law that the society as a whole has granted to everyone?

Lesbians and gay men are currently prevented from holding jobs as teachers, police officers, and firefighters in many states. These discriminatory laws are not terribly effective, but this is not the issue. The relative ineffectiveness of such prohibitions should not blind us to the social realities that these laws incorporate. What should be considered is that the gay man or lesbian can work under his or her own identity only if masked as heterosexual. The military policy of "don't ask, don't tell" is a perfect example of how the society as a whole forces certain of its citizens to hide their true selves. Is society ethical when it requires such concealment of identity?

◆ Is it ethical to try to persuade your friends to avoid interacting with Tom and Lisa because you think they are immoral? Because you are jealous of them? Because you feel they will have a bad influence on your friends?

◆ Is it ethical for a child to turn in his or her parents to the police for alcohol abuse? For smoking marijuana? For using cocaine? For child abuse?

◆ Is it ethical to forcibly prevent a friend who has had too much to drink (in your opinion) from driving? To forcibly prevent a friend from riding in a car driven by someone who has just smoked marijuana?

◆ What ethical guidelines would you propose for the censorship of interactions?

[The next ethics box appears in Unit 21, pages 407–408, and deals with gossip.]

Are there situations when withdrawal might be a wise communication strategy?

Deception

Deception increases as relationships break down. Sometimes this takes the form of clear-cut lies that may be used to avoid arguments over such things as staying out all night, not calling, or being seen in the wrong place with the wrong person. At other times, lies may be used because of a feeling of shame; you might not want the other person to think less of you. Perhaps you want to save the relationship and do not want to add another obstacle. One of the problems with deception is that it has a way of escalating. Eventually, a climate of distrust and disbelief comes to characterize the relationship.

Do men and women lie about the same things and at the same frequency? How would you go about collecting evidence bearing on this question?

Evaluative Behaviors

During deterioration, there is likely to be an increase in negative and a decrease in positive evaluation. Where once you may have praised the other's behaviors or ideas, you now criticize them. Often the behaviors have not changed significantly; what has changed is your way of looking at them. What was once a cute habit now becomes annoying; what was once seen as "different" now becomes inconsiderate. This negative evaluation frequently leads to outright fighting and conflict; although conflict is not necessarily bad, in deteriorating relationships the conflict is often left unresolved.

During relational deterioration, there is also a marked change in the types of requests made (Lederer 1984). When a relationship is deteriorating, requests for pleasurable behaviors decrease ("Will you fix me my favorite dessert?"). At the same time, requests to stop unpleasant or negative behaviors increase ("Will you stop monopolizing the phone every evening?").

Another symptom is the sometimes gradual, sometimes sudden decrease in the social niceties that accompany requests, a progression from "Would you please make me a cup of coffee, honey?" to "Get me some coffee, will you?" to "Where's my coffee?"

How do your communication patterns change during relationship deterioration? Do these changed patterns also create additional problems for your relationship? In what way?

Figure 17.1 summarizes the changes in communication (discussed in this unit and the previous two) that take place as you move toward or away from intimacy. The general and most important point this figure makes is that communication effectiveness and satisfaction increase as you move toward intimacy and decrease as you move away from intimacy.

What the Theories Say About Relationship Deterioration and Dissolution

In Unit 16 we looked at four basic relationship theories. Let's see what each of these theories has to say about relationship deterioration. Attraction theory holds that relationships deteriorate and may dissolve when the attraction you felt for each other fades significantly. When relationships break up, it is the more attractive person who leaves (Blumstein and Schwartz 1983). There is no denying the power of attractiveness in the development of relationships and the influence of its loss to the deterioration of relationships.

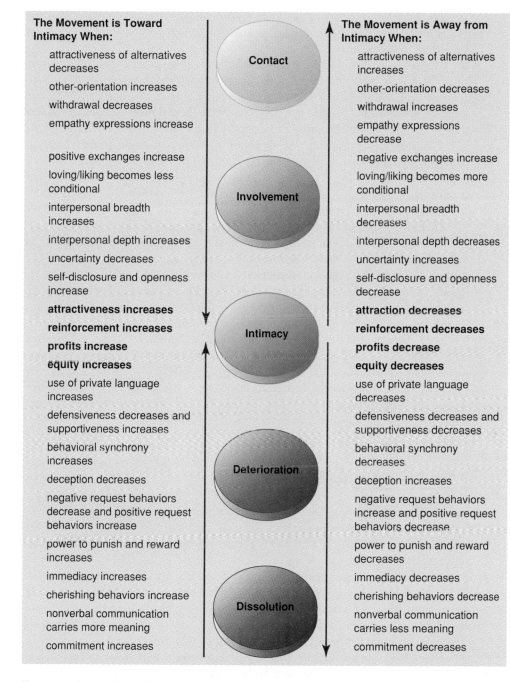

The Movement is Toward Intimacy When:

attractiveness of alternatives decreases

other-orientation increases

withdrawal decreases

empathy expressions increase

positive exchanges increase

loving/liking becomes less conditional

interpersonal breadth increases

interpersonal depth increases

uncertainty decreases

self-disclosure and openness increase

attractiveness increases

reinforcement increases

profits increase

equity increases

use of private language increases

defensiveness decreases and supportiveness increases

behavioral synchrony increases

deception decreases

negative request behaviors decrease and positive request behaviors increase

power to punish and reward increases

immediacy increases

cherishing behaviors increase

nonverbal communication carries more meaning

commitment increases

Contact

Involvement

Intimacy

Deterioration

Dissolution

The Movement is Away from Intimacy When:

attractiveness of alternatives increases

other-orientation decreases

withdrawal increases

empathy expressions decrease

negative exchanges increase

loving/liking becomes more conditional

interpersonal breadth decreases

interpersonal depth decreases

uncertainty increases

self-disclosure and openness decrease

attraction decreases

reinforcement decreases

profits decrease

equity decreases

use of private language decreases

defensiveness decreases and supportiveness decreases

behavioral synchrony decreases

deception increases

negative request behaviors increase and positive request behaviors decrease

power to punish and reward decreases

immediacy decreases

cherishing behaviors decrease

nonverbal communication carries less meaning

commitment decreases

Figure 17.1 Communication in Relationships.
This summary of some of the changes that accompany increased intimacy and some that accompany decreased intimacy contains many of the findings discussed here and in Units 15 and 16. The major theories discussed in Unit 16 are noted here in boldface. As you read down the list, try to identify examples from your own relationships. Did any factors listed here produce effects on your relationships different from that predicted here? For example, did one of the factors listed here as leading to greater intimacy actually result in decreased intimacy? What else happens as a relationship moves toward intimacy? Toward deterioration? How would you go about testing the validity of these movement predictions?

Reinforcement theory holds that relationships deteriorate when you no longer see the relationship as rewarding and may dissolve when you feel it is more punishing than rewarding.

According to social exchange theory, your relationship deteriorates when it is no longer profitable, when the costs exceed the rewards. If this happens, there is a tendency to reduce the rewards. For example, compliments, once given frequently and sincerely, are now rare; positive stroking is minimal; there is little eye contact and few smiles. This reduction in rewards further tips the scales toward deterioration.

Your present relationship may become unstable and begin to deteriorate if you see your alternatives (your available options) as more rewarding. However, even if your relationship is less than you expected it to be, you will probably not seek to dissolve it unless you perceive that another relationship (or being alone) will provide a greater profit.

According to equity theory, you stay in relationships in which you receive rewards in proportion to your costs. If you pay more of the costs, you should obtain more of the rewards. When a relationship becomes inequitable, that is, when one person derives a disproportionate share of the rewards or suffers an excessive share of the costs, the relationship suffers. Women are more likely to engage in extramarital affairs when they perceive their relationship as inequitable (Prins, Buunk, and VanYperen 1993). Perceptions of inequity by men, however, did not influence their likelihood of engaging in extramarital affairs. Further, women are more likely than men to break up a relationship as a result of their own extrarelational affair (Janus and Janus 1993).

When partners perceive their relationship to be equitable, they will continue to date, live together, or marry. When the relationship is not perceived to be equitable, the relationship suffers, and it may well deteriorate.

 Would you be unhappy in a relationship in which you and your partner contributed an equal share of the costs (that is, you each worked equally hard) but your partner derived significantly greater rewards? Why?

If the Relationship Ends

Some relationships, of course, do end. Sometimes there is simply not enough to hold the couple together. Sometimes there are problems that cannot be resolved. Sometimes the costs are too high and the rewards too few, or the relationship is recognized as destructive and escape is the only alternative. Regardless of the specific reason, relationship breakups are difficult to deal with; invariably, they cause stress.

You are likely to experience high levels of distress over the breakup of a relationship in which you were satisfied, were close to your partner, had dated your partner for a long time, and felt it would not be easy to replace the relationship with another one (Simpson 1987; Frazier and Cook 1993).

Given both the inevitability that some relationships will break up and the importance of such breakups, here are some suggestions to ease the difficulty that is sure to be experienced. These suggestions apply to the termination of any type of relationship—between friends or lovers, through death, separation, or breakup.

Break the Loneliness-Depression Cycle

The two most common feelings following the end of a relationship are loneliness and depression. These feelings are significant; treat them seriously. Realize that depression often leads to serious illness. In most cases, fortunately, loneliness and depression are temporary. Depression, for example, usually does not last longer than three or four days. Similarly, the loneliness that follows a breakup is generally linked to this specific situation and will fade when the situation changes. When depression does last, is especially deep, or disturbs your normal functioning, it's time for professional help.

Take Time Out

Resist the temptation to jump into a new relationship while the old one is still warm or before a new one can be assessed with some objectivity. At the same time, resist swearing off all relationships. Neither extreme works well.

Take time out for yourself. Renew your relationship with yourself. If you were in a long-term relationship, you probably saw yourself as part of a team, as part of a couple. Now get to know yourself as a unique individual, standing alone at present but fully capable of entering a meaningful relationship in the near future.

Bolster Self-Esteem

When relationships fail, self-esteem often declines. This seems especially true for those who did *not* initiate the breakup (Collins and Clark 1989). You may feel guilty for having caused the breakup or inadequate for not holding on to the relationship. You may feel unwanted and unloved. Your task is to regain the positive self-image needed to function effectively.

Recognize, too, that having been in a relationship that failed—even if you view yourself as the main cause of the breakup—does not mean that *you are a failure*. Neither does it mean that you cannot succeed in a new and different relationship. It does mean that something went wrong with this one relationship. And (ideally) it was a failure from which you have learned something important about yourself and about your relationship behavior.

Remove or Avoid Uncomfortable Symbols

After any breakup, there are a variety of reminders—photographs, gifts, and letters, for example. Resist the temptation to throw these out. Instead, remove them. Give them to a friend to hold or put them in a closet where you will not see them. If possible, avoid places you frequented together. These symbols will bring back uncomfortable memories. After you have achieved some emotional distance, you can go back and enjoy these as reminders of a once-pleasant relationship. Support for this suggestion comes from research showing that the more vivid your memory of a broken love affair—a memory greatly aided by these relationship symbols—the greater your depression is likely to be (Harvey, Flanary, and Morgan 1986).

Seek Support

Many people feel they should bear their burdens alone. Men, in particular, have been taught that this is the only "manly" way to handle things. But, seeking the support of others is one of the best antidotes to the unhappiness caused when a relationship ends. Tell your friends and family of your situation—in only general terms, if you prefer—and make it clear that you want support. Seek out people who are positive and nurturing. Avoid negative individuals who will paint the world in even darker tones. Make the distinction between seeking support and seeking advice. If you feel you need advice, seek out a professional.

Avoid Repeating Negative Patterns

Many people repeat their mistakes. They enter second and third relationships with the same blinders, faulty preconceptions, and unrealistic expectations with which they entered earlier ones. Instead, use the knowledge gained from your failed relationships to prevent repeating the same patterns.

At the same time, do not become a prophet of doom. Do not see in every relationship vestiges of the old. Do not jump at the first conflict and say, "Here it goes all over again." Treat the new relationship as the unique relationship it is. Don't evaluate it through past experiences. Use past relationships and experiences as guides, not filters.

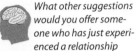
What other suggestions would you offer someone who has just experienced a relationship breakup? Would you offer different suggestions to men than you would to women?

Summary	U N I T I N B R I E F

A RETURN TO OBJECTIVES:

In this unit we focused on relationship deterioration and dissolution and specifically asked: (1) What is relationship deterioration and what stages does it pass through? (2) What causes relationships to deteriorate and break up? (3) What happens to communication during relationship deterioration? (4) How do the relationship theories deal with deterioration? (5) How can we best manage relationship dissolution?

Stages of Deterioration	Causes of Relational Deterioration	Communication Patterns in Deteriorating Relationships	Relationship Theories and Deterioration	Management Guidelines for Relational Dissolution
Breakdown phase Intrapsychic phase Dyadic phase Social phase Grave-dressing phase	Unrealistic beliefs about relationships Excessive intimacy claims Third-party relationships Relational changes Undefined expectations Sex-related problems Work-related problems Financial difficulties	Withdrawal Decline in self-disclosure Increased deception Change in evaluations	Relationships deteriorate when: ◆ Attraction fades ◆ The relationship is no longer rewarding ◆ The costs exceed the rewards or more rewarding alternatives are available ◆ The relationship is not equitable	Break the loneliness-depression cycle Take time out Bolster self-esteem Remove or avoid uncomfortable symbols Seek support Avoid repeating negative patterns

UNIT
18

Relationship Maintenance and Repair

Unit Topics	Unit Objectives
	After completing this unit, you should be able to:
Relationship Maintenance Reasons for Maintaining Relationships Maintenance Behaviors Interpersonal Maintenance and Rules	1. Explain the reasons for relationship maintenance 2. Explain how rules may be used to explain relationship maintenance 3. Identify at least five maintenance strategies
What the Theories Say About Maintenance	4. Describe how attraction, reinforcement, social exchange, and equity theories explain relationship maintenance
Relationship Repair General Relationship Repair Strategies Solo Relationship Repair Relationships in Cultural Context	5. Explain the relationship repair wheel 6. Explain how relationships may be repaired by only one person 7. Explain the influence of culture on interpersonal relationships

---

EXPERIENTIAL LEARNING VEHICLES

Experiential Learning Vehicle No. 20, "Relationship Repair from Advice Columnists," pp. 463–464, may be used to stimulate discussion on interpersonal relationship repair. No. 24, "The Television Relationship," pp. 467–468, may be used to focus on maintenance and repair.

After a relationship is established, it needs to be maintained and sometimes repaired; both topics are covered in this unit.

Relationship Maintenance

Relationship maintenance concerns what you do to continue (maintain, retain) your relationship. Maintenance behaviors can serve a variety of functions:

- to keep the relationship intact, to retain the semblance of a relationship, to prevent dissolution of the relationship;
- to keep the relationship at its present stage, to prevent it from moving too far toward either less or greater intimacy;
- to keep the relationship satisfying, to maintain an appropriate balance between rewards and penalties.

How would you go about investigating how different cultures view the importance of relationship maintenance? Do different cultures assign men and women different responsibilities for relationship maintenance?

Some people, after entering a relationship, assume that it will continue unless something catastrophic happens. Consequently, while they may seek to prevent any major mishaps, they are unlikely to engage in much maintenance behavior. Others will be ever on the lookout for something wrong and will seek to patch it up as quickly and effectively as possible. Most people lie in between. They will engage in maintenance behaviors when things are going wrong and when there is the possibility that the relationship can be improved. Behaviors directed at improving badly damaged or even broken relationships are considered under the topic of repair, in the second half of this unit.

Reasons for Maintaining Relationships

The reasons for maintaining relationships are as numerous and varied as the reasons for beginning them. Some of the more popular and frequently cited reasons are mentioned here.

Emotional Attachment Often you maintain a relationship because you love each other and want to preserve your relationship. You do not find alternative couplings as inviting or as potentially enjoyable—the individuals' needs are being satisfied, and so the relationship is maintained. In some cases, your needs are predominantly for love and mutual caring, but in other cases, the needs being met may not be quite so positive. For example, one individual may maintain a relationship because it provides a means of exercising control over another. Someone else may maintain a relationship because it provides ego gratification.

Do men and women maintain relationships for the same reasons? How would you go about collecting evidence bearing on this question?

Convenience Often the relationship is maintained because it's convenient. Both partners may jointly own a business or have mutual friends who are important to them. In these cases, it may be more convenient to stay together than to break up and go through the difficulties involved in finding another person to live with, another business partner, or another social escort. At times, both feel the same way about the relationship, and in such cases there is seldom any difficulty; neither person is "fooling" the other. At other times, the relationship is one of great love for one partner and one of convenience for the other.

Children   Relationships are often maintained because of children. Children are sometimes (fortunately or unfortunately) brought into the world to save a relationship. In some cases they do. The parents stay together because they feel, rightly or wrongly, that it is in the best interests of the children. In other instances, the children provide a socially acceptable excuse to mask the real reason—convenience, financial advantage, fear of being alone, and so on. In childless relationships, both parties can be more independent and can make life choices based more on individual needs and wants. As a result they are less likely to remain in relationships they find unpleasant or uncomfortable.

Fear   Fear motivates many couples to stay together. They may fear the outside world, being alone, facing others as "singles," or even of making it on one paycheck. They may remember the horrors of the singles bars, the one-night stands, and the lonely weekends. As a result, they may elect to preserve their current relationship as the better alternative. Sometimes the fear may be of social criticism: "What will our friends say? They'll think I'm a failure because I can't hold on to a relationship." Sometimes the fear concerns the consequences of violating a religious or parental tenet.

Inertia   Some relationships are maintained because of inertia, the tendency for a body at rest to remain at rest and a body in motion to remain in motion. Many people simply go along with the program, and it hardly occurs to them to consider changing their status; change seems too much trouble. Inertia is greatly aided by the media. It is easier for many individuals to remain in their present relationship and to seek vicarious satisfactions from situation comedies, dramas, and soap operas wherein the actors do all the things the viewer would do if he or she were not so resistant to change.

Commitment   An important factor influencing the course of relationship maintenance (as well as of relationship deterioration) is the degree of commitment you have toward each other and toward the relationship (Knapp and Taylor 1994; Kurdek 1995). Not surprisingly, young adults in satisfying relationships had greater feelings of commitment to each other than did those in less satisfying relationships. This was true for couples in the United States and in Taiwan and may suggest that commitment is a cultural universal (Lin and Rusbult 1995). Before reading any further examine your own commitment by taking the accompanying self-test, "How committed are you?"

Commitment can be divided into three types (Knapp and Taylor 1994, building on the work of Johnson 1973, 1982, 1991). "Want to" commitment is based on your positive feelings for the other person or the relationship; for example, you love your partner and therefore are committed to him or her and to the relationship. You *want to* stay together. "Ought to" commitment is based on your sense of moral obligation; for example, you made a promise to stay together or you would feel guilty if you broke up the relationship. You feel you *ought to* stay together. "Have to" commitment is based on your belief that you have no acceptable alternative; for example, your friends would disapprove or you would incur too many problems in breaking up. You feel you *have to* stay together.

All relationships are held together, in part, by one or a combination of these types of commitments. The strength of the relationship, including its resistance to

What factors maintain your own current friendship or romantic relationships? What is the most important factor?

Self Test

How Committed Are You?

Think about a current romantic relationship—long time and serious or short time and casual—and respond to each of the following questions according to the following scale: 1 = the statement is "absolutely" true, 7 = the statement is "absolutely not" true, and numbers 2–6 for statements that are sometimes true and sometimes not true.

_____1. I am likely to pursue another relationship or a single lifestyle.
_____2. I believe there will be a lot of future rewards associated with the relationship.
_____3. I feel a strong sense of "we" when thinking of my partner and me.
_____4. I am willing to exert a great deal of effort on behalf of this relationship.
_____5. I have a lot invested in this relationship.
_____6. I can image having an affair with another person and not having it affect my relationship with _____.
_____7. I expect to be with _____ for the rest of my life.
_____8. There is nothing holding me in this relationship except my own free choice.

Thinking Critically About Commitment
To compute your score follow these steps:

1. Add your scores from questions 2, 3, 4, 5, 7, and 8.
2. Add your score from items 1 and 6 and subtract this sum from 16 (the number 16 is chosen simply to eliminate negative numbers).
3. Add the totals from steps 1 and 2.

Your score should range somewhere between 8 and 56. Low scores indicate great commitment and high scores indicate less commitment. One of the purposes of including this self-test here is that it encourages you to look at your own commitment in very specific terms; it stimulates you to ask yourself the reasons for your own relationship commitment. Did it achieve this purpose or did you already have a good idea of the extent and reasons for your commitment in a relationship? Are there other items that you would add to this test? That is, are there other aspects of commitment that this test does not tap?

Think about both the type of commitment that exists in one of your relationships and also about the strength of the relationship. A good way of doing this is to consider such questions as the following (drawn from the research of Knapp and Taylor 1994):

◆ What kind of future do you see for the relationship? If you believe that the relationship will provide important rewards in the future, you will be more committed to preserving it. If you see few rewards or even punishments or costs, then you are likely to feel little commitment and perhaps will allow the relationship to dissolve. (Statement 2 in the self-test taps this dimension.)

◆ To what extent do you identify with the relationship? To what extent do you see yourself as a part of a pair? If your relationship identity is a strong one, then your commitment is also strong and you would be likely to try to preserve the relationship. (Statements 3 and 7 in the self-test get at this dimension.)

◆ Are you considering alternatives to the relationship? If you have a strong commitment to your relationship, then you are less likely to look for alternative relationships. If you are still on the lookout for alternatives, then your commitment is weak. (Statements 1 and 6 in the self-test refer to this dimension.)

◆ How willing are you to spend effort (energy and time, for example) on the relationship? The more willing you are to exert effort, the more committed you are to the relationship. (Statement 4 focuses on this factor.)

◆ How invested in the relationship are you? Increasing your investments in the relationship (for example, the more time you spend with a person or the more money you put into a relationship), usually means an increase in commitment. (Statement 5 taps this dimension.)

◆ Do you take personal responsibility for being in the relationship or do you feel you *have* to be in it? If you feel that your relationship involvement is due to your own free choice, then your commitment is likely to be stronger than if you feel you were forced or had to be in the relationship. (Statement 8 in the self-test reflects this dimension.)

From "Commitment and Its Communication in Romantic Relationships," by Mark L. Knapp and Eric H. Taylor. In Ann L. Weber and John H. Harvey, eds. *Perspectives on Close Relationships.* Boston: Allyn & Bacon, pp. 153–175. Reprinted by permission of Mark L. Knapp.

possible deterioration, is also related to this degree of commitment. When a relationship shows signs of deterioration and yet there is a strong commitment to preserving it, you may well surmount the obstacles and reverse the process. When commitment is weak and you doubt that there are good reasons for staying together, the relationship deteriorates faster.

What types of commitment hold your current relationships together? Do you and your friend or romantic partner feel the same type of commitment? The same degree?

Maintenance Behaviors

One reason relationships last is that you try to make them work. A number of researchers have focused on the maintenance strategies people use in their various relationships (Ayres 1983; Dindia and Baxter 1987; Dainton and Stafford 1993; Guerrero, Eloy, and Wabnik 1993; Canary, Stafford, Hause, and Wallace et al. 1993; Dainton and Stafford 1993; Canary and Stafford 1994). Here are some examples of how people maintain their relationships.

◆   Being nice (researchers call this prosocial behavior). It includes being polite, cheerful, and friendly; avoiding criticism; and compromising even when it involves self-sacrifice. Prosocial behaviors also include talking about sharing the future, taking a vacation, or buying a house together. It also includes acting affectionately and romantically.

◆   Communicating, including calling just to say, "How are you?" or sending cards or letters. Sometimes it's just "small talk" that is in itself insignificant but is engaged in because it preserves contact. Also included would be talking about the honesty and openness in the relationship and talking about shared feelings. Responding constructively in a conflict (even when your partner may act in ways harmful to the relationship) is another type of communicative maintenance strategy (Rusbult and Buunk 1993).

◆   Being open. You engage in direct discussion and listen to the other—for example, you self-disclose, talk about what you want from the relationship, give advice, and express empathy.

◆   Giving assurances. You assure the other person of the significance of the relationship—for example, you comfort the other, put your partner first, and express love.

◆   Sharing joint activities. You spend time with the other—for example, playing ball, visiting mutual friends, doing specific things as a couple (even cleaning the house), and sometimes just being together and talking with no concern for what is done. Controlling (eliminating or reducing) extrarelational activities would be another type of togetherness behavior (Rusbult and Buunk 1993). Also included here would be ceremonial behaviors, for example, celebrating birthdays and anniversaries, discussing past pleasurable times, and eating at a favorite restaurant.

◆   Being positive. You try to make interactions pleasant and upbeat—for example, holding hands, giving in to make your partner happy, and doing favors. At the same time, you would avoid certain issues that might cause arguments.

◆   Focusing on yourself, for example, making yourself look especially good and attractive to the other person.

Would you be more comfortable using some maintenance strategies rather than others? If so, which strategies would you find easy to use? Hard to use?

Interpersonal Maintenance and Rules

You gain an interesting perspective by looking at interpersonal relationships in terms of the rules that govern them. The general assumption of this perspective is that relationships—friendship and love in particular—are held together by mutual adherence to certain rules. When those rules are broken, the relationships may deteriorate and eventually dissolve.

Relationship rules help distinguish successful from destructive relationship behavior. They help pinpoint why relationships break up and how they may be repaired. Further, if you know what the rules are, you'll be better able to learn (and teach) the social skills involved in relationship development and maintenance.

Friendship Rules   The left half of Table 18.1 presents some of the most important rules of friendship (Argyle and Henderson 1984). When these rules are followed, the friendship is strong and mutually satisfying. When these rules are broken, the friendship suffers and may die. The right half of Table 18.1 presents the abuses that are most significant in breaking up a friendship (Argyle and Henderson 1984). Note that some of the rules for maintaining a friendship directly correspond to the abuses that break up friendships. For example, it is important to "demonstrate emotional support" to maintain a friendship; when emotional support is not shown, the friendship will prove less satisfying and may

Table 18.1	Maintaining and Breaking Up a Friendship

Have you seen these rules in operation in your own friendships? Are there other important rules that you would add to the list presented here?

Maintaining a Friendship	Breaking Up a Friendship
Stand up for the friend in his or her absence.	Be intolerant of the friend's friends.
Share information and feelings about successes.	Criticize the friend in public.
Demonstrate emotional support.	Discuss confidences between yourself and the friend with others.
Trust each other; confide in each other.	Don't display any positive regard for the friend.
Offer to help the friend in time of need.	Don't demonstrate any positive support for the friend.
Try to make the friend happy when the two of you are together.	Nag the friend.
Don't criticize in public.	Don't trust or confide in the friend.
Keep confidences.	Don't volunteer to help the friend in time of need.
Don't be jealous or negative about other relationships.	Be jealous or critical of the friend's other relationships.
Respect the friend's privacy.	Feel free to take up as much of friend's time as you want.

Can you identify any rules that help maintain one or more of your friendships? Your romantic relationships? How would you react if your friend or romantic partner broke these rules? How would your friend or romantic partner react if you broke these rules? What would happen to these relationships as a result of such rule-breaking?

well break up. The general assumption here is that friendships break down when a significant friendship rule is violated. The maintenance strategy depends on your knowing the rules and having the ability to apply the appropriate skills (Trower 1981; Blieszner and Adams 1992).

Romantic Rules   Other research has identified the rules that romantic relationships establish and follow. For example, here are rules that both keep the relationship together and, when broken, lead to deterioration and eventually to dissolution (Baxter 1986).

The general form for each rule, as Baxter phrases it, is "If parties are in a close relationship, they should . . . "

- acknowledge one another's individual identities and lives beyond the relationship;
- express similar attitudes, beliefs, values, and interests;
- enhance one another's self-worth and self-esteem;
- be open, genuine, and authentic with one another;
- remain loyal and faithful to one another;
- have substantial shared time together;
- reap rewards commensurate with their investments relative to the other party;
- experience a mysterious and inexplicable "magic" in one another's presence.

Can you describe a current or past friendship or romantic relationship in terms of the rules discussed here? What three rules are most important to one specific current relationship?

What the Theories Say About Maintenance

What predictions do the theories of interpersonal relationships make about relationship maintenance? Attraction theory holds that relationships are maintained when there is significant attraction, generally of the kind that led to the development of the relationship. Although both individuals, as well as their definitions of what constitutes attractiveness, may have changed, the importance of attraction—however defined—is likely to continue throughout the life of the relationship.

Reinforcement theory holds that you maintain relationships when you feel rewarded. Note, however, that this theory's predictions may not be intuitively obvious. For example, when a person gives many rewards, the power of future rewards to increase positive feelings actually decreases. However, the punishments given out by this (normally rewarding) person are likely to be extremely influential because of their infrequency. According to reinforcement theory, rewards should be somewhat unpredictable. Predictable rewards are less likely to influence a person than are unpredictable rewards. Reinforcement theory offers the following practical suggestions:

◆ Give rewards that are at times unpredictable; surprise your partner.
◆ Recognize that because you are liked or loved, your power to punish is considerable; limit it.

Social exchange theory holds that relationships will be maintained as long as the relationship is profitable, as long as the rewards exceed the costs,. Note, of course, that what constitutes a reward and how significant that reward is can only be defined by the individual.

More specifically, a relationship is likely to be maintained when it is more rewarding than what you expected (your comparison level) or what you feel you could get elsewhere (your comparison level for alternatives). Your relationship is also likely to be maintained when your present relationship falls short of your comparison level but is still higher than your comparison level for alternatives. That is, even though you may think you deserve more, if you can't get more, then you are likely to stay put. Maintenance is likely to be in jeopardy when your comparison level for alternatives is greater than your present level of rewards.

Equity theory holds that you maintain a relationship when you perceive relative equity. If you feel that you are getting rewards from the relationship proportional to the costs paid, then you are likely to maintain your relationship. If either person—but especially the person who is being shortchanged—perceives a lack of equity, the relationship may experience difficulty.

 Do any of these four theories offer any practical advice for effectively maintaining relationships? Do they offer any advice on relationship repair?

Relationship Repair

If you wish to save a relationship, you may try to do so by changing your communication patterns and, in effect, putting into practice the insights and skills learned in this course. First, let's look at some general ways to repair a relationship, and second we can examine ways to deal with repair when you are the only one who wants to change the relationship.

MEDIA & TECHNOLOGY

ONLINE RELATIONSHIP COMMUNICATION

In face-to-face interactions we form impressions more quickly than we do in computer mediated communication. For example, in one study participants (in both face-to-face and computer groups) were asked their impressions of the person they worked with to solve a problem over a five-week course (Walther 1993). In the beginning of their "relationship" those in the computer groups gave lots of "don't know" responses. With time, however, these responses decreased and gradually began to approach the level of face-to-face participants. Note that the fact that both groups became more sure of their impressions of the other person does not mean that they formed the same impressions or that their impressions were necessarily correct; it merely means that they gradually came to form impressions that were relatively clear to themselves.

One assumption that may logically be made is that when the number of communication cues is few the relationships based on such communication are likely to be more impersonal and to exist more on a surface level. As more cues are added, there is greater opportunity for a more personal communication. Thus, for example, in computer mediated communication you are likely to use fewer cues than you are in face-to-face interaction; thus, the assumption goes, computer mediated communication will result in more impersonal-type relationships, whereas face-to-face interaction will result in more personal type relationships (Parks and Floyd 1996).

Another way of looking at this is through uncertainty reduction. Recall that this theory holds that greater uncertainty will delay the development of interpersonal relationships; as uncertainty is reduced, the relationship will progress and develop toward greater intimacy. But this does not really seem to be the case. Many people who communicate through e-mail and in computer discussion groups have formed relationships that are personal and long lasting. Further, uncertainty is reduced through computer mediated communication. In fact, some may argue that people communicating via computer feel freer to reveal themselves and consequently reduce uncertainty even faster than would be the case in face-to-face interaction (Parks and Floyd 1996).

When researchers asked newsgroup users if they had formed new acquaintances, friendships, or other personal relationships as a result of communicating in newsgroups, almost two-thirds said that they had formed such relationships with someone they met on the Internet. Almost one-third said that they communicated with their partner at least 3 or 4 times a week; more than half communicated on a weekly basis (Parks and Floyd 1996).

Women, it seems, were more likely to have formed relationships on the Internet than men. Some 72 percent of women and about 55 percent of men had formed personal relationships (Parks and Floyd 1996). Not surprisingly, those who communicated more frequently formed more relationships.

As relationships develop on the Internet, network convergence occurs; that is, as a relationship between two people develops, they begin to share their network of other communicators with each other (Parks 1995; Parks and Floyd 1996). This, of course, is similar to relationships formed through face-to-face contact.

Of all those surveyed in this study (176 people responded to this extensive survey), approximately 40 percent had no personal relationships online, approximately 30 percent had a somewhat developed relationship, and about 30 percent had what the researchers refer to as "a highly developed personal relationship" (Parks and Floyd 1996, p. 92).

Once a relationship had formed, almost all subjects also communicated through the more private and direct channel of e-mail (98 percent), the telephone (35 percent), letter (28 percent), or face-to-face communication (33 percent) (Parks and Floyd 1996).

Do you communicate online in the same way you communicate face-to-face? Can you identify three major differences? Three major similarities?

p. 423

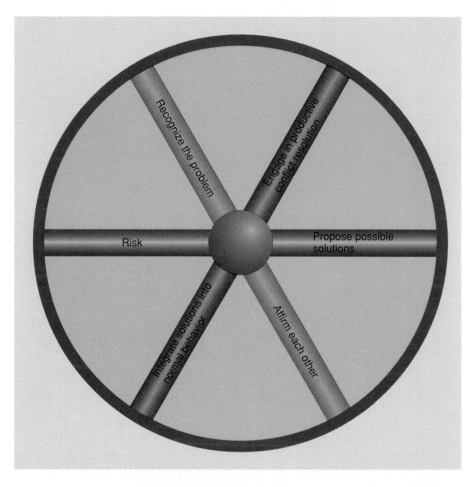

Figure 18.1   The Relationship Repair Wheel.
The wheel seems an apt metaphor for the repair process; the specific repair strategies—the spokes—all work together in constant process. The wheel is difficult to get moving, but once in motion it becomes easier to turn. It is easier to start when two people are pushing, but not impossible for one to move it in the right direction. What metaphor do you find helpful in thinking about relationship repair?

General Relationship Repair Strategies

We can look at the strategies for repairing a relationship in terms of the following six suggestions, which conveniently spell out the word REPAIR, a useful reminder that repair is not a one-step but a multistep process (Figure 18.1):

1. **R**ecognize the problem.
2. **E**ngage in productive conflict resolution.
3. **P**ose possible solutions.
4. **A**ffirm each other.
5. **I**ntegrate solutions into normal behavior.
6. **R**isk.

Recognize the Problem   Your first step is to identify the problem and to recognize it both intellectually and emotionally. Specify what is wrong with your present relationship (in concrete terms) and what changes would be needed to make it better (again, in specific terms). Create a picture of your relationship as you would want it to be, and compare that picture to the way the relationship looks now. Specify the changes that would have to take place if the ideal picture were to replace the present picture.

Try also to see the problem from your partner's point of view and to have your partner see the problem from yours. Exchange these perspectives, empathically and with open minds. Try, too, to be descriptive when discussing grievances, taking special care to avoid such troublesome terms as "always" and "never." Own your feelings and thoughts; use I-messages and take responsibility for your feelings instead of blaming your partner.

Engage in Productive Communication and Conflict Resolution   Interpersonal communication skills (such as openness, empathy, and other-orientation) are especially important during repair and are an essential part of any repair strategy. These skills were considered in detail in Unit 8 but appear throughout the text. Here is just a handful of suggestions designed to refresh your memory

- Look closely for relational messages that will help clarify motivations and needs. Respond to these messages as well as to the content messages.
- Exchange perspectives with your partner, and see the situation as your partner does.
- Practice empathic and positive responses, even in conflict situations.
- Own your feelings and thoughts. Use I-messages and take responsibility for these feelings.
- Use active listening techniques to help your partner explore and express relevant thoughts and feelings.
- Remember the principle of irreversibility. Think carefully before saying things you may later regret.
- Keep the channels of communication open. Be available to discuss problems, to negotiate solutions, and to practice new and more productive communication patterns.

Similarly, the skills of effective interpersonal conflict resolution are crucial in any attempt at relationship repair. If relationship problems are confronted with productive conflict resolution strategies, the difficulties may be resolved, and the relationship may actually emerge stronger and healthier. If, however, unproductive and destructive strategies are used, then the relationship may well deteriorate further. The nature and skills of conflict are considered in depth in Unit 20.

What other communication skills do you feel are especially important during relationship repair?

Pose Possible Solutions   After the problem is identified, you discuss solutions, the ways to lessen or eliminate the difficulty. Look for solutions that will enable both of you to win. Try to avoid "solutions" in which one person wins and the other loses. With such win-lose solutions, resentment and hostility are likely to fester.

Affirm Each Other   Any strategy of relationship repair should incorporate supportiveness and positive evaluations. For example, happy couples engage in greater positive behavior exchange; they communicate more agreement, approval, and positive affect than do unhappy couples (Dindia and Fitzpatrick 1985). Clearly, these behaviors result from the positive feelings the partners have for each other. However, it can also be argued that these expressions help to increase the positive regard each person has for the other.

One way to affirm another is to talk positively. Reverse negative communication patterns. For example, instead of withdrawing, talk about the causes of and the possible cures for your disagreements and problems. Reverse the tendency to hide your inner self. Disclose your feelings. Increase positive evaluations and decrease negative evaluations. Positive expressions and behaviors help to increase the positive regard each person has for his or her partner. Compliments, positive stroking, and all the nonverbals that say "I care" are especially important when you wish to reverse negative communication patterns.

Cherishing behaviors are an especially insightful way to affirm another person and to increase favor exchange (Lederer 1984). Cherishing behaviors are those small gestures you enjoy receiving from your partner (a smile, a wink, a squeeze, a kiss). Cherishing behaviors should be (1) specific and positive, (2) focused on the present and future rather than related to issues about which the partners have argued in the past, (3) capable of being performed daily, and (4) easily executed. People can make a list of the cherishing behaviors they each wish to receive and then exchange lists. Each person then performs the cherishing behaviors desired by the partner. At first, these behaviors may seem self-conscious and awkward. In time, however, they will become a normal part of interaction.

Integrate Solutions into Normal Behavior   Often solutions that are reached after an argument are followed for only a very short time; then the couple goes back to their previous, unproductive behavior patterns. Instead, integrate the solutions into your normal behavior; make them an integral part of your everyday relationship behavior. Make the exchange of favors, compliments, and cherishing behaviors a part of your normal relationship behavior.

Can you identify additional general repair strategies?

Risk   Take risks in trying to improve your relationship. Risk giving favors without any certainty of reciprocity. Risk rejection by making the first move to make up or say you're sorry. Be willing to change, to adapt, to take on new tasks and responsibilities.

Solo Relationship Repair

One of the most important implications for repair comes from the principle of punctuation (see Unit 2) and the idea that communication is circular rather than linear (see Unit 1; Duncan and Rock 1991). Let's consider an example involving Pat and Chris: Pat is highly critical of Chris; Chris is defensive and attacks Pat for being insensitive, overly negative, and unsupportive. If you view the communication process as beginning with Pat's being critical (that is, the stimulus) and with Chris's attacks being the response, you have a pattern such as occurs in Figure 18.2.

With this view, the only way to stop the unproductive communication pattern is for Pat to stop criticizing. But what if you are Chris and can't get Pat to stop being critical? What if Pat doesn't want to stop being critical?

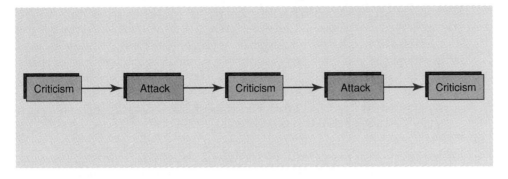

Figure 18.2 A Stimulus-Response View of Relationship Problems.
This view of the relationship process implies that one behavior is the stimulus and one behavior is the response. It implies that a pattern of behavior can only be modified if you change the stimulus, which will produce a different (more desirable) response.

You get a different view of the problem when you see communication as circular and apply the principle of punctuation. The result is a pattern such as appears in Figure 18.3.

Note that no assumptions are made about causes. Instead, the only assumption is that each response triggers another response; each response depends in part on the previous response. Therefore, the pattern can be broken at any point:

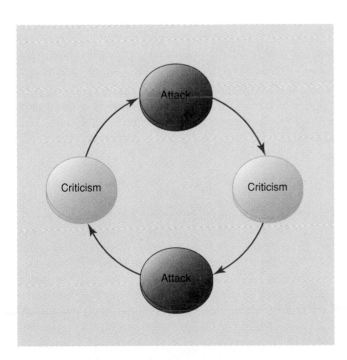

Figure 18.3 A Circular View of Relationship Problems.
Note that in this view of relationships, as distinguished from that depicted in Figure 18.2, relationship behaviors are seen in a circular pattern where no specific behavior is singled out as a stimulus and none as a response. The pattern can thus be broken by interference anywhere along the circle.

Pat's criticism, for example, may be stopped by Chris not responding with attacks. Similarly, Pat can stop Chris's attacks by not responding with criticism.

In this view, either person can break an unproductive circle. Clearly, relationship communication can be most effectively improved when both parties change their unproductive patterns. Nevertheless, communication can be improved even if only one person changes and begins to use a more productive pattern. This is true to the extent that Pat's criticism depends on Chris's attacks and to the extent that Chris's attacks depend on Pat's criticism.

Have you ever tried to repair a relationship by yourself? If so, what difficulties did you experience? How successful were you?

Whether expert or novice, each of us gives relationship repair advice and probably each of us seeks it from time to time from friends and sometimes from therapists. Here are a few situations which call for repair. Can you use what you've read about here (as well as your own experiences, readings, observations, and so on) to explain what is going on in these situations? What repair advice would you give to each of the people in these situations?

Friends and Colleagues

Mike and Jim, friends for 20 years, had a falling out over the fact that Mike supported another person for promotion over Jim. Jim is resentful and feels that Mike should have given him his support, which was tantamount to getting the promotion and a good raise which Jim and his large family could surely use. Mike feels that his first obligation was to the company and chose the person he felt would do the best job. Mike feels that if Jim feels this way and can't understand or appreciate his motives, then he no longer cares to be friends. Assuming that both Mike and Jim want the friendship to continue or will at some later time, what do you suggest Mike do? What do you suggest Jim do?

Coming Out

Tom, a junior in college—recently came out as gay to his family. Contrary to his every expectation, they went ballistic. His parents want him out of the house and his two brothers refuse to talk with him. In fact, they have now come to refer to him only in the third person and then with derogatory hate speech. Assuming that all parties will be sorry at some later time if the relationship is not repaired, what would you suggest Tom's mother and father do? What do you suggest Tom's brothers do? What do you suggest Tom do?

Betraying a Confidence

Pat and Chris have been best friends since elementary school and even now, in their twenties, speak every day and rely on each other for emotional and sometimes financial support. Recently, Pat betrayed a confidence and told several mutual friends that Chris had been having emotional problems and had been considering suicide. Chris found out and no longer wants to maintain the friendship; in fact, Chris refuses to even talk with Pat. Assuming that the friendship is more good than bad and that both parties will be sorry if they don't patch up the friendship, what would you suggest Pat do? What do you suggest Chris do? What should a mutual friend do?

Karen Ma (1996, pg. 18), in her The Modern Madam Butterfly: Fantasy and Reality in Japanese Cross-Cultural Relationships, *tells the story of a recently divorced Australian man who confided that the next time he married it would be to a Japanese woman. "This man," notes Ma, "had no prior experience in Japan nor did he speak a word of Japanese. Yet he presumed he would have a better marriage with a woman from a country he knew nothing about after failing in a relationship with someone from his own culture." If this man had said this to you, what would you say to him?*

Relationships in Cultural Context

The research and theory discussed throughout Units 15, 16, 17, and this one derive in great part from research conducted in the United States and on heterosexual couples. This research and the corresponding theory reflect the way most heterosexual relationships are viewed in the United States. And although we paused periodically to note cultural differences, it's helpful to bring the influence of culture together now that we've covered a major part of our relationship discussion.

For example, we assume in the model and in the discussion of relationship development (Unit 16) that we voluntarily choose our relationship partners. We choose to pursue certain relationships and not others. In some cultures, however, your romantic partner is chosen for you by your parents. In some cases, your husband or wife is chosen to solidify two families or to bring some financial advantage to your family or village. Such an arrangement may have been entered into by your parents when you were an infant.

In the United States, researchers study and textbook authors write about dissolving relationships and how to manage after a relationship breaks up. It is assumed that you have the right to exit an undesirable relationship. But, that is not always true. In some cultures, you simply cannot dissolve a relationship once it is formed or once there are children. In the practice of Roman Catholicism, once people are validly married, they are always married and cannot dissolve that relationship.

A similar assumption of choice is seen in the research and theory on friendships. In most of the United States, interpersonal friendships are drawn from a relatively large pool. Of all the people you come into regular contact with, you choose relatively few as friends. Now, with computer discussion groups, the number of friends you can have has increased enormously as has the range from which these friends can be chosen. In rural areas and in small villages throughout the world, however, you would have very few choices. The two or three other children your age become your friends; there is no real choice because these are the only possible friends you could make.

Some cultures consider sexual relationships to be undesirable outside of a formally sanctioned marriage whereas others consider it a normal part of relationships and view chastity as undesirable. Intercultural researchers Elaine Hatfield and Richard Rapson (1996, p. 36) recall a meeting of the International Academy of Sex Research where colleagues from Sweden and the United States were discussing ways of preventing AIDS. When members from the United States suggested teaching abstinence as a way of preventing AIDS, Swedish members asked, "How will teenagers ever learn to become loving, considerate sexual partners if they don't practice?" "The silence that greeted the question," note Hatfield and Rapson, "was the sound of two cultures clashing."

A cultural bias is also seen in the research on maintenance—a topic reviewed earlier in this unit. It is assumed that relationships should be permanent or at least long lasting. Consequently, it is assumed that people want to keep relationships together and will exert considerable energy to maintain relationships. Because of this bias, there is little research that has studied how to move effortlessly from one intimate relationship to another or that advises you how to do this more effectively and efficiently.

Culture influences heterosexual relationships by assigning different roles to men and to women. In the United States men and women are supposed to be equal—at least that is the stated ideal. As a result, both men and women can initiate relationships and both men and women can dissolve them. Both men and women are expected to derive satisfaction from their interpersonal relationships and when that satisfaction is not present, either may seek to exit the relationship. In Iran, on the other hand, only the man has the right to dissolve a marriage without giving reasons.

In some cultures gay and lesbian relationships are accepted and in others they are condemned. In some areas of the United States "domestic partnerships" may be registered and gay men, lesbians, and unmarried heterosexuals granted rights (such as health insurance benefits and the right to make decisions when one member is incapacitated) that were formerly reserved for married couples. In Norway, Iceland, Sweden, and Denmark, on the other hand, same sex marriage is legal.

What has your culture taught you about interpersonal relationships? Have these teachings influenced specific relationship behaviors?

Summary — UNIT IN BRIEF

A RETURN TO OBJECTIVES:

In this unit we explored the processes of relationship maintenance and relationship repair and focused on: (1) What is relationship maintenance? What behaviors do people use to maintain their behavior? (2) What do the relationship theories say about maintenance? (3) What is relationship repair and what strategies can one use to repair a relationship? (4) In what ways does culture influence interpersonal relationships?

Relationship Maintenance: The Process of Preventive Care	Relationship Theories and Maintenance	Relationship Repair: The Process of Corrective Care	Relationships in Cultural Context
Reasons for maintaining a relationship: ◆ Emotional attachment ◆ Convenience ◆ Children ◆ Fear ◆ Inertia ◆ Commimtent **Maintenance behaviors:** ◆ Being nice ◆ Communicating ◆ Being open ◆ Sharing activities **Relationship maintenance** can be achieved by following the rules for keeping the relationship together.	**Relationships are maintained when:** ◆ There is significant attraction ◆ The individuals feel rewarded ◆ When the rewards exceed the costs ◆ When the relationship is perceived as equitable	**General repair strategies:** ◆ Recognize the problem ◆ Engage in productive communication and conflict resolution ◆ Pose possible solutions ◆ Affirm each other ◆ Integrate solutions into normal behavior ◆ Risk Repair is not necessarily a two-person process.	**Culture influences all aspects of relationships:** ◆ The ways in which relationships are viewed ◆ The choice involved in developing and in dissolving relationships ◆ The perceived values of relationships ◆ The rules that relationships should follow ◆ The roles that are considered appropriate in relationships

UNIT

19

Power in Interpersonal Relationships

Unit Topics	Unit Objectives
	After completing this unit, you should be able to:

Principles of Power
Some People Are More Powerful
      Than Others
Some People are More Machiavellian
      Than Others
Power Can Be Increased or Decreased
Power Follows the Principle of Less
      Interest
Power Has a Cultural Dimension
Power is Frequently Used Unfairly
	1. Define *power* and explain its general principles

The Bases of Power Referent Power Legitimate Power Reward Power Coercive Power Expert Power Information or Persuasion Power	2. Define the six bases of power 3. Discuss at least six suggestions for making your speech more powerful
Communicating Power Speaking Power Nonverbal Power Listening Power	4. Explain how you can communicate power in speaking, in nonverbal communication, and in listening
Empowering Others	5. Explain the concept of *empowerment* and some of the ways you might empower others
Compliance Gaining and Compliance Resisting Compliance-Gaining Strategies Compliance-Resisting Strategies	6. Explain *compliance-gaining* and *compliance-resisting strategies*

EXPERIENTIAL LEARNING VEHICLES

Vehicle No. 21, "Power Plays," p. 464, explores several types of power plays and appropriate responses to them. No. 24, "The Television Relationship," pp. 467–468, can be used to identify the principles of power.

Power is a part of all interpersonal relationships and interactions. It influences what you do, when you do it, and with whom. It influences your choice of friends, your romantic and your family relationships—and how successful you feel they are. Interpersonal power is what enables one person to control the behavior of the other. Thus, if A has power over B, then A, by virtue of this power—through either its exercise or the threat of its being exercised—can control B's behaviors.

Principles of Power

Power in interpersonal relationships may best be introduced by a discussion of some of its most important principles. These principles explain how power operates interpersonally and how you may effectively manage its use.

Some People Are More Powerful than Others

In the United States, all people are considered equal under the law and therefore equal in their entitlement to education, legal protection, and freedom of speech. But all people are not equal when it comes to just about everything else. Some are born into wealth, others into poverty. Some are born physically strong, good-looking, and healthy; others are born weak, less attractive, and with a variety of inherited illnesses.

Some people are born into power and some who are not learn to acquire it. In short, some people control and others are controlled. Of course, the world is not quite that simple; some exert power in certain areas, some in others. Some exert power in many areas, some in just a few.

Some People Are More Machiavellian than Others

 Whom do you consider the three most interpersonally powerful people you have ever known? Why were these people so powerful? Which types of power did they possess? What types of power do you have?

Before reading about this fascinating concept, take the accompanying self-test, "How Machiavellian Are You?" It focuses on your beliefs about how easily you think people can be manipulated.

Niccolo Machiavelli (1469–1527) was a political philosopher and advisor and wrote his theory of political control in *The Prince*. The book took the position (in greatly simplified form) that the prince must do whatever is necessary to rule the people; the ends justified the means. The ruler was obligated to use power to gain more power and thus better achieve the desired goals (Steinfatt 1987). The term *Machiavellian* has thus come to refer to the techniques or tactics one person uses to control another. Research finds significant differences between those who score high and those who score low on the Mach scale. Low Machs are more easily susceptible to social influence; they are more easily persuaded. High Machs are more resistant to persuasion. Low Machs are more empathic while high Machs are more logical. Low Machs are more interpersonally oriented and involved with other people; high Machs are more assertive and more controlling. Business students (especially marketing students) score higher in Machiavellianism than do nonbusiness majors (McLean and Jones 1992).

High Machs are most effective at persuading others when the situation allows them to improvise (Christie 1970). High Machs are also rated higher on job per-

How Machiavellian Are You?

Self Test

For each statement record the number on the following scale which most closely represents your attitude:

1 = disagree a lot
2 = disagree a little
3 = neutral
4 = agree a bit
5 = agree a lot

_____ 1. The best way to handle people is to tell them what they want to hear.
_____ 2. When you ask someone to do something for you, it is best to give the real reasons rather than giving reasons that might carry more weight.
_____ 3. Anyone who completely trusts anyone else is asking for trouble.
_____ 4. It is hard to get ahead without cutting corners here and there.
_____ 5. It is safest to assume that all people have a vicious streak and it will come out when they are given a chance.
_____ 6. One should take action only when sure it is morally right.
_____ 7. Most people are basically good and kind.
_____ 8. There is no excuse for lying to someone.
_____ 9. Most people forget more easily the death of their parents than the loss of their property.
_____ 10. Generally speaking, people won't work hard unless they're forced to.

Thinking Critically About Machiavellianism
To compute your Mach score follow these steps:
1. Reverse the scores on items 2, 6, 7, and 8 according to the following scale:

If you responded with	Change it to
5	1
4	2
3	3
2	2
1	1

2. Add all ten scores, being sure to use the reversed numbers for 2, 6, 7, and 8.

Your Mach score is a measure of the degree to which you believe that people in general are manipulable and not necessarily the degree to which you would or do manipulate others. If you scored somewhere between 35 and 50 you would be considered a high Mach; if you scored between 10 and 15 you would be considered a low Mach. Most of us would score in between these extremes.

The concept of Machiavellianism is explained in the text. As you read the discussion try to visualize what you would do in the various situations described. See if your score on this test is a generally accurate description of your own Machiavellianism. You will also note a similarity between this concept and self-monitoring (discussed in Unit 8). Both high self-monitors and high Machs try to manipulate others and get his or her own way. The difference is that self-monitors change their own behaviors as a way of pleasing and manipulating others; Machiavellians try to change the behaviors of others to get what they want.

From "The Machiavellis Among Us," by Richard Christie, *Psychology Today,* November 1970. Copyright © 1970 by Sussex Publishers, Inc. Reprinted by permission of *Psychology Today Magazine.*

formance when they functioned within a loosely structured work environment that allowed them to improvise (Gable, Hollon, and Dangello 1992).

Machiavellianism seems in part at least to be culturally conditioned. Individualistic orientation, which favors competition and being Number One, seems more conducive to the development of Machiavellianism. Collectivist orientation, which favors cooperation and being one of a group, seems a less friendly environment for the development of Machiavellianism in its members. Some evidence of this comes from research showing that Chinese students attending a traditional Chinese (Confucian) school rated lower in Machiavellianism than similar Chinese students attending a Western-style school (Christie 1970).

How would you go about discovering differences in Machiavellianism between the women and the men at your school?

Interpersonally, your own level of Machiavellianism will influence the communication choices you make. For example, high Machs are more strategic and manipulative in their self-disclosures than are low Machs; that is, high Machs will self-disclose to influence the attitudes and behaviors of listeners (Steinfatt 1987). Machiavellianism influences the way you seek to gain the compliance of others (a topic discussed later in this unit). High Machs are more likely to be manipulative in their conflict resolving behavior than are low Machs. High Machs are generally more effective in just about all aspects studied (they even earn higher grades in communication courses that involve face-to-face interaction, Burgoon 1971). Low Mach women, however, are preferred as dating partners by both high and low Mach men (Steinfatt 1987).

Power Can Be Increased or Decreased

Although people differ greatly in the amount of power they wield at any time and in any specific area, all can increase their power in some ways. You can lift weights and increase your physical power. You can learn the techniques of negotiation and increase your power in group situations. You can learn the principles of communication and increase your persuasive power.

Power can also be decreased. Probably the most common way to lose power is by unsuccessfully trying to control another's behavior. For example, the person who threatens you with punishment and then fails to carry out the threat loses power. Another way to lose power is to allow others to control you, for example, to take unfair advantage of you. When you don't confront these power tactics of others, you lose power yourself.

Power Follows the Principle of Less Interest

In any interpersonal relationship, the person who holds the power is the one less interested in and less dependent on the rewards and punishments controlled by the other person. If, for example, Pat can walk away from the rewards Chris controls or can suffer the punishments Chris can mete out, Pat controls the relationship. If, on the other hand, Pat needs the rewards Chris controls or is unable or unwilling to suffer the punishments Chris can administer, Chris maintains the power and controls the relationship. Put differently, Chris holds the relationship power to the degree that Chris is not dependent upon the rewards and punishments under Pat's control.

The more a person needs a relationship, the less power that person has in it. The less a person needs a relationship, the greater that person's power. In a love

Another way of looking at the principle of less effort is in terms of social exchange theory (see Unit 16). From this perspective, power may be viewed as control of the significant rewards and costs in the relationship. The person who controls the rewards and punishments controls the relationship. The person who needs to receive the rewards and to avoid the costs or punishments controlled by the other person is less powerful. Alternatively, the person who can effectively ignore both the rewards and the costs is the less interested party and therefore possesses the controlling power in the relationship.

relationship, for example, the person who maintains greater power is the one who would find it easier to break up the relationship. The person who is unwilling (or unable) to break up has little power, precisely because he or she is dependent upon the relationship and the rewards provided by the other person.

Power Has a Cultural Dimension

Recall the concept of power distance discussed earlier (Unit 3). There it was pointed out that cultures differ in the amount of power that exists between people and in the attitudes that people have about power, its legitimacy and its desirability (Hofstede 1983). In many Asian, African, and Arab cultures (as well as in many European cultures such as Italian and Greek), there is a great power distance between men and women. Men have the greater power and women are expected to recognize this and abide by its implications. Men, for example, make the important decisions and have the final word in any difference of opinion (Hatfield and Rapson 1996).

In the United States the power structure is undergoing considerable changes. In many families men still have the greater power. Partly because they earn more money, they also make the more important decisions. As economic equality becomes more a reality than an ideal, this power difference may also change. In Arab cultures, the man makes the more important decisions not because he earns more money, but because he is the man and men are simply given greater power.

Does the statement that power follows the principle of less interest explain the balance of power as you see it at work in interpersonal relationships? Test this principle by examining your own interpersonal relationships to determine if the power is in fact held by the less interested party.

What has your culture taught you about power? Is power good? Is it bad? Does a person who has power also have obligations to those who have less power?

In some of these cultures, the power difference is perpetuated by granting men greater educational opportunities. Although college education for women is taken for granted in most of the United States, it is the exception in many other cultures throughout the world.

In some Asian cultures particularly, persons in positions of authority—for example, teachers—have unquestioned power. Students do not contradict, criticize, or challenge teachers. This can easily create problems in the typical college classroom. Students from cultures that taught that the teacher has unquestioned authority may have great difficulty meeting the United States teacher expectation that students interact critically with the material and with its interpretation.

Power Is Frequently Used Unfairly

Although it would be nice to believe that power is wielded for the good of all, it is often used selfishly and unfairly. Here are two rather extensive examples: sexual harassment and the use of power plays.

Sexual Harassment   One type of unfair use of power is sexual harassment. Sexual harassment may be defined as "bothering someone in a sexual way" (Bravo and Cassedy 1992). "Sexual harassment," note another team of researchers, "refers to conduct, typically experienced as offensive in nature, in which unwanted sexual advances are made in the context of a relationship of unequal power or authority. The victims are subjected to verbal comments of a sexual nature, unconsented touching and requests for sexual favors" (Friedman, Boumil, and Taylor 1992).

Attorneys note that under the law "sexual harassment is any unwelcome sexual advance or conduct on the job that creates an intimidating, hostile or offensive working environment" (Petrocelli and Repa 1992).

The Equal Employment Opportunity Commission (EEOC) has defined sexual harassment as follows:

> *Unwelcome sexual advances, requests for sexual favors and other verbal or physical conduct of a sexual nature constitute sexual harassment when (1) submission to such conduct is made either explicitly or implicitly a term or condition of an individual's employment, (2) submission to or rejection of such conduct by an individual is used as the basis for employment decisions affecting such individual, or (3) such conduct has the purpose or effect of unreasonably interfering with an individual's work performance or creating an intimidating, hostile, or offensive working environment. (Friedman, Boumil, and Taylor 1992)*

Behavior constitutes sexual harassment, according to attorneys Petrocelli and Repa (1992), when it is:

1. Sexual in nature—for example, sexual advances, showing pornographic pictures, telling jokes that revolve around sex, comments on anatomy.
2. Unreasonable—for example, behavior that a reasonable person would object to.
3. Severe or pervasive—for example, physical molestation or creating an intimidating environment.

Table 19.1	Sexual Harassment in High School		

Before looking at this table, which identifies the types of sexual harassment experienced by high school boys and girls, think back to your own high school days. Did you experience sexual harassment? Did you sexually harass others? What forms did the sexual harassment take? Data come from the American Association of University Women as reported in The New York Times, *June 2, 1993. Copyright © 1993 by* The New York Times. *Reprinted by permission.*

Behavior	Boys	Girls
Sexual comments or looks	56%	76%
Touched, grabbed, or pinched	42	65
Intentionally pushed up against	36	57
Sexual rumors spread about them	34	42
Clothing pulled at	28	38
Shown, given, or left sexual materials	34	31
Had sexual messages written about them in public places	16	20

4. Unwelcome and offensive—for example, behavior that you let others know offends you and that you want stopped.

In a Harris poll (*New York Times,* June 2, 1993) on sexual harassment in junior and senior high school, 56 percent of the boys and 75 percent of the girls said they were the target of some form of sexual harassment consisting of sexually explicit comments, jokes, or gestures. Forty-two percent of the boys and 66 percent of the girls said they were the victims of sexual touching, grabbing, or pinching. Table 19.1 presents the major behaviors and the percentage of students reporting that they were victims of such behaviors. All the behaviors are sexual in nature.

The students noted that among the effects of sexual harassment were not wanting to go to school, being reluctant to talk in class, finding it difficult to pay attention or to study, getting lower grades, and even considering changing schools. This is especially true for gay and lesbian youth. In New York City, a special high school has been established—the Harvey Milk School—to accommodate gay and lesbian teens who have been sexually harassed to the point where they cannot function effectively in the school environment. Lesbian and gay youth, for example experience such harassment in all social environments: family, school, work, and in the general community (Pilkington and D'Augelli 1995). In one study 77 percent of undergraduate lesbians and gay men reported that they experienced such harassment (D'Augelli 1992).

To determine whether behavior constitutes sexual harassment, Memory VanHyning (1993) suggests that you ask the following four questions to help you assess your own situation objectively rather than emotionally.

1. Is it real? Does this behavior have the meaning it seems to have?
2. Is it job related? Does this behavior have something to do with or will it influence the way you do your job?

Are these four questions sufficient for determining whether or not behavior constitutes sexual harassment? If not, what other questions would you add?

3. Did you reject this behavior? Did you make your rejection of unwanted messages clear to the other person?
4. Have these types of messages persisted? Is there a pattern, a consistency to these messages?

"Yes" answers to all four questions define the behavior as sexual harassment (VanHyning 1993).

Avoiding Sexual Harassment Behaviors   Three suggestions for avoiding behaviors that might be considered sexual harassment will help to clarify the concept further and to prevent the occurrence of harassment (Bravo and Cassedy 1992).

1. Begin with the assumption that others at work are not interested in your sexual advances, sexual stories and jokes, or sexual gestures.
2. Listen and watch for negative reactions to any sex-related discussion. Use the suggestions and techniques discussed throughout this book (for example, perception checking, critical listening) to become aware of such reactions. When in doubt, find out; ask questions, for example.
3. Avoid saying or doing what you think your parent, partner, or child would find offensive in the behavior of someone with whom she or he worked.

What to Do About Sexual Harassment   What should you do if you believe you are being sexually harassed and feel a need to do something about it? Here are a few suggestions recommended by workers in the field (Petrocelli and Repa 1992; Bravo and Cassedy 1992; Rubenstein 1993).

1. Talk to the harasser. Tell this person, assertively, that you do not welcome the behavior and that you find it offensive. Simply informing Fred that his sexual jokes are not appreciated and are seen as offensive may be sufficient to make him stop this joke telling. In some instances, unfortunately, such criticism goes unheeded, and the offensive behavior continues.
2. Collect evidence—perhaps corroboration from others who have experienced similar harassment at the hands of the same individual, perhaps a log of the offensive behaviors.
3. Use appropriate channels within the organization. Most organizations have established channels to deal with such grievances. This step will in most cases eliminate any further harassment. In the event that it doesn't, you may consider going further.
4. File a complaint with an organization or governmental agency or perhaps take legal action.
5. Don't blame yourself. Like many who are abused, you may tend to blame yourself, feeling that you are responsible for being harassed. You aren't; however, you may need to secure emotional support from friends or perhaps from trained professionals.

What would you add to the discussion of sexual harassment presented here?

Power Plays   Power plays are patterns (not isolated instances) of communication that take unfair advantage of another person (Steiner 1981). Put in terms of the notion of choice (Unit 1) power plays aim to rob us of our right to make our own choices, free of harassment or intimidation.

For example, in the power play *Nobody Upstairs* the individual refuses to acknowledge your request, regardless of how or how many times you make it. One common form is the refusal to take no for an answer. Sometimes "nobody upstairs" takes the form of pleading ignorance of common socially accepted (but unspoken) rules, such as knocking when you enter someone's room or refraining from opening another person's mail or wallet: "I didn't know you didn't want me to look in your wallet" or "Do you want me to knock the next time I come into your room?"

Another power play is *You Owe Me*. Here others do something for you and then demand something in return. They remind you of what they did for you and use this to get you to do what they want.

In *Yougottobekidding* one person attacks the other by saying "yougottobekidding" or some similar phrase: "You can't be serious." "You can't mean that." "You didn't say what I thought you said, did you?" The intention here is to express utter disbelief in the other's statement so as to make the statement and the person seem inadequate or stupid.

These power plays are just examples. There are, of course, many others that you have no doubt met on occasion. What do you do when you recognize such a power play? One commonly employed response is to ignore the power play and allow the other person to take control. Another response is to treat the power play as an isolated instance (rather than as a pattern of behavior) and object to it. For example, you might say quite simply, "Please don't come into my room without knocking first" or "Please don't look in my wallet without permission."

A third response is a cooperative one (Steiner 1981). In this response, you do the following.

- ◆ *Express your feelings.* Tell the person that you are angry, annoyed, or disturbed by his or her behavior.
- ◆ *Describe the behavior to which you object.* Tell the person—in language that describes rather than evaluates—the specific behavior you object to: for example, reading your mail, coming into your room without knocking, persisting in trying to hug you.
- ◆ *State a cooperative response you both can live with comfortably.* Tell the person—in a cooperative tone—what you want: for example: "I want you to knock before coming into my room." "I want you to stop reading my mail." "I want you to stop trying to hug me when I tell you to stop."

A cooperative response to "nobody upstairs" might go something like this: "I'm angry (*statement of feelings*) that you persist in opening my mail. You have opened my mail four times this past week alone (*description of the behavior to which you object*). I want you to allow me to open my own mail. If there is anything in it that concerns you, I will let you know immediately" (*statement of cooperative response*).

Bases of Power

Power is present in all relationships and in all communication interchanges. But the type of power varies greatly from one situation to another and from one person to another. Here we identify six types of power (French and Raven 1968; Raven, Centers, and Rodrigues 1975).

Have you ever been a party to or witnessed any of the power plays discussed in this unit? What led to their use? What effects did these power plays have on the people involved?

In what kinds of situations do you think it might be best simply to ignore the power play? In what situations might it be best to neutralize the power play (treat it as an isolated instance)? In what situations might it be best to employ a cooperative response to the power play?

Referent Power

You have **referent power** over others when they wish to be like you or be identi-fied with you. For example, an older brother may have power over a younger brother because the younger brother wants to be like the older one. The assump-tion made by the younger brother is that he will be more like his older brother if he behaves and believes as his brother does. Once he decides to do so, it takes lit-tle effort for the older brother to exert influence or power over the younger. Referent power depends greatly on attractiveness and prestige; as they increase, so does identification and consequently power. When you are well liked and well respected, of the same sex as the other person, and have the same attitudes and experiences as the other person, your referent power is especially great.

Legitimate Power

You have **legitimate power** over others when they believe you have the right—by virtue of your position—to influence or control their behavior. Legitimate power stems from our belief that certain people should have power over us, that they have a right to influence us because of who they are. Legitimate power usually de-rives from the roles people occupy. Teachers are often perceived to have legitimate power, and this is doubly true for religious teachers. Parents are seen as having le-gitimate power over their children. Employers, judges, managers, doctors, and police officers are others who hold legitimate power in different areas.

Reward Power

You have **reward power** over others if you have the ability to reward them. Rewards may be material (money, promotion, jewelry) or social (love, friendship, respect). If you are able to grant others some kind of reward, you have control over them to the extent that they want what you can give them. The degree of power you have is directly related to the desirability of the reward as seen by oth-ers. Teachers have reward power over students because they control grades, let-ters of recommendation, social approval, and so on. Students, in turn, have reward power over teachers because they control social approval, student evalua-tions of faculty, and various other rewards. Parents control rewards for children—food, television privileges, rights to the car, curfew times, and the like—and thus possess reward power.

Coercive Power

You have **coercive power** over others when you have the ability to administer punishments to or remove their rewards should they not yield to your influence. Usually, if you have reward power you also have coercive power. Teachers not only may reward with high grades, favorable letters of recommendation, and so-cial approval but also may punish with low grades, unfavorable letters, and social disapproval. Parents may deny as well as grant privileges to their children, and hence they possess coercive as well as reward power.

   The strength of coercive power depends on two factors: (1) the magnitude of the punishment that can be administered and (2) the likelihood that it will be ad-ministered as a result of noncompliance. When threatened by mild punishment or by punishment you think will not be administered, you are not as likely to do as directed as you would if the threatened punishment were severe and highly likely to be administered.

Reward Versus Coercive Power: Some Consequences   Reward and coercive power are opposite sides of a coin and the consequences of using them are quite different. First, if you have reward power, you are likely to be seen as more attractive. People like those who have the power to reward them and who do in fact reward them. Coercive power, on the other hand, decreases attractiveness; people dislike those who have the power to punish them or who threaten them with punishment, whether they actually follow through or not.

Second, when you use rewards to exert power you do not incur the same costs as when you use punishment. When you exert reward power, you are dealing with a contented and happy individual. When you use coercive punishments, however, you must be prepared to incur anger and hostility, which may well be turned against you in the future.

Third, when you give a reward, it signals that you effectively exercised power and that you gained the compliance of the other person. You give the reward because the person did as you wanted. In the exercise of coercive power, however, the reverse is true. When you administer punishment, it shows that you have been ineffective in using the threat of coercive power and that there has been no compliance.

Fourth, when you exert coercive power, other bases of power frequently are diminished. There seems to be a kind of boomerang effect in operation. People who exercise coercive power are seen as possessing less expert, legitimate, and referent power. (Expert power is discussed in the following section.) Alternatively, when reward power is exerted, other bases of power increase.

Fifth, the use of coercive power in the classroom leads to a decrease in cognitive learning and hinders effective learning generally (Richmond and McCroskey 1984; Kearney, Plax, Richmond, and McCroskey 1984, 1985). In classrooms where the teacher is seen by the students to exercise coercive (and legitimate) power, students learn less effectively; have more negative attitudes toward the course, the course content, and the teacher; are less likely to take similar courses; and are less likely to perform the behaviors taught in the course. Coercive power and legitimate power also have a negative impact when used by supervisors on subordinates in business settings (Richmond, Davis, Saylor and McCroskey 1984). All in all, coercive power seems a last resort, one whose potential negative consequences should be carefully weighed before it is used.

Will the discussion of the consequences of reward versus coercive power influence your own exercise of these two types of power?

Expert Power

You have **expert power** over others when they see you as having expertise or knowledge. Your knowledge—as seen by others—gives you expert power. Usually expert power is subject-specific. For example, when you are ill, you are influenced by the recommendation of someone with expert power related to your illness—say, a doctor. But you would not be influenced by the recommendation of someone to whom you do not attribute illness-related expert power—say, the mail carrier or a plumber. You give the lawyer expert power in matters of law and psychiatrists expert power in matters of the mind, but, ideally, you don't interchange them.

Your expert power increases when you are seen as unbiased and as having nothing to gain personally from influencing others. It decreases when you are seen as biased or as having something to gain from influencing others.

Information or Persuasion Power

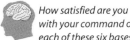

How satisfied are you with your command of each of these six bases of power? What might you do to increase those bases with which you are not satisfied?

You have **information** or **persuasion power** over others when they see you as having the ability to communicate logically and persuasively. If others believe that you have persuasive ability, then you have information power. If you are seen as possessing significant information and the ability to use that information in presenting a well-reasoned argument, then you have information power.

You rarely find only one base of power used to influence another person. Usually, a number of power bases are used in concert. If you possess expert power, it is likely that you also possess information power and perhaps legitimate power as well. If you want to control the behavior of another person, you would probably use all three bases of power rather than rely on just one. As you can appreciate,

What types of power might this teacher have in her Cherokee community in Tahlequah, Oklahoma? What types of power might this teacher have in, say, Chicago or Paris or Hong Kong?

certain individuals have a number of power bases at their disposal, whereas others seem to have few to none. This point brings us back to our first principle: Some people are more powerful than others.

Also, recognize that attempts to influence others may backfire. At times, negative power operates. Each of the six power bases may, at times, have such negative influence. For example, negative referent power occurs when a son rejects his father and wants to be his exact opposite. Negative coercive power may be seen when a child is warned against doing something under threat of punishment and then does exactly what he or she was told not to do; the threat of punishment may have made the forbidden behavior seem exciting or challenging.

Communicating Power

You can communicate power much as you communicate any other message. Here we consider how you can communicate power through speaking, through nonverbal communication, and through listening.

Speaking Power

The ways in which powerfulness and powerlessness are communicated through speech have received lots of research attention. A summary of some of the major characteristics of powerful and powerless speech is presented in Table 19.2 (Molloy 1981; Kleinke 1986; Johnson 1987).

Table 19.2	Toward More Powerful Speech	

As you read this table, think of your own speech and the power it communicates. Are you satisfied with the level of power your speech communicates?

Suggestions	Examples	Reasons
Avoid hesitations.	"I *er* want to say that *ah* this one is *er* the best, *you know.*"	Hesitations make you sound unprepared and uncertain.
Avoid too many intensifiers.	"*Really*, this was *the greatest*; it was *truly phenomenal.*"	Too many intensifiers make your speech sound the same and do not allow for intensifying what should be emphasized.
Avoid disqualifiers.	"*I didn't read the entire article*, but . . . ." "*I didn't actually see the accident*, but . . . ."	Disqualifiers signal a lack of competence and a feeling of uncertainty.
Avoid tag questions.	"That was a great movie, *wasn't it?*" "She's brilliant, *don't you think?*"	Tag questions ask for another's agreement and therefore signal your uncertainty.
Avoid self-critical statements.	"*I'm not very good at this.*" "*This is my first public speech.*"	Self-critical statements signal a lack of confidence.
Avoid slang and vulgar expressions.	"*##!!!///****!*" "*No problem!*"	Slang and vulgarity signal low social class and hence little power.

Nonverbal Power

Much nonverbal research has focused on the factors related to your ability to persuade and influence others (Burgoon, Buller, and Woodall 1995). For example, clothing and other artifactual symbols of authority help you to influence others. Research shows you would be more easily influenced by people in, for example, a respected uniform than in civilian clothes.

Affirmative nodding, facial expressions, and gestures help you express your concern for the other person and for the interaction and help you establish your charisma, an essential component of credibility. Self-manipulations (playing with your hair or touching your face, for example) and backward leaning will damage your persuasiveness.

Here are some popular suggestions most from Lewis (1989) for communicating power nonverbally in a business situation. As you read this list, try to provide specific examples of these suggestions and how they might work in business, at home, or at school. Are there situations in which these suggestions would have negative effects? How would you go about testing the validity of these suggestions?

- ◆ Be sure to respond in kind to another's eyebrow flash (raising the eyebrow as a way of acknowledging another person).
- ◆ Avoid adaptors—self, other, and object—especially when you wish to communicate confidence and control.
- ◆ Use consistent packaging; be especially careful that your verbal and nonverbal messages do not contradict each other.
- ◆ When sitting, select chairs you can get in and out of easily; avoid deep plush chairs which you sink into and have trouble getting out of.
- ◆ To communicate dominance with your handshake, exert more pressure than usual and hold the grip a bit longer than normal.
- ◆ Walk slowly and deliberately. To appear hurried is to appear as without power, as if you were rushing to meet the expectations of another person who had power over you.
- ◆ Maintain eye contact. People who maintain eye contact are judged to be more at ease and less afraid to engage in meaningful interaction than those who avoid eye contact. When you break eye contact, direct your gaze downward; otherwise you'll communicate a lack of interest in the other person.
- ◆ Avoid vocalized pauses—the -ers and -ahs—that frequently punctuate conversations when you are not quite sure of what to say next.
- ◆ Maintain reasonably close distances between yourself and those with whom you interact. If the distance is too far, you may be seen as fearful or uninvolved. If the distance is too close you may be seen as pushy or overly aggressive.

Listening Power

Much as you can communicate power and authority with words and nonverbal expression, you also communicate power through listening. Throughout your listening, you are communicating messages to others and these messages comment in some way on your power.

Powerful listeners listen actively. They focus and concentrate (with no real effort) on what is being said, especially on what people say they want or need (Fisher 1995). Listen to phrases such as "I want . . . ," or "It would help if I had," or "I'm looking for . . . ." Too, respond to what the others have said. For example, preface comments with "In light of what you said about . . ." or "If you feel strongly about . . . ." Powerless listeners, on the other hand, listen passively; they appear to be thinking about something else and only pretend to be listening. And they rarely refer to what the other person has said when they do respond.

Powerful listeners respond visibly but in moderation; an occasional nod of agreement or a facial expression that says "that's interesting" are usually sufficient. Responding with too little or too much reaction is likely to be perceived as powerless. Too little response says you aren't listening and too much response says you aren't listening critically. Powerful listeners also use backchanneling cues—head nods and brief oral responses that say "I'm listening, I'm following you"—when appropriate. When no backchanneling cues are given, the speaker comes to wonder if the other person is really listening.

Powerful listeners maintain more focused eye contact than do those seen to have less power. In conversation, normal eye contact is intermittent—you glance at the speaker's face, then away, then back again, and so on. In a small group or public speaking situation, eye contact with the speaker is normally greater.

Adaptors—playing with your hair or a pencil—give the appearance of discomfort. Because of this, adaptors communicate a lack of power. These body movements show the listener to be more concerned with himself or herself than with the speaker. The lack of adaptors, on the other hand, make the listener appear in control of the situation and comfortable in the role of listener.

Powerful listeners are more likely to maintain an open posture. When around a table or in an audience they resist covering their stomach or face with their hands. Persons who maintain a defensive posture with, for example, arms crossed around their stomach, may communicate a feeling of vulnerability and powerlessness.

Powerful listeners avoid interrupting the speaker in conversations or in small group situations. The reason is simple: Not interrupting is one of the rules of business communication that powerful people follow and powerless people don't. Completing the speaker's thoughts (or what the listener thinks is the speaker's thought) has a similar powerless effect.

How would you evaluate your own speaking, nonverbal, and listening power? In which area are you most powerful? In which are you least powerful? What might you do to increase your power?

You can also signal power through visual dominance behavior (Exline, Ellyson, and Long 1975), a consideration mentioned in the discussion of eye communication in Unit 12. For example, the average speaker maintains a high level of eye contact while listening and a lower level while speaking. When powerful individuals want to signal dominance, they may reverse this pattern. They may, for example, maintain a high level of eye contact while talking but a much lower level while listening.

Empowering Others

Empowerment involves helping others (your relational partner, an employee, another student, a sibling) to gain increased power over themselves and their environment. Empowerment is not just an altruistic gesture on the part of one relationship partner or of management (many of whom use it as a basic philosophy). The reason empowerment is so much discussed and so much a part of modern business practices is that it provides lots of benefits. Empowered people are more likely to take a more personal interest in the job or in the relationship. Empowered people will be proactive; they will act and not just react. They are more likely to take on decision-making responsibilities, are willing to take risks, and are willing to take responsibility for their actions, qualities that make both relationships and business exciting. In an interpersonal relationship (though the same would apply to a multinational organization), two empowered partners are more likely to effectively meet the challenges and difficulties most relationships will encounter.

Here are a few ways of empowering others.

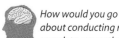

How would you go about conducting research to assess the effectiveness of these strategies of empowerment on, say, self-esteem or confidence?

◆ Raise the self-esteem of the other person. Resist fault-finding. It doesn't really benefit the fault-finder and certainly doesn't benefit the other person. Fault-finding disempowers others.

◆ Be open, positive, empathic, and supportive and treat the other person with an equality of respect. These of course are the humanistic qualities of effectiveness we pointed out in Unit 8.

◆ Be attentive, listen actively. Attentiveness and active listening tell the other person that he or she is important. After all, what greater praise could you pay than to give another person your time and energy?

◆ Avoid verbal aggressiveness and abusiveness. Resist the temptation to win an argument with unfair tactics, tactics that are going to hurt the other person.

◆ Share skills and share decision making. Be willing to relinquish control and allow the other person the freedom to make decisions.

◆ Be constructively critical. Be willing to offer your perspective, to lend an ear to a first singing effort or to listen to a new poem.

◆ Encourage growth in all forms, academic and relational. Growth, like empowerment, is not of limited supply that must be parceled out. Both persons can grow and develop and both persons can be empowered. The growth and empowerment of one person enhances the growth and power of the other.

Compliance Gaining and Compliance Resisting

These strategies are regarded as generally effective, though not necessarily moral or ethical. Which do you consider ethical? Which do you consider unethical?

The use of compliance strategies clearly illustrates the way power is exercised. **Compliance-gaining strategies** are the tactics that influence others to do what you want them to do. **Compliance-resisting strategies** are the tactics that enable you to say no and to resist another person's attempts to influence you.

Compliance-Gaining Strategies

Which of these strategies do you find most effective? Which strategies work best on you? What other strategies can you identify?

Sixteen compliance-gaining strategies are presented in Table 19.3. In reviewing these strategies, keep in mind that compliance gaining, like all interpersonal processes, involves two people in a transaction. Reading down the list may give the impression that these strategies are one-shot affairs, with one person using the strategy and the other person complying. Actually, compliance gaining is best viewed as a transactional, back-and-forth process. Conflict, compromise, renego-

Table 19.3	**Compliance-Gaining Strategies**

As you read this table realize that these strategies and the responses to them depend both on the personalities of the individuals and on their unique relationship. Which strategies you use, which strategies will work for you, and which strategies will backfire depend on who you are, on who the other person is, and on the interpersonal relationship between you. These compliance-gaining strategies come from the research of Marwell and Schmitt (1967, 1990; also see Miller and Parks 1982; Dillard 1990).

Compliance Strategy	Example
Pregiving. Pat rewards Chris and then requests compliance.	**Pat:** *I'm glad you enjoyed dinner. This really is the best restaur|ant in the city. How about going back to my place for a nightcap and whatever?*
Liking. Pat is helpful and friendly in order to get Chris in a good mood so that Chris will be more likely to comply with Pat's request.	**Pat:** [After cleaning up the living room and bedroom] *I'd really like to relax and bowl a few games with Terry. OK?*
Promise. Pat promises to reward Chris if Chris complies with Pat's request.	**Pat:** *I'll give you anything you want if you will just give me a divorce. You can have the house, the car, the stocks, the three kids; just give me my freedom.*
Threat. Pat threatens to punish Chris for noncompliance.	**Pat:** *If you don't give me a divorce, you'll never see the kids again.*
Aversive stimulation. Pat continuously punishes Chris and makes cessation of the punishment contingent upon compliance.	**Pat:** *demonstrates hysterical reactions* (for example, screaming and crying) *and stops only when Chris agrees to comply*
Positive expertise. Pat promises that Chris will be rewarded for compliance because of "the nature of things."	**Pat:** *It will be a lot easier for everyone involved if you don't contest the divorce.*
Negative expertise. Pat promises that Chris will be punished for noncompliance because of "the nature of things."	**Pat:** *If you don't listen to the doctor, you're going to wind up back in the hospital.*
Positive self-feelings. Pat promises that Chris will feel better if Chris complies with Pat's request.	**Pat:** *You'll see. You'll be a lot better off without me; you'll feel a lot better after the divorce.*
Negative self-feelings. Pat promises that Chris will feel worse if Chris does not comply with Pat's request.	**Pat:** *Only a selfish creep would force another person to stay in a relationship. You'll hate yourself if you don't give me this divorce.*
Positive altercasting. Pat casts Chris in the role of the "good" person and argues that Chris should comply because a person with "good" qualities would comply.	**Pat:** *Any intelligent person would grant a partner a divorce when the relationship had died.*
Negative altercasting. Pat casts Chris in the role of the "bad" person and argues that Chris should comply because only a person with "bad" qualities would not comply.	**Pat:** *Only a cruel and selfish neurotic could stand in the way of another's happiness.*
Positive esteem. Pat tells Chris that people will think more highly of Chris (relying on our need for the approval of others) if Chris complies with Pat's request.	**Pat:** *Everyone will respect your decision to grant me a divorce.*
Negative esteem. Pat tells Chris that people will think poorly of Chris if Chris does not comply with Pat's request.	**Pat:** *Everyone will think you're paranoid if you don't join the club.*
Moral appeals. Pat argues that Chris should comply because it is moral to comply and immoral not to comply.	**Pat:** *An ethical individual would never stand in the way of a partner's freedom and sanity.*
Altruism. Pat asks Chris to comply because Pat needs this compliance (relying on Chris's desire to help and be of assistance).	**Pat:** *I would feel so disappointed if you quit college now. Don't hurt me by quitting.*
Debt. Pat asks Chris to comply because of the past favors given to Chris.	**Pat:** *Look at how we sacrificed to send you to college.*

Which—if any—of the 16 compliance-gaining strategies have you used? Which—if any—have been used on you? How effective were these attempts?

tiation of the goal, rejection of the strategy, and a host of other responses—in addition to simple compliance—are possible.

Compliance-Resisting Strategies

Let's say that someone you know asks you to do something you don't want to do, for example, lend your term paper so this person can copy it and turn it in to another teacher. Research with college students shows that there are four principal ways of responding (McLaughlin, Cody, and Robey 1980; O'Hair, Cody, and O'Hair 1991).

In **identity management**, you resist by trying to manipulate the image of the person making the request. You might do this negatively or positively. In negative identity management, you might portray the person as unreasonable or unfair and say, for example, "That's really unfair of you to ask me to compromise my ethics." Or you might tell the person that it hurts that he or she would even think you would do such a thing.

You might also use positive identity management. Here you resist complying by making the other person feel good about himself or herself. For example, you might say, "You know this material much better than I do; you can easily do a much better paper yourself."

Another way to resist compliance is to use **nonnegotiation**, a direct refusal to do as asked. You might simply say, "No, I don't lend my papers out."

In **negotiation**, you resist compliance by, for example, offering a compromise ("I'll let you read my paper but not copy it") or by offering to help the person in some other way ("If you write a first draft, I'll go over it and try to make some comments"). If the request is a romantic one—for example, a request to go away for a ski weekend—you might resist by discussing your feelings and proposing an alternative: for example, "Let's double date first."

Another way to resist compliance is through **justification**. Here you justify your refusal by citing possible consequences of compliance or noncompliance. For example, you might cite a negative consequence if you complied ("I'm afraid that I'd get caught, and then I'd fail the course"). Or you might cite a positive consequence of your not complying ("You'll really enjoy writing this paper; it's a lot of fun").

Remember that compliance gaining and resisting—like all interpersonal communication—are transactional processes in which all elements are interdependent; each element influences each other. Your attempts to gain compliance, for example, will be influenced by the responses of the person you wish to influence. These responses in turn will influence your responses, and so on. Also, just as your relationship (its type, length, intimacy, for example) will influence the strategies you use, so will the strategies you use influence your relationship. Inappropriate strategies will have negative effects, just as positive strategies will have positive effects.

How would you use compliance-resisting strategies to say no to someone's romantic advances? How would you use compliance-gaining strategies to specify that there must be a particular condition for a romantic involvement?

A RETURN TO OBJECTIVES:

In this unit the importance of power in interpersonal relationships was considered where we emphasized: (1) What is power and what are its main principles? (2) What are the major types (or bases) of power? (3) How can you communicate power verbally, nonverbally, and in listening? (4) What are some of the power plays that people use to control the behavior of others and how can you effectively combat them? (5) What are the strategies for interpersonal compliance-gaining and compliance-resisting?

Principles of Power	Bases of Power	Communicating Power	Empowering Others	Compliance Gaining and Compliance Resisting
Some people are more powerful than others. Some people are more Machiavellian than others. Power can be increased or decreased. Power follows the principle of least interest. Power has a cultural dimension. Power is often used unfairly as in sexual harassment and power plays.	**Referent:** B wants to be like A. **Legitimate:** B believes that A has a right to influence or control B's behavior. **Reward:** A has the ability to reward B. **Coercive:** A has the ability to punish B. **Expert:** B regards A as having knowledge. **Information or persuasion:** B attributes to A the ability to communicate effectively.	**Speaking power:** Avoid hesitations, disqualifiers, and self-critical statements. **Nonverbal power:** Avoid adaptors, use consistent packaging, and avoid excessive movements. **Listening power:** Respond visibly, maintain eye contact and an open posture, avoid interrupting.	Helping the other person to gain in power and control over himself or herself and over the environment has numerous advantages. For example, empowered people are more proactive and more responsible. Empowering others involves such strategies as being positive, avoiding verbal aggressiveness and abusiveness, encouraging growth.	Tactics that influence others to do as you want (liking, promise, threat) or enable you to resist compliance (identify management, negotiation)

UNIT

20

Conflict in Interpersonal Relationships

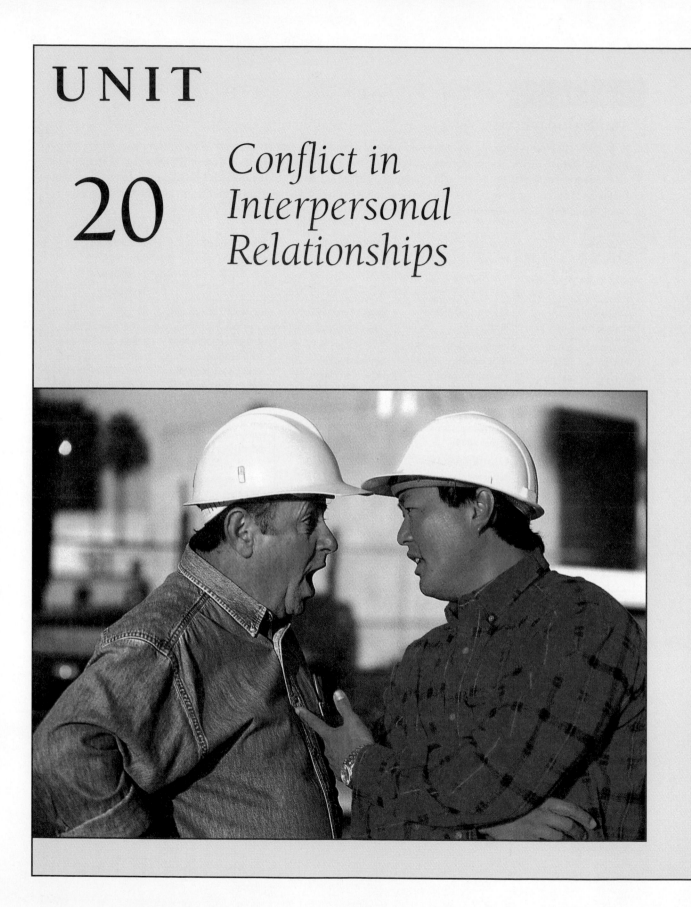

Unit Topics	Unit Objectives
	After completing this unit, you should be able to:
The Nature of Conflict Myths About Conflict The Negatives and Positives of Conflict Content and Relationship Conflicts Conflict and Culture	1. Define *interpersonal conflict* 2. Identify potentially negative and positive aspects of conflict 3. Distinguish between content and relationship conflict 4. Explain the relevance of culture to interpersonal conflict
A Model of Conflict Resolution Define the Conflict Examine Possible Solutions Test the Solution Evaluate the Solution Accept or Reject the Solution	5. Explain the model of *conflict resolution*

Conflict Management Strategies
Avoidance and Fighting Actively
Force and Talk
Blame and Empathy
Silencers and Facilitating Open Expression
Gunnysacking and Present Focus
Fighting Below and Above the Belt
Face-Detracting and Face-Enhancing
     Strategies
Verbal Aggressiveness, Verbal Abuse, and
     Argumentativeness
Dealing with Unfair Conflict Strategies
	6. Describe the major destructive and constructive *conflict management* strategies

Before and After the Conflict Before the Conflict After the Conflict	7. Explain the suggestions for preparing for and concluding conflict

---

EXPERIENTIAL LEARNING VEHICLES

Experiential Learning Vehicle No. 19, "Male and Female," p. 463, is useful in illustrating some of the causes of communication difficulties between men and women. No. 20, "Relationship Repair from Advice Columnists," pp. 463–464, can easily be focused on conflict. No. 22, "Analyzing a Conflict Episode," provides a script appropriate for analyzing productive and unproductive conflict strategies. Vehicle No. 24, "The Television Relationship," pp. 467–468, is useful for analyzing the numerous conflict episodes as they are developed and resolved on television.

In its most basic form, conflict refers to a disagreement. **Interpersonal conflict**, then, refers to a disagreement between or among connected individuals: for example, close friends, lovers, or family members. The word "connected" emphasizes the transactional nature of interpersonal conflict, that each person's position affects the other person. The positions in conflict are to some degree interrelated and incompatible.

Conflict is a part of every interpersonal relationship, between parents and children, brothers and sisters, friends, lovers, coworkers. As Louis Nizer put it, "Where there is no difference, there is only indifference."

The Nature of Conflict

Conflicts can center on a wide variety of issues:

- goals to be pursued ("We want you to go to college and become a teacher or a doctor, not a dancer");
- allocation of resources, such as money or time ("I want to spend the tax refund on a car, not on new furniture");
- decisions to be made ("I refuse to have the Jeffersons over to dinner");
- behaviors that are considered appropriate or desirable by one person and inappropriate or undesirable by the other ("I hate it when you get drunk, pinch me, ridicule me in front of others, flirt with others, dress provocatively, and so on").

Myths About Conflict

What do you believe about conflict? For example, do you think the following statements are true or false?

- If two people engage in relationship conflict, it means their relationship is a bad one.
- Conflict hurts an interpersonal relationship.
- Conflict is bad because it reveals our negative selves—for example, our pettiness, our need to be in control, our unreasonable expectations.

As with most things, simple answers are usually wrong. The three assumptions above may all be true or may all be false. It depends.

It is not so much the conflict that creates the problem as the way in which you approach and deal with the conflict. Some ways of approaching conflict can resolve difficulties and improve the relationship. Other ways can hurt the relationship; they can destroy self-esteem, create bitterness, and foster suspicion.

Similarly, it is not the conflict that reveals your negative side but the fight strategies you use. Thus, if you attack the other person personally or use force, you reveal your negative side. But you can also reveal your positive self—your willingness to listen to opposing points of view, to change unpleasant behaviors, and to accept imperfection in others.

 Do you hold any personal conflict myths? Do you entertain any beliefs about interpersonal conflict that might be untrue and self-defeating?

The Negatives and Positives of Conflict

Interpersonal conflict is inevitable because people are different and will necessarily see things differently. But it is neither good nor bad in itself. Conflict and the way you deal with it can, however, have both negative and positive effects.

Among the disadvantages of conflict is that it often leads to increased negative regard for the opponent. When this opponent is someone you love or care for, it can create serious problems. One problem is that many conflicts involve unfair fighting methods and focus largely on hurting the other person. If this happens, negative feelings are sure to increase. Conflict may also deplete energy better spent on other areas, especially when unproductive conflict strategies are used.

At times, conflict may lead you to close yourself off from the other individual. When you do this and hide your true feelings from an intimate, you prevent meaningful communication. Because the need for intimacy is so strong, one possible outcome is that one or both parties may seek this intimacy elsewhere. This often leads to further conflict, mutual hurt, and resentment—qualities that add heavily to the costs carried by the relationship. As these costs increase, the rewards may become more difficult to exchange. Here, then, is a situation in which costs increase and rewards decrease, one that often results in relationship deterioration and eventual dissolution.

One of the advantages of conflict is that it forces you to examine a problem and work toward a potential solution. If you use productive conflict strategies, your relationship may emerge from the encounter stronger, healthier, and more satisfying than before.

Conflict also enables you to state what you each want and—if the conflict is resolved effectively—perhaps to get it. For example, let's say that I want to spend our money on a new car (my old one is unreliable), and you want to spend it on a vacation (you feel the need for a change of pace). Through our conflict and its resolution, we can learn what each genuinely wants: in this case, a reliable car and a break from routine. We may then be able to figure out a way for each of us to get what we want. I might accept a good used car or a less expensive new car, and you might accept a shorter or less expensive vacation. Or we might buy a used car and take an inexpensive motor trip. Each of these solutions will satisfy both of us; they are win-win solutions—each of us wins, and each of us gets what we wanted.

Conflict often prevents hostilities and resentments from festering. Say I'm annoyed at your talking on the phone with your colleagues for two hours instead of giving that time to me. If I say nothing, my annoyance and resentment are likely to grow. Further, by saying nothing I have implicitly approved such behavior, and so it is likely that such phone calls will be repeated. Through your conflict and its resolution, you stop resentment from increasing. In the process, you also let your own needs be known—that I need lots of attention when I come home from work and that you need to review the day's work and gain the assurance that it has been properly completed. If you both can appreciate the legitimacy of these needs, then you stand a good chance of finding workable solutions. Perhaps you can make the phone call after my attention needs are met. Perhaps I can delay my need for attention until you get closure about work. Perhaps I can learn to provide for your closure needs and in doing so get my attention needs met. Again, we have win-win solutions; each of us gets our needs met.

What, if any, positive outcomes emerged from your previous interpersonal conflicts? What negative outcomes?

Consider, too, that when you try to resolve conflict within an interpersonal relationship, you are saying that the relationship is worth the effort; otherwise, you would walk away. Although there may be exceptions—as when you confront conflict to save face or to gratify some ego need—confronting a conflict usually indicates concern, commitment, and a desire to protect and preserve the relationship.

Content and Relationship Conflicts

Using concepts developed earlier (Unit 2), we may distinguish between content conflict and relationship conflict. Content conflict centers on objects, events, and persons in the world that are usually, but not always, external to the people involved in the conflict. These include the millions of issues that you argue and fight about every day—the value of a particular movie, what to watch on television, the fairness of the last examination or job promotion, and the way to spend your savings.

Relationship conflicts are equally numerous and include such conflict situations as a younger brother who does not obey his older brother, two partners who each want an equal say in making vacation plans, and the mother and daughter who each want to have the final word concerning the daughter's lifestyle. Here the conflicts are concerned not so much with some external object as with the relationships between the individuals, with such relationship issues as who is in charge, the equality of a primary relationship, and who has the right to establish rules of behavior.

Content conflicts are usually more easily identifiable. Relationship conflicts are often hidden and much more difficult to identify. Thus, a conflict over where you should vacation may, on the surface level, center on the advantages and disadvantages of Mexico versus Hawaii. On a relationship and often hidden level, however, it may center on who has the greater right to select the place to vacation, who should win the argument, who is the decision maker in the relationship, and so on.

Here are the results from three studies to give you some idea of what specific issues people argue about. In the first study gay, lesbian, and heterosexual couples were surveyed on the issues they argued about most; the findings are presented in Table 20.1 (Kurdek 1994).

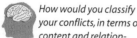

How would you classify your conflicts, in terms of content and relationship? With friends? With coworkers? With romantic partners? With family members? Which do you find easier to resolve? Which create the more lasting hurt?

Table 20.1	Interpersonal Conflict Issues		

This table presents the rank order of the six most frequently argued-about issues. Seventy-five gay men, 51 lesbians, and 108 heterosexuals participated in this survey. Note that these issues involve both content and relationship dimensions. Note also the striking similarity among all couples. It seems that affectional orientation has little to do with the topics people argue about. What issues do you argue about?

Issues Argued About	Gay	Lesbian	Hetero-sexual
Intimacy issues such as affection and sex	1	1	1
Power issues such as excessive demands or possessiveness, lack of equality in the relationship, friends, and leisure time	2	2	2
Personal flaws issues such as drinking or smoking, personal grooming, and driving style	3	3	4
Personal distance issues such as frequently being absent and school or job commitments	4	4	5
Social issues such as politics and social issues, parents, and personal values	5	5	3
Distrust issues such as previous lovers and lying	6	6	6

In another study four conditions led up to a couple's "first big fight" (Siegert and Stamp 1994): uncertainty over commitment, jealousy, violation of expectations, and personality differences.

In a study of conflict among top managers, the major source of conflict revolved around the issue of executive responsibility and coordination. Other conflicts focused on differences in organizational objectives, in how resources are to be allocated, and in what constitutes an appropriate management style (Morrill 1992).

Conflict and Culture

Culture influences conflict as it does all aspects of interpersonal communication. Culture influences the topics people fight about as well as what is considered appropriate and inappropriate ways of dealing with conflict. For example, cohabitating 18-year-olds are more likely to have conflict with the parents on their living style if they lived in the United States than if they lived in Sweden where cohabitation is much more accepted. Similarly, male infidelity is more likely to cause conflict among American couples than among Southern European couples. Students from the United States are more likely to pursue a conflict with another United States student than with someone from another culture. Chinese students, on the other hand, are more likely to pursue a conflict with another Chinese student than with a non-Chinese (Leung 1988).

Cultures also differ in how they define and evaluate a conflict strategy. In some cultures it is quite common for women to be referred to negatively and as less than equal. To most people in the United States this would constitute verbal abuse. To some Japanese women, however, this is not uncommon and is not perceived as abusive (*New York Times,* February 11, 1996, pp. 1, 12). As already noted, cultures also vary widely in their responses to abuse (physical and verbal). In some Asian and Hispanic cultures, for example, the fear of losing face or embarrassing the family is so great that they would rather not report or reveal any abuse. In much of the United States, and in many other cultures as well, such abuse would not be tolerated no matter who was embarrassed or insulted.

Cultures differ in the extent to which they think abuse takes place in relationships; for example, people from industrialized countries believe that abuse against women is higher than do people from less developed countries (Reichert 1991). Cultures differ in the extent of the occurrence of verbal abuse (Clark et al. 1994; Obujinrin 1993). In a study of 90 preliterate societies, for example, abuse was common in 84 percent of them and unknown or rare in only 16 percent. Husbands were the abusive partners in 84 percent of the societies studied; wives were the abusive partners in 27 percent (Levinson 1989; Hatfield and Rapson 1996).

The types of conflicts that arise will depend on the cultural orientation of the individuals. For example, it is likely that in high-context cultures conflicts are more likely to center on violating collective or group norms and values. Conversely, it is likely that in low-context cultures conflicts are more likely to arise when individual norms are violated (Ting-Toomey 1985).

 What has your culture taught you about conflict?

In Japan it is important that you not embarrass the person with whom you are in conflict, especially if that conflict occurs in public. This face-saving principle prohibits the use of such strategies as personal rejection or verbal aggressiveness. In the United States men and women, ideally at least, are both expected to express their desires and complaints openly and directly. Many Middle Eastern and Pacific Rim cultures would discourage women from such expressions. Rather, a more agreeable and permissive posture would be expected.

A similar concern for face saving operates among Asian women who, for example, will rarely report wife abuse because it would result in a loss of face for them, their husbands, and their entire family. When examining statistics, it may appear that there is little violence in Asian families. Yet, we know from research that wife beating is quite common in India and Taiwan, for example (Counts, Brown, and Campbell 1992; Hatfield and Rapson 1996). An estimated 60 to 70 percent of cases of domestic violence in Asian families are never reported (Dresser 1996). In Iran, where wife beating is also common, it is not reported, very likely because reporting it would result in greater abuse (cf. Hatfield and Rapson 1996).

African Americans and European Americans engage in conflict in very different ways (Kochman 1981). The issues which cause conflict and which aggravate conflict, the conflict strategies that are expected and accepted, and the entire attitude toward conflict vary from one group to the other.

Different cultures also view conflict management techniques differently. For example, in one study (Collier 1991) it was found that African American men preferred clear arguments and a focus on problem-solving. African American women, however, preferred assertiveness and respect. In another study African American females were found to use more direct controlling strategies (for example, assuming control over the conflict and arguing persistently for their point of view) than did white females. White females, on the other hand, used more problem solution-oriented conflict styles than did African American females. African American and white men were very similar in their conflict strategies; both tended to avoid or withdraw from relationship conflict. They preferred to keep quiet about their differences or make them seem insignificant (Ting-Toomey 1986).

Mexican American men emphasized mutual understanding achieved through discussing the reasons for the conflict while women focused on support for the relationship. Anglo-American men preferred direct and rational argument while women preferred flexibility. These, of course, are merely examples, but the underlying principle is that techniques for dealing with interpersonal conflict are viewed differently by different cultures.

The following brief dialogue (modeled on an idea by Crohn 1995) is designed to illustrate the issue of cultural differences in conflict and some of the problems these may create. As you read it try to explain what may be going on interculturally.

PAT: Why did you tell her I was home? I told you an hour ago that I didn't want to speak with her. You just don't listen.

CHRIS: I'm sorry. I completely forgot. But, you seemed to have had a nice talk. So, no harm done—right?

PAT: Wrong. You just don't understand. I didn't want to talk with her.

CHRIS: O.K. Sorry.

Chris withdraws to next room and remains silent. To Pat's repeated comments and criticisms, he says nothing. After about 2 hours:

PAT: I can't stand your silent treatment; you're making me the villain. You're the one who screwed up.

CHRIS: I'm sorry. [*Walks away*]

Recall your last few interpersonal conflicts. What role did face-saving play in these? How important was face-saving to you? How important was it to your partner? How do you know this?

Communication continued in this way for the rest of the evening—with Pat ranting and raving every several minutes and with Chris saying hardly anything and always trying to walk away. Pat comes from a culture where anger is regularly and expectedly expressed. Yelling and screaming are customary ways of dealing with conflict. Chris comes from a culture where anger is expressed by silence. The extent to which you remain silent is a measure of how angry you are.

Their different cultural beliefs about conflict can lead each to draw incorrect conclusions about the other. For example, from Chris's silence it is easy for Pat to conclude that Chris doesn't care about what happened and is indifferent to Pat's anger. From Pat's outburst Chris may easily conclude that Pat is unhappy in their relationship.

If Pat and Chris came from the same culture—with the same rules for expressing anger or had sufficient intercultural awareness—their argument would have been no less real. Don't let us fool ourselves into thinking that cultural awareness will resolve all conflicts or that culture is the only factor that can cause such differences; it won't and it isn't. But, it would have prevented a large part of the conflict—for example, the anger over the way the other person expressed anger—and would have prevented each from making inaccurate assumptions about the other. The problem is made even more difficult to resolve because these cultural rules are so deeply ingrained that we assume everyone has the same rules. Because we assume this underlying similarity, we never get to explore the problem from the point of view of intercultural communication differences

What has your culture taught you about interpersonal conflict? Have any of these teachings influenced your current conflict behavior? Have these cultural principles generally been effective in helping you deal with interpersonal conflict?

A Model of Conflict Resolution

We can explain conflict more fully and provide guidance for dealing with it effectively by referring to the model in Figure 20.1.

Define the Conflict

Define the obvious content issues (who should do the dishes, who should take the kids to school, who should take out the dog) as well as the underlying relationship issues (who has been avoiding household responsibilities, who has been neglecting responsibility toward the kids, whose time is more valuable).

Define the problem in specific terms. Conflict defined in the abstract is difficult to deal with and resolve. It is one thing for a husband to say that his wife is "cold and unfeeling" and quite another to say that she does not call him at the office, kiss him when he comes home, or hold his hand when they are at a party. These behaviors can be agreed upon and dealt with, but the abstract "cold and unfeeling" remains elusive.

Throughout this process, try to understand the nature of the conflict from the other person's point of view. Use your perspective-taking skills. Why is your partner disturbed that you are not doing the dishes? Why is your neighbor complaining about taking the kids to school? Why is your mother insisting you take out the dog?

Don't try to read the other person's mind. Ask questions to make sure you see the problem from the other person's point of view. Ask directly and simply: for example, "Why are you insisting that I take the dog out now when I have to call three clients before nine o'clock?"

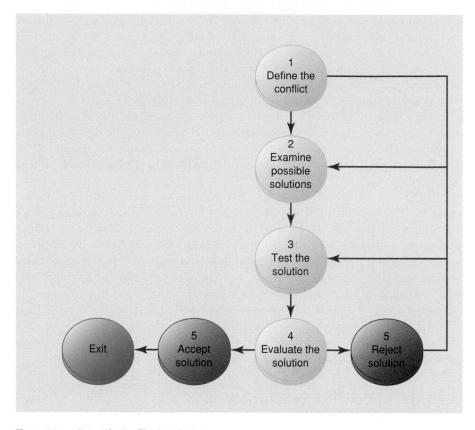

Figure 20.1   Stages in Conflict Resolution.
This model of conflict resolution is essentially John Dewey's problem-solving sequence. The assumption made here is that a conflict is essentially a problem to be solved and follows the same general sequence. As you read about this problem/conflict-solving sequence, try visualizing a specific conflict and how these steps might help to resolve it.

Let us select an example and work it through the remaining steps. This conflict revolves around Pat's not wanting to socialize with Chris's friends. Chris is devoted to them, but Pat actively dislikes them. Chris thinks they are wonderful and exciting; Pat thinks they are unpleasant and boring.

Examine Possible Solutions

Most conflicts can probably be resolved through a variety of solutions. At this stage, try to identify as many solutions as possible. Brainstorm by yourself or with your partner. Try generating as many solutions as possible, trying not to inhibit or censor yourself or your partner.

Once you have proposed a variety of solutions, look especially for solutions that will enable both parties to win—to get something each wants. Avoid win-lose solutions, in which one wins and one loses. They will cause difficulty for the relationship by engendering frustration and resentment.

In problem-solving discussion, from which this model derives, it is often helpful to decide on the criteria or standards you will use in evaluating the proposed solutions—the basis on which you will select one solution over another. This same technique can be used in dealing with interpersonal conflict; for example, you might decide before exploring solutions that the selected solution must be such that we both agree with it or that it won't cost more than we have in the bank. The disadvantage of doing this is that it may inhibit you from generating imaginative solutions. How do you feel about including this stage in the model?

In examining these potential solutions, carefully weigh the costs and the rewards that each solution entails. Most solutions will involve costs to one or both parties (after all, *someone* has to take the dog out). Seek solutions in which the costs and the rewards will be evenly shared.

Once you have examined all possible solutions, select one and test it out. Among the solutions that Pat and Chris might identify are these.

The suggestion to seek solutions in which the costs and the rewards will be evenly shared is an easy and logical one to offer. But, it is not so easy to act on. What difficulties would you have in implementing this suggestion?

1. Chris should not interact with these friends anymore.
2. Pat should interact with Chris's friends.
3. Chris should see these friends without Pat.

Clearly solutions 1 and 2 are win-lose solutions. In solution 1, Pat wins and Chris loses; in 2, Chris wins and Pat loses. Solution 3 has some possibilities. Both might win and neither must necessarily lose. This potential solution, then, needs to be looked at more closely.

Test the Solution

Test the solution mentally. How does it feel now? How will it feel tomorrow? Are you comfortable with it? Would Pat be comfortable with Chris's socializing with these friends alone? Some of Chris's friends are attractive; would this cause difficulty for Pat and Chris's relationship? Will Chris give people too much to gossip about? Will Chris feel guilty? Will Chris enjoy these friends without Pat?

Test the solution in practice. Put the solution into operation. How does it work? If it doesn't work, then discard it and try another solution. Give each solution a fair chance, but don't hang on to a solution when it is clear that it won't resolve the conflict.

Perhaps Chris might go out without Pat once to test this solution. How was it? Did these friends think there was something wrong with Chris's relationship with Pat? Did Chris feel guilty? Did Chris enjoy this new experience? How did Pat feel? Did Pat feel jealous? Lonely? Abandoned?

Evaluate the Solution

Did the solution help resolve the conflict? Is the situation better now than it was before the solution was tried? Share your feelings and evaluations of the solution.

Pat and Chris now need to share their perceptions of this possible solution. Would they be comfortable with this solution on a monthly basis? Is the solution worth the costs each will pay? Are the costs and rewards evenly distributed? Might other solutions be more effective?

Accept or Reject the Solution

If you accept the solution, you are ready to put it into more permanent operation. If you decide that this is not the right solution for the conflict, then you might test another solution or perhaps go back to redefine the conflict.

Let us say that Pat is actually quite happy with the solution. Pat was able to use that time to visit college friends. The next time Chris goes out with friends, Pat intends to go to wrestling with these people from college. Chris feels pretty good about seeing friends without Pat. Chris explains that they have both decided to see their friends separately and both are comfortable with this decision.

 Do you generally follow the pattern of conflict resolution identified in this five-step model? Can you trace a recent conflict resolution through the model? What additional suggestions can you offer for dealing with any of the five stages?

If, however, Pat or Chris was unhappy with this solution, they would have to try out another one or perhaps go back and redefine the problem and seek other ways to resolve it. Throughout this process, avoid the common but damaging conflict strategies that can destroy a relationship. At the same time, use those strategies that will help to resolve the conflict and even improve the relationship.

Conflict Management Strategies

The conflict management strategies that you choose will be influenced by a variety of considerations. Understanding these factors may help you select more appropriate and more effective strategies.

For example, the goals (short-term and long-term) you wish to achieve will influence what strategies seem appropriate to you. If you just want to save today's date, you might want to simply "give in" and basically ignore the difficulty. On the other hand, if you want to build a long-term relationship, you might want to fully analyze the cause of the problem and look for strategies that will enable both of you to win.

Your emotional state will influence your strategies. You are unlikely to select the same strategies when you are sad as when you are angry. Different strategies will be used if you are seeking to apologize or looking for revenge.

Your cognitive assessment of the situation will exert powerful influence. For example, your attitudes and beliefs about what is fair and equitable will influence your readiness to acknowledge the fairness in the other person's position. Your own assessment of who (if anyone) is the cause of the problem will also influence your conflict style. You might also assess the likely effects of your various strategies. For example, what do you risk if you fight with your boss by using blame or personal rejection? Do you risk alienating your teenager when you use force?

Your personality and level of communication competence will influence the way you engage in conflict. For example, if you are shy and unassertive, you may be more likely to avoid a conflict than fight actively. If you are extroverted and have a strong desire to state your position, then you may be more likely to fight actively and to argue forcefully.

Your cultural background will influence your strategies. As noted earlier, many Asian cultures emphasize the importance of saving face, of not embarrassing another person, especially in public. Consequently, Asians are probably less likely to use conflict strategies such as blame and personal rejection, since these are likely to result in a loss of face. And of course many Asians are more likely to use such strategies to preserve and enhance one's public image. Those from cultures which favor more open discussion of conflict might be more apt to use argumentativeness and to fight actively. If you are from a collective culture you are more likely to prefer mediation and bargaining as conflict resolution strategies than would those from individualistic cultures who prefer a more adversarial and confrontational conflict style (Leung 1987; Berry, Poortinga, Segall, and Dasen 1992).

Many cultures have different rules for men and women. These rules don't seem to vary on the basis of affectional orientation; gay men and lesbian couples use essentially the same conflict resolution strategies as do heterosexual men and women (Metz, Rosser, and Strapko 1994). For example, one study found that in the United States when men argue with other men they both use assertiveness and reason throughout. When women argue with women they begin with assertiveness, then reasoning, and then move to bargaining. When women and men argue they both use reason and bargaining throughout the discussion (Papa and Natalle 1989). Asian cultures are more strongly prohibitive of women's conflict strategies. Asian women are expected to be exceptionally polite; this is even more important when women are in conflict with men and when the conflict is public (Tannen 1994b). In the United States, there is a verbalized equality; men and women have equal rights when it comes to permissible conflict strategies. In reality, many expect women to be more polite and to pursue conflict in a nonargumentative way. Men are expected to argue forcefully and logically.

How would you go about discovering if the men and women at your college use different or similar conflict strategies?

We have already covered a wide variety of conflict resolution skills. For example, active listening is a skill that has wide application in conflict situations (see Unit 7). Similarly, using I-messages (rather than accusatory you-messages; see Unit 8) will contribute to effective interpersonal conflict resolution (Noller and Fitzpatrick 1993). Of course, the characteristics of interpersonal competence (Unit 8) are clear and effective conflict resolution techniques. The following discussion focuses on unproductive strategies that should be avoided, as well as their productive counterparts.

Avoidance and Fighting Actively

Avoidance may involve actual physical flight: for example, leaving the scene of the conflict (walking out of the apartment or going to another part of the office), falling asleep, or blasting the stereo to drown out all conversation. It may also take the form of emotional or intellectual avoidance, whereby you leave the conflict psychologically by not dealing with the issues raised.

Men are more likely to use this strategy, coupled with denial that anything is wrong (Haferkamp 1991–92). However, this does not mean that men are simply unfair in their approach to conflict. One theory is that men experience flooding (a sense of being out of control, of extreme negative feelings of anger or rage, for example) more easily and with less provocation than women (Gottman 1993, 1994; Goleman 1995). Physiologically, flooding occurs at 10 heart beats per minute more than normal; when the heart rate increases to about 100 beats per minute the distress level—because of the extra adrenaline pumped in—will remain high for some time, even after the conflict is "settled." The tendency to withdraw from an argument or to say nothing in response to a woman's desire to discuss the conflict may be due to a desire to avoid or reduce the effects of flooding.

Nonnegotiation is a special type of avoidance. Here you refuse to discuss the conflict or to listen to the other person's argument. At times, this nonnegotiation takes the form of hammering away at one's own point of view until the other person gives in.

Instead of avoiding the issues, take an active role in your interpersonal conflicts. This is not to say that a cooling-off period is not at times desirable. It is to say, instead, that if you wish to resolve conflicts, you need to confront them actively. Involve yourself on both sides of the communication exchange. Be an active participant as a speaker and as a listener; voice your own feelings and listen carefully to your partner's feelings.

Another part of active fighting involves taking responsibility for your thoughts and feelings. For example, when you disagree with your partner or find fault with her or his behavior, take responsibility for these feelings. Say, for example, "I disagree with . . ." or "I don't like it when you. . . ." Avoid statements that deny your responsibility: for example, "Everybody thinks you're wrong about . . ." or "Chris thinks you shouldn't. . . ."

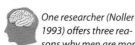

One researcher (Noller 1993) offers three reasons why men are more likely to withdraw from conflict: (1) because men have difficulty dealing with conflict; (2) because the culture has taught men to avoid it; (3) because withdrawal is an expression of power. What do you feel contributes most to the finding that men are more likely than women to avoid interpersonal conflict?

Force and Talk

When confronted with conflict, many people prefer not to deal with the issues but rather to force their position on the other person. The force may be emotional or physical. In either case, however, the issues are avoided, and the person who "wins" is the one who exerts the most force. This is the technique of warring nations, children, and even some normally sensible adults.

More than 50 percent of both single and married couples reported that they had experienced physical violence in their relationship. If we add symbolic violence (for example, threatening to hit the other person or throwing something), the percentages are above 60 percent for singles and above 70 percent for marrieds (Marshall and Rose 1987). In another study, 47 percent of a sample of 410 college students reported some experience with violence in a dating relationship (Deal and Wampler 1986). In most cases, the violence was reciprocal—each person in the relationship used violence.

In cases in which only one person was violent, the research results are conflicting. For example, the study involving the college students found that in cases in which one partner was violent, the aggressor was significantly more often the female (Deal and Wampler 1986). Earlier research found similar sex differences (for example, Cate, Henton, Koval, Christopher, and Lloyd 1982). These findings contradict the popular belief that males are more violent in heterosexual partnerships. One possible explanation is that in our society women are more likely to accept victimization as "normal," the implication being that they are therefore less likely to report it. Aggression by women on the other hand, being "unnatural," would stand out more and be remembered more. Since women are stereotypically seen as less aggressive than men, it may take less aggression on the part of a woman for her to be labeled aggressive. This may then lead to an over reporting of the woman's aggressive acts (Deal and Wampler 1986; also see Gelles 1981). Other research, however, has found that the popular conception of men being more likely than women to use force to achieve compliance is indeed true (DeTurck 1987).

One form of relational force is, of course, rape—a topic that revolves largely around power (see Unit 19). The studies in this area show alarming findings. According to Karen Kersten and Lawrence Kersten (1988), "forced sex on a date is probably one of the most common forms of all types of rape." In a study of force and violence on one college campus, more than half of the women students reported that they were verbally threatened, physically coerced, or physically abused; more than 12 percent indicated they had been raped (Barrett 1982; Kersten and Kersten 1988). In another investigation of sexual assault on college campuses, 45 percent of the women surveyed reported being victims of criminal sexual assault, criminal sexual abuse, and battery-intimidation (Illinois Coalition 1990). In yet another study, 42 percent of the men surveyed indicated they had engaged in coercive sexual relationships in which they were the coercing partners (Craig, Kalichman, and Follingstad 1989).

Findings such as these point to problems well beyond the prevalence of unproductive conflict strategies that we want to identify and avoid. They demonstrate the existence of underlying pathologies, which we are discovering are a lot more common than we previously thought when issues like these were never mentioned in college textbooks or lectures. Awareness is, of course, only the first step in understanding and eventually combating such problems.

The only real alternative to force is talk. Instead of using force, talk and listen. The qualities of openness, empathy, and positiveness (see Unit 8), for example, are suitable starting points.

One of the most puzzling findings on violence is that many victims interpret it as a sign of love. For some reason, they see being beaten or verbally abused as a sign that their partner is fully in love with them. Many victims also blame themselves for the violence instead of blaming their partners (Gelles and Cornell 1985). Why do you think this is so? What part does force or violence play in your own interpersonal relationship conflicts?

Blame and Empathy

Because most relationship conflicts are caused by a wide variety of factors, any attempt to single out one or two for **blame** is sure to fail. Yet a frequently used fight strategy is to blame someone. Consider, for example, the couple who fight over their child's getting into trouble with the police. The parents may—instead of dealing with the conflict itself—blame each other for the child's troubles. Such blaming, of course, does nothing to resolve the problem or to help the child.

Often when you blame someone you attribute motives to the person. Thus, if the person forgot your birthday and this oversight disturbs you, fight about the forgetting of the birthday (the actual behavior). Try not to mind read the motives of another person: "Well, it's obvious you just don't care about me. If you really cared, you could never have forgotten my birthday!"

Perhaps the best alternative to blame is empathy. Try to feel what the other person is feeling and to see the situation as the other person does. Try to see the situation as punctuated by the other person and how this punctuation may differ from your own.

Demonstrate empathic understanding. Once you have empathically understood your opponent's feelings, validate those feelings when appropriate. If your partner is hurt or angry and you believe such feelings are legitimate and justified, say so: "You have a right to be angry; I shouldn't have called your mother a slob. I'm sorry. But I still don't want to go on vacation with her." In expressing validation, you are not necessarily expressing agreement on the issue in conflict; you are merely stating that your partner has feelings that you recognize as legitimate.

Silencers and Facilitating Open Expression

Silencers are conflict techniques that literally silence the other individual. Among the wide variety that exists, crying is one frequently used silencer. When a person is unable to deal with a conflict or when winning seems unlikely, he or she may cry and thus silence the other person.

Another silencer is to feign extreme emotionalism—to yell and scream and pretend to be losing control of oneself. Still another is to develop some "physical" reaction—headaches and shortness of breath are probably the most popular. One of the major problems with silencers is that you can never be certain whether they are strategies to win the argument or real physical reactions to which you should pay attention. Regardless of what we do, however, the conflict remains unexamined and unresolved.

Grant the other person permission to express himself or herself freely and openly; grant permission to be oneself. Avoid power tactics that suppress or inhibit freedom of expression. Avoid, for example, tactics such as "nobody upstairs" or "you owe me," identified in Unit 19. These tactics are designed to put the other person down and to subvert true interpersonal equality.

Gunnysacking and Present Focus

Gunnysacking—a term derived from the large burlap bag called a gunnysack—refers to the practice of storing up grievances so they may be unloaded at another time. The immediate occasion may be relatively simple (or so it might seem at first), such as someone's coming home late without calling. Instead of arguing about this, the gunnysacker unloads all past grievances. The birthday you forgot, the time you arrived late for dinner, the hotel reservations you forgot to make are all thrown at you. As you may know from experience, gunnysacking begets gunnysacking. When one person gunnysacks, the other person gunnysacks. The result is two people dumping their stored-up grievances on one another. Frequently, the original problem never gets addressed. Instead, resentment and hostility escalate.

Focus your conflict on the here-and-now rather than on issues that occurred two months ago (as in gunnysacking). Similarly, focus your conflict on the person with whom you are fighting and not on the person's mother, child, or friends.

Fighting Below and Above the Belt

Much like prize fighters in a ring, each of us has a "belt line." When you hit someone below it, you can inflict serious injury. When you hit above the belt, however, the person is able to absorb the blow. With most interpersonal relationships, especially those of long standing, you know where the belt line is. You know, for example, that to hit Pat with the inability to have children is to hit below the belt. You know that to hit Chris with the failure to get a permanent job is to hit below the belt. Hitting below the belt line causes added problems for all persons involved. Keep blows to areas your opponent can absorb and handle.

The aim of relationship conflict is not to win and have your opponent lose. Rather, it is to resolve a problem and strengthen the relationship. Keep this ultimate goal always in clear focus, especially when you are angry or hurt.

Face-Detracting and Face-Enhancing Strategies

Another dimension of conflict strategies is that of face orientation. Face-detracting or face-attacking orientation involves treating the other person as incompetent or untrustworthy, as unable or bad (Donahue and Kolt 1992). Such attacks can vary from mildly embarrassing the other person to severely damaging his or her ego or reputation. When such attacks become extreme they may be similar to verbal aggressiveness—a tactic explained in the next section.

Face-enhancing techniques involve helping the other person to maintain a positive image, an image as competent and trustworthy, able and good. There is some evidence to show that even when you get what you want, say at bargaining, it is wise to help the other person retain positive face. This makes it less likely that future conflicts will arise (Donahue and Kolt 1992). Not surprisingly, people are more likely to make a greater effort to support the listener's "face" if they like the listener than if they didn't (Meyer 1994).

Generally, collectivist cultures place greater emphasis on face, especially on maintaining a positive image in public. Face is generally less crucial in individualist cultures such as the United States. Yet there are significant exceptions which require us to qualify any such broad generalization. For example, in parts of China, a highly collectivist culture where face-saving is extremely important, criminals are paraded publicly at rallies and humiliated before being put to death (Tyler 1996). You could of course argue that the importance of face-saving in China gives this particular punishment a meaning that it could not have in more individualistic cultures.

Confirming the other person's definition of self (Unit 4), avoiding attack and blame, and using excuses and apologies as appropriate are some generally useful face-positive strategies.

Can you identify examples of face-negative or face-positive strategies that were used during your last interpersonal conflict? Are you more likely to use one rather than the other type of strategy?

Verbal Aggressiveness, Verbal Abuse, and Argumentativeness

An especially interesting perspective on conflict is emerging from the work on verbal aggressiveness, verbal abuse, and argumentativeness (Infante and Rancer 1982; Infante and Wigley 1986; Infante 1988). Understanding these concepts will help in understanding some of the reasons things go wrong and some of the ways in which you can use conflict to improve your relationships.

Verbal Aggressiveness   **Verbal aggressiveness** is a method of winning an argument by inflicting psychological pain, by attacking the other person's self-concept. It is a type of disconfirmation (and the opposite of confirmation) in that it seeks to discredit the individual's view of self (see Unit 10). To explore this tendency further, take the accompanying self-test of verbal aggressiveness.

Character attack, perhaps because it is extremely effective in inflicting psychological pain, is the most popular tactic of verbal aggressiveness. Other tactics include attacking the person's abilities, background, and physical appearance; and cursing, teasing, ridiculing, threatening, swearing, and using various nonverbal emblems (Infante, Sabourin, Rudd, and Shannon 1990).

Some researchers have argued that "unless aroused by verbal aggression, a hostile disposition remains latent in the form of unexpressed anger" (Infante, Chandler, and Rudd 1989). There is some evidence to show that people in violent marriages are more often verbally aggressive than people in nonviolent marriages.

Because verbal aggressiveness does not help to resolve conflicts, results in loss of credibility for the person using it, and increases the credibility of the target of the aggressiveness (Infante, Hartley, Martin, Higgins, Bruning, and Hur 1992), you may wonder why people act verbally aggressive. What, if anything, would lead you to act in a verbally aggressive manner? Acting verbally aggressive as a response to the other person's aggressiveness is the most frequently cited reason. Other reasons are dislike for the other person, anger, feeling unable to argue effectively, responding to a degenerating discussion, being taught to respond this way, being reminded of being hurt, and being in a bad mood (Infante, Riddle, Horvath, and Tumlin 1992).

Communicating with an affirming style (smiling, pleasant facial expression, touching, physical closeness, eye contact, nodding, warm and sincere voice, vocal variety) leads others to perceive less verbal aggression in an interaction than when communicating with a nonaffirming style. That is, the assumption that people seem to make is that if your actions are affirming, your messages are also; and if your actions are nonaffirming, your messages are also (Infante, Rancer, and Jordan 1996).

Verbal Abuse   When verbal aggressiveness becomes a pattern and comes to define the relationships, we are dealing with verbal abuse and the verbally abusive relationship. The interpersonal patterns in verbal abuse may be spelled out more completely as violations of the humanistic qualities of interpersonal effectiveness. A lack of *openness* is seen in the person's:

♦ refusal to reveal feelings, discouragement of the partner's disclosures ("Let's not get morbid"; "Why must you always talk about feelings? Can't you just keep them to yourself?") and the mutual sharing of thoughts and feelings ("I'm really not in the mood to talk; watch the game.");

♦ refusal to admit there is a problem when his or her silence is questioned ("Nothing's wrong; I'm just quiet.");

♦ avoidance of taking responsibility for his or her own thoughts and feelings and instead attribute them to others ("Everyone thinks you should ask for a raise"; "No one likes the way you dress"; "Well, it was your decision that got us into this mess.").

Self Test ▶ *How Verbally Aggressive Are You?*

This scale is designed to measure how people try to obtain compliance from others. For each statement, indicate the extent to which you feel it is true for you in your attempts to influence others. Use the following scale:

1= almost never true
2= rarely true
3= occasionally true
4= often true
5= almost always true

_____ 1. I am extremely careful to avoid attacking individuals' intelligence when I attack their ideas.
_____ 2. When individuals are very stubborn, I use insults to soften the stubbornness.
_____ 3. I try very hard to avoid having other people feel bad about themselves when I try to influence them.
_____ 4. When people refuse without good reason to do a task I know is important, I tell them they are unreasonable.
_____ 5. When others do things I regard as stupid, I try to be extremely gentle with them.
_____ 6. If individuals I am trying to influence really deserve it, I attack their character.
_____ 7. When people behave in ways that are in very poor taste, I insult them in order to shock them into proper behavior.
_____ 8. I try to make people feel good about themselves even when their ideas are stupid.
_____ 9. When people simply will not budge on a matter of importance, I lose my temper and say rather strong things to them.
_____ 10. When people criticize my shortcomings, I take it in good humor and do not try to get back at them.
_____ 11. When individuals insult me, I get a lot of pleasure out of really telling them off.
_____ 12. When I dislike individuals greatly, I try not to show it in what I say or how I say it.
_____ 13. I like poking fun at people who do things which are very stupid in order to stimulate their intelligence.
_____ 14. When I attack a person's ideas, I try not to damage their self-concepts.
_____ 15. When I try to influence people, I make a great effort not to offend them.
_____ 16. When people do things which are mean or cruel, I attack their character in order to help correct their behavior.
_____ 17. I refuse to participate in arguments when they involve personal attacks.
_____ 18. When nothing seems to work in trying to influence others, I yell and scream in order to get some movement from them.
_____ 19. When I am not able to refute others' positions, I try to make them feel defensive in order to weaken their positions.
_____ 20. When an argument shifts to personal attacks, I try very hard to change the subject.

Thinking Critically About Verbal Aggressiveness
To compute your verbal aggressiveness score, follow these steps.
1. Add the scores on items 2, 4, 6, 7, 9, 11, 13, 16, 18, 19.
2. Add the scores on items 1, 3, 5, 8, 10, 12, 14, 15, 17, 20.
3. Subtract the sum obtained in step 2 from 60.
4. To compute your verbal aggressiveness score, add the total obtained in step 1 to the result obtained in step 3.

If you scored between 59 and 100, you are high in verbal aggressiveness; if you scored between 39 and 58, you are moderate in verbal aggressiveness; if you scored between 20 and 38, you are low in verbal aggressiveness.

In computing your score, make special note of the characteristics the statements identify in connection with the tendency to act verbally aggressive. Note those inappropriate behaviors you are especially prone to commit. High agreement (4 or 5 on the scale) with statements 2, 4, 6, 7, 9, 11, 13, 16, 18, and 19 and low agreement (1 and 2 on the scale) with statements 1, 3, 5, 8, 10, 12, 14, 15, 17, and 20 will help you highlight any significant verbal aggressiveness you might have. Review previous encounters when you acted verbally aggressive. What effect did such action have on your subsequent interaction? What effect did it have on your relationship with the other person? What alternative ways of getting your point across might you have used? Might these have proved more effective?

From "Verbal Aggressiveness: An Interpersonal Model and Measure" by Dominic Infante and C.J. Wigley, *Communication Monographs* 53, 1986, pp. 61–69. Reprinted by permission of the Speech Communication Association.

A lack of *empathy* is seen in the person's:

- becoming disturbed by the partner's disagreements or holding attitudes and beliefs different from his or her own ("How can you possibly say that?" "You've got to be kidding.");
- refusal to acknowledge any understanding of the partners' communications or to grant any validity to his or her feelings ("You're being silly"; "You're always complaining.");
- avoidance of checking or verifying his or her perceptions of the other person's feelings.

A lack of *supportiveness* is seen in the person's:

- being judgmental of the partner's accomplishments ("Now that was fine— much better than last time.") and critical of the shortcomings ("You never could fix the plumbing"; "You're afraid to try anything new, aren't you?");
- stating his or her own position as final, definitive, and unalterable ("Harrington is the best person for the job and that's it; there's no question about it.");
- assumption that the partner is at fault when something goes wrong ("What did you do wrong now?") and that the partner will fail even before trying ("Why bother? You know you'll never finish.").

A lack of *positiveness* is seen in the person's:

- emphasis on the negatives in the relationship and in the partner's behaviors, the refusal to compliment regardless of accomplishments, and the frequent indifference to the partner's thoughts and feelings;
- blaming the partners for difficulties ("How can I accomplish anything with you always nagging me?");
- use of derogatory names to describe partners or the partners' ways of behaving (often children) ("Hey, big ears, come here a minute"; "Clumsy must be your middle name.").

A lack of *equality* is seen in the person's:

- emphasis on his or her own superiority over the partners ("Look, I studied accounting; you can't even balance a checkbook.") and talking a great deal more than listening, often interrupting to interject his or her own thoughts;
- refusal to grant the partners' thoughts any credibility or value ("That's ridiculous"; "You're talking about economics?");
- giving ultimatums to get his or her way ("If you don't want to go to London, then let's forget about a vacation altogether.") and giving orders rather than making requests ("Get me coffee before you go out"; "Buy butter pecan; I hate that vanilla you always buy.").

Verbal abuse may be defined as a consistent pattern of attacking another person's self-concept and self-esteem through communication that is closed, nonempathic, unsupportive, negative, and unequal. It is in many ways similar to the concept of verbal aggressiveness, described elsewhere in this unit. Verbal aggressiveness, according to Infante (1988), is "the inclination to attack the self-concepts of individuals instead of, or in addition to, their positions on particular issues." Verbal aggressiveness is thus a way of approaching an argument or con-

What other types of messages might you identify as constituting verbal abuse?

flict; verbal abusiveness is a way of relating to another person, a way of treating another person. Both concepts highlight attacking the other person's self-concept.

Three essential characteristics are identified in this definition. First, to constitute verbal abuse, the behavior must be relatively *consistent*. Although isolated statements may prove abusive (cursing at someone, for example), verbal abuse as an interpersonal relationship problem is a repeated pattern: It is the consistency of such behavior that makes it so debilitating. (Verbal aggressiveness, in contrast, centers on the *specific message*—for example, a specific attack on a person's character or physical appearance [Infante 1993].)

Second, verbal abuse *attacks the person's concept of self*. It is not, for example, merely negative behaviors but negative behaviors that are directed at the self-image of the other person. Verbally abusive statements are relational rather than content oriented. It is relatively unimportant what content they address, and, in fact, they may frequently address quite trivial issues. Their defining characteristic is that they comment on the person's self-image (attacking and lowering it) and on the way the person is defined in the relationship (as of little competence, importance, or consequence, for example). This is a major reason such behaviors result in low relationship satisfaction (Kasian and Painter 1992).

Third, verbal abuse consists of a *variety of communication patterns* that can be grouped conveniently as violations of the five qualities of interpersonal effectiveness. This is not to imply that other patterns could not be identified. The five qualities focused on here are offered as an introductory description of this type of interpersonal behavior.

Just as physical abuse attacks and weakens the body, verbal abuse attacks and weakens self-image. Many would argue that verbal abuse is more damaging and more destructive than physical abuse. Physical abuse is, in many cases, relatively easy to recover from; verbal abuse is likely to leave scars for long periods, sometimes throughout one's life. In a study of 234 battered women aged 19 through 64, 159 reported that the verbal abuse (defined in this study as ridicule, jealousy, threats of abuse, threats to change the marriage, the imposing of restrictions, and the damaging of property) had a greater impact than the actual physical abuse (Follingstad et al. 1990).

Research finds, moreover, that wives who engage in verbal abuse—especially swearing and attacking the other's character and competency—also experience greater relationship violence (Infante, Sabourin, Rudd, and Shannon 1990). Verbal abuse of husbands contributes to wife battering and to the post traumatic stress that many battered women experience (Kemp, Green, Hovanitz, and Rawlings 1995; Rodenburg and Fantuzzo 1993). And, not surprisingly, verbal abuse among college students was related to actual courtship violence; the more verbal abuse, the more physical violence (Ryan 1995).

If you are in a verbally abusive relationship, it is difficult to feel good about yourself, to maintain a positive self-image, or to feel competent, successful, or worthwhile. Whether it is your physical appearance, intellectual abilities, relational expertise, or emotional stability that is being undermined, it is difficult to maintain a positive self-image when you are subjected to verbal abuse.

What would the theories of attraction, reinforcement, social exchange, and equity say about abusive relationships? For example, how would the theories account for the maintenance of such relationships? What predictions would the theories make as to the eventual course of such relationships?

Argumentativeness   Contrary to popular usage, the term "argumentativeness" refers to a quality to be cultivated rather than avoided. **Argumentativeness** is your willingness to argue for a point of view, your tendency to speak your mind

Persons with disabilities are often singled out for verbal abuse and physical violence. One study identifies some of this behavior as: physical violence, denying persons of their rights and opportunities, verbal abuse, and failure to respond to complaints about abuse (Roeher Institute 1995). What do you think contributes to abuse against persons with disabilities? Are these the same factors that contribute to abuse against women, against newly arrived immigrants, and against gay men and lesbians?

on significant issues. It is the mode of dealing with disagreements that is the preferred alternative to verbal aggressiveness. Before reading about ways to increase your argumentativeness, take the accompanying self-test, "How Argumentative Are You?"

Generally, those who score high in argumentativeness have a strong tendency to state their position on controversial issues and argue against the positions of others. A high scorer sees arguing as exciting, intellectually challenging, and as an opportunity to win a kind of contest.

The moderately argumentative person possesses some of the qualities of the high argumentative and some of the qualities of the low argumentative. The person who scores low in argumentativeness tries to prevent arguments. This person experiences satisfaction not from arguing, but from avoiding arguments. The low argumentative sees arguing as unpleasant and unsatisfying. Not surprisingly, this person has little confidence in his or her ability to argue effectively.

Can you identify a character in a television series who demonstrates verbal aggressiveness? One who demonstrates argumentativeness? What distinguishes these two characters? What can you do to more effectively regulate your own tendencies toward verbal aggressiveness and argumentativeness?

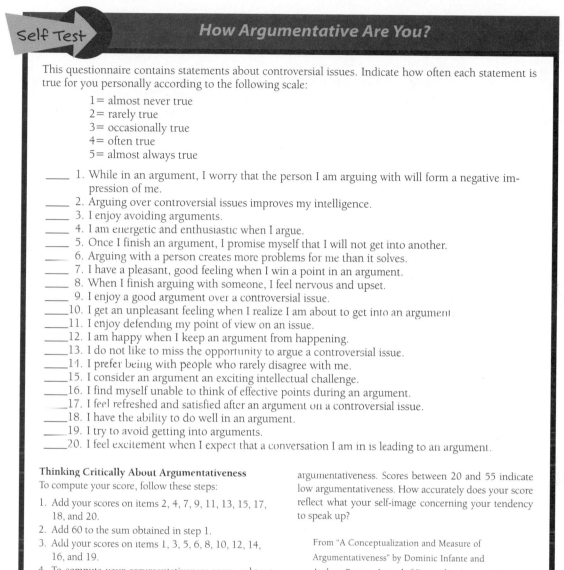

Self Test

How Argumentative Are You?

This questionnaire contains statements about controversial issues. Indicate how often each statement is true for you personally according to the following scale:

1 = almost never true
2 = rarely true
3 = occasionally true
4 = often true
5 = almost always true

_____ 1. While in an argument, I worry that the person I am arguing with will form a negative impression of me.
_____ 2. Arguing over controversial issues improves my intelligence.
_____ 3. I enjoy avoiding arguments.
_____ 4. I am energetic and enthusiastic when I argue.
_____ 5. Once I finish an argument, I promise myself that I will not get into another.
_____ 6. Arguing with a person creates more problems for me than it solves.
_____ 7. I have a pleasant, good feeling when I win a point in an argument.
_____ 8. When I finish arguing with someone, I feel nervous and upset.
_____ 9. I enjoy a good argument over a controversial issue.
_____10. I get an unpleasant feeling when I realize I am about to get into an argument.
_____11. I enjoy defending my point of view on an issue.
_____12. I am happy when I keep an argument from happening.
_____13. I do not like to miss the opportunity to argue a controversial issue.
_____14. I prefer being with people who rarely disagree with me.
_____15. I consider an argument an exciting intellectual challenge.
_____16. I find myself unable to think of effective points during an argument.
_____17. I feel refreshed and satisfied after an argument on a controversial issue.
_____18. I have the ability to do well in an argument.
_____19. I try to avoid getting into arguments.
_____20. I feel excitement when I expect that a conversation I am in is leading to an argument.

Thinking Critically About Argumentativeness

To compute your score, follow these steps:

1. Add your scores on items 2, 4, 7, 9, 11, 13, 15, 17, 18, and 20.
2. Add 60 to the sum obtained in step 1.
3. Add your scores on items 1, 3, 5, 6, 8, 10, 12, 14, 16, and 19.
4. To compute your argumentativeness score, subtract the total obtained in step 3 from the total obtained in step 2.

Scores between 73 and 100 indicate high argumentativeness. Scores between 56 and 72 indicate moderate argumentativeness. Scores between 20 and 55 indicate low argumentativeness. How accurately does your score reflect what your self-image concerning your tendency to speak up?

From "A Conceptualization and Measure of Argumentativeness" by Dominic Infante and Andrew Rancer, *Journal of Personality Assessment,* 1982, Vol. 46, pp. 72–80. Copyright © 1982 Lawrence Erlbaum Associates, Inc. Reprinted by permission of Lawrence Erlbaum Associates, Inc. and the authors.

Men generally score higher in argumentativeness (and in verbal aggressiveness) than women. Men are also more apt to be perceived (by both men and women) as more argumentative and verbally aggressive than women (Nicotera and Rancer 1994). High and low argumentatives also differ in the way in which they view argument (Rancer, Kosberg, and Baukus 1992). High argumentatives see arguing as enjoyable and its outcomes as pragmatic. They see arguing as having a positive impact on their self-concept, to have functional outcomes, and to be highly ego-involving. Low argumentatives, on the other hand, believe that arguing has a negative impact on their self-concept, that it has dysfunctional outcomes, and that it is not very ego-involving. They see arguing as having little enjoyment or pragmatic outcome.

The researchers who developed this test note that both high and low argumentatives may experience communication difficulties. The high argumentative, for example, may argue needlessly, too often, and too forcefully. The low argumentative, on the other hand, may avoid taking a stand even when it seems necessary.

Persons scoring somewhere in the middle are probably the most interpersonally skilled and adaptable, arguing when it is necessary but avoiding the many arguments that are needless and repetitive.

Here are some suggestions for cultivating argumentativeness and for preventing it from degenerating into aggressiveness (Infante 1988).

- Treat disagreements as objectively as possible; avoid assuming that because someone takes issue with your position or your interpretation he or she is attacking you as a person.
- Avoid attacking the other person (rather than the person's arguments) even if this would give you a tactical advantage—it will probably backfire at some later time and make your relationship more difficult. Center your arguments on issues rather than personalities.
- Reaffirm the other person's sense of competence; compliment the other person as appropriate.
- Avoid interrupting; allow the other person to state her or his position fully before you respond.
- Stress equality (see Unit 8) and stress the similarities that you have with the other person; stress your areas of agreement before attacking the disagreements.
- Express interest in the other person's position, attitude, and point of view.
- Avoid presenting your arguments too emotionally; using an overly loud voice or interjecting vulgar expressions will prove offensive and eventually ineffective.
- Allow the other person to save face; never humiliate the other person.

Dealing with Unfair Conflict Strategies

 Which unproductive conflict strategy do you resent the most? Which unproductive conflict strategy—if any—are you most ashamed of using? Why? Which of the unproductive conflict strategies, if any, have you used in the last two or three months? What effects—both immediate and long-term—did your use of these strategies have?

Perhaps the first step in dealing with any unfair conflict strategy is awareness. You first have to recognize it; you have to be able to see it in your own interpersonal interactions. In the case of verbal abuse, for example, it is necessary that it be identified by both individuals, the abuser and the one abused. Often, of course, both parties may function as both abuser and abused. George and Martha in Edward Albee's *Who's Afraid of Virginia Woolf?* are perfect examples of a couple who are equally abusive and equally abused. There is nothing in the definition of verbal abuse that excludes mutuality.

Unfair conflict strategies are frequently denied by the user, often because they are difficult to recognize in one's own behaviors. Distinguishing between criticizing because your partner made an important mistake and criticizing because your normal tendency is to look for things to criticize is not always easy. A useful guide is to look at the interpretation of the behavior by the other person. If the behavior is interpreted as unfair, then perhaps it is and bears inspection.

The second step is to recognize the significant consequences of unfair conflict strategies on your own behavior and on your relationship. For example, do frequent face-detracting strategies lead you to withdraw and fail to express yourself? Do they embarrass you and make you unhappy? Does frequent criticism prevent you from trying new things or expanding your talents and competencies? Does lack of empathy create self-doubt? Does negativity lead you to feel depressed?

Do recognize that there are potential dangers. Bringing unfair conflict strategies (especially abusive behavior) to the attention of the other person may itself lead not to rational discussion but to abusive behavior, perhaps even physical violence. You may wish to choose a safe place for such discussion—for example, one in which supportive others are nearby.

The third step is to change the behaviors. Assuming that the conflict patterns are not the product of a severely disturbed psyche, changing these behaviors should prove no more difficult than changing any other behaviors. The techniques for creating and increasing openness, empathy, supportiveness, positiveness, and equality, identified throughout this text (and especially in Unit 8), are especially relevant tools. Similarly, the skills of effective conflict resolution discussed here and the suggestions for dealing with power games (Unit 19) will prove helpful in confronting and eventually changing the destructive behavior patterns.

If the unfair strategies are personally destructive (as they are with verbal aggressiveness and verbal abuse) and if you are unable to change the behavior, you may wish to consider seeking professional help. College student services personnel will prove a useful source of information on available local facilities. Another alternative is to end the relationship, a topic considered in depth in Unit 17.

Think about the productive and unproductive conflict strategies as they might apply to these specific situations. Try developing an unproductive and an alternative productive strategy for each situation.

1. "You're late again. You're always late. Your lateness is so inconsiderate of my time and my interests. What is wrong with you?"
2. "I just can't bear another weekend of sitting home watching television. You never want to do anything. I'm just not going to do that again and that's final."
3. "Guess who forgot to phone for reservations again? Don't you remember anything?"
4. "You can't possibly go out with Pat. We're your parents and we simply won't allow it. And we don't want to hear any more about it. It's over."
5. "Why don't you stay out of the neighbor's business? You're always butting in and telling people what to do. Why don't you mind your own business and take care of your own family instead of trying to run everybody else's?"

Before and After the Conflict

If you are to make conflict truly productive, consider a few suggestions for preparing for conflict and for using it for relational growth.

Before the Conflict

Try to fight in private. When you air your conflicts in front of others, you create a variety of other problems. You may not be willing to be totally honest when third parties are present; you may feel you have to save face and therefore must win the fight at all costs. This may lead you to use strategies to win the argument rather than to resolve the conflict. You may become so absorbed by the image that others will have of you that you forget you have a relationship problem that needs to be resolved. Also, you run the risk of embarrassing your partner in front of others, and this embarrassment may create resentment and hostility.

Be sure you are both ready to fight. Although conflicts arise at the most inopportune times, you can choose the time to resolve them. Confronting your partner when she or he comes home after a hard day of work may not be the right time for resolving a conflict. Make sure you are both relatively free of other problems and ready to deal with the conflict at hand.

Know what you're fighting about. Sometimes people in a relationship become so hurt and angry that they lash out at the other person just to vent their own frustration. The problem at the center of the conflict (for example, the uncapped toothpaste tube) is merely an excuse to express anger. Any attempt to resolve this "problem" will be doomed to failure because the problem addressed is not what is causing the conflict. Instead, it is the underlying hostility, anger, and frustration that needs to be addressed.

Fight about problems that can be solved. Fighting about past behaviors or about family members or situations over which you have no control solves nothing; instead, it creates additional difficulties. Any attempt at resolution will fail because the problems are incapable of being solved. Often such conflicts are concealed attempts at expressing one's frustration or dissatisfaction.

After the Conflict

After the conflict is resolved, there is still work to be done. Often after one conflict is supposedly settled, another will emerge because, for example, one person feels harmed, with the need to retaliate and take revenge in order to restore self-worth (Kim and Smith 1993). So, it is especially important that the conflict be resolved and not allowed to generate other, perhaps more significant, conflicts.

Learn from the conflict and from the process you went through in trying to resolve it. Can you identify the fight strategies that merely aggravated the situation? Do you or your partner need a cooling-off period? Can you tell when minor issues are going to escalate into major arguments? Does avoidance make matters worse? What issues are particularly disturbing and likely to cause difficulties? Can they be avoided?

Keep the conflict in perspective. Be careful not to blow it out of proportion to the extent that you begin to define your relationship in terms of conflict. Avoid the tendency to see disagreement as inevitably leading to major blowups. Conflicts in most relationships actually occupy a very small percentage of the couple's time, and yet, in recollection, they often loom extremely large. Also, don't allow the conflict to undermine your own or your partner's self-esteem. Don't view yourself, your partner, or your relationship as failures just because you had an argument or even lots of arguments.

 Do you agree with the before and after suggestions made for dealing with conflict? Which do you find most useful? Would some suggestions be more useful for certain conflicts? What other suggestions would you offer?

Attack your negative feelings. Negative feelings frequently arise after an interpersonal conflict. They most often arise because unfair fight strategies were used to undermine the other person—for example, personal rejection, manipulation, or force. Resolve to avoid such unfair tactics in the future, but at the same time let go of guilt, of blame, for yourself and your partner. If you think it would help, discuss these feelings with your partner or even a therapist.

Increase the exchange of rewards and cherishing behaviors to demonstrate your positive feelings and to show you are over the conflict and want the relationship to survive and flourish.

What one principle from this unit will most influence your own conflict behavior?

Summary	**U N I T I N B R I E F**

A RETURN TO OBJECTIVES:

In this unit we focused on interpersonal conflict and considered the following: (1) What is the nature of conflict? (2) What pattern or general strategy for resolving conflicts might be followed? (3) What are the major productive and unproductive strategies for resolving an interpersonal conflict? (4) How can we prepare for and conclude an interpersonal conflict?

Nature of Conflict	Conflict Resolution Model	Conflict Strategies	Before and After the Conflict
Content and/or relationship: Disagreement between or among connected individuals resulting in negative or positive consequences. Conflict may have both **negative and positive** outcomes. Conflict and the strategies used to resolve it are **culturally influenced.**	Define the conflict. Examine possible solutions. Test the solution. Evaluate the solution. Accept or reject the solution.	Avoidance and active fighting Force and talk Blame and empathy Gunnysacking and present focus Fighting below and above the belt Face detracting and face enhancing Verbal aggressiveness, verbal abuse, and argumentativeness	**Before the conflict:** Try to fight in private, fight when you are ready, know what you are fighting about, and fight about problems that can be solved. **After the conflict:** Learn something from the conflict, keep the conflict in perspective, attack your negative feelings, and increase the exchange of rewards.

UNIT

21 *Friends and Lovers*

Unit Topics

Friends
The Nature of Friendship
The Needs of Friendship
Stages and Communication in Friendship
    Development
Cultural Differences in Friendship
Gender Differences in Friendship

Lovers
The Nature of Love
Types of Love
Cultural Differences in Loving
Gender Differences in Loving

Unit Objectives

After completing this unit, you should be able to:

1. Define *friendship* and its three types

2. Identify the three stages of friendship development and characterize the communications at each stage

3. Describe the cultural and gender differences in friendship

4. Identify the major elements that make up love

5. Define *ludus, storge, mania, pragma, eros,* and *agape*

6. Describe the cultural and gender differences in loving

EXPERIENTIAL LEARNING VEHICLES

Vehicle Nos. 23, "Friendship Behaviors," pp. 466–467, and 24, "The Television Relationship," pp. 467–468, are useful for illustrating the role of interpersonal communication in friendship and love.

Of all the interpersonal relationships you have, no doubt the most important are those with your friends, lovers, and family. In this unit, we cover friends and lovers and in the next, family. The combination of friends and lovers in one unit seems especially appropriate because many people see love as a natural progression from friendship. Both relationships also serve many of the same functions: for example, lessening loneliness and providing excitement and security.

Friends

Friendship has engaged the attention and imagination of poets, novelists, and artists of all kinds. In television, our most influential mass medium, friendships have become almost as important as romantic pairings. Friendship now engages the attention of a range of interpersonal communication researchers. Table 21.1 presents a selection of findings to illustrate the range of topics addressed. In reviewing the table, consider why the results were obtained and what implications they may have for developing, maintaining, and repairing friendship relationships.

Throughout your life, you will meet many people, but out of this wide array you'll develop relatively few relationships you would call friendships. Yet despite the low number of friendships you may form, their importance is great.

 Can you identify cultures in which these findings would not hold true?

Table 21.1	A Selection of Research Findings on Friendship

As you read through these findings, consider whether they seem consistent with your own friendship experience. These findings were taken from the extensive literature review in Blieszner and Adams (1992).

1. Young single men see their friends more often than young married men do (Farrell and Rosenberg 1981).
2. Women are more expressive in their friendships than are men. Men talk about business, politics, and sports, whereas women talk about feelings and relationship issues (Fox, Gibbs, and Auerbach 1985).
3. When women were asked about the most important benefit they derive from their friendships, conversation was highlighted and included listening in a supportive way, enhancing feelings of self-esteem, and validating their experiences (Johnson and Aries 1983).
4. Men and women did not differ in their rankings of the characteristics of personal relationships with friends (Albert and Moss 1990).
5. Similarity in personality was not found to be a strong basis for selecting friends, but similarity of needs and beliefs was (Henderson and Furnhan 1982). Friends with dissimilar attitudes were preferred in recent friendships, whereas in established friendships similar attitudes were preferred (McCarthy and Duck 1976).
6. The average number of friends of college students varies from 2.88 to 9.1 (Blieszner and Adams 1992); for older persons, the average varies between 1 and 12.2 (Adams 1987).

The Nature of Friendship

Friendship is an interpersonal relationship between two persons that is mutually productive and characterized by mutual positive regard.

Friendship is an interpersonal relationship; communication interactions must have taken place between the people. The interpersonal relationship involves a "personalistic focus" (Wright 1978, 1984). Friends react to each other as complete persons, as unique, genuine, and irreplaceable individuals.

Friendships must be mutually productive; this qualifier emphasizes that, by definition, they cannot be destructive either to oneself or to the other person. Once destructiveness enters into a relationship, it can no longer be characterized as friendship. Lover relationships, marriage relationships, parent-child relationships, and just about any other possible relationship can be either destructive or productive. But friendship must enhance the potential of each person and can only be productive.

Friendships are characterized by mutual positive regard. Liking people is essential if we are to call them friends. Three major characteristics of friends—trust, emotional support, and sharing of interests (Blieszner and Adams 1992)—testify to this positive regard.

The closer friends are the more *interdependent* they become; that is, when friends are especially close, the actions of one will impact more significantly on the other than they would if the friends were just casual acquaintances. At the same time, however, the closer friends are the more *independent* they are of, for example, the attitudes and behaviors of others. Also, they are less influenced by the societal rules that govern more casual relationships (see Unit 1 on the developmental definition of interpersonal communication). Close friends are likely to make up their own rules for interacting with each other; they decide what they will talk about and when, what they can say to each other without offending and what they can't, when and for what reasons you can call the other person, and so on.

In North America, friendships clearly are a matter of choice; you choose—within limits—who your friends will be. The density of the cities and the ease of communication and relocation makes friendships voluntary, a matter of choice. But, in many parts of the world—small villages miles away from urban centers, where people are born, live, and die without venturing much beyond their birthplace, for example—relationships are not voluntary. In these cases, you simply form relationships with those in your village. Here you do not have the luxury of selecting certain people to interact with and others to ignore. You must interact with and form relationships with members of the community simply because these people are the only ones you come into contact with regularly (Moghaddam, Taylor, and Wright 1993).

 Can you identify any other qualities you would consider defining of friendship?

Three Types of Friendships   Not all friendships are the same. But how do they differ? One way of answering this question is by distinguishing among the three major types of friendship: reciprocity, receptivity, and association (Reisman 1979, 1981).

The friendship of **reciprocity** is the ideal type, characterized by loyalty, self-sacrifice, mutual affection, and generosity. A friendship of reciprocity is based on equality: each individual shares equally in giving and receiving the benefits and rewards of the relationship. In the friendship of **receptivity**, in contrast, there is an imbalance in giving and receiving; one person is the primary giver and one the primary receiver. This imbalance, however, is a positive one because each person gains something from the relationship. The different needs of both the person who receives and the person who gives affection are satisfied. This is the friendship that may develop between a teacher and a student or between a doctor and a patient. In fact, a difference in status is essential for the friendship of receptivity to develop.

The friendship of **association** is a transitory one. It might be described as a friendly relationship rather than a true friendship. Associative friendships are the kind we often have with classmates, neighbors, or coworkers. There is no great loyalty, no great trust, no great giving or receiving. The association is cordial but not intense.

The definition and types of friendships may be seen in the responses of people who were asked to identify the qualities they felt were most important in a friend. The responses, presented in Table 21.2, are derived from a *Psychology Today* survey of 40,000 respondents (Parlee 1979). As you examine the list, you will find it easy to match each of these qualities to one of the types of friendship just described.

Of the three types of friendship identified in this unit—reciprocity, receptivity, and association—which type characterizes most of your friendships? Which type characterizes your closest friendships?

The Needs of Friendship

In the *Psychology Today* survey, the 40,000 respondents selected from a wide number of activities the ones they had shared with friends over the previous month. Table 21.3 presents the ten activities most frequently noted by these respondents. As can be appreciated from this list, friendship seems to serve the same needs that all relationships serve (lessening loneliness, providing stimulation, and encouraging self-knowledge).

You develop and maintain friendships to satisfy those needs that can only be satisfied by certain people. On the basis of your experiences or your predictions, you select as friends those who will help to satisfy your basic growth needs. Selecting friends on the basis of need satisfaction is similar to choosing a marriage partner, an employee, or any person who may be in a position to satisfy your needs. Thus, if you need to be the center of attention or to be popular, you might

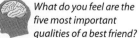

What do you feel are the five most important qualities of a best friend? How would your best friend answer this question about you? Which of these qualities is the most important in maintaining your friendship?

Table 21.2	**The Most Frequently Mentioned Qualities of a Friend**

Before reading this table, think about the qualities you look for in a friend and the qualities you offer to others as a friend. How similar are they to those noted here? The qualities are arranged in order of frequency of mention; No. 1, keeps confidences, was mentioned 89% of the time while No. 10, intelligence, was mentioned 57% of the time.

1. Keep confidences
2. Loyalty
3. Warmth, affection
4. Supportiveness
5. Frankness
6. Sense of humor
7. Willingness to make time for me
8. Independence
9. Good conversationalist
10. Intelligence

Table 21.3	The Ten Most Frequently Identified Activities Shared with Friends

Before reading this table, consider the activities you share with friends. How similar are the activities you engage in with those identified here? No. 1 = the most frequently identified activity.

1. Had an intimate talk
2. Had a friend ask you to do something for him or her
3. Went to dinner in a restaurant
4. Asked your friend to do something for you
5. Had a meal together at home or at your friend's home
6. Went to a movie, play, or concert
7. Went drinking together
8. Went shopping
9. Participated in sports
10. Watched a sporting event

select friends who allow you, and even encourage you, to be the center of attention or who tell you, verbally and nonverbally, that you are popular.

As your needs change, the qualities you look for in friendships also change. In many instances, old friends are dropped from your close circle to be replaced by new friends who better serve these new needs.

We can also look at needs in terms of the five values or rewards we seek to gain through our friendships (Wright 1978, 1984). First, friends have a **utility value.** A friend may have special talents, skills, or resources that prove useful to us in achieving our specific goals and needs. We may, for example, become friends with someone who is particularly bright because such a person might assist us in getting better grades, in solving our personal problems, or in getting a better job.

Second, friends have an **affirmation value.** A friend's behavior toward us acts as a mirror that affirms our personal value and helps us to recognize our attributes. A friend may, for example, help us to see more clearly our leadership abilities, athletic prowess, or sense of humor.

Third, friends have an **ego-support value.** By behaving in a supportive, encouraging, and helpful manner, friends help us to view ourselves as worthy and competent individuals.

Fourth, friends have a **stimulation value.** A friend introduces us to new ideas and new ways of seeing the world and helps us to expand our worldview. A friend brings us into contact with previously unfamiliar issues, concepts, and experiences—for example, modern art, foreign cultures, new foods.

Fifth, friends have a **security value.** A friend does nothing to hurt the other person or to emphasize or call attention to the other person's inadequacies or weaknesses. Because of this security value, friends can interact freely and openly without having to worry about betrayal or negative responses.

What values do you serve for your friends? What values do your friends serve for you?

Stages and Communication in Friendship Development

Friendships develop over time in stages. At one end of the friendship continuum are strangers, two persons who have just met, and at the other end are intimate friends. What happens between these two extremes?

As you progress from the initial contact stage to intimate friendship, the depth and breadth of communications increase (see Unit 15). You talk about issues that are closer and closer to your inner core. Similarly, the number of communication topics increases as your friendship becomes closer. As depth and breadth increase, so does the satisfaction you derive from the friendship.

Earlier (Unit 15), the concept of dynamic tension in relationships was discussed. It was pointed out that there is a tension between, for example, autonomy and connection—the desire to be an individual but also to be connected to another person. Interpersonal researcher William Rawlins (1983) argues that friendships are also defined by dynamic tensions. One tension is between the impulse to be open and to reveal personal thoughts and feelings on the one hand and the impulse to protect oneself by not revealing personal information on the other. There is also the tension between being open and candid with your friend and being discreet. These contradictory impulses make it clear that friendships do not follow a straight path of always increasing openness or candor. This is not to say that openness and candor do not increase as you progress from initial to casual to close friendships; they do. But the pattern does not follow a straight line; throughout the friendship development process, there are tensions that periodically restrict openness and candor.

Similarly, there are regressions that may temporarily pull the friendship back to a less intimate stage. And, of course, friendships stabilize at a level that is, ideally at least, comfortable to both persons; some friendships will remain as casual and others will remain as close. So, keep in mind that although friendship is presented in stages, the progression is not always a straight line to ever increasing intimacy.

With these qualifications in mind, we can discuss three stages of friendship development and integrate the ten characteristics of effective interpersonal communication identified earlier (Unit 8). The assumption made here is that as the friendship progresses from initial contact and acquaintanceship through casual friendship to close and intimate friendship, the qualities of effective interpersonal communication increase. However, there is no assumption made that close relationships are necessarily the preferred type or that they are better than casual or temporary relationships. We need all types.

As you read this section consider the differences between face-to-face friendships and online friendships. How do they follow similar development patterns? How do they follow different patterns?

Initial Contact and Acquaintanceship   The first stage of friendship development is obviously an initial meeting of some kind. This does not mean that what has happened prior to the encounter is unimportant—quite the contrary. Your prior history of friendships, your personal needs, and your readiness for friendship development are extremely important in determining whether the relationship will develop.

At the initial stage, the characteristics of effective interpersonal communication are usually present to only a small degree. You are guarded rather than open or expressive, lest you reveal aspects of yourself that might be viewed negatively. Because you do not yet know the other person, your ability to empathize with or to orient yourself significantly to the other is limited, and the "relationship"—at this stage, at least—is probably viewed as too temporary to be worth the effort. Because the other person is not well-known to you, supportiveness, positiveness, and equality would all be difficult to manifest in any meaningful sense. The characteristics demonstrated are probably more the result of politeness than any genuine expression of positive regard.

At this stage, there is little genuine immediacy; the people see themselves as separate and distinct rather than as a unit. The confidence that is demonstrated is probably more a function of the individual personalities than of the relationship. Because the relationship is so new and because the people do not know each other very well, the interaction is often characterized by awkwardness—for example, overlong pauses, uncertainty over the topics to be discussed, and ineffective exchanges of speaker and listener roles.

 After meeting someone for the first time, how long (on average) does it take you to decide whether this person will become a friend? What specific qualities do you look for?

Casual Friendship   In the second stage, there is a dyadic consciousness, a clear sense of "we-ness," of togetherness; communication demonstrates a sense of immediacy. At this stage, you participate in activities as a unit rather than as separate individuals. A casual friend is one we would go with to the movies, sit with in the cafeteria or in class, or ride home with from school.

At this casual friendship stage, the qualities of effective interpersonal interaction begin to be seen more clearly. You start to express yourself openly and become interested in the other person's disclosures. You begin to own your feelings and thoughts and respond openly to his or her communications. Because you are beginning to understand this person, you empathize and demonstrate significant other-orientation. You also demonstrate supportiveness and develop a genuinely positive attitude toward both the other person and mutual communication situations. As you learn this person's needs and wants, you can stroke more effectively.

There is an ease at this stage, a coordination in the interaction between the two persons. You communicate with confidence, maintain appropriate eye contact and flexibility in body posture and gesturing, and use few adaptors signaling discomfort.

Close and Intimate Friendship   At the stage of close and intimate friendship, there is an intensification of the casual friendship; you and your friend see yourselves more as an exclusive unit, and each of you derives greater benefits (for example, emotional support) from intimate friendship than from casual friendship (Hays 1989).

Because you know each other well (for example, you know one another's values, opinions, attitudes), your uncertainty about each other has been significantly reduced—you are able to predict each other's behaviors with considerable accuracy. This knowledge makes possible significant interaction management. Similarly, you can read the other's nonverbal signals more accurately and can use these signals as guides to your interactions—avoiding certain topics at certain times or offering consolation on the basis of facial expressions.

At this stage, you exchange significant messages of affection, messages that express fondness, liking, loving, and caring for the other person. Openness and expressiveness are more clearly in evidence.

You become more other-oriented and willing to make significant sacrifices for the other person. You will go far out of your way for the benefit of this friend, and the friend in turn does the same for you. You empathize and exchange perspectives a great deal more, and you expect in return that your friend will also empathize with you. With a genuinely positive feeling for this individual, your supportiveness and positive stroking become spontaneous. Because you see yourselves as an exclusive unit, both equality and immediacy are in clear evidence. You view this friend as one who is important in your life; as a result, conflicts—inevitable in all close relationships—become important to work out and resolve through compromise and empathic understanding rather than through, for example, refusal to negotiate or a show of force.

You are willing to respond openly, confidently, and expressively to this person and to own your feelings and thoughts. Your supportiveness and positiveness are genuine expressions of the closeness you feel for this person. Each person in an intimate friendship is truly equal; each can initiate and each can respond; each can be active and each can be passive; each speaks and each listens.

What other communication changes take place as a friendship progresses from casual to intimate? What communication changes take place when a friendship goes from intimate to casual?

Cultural Differences in Friendship

Your friendships and the way you look at friendships will be influenced by your culture. For example, in the United States you can be friends with someone, yet not really be expected to go much out of your way for this person. Many Middle Easterners, Asians, and Latin Americans would consider going out of their way (significantly) an absolute essential ingredient in friendship; if you are not willing to sacrifice for your friend, then this person is really not your friend (Dresser 1996).

Generally, friendships are closer in collectivist cultures than in individualistic cultures (see Unit 3). In their emphasis on the group and on cooperating, the collectivist cultures foster the development of close friendship bonds.

Members of collectivist culture are expected to help others in the group. When you help or do things for someone else, you increase your own attraction for this person (recall our discussion in Unit 16 on attraction and reinforcement) and this is certainly a good start for a friendship. Of course, the culture continues to reward these close associations. Members of individualistic cultures, on the other hand, are expected to look out for No. 1, themselves. Consequently, they are more likely to compete and to try to do better than each other—conditions that do not support, generally at least, the development of friendships. Recall as we noted earlier (Unit 3) that these characteristics are extremes; most people have both collectivist and individualistic values but have them to different degrees and that is what we are talking about here—differences in degree of collectivist and individualistic orientation.

What has your culture taught you about friendship? Were you taught different ideas about same-sex and opposite-sex friendships?

Gender Differences in Friendship

Perhaps the best-documented finding—already noted in our discussion of self-disclosure—is that women self-disclose more than do men (for example, Dolgin, Meyer, and Schwartz 1991). This difference holds throughout male and female friendships. Male friends self-disclose less often and with less intimate details than female friends do. Men generally do not view intimacy as a necessary quality of their friendships (Hart 1990).

Women engage in significantly more affectional behaviors with their friends than do males (Hays 1989). This difference, Hays notes, may account for the greater difficulty men experience in beginning and maintaining close friendships. Women engage in more casual communication; they also share greater intimacy and more confidences with their friends than do men. Communication, in all its

What do you see as the one major difference between a friendship between two women and a friendship between two men? How do same-sex friendships differ from opposite-sex friendships?

forms and functions, seems a much more important dimension of women's friendships.

When women and men were asked to evaluate their friendships, women rated their same-sex friendships higher in general quality, intimacy, enjoyment, and nurturance than did men (Sapadin 1988). Men, in contrast, rated their opposite-sex friendships higher in quality, enjoyment, and nurturance than did women. Both men and women rated their opposite-sex friendships similarly in intimacy. These differences may be due, in part, to our society's suspicion of male friendships; as a result, a man may be reluctant to admit to having close relationship bonds with another man.

Men's friendships are often built around shared activities—attending a ball game, playing cards, working on a project at the office. Women's friendships, on the other hand, are built more around a sharing of feelings, support, and "personalism." Similarity in status, in willingness to protect one's friend in uncomfortable situations, in academic major, and even in proficiency in playing Password were significantly related to the relationship closeness of male-male friends but not of female-female or female-male friends (Griffin and Sparks 1990). Perhaps similarity is a criterion for male friendships but not for female or mixed-sex friendships.

The ways in which men and women develop and maintain their friendships will undoubtedly change considerably—as will all sex-related variables—in the next several years. Perhaps there will be a further differentiation or perhaps an increase in similarities. In the meantime, given the present state of research in gender differences, we need to be careful not to exaggerate and to treat small differences as if they were highly significant. "Let us," warns one friendship researcher, "avoid stereotypes or, worse yet, caricatures" (Wright 1988).

Further, friendship researchers warn that even when we find differences, the reasons for them are not always clear (Blieszner and Adams 1992). An interesting example is the finding that middle-aged men have more friends than middle-aged women and that women have more intimate friendships (Fischer and Oliker 1983). But why is this so? Do men have more friends because they are friendlier than women or because they have more opportunities to develop such friendships? Do women have more intimate friends because they have more opportunities to pursue such friendships or because they have a greater psychological capacity for intimacy?

Do you find significant sex differences in your own friendships with men and women? In what ways are men and women different in their friendship behaviors?

Lovers

Of all the qualities of interpersonal relationships, none seems as important as love. "We are all born for love," noted famed British prime minister Disraeli; "It is the principle of existence and its only end." It is also an interpersonal relationship developed, maintained, and sometimes destroyed through communication.

The Nature of Love

Much research is currently devoted to identifying the ingredients of love. What makes up the love experience? What are its major parts? Here are two well-reasoned explanations.

Psychotherapist Albert Ellis has argued that love and infatuation are actually the same emotion; he claims that we use the term "infatuation" to describe relationships that did not work out and "love" to describe our current romantic relationships. Do you agree that infatuation and love are essentially the same emotion? If you disagree, in what specific ways are they different?

◆ Love is a combination of passion and caring (Davis 1985). Both of these emotions are looked at as clusters consisting of more specific emotions. The **passion cluster**, for example, consists of *fascination* (seen in the lovers' preoccupation with each other), *exclusiveness* (seen in their mutual commitment), and *sexual desire* (seen in their desire to touch). The **caring cluster** consists of *giving the utmost* (seen in sacrifice for the lover) and *serving as the lover's champion* or advocate (seen in support for the lover's interest and success).

◆ Love is a combination of intimacy, passion, and commitment (Sternberg 1986, 1988). **Intimacy** (corresponding to part of Davis's caring cluster) is the emotional aspect of love and includes sharing, communicating, and mutual support; it is a sense of closeness and connection. **Passion** is the motivational aspect (corresponding to the passion cluster) and consists of physical attraction and romantic passion. **Commitment** (corresponding to part of the caring cluster) is the cognitive aspect and consists of the decisions you make con-

INTERPERSONAL ETHICS

Gossip

Frank: father
Jeff: son
Laura: mother

Jeff: Listen, everyone. Kim told me something today that I want to tell you. I promised her I wouldn't tell anyone but I just have to tell you.

Laura: Well, maybe you shouldn't. I mean, if you promised Kim, maybe you shouldn't tell us.

Jeff: No, no, I really want to—I have to.

Frank: Your mother's right. If you promised to keep a secret, then keep it. You'll be the better person for it.

Jeff: Well, if you all promise to keep it a secret, it'll be OK.

Would it be wrong for Jeff to reveal the secret? Would your answer depend on the kind of secret? If so, what would you have to know about the secret to answer this question? What would you answer if the secret was that Kim broke up with her boyfriend yesterday for the third time this month (and they are both 14 years old)? If Kim, who has been having mental problems, plans to kill her father? If Kim, 17 years old, plans to commit suicide? If Kim is heavily into drugs?

Would your answer be different if Kim was 4 and Jeff was 5? Kim was 4 and Jeff was 32? Kim and Jeff were both 19? If the family members kept the secret confidential?

Gossip is talk about a person who is not present during the communication (Eder and Enke 1991). If you are like most people, you spend at least some of your time gossiping about others. Gossip seems universal among all cultures (Laing 1993) and among some it is a commonly accepted ritual (Hall 1993). Gossip generally occurs when two people talk about a third party and profit in some way. Among the rewards or benefits of gossip is that it helps us to make social comparisons (Leaper and Holliday 1995; Westen 1996). By hearing about others, their accomplishments and their problems, you can better see how you stand in comparison with your peers.

Another benefit is that gossip humanizes people (Westen 1996). It lets you see a little bit of the inside of people. It puts you into a network of people, cements the bonds between you (Rosnow 1977; Miller and Wilcox 1986). It gives you social status. Just think of your social standing if no one talked to you about others and, maybe more important, if no one talked about you to others. As Oscar Wilde put it, "There is only one thing in the world worse than being talked about, and that is not being talked about."

Gossip also tells you the norms of the culture or society. When a supervisor tells you that Mason took off too many Mondays and wasn't promoted because of it, you are hearing (and learning) the rules or norms of the organization. You know that you should try especially hard to avoid taking off on Mondays or you too will not get promoted.

Nevertheless, gossip does create serious problems when not managed fairly. When you tell someone your feelings for some third party, say, you expect that the conversation will be held in confidence. You do not expect it to be relayed to others, especially not to the individual discussed. If you had wanted it relayed, you probably would have done so yourself. When such a conversation is passed on without your knowledge or approval, you feel that your confidence has been betrayed.

In *Secrets* (1983), ethicist Sissela Bok identifies three kinds of gossip that she considers unethical. First, it is unethical to reveal information that you have promised to keep secret. In situations in which that is impossible (Bok offers the example of a teenager who confides a suicide plan), the information should be revealed only to those required to know it and not to the world at large.

Second, gossip is unethical when we know it to be false and pass it on nevertheless. When we try to deceive our listeners by spreading gossip we know to be false, our communications are unethical.

Third, gossip is unethical when it invades the privacy to which everyone has a right. Invasive gossip is especially unethical when the gossip can hurt the individual involved. These conditions are not easy to identify in any given instance, but they do provide us with excellent starting points for asking ourselves whether or not a discussion of another person is ethical.

◆ Under what conditions would revealing another person's secrets be ethical? Under what conditions would it be unethical? Are there times when the failure to reveal such secrets would be unethical?

◆ What is your obligation as a listener, when you hear gossip being repeated that you know to be false?

◆ Is it ethical for you to observe someone (without his or her knowledge) and report your observations to others? For example, would it be ethical to observe your communication professor on a date with a student or smoking marijuana and then report these observations back to your classmates?

◆ What ethical guidelines would you propose for revealing secrets?

[The next ethics box appears in Unit 22, page 428, and deals with developing your own ethic of interpersonal communication.]

cerning your lover. When you have a relationship characterized by intimacy only, you have essentially a **liking** relationship. When you have only passion, you have a relationship of **infatuation**. When you have only commitment, you have **empty love**. When you have all three components to about equal degrees, you have **complete or consummate love**.

Types of Love

Although there are many theories about love, the one that has captured the attention of interpersonal researchers was the proposal that there is not one, but six types of love (Lee 1976). View the descriptions of each type that follow as broad characterizations that are generally but not always true. As a preface to this discussion of the types of love, you may wish to respond to the self-test "What Kind of Lover Are You?"

Eros: Beauty and Sexuality   Like Narcissus, who fell in love with the beauty of his own image, the **erotic** lover focuses on beauty and physical attractiveness, sometimes to the exclusion of qualities you might consider more important and more lasting. Also like Narcissus, the erotic lover has an idealized image of beauty that is unattainable in reality. Consequently, the erotic lover often feels unfulfilled. Not surprisingly, erotic lovers are particularly sensitive to physical imperfections in the ones they love.

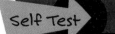

What Kind of Lover Are You?

Respond to each of the following statements with T if you believe the statement to be a generally accurate representation of your attitudes about love or F if you believe the statement does not adequately represent your attitudes about love.

_____ 1. My lover and I have the right physical "chemistry" between us.
_____ 2. I feel that my lover and I were meant for each other.
_____ 3. My lover and I really understand each other.
_____ 4. My lover fits my ideal standards of physical beauty/handsomeness.
_____ 5. I try to keep my lover a little uncertain about my commitment to him/her.
_____ 6. I believe that what my lover doesn't know about me won't hurt him/her.
_____ 7. My lover would get upset if he/she knew of some of the things I've done with other people.
_____ 8. When my lover gets too dependent on me, I want to back off a little.
_____ 9. To be genuine, our love first required caring for awhile.
_____10. I expect to always be friends with my lover.
_____11. Our love is really a deep friendship, not a mysterious, mystical emotion.
_____12. Our love relationship is the most satisfying because it developed from a good friendship.
_____13. In choosing my lover, I believed it was best to love someone with a similar background.
_____14. A main consideration in choosing my lover was how he/she would reflect on my family.
_____15. An important factor in choosing a partner is whether or not he/she would be a good parent.
_____16. One consideration in choosing my lover was how he/she would reflect on my career.
_____17. When things aren't right with my lover and me, my stomach gets upset.
_____18. Sometimes I get so excited about being in love with my lover that I can't sleep.
_____19. When my lover doesn't pay attention to me, I feel sick all over.
_____20. I cannot relax if I suspect that my lover is with someone else.
_____21. I try to always help my lover through difficult times.
_____22. I would rather suffer myself than let my lover suffer.
_____23. When my lover gets angry with me, I still love him/her fully and unconditionally.
_____24. I would endure all things for the sake of my lover.

Thinking Critically About Love

This scale is designed to enable you to identify those styles that best reflect your own beliefs about love. The statements refer to the six types of love that we discuss below: eros, ludus, storge, pragma, mania, and agape. "True" answers represent your agreement and "false" answers represent your disagreement with the type of love to which the statements refer. Statements 1–4 are characteristic of the eros lover. If you answered "true" to these statements, you have a strong eros component to your love style. If you answered "false," you have a weak eros component. Statements 5–8 refer to ludus love, 9–12 to storge love, 13–16 to pragma love, 17–20 to manic love, and 21–24 to agapic love.

This scale comes from Hendrick and Hendrick (1990) and is reprinted by permission. (Adapted from "A Relationship-Specific Version of the Love Attitudes Scale," by C. Hendrick and S. Hendrick, 1990, from *Journal of Social Behavior and Personality* 5 (1990):239–254.) It is based on the work of Lee (1976), as is our discussion of the six types of love.

Ludus: Entertainment and Excitement **Ludus** love is experienced as a game, as fun. The better he or she can play the game, the greater the enjoyment. Love is not to be taken too seriously; emotions are to be held in check lest they get out of hand and make trouble; passions never rise to the point where they get out of control. A ludic lover is self-controlled, always aware of the need to manage love rather than allow it to be in control. Perhaps because of this need to control love, some researchers have proposed that ludic love tendencies may reveal tendencies to sexual aggression (Sarwer, Kalichman, Johnson, Earl et al. 1993). Not surprisingly, the ludic lover retains a partner only as long as he or she is interesting and

What type of lover are you, according to this love-style test? Does this correspond to (or contradict) your self-image? Which type of love relationship (ludus, storge, mania, pragma, eros, or agape) do you think stands the best chance for survival? What type do you consider the most satisfying?

amusing. When interest fades, it is time to change partners. Perhaps because love is a game, sexual fidelity is of little importance.

Storge: Peaceful and Slow   **Storge** lacks passion and intensity. Storgic lovers do not set out to find lovers but to establish a companionable relationship with someone they know and with whom they can share interests and activities. Storgic love is a gradual process of unfolding thoughts and feelings; the changes seem to come so slowly and so gradually that it is often difficult to define exactly where the relationship is at any point in time. Sex in storgic relationships comes late, and when it comes it assumes no great importance.

Pragma: Practical and Traditional   The **pragma** lover is practical and seeks a relationship that will work. Pragma lovers want compatibility and a relationship in which their important needs and desires will be satisfied. They are concerned with the social qualifications of a potential mate even more than with personal qualities; family and background are extremely important to the pragma lover, who relies not so much on feelings as on logic. The pragma lover views love as a useful relationship, one that makes the rest of life easier. So the pragma lover asks such questions of a potential mate as "Will this person earn a good living?" "Can this person cook?" "Will this person help me advance in my career?" Pragma lovers' relationships rarely deteriorate. This is partly because pragma lovers choose their mates carefully and emphasize similarities. Another reason is that they have realistic romantic expectations.

Mania: Elation and Depression   **Mania** is characterized by extreme highs and extreme lows. The manic lover loves intensely and at the same time intensely worries about the loss of the love. This fear often prevents the manic lover from deriving as much pleasure as possible from the relationship. With little provocation, the manic lover may experience extreme jealousy. Manic love is obsessive; the manic lover has to possess the beloved completely. In return, the manic lover wishes to be possessed, to be loved intensely. The manic lover's poor self-image seems capable of being improved only by being loved; self-worth comes from being loved rather than from any sense of inner satisfaction. Because love is so important, danger signs in a relationship are often ignored; the manic lover believes that if there is love, then nothing else matters.

 Can you identify a character from literature who exemplifies one of these types of lovers? What fate does each of these lovers experience?

Agape: Compassionate and Selfless   **Agape** (ah-guh-pay) is a compassionate, egoless, self-giving love. The agapic lover loves even people with whom he or she has no close ties. This lover loves the stranger on the road even though they will probably never meet again. Agape is a spiritual love, offered without concern for personal reward or gain. This lover loves without expecting that the love will be reciprocated. Jesus, Buddha, and Gandhi practiced and preached this unqualified love, agape (Lee 1976). In one sense, agape is more a philosophical kind of love than a love that most people have the strength to achieve.

Love Styles and Personality   In reading about the love styles, you may have felt that there are certain personality types who are likely to favor one type of love over another. Here are personality traits that research finds people assign to each love style. Try identifying which personality traits people think go with each of the six love styles: eros, ludus, storge, pragma, mania, and agape.

1. ____ inconsiderate, secretive, dishonest, selfish, and dangerous
2. ____ honest, loyal, mature, caring, loving, and understanding
3. ____ jealous, possessive, obsessed, emotional, and dependent
4. ____ sexual, exciting, loving, happy, optimistic
5. ____ committed, giving, caring, self-sacrificing, and loving
6. ____ family-oriented, planning, careful, hard-working, and concerned

Very likely you perceived these personality factors in the same way as did the participants in research from which these traits were drawn (Taraban and Hendrick 1995): 1 = ludus, 2 = storge, 3 = mania, 4 = eros, 5 = agape, and 6 = pragma. Note, of course, that these results do not imply that ludus lovers are inconsiderate, secretive, and dishonest. They merely mean that people *think* of ludus lovers as inconsiderate, secretive, and dishonest.

Love Styles in Combination   Each of these varieties of love can combine with others to form new and different patterns (for example, manic and ludic or storge and pragma). These six, however, identify the major types of love and illustrate the complexity of any love relationship. The six styles should also make it clear that different people want different things, that each person seeks satisfaction in a unique way. The love that may seem lifeless or crazy or boring to you may be ideal for someone else. At the same time, another person may see these same negative qualities in the love you are seeking.

Love changes. A relationship that began as pragma may develop into ludus or eros. A relationship that began as erotic may develop into mania or storge. One approach sees this as a developmental process having three major stages (Duck 1986):

♦ First stage: Initial attraction—eros, mania, and ludus.
♦ Second stage: Storge (as the relationship develops).
♦ Third stage: Pragma (as relationship bonds develop).

Love Styles and Communication   How do you communicate when you are in love? What do you say? What do you do nonverbally? How closely do the research findings describe you? According to research, you exaggerate your beloved's virtues and minimize his or her faults. You share emotions and experiences and speak tenderly, with an extra degree of courtesy, to each other; "please," "thank you," and similar politenesses abound. You frequently use "personalized communication." This type of communication includes secrets you keep from other people and messages that have meaning only within your specific relationship (Knapp, Ellis, and Williams 1980). You also create and use personal idioms—those words, phrases, and gestures that carry meaning only for the particular relationship and that say you have a special language that signifies your special bond (Hopper, Knapp, and Scott 1981). When outsiders try to use personal idioms—as they sometimes do—the expressions seem inappropriate, at times even an invasion of privacy.

You engage in significant self-disclosure. There is more confirmation and less disconfirmation among lovers than among either nonlovers or those who are going through romantic breakups. You are also highly aware of what is and is not appropriate to the one you love. You know how to reward but also how to punish each other. In short, you know what to do to obtain the reaction you want.

Among your most often used means for communicating love are telling the person face to face or by telephone (in one survey 79 percent indicated they did it this way), expressing supportiveness, and talking things out and cooperating (Marston, Hecht, and Robers 1987).

Nonverbally, you also communicate your love. Prolonged and focused eye contact is perhaps the clearest nonverbal indicator of love. So important is eye contact that its avoidance almost always triggers a "what's wrong?" response.

You grow more aware not only of your loved one but also of your own physical self. Your muscle tone is heightened, for example. When you are in love you engage in preening gestures, especially immediately prior to meeting your lover, and you position your body attractively—stomach pulled in, shoulders square, legs arranged in appropriate masculine or feminine positions.

Your speech may even have a somewhat different vocal quality. There is some evidence to show that sexual excitement enlarges the nasal membranes, which introduces a certain nasal quality into the voice (M. Davis 1973).

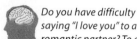

Do you have difficulty saying "I love you" to a romantic partner? To a family member? To a same-sex friend? To an opposite-sex friend? Do you find that one sex has greater difficulty saying "I love you," or are men and women equally comfortable or uncomfortable?

You eliminate socially taboo adaptors, at least in the presence of the loved one. You would curtail, for example, scratching your head, picking your teeth, cleaning your ears, and passing wind. Interestingly enough, these adaptors often return after the lovers have achieved a permanent relationship.

You touch more frequently and more intimately. You also use more "tie signs," nonverbal gestures that show that you are together, such as holding hands, walking with arms entwined, kissing, and the like. You may even dress alike. The styles of clothes and even the colors selected by lovers are more similar than those worn by nonlovers.

Cultural Differences in Loving

Although most of the research on these love styles has been done in the United States, some research has been conducted in other cultures. Here is a sampling of the research findings—just enough to illustrate that culture is an important factor in love. The test and the love styles have been found to have validity among Germans (Bierhoff and Klein 1991). Asians have been found to be more friendship oriented in their love style than are Europeans (Dion and Dion 1993b). Members of individualistic cultures (for example, Europeans) are likely to place greater emphasis on romantic love and on individual fulfillment. Members of collectivist cultures are likely to spread their love over a large network of relatives (Dion and Dion 1993a)

One study finds a love style among Mexicans characterized as calm, compassionate, and deliberate (Leon, Philbrick, Parra, Escobedo et al. 1994). In comparisons between loves styles in the United States and France, it was found that subjects from the United States scored higher on storge and mania than the French; in contrast, the French scored higher on agape (Murstein, Merighi, and Vyse 1991). Caucasian women, compared to African-American women, scored higher on mania whereas African-American women scored higher on agape. Caucasian and African-American men, however, scored very similarly; no statistically significant differences have been found (Morrow, Clark, and Brock 1995).

What has your culture taught you about love? How would you characterize these teaching in terms of "psychological healthiness"?

Gender Differences in Loving

In the United States, the differences between men and women in love are considered great. In poetry, novels, and the mass media, women and men are depicted as acting very differently when falling in love, being in love, and ending a love relationship. As Lord Byron put it in *Don Juan,* "Man's love is of man's life a thing apart, / 'Tis woman's whole existence." Women are portrayed as emotional, men as logical. Women are supposed to love intensely; men are supposed to love with detachment.

Women and men seem to experience love to a similar degree (Rubin 1973). However, women indicate greater love than men do for their same-sex friends. This may reflect a real difference between the sexes, or it may be a function of the greater social restrictions on men. A man is not supposed to admit his love for another man. Women are permitted greater freedom to communicate their love for other women.

Men and women also differ in the types of love they prefer (Hendrick, Hendrick, Foote, and Slapion-Foote 1984). For example, on one version of the love self-test presented earlier, men have been found to score higher on erotic and ludic love, whereas women score higher on manic, pragmatic, and storgic love. No difference has been found for agapic love.

Another gender difference frequently noted is that of romanticism. Before reading about this topic, you may wish to take the accompanying self-test, "How Romantic Are You?"

Women have their first romantic experiences earlier than men. The median age of first infatuation for women was 13 and for men 13.6; the median age for first time in love for women was 17.1 and for men 17.6 (Kirkpatrick and Caplow 1945; Hendrick, Hendrick, Foote, and Slapion-Foote 1984).

Men were found to place more emphasis on romance than women (Kirkpatrick and Caplow 1945). For example, when college students were asked the question posed in the photo caption below, approximately two-thirds of the men responded no, which seems to indicate that a high percentage were concerned with love and romance. However, less than one-third of the women responded no. Further, when men and women were surveyed concerning their view

Do you think that the love in a man and in a woman develop in essentially the same way? In a heterosexual relationship and in a homosexual relationship? How would you go about finding evidence to help answer these questions?

In an interesting study on love, men and women from different cultures were asked the following question: "If a man (woman) has all the other qualities you desired, would you marry this person if you were not in love with him (her)?" Results varied greatly from one culture to another (Levine, Sato, Hashimoto, & Verma 1994). For example, 50.4 percent of the respondents from Pakistan said, "yes," 49 percent of those from India said "yes," and 18.8 percent of those from Thailand said "yes." At the other extreme were those from Japan (only 2.3 percent said "yes."), the United States (only 3.5 percent said "yes"), and Brazil (only 4.3 percent said "yes"). How would you answer this question?

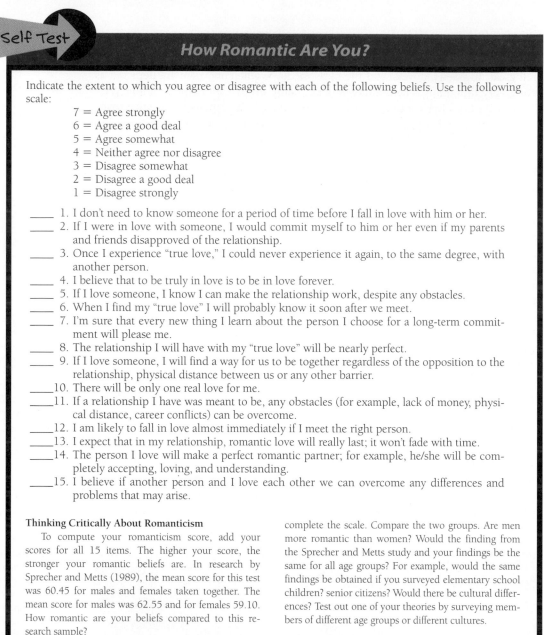

Self Test

How Romantic Are You?

Indicate the extent to which you agree or disagree with each of the following beliefs. Use the following scale:

7 = Agree strongly
6 = Agree a good deal
5 = Agree somewhat
4 = Neither agree nor disagree
3 = Disagree somewhat
2 = Disagree a good deal
1 = Disagree strongly

_____ 1. I don't need to know someone for a period of time before I fall in love with him or her.
_____ 2. If I were in love with someone, I would commit myself to him or her even if my parents and friends disapproved of the relationship.
_____ 3. Once I experience "true love," I could never experience it again, to the same degree, with another person.
_____ 4. I believe that to be truly in love is to be in love forever.
_____ 5. If I love someone, I know I can make the relationship work, despite any obstacles.
_____ 6. When I find my "true love" I will probably know it soon after we meet.
_____ 7. I'm sure that every new thing I learn about the person I choose for a long-term commitment will please me.
_____ 8. The relationship I will have with my "true love" will be nearly perfect.
_____ 9. If I love someone, I will find a way for us to be together regardless of the opposition to the relationship, physical distance between us or any other barrier.
_____10. There will be only one real love for me.
_____11. If a relationship I have was meant to be, any obstacles (for example, lack of money, physical distance, career conflicts) can be overcome.
_____12. I am likely to fall in love almost immediately if I meet the right person.
_____13. I expect that in my relationship, romantic love will really last; it won't fade with time.
_____14. The person I love will make a perfect romantic partner; for example, he/she will be completely accepting, loving, and understanding.
_____15. I believe if another person and I love each other we can overcome any differences and problems that may arise.

Thinking Critically About Romanticism

To compute your romanticism score, add your scores for all 15 items. The higher your score, the stronger your romantic beliefs are. In research by Sprecher and Metts (1989), the mean score for this test was 60.45 for males and females taken together. The mean score for males was 62.55 and for females 59.10. How romantic are your beliefs compared to this research sample?

In the discussion of gender differences, research was cited showing that men are more romantic than women. The test presented above was developed for and used in that research (Sprecher and Metts 1989).

Test out the finding showing that men are more romantic by asking at least ten men and ten women to complete the scale. Compare the two groups. Are men more romantic than women? Would the finding from the Sprecher and Metts study and your findings be the same for all age groups? For example, would the same findings be obtained if you surveyed elementary school children? senior citizens? Would there be cultural differences? Test out one of your theories by surveying members of different age groups or different cultures.

From "Romantic Beliefs Scale" and "Examination of the Effects of Gender and Gender-Role Orientation," Journal of Social and Personal Relationships 6:387–411. Copyright © 1989 Sage Publications Ltd. Reprinted by permission of Sage Publications Ltd.

How would you go about finding evidence bearing on the differences (if any) between men or women in the breakup of friendships? For example, would a pattern similar to that found for love, be found for friendship breakups?

on love—whether it is basically realistic or basically romantic—it was found that married women had a more realistic (less romantic) conception of love than did married men (Knapp 1984).

More recent research (based on the romanticism questionnaire presented here) confirms this view that men are more romantic. For example, "Men are more likely than women to believe in love at first sight, in love as the basis for marriage and for overcoming obstacles, and to believe that their partner and relationship will be perfect" (Sprecher and Metts 1989). This difference seems to increase as the romantic relationship develops: Men become more romantic and women less romantic (Fengler 1974).

One further gender difference may be noted and that is differences between men and women in breaking up a relationship (Blumstein and Schwartz 1983; cf. Janus and Janus 1993). Popular myth would have us believe that love affairs break up as a result of the man's outside affair. But the research does not support this. When surveyed as to the reason for breaking up, only 15 percent of the men indicated that it was their interest in another partner, whereas 32 percent of the women noted this as a cause of the breakup. These findings are consistent with their partners' perceptions as well: 30 percent of the men (but only 15 percent of the women) noted that their partner's interest in another person was the reason for the breakup.

In their reactions to broken romantic affairs, women and men exhibit both similarities and differences. For example, the tendency for women and men to recall only pleasant memories and to revisit places with past associations was about equal. However, men engaged in more dreaming about the lost partner and in more daydreaming generally as a reaction to the breakup than did women.

Summary — UNIT IN BRIEF

A RETURN TO OBJECTIVES:

In this unit we explored friendship and love, two of our most important interpersonal relationships, and considered: (1) What is friendship? What needs does it serve? What stages does it pass through? How does friendship differ in different cultures and between men and women? (2) What is love? What are the major kinds of love? How does love vary in different cultures and between men and women?

Friendship: An interpersonal relationship (rule-governed?) between two persons that is mutually productive, and characterized by mutual positive regard.	Love: A feeling characterized by passion and caring (Davis) and by intimacy, passion, and commitment (Sternberg)
Types of friendships: ◆ Reciprocity ◆ Receptivity ◆ Association	**Types of love:** ◆ Eros: Love as sensuous and erotic. ◆ Ludus: Love as a game. ◆ Storge: Love as companionship. ◆ Pragma: Love as a practical relation. ◆ Mania: Love as obsession and possession. ◆ Agape: Love as self-giving, altruistic.
Purposes of friendships: ◆ Utility value ◆ Affirmation value ◆ Ego-support value ◆ Stimulation value ◆ Security value	
Culture and gender differences: ◆ Friendship demands vary between collectivist and individualistic cultures. ◆ Women share more and are more intimate with same-sex friends. ◆ Men's friendships are built around shared activities.	**Culture and gender differences:** ◆ Members of individualistic cultures are likely to place greater emphasis on romantic love than are members of collectivist cultures. ◆ Men score higher on erotic and ludic love; women score higher on manic, pragmatic, and storgic love. ◆ Men score higher on romanticism.

UNIT

22 Primary and Family Relationships

Unit Topics	Unit Objectives
	After completing this unit, you should be able to:
Primary Relationships and Families: Nature and Characteristics Defined Roles Recognition of Responsibilities Shared History and Future Shared Living Space Established Rules	1. Define *family* and *primary relationship* 2. Identify five characteristics common to all primary relationships
Types of Relationships Traditionals Independents Separates	3. Define and distinguish among *traditionals, independents,* and *separates*
Communication Patterns in Primary Relationships and Families The Equality Pattern The Balanced Split Pattern The Unbalanced Split Pattern The Monopoly Pattern Reflections on Types and Patterns of Primary Relationships	4. Explain the four communication patterns that characterize primary relationships
Improving Communication Within Primary Relationships and Families Empathic Understanding Self-Disclosures Openness to Change Fair Fighting Reasonableness	5. Describe the five suggestions for improving communication within the primary relationship and the family

EXPERIENTIAL LEARNING VEHICLES

Experiential Vehicle No. 24, "The Television Relationship," pp. 467–468, may be used to illustrate any of a number of family communication issues. Vehicle No. 1, "Analyzing an Interaction," pp. 437–440, can be used to focus on family communication or, if already used, can be returned to as a summary of the entire course or to illustrate a more sophisticated analysis than was possible at the beginning of the semester. Vehicle Nos. 20, "Relationship Repair from Advice Columnists," pp. 463–464, may be used to illustrate family problems and solutions, and No. 21, "Power Plays," p. 464, to illustrate the role of power in the family.

All of us are now or were at one time part of a family. Some of our experiences have been pleasant and positive and are recalled with considerable pleasure. Other experiences have been unpleasant and negative and are recalled only with considerable pain. Part of the reason for this lies in the interpersonal communication patterns that operate within the family. This unit is designed to provide a better understanding of these patterns as well as insight into how family interactions can be made more effective, more productive, and more pleasant.

Primary Relationships and Families: Nature and Characteristics

 How would you define "family"? What types of relationships would be included in your definition? What types would be excluded? What advantages does your definition have?

If you had to define "family," you would probably note that a family consists of a husband, a wife, and one or more children. When pressed, you might add that some of these families also consist of other relatives-in-law, brothers and sisters, grandparents, aunts and uncles, and so on. But there are other types of relationships that are, to its own members, "families."

One obvious example is the family with one parent. There are now over 10 million single-parent households in the United States (Wright 1995). If current trends continue, notes *American Demographic* magazine (July 1992), 61 percent of all children (up to age 18) will spend part of their time in a single-parent home (Wright 1995).

Another obvious example is people living together in an exclusive relationship who are not married. For the most part, these cohabitants live as if they were married: there is an exclusive sexual commitment; there may be children; there are shared financial responsibilities, shared time, and shared space; and so on. These relationships mirror traditional marriages, except that in marriage the union is recognized by a religious body, the state, or both and in a relationship of cohabitants it generally is not. In their comprehensive study *American Couples* (1983), sociologists Philip Blumstein and Pepper Schwartz report that although cohabiting couples represent only about 2 percent to 3.8 percent of all couples, their number is increasing: One bit of supporting evidence for increase is that among couples in which the male is under age 25, the percentage of cohabiting couples is 7.4 percent. In Sweden, a country that often leads in sexual trends, 12 percent of all couples are cohabitants.

Another example is the gay male or lesbian couple who live together as "domestic partners"—a relatively new term for people living together—and have all the characteristics of a "family." Many of these couples have children from previous heterosexual unions, through artificial insemination, or by adoption. Although accurate statistics are difficult to secure, primary relationships among gays and lesbians seem more common than the popular media lead us to believe. Research estimates the number of gay and lesbian couples to be 70 percent to more than 80 percent of the gay population (itself estimated variously at between 4 percent and 16 percent of the total population, depending on the definitions used and the studies cited). In summarizing these previous studies and their own research, Blumstein and Schwartz (1983) conclude, "'Couplehood,' either as a reality or as an aspiration, is as strong among gay people as it is among heterosexuals."

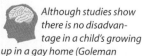 *Although studies show there is no disadvantage in a child's growing up in a gay home (Goleman 1992), the major argument made against granting adoption rights to gay men and lesbians is that the child will suffer. How do you account for this?*

The communication principles that apply to the traditional nuclear family (the mother-father-child family) also apply to these relationships. In the following discussion, the term **primary relationship** denotes the relationship between

Table 22.1	Definitions of Family

Here are several definitions of family that researchers in family communication use. You may find it interesting to formulate your own definition first and then compare it with those presented here. What relationships does your definition include that these definitions exclude? What relationships does your definition exclude that these definitions include?

"Any number of persons who live in relationship with one another and are usually, but not always, united by marriage and kinship."

—*Family Talk: Interpersonal Communication in the Family* (Beebe and Masterson 1986)

"Networks of people who share their lives over long periods of time bound by ties of marriage, blood, or commitment, legal or otherwise, who consider themselves as family and who share a significant history and anticipated future of functioning in a family relationship."

—*Family Communication: Cohesion and Change* (Galvin and Brommel 1996)

"A group of intimates, who generate a sense of home and group identity, complete with strong ties of loyalty and emotion, and an experience of a history and a future."

—*Communication in Family Relationships* (Noller and Fitzpatrick 1993)

"An organized, relational transaction group, usually occupying a common living space over an extended time period, and possessing a confluence of interpersonal images that evolve through the exchange of meaning over time."

—*Communication in the Family* (Pearson 1993)

"A multigenerational social system consisting of at least two interdependent people bound together by a common living space (at one time or another) and a common history, and who share some degree of emotional attachment to or involvement with one another."

—*Understanding Family Communication* (Yerby, Buerkel-Rothfuss, and Bochner 1990)

One researcher, looking at the family from an evolutionary-Darwinian point of view, concludes that families are "inherently unstable" and that it is necessity, not choice, that keeps them together. If they had better opportunities elsewhere they would leave immediately (Goleman 1995). What do you think of this position?

the two principal parties—the husband and wife, the lovers, the domestic partners, for example—and the term **family** denotes the broader constellation that includes children, relatives, and assorted significant others. Table 22.1 provides a variety of definitions of "family" by the authors of works on family communication. All primary relationships and families have several characteristics that further define this relationship type: defined roles, recognition of responsibilities, shared history and future, shared living space, and established rules.

Defined Roles

Primary relationship partners have a relatively clear perception of the roles each person is expected to play in relation to the other and to the relationship as a whole. Each acquired the rules of the culture and social group; each knows approximately what his or her obligations, duties, privileges, and responsibilities are. The partners' roles might include wage earner, cook, house cleaner, child care giver, social secretary, home decorator, plumber, carpenter, food shopper, money manager, and so on. At times, the roles may be shared, but even then it is generally assumed that one person has primary responsibility for certain tasks and the other person for others.

Most heterosexual couples divide the roles rather traditionally, with the man as primary wage earner and maintenance person and the woman as primary cook, child rearer, and housekeeper. This is less true among the more highly educated and those in the higher socioeconomic classes, where changes in traditional role assignments are first seen. However, among gay male and lesbian couples, clear-cut, stereotypical male and female roles are not found. In her review of the research literature, psychologist Letitia Anne Peplau (1988) notes that scientific studies "have consistently debunked this myth. Most contemporary gay relationships do not conform to traditional 'masculine' and 'feminine' roles; instead, role flexibility and turn-taking are more common patterns. . . . In this sense, traditional heterosexual marriage is not the predominant model or script for current homosexual couples."

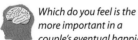

What roles do you play in your family system? If you are in a primary relationship, what roles do you play in it? What roles do you play in your friendship relationships? How satisfied are you with these roles?

Recognition of Responsibilities

Family members see themselves as having certain obligations and responsibilities to each other. A single person does not have the same kinds of obligations to another as someone in a primary relationship. For example, individuals have an obligation to help each other financially. There are also emotional responsibilities: to offer comfort when our family members are distressed, to take pleasure in their pleasures, to feel their pain, to raise their spirits. Each person also has a temporal obligation to reserve some large block of time for the other. Time sharing seems important to all relationships, although each couple will define it differently.

Shared History and Future

Primary relationships have a shared history and the prospect of a shared future. For a relationship to become a primary one, there must be some history, some significant past interaction. This interaction enables the members to get to know each other, to understand each other a little better, and ideally to like and even love each other. Similarly, the individuals view the relationship as having a potential future.

Despite researchers' prediction that 50 percent of those couples now entering first marriages will divorce (the rate is higher for second marriages) and that 41 percent of all persons of marriageable age will experience divorce, most couples entering a relationship such as marriage view it—ideally, at least—as permanent.

Which do you feel is the more important in a couple's eventual happiness: a shared history or the expectation of a shared future? Would men and women answer this question differently? How would you go about accumulating evidence bearing on this question?

Shared Living Space

In general American culture, persons in primary interpersonal relationships usually share the same living space. When living space is not shared, the situation is generally seen as an "abnormal" or temporary one both by the culture as a whole and by the individuals involved in the relationship. Even those who live apart for significant periods probably perceive a shared space as the ideal and, in fact, usually do share some special space at least part of the time. In some cultures, men and women do not share the same living space; the women may live with the children while the men live together in a communal arrangement (Harris 1993).

Although shared-living space is generally a goal of most primary relationships, the number of long distance relationships is increasing. Further, although

*Family history (as opposed to the history of two people in a relationship discussed in the text) is an extremely important factor in influencing the way in which the family operates. For example, understanding the history of your parents' families may help explain values, beliefs, and traditions considered important (or unimportant) in your home as well as the reasons for differences and conflicts. Books on genealogy—the science of tracing your family history—can be found in any bookstore. More interesting sources are on the Internet—***http://members.aol.com/johnfl4246/internet/html** *will provide you with a list of cultural mailing lists (Weitzman 1996). Or you can go to any search engine such as Yahoo or WebCrawler or Lycos and ask it to search genealogy [your last name] or genealogy [cultural identifiers, i.e. nationality, religion]. What information about your family history would you like to know? Why?*

living together is a goal, this does not mean that long-distance relationships are necessarily less satisfying. After a thorough review of the research, one researcher concludes that "there is little, if any, decrease in relationship satisfaction, intimacy, and commitment as long as lovers are able to reunite with some frequency (approximately once a month)" (Rohlfing 1995, pp. 182–183).

Not surprisingly, research finds that lovers employ a variety of strategies to maintain long distance relationships, acknowledging in their use of strategies that something extra has to be done to keep the relationships satisfying and together. Among these strategies are: recognizing that long distance relationships are common, establishing support systems while apart, and communicating in creative ways (for example, sending cards or videos) (Westefeld and Lidddell 1982).

How would you go about discovering how important a shared living space is to the health of a relationship? Do couples who live together stay together longer? Are they happier?

Established Rules

Relying on the insights of family communication researchers, Kathleen Galvin and Bernard Brommel (1996) we note the importance of family rules. You can view rules as concerning three main interpersonal communication issues (Satir 1983): (1) What can you talk about? Can you talk about the family finances? Grandpa's drinking? Your sister's life style? (2) How can you talk about something? Can you joke about your brother's disability? Can you address directly questions of family history or family skeleton? (3) To whom can you talk? Can you talk openly to extended family members such as cousins and aunts and uncles? Can you talk to close neighbors about family health issues?

All families teach rules for communication. Some of these are explicit: Never contradict the family in front of outsiders. Never talk finances with outsiders. Other rules are unspoken and which you deduce as you learn the communication style of your family. For example, if financial issues are always discussed in secret and in hushed tones, then you can infer that you shouldn't tell other more distant family members or neighbors about family finances.

These rules tell you which behaviors will be rewarded (and therefore what you should do) and which will be punished (and therefore what you should not do). Rules tell you what moves are permissible and what moves are not permissible. Rules also provide a kind of structure that defines the family as a cohesive unit and that distinguish it from other similar families.

Not surprisingly, the rules a family develops are greatly influenced by the culture. For example, members of collectivist cultures are more likely to restrict family information from outsiders as a way of protecting the family than are members of individualistic cultures. As already noted, this tendency to protect the family can create serious problems in cases of wife abuse. Many women will not report spousal abuse due to the desire to protect the family image and not let others know that things are not perfect at home (Dresser 1996).

Family communication theorists argue that rules should be flexible so that special circumstances can be accommodated; there are situations that necessitate changing the family dinner time or vacation plans or savings goals (Noller and Fitzpatrick 1993). Rules should be negotiable so that all members can participate in their modification and feel a part of family government.

Of the characteristics of primary relationships and families discussed in this unit (defined roles, recognition of responsibilities, shared history and future, shared living space, and established rules), which do you feel is the most important in keeping a relationship or family together? Which one—when absent—will contribute most to the breakup of the relationship?

What single rule of communication is most often abused in primary relationships and families? What one suggestion would you give your best friend for improving his or her relationship communication?

Types of Relationships

Although each relationship is unique, a few basic types of primary relationships can be identified (Fitzpatrick 1983, 1988, 1991; Noller and Fitzpatrick 1993). This typology was derived from a series of studies, including cross-cultural ones (for example, Noller and Hiscock 1989), that investigated eight significant aspects of relational life:

1. **Ideology of traditionalism**, the extent to which the individuals believe in the traditional sex roles for couples.
2. **Ideology of uncertainty and change**, the extent to which unpredictability and change are tolerated or welcomed.
3. **Sharing**, the extent to which the individuals share their feelings for each other and engage in significant self-disclosure.
4. **Autonomy**, the extent to which each retains his or her own identity and autonomy.
5. **Undifferentiated space**, the extent to which the individuals have their own space and privacy.
6. **Temporal regularity**, the extent to which the individuals spend time together.

MEDIA & TECHNOLOGY

NEW DIRECTIONS

At this point in the text you have a pretty firm grasp on interpersonal communication—what it is, how it works, and how it can be made more effective. Similarly, you have a good command of interpersonal relationships—what they are, how they develop and some-times deteriorate, how they can be maintained, how they can be productive, and how they can be destructive, and so on. You also have been thinking about some of the points at which media and technology on the one hand and interpersonal communication on the other come into contact.

Use whatever you have learned in this course along with your experiences in living in a world dominated by media and technology (as well as any technical knowledge you may have) to write your own media and technology box. Focus on any aspect of interpersonal communication and relationships you wish—look through the glossary for suitable concepts—and illustrate how it is influenced by or influences some aspect of media and technology.

Here are a few suggestions.

- People perception in cyberspace
- Self-concept, media exposure, and computer competence
- Self-disclosure on the Internet
- Electronic communication apprehension
- The Internet and the long-distance relationship
- Breaking up relationships over the Internet
- Conflict on the Internet—causes and cures
- Verbal aggressiveness and argumentativeness in television sitcoms or on the Internet
- Power strategies in comic books and in real life
- The computer family

7. **Conflict avoidance**, the extent to which the individuals seek to avoid conflict and confrontation.
8. **Assertiveness**, the extent to which each asserts his or her own rights.

At this point, you may wish to examine your own relational attitudes and style by taking the "Perceptions of Relationships" self-test. If you have a relational partner, you might wish to have him or her also complete the test and then compare your results.

Based on responses from more than 1,000 couples to questions covering these eight dimensions, three major types of primary relationships were identified: traditionals, separates, and independents.

Traditionals

Traditional couples are, as the term implies, traditional in several ways. For example, they share a basic belief system and philosophy of life. They see themselves as a blending of two persons into a single couple rather than as two separate individuals. They are interdependent and believe that an individual's independence must be sacrificed for the good of the relationship.

Self Test   *Perceptions of Relationships*

Respond to each of the following 24 statements by indicating the degree to which you agree with each. Encircle *high* if you agree strongly, *med* if you agree moderately (medium), and *low* if you feel little agreement. For now, do not be concerned that these terms appear in different positions in the columns to the right. Note that in some cases there are only two alternatives. When you agree with an alternative that appears twice, circle it both times.

Ideology of Traditionalism	Col 1	Col 2	Col 3
1. A woman should take her husband's last name when she marries.	High	Low	Med
2. Our wedding ceremony was (will be) very important to us.	High	Low	Med
3. Our society, as we see it, needs to regain faith in the law and in our institutions.	High	Low	Med

Ideology of Uncertainty and Change			
4. In marriage/close relationships, there should be no constraints or restrictions on individual freedom.	Low	High	Med
5. The ideal relationship is one marked by novelty, humor, and spontaneity.	Low	High	Med
6. In a relationship, each individual should be permitted to establish the daily rhythm and time schedule that suits him/her best.	Low	High	Med

Sharing			
7. We tell each other how much we love or care about each other.	High	Med	Low
8. My spouse/mate reassures and comforts me when I am feeling low.	High	Med	Low
9. I think that we joke around and have more fun than most couples.	High	Med	Low

Autonomy			
10. I have my own private work space (study, workshop, utility room, etc.).	Low	High	High
11. My spouse has his/her own private work space (workshop, utility, etc.).	Low	High	High
12. I think it is important for one to have some private space which is all his/her own and separate.	Low	High	High

Undifferentiated Space			
13. I feel free to interrupt my spouse/mate when he/she is concentrating on something if he/she is in my presence.	High	High	Low
14. I open my spouse/mate's personal mail without asking permission.	High	Med	Low
15. I feel free to invite guests home without informing my spouse/mate.	High	High	Low

Temporal Regularity	Col 1	Col 2	Col 3
16. We eat our meals (i.e., the ones at home) at the same time every day.	High	Low	High
17. In our house, we keep a fairly regular daily time schedule.	High	Low	High
18. We serve the main meal at the same time every day.	High	Low	High
Conflict Avoidance			
19. If I can avoid arguing about some problems, they will disappear.	Med	Low	High
20. In our relationships, we feel it is better to engage in conflicts than to avoid them.	Med	Low	High
21. It is better to hide one's true feelings in order to avoid hurting your spouse/mate.	Med	Low	High
Assertiveness			
22. My spouse/mate forces me to do things I do not want to do.	Low	Med	Med
23. We are likely to argue in front of friends or in public places.	Low	Med	Med
24. My spouse/mate tries to persuade me to do something I do not want to do.	Low	Med	Med

Thinking Critically About Perceptions of Relationships

The responses noted in column 1 are characteristic of traditionals. The number of circled items in this column, then, indicates your agreement with and similarity to those considered "traditionals." Responses noted in column 2 are characteristic of independents; those noted in column 3 are characteristic of separates. How accurately do you think this test measures these three kinds of relationships? Do you find this classification a useful one for talking about relationships?

These statements are from Mary Anne Fitzpatrick's *Relational Dimensions Instrument* and are reprinted by permission of Mary Anne Fitzpatrick.

Traditionals believe in mutual sharing and do little separately. For example, they spend a lot of time together, eat their meals together, place considerable emphasis on the home, and, perhaps most important, present themselves to others as a unified couple. This couple holds to the traditional sex roles, and there are seldom any role conflicts. There are few power struggles and few conflicts because each person knows and adheres to a specified role within the relationship. Perhaps as a result of the relative serenity of their lives, traditionals view their relationship as well-adjusted and permanent. Traditionals rarely even think of separation or divorce.

In their communications, traditionals are highly responsive to each other. Traditionals lean toward each other, smile, talk a lot, interrupt each other, and finish each other's sentences. Although they claim to be open with each other and free to express their vulnerabilities and weaknesses, their self-disclosures actually involve relatively low-risk rather than high-risk, and positive rather than negative, items.

Independents

In contrast to traditionals, independents stress their individuality. The relationship is important but never more important than each person's individual identity—identities they frequently discuss. A strong sense of self is essential to independents. The relationship exists to provide satisfaction for each individual. Although independents spend a great deal of time together, they do not ritualize it, for example, with schedules. Each individual spends time with outside friends.

Independents see themselves as relatively androgynous, as individuals who combine the traditionally feminine and the traditionally masculine roles and qualities. The communication between independents is responsive. Although they do not finish each other's sentences, they do interrupt with questions. They engage in conflict openly and without fear. Their disclosures are quite extensive and include high-risk and negative disclosures that are typically absent among traditionals. This couple sees their relationship as relatively well-adjusted.

Separates

Separates live together but view their relationship as more a matter of convenience than a result of their mutual love or closeness. They seem to have little desire to be together and, in fact, usually are so only at ritual functions, such as mealtime or holiday get-togethers. It is important to these separates that each has his or her own physical as well as psychological space. Separates share little; each seems to prefer to go his or her own way. They try to avoid conflict and the expression of negative feelings, but when conflict does emerge, it frequently takes the form of personal attack.

 Can you describe couples you know as being traditionals, independents, or separates? With what type of relationship (traditional, independent, or separate) do you most identify?

Separates hold relatively traditional values and beliefs about sex roles, and each person tries to follow the behaviors normally assigned to each role. They see their relationship as a part of normal life rather than as created out of a strong emotional attachment or love. What best characterizes this type, however, is that each person sees himself or herself as a separate individual and not as a part of a "we."

In addition to these three pure types, there are combinations. For example, in the separate-traditional couple one individual is a separate and one a traditional. Another common pattern is the traditional-independent, in which one individual believes in the traditional view of relationships and one in autonomy and independence.

Communication Patterns in Primary Relationships and Families

Another way to gain insight into primary relationships is to focus on communication patterns rather than on attitudes and beliefs, as in the previous discussion. Four general communication patterns are identified here; each interpersonal relationship may then be viewed as a variation on one of these basic patterns.

The Equality Pattern

The equality pattern probably exists more in theory than in practice, but it is a good starting point for looking at communication in primary relationships. It does exist more among same-sex couples than it does in opposite sex couples, however (Huston and Schwartz 1995). In the **equality pattern**, each person shares equally in the communication transactions; the roles played by each are equal. Thus, each person is accorded a similar degree of credibility; each is equally open to the ideas, opinions, and beliefs of the other; each engages in self-disclosure on a more or less equal basis. The communication is open, honest, direct, and free of the power plays that characterize so many other interpersonal relationships. There is no leader or follower, no opinion giver or opinion seeker; rather, both parties play these roles equally. Because of this basic equality, the communication exchanges themselves, over a substantial period, are equal. For example, the number of questions asked, the depth and frequency of self-disclosures, and the nonverbal behaviors of touching and eye gaze would all be about the same for both people.

Both parties share equally in the decision-making processes—the insignificant ones, such as which movie to attend, as well as the significant ones, such as where to send the child to school, whether to attend religious services, what house to buy, and so on. Conflicts in equality relationships may occur with some frequency, but they are not seen as threatening to the individuals or to the relationship. They are viewed, rather, as exchanges of ideas, opinions, and values. These conflicts are content rather than relational in nature (Unit 20), and the couple has few power struggles within the relationship domain.

Equal relationships are also equitable. According to equity theory, family or relationship satisfaction will be highest when there is equity, when the rewards are distributed in proportion to the costs one pays into the relationship (Unit 16). Dissatisfaction over inequities can lead to a balancing of the scales reaction. For example, an underbenefitted partner may seek outside affairs as a way to get more relationship benefits—more love, more consideration, more support (Walster, Walster, and Traupmann 1978; Noller and Fitzpatrick 1993).

The Balanced Split Pattern

In the **balanced split pattern** an equality relationship is maintained, but here each person has authority over different domains. Each person is seen as an expert or a decision-maker in different areas. For example, in the traditional nuclear family, the husband maintains high credibility in business matters and perhaps in politics. The wife maintains high credibility in such matters as child care and cooking. These sex roles are, in many cultures, breaking down, though they still define lots of families throughout the world (Hatfield and Rapson 1996).

Conflict is generally viewed as nonthreatening by these individuals because each has specified areas of expertise. Consequently, the outcome of the conflict is almost predetermined.

The Unbalanced Split Pattern

In the **unbalanced split pattern** one person dominates; one person is seen as an expert in more than half the areas of mutual communication. In many unions, this expertise takes the form of control. Thus, in the unbalanced split, one person is more or less regularly in control of the relationship. In some cases, this person is the more intelligent or more knowledgeable, but in many cases he or she is the more physically attractive or the higher wage earner. The less attractive or lower-income partner compensates by giving in to the other person, allowing the other to win the arguments or to have his or her way in decision making.

The person in control makes more assertions, tells the other person what should or will be done, gives opinions freely, plays power games to maintain control, and seldom asks for opinions in return. The noncontrolling person, conversely, asks questions, seeks opinions, and looks to the other for decision-making leadership.

The Monopoly Pattern

In a **monopoly pattern**, one person is seen as the authority. This person lectures rather than communicates. Rarely does this person ask questions to seek advice, and he or she always reserves the right to have the final say. In this type of couple, the arguments are few because both individuals already know who is boss and who will win the argument should one arise. When the authority is challenged, there are arguments and bitter conflicts. One reason the conflicts are so bitter is that these individuals have had no rehearsal for adequate conflict resolution. They do not know how to argue or how to disagree agreeably, so their arguments frequently take the form of hurting the other person.

The controlling person tells the partner what is and what is not to be. The controlling person talks more and talks more about matters independent of the other person's remarks than does the noncontrolling partner (Palmer 1989). The noncontrolling person looks to the other to give permission, to voice opinion leadership, and to make decisions, almost as a child looks to an all-knowing, all-powerful parent.

What communication pattern (equality, balanced split, unbalanced split, or monopoly) characterizes your primary relationship? How effective is it in keeping the relationship together? How personally satisfying is it?

INTERPERSONAL ETHICS

A PERSONAL ETHIC OF INTERPERSONAL COMMUNICATION

Ethical issues were raised throughout this book to encourage you to think about some of the ethical issues in interpersonal communication. Try formulating a general theory of ethics in interpersonal communication or, if you prefer, a theory built around one aspect of interpersonal communication. You can do this in lots of ways. Here are a few suggestions:

- The 10 rights of the interpersonal communicator
- The ethical obligations of self-disclosure
- The interpersonal listener's obligations
- The obligations of those with power
- The ethical friend
- Parents' ethical responsibilities to children
- Children's ethical responsibilities to parents
- The health professional's responsibility to the patient
- A bill of rights for friends and lovers
- The ethics of empowerment

What did you learn about the effective family from observing the family in which you grew up? What did you learn from television families?

Reflections on Types and Patterns of Primary Relationships

In thinking about the three types and four patterns of primary relationships, it is easy to identify with, say, those who are independents or those in the equality pattern. But many of our decisions are based on subconscious factors, and our motivations are not always "logical" and "mature." What makes for happiness, satisfaction, and productivity in a relationship varies with the individuals involved. For example, an equality pattern that might give satisfaction in one relationship may lead to dissatisfaction among individuals who need either to control another person or to be controlled. The type and pattern of relationship that makes you happy might make your father and mother or your son and daughter unhappy. A clear recognition of this factor of relativity is essential to understanding and appreciating your own and other people's relationships.

Improving Communication Within Primary Relationships and Families

Communication in primary interpersonal relationships can be improved by applying the same principles that improve communication in any other context. To be most effective, however, these principles need to be adapted to the unique context of the primary relationship. The purpose of this section is to suggest how the general principles of effective communication may be best applied to primary and family relationships. Additional suggestions for improving communication within relationships are presented in Unit 17 (see the section "Communication Patterns in Relationship Deterioration").

Can you describe your family communication in terms of these five characteristics? Which is strongest? Weakest? How might you go about improving your family's communication?

Empathic Understanding

If meaningful communication is to be established, we must learn to see the world from the other person's point of view, to feel that person's pain and insecurity, to experience the other person's love and fear. Empathy is an essential ingredient if a primary relationship or a family is to survive as a meaningful and productive

How would you define "family"? How does your definition compare with those presented in Table 22.1?

union. It is essential, for example, that the individuals be allowed—and in fact encouraged—to explain how and why they see the world, their relationship, and their problems as they do.

Self-Disclosures

The importance of self-disclosure in the development and maintenance of a meaningful interpersonal relationship has been noted repeatedly. Recall that total self-disclosure may not always be effective (Noller and Fitzpatrick 1993). At times, it may be expedient to omit, for example, past indiscretions, certain fears, and perceived personal inadequacies if these disclosures may lead to negative perceptions or damage the relationship in some way. In any decision concerning self-disclosure, the possible effects on the relationship should be considered. But it is also necessary to consider the ethical issues involved, specifically the other person's right to know about behaviors and thoughts that may influence the choices he or she will make. Most relationships would profit from greater self-disclosure of present feelings rather than details of past sexual experiences or past psychological problems. The sharing of present feelings also helps a great deal in enabling each person to empathize with the other; each comes to understand better the other's point of view when these self-disclosures are made.

Openness to Change

Throughout any significant relationship, there will be numerous and significant changes in each of the individuals and in the relationship. Because persons in relationships are interconnected, with each having an impact on the other, changes in one person may demand changes in the other person. Frequently asked-for changes include, giving more attention, complimenting more often, and expressing feelings more openly (Noller 1982). Willingness to be responsive to such changes, to be adaptable and flexible, is likely to enhance relationship satisfaction (Noller and Fitzpatrick 1993).

Fair Fighting

Conflict, we know, is inevitable; it is an essential part of every meaningful interpersonal relationship. Perhaps the most general rule to follow is to fight fair. Winning at all costs, beating down the other person, getting one's own way, and the like have little use in a primary relationship or family. Instead, cooperation, compromise, and mutual understanding must be substituted. If we enter into conflict with a person we love with the idea that we must win and the other must lose, the conflict has to hurt at least one partner, very often both. In these situations, the loser gets hurt and frequently retaliates, so no one truly wins in any meaningful sense. However, if we enter a conflict with the aim of resolving it by reaching some kind of mutual understanding, neither party need be hurt, and both parties may benefit from the clash of ideas or desires and from the airing of differences.

 How would you define fair fighting?

Reasonableness

Some people expect their relationship to be perfect. Whether influenced by the media, by a self-commitment to have a relationship better than one's parents', or by a mistaken belief that other relationships are a lot better than one's own, many people expect and look for perfection. Of course, this quest is likely to result in disappointment and dissatisfaction with existing relationships. Psychologist John DeCecco (1988) argues that relationships should be characterized by reasonableness: "*reasonableness* of need and expectation, avoiding the wasteful pursuit of the extravagant fantasy that *every* desire will be fulfilled, so that the relationship does not consume its partners or leave them chronically dissatisfied."

Family communication theorists Galvin and Brommel (1996, p. 412) state their belief about what constitutes a healthy family. As you read their statement, try to formulate your own. What type of family would be a healthy one to you?

 What other suggestions for improving family communication would you add to this list?

> *A healthy family recognizes the interdependence of all members of the system and attempts to provide for growth of the system as a whole, as well as the individual members involved. Such families develop a capacity for adaptation and cohesion that avoids the extremes of the continuum; it welcomes each life stage, tries to find some joy in the present, and creates a personal network to provide support during crises. Such families exhibit levels of cohesion which allow members to feel cared for but not smothered. Family members make an effort to understand the underlying meanings of messages expressed by other members. All members find a sense of connections in the family's stories and rituals.*

Summary	U N I T I N B R I E F

A RETURN TO OBJECTIVES:

In this unit we looked at primary relationships and families and considered: (1) What is a primary relationship? What is a family? What are the characteristics that families have in common? (2) How can the various types of families by classified? How do families differ from each other? (3) What are the major communication patterns that can be identified? (4) How can we improve family communication?

Characteristics of Primary Relationships and Families	Types of Primary Relationships and Families	Communication Patterns	Communication Improvement
Defined roles	Traditionals	Equality	Empathy
Recognition of responsibilities	Independents	Balanced split	Self-disclosure
Shared history and future	Separates	Unbalanced split	Openness to change
Shared living space		Monopoly	Fair fighting
Established rules			Reasonableness

Handbook of Experiential Learning Vehicles

The following twenty-four interpersonal communication experiences represent a broad selection of exercises that may be used to illustrate the concepts discussed in the text. Because many experiences are integrated into the text, these exercises are presented as supplements to those interactive text discussions. Most of the experiences in this Handbook are also more suited to small group interaction whereas those in the text may be completed alone (as well as in groups). Additional experiences may be found in the Instructor's Manual to this text, in *Messages: Building Interpersonal Communication Skills,* and in *Brainstorms: How to Think More Creatively About Communication (or about anything else).*

Interpersonal Communication Experiences	Units/Topics
1. Analyzing an Interaction	Unit 2/The Axioms of Interpersonal Communication
	Unit 22/Primary and Family Relationships
2. Matching Pairs	Unit 3/Culture in Interpersonal Communication
3. I'd Prefer to Be	Unit 1/Universals of Interpersonal Communication
	Unit 4/The Self in Interpersonal Communication/Self-Awareness/Self-Esteem/Self-Disclosure
	Unit 6/Perception in Interpersonal Communication
4. Disclosing your Hidden Self	Unit 4/The Self in Interpersonal Communication/Self-Awareness/Self-Esteem/Self-Disclosure
5. Time for Self-Disclosure	Unit 4/The Self in Interpersonal Communication/Self-Disclosure
6. Analyzing Assertiveness	Unit 5/Apprehension and Assertiveness/Assertiveness
7. Perceiving My Selves	Unit 4/The Self in Interpersonal Communication/Self-Awareness/Self-Esteem
	Unit 6/Perception in Interpersonal Communication
8. Sequential Communication	Unit 7/Listening in Interpersonal Communication
	Unit 14/Messages and Conversation

Interpersonal Communication Experiences	Units/Topics
9. Facial Expressions	Unit 9/Universals of Verbal and Nonverbal Messages
	Unit 12/Nonverbal Messages: Body and Sound/Facial Communication
10. Eye Contact	Unit 9/Universals of Verbal and Nonverbal Messages
	Unit 12/Nonverbal Messages: Body and Sound/Eye Communication
11. Interpersonal Interactions and Space	Unit 9/Universals of Verbal and Nonverbal Messages
	Unit 13/Nonverbal Messages: Space and Time/Spatial Messages
12. Who?	Unit 1/Universals of Interpersonal Communication
	Unit 4/The Self in Interpersonal Communication
	Unit 6/Perception in Interpersonal Communication
	Unit 9/Universals of Verbal and Nonverbal Messages
	Unit 12/Nonverbal Messages: Body and Sound
	Unit 13/Nonverbal Messages: Space and Time
13. The Meanings of Color	Unit 13/Nonverbal Messages: Space and Time/Artifactual Communication/Color Communication
14. Conversational Analysis: A Chance Meeting	Unit 10/Verbal Messages: Principles and Pitfalls
	Unit 11/Verbal Messages: Barriers to Interaction
	Unit 14/Messages and Conversation
15. Giving and Taking Directions	Unit 1/Universals of Interpersonal Communication
	Unit 7/Listening in Interpersonal Communication
	Unit 10/Verbal Messages: Principles and Pitfalls
	Unit 11/Verbal Messages: Barriers to Interaction
	Unit 14/Messages and Conversation
16. Analyzing Stage Talk	Unit 14/Messages and Conversation
	Unit 15/Universals of Interpersonal Relationships
17. Interpersonal Relationships in Songs and Greeting Cards	Unit 3/Culture in Interpersonal Communication
	Unit 15/Universals of Interpersonal Relationships
18. Mate Preferences: I Prefer Someone Who …	Unit 3/Culture in Interpersonal Communication
	Unit 15/Universals of Interpersonal Relationships
	Unit 16/Relationship Development and Involvement
19. Male and Female	Unit 3/Culture in Interpersonal Communication
	Unit 15/Universals of Interpersonal Relationships
	Unit 16/Relationship Development and Involvement
	Unit 17/Relationship Deterioration and Dissolution
	Unit 20/Conflict in Interpersonal Relationships

Interpersonal Communication Experiences	Units/Topics
20. Relationship Repair from Advice Columnists	Unit 15/Universals of Interpersonal Relationships
	Unit 17/Relationship Deterioration and Dissolution
	Unit 18/Relationship Maintenance and Repair
	Unit 20/Conflict in Interpersonal Relationshipss
	Unit 22/Primary and Family Relationship
21. Power Plays	Unit 3/Culture in Interpersonal Communication
	Unit 19/Power in Interpersonal Relationships
	Unit 22/Primary and Family Relationships
22. Analyzing a Conflict Episode	Unit 20/Conflict in Interpersonal Relationships
	Unit 22/Primary and Family Relationships
23. Friendship Behaviors	Unit 21/Friends and Lovers/Friends
24. The Television Relationship	Unit 15/Universals of Interpersonal Relationships
	Unit 16/Relationship Development and Involvement
	Unit 17/Relationship Deterioration and Dissolution
	Unit 18/Relationship Maintenance and Repair
	Unit 19/Power in Interpersonal Relationships
	Unit 20/Conflict in Interpersonal Relationships
	Unit 21/Friends and Lovers
	Unit 22/Primary and Family Relationships

1. Analyzing an Interaction

The axioms of human communication discussed in Unit 2 should prove useful in analyzing any communication interaction. To help illustrate these principles and to provide some practice in applying them to a real-life situation, the following interaction is presented. Read it carefully, and analyze each of the axioms of communication identified following the interaction.

As an alternative to analyzing this interaction, the entire class may watch a situation comedy show, television drama, or film and explore the communication axioms in these presentations. The questions used in this exercise should prove useful in formulating parallel questions for the television program or film. Another way of approaching this topic is for all students to watch the same television programs for an entire evening, with groups of students focusing on the operation of different axioms. Thus, one group would focus on examples and illustrations of the impossibility of not communicating, another group would focus on the content and relationship dimensions of messages, and so on. Each group can then report its findings and insights to the entire class.

AN INTERPERSONAL TRANSACTION

MARGARET: mother, housewife, junior high school history teacher; 41 years old

FRED: father, gas station attendant; 46 years old

DIANE: daughter, receptionist in an art gallery; 22 years old

STEPHEN: son, college freshman; 18 years old

Margaret is in the kitchen finishing preparations for dinner—lamb chops, Fred's favorite, though she does not much care for them. Diane is going through some CDs. Stephen is reading one of his textbooks. Fred comes in from work and throws his jacket over the couch; it falls to the floor.

FRED: [*Bored but angry, looking at Stephen*] What did you do with the car last night? It stunk like hell. And you left all your damn school papers all over the back seat.

STEPHEN: [*As if expecting the angry remarks*] What did I do now?

FRED: You stunk up the car with your damn pot or whatever you kids smoke, and you left the car looking like hell. Can't you hear?

[Stephen says nothing; goes back to looking at his book but without really reading.]

MARGARET: Dinner's almost ready. Come on. Wash up and sit down.

[At dinner]

DIANE: Mom, I'm going to go to the shore for the weekend with some friends from work.

MARGARET: OK. When will you be leaving?

DIANE: Friday afternoon, right after work.

FRED: Like hell you're going. No more going to the shore with that group.

MARGARET: Fred, they're nice people. Why shouldn't she go?

FRED: Because I said so, OK? Finished. Closed.

DIANE: [*Mumbling*] I'm 22 years old and he gives me problems. You make me feel like a kid, like some stupid little kid.

FRED: Get married and then you can tell your husband what to do.

DIANE: I wish I could.

STEPHEN: But nobody'll ask her.

MARGARET: Why should she get married? She's got a good life—good job, nice friends, good home. Listen, I was talking with Elizabeth and Cara this morning, and they both feel they've just wasted their lives. They raised a family and what have they got? They got *nothing*. [*To Diane*] And don't think sex is so great either; it isn't, believe me.

FRED: Well, they're idiots.

MARGARET: [*Snidely*] They're idiots? Yeah, I guess they are.

DIANE: Joanne's getting married.

MARGARET: Who's Joanne?

STEPHEN: That creature who lives with that guy Michael.

FRED: Watch your mouth, wiseass. Don't be disrespectful to your mother or I'll teach you how to act right.

MARGARET: Well, how do you like the dinner?

[Prolonged silence]

DIANE: Do you think I should be in the wedding party if Joanne asks me? I think she will; we always said we'd be in each other's wedding.
MARGARET: Sure, why not. It'll be nice.
FRED: I'm not going to no wedding, no matter who's in it.
STEPHEN: Me neither.
DIANE: I hope you'll both feel that way when I get married.
STEPHEN: By then I'll be too old to remember I got a sister.
MARGARET: How's school, Stephen?
STEPHEN: I hate it. It's so big. Nobody knows anyone. You sit in these big lecture halls and listen to some creep talk. I really feel lonely and isolated, like nobody knows I'm alive.
FRED: Listen to that college-talk garbage. Get yourself a woman and you won't feel lonely, instead of hanging out with those pothead faggots.

[Diane looks to Margaret, giving a sigh as if to say, "Here we go again."]

MARGARET: *[To Diane, in whisper]* I know.
DIANE: Mom? Do you think I'm getting fat?
STEPHEN: Yes.
FRED: Just don't get fat in the stomach or you'll get thrown out of here.
MARGARET: No, I don't notice it.
DIANE: Well, I just thought I might be.
STEPHEN: *[Pushing his plate away]* I'm finished; I'm going out.
FRED: Sit down and finish your damn supper. You think I work all day for you to throw the food away? You wanna go smoke your dope?
STEPHEN: No. I just want to get away from you—forever.
MARGARET: You mean we both work all day; it's just that I earn a lot more than you do.
FRED: No, I mean I work and you baby-sit.
MARGARET: Teaching junior high school history isn't baby sitting.
FRED: What the hell is it then? You don't teach them anything.
MARGARET: *[To Diane]* You see? You're better off single. I should've stayed single. Instead. . . Oh, well. I was young and stupid. It was my own fault for getting involved with a loser. Just don't you make the same mistake.
FRED: *[To Stephen]* Go ahead. Leave the table. Leave the house. Who cares what you do?

Thinking Critically About an Interpersonal Transaction

Here are some questions, built around the axioms discussed in Unit 2, to guide your analysis.

1. Interpersonal communication is transactional.
   a. How is the process nature of communication illustrated in this interaction? For example, why is it impossible to identify specific beginnings and

specific endings for any of the varied interactions? Are there instances in which individual characters attempt to deny the process nature of inter-personal interaction?

  b. Can you illustrate how the messages of the different characters are inter-dependent?

2. Interpersonal communication is inevitable, irreversible, and unrepeatable.

  a. Do the characters communicate significant messages, even though they may attempt not to communicate? For example, in what ways do the characters communicate simply by their physical presence or by the role they occupy in the family? Do the characters attempt not to communicate? Why do these attempts fail?

  b. Are any messages being communicated that you think the characters will later wish they had not communicated? Why do you think so? Do any of the characters try to reverse the communication process—that is, to "un-communicate"?

  c. What evidence can you offer to illustrate that communication is unrepeatable?

3. Interpersonal communication is a process of adjustment.

  a. Can any of the failures to communicate be traced to the lack of adjust-ment?

  b. Throughout the interaction, how do the characters adjust to one another?

  c. What suggestions would you offer this family for increasing their abilities to adjust to one another?

4. Interpersonal communication sequences are punctuated for processing.

  a. Select any two characters and indicate how they differ in their punctua-tion of any specific sequence of events. Do the characters realize that they are each punctuating differently?

  b. What problems might a failure to recognize the arbitrary nature of punc-tuation create?

5. Interpersonal communication involves symmetrical and complementary transactions.

  a. What type of relationship do you suppose exists between Fred and Margaret? Between Fred and Diane? Between Fred and Stephen? Between Diane and Stephen? Between Margaret and Stephen?

  b. Can any instances of inappropriate complementarity be found? Inappropriate symmetry? What problems might these cause this particu-lar family?

  c. Can you find any of the nine patterns of interaction identified here: sym-metry (competitive, submissive, or neutralized); complementarity (one-up followed by one-down or one-down followed by one-up messages); and transitions (one-up plus one-across, one-down plus one-across, one-across plus one-up, and one-across plus one-down)? What added insights does this analysis provide?

6. Communication involves both content and relationship dimensions.

  a. How does each of the characters deal with the self-definitions of the other characters? For example, how does Fred deal with the self-definition of Margaret? How does Margaret deal with the self-definition of Fred?

  b. Are any problems caused by failure to recognize the distinction between the content and the relationship levels of communication?

  c. Select one topic of conversation and identify both the content and the re-lationship messages communicated.

2. Matching Pairs

This exercise is designed to provide an opportunity to analyze communication and particularly intercultural communication in terms of the concepts considered in this text. The procedures are simple:

- Select a five number code, e.g., 1–3–9–14–10—consisting of all *different* numbers—without reference to the table below. Choose numbers from 1–15. After selecting your code, refer to the table to get your basic communication act: Source (plus identifiers)-Message-Receiver (plus identifiers).
- Explain the communication and cultural factors operating in this basic interpersonal communication act *as you see it*. Consider, for example, are there likely to be significant self-concept differences? Is apprehension likely to be a factor? Is self-disclosure relevant here? Are certain perceptual or listening barriers especially likely to create problems?
- If you were asked to give these two people advice to make their communications more effective—even before they begin to speak—what would it be? What one rule would you ask them to follow?
- How likely is this communication dyad to succeed? To fail? What reasons can you offer for your prediction?

Source-Sender	Further Identifiers	Message Situation	Receiver-Audience	Further Identifiers
1. Australian	1. Male MBA	1. Applying for an entry-level office job	1. Australian	1. Male MBA
2. African American	2. Female, sightless and uneducated	2. Giving a speech to support a politician	2. African American	2. Female, sightless and uneducated
3. Latino	3. Male nursery school teacher	3. Asking for a date	3. Latino	3. Male nursery school teacher
4. Native American	4. Female PhD in physics	4. Giving a compliment	4. Native American	4. Female PhD in physics
5. Mexican	5. Male lawyer earning $400,000	5. Asking directions on a subway late at night	5. Mexican	5. Male lawyer earning $400,000
6. Jewish	6. Father who owes three years child support	6. Asking for a sizable favor	6. Jewish	6. Father who owes three years child support
7. American	7. Gay male, uneducated	7. Working together on a project	7. American	7. Gay male, uneducated
8. European white	8. Lesbian, MD, mother of 4	8. Planning to marry	8. European white	8. Lesbian, MD, mother of 4
9. South African	9. Male welfare recipient	9. Competing for leadership in an organization	9. South African	9. Male welfare recipient
10. Japanese	10. Hearing-impaired male, recent college graduate	10. Firing someone for incompetence	10. Japanese	10. Hearing-impaired male, recent college graduate
11. Chinese	11. Female ex-convict (armed robber)	11. Asking for a handout	11. Chinese	11. Female ex-convict (armed robber)
12. Iranian	12. Homeless male, 25 years old	12. Complaining about poor service	12. Iranian	12. Homeless male, 25 years old
13. Ugandan	13. Male model	13. Buying an expensive sweater	13. Ugandan	13. Male model
14. German	14. Rap singer	14. Self-disclosing past indiscretions	14. German	14. Rap singer
15. Northern Irelander	15. Female HIV+ drug user	15. Opening a conversation	15. Northern Irelander	15. Female HIV+ drug user

3. I'd Prefer to Be

This exercise should enable you to get to know each other better and at the same time get to know yourself better. It's a useful exercise for getting strangers to talk about themselves and then to talk about their talk. It is best played in groups of 5 or 6 members.

First, each group member should rank each of the three traits in the 15 groupings listed, using 1 for the most preferred and 3 for the least preferred. After the traits are ranked by each person, discuss your rankings with other group members.

Any member may refuse to reveal his or her rankings for any category by saying "I pass." The group is not permitted to question the reasons for any member's passing. When a member reveals rankings for a category, the group members may ask questions relevant to that category. These questions may be asked after any individual member's response or may be reserved until all members have given their rankings for a particular category.

"I'd Prefer to Be"

1. ___ intelligent
    ___ wealthy
    ___ physically attractive
2. ___ a movie star
    ___ a senator
    ___ a successful businessperson
3. ___ blind
    ___ deaf
    ___ mute
4. ___ on an average date
    ___ reading an average book
    ___ watching average television
5. ___ loved
    ___ feared
    ___ respected
6. ___ bisexual
    ___ heterosexual
    ___ homosexual
7. ___ applying for a job by letter
    ___ applying by face-to-face interview
    ___ applying by telephone interview
8. ___ adventurous
    ___ scientific
    ___ creative
9. ___ successful in social life
    ___ successful in family life
    ___ successful in business life
10. ___ a traitor to my friend
    ___ a traitor to my country
    ___ a traitor to myself

11. ___ angry
    ___ guilty
    ___ fearful
12. ___ an introvert
    ___ an extrovert
    ___ an ambivert
13. ___ the loved
    ___ the lover
    ___ the good friend
14. ___ a leader
    ___ a follower
    ___ a loner
15. ___ more open, more disclosive
    ___ more flexible, more willing to try new things
    ___ more supportive, more giving of myself

Thinking Critically About Your Preferences

After all categories have been discussed or after a certain time limit has been reached, consider the following questions:

◆ How would you rate this experience in terms of enjoyment? In terms of the openness of group members? Are these related?
◆ How supportive or accepting was the group of the individual choices of members? Were some choices more acceptable than others?
◆ Did the gender or culture of the group members influence the choices made? The openness of the discussion?
◆ What one principle of communication would you draw from this experience?

4. Disclosing Your Hidden Self

This experience is an extremely powerful one for exploring some of the dimensions of self-disclosure and is based on a suggestion by Gerard Egan (1970). The procedure is simple: Write on an index card a statement of information that is currently in your hidden self (that is, currently undisclosed to all or most of the others in this class). Do not put your name on the card. The statements are dealt with anonymously. The cards should be collected and read aloud to the entire group.

No comments should be made as the cards are read; no indication of evaluation should be made. The comments are to be dealt with in a totally supportive atmosphere. After the cards are read, you may wish to consider some or all of the following issues:

◆ What topics did the statements deal with? Are they generally the topics about which you too keep information hidden?
◆ Why do you suppose this type of information is kept in the hidden self? What advantages might there be in keeping it hidden? What disadvantages?
◆ How would you react to people who disclosed such statements to you? For example, what difference, if any, would these types of disclosures make in your closest interpersonal relationships?

5. Time for Self-Disclosure

Relationship self-disclosures occur throughout a relationship, but not always at what you may think is the right time. Some disclosures seem to occur too early and signal an intimacy in disclosure that is not echoed in the relationship. The disclosures seem prematurely and inappropriately intimate. Some disclosures, on the other hand, occur too late; we feel we should have been told something earlier and resent not learning of it sooner. Of course, some disclosures seem to occur at exactly the right time. This exercise explores the timeliness of self-disclosures.

Another way of looking at this exercise is from an ethical perspective, from the point of view of your right to know certain information about a person with whom you become relationally involved. At what point in the relationship do you have a right to know this type of information?

Listed below are 10 items of personal information. Next to each item indicate the stage at which you would expect the persons to disclose this type of information. Use X for any item you feel should not have been disclosed at any time. Use the following shorthand for those items you feel should be disclosed.

> Cp = Contact (perceptual)
> Ci = Contact (interactional)
> It = Involvement (testing)
> Ii = Involvement (intensifying)
> Iic = Intimacy (interpersonal commitment)
> Isb = Intimacy (social bonding)

_____ 1. Correct age
_____ 2. History of family mental illness or genetic disorders
_____ 3. Relationship history (previous involvements, children)
_____ 4. Annual income, assets, and debts
_____ 5. Cultural background (race and nationality) and beliefs (for example, prejudices, ethnocentrism)
_____ 6. Sexual orientation and inclinations
_____ 7. Religion and religious beliefs
_____ 8. HIV status
_____ 9. Attitudes toward commitment, fidelity, relationship expectations
_____ 10. Political beliefs and attitudes

Thinking Critically About the Appropriateness of Self-disclosure

After you have labeled all ten items, consider some or all of the following questions, alone, in groups, or with the class as a whole:

- ◆ Does age influence appropriateness? For example, are certain items important at 18 but unimportant at 50? Important at 50 but unimportant at 18?
- ◆ Do men and women expect the same level of self-disclosure from their partners? If you have the opportunity you may wish to compare your responses with others in your group or class. Are there noticeable sex differences?

◆ Do men and women follow different norms or rules in self-disclosing? How would you state these rules?

◆ In what kind of relationship would you expect self-disclosure to be highest? Lowest? Heterosexual? Gay male? Lesbian? What reasons can you advance to support your prediction? How would you go about testing your prediction?

◆ Does the future of the relationship (as envisioned by each person) influence the timing of self-disclosures?

◆ Do cultures vary in the way their members disclose? What implications might these differences have for intercultural communication? For example, can you identify potential problems that different cultural time schedules for self-disclosure might create?

6. Analyzing Assertiveness

Read each of the following five situations. Consider all or some of the following questions, either individually, in small groups, or with the class as a whole:

1. How might an aggressive, a nonassertive, and an assertive person deal with each of these situations?
2. What obstacles might you anticipate if you choose to respond assertively?
3. What suggestions might you offer the person who wants to respond assertively but is having difficulty putting the principles into practice?

Cheating on an Examination

You and another student turn in examination papers that are too similar to be the result of mere coincidence. The instructor accuses you of cheating by allowing the student behind you to copy your answers. You were not aware that anyone saw your paper.

Decorating Your Apartment

You have just redecorated your apartment, expending considerable time and money in making it exactly as you want it. A good friend of yours brings you a house gift—the ugliest poster you have ever seen. Your friend insists that you hang it over your fireplace, the focal point of your living room.

Borrowing Money

A friend borrows $30 and promises to pay you back tomorrow. But tomorrow passes, as do 20 other tomorrows, and there is no sign of the money. You know that the person has not forgotten about it, and you also know that the person has more than enough money to pay you back.

Neighbor Intrusions

A neighbor has been playing a stereo at an extremely high volume late into the night. This makes it difficult for you to sleep.

Sexual Harassment

Your supervisor at work has been coming on to you and has asked repeatedly to go out with you. You have refused each time. Brushing up against you, touching you in passing, and staring at you in a sexual way are common occurrences. You have no romantic interest in your supervisor and simply want to do your job, free from this type of harassment.

7. Perceiving My Selves

The purpose of this exercise is to explore how you perceive yourself, how you think others perceive you, and how you would like to be perceived (ideally). In some instances and for some people, these three perceptions will be the same; in most cases and for most people, however, they will be different.

Following this brief introduction are nine lists of items (animals, birds, colors, communications media, dogs, drinks, music, transportation, and sports). Read over each list carefully, trying to look past the purely physical characteristics of the objects to their "personalities" or "psychological meanings."

1. For each of the nine lists, indicate the one item that best represents how you perceive yourself—not your physical self, but your psychological and philosophical self. Mark these items *MM* (Myself to Me).
2. In each of the nine lists, select the one item that best represents how you feel others perceive you. By "others" is meant acquaintances—neither passing strangers nor close friends, but people you meet and talk with for some time—for example, people in this class. Mark these items *MO* (Myself to Others).
3. In each of the nine lists, select the one item that best represents how you would like to be. Put differently, what items would your ideal self select? Mark these items *MI* (Myself as Ideal).

Thinking Critically About Self-perception

After all nine lists are marked three times, discuss your choices in groups of five or six in any way you feel is meaningful. Your objective is to get a better perspective on how your self-perception compares with both the perceptions of you by others and your own ideal perception. In these discussions, state as clearly as possible why you selected the items you did and specifically what each selected item means to you at this time. Welcome suggestions from group members as to why they think you selected the items you did. You might also wish to integrate consideration of some or all of the following questions into your discussion:

- How different are the items marked *MM* from those marked *MO*? Why do you suppose this is so? Which is the more positive? Why?
- How different are the items marked *MM* from those marked *MI*? Why do you suppose this is so?

- ◆ What do the number of differences between the items marked *MM* and the items marked *MI* mean for personal happiness?
- ◆ How accurate were you in the items you marked *MO*? Ask members of the group which items they would have selected for you.
- ◆ Would you show these forms to your best same-sex friend? Your best opposite-sex friend? Your parents? Your children? Explain.

Animals

____ bear
____ deer
____ fox
____ lion
____ monkey
____ rabbit
____ turtle

Birds

____ chicken
____ eagle
____ ostrich
____ owl
____ parrot
____ swan
____ turkey

Colors

____ black
____ blue
____ gray
____ pink
____ red
____ white
____ yellow

Communications Media

____ book
____ film
____ fourth-class mail
____ radio
____ special delivery
____ telephone
____ television

Dogs

____ boxer
____ Doberman
____ greyhound
____ husky
____ mutt
____ poodle
____ St. Bernard

Drinks

____ beer

____ champagne

____ milk

____ prune juice

____ water

____ wine

____ hot chocolate

Sports

____ auto racing

____ baseball

____ boxing

____ bullfighting

____ chess

____ ice skating

____ tennis

Transportation

____ bicycle

____ jet plane

____ horse and wagon

____ motorcycle

____ Rolls-Royce

____ van

____ Volkswagen

Music

____ rap

____ country/western

____ folk

____ jazz

____ opera

____ popular

____ rock

8. Sequential Communication

This exercise is designed to illustrate some of the processes involved in what might be called "sequential communication"—communication that is passed on from one person to another. Six volunteers participate. Five of the volunteers should leave the room so they cannot hear what is being said. The sixth volunteer is then read a statement once, twice, or even three times until he or she fully understands it. The second person then enters the room and listens carefully to the first subject's restatement of the message. This second person then repeats it to the third person, and so on, until all volunteers have restated the communication. The last restatement and the original are then compared on the basis of the processes listed on the next page.

Members of the class not serving as volunteers should record the changes made in the various restatements. Special attention should be given to the following basic processes in sequential communication:

1. *Omissions*. What kinds of information are omitted? At what point in the chain of communication are such omissions introduced? Do the omissions follow any pattern?
2. *Additions*. What kinds of information are added? When? Can patterns be discerned here, or are the additions totally random?
3. *Distortions*. What kinds of information are distorted? When? Are there any patterns? Can the distortions be classified in any way? Are the distortions in the direction of increased simplicity? Increased complexity? Can the sources of or reasons for the distortions be identified?

A verbal communication that works well comes from William Haney (1981).

> *Every year at State University, the eagles in front of the Psi Gamma fraternity house were mysteriously sprayed during the night. Whenever this happened, it cost the Psi Gams from $75 to $100 to have the eagles cleaned. The Psi Gams complained to officials and were promised by the president that if ever any students were caught painting the eagles, they would be expelled from school.*

9. Facial Expressions

The objective of this exercise is to gain a greater understanding of the role of facial features in communicating different emotions. Draw faces, depicting only eyebrows, eyes, and mouth, to illustrate the primary emotions: happiness (provided as an example), surprise, fear, anger, sadness, disgust, contempt, and interest. In the space provided, write a verbal description of how one would facially express each of these emotions. Follow the format provided in the happiness example.

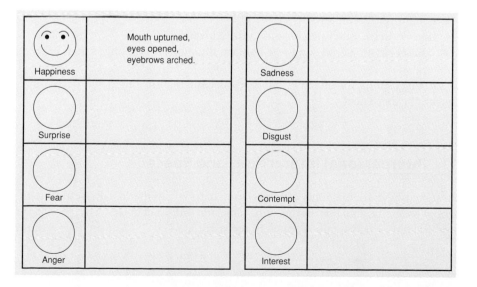

Compare your faces and descriptions with those done by others. What do the several faces for each emotion have in common? How do they differ? What do the verbal descriptions have in common? How do they differ?

10. Eye Contact

Form dyads and talk about any topic of mutual interest—sports, film, politics. For the first two minutes, the conversation should be conducted without any special rules. At an agreed-upon signal, eye-face contact is to cease. The conversation should continue for another two minutes, as before, ideally without interruption. At another signal, focused eye-to-eye contact is to be established. Each person is to maintain direct focused eye contact for two minutes and continue the conversation. At another signal, the participants should return to their customary means of communication for the final two minutes. Each person should share her or his feelings during the four periods:

1. Normal interaction situation
2. No-eye-contact situation
3. Focused eye contact
4. Normal situation but with heightened awareness and perhaps some awkwardness carried over from the two periods of abnormal interaction

Thinking Critically About Eye Contact and Its Role in Interpersonal Communication

What influences do changes in eye contact have on such variables as:

◆ fluency, nonfluencies, and silences
◆ general body movements, especially of the head, hands, and legs
◆ comfort or discomfort
◆ interest in the other person and in the conversation
◆ time perception (did some eye-contact situations seem longer than others?)

What suggestions for effective interpersonal interaction might we derive from this brief experience?

11. Interpersonal Interactions and Space

Presented here are diagrams of tables and chairs. Imagine that the setting is the school cafeteria and this is the only table not fully occupied. The person described above the diagram is seated in the space marked X. Place another X in the circle where you would sit.

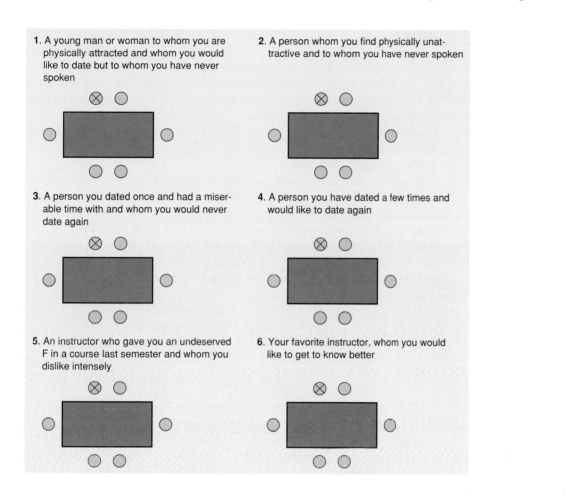

1. A young man or woman to whom you are physically attracted and whom you would like to date but to whom you have never spoken

2. A person whom you find physically unattractive and to whom you have never spoken

3. A person you dated once and had a miserable time with and whom you would never date again

4. A person you have dated a few times and would like to date again

5. An instructor who gave you an undeserved F in a course last semester and whom you dislike intensely

6. Your favorite instructor, whom you would like to get to know better

Thinking Critically About Interpersonal Interactions and Space

After completing all six situations, consider some or all of the following issues:

1. Why did you select the position you did? How does the position you selected better enable you to achieve your purpose?
2. Assume that you were already seated in the position marked *X*. Do you think the person described would sit where you indicated you would? Why? Does the sex or status or your liking for the other person influence your choice of seat?
3. What does the position you selected communicate to the person already seated? In what ways might this nonverbal message be misinterpreted?
4. Do you notice cultural influences on seating preferences? For example, in the United States seating arrangements would unite men and women; in Taiwan, however, seating arrangements would separate the sexes (Cline and Puhl 1984).

12. Who?

The purpose of this exercise is to explore some of the verbal and nonverbal cues you give that others use in forming assumptions about you. The exercise should serve as a useful summary of the concepts and principles both of verbal and non-verbal communication and of perception.

The entire class should form a circle so that each member may see all other members without straining. If members do not know each others' names, some system of name tags should be used.

Each member should examine the following list of phrases and write in the column labeled *Who?* the name of one student to whom he or she feels each statement applies. Be certain to respond to all statements. Although one name may be used more than once, the experience will prove more effective if a wide variety of names are chosen. Unless the class is very small, no name should be used more than four times.

After the names have been recorded for *each* statement by *each* student, the following procedure may prove useful. The instructor or group leader selects a statement and asks someone specifically, or the class generally, what names were written down. (There is no need to tackle the statements in order.) Before the person whose name was selected is asked whether the phrase is correctly or incorrectly attributed to him or her, some or all of the following questions may be considered:

1. Why did you select the name you did? What was there about this person that led you to think that this phrase applied to him or her? What specific verbal or nonverbal cues led you to your conclusion?
2. Is your response all a function of a stereotype you might have of this individual's ethnic, religious, racial, or sexual identification? For example, how many women's names were written next to the statements about the saws (No. 13)? How many men's names were written for the statement on cooking (No. 3)?
3. Did anyone give off contradictory cues such that some cues were appropriate for a specific phrase and others were not? Explain these contradictory cues.
4. How accurate were the predictions? Why are some people easier to predict than others?
5. How do you communicate your "self" to others? How do you communicate what you know, think, feel, and do to your peers?

Who?

_____ 1. goes to the professional theater a few times a year.
_____ 2. has taken a vacation outside the country in the last 12 months.
_____ 3. likes to cook.
_____ 4. watches soap operas on a fairly regular basis.
_____ 5. wants lots of children.
_____ 6. has seen a pornographic (XXX-rated) movie within the last three months.
_____ 7. surfs the Net almost daily.
_____ 8. has lots of associations with people from different cultures.

_____ 9. has cried over a movie in the last few months.

_____ 10. has many close friends.

_____ 11. knows how potatoes should be planted.

_____ 12. knows the difference between ROM and RAM.

_____ 13. knows the differences among a hacksaw, a jigsaw, and a coping saw.

_____ 14. knows the ingredients for a Bloody Mary.

_____ 15. knows the function of the spleen.

_____ 16. knows what an armoire is.

_____ 17. can name all 12 signs of the zodiac.

_____ 18. has a car in his or her immediate family costing over $40,000.

_____ 19. is frequently infatuated (or in love).

_____ 20. would like, perhaps secretly, to be a movie star.

_____ 21. knows the legal status of Puerto Rico.

_____ 22. keeps a diary or a journal.

_____ 23. knows what NAFTA stands for.

_____ 24. knows what the prime rate means and approximately how much it is today.

_____ 25. is very religious.

_____ 26. has a state-of-the-art personal computer.

_____ 27. would vote in favor of gay rights legislation.

_____ 28. is going to make a significant contribution to society.

_____ 29. is going to be a millionaire.

_____ 30. would emerge as a leader in a small-group situation.

13. The Meanings of Color

This exercise raises questions about the meanings colors communicate and focuses on the ways advertisers and marketers use colors to influence your perception of a product. The color spectrum is presented below, with numbers from 1 to 25 to help you identify the colors you select for the objects noted below.

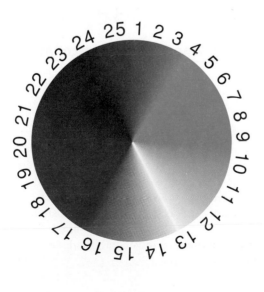

Assume that you are working for an advertising agency and that your task is to select colors for the objects in the following list. For each object, select the major color as well as any secondary colors you would use in its packaging. Record these choices in the spaces provided by selecting the numbers corresponding to the colors of the spectrum.

Objects	Major Color	Secondary Colors
Coffee can for rich Colombian coffee	_____	_____
A children's cereal	_____	_____
An especially rich ice cream	_____	_____
Expensive freshly squeezed orange juice	_____	_____
Packaging for upscale jewelry store	_____	_____
Dietetic TV dinners	_____	_____
Microwave popcorn	_____	_____
Shampoo for gray hair	_____	_____
Liquid detergent for heavy-duty washing	_____	_____
A textbook in interpersonal communication	_____	_____

Thinking Critically About the Meanings of Color

After each person has recorded his or her decisions, discuss them in small groups of five or six or with the class as a whole. You may find it helpful to consider the following questions:

- ◆ What meanings did you wish to communicate for each of the objects?
- ◆ How much agreement is there among the group members that these meanings are the appropriate ones for these products?
- ◆ How much agreement is there among the group members on the meanings that the different colors communicate?
- ◆ How effectively do the colors selected communicate the desired meanings?
- ◆ Pool the insights of all group members and recolor the products. Are these group designs superior to those developed individually? If a number of groups are working on this project at the same time, it may be interesting to compare the final group colors for each of the products.

14. Conversational Analysis: A Chance Meeting

Read the following dialogue, "A Chance Meeting." As you read it, keep the following questions in mind:

1. How would you describe the conversational styles of each of the four participants? (For the purposes of this exercise, assume that each person speaks this way all the time. Although this assumption is certainly false—no one talks the same way all the time—most people do have a style of conversation that is consistent across a wide variety of situations.)
2. Which person do you think is, in general, the most effective communicator? Why?
3. Which person do you think is, in general, the least effective communicator? Why?

Then select one of the four participants, and analyze that person's conversational style in depth:

1. Describe the person's style, especially as it relates to appropriateness for this particular communication situation.
2. Describe the rules of conversation that this person is following. What specific lines of dialogue can you point to in support of your analysis?
3. Describe the rules of conversation that you feel this person *should* follow. On what basis do you make these recommendations?
4. Would this dialogue seem more realistic if you assumed that certain characters are men and others are women? If you assumed they are all men? All women? Why?

A CHANCE MEETING

PAT: Hi!

SMITTY: Hi, Pat.

CHRIS: What's up?

SMITTY: You look horrible. What's happened to you?

PAT: Nothing.

SMITTY: Oh, good. Just the day? I have days like that, too.

LEE: You make the day you have, you know. I mean, expect the worst and you'll get it. Cheer up, Pat. Things will change, once you change yourself, of course. You know: Smile and the world smiles with you.

CHRIS: Nothing? You seem upset.

PAT: No, it's just my job. Kind of, but not exactly.

SMITTY: I wish I could forget my job, too. Now I gotta work Saturdays.

LEE: Try running an ice cream parlor. Seven days a week of pure torture.

CHRIS: You sound really disturbed, Pat. Are they cutting back? Is your job in danger?

PAT: In danger? No, it's not in danger. It's dead. I was let go three weeks ago.

SMITTY: Oh, bummer. Big bummer.

LEE: You screwed up again, didn't you?

CHRIS: And you didn't say anything? What's wrong with you? We talked three or four times since then, and you never said anything. Let's go for coffee.

PAT: No, I gotta get home.

SMITTY: Yeah, me too.

CHRIS: I know you do, Pat. But ten minutes for coffee won't hurt.

LEE: Okay. Ten minutes. Let's go.

[At coffee]

CHRIS: Now, what happened?

PAT: Nothing. I got fired. Cutbacks, same as everyone else. They let 35 of us go—all at once.

LEE: Thirty-five? Wow! Did Trainer get the ax, too?

PAT: I don't know. I think so.

LEE: Wow, I wonder what Trainer will do now.

CHRIS: What's your next step?

SMITTY: Unemployment! I've been on it more than off it.

PAT: Unfortunately, he's right. I'm on unemployment. I hate it.

SMITTY: I love it.

LEE: Yeah, that's because you try to avoid responsibilities. Pat is trying to face them, and I think that's good. If we don't face our problems, we'll never solve them.

CHRIS: Yeah, but you won't be for long. There are lots of places you could work.

SMITTY: That's not what the papers said. Everyone's cutting back.

LEE: I have the classified section right here. You can have it. It'll give you some leads.

PAT: I'd have to relocate to stay at my present job, and I really don't want to do that.

CHRIS: What do you mean?

PAT: I'm not qualified to do anything more than I'm doing. The market has changed; there's no place for my skills anymore.

LEE: Is that what happened to Tommy? No skills?

PAT: I don't know. I never hung out with Tommy.

SMITTY: That's what everybody's saying; computers can do it better. Soon they'll have robots, and we'll all be up the creek.

CHRIS: What about retraining?

PAT: Me? At 31?

SMITTY: Are you 31? I thought you were a lot older. Really? You look good.

LEE: Yeah, 31 is kind of old to start all over again.

CHRIS: Yes, you at 31. And 31 is not to old to retrain. And you might like it. You've got enough money to take a year off, retool, and get back in the game.

SMITTY: Back to school, like Rodney Dangerfield.

LEE: I'm not sure that's the answer. I think you gotta get your act together. You've got this defeatist attitude. You've got to get rid of that. You want the name of my shrink? He's great. Deals with all sorts of problems.

PAT: I don't really want to see your shrink, much as I should, I know. I guess with unemployment I can make it. Yeah, I could do it.

CHRIS: And you might even like it. You enjoyed college.

PAT: And I know exactly what I'd train for.

LEE: How can you know with such certainty? Have you looked at the predictions for the growth in different jobs?

SMITTY: Hey, how about getting out of here? I have to get home and take the kid to Little League. Talk about problems. Little League. That's a problem.

CHRIS: What would you train for?

PAT: What do you think of this idea?

15. Giving and Taking Directions

This exercise is designed to illustrate the difficulties in giving and taking directions. It will also provide practice in the much needed skills for giving and taking directions. Presented below is a diagram of Commville. Each circle with a single letter is a starting point. Double- and triple-lettered circles are destinations. A much larger number of destinations than will be used in the exercise are included so that no one will be able to memorize the locations.

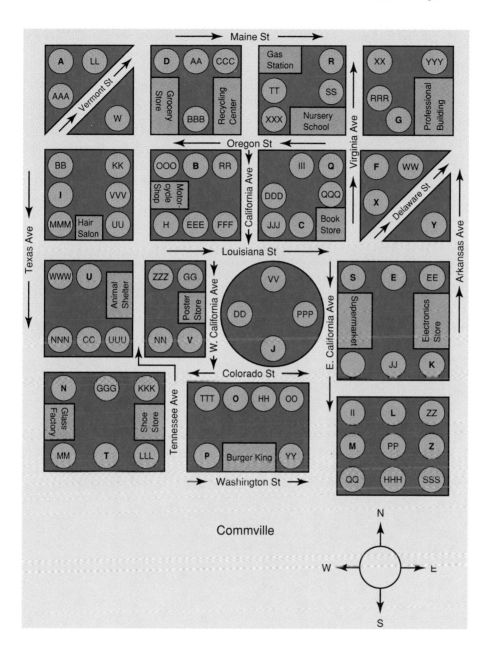

Commville

1. The diagram of Commville with all the circles but without the double and triple letters should be put on the chalkboard or projected onto a screen. (A transparency master for this purpose is provided in the *Instructor's Manual.*)
2. Two students participate in each round; one is the direction giver and the other the direction taker. The direction giver should select one of the directions provided below and tell the direction taker how to get there. At this time, only the direction giver may look at the complete diagram in the text. Assume that the direction taker is driving and so must observe the one-way signs. The direction taker may ask any questions at this point (but only at this point) but may not take any notes. After the complete direction is given,

the direction taker should follow the directions by tracing the path on the chalkboard or transparency.

3. This procedure should be continued for at least three to five rounds.
4. Discussion may focus on some or all of the following issues. These issues identify the qualities of a good direction: easy to remember, specific, and efficient.

   ◆ Were the directions easy to remember? In what ways might they have been made easier to remember?
   ◆ Were the directions specific? Did the directions specify one and only one location?
   ◆ Were the directions efficient? Did the directions enable the direction taker to get to the location with the least amount of effort, in this case, the least number of blocks traveled? Can you identify an easier way to get from the starting point to the location? Note that in some cases you may find that ease of remembering and maximum efficiency cannot both be achieved. It will then be necessary to sacrifice one of these qualities and give either a direction that is easy to remember but inefficient or a direction that is efficient but difficult to remember.

Guidelines in Giving Directions   You may find the following guidelines helpful in giving directions:

1. Use guide phrases such as "first" or "after you get to Maine Street" to help the listener follow your plan for directions.
2. Include internal summaries with complex directions: for example, "You should now be on East California Avenue in front of a supermarket."
3. Don't assume that the other person knows the area or its landmarks. "It's next to the recycling center" does not help the person who doesn't know where the recycling center is.
4. Include relevant details but, equally important, omit irrelevant details.
5. Ask the person if your directions are clear. Give the person an opportunity to ask questions or to confirm his or her understanding of your directions.

Sample Directions   Explain how to get from:

1. J to WW	11. B to EEE
2. T to YYY	12. M to LL
3. U to MMM	13. Z to ZZZ
4. G to SSS	14. D to PPP
5. C to UU	15. H to YY
6. L to OOO	16. I to SS
7. A to HHH	17. E to LLL
8. Y to CC	18. K to AAA
9. V to AA	19. N to VV
10. F to GGG	20. O to RRR

16. Analyzing Stage Talk

The table gives examples of the kinds of messages you might compose at each of the six relationship stages discussed in Unit 15. Notice that some messages ("How are you?" is a good example) may be said at several stages. Although the words are the same, the meaning they communicate differs depending on the stage. At the contact stage, "How are you?" may simply mean "Hello." At the involvement stage, it may mean "Tell me what has been going on." At the intimate stage, it may be a request for highly personal information about the person's feelings.

Although the examples here are obviously incomplete, know that research finds that as the relationship becomes more intimate, the messages communicating immediacy and affection, similarity and depth, trust, and composure also increase (Hale, Lundy, and Mongeau 1989).

Contact

Hello.	
Hi.	Surface-level messages that we use with just about everyone to acknowledge them.
How are you?	Just another way of saying hello. We really don't want to hear about Sam's last operation.
Didn't I see you here last week?	Phatic communion, an indirect attempt to make contact.
May I join you for coffee?	A direct statement expressing the desire to make contact.

Involvement

I like to cook too.	Establishing and talking about common interests.
How are you?	A request for some (mostly positive) information, but not in too great detail.
I'm having some difficulties at home; nothing really serious.	Low- to mid-level self-disclosures; nothing too serious will be discussed here.
I'd like to take you to dinner.	
I'd like to get to know you.	Direct statements expressing the desire for involvement.

Intimacy

We might go dancing.	Expression of togetherness ("we-ness").
How are you?	A request for significant information about health or feelings, especially if there's reason to believe there's been a recent change; a way of saying, "I care."
I'm really depressed.	Significant self-disclosure.
I love you.	A direct expression of intimacy.

Deterioration

I can't stand. . . .	Negative evaluations increase.
I'd like to start seeing others.	Direct statement expressing desire to reduce the present level of intimacy.
Why don't you go to Kate and Allie's by yourself?	Expression of desire to separate in the eyes of others.
You never listen to my needs. It was all your fault.	Fault-finding, criticism, and blaming.

Repair

Is this relationship worth saving?	Self-analysis; assessing the value of repair.
We need to talk; our lives are falling apart.	Opening the issue of repair.
Will you give up seeing Pat?	Negotiation; identifying what you want if the relationship is to survive.

Dissolution	
Good-bye.	The ultimate expression of dissolution.
I want to end this relationship.	A direct statement expressing the desire to dissolve the relationship formally.
I tried but I guess it wasn't enough.	Attempt to gain "social credit," approval from others.

Learning to Hear Stage Talk   Learning to hear stage-talk messages—messages that express a desire to move the relationship in a particular way or to stabilize the relationship at a particular stage—will help you understand and manage your own interpersonal relationships. Over the next few days listen carefully to all stage-talk messages. Listen to those messages referring to your own relationships as well as those messages that friends or acquaintances disclose to you about their relationships. Collect these messages and classify them into the following categories.

1. **Contact messages** express a desire for contact: *Hi, my name is Joe.*
2. **Closeness messages** express a desire to increased closeness, involvement, or intimacy: *I'd like to see you more often.*
3. **Stabilizing messages** express a desire to stabilize the relationship at one stage: *Let's keep it like this for a while. I'm afraid to get more involved at this point in my life.*
4. **Distancing messages** express a desire to distance oneself from a relationship. *I think we should spend a few weeks apart.*
5. **Repair messages** express a desire to repair the relationship: *Couldn't we discuss this and work it out? I didn't mean to be so dogmatic.*
6. **Dissolution messages** express a desire to break up or dissolve the existing relationship: *Look, it's just not working out as we planned; let's each go our own way.*

Share these collected messages with others in small groups or with the class as a whole. Consider, for example:

- What types of messages are used to indicate the six different desires noted above?
- Do people give reasons for their desire to move from one stage to another or to stabilize their relationship? If so, what types of reasons do they give?
- Do men and women talk about relationship stages in the same way? In different ways?

17. Interpersonal Relationships in Songs and Greeting Cards

The objectives of this exercise are (1) to become familiar with some of the popular sentiments concerning interpersonal relationships as they are expressed in songs and greeting cards and (2) to provide a stimulus for considering significant concepts and theories in interpersonal relationships.

Bring to class a recording of one song or a greeting card that expresses a sentiment that is significant to the study of interpersonal relationships for any one of the following reasons:

- It expresses a sentiment that can assist us in understanding interpersonal relationships.
- It illustrates a concept or theory that is important in the study of interpersonal relationships.
- It suggests a useful question concerning interpersonal relationships.
- It illustrates a popular relational problem or difficulty.
- It illustrates a method for dealing with some kind of relationship problem or difficulty.

Explain the relevance of the song or greeting card to the study of interpersonal relationships. What one principle of interpersonal communication does this song or card best express?

18. Mate Preferences: I Prefer Someone Who . . .

This exercise is designed to stimulate a sharing of perspectives on what we want in a mate. Each of the choices here concerns issues considered throughout this text. In a gamelike setting, the importance of money, similarity, self-disclosure, and conflict strategies to relational desirability is explored.

"I Prefer Someone Who . . ." is played in a group of five to seven people. The general procedure is as follows. Each member individually ranks each of the three alternatives in the 15 groupings listed, using 1 for the most preferred and 3 for the least preferred choice. Then the group considers each of the 15 categories, with each member giving her or his rank order. As always, members may refuse to reveal their rankings for any category by saying "I pass." The group is not permitted to question the reasons for any member's passing. When a member has revealed rankings for a category, the group members may ask questions relevant to that category. These questions may be asked after any individual member's response or may be reserved until all members have given their rankings for a particular category.

I prefer someone who . . .
1. ___ is similar to me in race, religion, and nationality.
   ___ is similar to me in attitudes, values, and opinions.
   ___ is similar to me in personality.
2. ___ reduces my loneliness.
   ___ enhances my self-esteem.
   ___ increases my self-knowledge and self-growth.
3. ___ is deceptive.
   ___ is jealous.
   ___ is boring.
4. ___ reveals his or her innermost secrets to me.
   ___ reveals some secrets but keeps an equal number hidden from me.
   ___ reveals hardly anything about his or her innermost secrets.

5. ___ keeps confidences.
    ___ has a sense of humor.
    ___ is intelligent.
6. ___ thinks money is most important.
    ___ thinks friendship is most important.
    ___ thinks job satisfaction is most important.
7. ___ talks more than listens.
    ___ talks and listens about equally.
    ___ listens more than talks.
8. ___ dresses at the cutting edge of fashion.
    ___ dresses conventionally.
    ___ dresses very conservatively.
9. ___ is empathic.
    ___ is supportive.
    ___ is confident.
10. ___ wants to make most of the major decisions.
    ___ wants to share equally in making the major decisions.
    ___ wants me to make most of the major decisions.
11. ___ is unattractive.
    ___ is unemotional.
    ___ is uncommunicative.
12. ___ stands up for me in my absence.
    ___ trusts me.
    ___ tries to make me happy when I'm sad.
13. ___ views love as a game, as fun; focuses on entertainment and excitement.
    ___ views love as peaceful and slow; focuses on friendship and companionship.
    ___ views love as physical and erotic; focuses on beauty and sexuality.
14. ___ has great sex appeal.
    ___ has great intellectual appeal.
    ___ has lots of money.
15. ___ is like a tiger.
    ___ is like a puppy dog.
    ___ is like a farm horse.

Thinking Critically About Mate Preferences

In discussing the choices of the group members, consider some or all of the following issues:

1. What are the reasons for the choices? Where did these reasons come from? Were they acquired from parents, an older sibling, a teacher? How has your culture influenced your choices? What has your culture taught you about the "ideal" partner? Be sure to consider the reasons for the least preferred choices as well as the most preferred. Both are revealing.
2. Do men and women make similar choices? Explain.
3. Does an ideal man or an ideal woman emerge from the composite rankings? Does a least preferred man or a least preferred woman emerge? If so, describe these types as specifically as possible.

4. If the title of this exercise were "I am someone who . . . ", how similarly or differently would you respond to these choices? How close to yourself is your ideal mate?

19. Male and Female

This exercise is designed to increase your awareness of matters that may prevent meaningful interpersonal communication between the sexes. It will also encourage dialogue among class members.

The women and the men are separated, and one group goes into another classroom. The task of each group is to write on the chalkboard all the things that members of the opposite sex think, believe, say, or do in reference to them that they dislike and that prevent meaningful interpersonal communication from taking place.

After this is done, the groups should change rooms. The men discuss what the women wrote, and the women discuss what the men wrote. After satisfactory discussion has taken place, the groups should get together in the original room.

Thinking Critically About Male-female Differences and Similarities

Discussion might center on such questions as the following:

1. Were there any surprises?
2. Were there any disagreements? That is, did the members of one sex write anything that the members of the other sex argued they do not believe, think, do, or say?
3. How do you suppose the ideas about the other sex got started?
4. Is there any reliable evidence in support of the men's beliefs about the women or the women's about the men?
5. In what specific ways do these beliefs, thoughts, actions, and statements prevent meaningful interpersonal communication?

20. Relationship Repair from Advice Columnists

Select a specific relationship-oriented question and answer from an advice column in a newspaper or magazine. Bring this column to class and discuss it, covering such issues as these:

1. Is the advice generally good? Bad? Is there any evidence to support the usefulness or validity of the answer given?
2. What relationship rule is the advice columnist using in answering this question?
3. To what other situations might this relationship rule apply? That is, what other applications might you find for this specific rule?
4. What are the limitations of this rule? That is, are there situations where this rule should not be used?

5. Can you identify any difficulties in applying the advice offered by the columnist? What additional advice would you like to see accompany the columnist's answer?

21. Power Plays

Here are some examples of power plays. Try identifying the power play and providing an appropriate three-part management strategy as identified here. Recall that the three-part cooperative management strategy consists of the following:

- Expression of your feelings. Tell the person how you feel and why you feel as you do.
- Description of the behavior to which you object. Tell the person what you object to in specific terms.
- Statement of a cooperative response you and the other person would be comfortable with. Tell the other person what you want him or her to do differently.

1. Fred continually interrupts you. Whenever you want to say something, Fred breaks in, finishes what he thinks you were saying, and then says what he wants to say.
2. One of your coworkers responds to your ideas, plans, and suggestions with statements like "yougottobekidding," "you can't mean that," and "you can't possibly be serious." So when you say you are going to date Harry, she says, "You can't be serious! Harry!" When you say you are going to apply for a promotion, she says, "Promotion! You got to be kidding! You've only been with the company six months."
3. Your close friend has helped you get a job in his company. Now, whenever he wants you to do something, he reminds you that he got you the job. Whenever you object that you have your own work to do, he reminds you that you wouldn't have any work to do if it wasn't for his getting you the job in the first place.
4. Your supervisor is compulsive about neatness and frequently goes around telling the workers to clean up their areas. This supervisor often uses the power play metaphor: "Clean up this crap before you leave tonight" or "Make sure this junk is put away."
5. Your friend Amida sits next to you in class but rarely listens to the instructor. Instead, she waits until you copy something down in your notes, and then she copies what you have written. In doing this, she frequently distracts you, and you miss a great deal of what the instructor has said. You have told her repeatedly that you object to this, but she acts as though she doesn't hear you.

22. Analyzing a Conflict Episode

Here is a brief dialogue written to illustrate the unproductive conflict strategies discussed in the text (avoidance, force, blame, silencers, gunnysacking, fighting below the belt, face-detracting, verbal aggressiveness, and verbal abuse) as well as the failure to use their more productive counterparts (active fighting, talk, empathy, open expression, present focus, fighting above the belt, face-enhancing, and argumentativeness).

Identify the conflict strategies used by Pat and Chris so you can see the strategies as they operate in an interactional context. You may also find it profitable to write a continuation of the dialogue. Assume, for example, that Pat and Chris meet a few weeks later and wish to patch things up. How might the dialogue go if they used the principles of effective interpersonal communication and conflict management?

PAT: It's me. Just came in to get my papers for the meeting tonight.

CHRIS: You're not going to another meeting, are you?

PAT: I told you last month that I had to give a lecture to the new managers on how to use some new research methods. What do you think I've been working on for the past two weeks? If you cared about what I do, you'd know that I was working on this lecture and that it was especially important that it go well.

CHRIS: What about shopping? We always do the shopping on Friday night.

PAT: The shopping will have to wait; this lecture is important.

CHRIS: Shopping is important, too, and so are the children and so is my job and so is the leak in the basement that's been driving me crazy for the past week and that I've asked you to look at every day since I found it.

PAT: Get off it. We can do the shopping anytime. Your job is fine and the children are fine and we'll get a plumber just as soon as I get the name from the Johnsons.

CHRIS: You always do that. You always think only you count, only you matter. Even when we were in school, your classes were the important ones, your papers, your tests were the important ones. Remember when I had that chemistry final and you had to have your history paper typed? We stayed up all night typing *your* paper. I failed chemistry, remember? That's not so good when you're pre-med! I suppose I should thank you for my not being a doctor? But you got your A in history. It's always been that way. You never give a damn about what's important in my life.

PAT: I really don't want to talk about it. I'll only get upset and bomb out with the lecture. Forget it. I don't want to hear any more about it. So just shut up before I do something I should do more often.

CHRIS: You hit me and I'll call the cops. I'm not putting up with another black eye or another fat lip—never, never again.

PAT: Well, then, just shut up. I just don't want to talk about it anymore. Forget it. I have to give the lecture and that's that.

CHRIS: The children were looking forward to going shopping. Johnny wanted to get a new record, and Jennifer needed to get a book for school. You promised them.

PAT: I didn't promise anyone anything. You promised them, and now you want me to take the blame. You know, you promise too much. You should only promise what you can deliver—like fidelity. Remember you promised to be faithful? Or did you forget that promise? Why don't you tell the kids that? Or do they already know? Were they here when you had your sordid affair? Did they see their loving parent loving some stranger?

CHRIS: I thought we agreed not to talk about that. You know how bad I feel about what happened. And anyway, that was six months ago. What has that to do with tonight?

PAT: You're the one who brought up promises, not me. You're always bringing up the past. You live in the past.

CHRIS: Well, at least the kids would have seen me enjoying myself—one enjoyable experience in eight years isn't too much, is it?

PAT: I'm leaving. Don't wait up.

23. Friendship Behaviors

For each of the following three situations indicate (1) how you, as a friend, would respond, by writing the word "would" in the appropriate space; (2) how you think a good friend should respond, by writing "should" in the appropriate space; and (3) the qualities or characteristics you feel a good friend should have relevant to the situation, by completing the sentence "because a good friend should. . . ."
After completing your responses for all three situations, answer the questions presented at the end of this exercise—alone, in dyads, or in small groups of five, six, or seven persons.

Friendship and Money Your closest friend has just gotten into serious debt through some misjudgment. You have saved $5000 over the past few years and plan to buy a car upon being graduated from college. Your friend asks to borrow the money, which could not be repaid for at least four or possibly five years. Although you do not need the car for work or for any other necessity, you have been looking forward to the day when you could get one. You've worked hard for it and feel you deserve the car, but you are also concerned about the plight of your friend, who would be in serious trouble without the $5000 loan. You wonder what you should do.

_____ Lend your friend the money.

_____ Tell your friend that you have been planning to buy the car for the last few years and that you cannot lend him or her the money.

_____ Give your friend the money and tell your friend that there is no need to pay it back; after all, your friend already has enough problems without having to worry about paying money back.

_____ Tell your friend that you already gave the $5000 to your brother but that you would certainly have lent him or her the money if you still had it.

_____ (Other—you suggest an alternative.)

because a good friend should _____

Friendship and Advice Two friends, Pat and Chris, have been dating for the past several months. They will soon enter into a more permanent relationship after graduation from college. Pat is now having second thoughts and is currently having an affair with another friend, Lee. Chris tells you that there is probably an affair going on (which you know to be true) and seeks your advice. You are the only one who is friendly with all three parties. You wonder what you should do.

_____ Tell Chris everything you know.

_____ Tell Pat to be honest with Chris.

_____ Say nothing; don't get involved.

_____ Suggest to Chris that the more permanent relationship plan should be reconsidered, but don't be specific.

_____ (Other—you suggest an alternative.)

because a good friend should _____

Friendship and Cheating   Your anthropology instructor is giving a midterm and is grading it on a curve. Your close friend somehow manages to secure a copy of the examination a few days before it is scheduled to be given. Because you are a close friend, the examination is offered to you as well. You refuse to look at it.

The examination turns out to be even more difficult than you had anticipated, the highest grade being a 68 (except for your friend's, which was a 96). According to the system of curving used by this instructor, each grade will be raised by 4 points. But this means that the highest grade (aside from your friend's) will be only a 72, or a C−. A few students will receive C−, about 30 percent to 40 percent will receive D, and the rest (more than 50 percent) will receive F. Although only you and your friend know what happened, you know that the instructor and the entire class are wondering why this one student, never particularly outstanding, did so well. After curving, your grade is 70 (C−). You wonder what you should do.

_____ Tell your friend to confess or you will tell the instructor yourself.

_____ Tell the instructor what happened.

_____ Say nothing; don't get involved.

_____ (Other—you suggest an alternative.)

because a good friend should _____

Thinking Critically About Friendship

After you have marked your choices, consider such questions as these:

1. Were there significant differences between the "would" and the "should" responses? How do you account for these differences?
2. What values, standards, or models did you use in making the "should" responses? Why did you choose them?
3. With which situation did you experience the greatest difficulty deciding what you would do? Can you explain why?
4. Does friendship necessarily entail the willingness to make sacrifices?
5. How would you define "friend"?

24. The Television Relationship

This exercise can be used to focus on any interpersonal concept, for example, conflict, power, relationship development, communication effectiveness, assertiveness, or any number of other topics considered throughout this text. The class should be separated into several small groups. The groups may each watch a different sitcom or drama or soap opera or may watch the same program but focus on different concepts.

One procedure is to have each group select a topic (say, conflict). The group should meet briefly to work up a list of questions or "viewing guides" to help focus their attention and to make sure that the concept is covered fully. Each member should then watch and analyze a television program for the way in which it portrays and deals with the concept. To illustrate the type of questions that might prove helpful, here are some on the concept of conflict:

- How is conflict illustrated in this television relationship?
- What principles about conflict can you derive solely on the basis of this television relationship? How would you use this television episode to illustrate one or more principles of conflict?
- Does this television relationship illustrate the differences between productive and unproductive conflict management skills? Can you cite specific examples?
- Does this television episode try to teach a lesson or moral? Did the episode persuade or influence you in any way? For example, did it strengthen a belief you already had?
- Does the treatment of conflict in this episode reflect cultural values and beliefs?

Glossary of Interpersonal Communication Concepts and Skills

Listed here are definitions of the technical terms of interpersonal communication—the words that are peculiar or unique to this discipline—and, where appropriate, the corresponding skills. These definitions and statements of skills should make new or difficult terms a bit easier to understand and should help to place the skill in context. The statements of skills appear in italics. All boldface terms within the definitions appear as separate entries in the glossary.

acculturation. The process by which a person's culture is modified or changed through contact with or exposure to another culture.

active listening. A process of putting together into some meaningful whole the listener's understanding of the speaker's total message—the verbal and the nonverbal, the content and the feelings. *Listen actively by paraphrasing the speaker's meanings, expressing an understanding of the speaker's feelings, and asking questions to enable you to check the accuracy of your understanding of the speaker. Express acceptance of the speaker's feelings, and encourage the speaker to explore further his or her feelings and thoughts and thereby increase meaningful sharing.*

active listening and self-disclosure. *In responding to the disclosures of others, listen actively: Paraphrase the speaker's thoughts and feelings, express understanding of the speaker's feelings, and ask relevant questions to ensure understanding and to signal attention and interest.*

adaptors. Nonverbal behaviors that, when engaged in either in private or in public without being seen, serve some kind of need and occur in their entirety—for example, scratching one's head until the itch is relieved. *Adaptor interference: Avoid adaptors that interfere with effective communication and reveal your discomfort or anxiety.*

adjustment (principle of). The principle of verbal interaction that claims that communication may take place only to the extent that the parties communicating share the same system of signals. *Expand the common areas between you and significant others; learn each other's system of com-*munication signals and meanings in order to increase understanding and interpersonal communication effectiveness.

aesthetics. The appeal, tastefulness, or beauty of an object or situation. *Make the physical context of communication as aesthetically pleasing as possible in order to make interpersonal interactions more effective and satisfying.*

affect displays. Movements of the facial area that convey emotional meaning—for example, anger, fear, and surprise.

affinity-seeking strategies. Behaviors designed to increase our interpersonal attractiveness. *Use the various affinity-seeking strategies (for example, listening, openness, and dynamism), as appropriate to the interpersonal relationship and the situation, to increase your own interpersonal attractiveness.*

affirmation. The communication of support and approval. *Use affirmation to express your supportiveness and to raise esteem.*

allness. The assumption that all can be known or is known about a given person, issue, object, or event. *End statements with an implicit "etc." ("et cetera") to indicate that more could be known and said; avoid allness terms and statements.*

alter-adaptors. Body movements you make in response to your current interactions, for example, crossing your arms over your chest when someone unpleasant approaches or moving closer to someone you like.

altercasting. Placing the listener in a specific role for a specific purpose and asking that the listener approach the question or problem from the perspective of this specific role.

ambiguity. The condition in which a message may be interpreted as having more than one meaning.

apprehension. See **communication apprehension**.

arbitrariness. The feature of human language that reflects the absence of a real or inherent relationship between the form of a word and its meaning. If we do not know anything of a particular language, we cannot examine the form of a word and thereby discover its meaning.

argot. A kind of sublanguage; **cant** and **jargon** of a particular class, generally an underworld or a criminal class, which is difficult and sometimes impossible for outsiders to understand.

argumentativeness. A willingness to argue for a point of view, to speak one's mind. *Cultivate your argumentativeness, your willingness to argue for what you believe, by, for example, treating disagreements as objectively as possible,* *reaffirming the other, stressing equality, expressing interest in the other's position, and allowing the other person to save face.* Distinguished from **verbal aggressiveness.**

arrangement of physical setting. *Arrange the physical setting of communication to stimulate effective and satisfying interactions; avoid creating spaces that make communication difficult and tedious (for example, seats that are too far apart or awkwardly aligned); arrange seating positions that are most conducive to the task at hand.*

assertiveness. A willingness to stand up for one's rights but with respect for the rights of others. *Increase assertiveness (if desired) by analyzing the assertive and nonassertive behaviors of others, analyzing your own behaviors in terms of assertiveness, recording your behaviors, rehearsing assertive behaviors, and acting assertively in appropriate situations. Secure feedback from others for further guidance in increasing assertiveness.*

assimilation. A process of message distortion in which messages are reworked to conform to our own attitudes, prejudices, needs, and values.

attention. The process of responding to a stimulus or stimuli; usually some consciousness of responding is implied.

attitude. A predisposition to respond for or against an object, person, or position.

attitudinal similarity. *Identify those attitudes for which you feel similarity is important and those for which it is unimportant.*

attraction. The state or process by which one individual is drawn to another, by having a highly positive evaluation of that other person.

attractiveness. The degree to which one is perceived to be physically attractive and to possess a pleasing personality.

attribution theory. A theory concerned with the processes involved in attributing causation or motivation to a person's behavior. *In attempting to identify the motivation for behaviors, examine consensus, consistency, distinctiveness, and controllability. Generally, low consensus, high consistency, low distinctiveness, and high controllability identify internally motivated behavior; high consensus, low consistency, high distinctiveness, and low controllability identify externally motivated behavior.*

avoidance. An unproductive **conflict** strategy in which a person takes mental or physical flight from the actual conflict.

backchanneling cues. Listener responses to a speaker which do not ask for the speaking role. *Respond to backchanneling cues as appropriate to the conversation. Use back-channeling cues to let the speaker know you are listening.*

barriers to intercultural communication. Those factors (physical or psychological) that prevent or hinder effective communication. *Avoid the major barriers to intercultural communication: ignoring differences between yourself and the culturally different, ignoring differences among the culturally different, ignoring differences in meaning, violating cultural rules and customs, and evaluating differences negatively.*

behavioral synchrony. The similarity in the behavior, usually nonverbal, of two persons. Generally, it is taken as an index of mutual liking.

belief. Confidence in the existence or truth of something; conviction. *Weigh both verbal and nonverbal messages before making believability judgments; increase your own sensitivity to nonverbal (and verbal) deception cues—for example, too little movement, long pauses, slow speech, increased speech errors, mouth guard, nose touching, eye rubbing, or the use of few words, especially monosyllabic answers. Use such cues to formulate hypotheses rather than conclusions concerning deception.*

beltlining. An unproductive **conflict** strategy in which one hits at the level at which the other person cannot withstand the blow. *Avoid beltlining.*

blame. An unproductive **conflict** strategy in which we attribute the cause of the conflict to the other person or devote our energies to discovering who is the cause and avoid talking about the issues causing the conflict. *Avoid using blame to win an argument, especially with those with whom you are in close relationships.*

boundary marker. A marker that sets boundaries that divide one person's territory from another's—for example, a fence.

breadth. The number of topics about which individuals in a relationship communicate.

cant. The conversational language of a special group (usually, a lower-social-class group), generally understood only by members of that group.

censorship. Legal restriction imposed on one's right to produce, distribute, or receive various communications.

central marker. A marker or item that is placed in a territory to reserve it for a specific person—for example, the sweater thrown over a library chair to signal that the chair is taken.

certainty. An attitude of closed-mindedness that creates a defensiveness among communication participants; opposed to **provisionalism.**

channel. The vehicle or medium through which signals are sent.

cherishing behaviors. Small behaviors we enjoy receiving from others, especially from our relational partner—for example, a kiss before leaving for work.

chronemics. The study of the communicative nature of time—the way you treat time and use it to communicate. Two general areas of chronemics are **cultural** and **psychological time.**

civil inattention. Polite ignoring of others so as not to invade their privacy.

cliché. An expression whose overuse calls attention to itself; "tall, dark, and handsome" as a description of a man would be considered a cliché.

closed-mindedness. An unwillingness to receive certain communication messages.

code. A set of symbols used to translate a message from one form to another.

collectivist culture. A culture in which the group's goals rather than the individual's are given greater importance and where, for example, benevolence, tradition, and conformity are given special emphasis. Opposed to **individualistic culture.**

color communication. *Use colors (in clothing and in room decor, for example) to convey desired meanings.*

communication. (1) The process or act of communicating; (2) the actual message or messages sent and received; (3) the study of the processes involved in the sending and receiving of messages. (The term **communicology** is suggested for the third definition.)

communication adjustment. *Adjust your communications as appropriate to the stage of your interpersonal relationship.*

communication apprehension. Fear or anxiety over communicating; "trait apprehension" refers to fear of communication generally, regardless of the specific situation; "state apprehension" refers to fear that is specific to a given communication situation. **apprehension causes.** *Identify the causes of your own apprehension, considering, for example, lack of communication skills and experience, fear of evaluation, conspicuousness, unpredictability of the situation (ambiguity, newness), and your history of prior successes or failures in similar and related situations.* **apprehension management.** *Manage your own communication apprehension by acquiring the necessary communication skills and experience, preparing and practicing for relevant communication situations, focusing on success, familiarizing yourself with the communication situations important to you, using physical activity and deep breathing to relax, and putting communication apprehension in perspective. In cases of extreme communication apprehension, seek professional help.*

communicology. The study of communication, particularly the subsection concerned with human communication.

competence. "Language competence" is a speaker's ability to use the language; it is a knowledge of the elements and rules of the language. "Communication competence" refers to the rules of the social or interpersonal dimensions of communication and is often used to denote the qualities that make for effectiveness in interpersonal communication.

complementarity. A principle of **attraction** holding that one is attracted by qualities one does not possess or one wishes to possess and to people who are opposite or different from oneself; opposed to **similarity.** *Identify the characteristics that you do not find in yourself but admire in others and that therefore might be important in influencing your perception of complementarity.*

complementary relationship. A relationship in which the behavior of one person serves as the stimulus for the complementary behavior of the other; in complementary relationships, behavioral differences are maximized.

compliance-gaining strategies. Behaviors that are directed toward gaining the agreement of others; behaviors designed to persuade others to do as we wish. *Use the various compliance-gaining strategies to increase your own persuasive power.*

compliance-resisting strategies. Behaviors directed at resisting the persuasive attempts of others. *Use such strategies as identity management, nonnegotiation, negotiation, and justification as appropriate in resisting compliance.*

confidence. A quality of interpersonal effectiveness; a comfortable, at-ease feeling in interpersonal communication situations. *Communicate a feeling of being comfortable and at ease with the interaction through appropriate verbal and nonverbal signals.*

confidentiality. *Keep the disclosures of others confidential.*

confirmation. A communication pattern that acknowledges another person's presence and also indicates an acceptance of this person, this person's definition of self, and the relationship as defined or viewed by this other person; opposed to **disconfirmation.** *Avoid those verbal and nonverbal behaviors that disconfirm another person. Substitute confirming behaviors, behaviors that acknowledge the presence and the contributions of the other person.*

conflict. An extreme form of competition in which a person attempts to bring a rival to surrender; a situation in which one person's behaviors are directed at preventing something or at interfering with or harming another individual. *See also* **interpersonal conflict.**

congruence. A condition in which both verbal and nonverbal behaviors reinforce each other.

connotation. The feeling or emotional aspect of meaning, generally viewed as consisting of the evaluative (for example, good-bad), potency (strong-weak), and activity (fast-slow) dimensions; the associations of a term. *See also* **denotation.**

consistency. A perceptual process that influences us to maintain balance among our perceptions; a process that makes us tend to see what we expect to see and to be uncomfortable when our perceptions run contrary to our expectations. *Recognize the human tendency to seek and to see consistency even where it does not exist—to see our friends as all positive and our enemies as all negative, for example.*

content and relationship dimensions. A principle of communication that messages refer both to content (the world external to both speaker and listener) and to the relationship existing between the individuals who are interacting.

context of communication. The physical, psychological, social, and temporal environment in which communication takes place. *Assess the context in which messages are communicated and interpret that communication behavior accordingly; avoid seeing messages as independent of context.*

conversation. Two-person communication usually possessing an opening, feedforward, a business stage, feedback, and a closing.

conversational maxims. Principles that are followed in conversation to ensure that the goal of the conversation is achieved. *Discover, try not to violate, and, if appropriate, follow the conversational maxims of the culture in which you are communicating.*

conversational turns. The process of passing the speaker and listener roles during conversation. *Become sensitive to and respond appropriately to conversational turn cues, such as turn-maintaining, turn-yielding, turn-requesting, and turn-denying cues.*

cooperation. An interpersonal process by which individuals work together for a common end; the pooling of efforts to produce a mutually desired outcome.

cooperation principle. An implicit agreement between speaker and listener to cooperate in trying to understand what each is communicating.

conversational management. Respond to conversational turn cues from the other person, and use conversational cues to signal your own desire to exchange (or maintain) speaker or listener roles.

conversational processes. Use the general five-step process in conversation, and avoid the several barriers that can be created when the normal process is distorted.

credibility. The degree to which a receiver perceives the speaker to be believable; competence, character, and charisma (dynamism) are its major dimensions.

critical thinking. The process of logically evaluating reasons and evidence and reaching a judgment on the basis of this analysis.

cultural display. Signs that communicate one's cultural identification, for example, clothing or religious jewelry.

cultural rules. Rules that are specific to a given culture. *Respond to messages according to the cultural rules of the sender; avoid interpreting the messages of others exclusively through the perspective of your own culture in order to prevent misinterpretation of the intended meanings.*

cultural time. The meanings given to time communication by a particular culture.

date. An extensional device used to emphasize the notion of constant change and symbolized by a subscript: for example, John Smith$_{1988}$ is not John Smith$_{1998}$.

decoder. Something that takes a message in one form (for example, sound waves) and translates it into another code (for example, nerve impulses) from which meaning can be formulated. In human communication, the decoder is the auditory mechanism; in electronic communication, the decoder is, for example, the telephone ear piece. *See* **Encoder.**

decoding. The process of extracting a message from a code—for example, translating speech sounds into nerve impulses. *See* **Encoding.**

defensiveness. An attitude of an individual or an atmosphere in a group characterized by threats, fear, and domination; messages evidencing evaluation, control, strategy, neutrality, superiority, and certainty are assumed to lead to defensiveness; opposed to **supportiveness.**

delayed reactions. Reactions that are consciously delayed while a situation is analyzed.

denial. One of the obstacles to the expression of emotion; the process by which we deny our emotions to ourselves or to others.

denotation. Referential meaning; the objective or descriptive meaning of a word. See also **connotation.**

depenetration. A reversal of penetration; a condition in which the **breadth** and **depth** of a relationship decrease.

depth. The degree to which the inner personality—the inner core of an individual—is penetrated in interpersonal interaction.

determinism (principle of). The principle of verbal interaction that holds that all verbalizations are to some extent purposeful, that there is a reason for every verbalization.

dialogic conversation. *Treat conversation as a dialogue rather than a monologue; show concern for the other person, and for the relationship between you, with other-orientation.*

dialogue. A form of **communication** in which each person is both speaker and listener; communication characterized by involvement, concern, and respect for the other person; opposed to **monologue.**

direct speech. Speech in which the speaker's intentions are stated clearly and directly. *Use direct requests and responses (1) to encourage compromise, (2) to acknowledge responsibility for your own feelings and desires, and (3) to state your own desires honestly so as to encourage honesty, openness, and supportiveness in others.*

disclaimer. Statement that asks the listener to receive what the speaker says as intended without its reflecting negatively on the image of the speaker. *Avoid using disclaimers that may not be accepted by your listeners (they may raise the very doubts you wish to put to rest), but do use disclaimers when you think your future messages might offend your listeners.*

disclosure responses. Feedback given by the listener in response to the disclosure of another. *In responding to the disclosures of others, demonstrate the skills of effective listening, express support for the discloser (but resist evaluation), reinforce the disclosing behavior, keep the disclosures confidential, and avoid using the disclosures against the person.*

disconfirmation. The process by which one ignores or denies the right of the individual even to define himself or herself; opposed to **confirmation.**

discriminating. Being sensitive to differences *among* individuals prevents discrimination against individuals.

dyadic coalition. A two-person group formed from some larger group to achieve a particular goal.

dyadic communication. Two-person communication.

dyadic consciousness. An awareness of an interpersonal relationship or pairing of two individuals; distinguished from situations in which two individuals are together but do not perceive themselves as being a unit or twosome.

dyadic effect. The tendency for the behaviors of one person to stimulate behaviors in the other interactant; usually used to refer to the tendency of one person's self-disclosures to prompt the other to self-disclose, also. *Be responsive to the dyadic effect; if it is not operating, consider why.*

dyadic primacy. The significance or centrality of the two-person group, even when there are many more people interacting.

ear marker. A marker that identifies an item as belonging to a specific person—for example, a nameplate on a desk or initials on an attaché case.

effect. The outcome or consequence of an action or behavior; communication is assumed always to have some effect.

effectiveness characteristics. *Use the characteristics of interpersonal effectiveness as general guidelines, and modify them as the different cultural orientations warrant.*

emotional expression. *Before expressing your emotions, understand them, decide whether you wish to express them, and assess your communication options. In expressing your emotions, describe your feelings as accurately as possible, identify the reasons for them, anchor your feelings and their expression to the present time, and own your feelings.*

emblems. Nonverbal behaviors that directly translate words or phrases—for example, the signs for "OK" and "peace."

emotion. The feelings we have—for example, our feelings of guilt, anger, or sorrow.

empathy. The feeling of another person's feeling; feeling or perceiving something as does another person. *empathic understanding. Increase empathic understanding for your primary partner by sharing experiences, role-playing, and seeing the world from his or her perspective. Empathize with others, and express this empathic understanding verbally and nonverbally.*

encoder. Something that takes a message in one form (for example, nerve impulses) and translates it into another form (for example, sound waves). In human communication the encoder is the speaking mechanism; in electronic communication the encoder is, for example, the telephone mouthpiece. *See* **Decoder.**

encoding. The process of putting a message into a code—for example, translating nerve impulses into speech sounds. *See* **Decoding.**

enculturation. The process by which culture is transmitted from one generation to another.

E-prime. A form of the language that omits the verb "to be" except when used as an auxiliary or in statements of existence. Designed to eliminate the tendency toward **projection.**

equality. An attitude that recognizes that each individual in a communication interaction is equal, that no one is superior to any other; encourages supportiveness; opposed to **superiority.** *Talk neither down nor up to others but communicate as an equal to increase interpersonal satisfaction and efficiency; share the speaking and the listening; recognize that all parties in communication have something to contribute.*

equilibrium theory. A theory of proxemics holding that intimacy and physical closeness are positively related; as relationship becomes more intimate, the individuals will use shorter distances between them.

equity theory. A theory claiming that we experience relational satisfaction when there is an equal distribution of rewards and costs between the two persons in the relationship.

etc. A safety device to remind you that not everything is known, not everything has been said. *Use it as a mental reminder that there is more to learn, more that could be said.*

ethics. The branch of philosophy that deals with the rightness or wrongness of actions; the study of moral values.

ethnocentrism. The tendency to see others and their behaviors through our own cultural filters, often as distortions of our own behaviors; the tendency to evaluate the values and beliefs of one's own culture more positively than those of another culture.

euphemism. A polite word or phrase used to substitute for some taboo or otherwise offensive term.

evaluation. A process whereby a value is placed on some person, object, or event. *Avoid premature evaluation; amass evidence before making evaluations, especially of other people.*

excuse. An explanation designed to lessen the negative consequences of something done or said. **Avoid excessive excuse making. Too many excuses may backfire and create image problems for the excuse maker.**

expectancy violations theory. A theory of proxemics holding that people have a certain expectancy for space relationships. When that is violated (say, a person stands too close to you or a romantic partner maintains abnormally large distances from you), the relationship comes into clearer focus and you wonder why this "normal distance" is being violated.

expectations. *Define and discuss the expectations each relationship partner has of the other, the nature of sexual satisfaction as each sees it, and the role and function of work and money in the relationship as a way of preventing unrealistic and unfulfilled expectations from creating conflicts.*

experiential limitation. The limit of an individual's ability to communicate, as set by the nature and extent of that individual's experiences.

expressiveness. A quality of interpersonal effectiveness; genuine involvement in speaking and listening, conveyed verbally and nonverbally. *Communicate involvement and interest in the interaction by providing appropriate feedback, by assuming responsibility for your thoughts and feelings and your role as speaker and listener, and by appropriate expressiveness, variety, and flexibility in voice and bodily action.*

extensional devices. Linguistic devices proposed by Alfred Korzybski to keep language a more accurate means for talking about the world. The extensional devices include **etc.**, **date**, and **index** (the working devices) and the **hyphen** and **quotes** (the safety devices).

extensional orientation. A point of view in which the primary consideration is given to the world of experience and only secondary consideration is given to labels. *See also* **intensional orientation.**

eye gaze. *Use eye contact effectively to monitor feedback, to signal conversational turns, to signal the nature of a relationship, and to compensate for physical distance.*

facial feedback hypothesis. The hypothesis or theory that your facial expressions can produce physiological and emotional effects.

facial management techniques. Techniques used to mask certain emotions and to emphasize others, for example, intensifying your expression of happiness to make a friend feel good about a promotion.

fact-inference confusion. A misevaluation in which one makes an inference, regards it as a fact, and acts upon it as if it were a fact. *Distinguish facts from inferences; respond to inferences as inferences and not as facts.*

factual statement. A statement made by the observer after observation and limited to what is observed. *See also* **inferential statement.**

family. A group of people who consider themselves related and connected to one another and where the actions of one have consequences for others.

fear appeal. The appeal to fear to persuade an individual or group of individuals to believe or to act in a certain way.

feedback. Information that is given back to the source. Feedback may come from the source's own messages (as when we hear what we are saying) or from the receiver(s) in the form of applause, yawning, puzzled looks, questions, letters to the editor of a newspaper, increased or decreased subscriptions to a magazine, and so forth. *See also* **negative feedback, positive feedback.** *Give clear feedback to others, and respond to others' feedback, either through corrective measures or by continuing current performance, to increase communication efficiency and satisfaction.*

feedforward. Information that is sent prior to the regular messages telling the listener something about what is to follow. *Feedforward appropriately. When appropriate, preface your messages in order to open the channels of communication, to preview the messages to be sent, to disclaim, and to altercast. In your use of feedforward, be brief, use feedforward sparingly, and follow through on your feedforward promises. Also, be sure to respond to the feedforward as well as the content messages of others.*

flexibility. The ability to adjust communication strategies on the basis of the unique situation. *Apply the principles of interpersonal communication with flexibility; remember that each situation calls for somewhat different skills.*

force. An unproductive **conflict** strategy in which you try to win an argument by physically overpowering the other person either by threat or by actual behavior. *Avoid it.*

free information. Information that is revealed implicitly and that may be used as a basis for opening or pursuing conversations.

friendship. An interpersonal relationship between two persons that is mutually productive, established and maintained through perceived mutual free choice, and characterized by mutual positive regard. *Adjust your verbal and nonverbal communication as appropriate to the stages of your various friendships. Learn the rules that govern your friendships; follow them or risk damaging the relationship.*

game. A simulation of some situation with rules governing the behaviors of the participants and with some payoff for winning; in transactional analysis, "game" refers to a series of ulterior transactions that lead to a payoff; the term also refers to a basically dishonest kind of transaction in which participants hide their true feelings.

General Semantics. The study of the relationships among language, thought, and behavior.

gossip. **Communication** about someone not present, some third party, usually about matters that are private to this third party. *Avoid gossip that breaches confidentiality, is known to be false, and is unnecessarily invasive.*

gunnysacking. An unproductive **conflict** strategy of storing up grievances—as if in a gunnysack—and holding them in readiness to dump on the person with whom one is in conflict. *Avoid it.*

halo effect. The tendency to generalize an individual's virtue or expertise from one area to another.

haptics. Technical term for the study of touch communication.

heterosexist language. Language that assumes all people are heterosexual and thereby denigrates lesbians and gay men. *Avoid it.*

high-context culture. A culture in which much of the information in communication is in the context or in the person rather than explicitly coded in the verbal messages. **Collectivist cultures** are generally high context. Opposed to **low-context culture**.

home field advantage. The increased power that comes from being in your own territory.

home territories. Territories for which individuals have a sense of intimacy and over which they exercise control—for example, a teacher's office.

hyphen. An **extensional device** used to illustrate that what may be separated verbally may not be separable on the event level or on the nonverbal level; although one may talk about body and mind as if they were separable, in reality they are better referred to as body-mind.

illustrators. Nonverbal behaviors that accompany and literally illustrate verbal messages—for example, upward movements that accompany the verbalization "It's up there."

I-messages. Messages in which the speaker accepts responsibility for personal thoughts and behaviors; messages in which the speaker's point of view is stated explicitly; opposed to **you-messages**. *Generally, I-messages are more effective than you-messages.*

immediacy. A quality of interpersonal effectiveness; a sense of contact and togetherness; a feeling of interest and liking for the other person. *Communicate immediacy through appropriate word choice, feedback, eye contact, body posture, and physical closeness.*

implicit personality theory. A theory of personality that each individual maintains, complete with rules or systems, through which others are perceived. *Be conscious of your implicit personality theories; avoid drawing firm conclusions about other people on the basis of these theories.*

inclusion principle. In verbal interaction, the principle that all members should be a part of (included in) the interaction. *Include everyone present in the interaction (both verbally and nonverbally) so you do not exclude or offend others or fail to profit from their contributions.*

increasing accuracy in perception. *Increase your accuracy in interpersonal perception by looking for a variety of cues that point in the same direction, formulating hypotheses (not conclusions), being especially alert to contradictory cues that may refute your initial hypotheses, avoiding the assumption that others will respond as you would, and being careful not to perceive only the positive in those you like and the negative in those you dislike.*

index. An **extensional device** used to emphasize the notion of nonidentity (no two things are the same) and symbolized by a subscript—for example, politician$_1$ is not politician$_2$.

indirect speech. Speech that hides the speaker's true intentions; speech in which requests and observations are made indirectly. *Use indirect speech (1) to express a desire without insulting or offending anyone, (2) to ask for compli-*

ments in a socially acceptable manner, and (3) to disagree without being disagreeable.

indiscrimination. A misevaluation caused by categorizing people, events, or objects into a particular class and responding to them only as members of the class; a failure to recognize that each individual is unique; a failure to apply the **index**. *Index your terms and statements to emphasize that each person and event is unique; avoid treating all individuals the same way because they are covered by the same label or term.*

individualistic culture. A culture in which the individual's rather than the group's goals and preferences are given greater importance. Opposed to **collectivist culture.**

inevitability. A principle of communication holding that communication cannot be avoided; all behavior in an interactional setting is communication. *Remember that all behavior in an interactional situation communicates; seek out nonobvious messages and meanings.*

inferential statement. A statement that can be made by anyone, is not limited to what is observed, and can be made at any time. *See also* **factual statement.**

informal-time terms. Terms that are approximate rather than exact, for example, "soon," "early," and "in a while." *Recognize that informal-time terms (for example, are often the cause of interpersonal difficulties. When misunderstanding is likely, use more precise terms.*

information overload. A condition in which the amount of information is too great to be dealt with effectively or the number or complexity of messages is so great that the individual or organization is not able to deal with them.

in-group talk. Talk about a subject or in a vocabulary that only certain people understand; such talk often occurs in the presence of someone who does not belong to the group and therefore does not understand.

initiating relationships. *In initiating relationships, remember the following steps: examine the qualifiers, determine clearance, open the encounter, select and put into operation an integrating topic, create a favorable impression, and establish a second meeting.*

insulation. A reaction to **territorial encroachment** in which you erect some sort of barrier between yourself and the invaders.

intensional orientation. A point of view in which primary consideration is given to the way things are labeled and only secondary consideration (if any) to the world of experience. *See also* **extensional orientation.** *Respond first to things; avoid responding to labels as if they were things; do not let labels distort your perception of the world.*

interaction management. A quality of interpersonal effectiveness; the control of interaction to the satisfaction of both parties; managing conversational turns, fluency, and message consistency. *Manage the interaction to the satisfaction of both parties by sharing the roles of speaker and listener, avoiding long and awkward silences, and being consistent in your verbal and nonverbal messages.*

intercultural communication. Communication that takes place between persons of different cultures or persons who have different cultural beliefs, values, or ways of behaving.

interpersonal conflict. A disagreement between two connected persons.

interpersonal communication. Communication between two persons or among a small group of persons and distinguished from public or mass communication; communication of a personal nature and distinguished from impersonal communication; communication between or among connected persons or those involved in a close relationship.

interpersonal perception. The perception of people; the processes through which we interpret and evaluate people and their behavior.

interpreting time cues. *Interpret time cues from the point of view of the other's culture rather than your own.*

intimacy. The closest interpersonal relationship; usually used to denote a close primary relationship.

intimacy claims. Obligations incurred by virtue of being in a close and intimate relationship. *Reduce the intensity of intimacy claims when things get rough; give each other space as appropriate.*

intimate distance. The closest proxemic distance, ranging from touching to 18 inches. *See also* **proxemics.**

intrapersonal communication. Communication with oneself.

irreversibility. A principle of communication holding that communication cannot be reversed; once something has been communicated, it cannot be uncommunicated. *Avoid saying things (for example, in anger) or making commitments that you may wish to retract (but will not be able to) in order to prevent resentment and ill feeling.*

jargon. The technical language of any specialized group, often a professional class, which is unintelligible to individuals not belonging to the group; "shop talk."

Johari window. A diagram of the four selves: *open, blind, hidden,* and *unknown.*

kinesics. The study of the communicative dimensions of facial and bodily movements.

language fairness. Use language fairly; avoid language that offends or demeans, for example, language that excludes others from full participation.

language relativity hypothesis. The theory that the language we speak influences our behaviors and our perceptions of the world and that therefore persons speaking widely differing languages will perceive and behave differently as a result of the language differences. Also referred to as the Sapir-Whorf hypothesis and the Whorfian hypothesis.

leave-taking cues. Verbal and nonverbal cues that indicate a desire to terminate a conversation. *Increase your sensitivity to leave-taking cues; pick up on the leave-taking cues of others, and communicate such cues tactfully so as not to insult or offend others.*

leveling. A process of message distortion in which a message is repeated but the number of details is reduced, some details are omitted entirely, and some details lose their complexity.

linguistic relativity hypothesis. A theory holding that since the language you speak influences your thoughts and behaviors and since the languages of the world differ greatly in semantics and syntax, people speaking widely different languages would also differ in how they viewed and thought about the world. *Because most research does not support such influence or such wide differences, the belief in this hypothesis is likely to cause undue concentration on differences when similarities really exist.*

listening. An active process of receiving aural stimuli; this process consists of five stages: receiving, understanding, remembering, evaluating, and responding. *Adjust your listening perspective, as the situation warrants, between active and passive, judgmental and nonjudgmental, surface and depth, and empathic and objective listening.*

loving. An interpersonal process in which one feels a closeness, a caring, a warmth, and an excitement for another person.

low-context culture. A culture in which most of the information in communication is explicitly stated in the verbal messages. **Individualistic cultures** are usually low-context cultures. Opposed to **high-context culture.**

machiavellianism. The belief that people can be manipulated easily; often used to refer to the techniques or tactics one person uses to control another.

maintenance. A stage of relationship stability at which the relationship does not progress or deteriorate significantly; a continuation as opposed to a dissolution of a relationship.

maintenance strategies. Specific behaviors designed to preserve an interpersonal relationship. *See also* **repair strategies.** *Use appropriate maintenance strategies (for example, openness, sharing joint activities, and acting positively) to preserve a valued relationship.*

manipulation. An unproductive **conflict** strategy that avoids open conflict; instead, attempts are made to divert the conflict by being especially charming and getting the other person into a noncombative frame of mind. *Avoid it.*

manner maxim. A principle of conversation that holds that speakers cooperate by being clear and by organizing their thoughts into some meaningful and coherent pattern. *Use it.*

markers. Devices that signify that a certain territory belongs to a particular person. *See also* **boundary marker, central marker,** and **ear marker.** *Become sensitive to the markers (central, boundary, and ear) of others, and learn to use these markers to define your own territories and to communicate the desired impression.*

matching hypothesis. An assumption that we date and mate with people who are similar to ourselves—who match us—in physical attractiveness.

meaning interpretation. Assess meaning as a function of both the messages sent and the speaker's (and your own) attitudes and values to account for the influence of personality, past experiences, attitudes, and the like.

meaningfulness. A principle of perception holding that we assume that the behavior of people is sensible, stems from some logical antecedent, and is consequently meaningful rather than meaningless.

mere exposure hypothesis. The theory that repeated or prolonged exposure to a stimulus may result in a change in attitude toward the stimulus object, generally in the direction of increased positiveness.

message. Any signal or combination of signals that serves as a **stimulus** for a receiver.

metacommunication. Communication about communication. *Metacommunicate to ensure understanding of the other person's thoughts and feelings: give clear feedforward, explain feelings as well as thoughts, paraphrase your own complex thoughts, and ask questions.*

metalanguage. Language used to talk about language.

metamessage. A message that makes reference to another message, for example, the statements "Did I make myself clear?" or "That's a lie" refer to other messages and are therefore considered metamessages. *Use metamessages to clarify your understanding of what another thinks and feels.*

micromomentary expressions. Extremely brief movements that are not consciously controlled or recognized and that are thought to be indicative of an individual's true emotional state.

mindfulness and mindlessness. States of relative awareness. In a mindful state, we are aware of the logic and rationality of our behaviors and the logical connections existing among elements. In a mindless state, we are unaware of this logic and rationality. *Apply the principles of interpersonal communication mindfully rather than mindlessly. Increase mindfulness by creating and re-creating categories, being open to new information and points of view, and being careful of relying too heavily on first impressions.*

mirroring destructive behavior. *Beware of mirroring destructive behavior and creating a spiral wherein the unproductive behavior of one person stimulates similarly unproductive behavior in the other; the result of such a pattern is that conflict and differences are maximized and agreements and similarities are minimized.*

mixed message. A message that contradicts itself; a message that asks for two different (often incompatible) responses. Avoid emitting mixed messages by focusing clearly on your purposes when communicating and by increasing conscious control over your verbal and nonverbal behaviors. *Detect mixed messages in other people's communications and avoid being placed in double-bind situations by seeking clarification from the sender.*

model. A representation of an object or process.

monochronic time orientation. A view of time in which things are done sequentially; one thing is scheduled at a time. Opposed to **polychronic time orientation.**

monologue. A form of **communication** in which one person speaks and the other listens; there is no real interaction among participants. *Avoid it, at least generally.* Opposed to **dialogue.**

negative allness and conflict. *Avoid negative allness terms and statements in conflict situations.*

negative feedback. Feedback that serves a corrective function by informing the source that his or her message is not being received in the way intended. Negative feedback serves to redirect the source's behavior. Looks of boredom, shouts of disagreement, letters critical of newspaper policy, and teachers' instructions on how better to approach a problem would be examples of negative feedback.

neutrality. A response pattern lacking in personal involvement; encourages defensiveness; opposed to **empathy.**

noise. Anything that interferes with a person's receiving a message as the source intended the message to be received. Noise is present in a communication system to the extent that the message received is not the message sent. *Combat the effects of physical, semantic, and psychological noise by eliminating or lessening the sources of physical noise, securing agreement on meanings, and interacting with an open mind in order to increase communication accuracy.*

nonallness. An attitude or point of view in which it is recognized that one can never know all about anything and that what we know, say, or hear is only a part of what there is to know, say, or hear.

nondirective language. Language that does not direct or focus our attention on certain aspects; neutral language.

nonnegotiation. An unproductive **conflict** strategy in which the individual refuses to discuss the conflict or to listen to the other person.

nonverbal communication. Communication without words; communication by means of space, gestures, facial expressions, touching, vocal variation, and silence, for example.

nonverbal dominance. Nonverbal behavior that allows one person to achieve psychological dominance over another. *Resist (as sender and receiver) nonverbal expressions of dominance when they are inappropriate—for example, when they are sexist.*

nonverbal encounter. *In initiating relationships, keep the following nonverbal guidelines in mind: establish eye contact, signal interest and positive responses, concentrate your focus, establish physical closeness, maintain an open posture, respond visibly, reinforce positive behaviors, and avoid overexposure.*

object-adaptors. Movements that involve your manipulation of some object, for example, punching holes in or drawing on the styrofoam coffee cup, clicking a ball point pen, or chewing on a pencil. *Avoid them; they generally communicate discomfort and a lack of control over the communication situation.*

object language. Language used to communicate about objects, events, and relations in the world; the structure of the object language is described in a **metalanguage**; the display of physical objects—for example, flower arranging and the colors of the clothes we wear.

olfactics. The study of communication by smell.

olfactory communication. Communication by smell.

openness. A quality of interpersonal effectiveness encompassing (1) a willingness to interact openly with others, to self-disclose as appropriate; (2) a willingness to react honestly to incoming stimuli; and (3) a willingness to own one's feelings and thoughts.

opinion. A tentative conclusion concerning some object, person, or event.

other talk. Talk about the listener or some third party.

other-orientation. A quality of interpersonal effectiveness involving attentiveness, interest, and concern for the other person. *Convey concern for and interest in the other person by means of empathic responses, appropriate feedback, and attentive listening responses.*

outing. The process whereby a person's affectional orientation is made public by another person and without the gay man or lesbian's consent.

ownership of feelings. Own your feelings; use I-messages; acknowledge responsibility for your own thoughts and feelings to increase honest sharing.

owning feelings. The process by which we take responsibility for our own feelings instead of attributing them to others.

packaging. *See* **reinforcement.**

packages or clusters. *Assess the entire package or cluster of message behaviors, and interpret any message as part of the cluster; avoid interpreting messages in isolation.*

paralanguage. The vocal (but nonverbal) aspect of speech. Paralanguage consists of voice qualities (for example, pitch range, resonance, tempo), vocal characterizers (laughing or crying, yelling or whispering), vocal qualifiers (intensity, pitch height), and vocal segregates ("uh-uh," meaning "no," or "sh" meaning "silence"). *Vary paralinguistic elements, such as rate, volume, and stress, to add variety and emphasis to your communications, and be responsive to the meanings communicated by others' variation of paralanguage features.*

passive listening. **Listening** that is attentive and supportive but occurs without talking and without directing the speaker in any nonverbal way; also used negatively to refer to inattentive and uninvolved listening.

pauses. Silent periods in the normally fluent stream of speech. Pauses are of two major types: filled pauses (interruptions in speech that are filled with such vocalizations as "er" or "um") and unfilled pauses (silences of unusually long duration).

perception. The process of becoming aware of objects and events through the senses.

perception checking. The process of verifying your understanding of some message or situation or feeling. *Use perception checking to get more information about your impressions: (1) describe what you think is happening, and (2) ask whether this is correct or in error.*

perceptual accentuation. A process that leads you to see what you expect to see and what you want to see—for example, seeing people you like as better looking and smarter than people you do not like. *Be aware of the influence your own needs, wants, and expectations have on your perceptions. Recognize that what you perceive is a function both of what exists in reality and what is going on inside your own head.*

personal rejection. An unproductive **conflict** strategy in which the individual withholds love and affection and seeks to win the argument by getting the other person to break down under this withdrawal.

personal distance. The second-closest proxemic distance, ranging from 18 inches to 4 feet. *See also* **proxemics.**

persuasion. The process of influencing attitudes and behavior.

phatic communication. Communication that is primarily social; communication designed to open the channels of communication rather than to communicate something about the external world; "Hello" and "How are you?" in everyday interaction are examples.

pitch. The highness or lowness of the vocal tone.

polarization. A form of fallacious reasoning by which only two extremes are considered; also referred to as "black-or-white" and "either-or" thinking or two-valued orientation. *Use middle terms and qualifiers when describing the world; avoid talking in terms of polar opposites (black and white, good and bad) in order to describe reality more accurately.*

Pollyanna effect. The condition in which one makes a prediction and then proceeds to fulfill it; a type of self-fulfilling prophecy, but one that refers to others and to your evaluation of others rather than to yourself. *Be aware of your own tendency to fulfill such prophecies and of others' tendencies to fulfill their prophecies of you.*

polychronic time orientation. A view of time in which several things may be scheduled or engaged in at the same time. Opposed to **monochronic time orientation.**

positive feedback. Feedback that supports or reinforces the continuation of behavior along the same lines in which it is already proceeding—for example, applause during a speech.

positiveness. A characteristic of effective communication involving positive attitudes toward oneself and toward the interpersonal interaction. Also used to refer to complimenting another and expressing acceptance and approval. *Verbally and nonverbally communicate a positive attitude toward yourself, others, and the situation with* *smiles, positive facial expressions, attentive gestures, positive verbal expressions, and the elimination or reduction of negative appraisals.*

power. The ability to control the behaviors of others.

power bases. *Increase your sources or bases of power (referent, legitimate, reward, coercive, expert, and information).*

power communication. *Communicate power through forceful speech. Avoid weak modifiers and excessive body movement, and demonstrate your knowledge, preparation, and organization in the matters at hand.*

power play. A consistent pattern of behavior in which one person tries to control the behavior of another. *Identify the power plays people use on you and respond to these power plays so as to stop them. Use an effective management strategy, for example, express your feelings, describe the behavior you object to, and state a cooperative response.*

pragmatic implication. An assumption that seems logical but is not necessarily true. *Identify your own pragmatic implications, and distinguish these from logical implications (those that are necessarily true) and recognize that memory often confuses the two. In recalling situations and events, ask yourself whether your conclusions are based on pragmatic or logical implications.*

pragmatics. In communication, an approach that focuses on behaviors, especially on the effects or consequences of communication.

praise and criticism. *Say what you feel without excessive and unjustified praise or criticism.*

premature self-disclosures. Disclosures that are made before the relationship has developed sufficiently. *Resist too intimate or too negative self-disclosures early in the development of a relationship.*

primacy effect. The condition in which what comes first exerts greater influence than what comes later. *See also* **recency effect.**

primacy and recency. Primacy refers to giving more credence to that which occurs first; recency refers to giving more credence to that which occurs last (that is, most recently). *Be aware that first impressions can serve as filters that prevent you from perceiving others' contradictory behaviors, changes in situations, and, especially, changes in people. Recognize the normal tendency for first impressions to leave lasting impressions and to color both what we see later and the conclusions we draw. Be at your very best in first encounters. Also, take the time and effort to revise your impressions of others on the basis of new information.*

primary affect displays. The communication of the six primary emotions: happiness, surprise, fear, anger, sadness, and disgust/contempt.

primary relationship. The relationship between two people that they consider their most (or one of their most) important—for example, the relationship between husband and wife or domestic partners.

primary territory. Areas that one can consider one's exclusive preserve—for example, one's room or office.

process. Ongoing activity; communication is referred to as a process to emphasize that it is always changing, always in motion.

productive conflict. *Follow these guidelines to fight more productively: (1) state your position directly and honestly; (2) react openly to the messages of your combatant; (3) own your thoughts and feelings; (4) address the real issues causing the conflict; (5) listen with and demonstrate empathic understanding; (6) validate the feelings of your interactant; (7) describe the behaviors causing the conflict; (8) express your feelings spontaneously rather than strategically; (9) state your position tentatively; (10) capitalize on agreements; (11) view conflict in positive terms to the extent possible; (12) express positive feelings for the other person; (13) be positive about the prospects of conflict resolution; (14) treat your combatant as an equal, avoiding ridicule or sarcasm, for example; (15) involve yourself in the conflict; play an active role as both sender and receiver; (16) grant the other person permission to express himself or herself freely; and (17) avoid power tactics that may inhibit freedom of expression.*

progressive differentiation. A relational problem caused by the exaggeration or intensification of differences or similarities between individuals.

projection. A psychological process whereby we attribute characteristics or feelings of our own to others; often used to refer to the process whereby we attribute our own faults to others.

pronouncements. Authoritative statements that imply that the speaker is in a position of authority and that the listener is in a childlike or learner role.

protection theory. A theory of proxemics holding that people establish a body-buffer zone to protect themselves from unwanted closeness, touching, or attack.

provisionalism. An attitude of open-mindedness that leads to the creation of supportiveness; opposed to **certainty.**

proxemic distances. The spatial distances that are maintained in communication and social interaction. *Adjust spatial (proxemic) distances as appropriate to the specific interaction; avoid distances that are too far, too close, or otherwise inappropriate, as they might falsely convey, for example, aloofness or aggression.*

proxemics. The study of the communicative function of space; the study of how people unconsciously structure their space—the distance between people in their interactions, the organization of space in homes and offices, and even the design of cities.

proximity. As a principle of perception, the tendency to perceive people or events that are physically close as belonging together or representing some unit; physical closeness; one of the qualities influencing interpersonal **attraction**. *Use physical proximity to increase interpersonal attractiveness.*

psychological time. The importance you place on past, present, or future time. *Recognize the significance of your own time orientation to your ultimate success, and make whatever adjustments you think desirable.*

public distance. The farthest proxemic distance, ranging from 12 feet to more than 25 feet.

public territory. Areas that are open to all people—for example, restaurants or parks.

punctuation of communication. The breaking up of continuous communication sequences into short sequences with identifiable beginnings and endings or stimuli and responses. *See the sequence of events punctuated from perspectives other than your own in order to increase empathy and mutual understanding.*

punishment. Noxious or aversive stimulation.

pupil dilation. *Detect pupil dilation and constriction, and formulate hypotheses concerning their possible meanings.*

pupillometrics. The study of communication through changes in the size of the pupils of the eyes.

Pygmalion effect. The condition in which one makes a prediction and then proceeds to fulfill it; a type of self-fulfilling prophecy but one that refers to others and to our evaluation of others rather than to ourselves.

quality maxim. A principle of **conversation** that holds that speakers cooperate by saying what they know or think is true and by not saying what they know or think is false. *Use it.*

quantity maxim. A principle of **conversation** that holds that speakers cooperate by being only as informative as necessary to communicate their intended meanings. *Use it.*

quotes. An **extensional device** to emphasize that a word or phrase is being used in a special sense and should therefore be given special attention.

racist language. Language that denigrates a particular race. *Avoid racist language—any language that demeans or is derogatory toward members of a particular race—so as not to offend or alienate others or reinforce stereotypes.*

rate. The speed with which we speak, generally measured in words per minute.

receiver. Any person or thing that takes in messages. Receivers may be individuals listening to or reading a message, a group of persons hearing a speech, a scattered television audience, or machines that store information.

recency effect. The condition in which what comes last (that is, most recently) exerts greater influence than what comes first. *See also* **primacy effect.**

reconciliation strategies. Behaviors designed to re-create a broken relationship. *Consider using such reconciliation strategies as third-party intervention, tacit persistence, and mutual interaction to patch up a broken relationship.*

redundancy. The quality of a message that makes it totally predictable and therefore lacking in information. A message of zero redundancy would be completely unpredictable; a message of 100 percent redundancy would be completely predictable. All human languages contain some degree of built-in redundancy, generally estimated to be about 50 percent.

reflexiveness. The feature of human language that makes it possible for that language to be used to refer to itself; that is, we can talk about our talk and create a **metalanguage**, a language for talking about language.

regulators. Nonverbal behaviors that regulate, monitor, or control the communications of another person.

reinforcement theory. A theory of behavior that when applied to relationships holds (essentially) that relationships develop because they are rewarding and end because they are punishing. *Reinforce others as a way to increase interpersonal attractiveness and general interpersonal satisfaction.*

reinforcement or packaging (principle of). The principle of verbal interaction that holds that in most interactions, messages are transmitted simultaneously through a number of different channels that normally reinforce each other; messages come in packages.

rejection. A response to an individual that rejects or denies the validity of that individual's self-view.

relational communication. Communication between or among intimates or those in close relationships; used by some theorists as synonymous with interpersonal communication.

relation maxim. A principle of **conversation** that holds that speakers cooperate by talking about what is relevant to the conversation and by not talking about what is not relevant.

relationship deterioration. The stage of a relationship during which the connecting bonds between the partners weaken and the partners begin drifting apart.

relationship dialectics theory. A theory that describes relationships among a series of opposites representing competing desires or motivations, such as the desire for autonomy and the desire to belong to someone, for novelty and predictability, and for closedness and openness.

relationship dissolution. The breaking of relationship bonds; relationship termination. *If the relationship ends: (1) break the loneliness-depression cycle, (2) take time out to get to know yourself as an individual, (3) bolster your self-esteem, (4) remove or avoid uncomfortable symbols that may remind you of your past relationship and may make you uncomfortable, (5) seek the support of friends and relatives, and (6) avoid repeating negative patterns.*

relationship improvement. *If you wish to preserve or repair a deteriorating relationship, take positive action by specifying what is wrong with the relationship, applying the skills and insights you have acquired to the task of relationship improvement, and taking risks in attempting to find a satisfactory solution to the relationship difficulty.*

relationship messages. Messages that comment on the relationship between the speakers rather than on matters external to them. *Recognize and respond to relationship as well as content messages in order to ensure a more complete understanding of the messages intended.*

relationship repair. *Consider the following steps when you wish to repair a relationship: (1) avoid withdrawal, keep the channels of communication open at all times, (2) avoid the sudden decrease in self-disclosure that often signals distrust, (3) increase supportiveness, (4) avoid deception, (5) avoid excessive negative responses, and (6) increase cherishing behaviors to create an environment conducive to compromise and rebuilding.*

relationship stimulation. Keep a relationship stimulating by changing routines and exposing yourselves to new experiences.

repair. A relationship stage in which one or both parties seek to improve the relationship.

repair strategies. Behaviors designed to improve a deteriorating relationship. *Relationship repair may be accomplished by recognizing the problem, engaging in productive conflict resolution, posing possible solutions, affirming each other, integrating solutions into everyday behavior, and taking relational risks. See also* **maintenance strategies.**

resemblance. As a principle of perception, the tendency to perceive people or events that are similar in appearance as belonging together.

response. Any bit of overt or covert behavior.

rigid complementarity. The inability to break away from the complementary type of relationship that was once appropriate and now is no longer.

role. The part an individual plays in a group; an individual's function or expected behavior.

romantic rules. The rules or norms that regulate and define romantic relationships. *Learn the romantic rules that govern your relationship, and follow them or risk damaging the relationship.*

rules theory. A theory that describes relationships as interactions governed by a series of rules that a couple agrees to follow. When the rules are followed, the relationship is maintained and when they are broken, the relationship experiences difficulty.

secondary territory. Areas that do not belong to a particular person but have been occupied by that person and are therefore associated with her or him—for example, the seat you normally take in class.

selective exposure (principle of). A principle of persuasion that states that listeners actively seek out information that supports their opinions and actively avoid information that contradicts their existing opinions, beliefs, attitudes, and values.

self-acceptance. Being satisfied with ourselves, our virtues and vices, and our abilities and limitations.

self-adaptors. Movements that usually satisfy a physical need, especially to make you more comfortable, for example, scratching your head to relieve an itch, moistening your lips because they feel dry, or pushing your hair out of your eyes. *Because these often communicate your nervousness or discomfort, they are best avoided.*

self-appreciation. *Appreciate yourself; identify your positive qualities; think positively about yourself.*

self-attribution. A process through which we seek to account for and understand the reasons and motivations for our own behaviors.

self-awareness. The degree to which a person knows himself or herself. *Increase self-awareness by asking yourself about yourself and listening to others; actively seek information about yourself from others by carefully observing their interactions with you and by asking relevant questions. See yourself from different perspectives (see your different selves), and increase your open self.*

self-concept. An individual's self-evaluation; an individual's self-appraisal.

self-disclosure. The process of revealing something about ourselves to another, usually used to refer to information that would normally be kept hidden.

self-disclosure guidelines. *Self-disclose when the motivation is to improve the relationship, when the context and the relationship are appropriate for the self-disclosure, when there is* *an opportunity for open and honest responses, when the self-disclosures will be clear and direct, when there are appropriate reciprocal disclosures, and when you have examined and are willing to risk the possible burdens that self-disclosure might entail. Self-disclose selectively; regulate your self-disclosures as appropriate to the context, topic, audience, and potential rewards and risks to secure the maximum advantage and reduce the possibility of negative effects.*

self-esteem. The value you place on yourself; your self-evaluation; usually used to refer to the positive value placed on oneself. *Increase your self-esteem by attacking destructive beliefs, engaging in self-affirmation, seeking out nourishing people, and working on projects that will result in success.*

self-fulfilling prophecy. The situation in which we make a prediction or prophecy and fulfill it ourselves—for example, expecting a class to be boring and then fulfilling this expectation by perceiving it as boring. *Avoid fulfilling your own negative prophecies and seeing only what you want to see. Be especially careful to examine your perceptions when they conform too closely to your expectations; check to make sure that you are seeing what exists in real life, not just in your expectations or predictions.*

self-monitoring. The manipulation of the image one presents to others in interpersonal interactions so as to give the most favorable impression of oneself. *Monitor your verbal and nonverbal behavior as appropriate to communicate the desired impression.*

self-serving bias. A bias that operates in the self-attribution process and leads us to take credit for the positive consequences and to deny responsibility for the negative consequences of our behaviors. *In examining the causes of your own behavior, beware of the tendency to attribute negative behaviors to external factors and positive behaviors to internal factors. In self-examinations, ask whether and how the self-serving bias might be operating.*

self-talk. Talk about oneself. *Balance talk about yourself with talk about the other; avoid excessive self-talk or extreme avoidance of self-talk to encourage equal sharing and interpersonal satisfaction.*

semantics. The area of language study concerned with meaning.

sexist language. Language derogatory to one sex, generally women. *Whether man or woman, avoid sexist language—for example, terms that presume maleness as the norm ("policeman" or "mailman"). Avoid it.*

sexual harassment. Unsolicited and unwanted sexual messages. *If confronted with sexual harassment, consider talking to the harasser, collecting evidence, using appropriate channels within the organization, or filing a complaint.*

Avoid any indication of sexual harassment by beginning with the assumption that others at work are not interested in sexual advances and stories; listen for negative reactions to any sexually explicit discussions, and avoid behaviors you think might prove offensive.

sharpening. A process of message distortion in which the details of messages, when repeated, are crystallized and heightened.

shyness. The condition of discomfort and uneasiness in interpersonal situations.

signal reaction. A conditioned response to a signal; a response to some signal that is immediate rather than delayed.

signal and noise (relativity of). The principle of verbal interaction that holds that what is signal (meaningful) and what is noise (interference) is relative to the communication analyst, the participants, and the context.

silence. The absence of vocal communication; often misunderstood to refer to the absence of any and all communication. *Use silence to communicate feelings or to prevent communication about certain topics. Interpret silences of others through their culturally determined rules rather than your own.*

silencers. A tactic (such as crying) that literally silences one's opponent—an unproductive **conflict** strategy.

similarity. A principle of **attraction** holding that one is attracted to qualities similar to those possessed by oneself and to people who are similar to oneself; opposed to **complementarity**.

slang. The language used by special groups that is not considered proper by the general society; language made up of the **argot**, **cant**, and **jargon** of various groups and known by the general public.

social comparison processes. The processes by which you compare yourself (for example, your abilities, opinions, and values) with others and then assess and evaluate yourself; one of the sources of self-concept.

social penetration theory. A theory concerned with relationship development from the superficial to the intimate levels and from few to many areas of interpersonal interaction.

social exchange theory. A theory hypothesizing that we develop relationships in which our rewards or profits will be greater than our costs and that we avoid or terminate relationships in which the costs exceed the rewards.

social distance. The third proxemic distance, ranging from 4 feet to 12 feet; the distance at which business is usually conducted. *See also* **proxemics**.

source. Any person or thing that creates messages. A source may be an individual speaking, writing, or gesturing or a computer solving a problem.

spatial distance. Use spatial distance to signal the type of relationship you are in: intimate, personal, social, or public. Let your spatial relationships reflect your interpersonal relationships.

speaker apprehension. A fear of engaging in communication transactions; a decrease in the frequency, strength, and likelihood of engaging in communication transactions.

speech. Messages conveyed via a vocal-auditory channel.

speech rate. *Use variations in rate to increase communication efficiency and persuasiveness as appropriate.*

spontaneity. The communication pattern in which one verbalizes what one is thinking without attempting to develop strategies for control; encourages **supportiveness**; opposed to **strategy**.

stability. The principle of perception that refers to the fact that our perceptions of things and of people are relatively consistent with our previous conceptions.

state apprehension. Speaker apprehension for specific types of communication situations—for example, public speaking or interview situations. *See* **trait apprehension.**

static evaluation. An orientation that fails to recognize that the world is characterized by constant change; an attitude that sees people and events as fixed rather than as constantly changing. *Date your statements to emphasize constant change; avoid the tendency to think of and describe things as static and unchanging.*

status. The relative level one occupies in a hierarchy; status always involves a comparison, and is only relative to the status of another. In our culture, occupation, financial position, age, and educational level are significant determinants of status. *Avoid inappropriate use of time cues in establishing and maintaining status differences.*

stereotype. In communication, a fixed impression of a group of people through which we then perceive specific individuals; stereotypes are most often negative (Martians are stupid, uneducated, and dirty) but may also be positive (Venusians are scientific, industrious, and helpful). *Avoid stereotyping others; instead, see and respond to each person as a unique individual.*

stimulus. Any external or internal change that impinges on or arouses an organism.

stimulus-response models of communication. Models of communication that assume that the process of communication is linear, beginning with a stimulus that leads to a response.

strategy. The use of some plan for control of other members of a communication interaction that guides one's own communications; encourages defensiveness; opposed to spontaneity.

subjectivity. The principle of perception that refers to the fact that one's perceptions are not objective but are influenced by one's wants and needs and one's expectations and predictions.

superiority. A point of view or attitude that assumes that others are not equal to oneself; encourages **defensiveness**; opposed to **equality**.

supportiveness. An attitude of an individual or an atmosphere in a group that is characterized by openness, absence of fear, and a genuine feeling of equality. *Exhibit supportiveness to others by being descriptive rather than evaluative, spontaneous rather than strategic, and provisional rather than certain.*

supportiveness in self-disclosure. *Express support for the discloser. Resist evaluation. Do not rush the discloser. Express support verbally and nonverbally: nod in agreement, maintain appropriate eye contact, smile, ask for relevant elaboration, and maintain physical closeness and directness.*

symmetrical relationship. A relation between two or more persons in which one person's behavior serves as a stimulus for the same type of behavior in the other person(s). Examples of such relationships include those in which anger in one person encourages or serves as a stimulus for anger in another person or in which a critical comment by the person leads the other person to respond in like manner.

taboo. Forbidden; culturally censored. Taboo language is language that is frowned upon by "polite society." Topics and specific words may be considered taboo—for example, death, sex, certain forms of illness, and various words denoting sexual activities and excretory functions. *Avoid taboo expressions so that others do not make negative evaluations; substitute more socially acceptable expressions or euphemisms where and when appropriate.*

tactile communication. Communication by touch; communication received by the skin.

temporal communication. The messages that one's time orientation and treatment of time communicates.

territorial encroachment. The trespassing on, use of, or appropriation of one's territory by another. *Generally, avoid territorial encroachment; give others the space they need; remember, for example, that people who are angry or disturbed need more space than usual.*

territoriality. A possessive or ownership reaction to an area of space or to particular objects. *Establish and maintain territory nonverbally by marking or otherwise indicating temporary or permanent ownership. Become sensitive to the territorial behavior of others.*

theory. A general statement or principle applicable to a number of related phenomena.

touch. *Use touch when appropriate to express positive effect, playfulness, control, and ritualistic meanings and to serve task-related functions. See haptics.*

touch avoidance. The tendency to avoid touching and being touched by others. *Recognize that some people may prefer to avoid touching and being touched. Avoid drawing too many conclusions about people from the way they treat interpersonal touching.*

touch rules. *Respond to the touch patterns of others in light of their gender and culture and not exclusively on the basis of your own.*

trait apprehension. Speaker apprehension for communication generally; a fear of communication situations regardless of their context. *See **state apprehension.***

transactional. Characterizing the relationship among elements whereby each influences and is influenced by each other element; communication is a transactional process because no element is independent of any other element.

uncertainty reduction strategies. *Increase your accuracy in interpersonal perception by using all three uncertainty reduction strategies: passive, active, and interactive strategies.*

uncertainty reduction theory. The theory holding that as relationships develop, uncertainty is reduced; relationship development is seen as a process of reducing uncertainty about one another.

universal of interpersonal communication. A feature of communication common to all interpersonal communication acts.

unproductive conflict strategies. *Avoid unproductive conflict strategies such as avoidance, force, blame, silencers, gunnysacking, manipulation, personal rejection, and fighting below the belt.*

value. Relative worth of an object; a quality that makes something desirable or undesirable; ideals or customs about which we have emotional responses, whether positive or negative.

verbal abuse. In dealing with verbal abuse, first recognize it for what it is; second, recognize the significant consequences, and try to change the behavior.

verbal aggressiveness. A method of winning an argument by attacking the other person's **self-concept.** Avoid inflicting psychological pain on the other person to win an argument.

verbal encounter. *In initiating relationships, keep the following verbal guidelines in mind: introduce yourself, focus the conversation on the other person, exchange favors-rewards, be energetic, stress the positives, avoid negative and too intimate self-disclosures, establish commonalities, avoid yes-no questions and answers, and avoid rapid-fire questions.*

visual dominance. The use of your eyes to maintain a superior or dominant position, for example, when making an especially important point, you might look intently at the other person. *Use visual dominance behavior when you wish to emphasize certain messages.ice qualities. Aspects of paralanguage—specifically, pitch range, vocal lip control, glottis control, pitch control, articulation control, rhythm control, resonance, and tempo.*

volume. The relative loudness of the voice.

you-messages. Messages in which the speaker denies responsibility for his or her own thoughts and behaviors; messages that attribute the speaker's perception to another person; messages of blame; opposed to **I-messages.**

Photo Acknowledgments

Unless otherwise acknowledged, all photographs are the property of Scott, Foresman and Company.

2: David R. Frazier Photolibrary; 4: Elena Roonaid/PhotoEdit; 9: Stephen Frisch/STOCK BOSTON; 23: Jeff Greenberg/Unicorn Stock Photos; 26: Granitsas/The Image Works; 33: Richard Hutchins/PhotoEdit; 41: Bob Daemmrich/The Image Works; 46: Penny Tweedie/Tony Stone Images,. Inc.; 55: Michael Newman/PhotoEdit; 53: Bruce Ayers/Tony Stone Images, Inc.; 64: Copyright 1996, USA TODAY. Reprinted with permission.; 68: SUPERSTOCK; 75: Jeff Greenberg/Unicorn Stock Photos; 83: David Young-Wolff/PhotoEdit; 90: Bob Daemmrich/STOCK BOSTON; 95: Michael Newman/PhotoEdit; 100: Chip Henderson/Tony Stone Images, Inc.; 106: Elsa Peterson/STOCK BOSTON; 111: W. Hill, Jr./The Image Works; 116: Christopher Brown/STOCK BOSTON; 130: SUPERSTOCK; 136: Elizabeth Crews/The Image Works; 149: Holt Confer/The Image Works; 152: Karen Kasmauski/Woodfin Camp & Assocaites; 158: Michael Newman/PhotoEdit; 162: David Young-Wolff/Tony Stone Images, Inc.; 172: Stewart Cohen/Tony Stone Images, Inc.; 174: Bob Daemmrich/The Image Works; 178: Peter L. Chapman/STOCK BOSTON; 181: Photofest; 193: Lee Snider/The Image Works; 100: Mike Douglas/The Image Works; 205: Stacy Pick/STOCK BOSTON; 208: Bob Daemmrich/The Image Works; 212: Laima Druskis/STOCK BOSTON; 220: Mark C. Burnett/STOCK BOSTON; 226: Amy Zuckerman/Impact Visuals; 232: SUPERSTOCK; 234: Ed Bock/Frozen Images; 246: Lauren Greenfield/SYGMA; 256: Paul Chesley/Tony Stone Images, Inc.; 264: Robert Brenner/PhotoEdit; 270: Stephanie Maze/Woodfin Camp & Associates; 274: David R. Frazier Photolibrary; 284: N. Antman/The Image Works; 286: Lawrence Migdale; 289: Rick Gerharter/Impact Visuals; 300: Alon Reininger/Contact Press Images; 304: Sepp Seitz/Woodfin Camp & Associates; 314: Barry King/Gamma-Liaison; 322: Charles Thatcher/Tony Stone Images, Inc.; 325: George Gardner/The Image Works; 332: SUPERSTOCK; 339: Cary Wolinsky/STOCK BOSTON; 347: Photofest; 350: David Joel/Tony Stone Images, Inc.; 355: Walter Hodges/Tony Stone Images, Inc.; 362: Lawrence Migdale/STOCK BOSTON; 370: Esbin-Anderson/The Image Works; 379: Mary Conner/PhotoEdit; 390: David R. Frazier Photolibrary; 396: Lee Snider/The Image Works; 405: Jeff Greenberg/PhotoEdit; 413: Esbin-Anrs/The Image Works; 416: Stephen McBrody/PhotoEdit ; 421: SUPERSTOCK; 429: Bob Daemmrich/STOCK BOSTON; 430: Zigy Kaluzny/Tony Stone Images, Inc.

Bibliography

Acuff, Frank L. (1993). *How to Negotiate Anything with Anyone Anywhere Around the World.* New York: American Management Association.

Adams, Linda, with Elinor Lenz (1989). *Be Your Best.* New York: Putnam.

Adams, R. G. (1987). Patterns of Network Change: A Longitudinal Study of Friendships of Elderly Women. *The Gerontologist* 27:222–227.

Addeo, Edmond G. and Robert E. Burger (1973). *Egospeak: Why No One Listens to You.* New York: Bantam.

Adler, Mortimer J. (1983). *How to Speak, How to Listen.* New York: Macmillan.

Adler, Ronald B. (1977). *Confidence in Communication: A Guide to Assertive and Social Skills.* New York: Holt, Rinehart and Winston.

Adler, Ronald B., Lawrence B. Rosenfeld, and Neil Towne (1989). *Interplay: The Process of Interpersonal Communication.* 4th ed. New York: Holt, Rinehart and Winston.

Akmajian, A., R. A. Demers, and R. M. Harnish (1979). *Linguistics: An Introduction to Language and Communication.* Cambridge, MA: MIT Press.

Albert, Rosita and Gayle L. Nelson (1993). Hispanic/Anglo American Differences in Attributions to Paralinguistic Behavior, *International Journal of Intercultural Relations* 17 (winter): 19–40.

Albert, S. M., and M. Moss (1990). Consensus and the Domain of Personal Relationships Among Older Adults. *Journal of Social and Personal Relationships* 7:353–369.

Alberti, Robert E., and Michael L. Emmons (1970). *Your Perfect Right: A Guide to Assertive Behavior.* San Luis Obispo, CA: Impact.

Alberti, Robert E., ed. (1977). *Assertiveness: Innovations, Applications, Issues.* San Luis Obispo, CA: Impact.

Alberts, J. K. (1988). An Analysis of Couples' Conversational Complaints. *Communication Monographs* 55:184–197.

Alessandra, Tony (1986). How to Listen Effectively, *Speaking of Success* (Video Tape Series). San Diego, CA: Levitz Sommer Productions.

Altman, Irwin (1975). *The Environment and Social Behavior.* Monterey, CA: Brooks/Cole.

Altman, Irwin, and Dalmas Taylor (1973). *Social Penetration: The Development of Interpersonal Relationships.* New York: Holt, Rinehart and Winston.

Amato, Paul R. (1994). The Impact of Divorce on Men and Women in India and the United States. *Journal of Comparative Family Studies* 25 (Summer):207–221.

Andersen, Peter (1991). Explaining Intercultural Differences in Nonverbal Communication. In Larry A. Samovar and Richard E. Porter, eds., *Intercultural Communication: A Reader,* 6th ed. Belmont, CA: Wadsworth, pp. 286–296.

Andersen, Peter A., and Ken Leibowitz (1978). The Development and Nature of the Construct Touch Avoidance. *Environmental Psychology and Nonverbal Behavior* 3:89–106. Reprinted in DeVito and Hecht (1990).

Angier, Natalie (1995a). Powerhouse of Senses: Smell, at Last, Gets Its Due, *New York Times* (February 14): C1, C6.

Angier, Natalie (1995b). New View of Family: Unstable but Wealth Helps. *New York Times* (August 29): C1, C5.

Ardrey, Robert (1966). *The Territorial Imperative.* New York: Atheneum.

Argyle, Michael (1983). *The Psychology of Interpersonal Behavior.* 4th ed. New York: Penguin.

Argyle, Michael (1988). *Bodily Communication.* 2d ed. New York: Methuen.

Argyle, Michael and J. Dean (1965). Eye Contact, Distance and Affiliation. *Sociometry* 28:289–304.

Argyle, Michael and Monika Henderson (1984). The Rules of Friendship. *Journal of Social and Personal Relationships* 1 (June): 211–237.

Argyle, Michael and Monika Henderson (1985). *The Anatomy of Relationships: And the Rules and Skills Needed to Manage Them Successfully.* London: Heinemann.

Argyle, Michael, and R. Ingham (1972). Gaze, Mutual Gaze, and Distance. *Semiotica* 1:32–49.

Arliss, Laurie P. (1991). *Gender Communication.* Englewood Cliffs, NJ: Prentice-Hall.

Armstrong, Cameron B. and Alan M. Rubin (1989). Talk Radio as Interpersonal Communication. *Journal of Communication* 39 (spring): 84–94.

Arnold, Carroll C., and John Waite Bowers, eds. (1984). *Handbook of Rhetorical and Communication Theory.* Boston: Allyn and Bacon.

Aronson, Elliot (1980). *The Social Animal.* 3d ed. San Francisco: W. H. Freeman.

Aronson, Elliot, Timothy D. Wilson, and Robin M. Akert (1994). *Social Psychology: The Heart and the Mind.* New York: HarperCollins.

Asch, Solomon (1946). Forming Impressions of Personality. *Journal of Abnormal and Social Psychology* 41:258–290.

Aune, R. Kelly and Toshiyuki Kikuchi (1993). Effects of Language Intensity Similarity on Perceptions of Credibility, Relational Attributions, and Persuasion. *Journal of Language and Social Psychology* 12 (September): 224–238.

Auter, Philip J. and Roy L. Moore (1993). Buying from a Friend: A Content Analysis of Two Teleshopping Programs. *Journalism Quarterly* 70 (summer): 425–436.

Authier, Jerry, and Kay Gustafson (1982). Microtraining: Focusing on Specific Skills. In *Interpersonal Helping Skills: A Guide to Training Methods, Programs, and Resources,* edited by Eldon K. Marshall, P. David Kurtz, and Associates. San Francisco: Jossey-Bass, pp. 93–130.

Axtell, Roger E. (1990a). *Do's and Taboos Around the World.* 2nd ed. New York: Wiley.

Axtell, Roger E. (1990b). *Do's and Taboos of Hosting International Visitors.* New York: Wiley.

Axtell, Roger E. (1993). *Do's and Taboos Around the World.* 3d ed. New York: Wiley.

Aylesworth, Thomas G., and Virginia L. Aylesworth (1978). *If You Don't Invade My Intimate Zone or Clean Up My Water Hole, I'll Breathe in Your Face, Blow on Your Neck, and Be Late for Your Party.* New York: Condor.

Ayres, Joe (1983). Strategies to Maintain Relationships: Their Identification and Perceived Usage. *Communication Quarterly* 31:62–67.

Ayres, Joe (1986). Perceptions of Speaking Ability: An Explanation for Stage Fright. *Communication Education* 35:275–287.

Ayres, Joe, Debbie M. Ayres, Gary Grudzinskas, Tim Hopf, Erin Kelly, and A. Kathleen Wilcox (1995). A Component Analysis of Performance Visualization. *Communication Reports* 8 (summer): 185–192.

Ayres, Joe and Tim Hopf (1993). *Coping with Speech Anxiety.* Norwood, NJ: Ablex Publishing Company.

Ayres, Joe and Tim Hopf (1995). An Assessment of the Role of Communication Apprehension in Communicating with the Terminally Ill. *Communication Research Reports* 12 (fall): 227–234.

Ayres, Joe, Tim Hopf, and Debbie M. Ayres (1994). An Examination of Whether Imaging Ability Enhances the Effectiveness of an Intervention Designed to Reduce Speech Anxiety. *Communication Education* 43 (July): 252–258.

Bach, George R., and Ronald M. Deutsch (1979). *Stop! You're Driving Me Crazy.* New York: Berkeley.

Bach, George R., and Peter Wyden (1968). *The Intimacy Enemy.* New York: Avon.

Backrack, Henry M. (1976). Empathy. *Archives of General Psychiatry* 33:35–38.

Balswick, J. O., and C. Peck (1971). The Inexpressive Male: A Tragedy of American Society? *The Family Coordinator* 20:363–368.

Banks, Stephen P., Dayle M. Altendorf, John O. Greene, and Michael J. Cody (1987). An Examination of Relationship Disengagement:

Perceptions, Breakup Strategies, and Outcomes. *Western Journal of Speech Communication* 51 (winter): 19–41.

Barker, Larry L. and Deborah A. Gaut (1996). *Communication.* 7th ed. Boston: Allyn and Bacon.

Barker, Larry, R. Edwards, C. Gaines, K. Gladney, and F. Holley (1980). An Investigation of Proportional Time Spent in Various Communication Activities by College Students. *Journal of Applied Communication Research* 8:101–109.

Barker, Randolph T., et al (1992). An Investigation of Perceived Managerial Listening Ability. *Journal of Business and Technical Communication* 6 (October): 438–457.

Barna, LaRay M. (1985). Stumbling Blocks in Intercultural Communication, in Larry A. Samovar and Richard E. Porter, eds., *Intercultural Communication: A Reader,* 4th ed. Belmont, Calif.: Wadsworth, pp. 330–338.

Barnlund, Dean C. (1970). A Transactional Model of Communication. In *Language Behavior: A Book of Readings in Communication,* compiled by J. Akin, A. Goldberg, G. Myers, and J. Stewart. The Hague: Mouton.

Barnlund, Dean C. (1975). Communicative Styles in Two Cultures: Japan and the United States. In *Organization of Behavior in Face-to-Face Interaction,* edited by A. Kendon, R. M. Harris, and M. R. Key. The Hague: Mouton.

Baron, Robert (1990). Countering the Effects of Destructive Criticism: The Relative Efficacy of Four Interventions. *Journal of Applied Psychology* 75 (3): 235–245.

Baron, Robert A., and Donn Byrne (1984). *Social Psychology: Understanding Human Interaction.* 4th ed. Boston: Allyn and Bacon.

Barrett, Karen (1982). Date Rape. *Ms.* (September): 48–51.

Barron, James (1995). It's Time to Mind Your E-Manners. *New York Times* (January 11): C1.

Bartholomew, Kim (1990). Avoidance of Intimacy: An Attachment Perspective. *Journal of Social and Personal Relationships* 7:147–178.

Basso, K. H. (1972). To Give Up on Words: Silence in Apache Culture. In *Language and Social Context,* edited by Pier Paolo Giglioli. New York: Penguin.

Bate, Barbara (1988). *Communication and the Sexes.* New York: Harper and Row.

Bateson, Gregory (1972). *Steps to an Ecology of Mind.* New York: Ballantine.

Bavelas, Janet Beavin (1990). Can One Not Communicate? Behaving and Communicating: A Reply to Motley. *Western Journal of Speech Communication* 54 (fall): 593–602.

Baxter, Leslie A. (1983). Relationship Disengagement: An Examination of the Reversal Hypothesis. *Western Journal of Speech Communication* 47:85–98.

Baxter, Leslie A. (1986). Gender Differences in the Heterosexual Relationship Rules Embedded in Break-up Accounts. *Journal of Social and Personal Relationships* 3:289–306.

Baxter, Leslie A. (1988). A Dialectical Perspective on Communication Strategies in Relationship Development. In *Handbook of Personal Relationships,* edited by Steve W. Duck. New York: Wiley.

Baxter, Leslie A. (1990). Dialectical Contradictions in Relationship Development. *Journal of Social and Personal Relationships* 7 (February): 69–88.

Baxter, Leslie A. (1992). Root Metaphors in Accounts of Developing Romantic Relationships. *Journal of Social and Personal Relationships* 9 (May): 253–275.

Baxter, Leslie A. and C. Bullis (1986). Turning Points in Developing Romantic Relationships. *Human Communication Research* 12 (summer): 469–493.

Baxter, Leslie A. and Eric P. Simon (1993). Relationship Maintenance Strategies and Dialectical Contradictions in Personal Relationships. *Journal of Social and Personal Relationships* 10 (May): 225–242.

Baxter, Leslie A., and W. W. Wilmot (1984). Secret Tests: Social Strategies for Acquiring Information About the State of the Relationship. *Human Communication Research* 11:171–201.

Beach, Wayne A. (1990). On (Not) Observing Behavior Interactionally. *Western Journal of Speech Communication* 54 (fall): 603–612.

Beattie, Melody (1987). *Co-Dependent No More.* New York: HarperCollins.

Beatty, M. (1988). Situational and Predispositional Correlates of Public Speaking Anxiety. *Communication Education* 37:28–39.

Beatty, Michael J. (1986). *Romantic Dialogue: Communication in Dating and Marriage.* Englewood, Colo.: Morton Publishing Co.

Beck, A. T. (1988). *Love Is Never Enough.* New York: Harper and Row.

Becker, Samuel L. and Churchill L. Roberts (1992). *Discovering Mass Communication.* 3rd ed. New York: HarperCollins.

Beebe, Steven A. and John T. Masterson (1986). *Family Talk: Interpersonal Communication in the Family.* New York: Random House.

Beier, Ernst (1974). How We Send Emotional Messages. *Psychology Today* 8:53–56.

Bell, Robert A., and N. L. Buerkel-Rothfuss (1990). S(he) Loves Me, S(he) Loves Me Not: Predictors of Relational Information-Seeking in Courtship and Beyond. *Communication Quarterly* 38:64–82.

Bell, Robert A., and John A. Daly (1984). The Affinity-Seeking Function of Communication. *Communication Monographs* 51:91–115.

Bennett, Mark (1990). Children's Understanding of the Mitigating Function of Disclaimers. *Journal of Social Psychology* 130 (February): 29–37.

Berg, John H., and Richard L. Archer (1983). The Disclosure-Liking Relationship. *Human Communication Research* 10:269–281.

Berg-Cross, Linda, Frank Kidd, and Peggy Carr (1990). Cohesion, Affect, and Self-Disclosure in African-American Adolescent Families. *Journal of Family Psychology* 4 (December): 235–250.

Berger, Charles R. and Richard J. Calabrese (1975). Some Explorations in Initial Interaction and Beyond: Toward a Theory of Interpersonal Communication. *Human Communication Research* 1 (winter): 99–112.

Berger, Charles R., and James J. Bradac (1982). *Language and Social Knowledge: Uncertainty in Interpersonal Relations.* London: Edward Arnold.

Berger, Charles R., and Steven H. Chaffee, eds. (1987). *Handbook of Communication Science.* Thousand Oaks, CA: Sage.

Berger, P. L. and T. Luckmann (1980). *The Social Construction of Reality.* New York: Irvington.

Berman, J. J., V. Murphy-Berman, and P. Singh (1985). Cross-Cultural Similarities and Differences in Perceptions of Fairness. *Journal of Cross-Cultural Psychology* 16:55–67.

Bernstein, W. M., W. G. Stephan, and M. H. Davis (1979). Explaining Attributions for Achievement: A Path Analytic Approach. *Journal of Personality and Social Psychology* 37:1810–1821.

Berry, John W., Ype H. Poortinga, Marshall H. Segall, and Pierre R. Dasen (1992). *Cross-Cultural Psychology: Research and Applications.* Cambridge: Cambridge University Press.

Berscheid, Ellen (1985). Interpersonal Attraction. In *Handbook of Social Psychology,* edited by G. Lindzey and E. Aronson, pp. 413–484. New York: Random House.

Berscheid, Ellen, and Elaine Hatfield Walster (1974). A Little Bit About Love. In *Foundations of Interpersonal Attraction,* edited by T. L. Huston. New York: Academic Press.

Berscheid, Ellen, and Elaine Hatfield Walster (1978). *Interpersonal Attraction.* 2d ed. Reading, MA: Addison-Wesley.

Bibby, Cyril (1967). The Art of Love. In *The Encyclopedia of Sexual Behavior,* edited by Albert Ellis and Albert Abarbanel. New York: Hawthorn.

Bierhoff, Hans W. and Renate Klein (1991). "Dimensionen der Liebe: Entwicklung einer Deutschsprachigen Skala zur Erfassung von Liebesstilen," *Zeitschrift for Differentielle und Diagnostische Psychologie* 12 (March): 53–71.

Birdwhistell, Ray L. (1970). *Kinesics and Context: Essays on Body Motion Communication.* New York: Ballantine.

Bishop, Jerry E. (1993). New Research Suggests that Romance Begins by Falling Nose Over Heels in Love. *Wall Street Journal* (April 7): B1.

Blieszner, Rosemary, and Rebecca G. Adams (1992). *Adult Friendship.* Thousand Oaks, CA: Sage.

Blood, Robert O., Jr. (1973). Resolving Family Conflicts. In *Conflict Resolution Through Communication,* edited by Fred E. Jandt. New York: Harper and Row, pp. 221–239.

Blumstein, Philip, and Pepper Schwartz (1983). *American Couples: Money, Work, Sex.* New York: Morrow.

Bochner, Arthur (1978). On Taking Ourselves Seriously: An Analysis of Some Persistent Problems and Promising Directions in Interpersonal Research. *Human Communication Research* 4:179–191.

Bochner, Arthur (1984). The Functions of Human Communication in Interpersonal Bonding. In Arnold and Bowers (1984), pp. 544–621.

Bochner, Arthur, and Clifford Kelly (1974). Interpersonal Competence: Rationale, Philosophy, and Implementation of a Conceptual Framework. *Communication Education* 23:279–301.

Bochner, Arthur, and Janet Yerby (1977). Factors Affecting Instruction in Interpersonal Competence. *Communication Education* 26:91–103.

Bochner, Stephen (1994). Cross-Cultural Differences in the Self-concept: A Test of Hofstede's Individualism/Collectivism Distinction. *Journal of Cross Cultural Psychology* 25 (June): 273–283.

Bochner, Stephen and Beryl Hesketh (1994). Power Distance, Individualism/Collectivism, and Job-related Attitudes in a Culturally Diverse Work Group. *Journal of Cross Cultural Psychology* 25 (June): 233–257.

Bok, Sissela (1978). *Lying: Moral Choice in Public and Private Life.* New York: Pantheon.

Bok, Sissela (1983). *Secrets.* New York: Vintage.

Borden, George A. (1991). *Cultural Orientation: An Approach to Understanding Intercultural Communication.* Englewood Cliffs, NJ: Prentice-Hall.

Borisoff, Deborah, and Lisa Merrill (1985). *The Power to Communicate: Gender Differences as Barriers.* Prospect Heights, IL: Waveland Press.

Bosmajian, Haig (1974). *The Language of Oppression.* Washington, DC: Public Affairs Press.

Bourland, D. David, Jr. (1965–66). A Linguistic Note: Writing in E-prime. *General Semantics Bulletin* 32–33:111–114.

Bourland, D. David, Jr. (1992). E-Prime and Un-Sanity. *Etc.: A Review of General Semantics* 49 (summer): 213–223.

Bradac, James J., John Waite Bowers, and John A. Courtright (1979). Three Language Variables in Communication Research: Intensity, Immediacy, and Diversity. *Human Communication Research* 5:256–269.

Bravo, Ellen and Ellen Cassedy (1992). *The 9 to 5 Guide to Combating Sexual Harassment.* New York: Wiley.

Brecher, Edward M. (1969). *The Sex Researchers.* Boston: Little, Brown.

Breidenstein-Cutspec, Patricia and Elizabeth Goering (1989). Exploring Cultural Diversity: A Network Analysis of the Communicative Correlates of Shyness Within the Black Culture. *Communication Research Reports* 6 (June): 37–46.

Brommel, Bernard (1990). Personal communication.

Brougher, Toni (1982). *A Way with Words.* Chicago: Nelson-Hall.

Brown, Charles T., and Paul W. Keller (1979). *Monologue to Dialogue: An Exploration of Interpersonal Communication.* 2d ed. Englewood Cliffs, NJ: Prentice Hall.

Brown, Penelope (1980). How and Why Are Women More Polite: Some Evidence from a Mayan Community. In Sally McConnell-Ginet, Ruth Borker, and Mellie Furman, eds., *Women and Language in Literature and Society.* New York: Praeger, pp. 111–136.

Brown, Penelope and S. C. Levinson (1987). *Politeness: Some Universals of Language Usage.* Cambridge: Cambridge University Press.

Brownell, Judi (1987). Listening: The Toughest Management Skill. *Cornell Hotel and Restaurant Administration Quarterly* 27:64–71.

Bruneau, Tom (1985). The Time Dimension in Intercultural Communication. In Samovar and Porter (1985), pp. 280–289.

Bruneau, Tom (1990). Chronemics: The Study of Time in Human Interaction. In DeVito and Hecht (1990), pp. 301–311.

Bugental, J., and S. Zelen (1950). Investigations into the "Self-Concept." I. The W-A-Y Technique. *Journal of Personality* 18:483–498.

Bull, Peter (1983). *Body Movement and Interpersonal Communication.* New York: Wiley.

Bull, R. and N. Rumsey (1988). *The Social Psychology of Facial Appearance.* New York: Springer-Verlag.

Buller, David B. and R. Kelly Aune (1992). The Effects of Speech Rate Similarity on Compliance: Application of Communication Accommodation Theory. *Western Journal of Communication* 56 (winter): 37–53.

Buller, David B., Beth A. LePoire, R. Kelly Aune, and Sylvie Eloy (1992). Social Perceptions as Mediators of the Effect of Speech Rate Similarity on Compliance. *Human Communication Research* 19 (December): 286–311.

Burgoon, Judee K. (1991). Relational Message Interpretations of Touch, Conversational Distance, and Posture. *Journal of Nonverbal Behavior* 15 (winter): 233–259.

Burgoon, Judee K., David B. Buller, and W. Gill Woodall (1995). *Nonverbal Communication: The Unspoken Dialogue.* 2d ed. New York: McGraw-Hill.

Burgoon, Judee K., David B. Buller, Amy S. Ebesu, and Patricia Rockwell (1994). Interpersonal Deception: V. Accuracy in Deception Detection. *Communication Monographs* 61 (December): 303–325.

Burgoon, Judee K., and Jerold L. Hale (1988). Nonverbal Expectancy Violations: Model Elaboration and Application to Immediacy Behaviors. *Communication Monographs* 55:58–79.

Burgoon, Michael (1971). The Relationship Between Willingness to Manipulate Others and Success in Two Different Types of Basic Speech Communication Courses. *Communication Education* 20:178–183.

Burns, D. D. (1980). *Feeling Good.* New York: New American Library.

Burns, D. D. (1985). *Intimate Connections.* New York: Morrow.

Burr, Chandler (1996). *A Separate Creation: The Search for the Biological origins of Sexual Orientation.* New York: Hyperion.

Buss, David (1989). Sex Differences in Human Mate Preferences: Evolutionary Hypotheses Tested in 37 Cultures. *Behavioral and Brain Sciences* 12:1–49.

Buss, David M., and David P. Schmitt (1993). Sexual Strategies Theory: An Evolutionary Perspective on Human Mating. *Psychological Review* 100 (April): 204–232.

Butler, Pamela E. (1981). *Talking to Yourself: Learning the Language of Self-Support.* New York: Harper and Row.

Cabello, B. and R. Terrell (1994). Making Students Feel Like Family: How Teachers Create Warm and Caring Classroom Climates. *Journal of Classroom Interaction* 29:17–23.

Camden, Carl, Michael T. Motley, and Ann Wilson (1984). White Lies in Interpersonal Communication: A Taxonomy and Preliminary Investigation of Social Motivations. *Western Journal of Speech Communication* 48:309–325.

Canary, D. J., and L. Stafford (1994). Maintaining Relationships Through Strategic and Routine Interaction. In *Communication and Relational Maintenance,* edited by D. J. Canary and L. Stafford. New York: Academic Press.

Canary, Daniel J. and Laura Stafford (1994). *Communication and Relational Maintenance.* Orlando, Fla.: Academic Press.

Canary, Daniel J., Laura Stafford, Kimberley S. Hause, and Lise A. Wallace (1993). An Inductive Analysis of Relational Maintenance Strategies: Comparisons Among Lovers, Relatives, Friends, and Others. *Communication Research Reports* 10 (June): 5–14.

Cappella, Joseph N. (1987). Interpersonal Communication: Definitions and Fundamental Questions. In Berger and Chaffee (1987), 184–238.

Cappella, Joseph N. (1993). The Facial Feedback Hypothesis in Human Interaction: Review and Speculation. *Journal of Language and Social Psychology* 12 (March–June): 13–29.

Carducci, Bernardo J. with Philip G. Zimbardo (1995). Are You Shy? *Psychology Today* 28 (November–December): 34–41, 64–70, 78–82.

Carpenter, David, and David Knox (1986). Relationship Maintenance of College Students Separated During Courtship. *College Student Journal*

20 (spring): 86–88.

Carroll, John B., ed (1956). *Language, Thought, and Reality: Selected Writings of Benjamin Lee Whorf.* New York: Wiley.

Cate, R., J. Henton, J. Koval, R. Christopher, and S. Lloyd (1982). Premarital Abuse: A Social Psychological Perspective. *Journal of Family Issues* 3:79–90.

Cegala, Donald J., Grant T. Savage, Claire C. Brunner, and Anne B. Conrad (1982). An Elaboration of the Meaning of Interaction Involvement. *Communication Monographs* 49:229–248.

Chadwick-Jones, J. K. (1976). *Social Exchange Theory: Its Structure and Influence in Social Psychology.* New York: Academic Press.

Chaikin, A. L., and V. J. Derlega (1974). Variables Affecting the Appropriateness of Self-Disclosure. *Journal of Consulting and Clinical Psychology* 42:588–628.

Chaney, Robert H., Carolyne A. Givens, Melanie F. Aoki, and Michael L. Gombiner (1989). Pupillary Responses in Recognizing Awareness in Persons with Profound Mental Retardation. *Perceptual and Motor Skills* 69 (October): 523–528.

Chang, Hui-Ching and G. Richard Holt (1996). The Changing Chinese Interpersonal World: Popular Themes in Interpersonal Communication Books in Modern Taiwan. *Communication Quarterly* 44 (winter): 85–106.

Chanowitz, B. and E. Langer (1981). Premature Cognitive Commitment. *Journal of Personality and Social Psychology* 41:1051–1063.

Chen, Guo-Ming (1990). Intercultural Communication Competence: Some Perspectives of Research. *The Howard Journal of Communication* 2 (summer): 243–261.

Chen, Guo-Ming (1992). "Differences in Self-Disclosure Patterns Among Americans versus Chinese: A Comparative Study." Paper presented at the annual meeting of the Eastern Communication Association (Portland, ME).

Cherry, Kittredge (1991). *Hide and Speak: How to Free Ourselves from Our Secrets.* San Francisco, CA: HarperSanFrancisco.

Chesebro, James, ed. (1981). *Gayspeak.* New York: Pilgrim Press.

Christie, Richard (1970). Scale Construction. In R. Christie and F. L. Geis, eds., *Studies in Machiavellianism,* pp. 35–52. New York: Academic Press.

Cialdini, Robert T. (1984). *Influence: How and Why People Agree to Things.* New York: Morrow.

Clark, Herbert (1974). The Power of Positive Speaking. *Psychology Today* 8:102, 108–111.

Clark, M. L., et al. (1994). Courtship Violence Among African American College Students. *Journal of Black Psychology* 20 (August): 264–281.

Clark, Ruth Anne (1991). *Studying Interpersonal Communication: The Research Experience.* Thousand Oaks, CA: Sage.

Clement, Donald A., and Kenneth D. Frandsen (1976). On Conceptual and Empirical Treatments of Feedback in Human Communication. *Communication Monographs* 43:11–28.

Cline, M. G. (1956). The Influence of Social Context on the Perception of Faces. *Journal of Personality* 2:142–185.

Cline, Rebecca J. and Carol A. Puhl (1984). Culture and Geography: A Comparison of Seating Arrangements in the United States and Taiwan. *Journal of International Relations* 8:199–219.

Cody, Michael J. (1982). A Typology of Disengagement Strategies and an Examination of the Role Intimacy, Reactions to Inequity, and Relational Problems Play in Strategy Selection. *Communication Monographs* 49:148–170.

Cody, Michael J., P. J. Marston, and M. Foster (1984). Deception: Paralinguistic and Verbal Leakage. In *Communication Yearbook 7,* edited by R. N. Bostrom. Thousand Oaks, CA: Sage, pp. 464–490.

Collier, Mary Jane (1991). Conflict Competence Within African, Mexican, and Anglo American Friendships. In *Cross-Cultural Interpersonal Communication,* edited by Stella Ting-Toomey and Felipe Korzenny. Thousand Oaks, CA: Sage, pp. 132–154.

Collins, B. E., and B. H. Raven (1969). Group Structure: Attraction, Coalitions, Communication, and Power. In *The Handbook of Social Psychology,* 2d ed., edited by Gardner Lindzey and Elliot Aronson Reading, MA: Addison-Wesley, pp. 102–204.

Collins, James E. and Leslie F. Clark (1989). Responsibility and Rumination: The Trouble with Understanding the Dissolution of a Relationship. *Social Cognition* 7 (summer): 152–173.

Condon, John C. (1974). *Semantics and Communication.* 2d ed. New York: Macmillan.

Condon, John C., and Yousef Fathi (1975). *An Introduction to Intercultural Communication.* Indianapolis, IN.: Bobbs-Merrill.

Cook, Anthony (1993). How Couples Can Avoid Money Misunderstandings. *Money* (July): 92.

Cook, Mark (1971). *Interpersonal Perception.* Baltimore: Penguin.

Cook, Mark, ed. (1984). *Issues in Person Perception.* New York: Methuen.

Cooley, Charles Horton (1922). *Human Nature and the Social Order.* Rev. ed. New York: Scribner's.

Counts, D. A., J. K. Brown, and J. C. Campbell (1992). *Sanctions and Sanctuary: Cultural Perspectives on the Beating of Wives.* Boulder, CO: Westview Press.

Cozby, Paul (1973). Self-Disclosure: A Literature Review. *Psychological Bulletin* 79:73–91.

Craig, Mary E., Seth C. Kalichman, and Diane R. Follingstad (1989). Verbal Coercive Sexual Behavior Among College Students. *Archives of Sexual Behavior* 18 (October): 421–434.

Crohn, Joel (1995). *Mixed Matches: How to Create Successful Interracial, Interethnic, and Interfaith Relationships.* New York: Fawcett Columbine.

Crusco, April H. and Christopher G. Wetzel (1984). The Midas Touch: The Effects of Interpersonal Touch on Restaurant Tipping. *Personality and Social Psychology Bulletin* 10 (December): 512–517.

Cupach, William R., and Sandra Metts (1986). Accounts of Relational Dissolution: A Comparison of Marital and Non-Marital Relationships. *Communication Monographs* 53 (December): 311–334.

Dainton, M., and L. Stafford (1993). Routine Maintenance Behaviors: A Comparison of Relationship Type, Partner Similarity, and Sex Differences. *Journal of Social and Personal Relationships* 10:255–272.

Daly, John A., and James C. McCroskey, eds. (1984). *Avoiding Communication: Shyness, Reticence, and Communication Apprehension.* Thousand Oaks: CA: Sage.

D'Augelli, Anthony R. (1992). Lesbian and Gay Male Undergraduates' Experiences of Harassment and Fear on Campus. *Journal of Interpersonal Violence* 7 (September): 383–395.

Davidson, A. G. (1995). Looking for Love in the Age of AIDS: The Language of Gay Personals 1978–1988. *Journal of Sex Research* 28:125–137.

Davis, Flora (1973). *Inside Intuition.* New York: New American Library.

Davis, Keith E. (1985). Near and Dear: Friendship and Love Compared. *Psychology Today* 19:22–30.

Davis, Murray S. (1973). *Intimate Relations.* New York: Free Press.

Davis, Ossie (1973). The English Language Is My Enemy. In *Language: Concepts and Processes,* edited by Joseph A. DeVito. Englewood Cliffs, NJ: Prentice-Hall, pp. 164–170.

Davitz, Joel R., ed. (1964). *The Communication of Emotional Meaning.* New York: McGraw-Hill.

Deal, James E., and Karen Smith Wampler (1986). Dating Violence: The Primacy of Previous Experience. *Journal of Social and Personal Relationships* 3:457–471.

deBono, Edward (1987). *The Six Thinking Hats.* New York: Penguin.

DeCecco, John (1988). Obligation versus Aspiration. In *Gay Relationships,* edited by John DeCecco. New York: Harrington Park Press.

Deetz, Stanley, and Sheryl Stevenson (1986). *Managing Interpersonal Communication.* New York: Harper and Row.

DeFrancisco, Victoria (1991). The Sound of Silence: How Men Silence Women in Marital Relations. *Discourse and Society* 2: 413–423.

Delia, Jesse G. (1977). Constructivism and the Study of Human Communication. *Quarterly Journal of Speech* 63:66–83.

Delia, Jesse G., Barbara J. O'Keefe, and Daniel J. O'Keefe (1982). The Constructivist Approach to Communication. In Frank E. X. Dance, ed., *Human Communication Theory: Comparative Essays*. New York: Harper and Row, pp. 147–191.

Derlega, Valerian J., and J. H. Berg, eds. (1987). *Self-Disclosure: Theory, Research, and Therapy*. New York: Plenum Press.

Derlega, Valerian J., Stephen T. Margulis, and Barbara A. Winstead (1987). A Social-Psychological Analysis of Self-Disclosure in Psychotherapy. *Journal of Social and Clinical Psychology* 5:205–215.

Derlega, Valerian J., Barbara A. Winstead, Paul T. P. Wong, and Michael Greenspan (1987). Self-Disclosure and Relationship Development: An Attributional Analysis. In *Interpersonal Processes: New Directions in Communication Research*, edited by Michael E. Roloff and Gerald R. Miller. Thousand Oaks, CA: Sage, pp. 172–187.

Deturck, Mark A. (1987). When Communication Fails: Physical Aggression as a Compliance-Gaining Strategy. *Communication Monographs* 54:106–112.

DeTurck, Mark A. and Gerald R. Miller (1985). Deception and Arousal: Isolating the Behavioral Correlates of Deception. *Human Communication Research* 12 (winter): 181–201.

DeVito, Joseph A. (1970). *The Psychology of Speech and Language: An Introduction to the Study of Psycholinguistics*. New York: Random House.

DeVito, Joseph A. (1974). *General Semantics: Guide and Workbook*. Rev. ed. DeLand, FL: Everett/Edwards.

DeVito, Joseph A. (1986a). *The Communication Handbook: A Dictionary*. New York: Harper and Row.

DeVito, Joseph A. (1986b). Teaching as Relational Development. In *Communicating in College Classrooms*, edited by Jean Civikly. New Directions for Teaching and Learning, no. 26. San Francisco: Jossey Bass, pp. 51–60.

DeVito, Joseph A. (1989). *The Nonverbal Communication Workbook*. Prospect Heights, IL: Waveland Press.

DeVito, Joseph A. (1990). *Messages: Building Interpersonal Communication Skills*. New York: Harper and Row.

DeVito, Joseph A. (1996). *Brainstorms: How to Think More Creatively About Communication (or About Anything Else)*. New York: Longman.

DeVito, Joseph A., and Michael L. Hecht, eds. (1990). *The Nonverbal Communication Reader*. Prospect Heights, IL: Waveland Press.

DeVito, Joseph A., ed. (1973). *Language: Concepts and Processes*. 3d ed. Englewood Cliffs, NJ: Prentice Hall.

DeVito, Joseph A., ed. (1981). *Communication: Concepts and Processes*. 3d ed. Englewood Cliffs, NJ: Prentice Hall.

DeVries, Mary A. (1994). *International Yours: Writing and Communicating Successfully in Today's Global Marketplace*. Boston: Houghton Mifflin.

Dickson-Markman, Fran (1984). How Important Is Self-Disclosure in Marriage? *Communication Research Reports* 1:7–14.

Dillard, James Price (1988). Compliance-Gaining Message-Selection: What Is Our Dependent Variable? *Communication Monographs* 55:162–183.

Dillard, James Price, ed. (1990). *Seeking Compliance: The Production of Interpersonal Influence Messages*. Scottsdale, AZ: Gorsuch Scarisbrick.

Dindia, Kathryn (1987). The Effects of Sex of Subject and Partner on Interruptions. *Human Communication Research* 13:345–371.

Dindia, Kathryn, and Leslie A. Baxter (1987). Strategies for Maintaining and Repairing Marital Relationships. *Journal of Social and Personal Relationships* 4:143–158.

Dindia, Kathryn and Daniel J. Canary (1993). Definitions and Theoretical Perspectives on Maintaining Relationships. *Journal of Social and Personal Relationships* 10 (May): 163–174.

Dindia, Kathryn, and Mary Anne Fitzpatrick (1985). Marital Communication: Three Approaches Compared. In *Understanding Personal Relationships: An Interdisciplinary Approach*, edited by Steve Duck and Daniel Perlman. Thousand Oaks, CA: Sage, pp. 137–158.

Dion, K., E. Berscheid, and E. Walster (1972). What Is Beautiful Is Good. *Journal of Personality and Social Psychology* 24:285–290.

Dion, Karen K. and Kenneth L. Dion (1993a). Individualistic and Collectivist Perspectives on Gender and the Cultural Context of Love and Intimacy. *Journal of Social Issues* 49 (fall): 53–69.

Dion, Kenneth L. and Karen K. Dion (1993b). Gender and Ethnocultural Comparisons in Styles of Love. *Psychology of Women Quarterly* 17 (December): 464–473.

Dodd, Carley H. (1982). *Dynamics of Intercultural Communication*. Dubuque, IA: William C. Brown.

Dodd, David H., and Raymond M. White, Jr. (1980). *Cognition: Mental Structures and Processes*. Boston: Allyn and Bacon.

Dolgin, Kim G., Leslie Meyer, and Janet Schwartz (1991). Effects of Gender, Target's Gender, Topic, and Self-Esteem on Disclosure to Best and Midling Friends. *Sex Roles* 25 (September): 311–329.

Donohue, William A. with Robert Kolt (1992). *Managing Interpersonal Conflict*. Thousand Oaks, CA: Sage.

Dosey, M. and M. Meisels (1976). Personal Space and Self-Protection. *Journal of Personality and Social Psychology* 38:959–965.

Dosser, David A., Jr., Jack O. Balswick, and Charles F. Halverson, Jr. (1986). Male Inexpressiveness and Relationships. *Journal of Social and Personal Relationships* 3:241–258.

Douglas, William (1994). The Acquaintanceship Process: An Examination of Uncertainty, Information Seeking, and Social Attraction during Initial Conversation. *Communication Research* 21 (April): 154–176.

Drass, Kriss A. (1986). The Effect of Gender Identity on Conversation. *Social Psychology Quarterly* 49 (December): 294–301.

Dresser, Norine (1996). *Multicultural Manners: New Rules of Etiquette for a Changing Society*. New York: Wiley.

Dreyfuss, Henry (1971). *Symbol Sourcebook*. New York: McGraw–Hill.

Driscoll, R., K. E. Davis, and M. E. Lipetz (1972). Parental Interference and Romantic Love: The Romeo and Juliet Effect. *Journal of Personality and Social Psychology* 24:1–10.

Drummond, Kent and Robert Hopper (1993). Acknowledgment Tokens in Series. *Communication Reports* 6 (winter): 47–53.

Dubois, Betty Lou, and Isabel Crouch (1975). The Question of Tag Questions in Women's Speech: They Don't Really Use More of Them, Do They? *Language and Society* 4:289–294.

Duck, Steve (1986). *Human Relationships*. Thousand Oaks, CA: Sage.

Duck, Steve (1988). *Relating to Others*. Milton Keynes, England: Open University Press.

Duck, Steve, ed. (1982). *Personal Relationships. 4: Dissolving Personal Relationships*. New York: Academic Press.

Duck, Steve, and Robin Gilmour, eds. (1981). *Personal Relationships. 1: Studying Personal Relationships*. New York: Academic Press.

Dullea, Georgia (1981). Presents: Hidden Messages. *New York Times*, 14 December, D12.

Duncan, Barry L. and Joseph W. Rock (1991). *Overcoming Relationship Impasses: Ways to Initiate Change When Your Partner Won't Help*. New York: Plenum Press/Insight Books.

Duncan, S. D., Jr. (1972). Some Signals and Rules for Taking Speaking Turns in Conversation. *Journal of Personality and Social Psychology* 23:283–292.

Duran, R. L., and L. Kelly (1988). The Influence of Communicative Competence on Perceived Task, Social, and Physical Attraction. *Communication Quarterly* 36:41–49.

Eakins, Barbara, and R. Gene Eakins (1978). *Sex Differences in Communication*. Boston: Houghton Mifflin.

Eden, Dov (1992). Leadership and Expectations: Pygmalion Effects and Other Self-Fulfilling Prophecies in Organizations. *Leadership Quarterly* 3 (winter): 271–305.

Eder, D. and J. L. Enke (1991). The Structure of Gossip: Opportunities and Constraints on Collective Expression among Adolescents. *American Sociological Review* 56:494–508.

Edgar, T., and M. A. Fitzpatrick (1988). Compliance-Gaining in Relational Interactions: When Your Life Depends on It. *Southern Speech Communication Journal* 53 (summer): 385–405.

Egan, Gerard (1970). *Encounter: Group Processes for Interpersonal Growth.* Belmont, CA: Brooks/Cole.

Ehrenhaus, Peter (1988). Silence and Symbolic Expression. *Communication Monographs* 55 (March): 41–57.

Ekman, Paul (1965). Communication Through Nonverbal Behavior: A Source of Information About an Interpersonal Relationship. In *Affect, Cognition and Personality,* edited by S. S. Tomkins and C. E. Izard. New York: Springer.

Ekman, Paul (1985). *Telling Lies: Clues to Deceit in the Marketplace, Politics, and Marriage.* New York: W. W. Norton.

Ekman, Paul, and Wallace V. Friesen (1969). The Repertoire of Nonverbal Behavior: Categories, Origins, Usage, and Coding. *Semiotica* 1:49–98.

Ekman, Paul and Wallace V. Friesen (1978). *The Facial Action Coding System.* Palo Alto, CA: Consulting Psychologists Press.

Ekman, Paul, Wallace V. Friesen, and Phoebe Ellsworth (1972). *Emotion in the Human Face: Guidelines for Research and an Integration of Findings.* New York: Pergamon Press.

Ekman, Paul, Wallace V. Friesen, and S. S. Tomkins (1971). Facial Affect Scoring Technique: A First Validity Study. *Semiotica* 3:37–58.

Ellis, Albert (1988). *How to Stubbornly Refuse to Make Yourself Miserable About Anything, Yes Anything.* Secaucus, NJ: Lyle Stuart.

Ellis, Albert, and Robert A. Harper (1975). *A New Guide to Rational Living.* Hollywood, CA: Wilshire Books.

Elmes, Michael B., and Gary Gemmill (1990). The Psychodynamics of Mindlessness and Dissent in Small Groups. *Small Group Research* 21 (February): 28–44.

Epstein, N., J. L. Pretzer, and B. Fleming (1987). The Role of Cognitive Appraisal in Self-Reports of Marital Communication. *Behavior Therapy* 18:51–69.

Exline, R. V., S. L. Ellyson, and B. Long (1975). Visual Behavior as an Aspect of Power Role Relationships. In *Nonverbal Communication of Aggression,* edited by P. Pliner, L. Krames, and T. Alloway. New York: Plenum Press.

Faber, Adele, and Elaine Mazlish (1980). *How to Talk so Kids Will Listen and Listen so Kids Will Talk.* New York: Avon.

Falk, Dennis R., and Pat N. Wagner (1985). Intimacy of Self-Disclosure and Response Processes as Factors Affecting the Development of Interpersonal Relationships. *Journal of Social Psychology* 125:557–570.

Farrell, M. P., and S. D. Rosenberg (1981). *Men at Midlife.* Westport, CT: Auburn House.

Feeley, Thomas H. and Mark A. deTurck (1995). Global Cue Usage in Behavioral Lie Detection. *Communication Quarterly* 43 (fall): 420–430.

Fengler, A. P. (1974). Romantic Love in Courtship: Divergent Paths of Male and Female Students. *Journal of Comparative Family Studies* 5:134–139.

Fernald, C. D. (1995). When in London . . .: Differences in Disability Language Preferences Among English-Speaking Countries. *Mental Retardation* 33 (April): 99–103.

Festinger, L., S. Schachter, and K. W. Back (1950). *Social Pressures in Informal Groups: A Study of Human Factors in Housing.* New York: Harper and Row.

Field, R. H. G. (1989). The Self-Fulfilling Prophecy Leader: Achieving the Metharme Effect. *Journal of Management Studies* 26 (March): 151–175.

Filley, Alan C. (1975). *Interpersonal Conflict Resolution.* Glenview, IL: Scott, Foresman.

Fischer, C. S., and S. J. Oliker (1983). A Research Note on Friendship, Gender, and the Life Cycle. *Social Forces* 62:124–133.

Fisher, Donna (1995). *People Power: 12 Power Principles to Enrich Your Business, Career, and Personal Networks.* Austin, TX: Bard and Stephen.

Fishman, Joshua (1960). A Systematization of the Whorfian Hypothesis. *Behavioral Science* 5:323–339.

Fishman, Joshua A. (1972). *The Sociology of Language.* Rowley, MA: Newbury House.

Fiske, Susan T., and Shelley E. Taylor (1984). *Social Cognition.* Reading, MA: Addison-Wesley.

Fitzpatrick, Mary Anne (1983). Predicting Couples' Communication from Couples' Self-Reports. In *Communication Yearbook 7,* edited by R. N. Bostrom. Thousand Oaks, CA: Sage, pp. 49–82.

Fitzpatrick, Mary Anne (1988). *Between Husbands and Wives: Communication in Marriage.* Thousand Oaks, CA: Sage.

Fitzpatrick, Mary Anne (1991). Sex Differences in Marital Conflict: Social Psychophysiological versus Cognitive Explanations. *Text* 11:341–364.

Floyd, James J. (1985). *Listening: A Practical Approach.* Glenview, IL: Scott, Foresman.

Folger, Joseph P., and Marshall Scott Poole (1984). *Working Through Conflict: A Communication Perspective.* Glenview, IL: Scott, Foresman.

Follingstad, Diane R., et al. (1990). The Role of Emotional Abuse in Physically Abusive Relationships. *Journal of Family Violence* 5 (June): 107–120.

Fox, M., M. Gibbs, and D. Auerbach (1985). Age and Gender Dimensions of Friendship. *Psychology of Women Quarterly* 9:489–501.

Fraser, Bruce (1990). Perspectives on Politeness. *Journal of Pragmatics* 14 (April): 219–236.

Frazier, P. A. and S. W. Cook (1993). Correlates of Distress Following Heterosexual Relationship Dissolution. *Journal of Social and Personal Relationships* 10:55–67.

Freedman, Jonathan (1978). *Happy People: What Happiness Is, Who Has It, and Why.* New York: Ballantine.

French, J. R. P., Jr., and B. Raven (1968). The Bases of Social Power. In *Group Dynamics: Research and Theory,* 3d ed., edited by Dorwin Cartwright and Alvin Zander. New York: Harper and Row, pp. 259–269.

Frentz, Thomas (1976). A General Approach to Episodic Structure. Paper presented at the Western Speech Association Convention, San Francisco. Cited in Reardon (1987).

Friedman, Joel, Marcia Mobilia Boumil, and Barbara Ewert Taylor (1992). *Sexual Harassment.* Deerfield Beach, FL: Health Communications, Inc.

Friedman, Meyer, and Ray Rosenman (1974). *Type A Behavior and Your Heart.* New York: Fawcett Crest.

Frye, Jerry K. (1980). *FIND: Frye's Index to Nonverbal Data.* Duluth: University of Minnesota Computer Center.

Fuller, Linda K. (1995). *Media-Mediated Relationships: Straight and Gay, Mainstream and Alternative Perspectives.* New York: Harrington Park Press.

Furlow, F. Bryant (1996). The smell of love. *Psychology Today* 29 (March/April): 38–45.

Furnham, Adrian and Nadine Bitar (1993). The Stereotyped Portrayal of Men and Women in British Television Advertisements. *Sex Roles* 29 (August): 297–310.

Furnham, Adrian, and Stephen Bochner (1986). *Culture Shock: Psychological Reactions to Unfamiliar Environments.* New York: Methuen.

Gable, Myron, Charles Hollon, and Frank Dangello (1992). Managerial Structuring of Work as a Moderator of the Machiavellianism and Job Performance Relationship. *Journal of Psychology* 126 (May): 317–325.

Gabor, Don (1989). *How to Talk to the People You Love.* New York: Simon and Schuster.

Gabrenya, W. K., Jr., Y. E. Wang, and B. Latane (1985). Social Loafing on an Optimizing Task: Cross-Cultural Differences among Chinese and Americans. *Journal of Cross-Cultural Psychology* 16:223–242.

Galbraith, J. K. (1983). *The Anatomy of Power.* Boston: Houghton Mifflin.

Galvin, Kathleen, and Bernard J. Brommel (1991). *Family Communication: Cohesion and Change.* 3d ed. Glenview, IL: Scott, Foresman.

Gangestad, S. and M. Snyder (1985). To Carve Nature at Its Joints: On the Existence of Discrete Classes in Personality. *Psychological Review* 92:317–349.

Gao, Ge and William B. Gudykunst (1995). Attributional Confidence, Perceived Similarity, and Network Involvement in Chinese and American Romantic Relationships. *Communication Quarterly* 43 (fall): 431–445.

Garner, Alan (1981). *Conversationally Speaking.* New York: McGraw-Hill.

Gelles, R. (1981). The Myth of the Battered Husband. In *Marriage and Family 81/82,* edited by R. Walsh and O. Pocs. Guildford: Dushkin.

Gelles, R., and C. Cornell (1985). *Intimate Violence in Families.* Thousand Oaks, CA: Sage.

Gergen, K. J., M. S. Greenberg, and R. H. Willis (1980). *Social Exchange: Advances in Theory and Research.* New York: Plenum Press.

Gibb, Jack (1961). Defensive Communication. *Journal of Communication* 11:141–148.

Gilbert, Shirley (1975). Empirical and Theoretical Extension of Self-Disclosure. In *Interpersonal Communication,* edited by Gerald R. Miller. Thousand Oaks, CA: Sage, pp. 197–215.

Giles, Howard, Anthony Mulac, James J. Bradac, and Patricia Johnson (1987). Speech Accommodation Theory: The First Decade and Beyond, in Margaret L. McLaughlin, ed., *Communication Yearbook 10.* Thousand Oaks, CA: Sage, pp. 13–48.

Gilmour, Robin, and Steve Duck, eds. (1986). *The Emerging Field of Personal Relationships.* Hillsdale, NJ: Lawrence Erlbaum.

Gladstein, Gerald A., et al. (1987). *Empathy and Counseling: Explorations in Theory and Research.* New York: Springer–Verlag.

Glucksberg, Sam and Joseph H. Danks (1975). *Experimental Psycholinguistics: An Introduction.* Hillsdale, NJ: Lawrence Erlbaum.

Goffman, Erving (1967). *Interaction Ritual: Essays on Face-to-Face Behavior.* New York: Pantheon.

Goffman, Erving (1971). *Relations in Public: Microstudies of the Public Order.* New York: Harper Colophon.

Goldberg, Philip (1968). Are Women Prejudiced Against Women? *Trans-action* 6.528–530.

Goleman, Daniel (1992). Studies Find No Disadvantage in Growing Up in a Gay Home. *New York Times,* (December 2): C14.

Goleman, Daniel (1995a). *Emotional Intelligence.* New York: Bantam.

Goleman, Daniel (1995b). For Man and Beast, Language of Love Shares Many Traits. *New York Times* (February 14): C1, C9.

Gonzalez, Alexander, and Philip G. Zimbardo (1985). Time in Perspective. *Psychology Today* 19:20–26. Reprinted in DeVito and Hecht (1990).

Goodwin, Robin and Iona Lee (1994). Taboo Topics Among Chinese and English Friends: A Cross-Cultural Comparison. *Journal of Cross Cultural Psychology* 25 (September): 325–338.

Gordon, Thomas (1975). *P.E.T.: Parent Effectiveness Training.* New York: New American Library.

Goss, Blaine (1985). *The Psychology of Communication.* Prospect Heights, IL: Waveland Press.

Goss, Blaine, M. Thompson, and S. Olds (1978). Behavioral Support for Systematic Desensitization for Communication Apprehension. *Human Communication Research* 4:158–163.

Gottman, John (1993). *What Predicts Divorce: The Relationships between Marital Processes and Marital Outcomes.* Hillsdale, NJ: Lawrence Erlbaum Associates.

Gottman, John (1994). *Why Marriages Succeed or Fail.* New York: Simon and Schuster.

Gould, Stephen Jay (1995). No More 'Wretched Refuse'. *New York Times* (June 7): A27.

Graham, E. E. (1994). Interpersonal Communication Motives Scale. In R. B. Rubin, P. Palmgreen, and H. E. Sypher, eds., *Communication Research Measures: A Sourcebook.* New York: Guilford, pp. 211–216.

Graham, E. E., C. A. Barbato, and E. M. Perse (1993). The Interpersonal Communication Motives Model. *Communication Quarterly* 41:172–186.

Graham, Jean Ann, and Michael Argyle (1975). The Effects of Different Patterns of Gaze, Combined with Different Facial Expressions, on Impression Formation. *Journal of Movement Studies* 1 (December): 178–182.

Graham, Jean Ann, Pio Ricci Bitti, and Michael Argyle (1975). A Cross-Cultural Study of the Communication of Emotion by Facial and Gestural Cues. *Journal of Human Movement Studies* 1 (June): 68–77.

Grant, August E. and K. Kendall Guthrie (1991). Television Shopping: A Media System Dependency Perspective. *Communication Research* 18 (December): 773–798.

Greif, Esther Blank (1980). Sex Differences in Parent-Child Conversations. *Women's Studies International Quarterly* 3:253–258.

Grice, H. P. (1975). Logic and Conversation. In *Syntax and Semantics.* Vol. 3, *Speech Acts,* edited by P. Cole and J. L. Morgan. New York: Seminar Press, pp. 41–58.

Griffin, Em (1997). *A First Look at Communication Theory.* 2d ed. New York: McGraw-Hill.

Griffin, Em, and Glenn G. Sparks (1990). Friends Forever: A Longitudinal Exploration of Intimacy in Same-Sex Friends and Platonic Pairs. *Journal of Social and Personal Relationships* 7:29–46.

Gross, Larry (1991). The Contested Closet: The Ethics and Politics of Outing. *Critical Studies in Mass Communication* 8 (September): 352–388.

Gross, Larry (1993). *Contested Closets: The Politics and Ethics of Outing.* New York: Oxford University Press

Gu, Yueguo (1990). Polite Phenomena in Modern Chinese. *Journal of Pragmatics* 14 (April): 237–257.

Gudykunst, W. and T. Nishida (1984). Individual and Cultural Influence on Uncertainty Reduction. *Communication Monographs* 51:23–36.

Gudykunst, W., S. Yang and T. Nishida (1985). A Cross-Cultural Test of Uncertainty Reduction Theory: Comparisons of Acquaintance, Friend, and Dating Relationships in Japan, Korea, and the United States. *Human Communication Research* 11:407–454.

Gudykunst, W. B. (1989). Culture and the Development of Interpersonal Relationships. In *Communication Yearbook 12,* edited by J. A. Anderson. Thousand Oaks, CA: Sage, pp. 315–354.

Gudykunst, W. B., ed. (1983). *Intercultural Communication Theory: Current Perspectives.* Thousand Oaks, CA: Sage.

Gudykunst, W. B., and Y. Y. Kim (1984). *Communicating with Strangers: An Approach to Intercultural Communication.* New York: Random House.

Gudykunst, William B. (1991). *Bridging Differences: Effective Intergroup Communication.* Thousand Oaks, CA: Sage.

Gudykunst, William B. and Stella Ting-Toomey with Elizabeth Chua (1988). *Culture and Interpersonal Communication.* Thousand Oaks, CA: Sage.

Guerrero, L. K., S. V. Eloy, and A. I. Wabnik (1993). Linking Maintenance Strategies to Relationship Development and Disengagement: A Reconceptualization. *Journal of Social and Personal Relationships* 10:273–282.

Guerrero, Laura K. and Peter A. Andersen (1991). The Waxing and Waning of Relational Intimacy: Touch as a Function of Relational Stage, Gender and Touch Avoidance. *Journal of Social and Personal Relationships* 8 (May): 147–165.

Guerrero, Laura K. and Peter A. Andersen (1994). Patterns of Matching and Initiation: Touch Behavior and Touch Avoidance Across Romantic Relationship Stages. *Journal of Nonverbal Behavior* 18 (summer): 137–153.

Gupta, U., and P. Singh (1982). Exploratory Studies in Love and Liking and Types of Marriages. *Indian Journal of Applied Psychology* 19:92–97.

Haferkamp, Claudia J. (1991–92). Orientations to Conflict: Gender, Attributes, Resolution Strategies, and Self-Monitoring. *Current Psychology: Research and Reviews* 10 (winter): 227–240.

Haga, Yasushi (1988). Traits de Langage et Caractere Japonais. *Cahiers de Sociologie Economique et Culturelle* 9 (June): 105–109.

Haggard, E. A., and K. S. Isaacs (1966). Micromomentary Facial Expressions as Indicators of Ego Mechanisms in Psychotherapy. In *Methods of Research in Psychotherapy,* edited by L. A. Gottschalk and A. H. Auerbach. Englewood Cliffs, NJ: Prentice Hall.

Hale, Jerold, James C. Lundy, and Paul A. Mongeau (1989). Perceived Relational Intimacy and Relational Message Content. *Communication Research Reports* 6 (December): 94–99.

Hall, Edward T. (1959). *The Silent Language.* Garden City, NY: Doubleday.

Hall, Edward T. (1963). System for the Notation of Proxemic Behavior. *American Anthropologist* 65:1003–1026.

Hall, Edward T. (1966). *The Hidden Dimension.* Garden City, NY: Doubleday.

Hall, Edward T. (1976). *Beyond Culture.* Garden City, NY: Anchor Press.

Hall, Edward T. (1983). *The Dance of Life: The Other Dimension of Time.* New York: Anchor Books/Doubleday.

Hall, Edward T., and Mildred Reed Hall (1987). *Hidden Differences: Doing Business with the Japanese.* New York: Anchor Books.

Hall, J. A. (1984). *Nonverbal Sex Differences.* Baltimore: Johns Hopkins University Press.

Hall, Joan Kelly (1993). Tengo una Bomba: The Paralinguistic and Linguistic Conventions of the Oral Practice *Chismeando. Research on Language and Social Interaction* 26:55–83.

Hamachek, Don E. (1982). *Encounters with Others: Interpersonal Relationships and You.* New York: Holt, Rinehart and Winston.

Han, Sang-pil and Shavitt, Sharon (1994). Persuasion and Culture: Advertising Appeals in Individualistic and Collectivistic Societies. *Journal of Experimental Social Psychology* 30 (July): 326–350.

Haney, William (1973). *Communication and Organizational Behavior: Text and Cases.* 3d ed. Homewood, IL: Irwin.

Haney, William (1981). Serial Communication of Information in Organizations. In DeVito (1981), pp. 169–182.

Harrell, W. Andrew (1990). Husband's Masculinity, Wife's Power, and Marital Conflict. *Social Behavior and Personality* 18:207–215.

Harris, Judy (1995). Educational Telecomputing Projects: Interpersonal Exchanges. *Computing Teacher* 22 (March): 60–64.

Harris, Marvin (1993). *Culture, People, Nature: An Introduction to General Anthropology.* 6th ed. New York: Longman.

Hart, Fiona (1990). The Construction of Masculinity in Men's Friendships: Misogyny, Heterosexism and Homophobia. *Resources for Feminist Research* 19 (September–December): 60–67.

Hart, R. P., and D. M. Burks (1972). Rhetorical Sensitivity and Social Interaction. *Communication Monographs* 39:75–91.

Hart, R. P., R. E. Carlson, and W. F. Eadie (1980). Attitudes Toward Communication and the Assessment of Rhetorical Sensitivity. *Communication Monographs* 47:1–22.

Hart, Russell D. and David E. Williams (1995). Able-Bodied Instructors and Students with Physical Disabilities: A Relationship Handicapped by Communication. *Communication Education* 44 (April): 140–154.

Harvey, John H., Rodney Flanary, and Melinda Morgan (1986). Vivid Memories of Vivid Loves Gone By. *Journal of Social and Personal Relationships* 3:359–373.

Hasart, Julie K. and Kevin L. Hutchinson (1993). The Effects of Eyeglasses on Perceptions of Interpersonal Attraction. *Journal of Social Behavior and Personality* 8:521–528.

Hastorf, Albert, David Schneider, and Judith Polefka (1970). *Person Perception.* Reading, MA: Addison-Wesley.

Hatfield, Elaine and Richard L. Rapson (1992). Similarity and Attraction in Close Relationships. *Communication Monographs* 59:209–212.

Hatfield, Elaine and Richard L. Rapson (1996). *Love and Sex: Cross Cultural Perspectives.* Boston: Allyn and Bacon.

Hatfield, Elaine, and Jane Traupman (1981). Intimate Relationships: A Perspective from Equity Theory. In Duck and Gilmour (1981), pp. 165–178.

Hayakawa, S. I., and A. R. Hayakawa (1989). *Language in Thought and Action.* 5th ed. New York: Harcourt Brace Jovanovich.

Hays, Robert B. (1989). The Day-to-Day Functioning of Close Versus Casual Friendships. *Journal of Social and Personal Relationships* 6:21–37.

Hecht, Michael (1978a). The Conceptualization and Measurement of Interpersonal Communication Satisfaction. *Human Communication Research* 4:253–264.

Hecht, Michael (1978b). Toward a Conceptualization of Communication Satisfaction. *Quarterly Journal of Speech* 64:47–62.

Hecht, Michael L., Mary Jane Collier, and Sidney Ribeau (1993). *African American Communication: Ethnic Identity and Cultural Interpretation.* Thousand Oaks, CA: Sage.

Hecht, Michael, and Sidney Ribeau (1984). Ethnic Communication: A Comparative Analysis of Satisfying Communication. *International Journal of Intercultural Relations* 8:135–151.

Hegstrom, Timothy (1979). Message Impact: What Percentage Is Nonverbal? *Western Journal of Speech Communication* 43:134–142.

Heiskell, Thomas L., and Joseph F. Rychiak (1986). The Therapeutic Relationship: Inexperienced Therapists' Affective Preference and Empathic Communication. *Journal of Social and Personal Relationships* 3:267–274.

Henderson, M., and A. Furnham (1982). Similarity and Attraction: The Relationship Between Personality, Beliefs, Skills, Needs, and Friendship Choice. *Journal of Adolescence* 5:111–123.

Hendrick, Clyde, and Susan Hendrick (1990). A Relationship-Specific Version of the Love Attitudes Scale. In *Handbook of Replication Research in the Behavioral and Social Sciences* (special issue), edited by J. W. Heulip, *Journal of Social Behavior and Personality* 5:239–254.

Hendrick, Clyde, Susan Hendrick, Franklin H. Foote, and Michelle J. Slapion-Foote (1984). Do Men and Women Love Differently? *Journal of Social and Personal Relationships* 1:177–195.

Henley, Nancy M. (1977). *Body Politics: Power, Sex, and Nonverbal Communication.* Englewood Cliffs, NJ: Prentice Hall.

Hertzler, J. O. (1965). *A Sociology of Language.* New York: Random House.

Heseltine, Olive (1927). *Conversation.* London: Methuen.

Hess, Eckhard H. (1975). *The Tell-Tale Eye.* New York: Van Nostrand Reinhold.

Hess, Ursula, Arvid Kappas, Gregory J. McHugo, John T. Lanzetta, et al (1992). The Facilitative Effect of Facial Expression on the Self-Generation of Emotion. *International Journal of Psychophysiology* 12 (May): 251–265.

Hess, Eckhard H., Allan L. Seltzer, and John M. Schlien (1965). Pupil Response of Hetero- and Homosexual Males to Pictures of Men and Women: A Pilot Study. *Journal of Abnormal Psychology* 70:165–168.

Hewitt, John, and Randall Stokes (1975). Disclaimers. *American Sociological Review* 40:1–11.

Hickson, Mark L., and Don W. Stacks (1989). *NVC: Nonverbal Communication: Studies and Applications.* 2d ed. Dubuque, Iowa: William. C. Brown.

Hocker, Joyce L., and William W. Wilmot (1985). *Interpersonal Conflict.* 2d ed. Dubuque, Iowa: William C. Brown.

Hockett, Charles F. (1977). *The View from Language: Selected Essays, 1948–1974.* Athens: University of Georgia Press.

Hofstede, Geert (1983). National Culture Revisited. *Behavior Science Research* 18:285–305.

Hofstede, Geert (1984). *Culture's Consequences: International Differences in Work-Related Values.* Thousand Oaks, CA: Sage.

Hofstede, Geert (1997). *Cultures and Organizations: Software of the Mind.* New York: McGraw-Hill.

Hoft, Nancy L. (1995). *International Technical Communication: How to Export Information about High Technology.* New York: Wiley.

Hoijer, Harry, ed. (1954). *Language in Culture.* Chicago: University of Chicago

Holden, Janice M. (1991). The Most Frequent Personality Priority Pairings in Marriage and Marriage Counseling. *Individual Psychology Journal of Adlerian Theory, Research, and Practice* 47 (September): 392–398.

Hollender, Marc, and Alexander Mercer (1976). Wish to Be Held and Wish to Hold in Men and Women. *Archives of General Psychiatry* 33:49–51.

Holmes, Janet (1986). Compliments and Compliment Responses in New Zealand English. *Anthropological Linguistics* 28:485–508.

Holmes, Janet (1995). *Women, Men and Politeness.* New York: Longman.

Honeycutt, James (1986). A Model of Marital Functioning Based on an Attraction Paradigm and Social Penetration Dimensions. *Journal of Marriage and the Family* 48 (August): 51–59.

Hopper, Robert, Mark L. Knapp, and Lorel Scott (1981). Couples' Personal Idioms: Exploring Intimate Talk. *Journal of Communication* 31:23–33.

Hosman, Lawrence A. (1989). The Evaluative Consequences of Hedges, Hesitations, and Intensifiers: Powerful and Powerless Speech Styles. *Human Communication Research* 15:383–406.

Huffines, LaUna (1986). *Connecting with All the People in Your Life.* New York: Harper and Row.

Huston, Michelle and Pepper Schwartz (1995). The Relationships of Lesbians and Gay Men. In Wood, Julia T. and Steve Duck (1995). *Under-Studied Relationships: Off the Beaten Track.* Thousand Oaks, CA: Sage, pp. 89–121.

Hymes, Dell (1974). *Foundations in Sociolinguistics: An Ethnographic Approach.* Philadelphia: University of Pennsylvania Press.

Ilinois Coalition Against Sexual Assault (spring 1990). *Coalition Commentary.* Urbana: Ilinois Coalition Against Sexual Assault.

Infante, Dominic A. (1988). *Arguing Constructively.* Prospect Heights, IL: Waveland Press.

Infante, Dominic A. (1993). Personal communication.

Infante, Dominic A., Teresa A. Chandler, and Jill E. Rudd (1989). Test of an Argumentative Skill Deficiency Model of Interspousal Violence. *Communication Monographs* 56 (June): 163–177.

Infante, Dominic A., Karen C. Hartley, Matthew M. Martin, Mary Anne Higgins, Stephen D. Bruning, and Gyeongho Hur (1992). Initiating and Reciprocating Verbal Aggression: Effects on Credibility and Credited Valid Arguments. *Communication Studies* 43 (fall): 182–190.

Infante, Dominic and Andrew Rancer (1982). A Conceptualization and Measure of Argumentativeness. *Journal of Personality Assessment* 46:72–80.

Infante, Dominic A., Andrew S. Rancer, and Felecia F. Jordan (1996). Affirming and Nonaffirming Style, Dyad Sex, and the Perception of Argumentation and Verbal Aggression in an Interpersonal Dispute. *Human Communication Research* 22 (March): 315–334.

Infante, Dominic A., Andrew S. Rancer, and Deanna F. Womack (1993). *Building Communication Theory,* 2nd ed. Prospect Heights, IL: Waveland Press.

Infante, Dominic A., Bruce L. Riddle, Cary L. Horvath, and S. A. Tumlin (1992). Verbal Aggressiveness: Messages and Reasons. *Communication Quarterly* 40 (spring): 116–126.

Infante, Dominic A., Teresa Chandler Sabourin, Jill E. Rudd, and Elizabeth A. Shannon (1990). Verbal Aggression in Violent and Nonviolent Marital Disputes. *Communication Quarterly* 38 (fall): 361–371.

Infante, Dominic and C. J. Wigley (1986). Verbal Aggressiveness: An Interpersonal Model and Measure. *Communication Monographs* 53:61–69.

Insel, Paul M., and Lenore F. Jacobson, eds. (1975). *What Do You Expect? An Inquiry into Self-Fulfilling Prophecies.* Menlo Park, CA: Cummings.

Jacobson, W. D. (1972). *Power and Interpersonal Relations.* Belmont, CA: Wadsworth.

Jaksa, James A. and Michael S. Pritchard (1994). *Communication Ethics: Methods of Analysis.* 2d ed. Belmont, CA: Wadsworth.

James, David L. (1995). *The Executive Guide to Asia-Pacific Communications.* New York: Kodansha International.

James, Phil and Jan Weingarten (1995). *Internet Guide for Windows 95.* Research Triangle Park, NC: Ventana.

Jandt, Fred E. (1995). *Intercultural Communication.* Thousand Oaks, CA: Sage.

Janus, Samuel S., and Cynthia L. Janus (1993). *The Janus Report on Sexual Behavior.* New York: Wiley.

Jaworski, Adam (1993). *The Power of Silence: Social and Pragmatic Perspectives.* Thousand Oaks, CA: Sage.

Jecker, Jon, and David Landy (1969). Liking a Person as a Function of Doing Him a Favor. *Human Relations* 22:371–378.

Jensen, J. Vernon (1985). Perspectives on Nonverbal Intercultural Communication. In Samovar & Porter (1985), 256–272.

Johannesen, Richard L. (1971). The Emerging Concept of Communication as Dialogue. *Quarterly Journal of Speech* 57:373–382.

Johannesen, Richard L. (1990). *Ethics in Human Communication.* 4th ed. Prospect Heights, IL: Waveland Press.

Johnson, C. E. (1987). An Introduction to Powerful and Powerless Talk in the Classroom. *Communication Education* 36:167–172.

Johnson, F. L., and E. J. Aries (1983). The Talk of Women Friends. *Women's Studies International Forum* 6:353–361.

Johnson, Frank A. and Anthony J. Marsella (1978). Differential Attitudes toward Verbal Behavior in Students of Japanese and European Ancestry. *Genetic Psychology Monographs* 97 (February): 43–76.

Johnson, M. P. (1973). Commitment: A Conceptual Structure and Empirical Application. *Sociological Quarterly* 14:395–406.

Johnson, M. P. (1982). Social and Cognitive Features of the Dissolution of Commitment to Relationships. In *Personal Relationships 4: Dissolving Personal Relationships,* edited by Steve Duck. New York: Academic Press, pp. 51–73.

Johnson, M. P. (1991). Commitment to Personal Relationships. In *Advances in Personal Relationships,* edited by W. H. Jones and D. Perlman, vol. 3. London: Jessica Kingsley, pp. 117–143.

Johnson, Otto, ed. (1994). *The 1994 Information Please Almanac.* New York: Houghton Mifflin.

Johnson, Scott A. (1993). *When "I Love You" Turns Violent: Emotional and Physical Abuse in Dating Relationships.* Far Hills, NJ: New Horizon Press.

Johnson, Wendell (1951). The Spoken Word and the Great Unsaid. *Quarterly Journal of Speech* 37:419–429.

Jones, E. E., et al. (1984). *Social Stigma: The Psychology of Marked Relationships.* New York: W. H. Freeman.

Jones, E. E., and K. E. Davis (1965). From Acts to Dispositions: The Attribution Process in Person Perception. In *Advances in Experimental Social Psychology,* edited by L. Berkowitz, vol. 2. New York: Academic Press, pp. 219–266.

Jones, E. E., Leslie Rock, Kelley G. Sharver, and Lawrence M. Wad (1968). Pattern of Performance and Ability Attribution: An Unexpected Primacy Effect. *Journal of Personality and Social Psychology* 10:317–340.

Jones, Stanley (1986). Sex Differences in Touch Communication. *Western Journal of Speech Communication* 50:227–241.

Jones, Stanley, and A. Elaine Yarbrough (1985). A Naturalistic Study of the Meanings of Touch. *Communication Monographs* 52:19–56. A version of this paper appears in DeVito and Hecht (1990).

Jourard, Sidney M. (1966). An Exploratory Study of Body-Accessibility. *British Journal of Social and Clinical Psychology* 5:221–231.

Jourard, Sidney M. (1968). *Disclosing Man to Himself.* New York: Van Nostrand Reinhold.

Jourard, Sidney M. (1971a). *Self-Disclosure.* New York: Wiley.

Jourard, Sidney M. (1971b). *The Transparent Self.* Rev. ed. New York: Van Nostrand Reinhold.

Joyner, Russell (1993). An Auto-Interview on the Need for E-Prime. *Etc.: A Review of General Semantics* 50 (fall): 317–325.

Kanner, Bernice (1989). Color Schemes. *New York Magazine* (April 3): 22–23.

Kapoor, Suraj, Arnold Wolfe, and Janet Blue (1995). Universal Values Structure and Individualism-Collectivism: A U.S. Test. *Communication Research Reports* 12 (spring): 112–123.

Kasian, Marilyn and Susan L. Painter (1992). Frequency and Severity of Psychological Abuse in a Dating Population. *Journal of Interpersonal Violence* 7 (September): 350–364.

Kazoleas, Dean (1993). The Impact of Argumentativeness on Resistance to Persuasion. *Human Communication Research* 20 (September): 118–137.

Kearney, P., T. G. Plax, V. P. Richmond, and J. C. McCroskey (1984). Power in the Classroom IV: Alternatives to Discipline. In *Communication Yearbook 8,* edited by R. N. Bostrom. Thousand Oaks, CA: Sage, pp. 724–746.

Kearney, P., T. G. Plax, V. P. Richmond, and J. C. McCroskey (1985). Power in the Classroom III: Teacher Communication Techniques and Messages. *Communication Education* 34:19–28.

Keating, Caroline F., Alan Mazur, and Marshall H. Segall (1977). Facial Gestures Which Influence the Perception of Status. *Sociometry* 40 (December): 374–378.

Keenan, Elinor Ochs (1976). The Universality of Conversational Postulates. *Language in Society* 5 (April): 67–80.

Kelley, H. H. (1967). Attribution Theory in Social Psychology. In *Nebraska Symposium on Motivation,* edited by D. Levine. Lincoln: University of Nebraska Press, pp. 192–240.

Kelley, H. H. (1973). The Process of Causal Attribution. *American Psychologist* 28:107–128.

Kelley, H. H. (1979). *Personal Relationships: Their Structures and Processes.* Hillsdale, NJ: Lawrence Erlbaum.

Kelley, H. H., and J. W. Thibaut (1978). *Interpersonal Relations: A Theory of Interdependence.* New York: Wiley/Interscience.

Kemp, Anita, Bonnie L. Green, Christine Hovanitz, and Edna I. Rawlings (1995). Incidence and Correlates of Posttraumatic Stress Disorder in Battered Women: Shelter and Community Samples. *Journal of Interpersonal Violence* 10 (March): 43–55.

Kennedy, C. W., and C. T. Camden (1988). A New Look at Interruptions. *Western Journal of Speech Communication* 47:45–58.

Kersten, K., and L. Kersten (1988). *Marriage and the Family: Studying Close Relationships.* New York: Harper & Row.

Keyes, Ken, Jr., and Penny Keyes (1987). *Gathering Power Through Insight and Love.* St. Mary, KY: Living Love.

Kiesler, Sara and Lee Sproull (1992). Group Decision Making and Communication Technology. Special Issue: Group Decision Making. *Organizational Behavior and Human Decision Processes* 52 (June): 96–123.

Kim, Min-Sun and William F. Sharkey (1995). Independent and Interdependent Contruals of Self: Explaining Cultural Patterns of Interpersonal Communication in Multi-Cultural Organizational Settings. *Communication Quarterly* 43 (winter): 20–38.

Kim, Sung Hee and Richard H. Smith (1993). Revenge and Conflict Escalation. *Negotiation Journal* 9 (January): 37–43.

Kim, Young Yun (1988). Communication and Acculturation. In Samovar and Porter (1988), pp. 344–354.

Kim, Young Yun (1991). Intercultural Communication Competence. In *Cross-Cultural Interpersonal Communication,* edited by Stella Ting-Toomey and Felipe Korzenny. Thousand Oaks, CA: Sage, pp. 259–275.

Kim, Young Yun, ed. (1986). *Interethnic Communication: Current Research.* Thousand Oaks, CA: Sage.

Kim, Young Yun, and William B. Gudykunst, eds. (1988). *Theories in Intercultural Communication.* Thousand Oaks, CA: Sage.

King, Robert and Eleanor DiMichael (1992). *Voice and Diction.* Prospect Heights, IL: Waveland Press.

Kirkpatrick, C., and T. Caplow (1945). Courtship in a Group of Minnesota Students. *American Journal of Sociology* 51:114–125.

Kleinfield, N. R. (1992). The Smell of Money. *New York Times* (October 25):1, 8.

Kleinke, Chris L. (1978). *Self-Perception: The Psychology of Personal Awareness.* San Francisco: W. H. Freeman.

Kleinke, Chris L. (1986). *Meeting and Understanding People.* New York: W. H. Freeman.

Klineberg, O. and W. F. Hull (1979). *At a Foreign University: An International Study of Adaptation and Coping.* New York: Praeger.

Knapp, Mark L. (1984). *Interpersonal Communication and Human Relationships.* Boston: Allyn and Bacon.

Knapp, Mark L., and Mark Comadena (1979). Telling It Like It Isn't: A Review of Theory and Research on Deceptive Communication. *Human Communication Research* 5:270–285.

Knapp, Mark L., Donald Ellis, and Barbara A. Williams (1980). Perceptions of Communication Behavior Associated with Relationship Terms. *Communication Monographs* 47:262–278.

Knapp, Mark L., and Judith Hall (1992). *Nonverbal Behavior in Human Interaction.* 3d ed. New York: Holt, Rinehart and Winston.

Knapp, Mark L. and Eric H. Taylor (1995). Commitment and Its Communication in Romantic Relationships. In Ann L. Weber and John H. Harvey, eds., *Perspectives on Close Relationships.* Boston: Allyn and Bacon, pp. 153–175.

Knapp, Mark L., and Anita Vangelisti (1992). *Interpersonal Communication and Human Relationships.* 2d ed. Boston: Allyn and Bacon.

Knapp, Mark L., and G. R. Miller, eds. (1985). *Handbook of Interpersonal Communication.* Thousand Oaks, CA: Sage.

Kochman, Thomas (1981). *Black and White: Styles in Conflict.* Chicago: University of Chicago Press.

Komarovsky, M. (1964). *Blue Collar Marriage* (New York: Random House).

Korda, M. (1975). *Power! How to Get It, How to Use It.* New York: Ballantine.

Korzybski, A. (1933). *Science and Sanity.* Lakeville, CT: The International Non-Aristotelian Library.

Kramarae, Cheris (1981). *Women and Men Speaking.* Rowley, MA: Newbury House.

Kramer, Ernest (1963). Judgment of Personal Characteristics and Emotions from Nonverbal Properties. *Psychological Bulletin* 60:408–420.

Kraut, R. (1978). Verbal and Nonverbal Cues in the Perceptions of Lying. *Journal of Personality and Social Psychology* 40:312–320.

Kristof, Nicholas D. (1996). Who Needs Love! In Japan, Many Couples Don't. *New York Times* (February 11): 1, 12.

Krug, Linda (1982). Alternative Lifestyle Dyads: An Alternative Relationship Paradigm. *Alternative Communications* 4:32–52.

Kurdek, Lawrence A. (1994). Areas of Conflict for Gay, Lesbian, and Heterosexual Couples: What Couples Argue About Influences Relationship Satisfaction. *Journal of Marriage and the Family* 56 (November): 923–934.

Kurdek, Lawrence A. (1995). Developmental Changes in Relationship Quality in Gay and Lesbian Cohabiting Couples. *Developmental Psychology* 31 (January): 86–93.

LaBarre, W. (1964). Paralinguistics, Kinesics, and Cultural Anthropology. In *Approaches to Semiotics,* edited by T. A. Sebeok, A. S. Hayes, and M. C. Bateson. The Hague: Mouton, pp. 191–220.

LaFrance, M., and C. Mayo (1978). *Moving Bodies: Nonverbal Communication in Social Relationships.* Monterey, CA: Brooks/Cole.

Lahey, B. B. (1989). *Psychology.* Dubuque, IA: William C. Brown.

Laing, Milli (1993). Gossip: Does It Play a Role in the Socialization of Nurses? *Journal of Nursing Scholarship* 25 (spring): 37–43.

Laing, Ronald D., H. Phillipson, and A. Russell Lee (1966). *Interpersonal Perception.* New York: Springer.

Lakoff, Robin (1975). *Language and Woman's Place.* New York: Harper and Row.

Lambdin, William (1981). *Doublespeak Dictionary.* Los Angeles: Pinnacle Books.

Langer, Ellen J. (1978). Rethinking the Role of Thought in Social Interaction. In *New Directions in Attribution Research,* vol. 2, edited by J. H. Harvey, W. J. Ickes, and R. F. Kidd. Hillsdale, NJ: Lawrence Erlbaum, pp. 35–58.

Langer, Ellen J. (1989). *Mindfulness.* Reading, MA: Addison-Wesley.

Lanzetta, J. T., J. Cartwright-Smith, and R. E. Kleck (1976). Effects of Nonverbal Dissimulations on Emotional Experience and Autonomic Arousal. *Journal of Personality and Social Psychology* 33:354–370.

Larsen, Randy J., Margaret Kasimatis, and Kurt Frey (1992). Facilitating the Furrowed Brow: An Unobtrusive Test of the Facial Feedback Hypothesis Applied to Unpleasant Affect. *Cognition and Emotion* 6 (September): 321–338.

Latane, B., K. Williams, and S. Harkins (1979). Many Hands Make Light the Work: Causes and Consequences of Social Loafing. *Journal of Personality and Social Psychology* 37:822–832.

Lea, Martin and Russell Spears (1995). Love at First Byte? Building Personal Relationships over Computer Networks. In Wood, Julia T. and Steve Duck (1995). *Under-Studied Relationships: Off the Beaten Track.* Thousand Oaks, CA: Sage, pp. 197–233.

Leaper, Campbell and Heithre Holliday (1995). Gossip in Same-Gender and Cross-Gender Friends' Conversations. *Personal Relationships* 2 (September): 237–246.

Leathers, Dale G. (1986). *Successful Nonverbal Communication: Principles and Applications.* New York: Macmillan.

LeBlanc, Dee-Ann and Robert LeBlanc (1995). *Using Eudora.* Indianapolis, IN: QUE.

Lederer, William J. (1984). *Creating a Good Relationship.* New York: W. W. Norton.

Lederer, William J., and D. D. Jackson (1968). *The Mirages of Marriage.* New York: W. W. Norton.

Lee, Alfred McClung and Elizabeth Briant Lee (1972). *The Fine Art of Propaganda.* San Francisco, CA: Interpersonal Society for General Semantics.

Lee, Alfred McClung and Elizabeth Briant Lee (1995). The Iconography of Propaganda Analysis. *Etc.: A Review of General Semantics* 52 (spring): 13–17.

Lee, Fiona (1993). Being Polite and Keeping MUM: How Bad News Is Communicated in Organizational Hierarchies. *Journal of Applied Social Psychology* 23 (July): 1124–1149.

Lee, John Alan (1973). Styles of Loving. *Psychology Today* 8:43–51.

Lee, John Alan (1976). *The Colors of Love.* New York: Bantam.

Leon, Joseph J., Joseph L. Philbrick, Fernando Parra, Emma Escobedo, et al. Love Styles among University Students in Mexico. *Psychological Reports* 74 (February): 307–310.

Leung, K. (1987). Some Determinants of Reactions to Procedural Models for Conflict Resolution: A Cross-National Study. *Journal of Personality and Social Psychology* 53:898–908.

Leung, Kwok (1988). Some Determinants of Conflict Avoidance. *Journal of Cross Cultural Psychology* 19 (March): 125–136.

LeVay, Simon (1996). *Queer Science: The Use and Abuse of Research Into Homosexuality.* Cambridge, MA: MIT Press.

Lever, Janet (1995). The 1995 Advocate Survey of Sexuality and Relationships: The Women, Lesbian Sex Survey. *The Advocate* 687/688 (August 22): 22–30.

LeVine, R., and K. Bartlett (1984). Pace of Life, Punctuality, and Coronary Heart Disease in Six Countries. *Journal of Cross-Cultural Psychology* 15:233–255.

LeVine, R., S. Sato, T. Hashimoto, and J. Verma (1994). *Love and Marriage in Eleven Cultures.* Unpublished manuscript. California State University, Fresno, CA, cited in Hatfield and Rapson (1996).

Levinger, George (1983). The Embrace of Lives: Changing and Unchanging. In *Close Relationships: Perspectives on the Meaning of Intimacy,* edited by George Levinger and Harold L. Raush. Amherst: University of Massachusetts Press, pp. 1–16.

Levinson, D. (1989). *Family Violence in Cross-Cultural Perspective.* Thousand Oaks, CA: Sage.

Lewis, David (1989). *The Secret Language of Success.* New York: Carroll and Graf.

Lin, Yuan-Huei W. and Caryl E. Rusbult (1995). Commitment to Dating Relationships and Cross-Sex Friendships in America and China. *Journal of Social and Personal Relationships* 12 (February): 7–26.

Lips, H. M. (1981). *Women, Men, and the Psychology of Power.* Englewood Cliffs, NJ: Prentice Hall.

Littlejohn, Stephen W. (1996). *Theories of Human Communication.* 5th ed. Belmont, CA: Wadsworth.

Loftus, Elizabeth F. (1979). *Eyewitness Testimony.* Cambridge, MA: Harvard University Press.

Loftus, Elizabeth F., and J. Monahan (1980). Trial by Data: Psychological Research as Legal Evidence. *American Psychologist* 35:270–283.

Loftus, Elizabeth F., and J. C. Palmer (1974). Reconstruction of Automobile Destruction: An Example of the Interaction Between Language and Memory. *Journal of Verbal Learning and Verbal Behavior* 13:585–589.

Lorenz, Konrad (1937). Imprinting. *The Auk* 54:245–273.

Luce, Gay Gaer (1971). *Body Time: Physiological Rhythms and Social Stress.* New York: Pantheon.

Luft, Joseph (1969). *Of Human Interaction.* Palo Alto, CA: Mayfield Publishing Co.

Luft, Joseph (1984). *Group Processes: An Introduction to Group Dynamics.* 3d ed. Palo Alto, CA: Mayfield Publishing Co.

Lujansky, H. and G. Mikula (1983). Can Equity Theory Explain the Quality and Stability of Romantic Relationships? *British Journal of Social Psychology* 22:101–112.

Lukens, J. (1978). Ethnocentric Speech. *Ethnic Groups* 2:35–53.

Lurie, Alison (1983). *The Language of Clothes.* New York: Vintage.

Lustig, Myron W. and Jolene Koester (1996). *Intercultural Competence: Interpersonal Communication Across Cultures.* 2d ed. New York: Longman.

Lyman, Stanford M., and Marvin B. Scott (1967). Territoriality: A Neglected Sociological Dimension. *Social Problems* 15:236–249.

Ma, Karen (1996). *The Modern Madame Butterfly: Fantasy and Reality in Japanese Cross-Cultural Relationships.* Rutland, VT: Charles E. Tuttle.

Ma, Ringo (1992). The Role of Unofficial Intermediaries in Interpersonal Conflicts in the Chinese Culture. *Communication Quarterly* 40 (summer): 269–278.

MacLachlan, James (1979). What People Really Think of Fast Talkers. *Psychology Today* 13:113–117.

Mahl, George F. and Gene Schulze (1964). Psychological Research in the Extralinguistic Area. In *Approaches to Semiotics,* edited by T. A. Sebeok, A. S. Hayes, and M. C. Bateson. The Hague: Mouton.

Main, Frank and Ronald Oliver (1988). Complementary, Symmetrical, and Parallel Personality Priorities as Indicators of Marital Adjustment. *Individual Psychology Journal of Adlerian Theory, Research, and Practice* 44 (September): 324–332.

Majeski, William J. (1988). *The Lie Detection Book.* New York: Ballantine.

Malandro, Loretta A., Larry Barker, and Deborah Ann Barker (1989). *Nonverbal Communication.* 2d ed. New York: Random House.

Malinowski, Bronislaw (1923). The Problem of Meaning in Primitive Languages. In *The Meaning of Meaning,* edited by C. K. Ogden and I. A. Richards. New York: Harcourt Brace Jovanovich, pp. 296–336.

Mallardi, Vincent (1978). *Biorhythms and Your Behavior.* Rev. ed. Philadelphia, PA: Running Press.

Manes, Joan and Nessa Wolfson (1981). The Compliment Formula. In Florian Coulmas, ed., *Conversational Routine.* The Hague: Mouton, pp. 115–132.

Mao, LuMing Robert (1994). Beyond Politeness Theory: 'Face' Revisited and Renewed. *Journal of Pragmatics* 21 (May): 451–486.

Markway, Barbara G., Cheryl N. Carmin, C. Alex Pollard, and Teresa Flynn (1992). *Dying of Embarrassment: Help for Social Anxiety and Phobia.* Oakland, CA: New Harbinger Publications.

Marsh, Peter (1988). *Eye to Eye: How People Interact.* Topside, MA: Salem House.

Marshall, Evan (1983). *Eye Language: Understanding the Eloquent Eye.* New York: New Trend.

Marshall, Linda L., and Patricia Rose (1987). Gender, Stress, and Violence in the Adult Relationships of a Sample of College Students. *Journal of Social and Personal Relationships* 4:229–316.

Marston, Peter J., Michael L. Hecht, and Tia Robers (1987). True Love Ways: The Subjective Experience and Communication of Romantic Love. *Journal of Personal and Social Relationships* 4:387–407.

Martel, Myles (1989). *The Persuasive Edge.* New York: Fawcett.

Martin, Matthew M. and Carolyn M. Anderson (1995). Roommate Similarity: Are Roommates Who Are Similar in Their Communication Traits More Satisfied? *Communication Research Reports* 12 (spring): 46–52.

Martin, Scott L. and Richard J. Klimoski (1990). Use of Verbal Protocols to Trace Cognitions Associated with Self- and Supervisor Evaluations of Performance. *Organizational Behavior and Human Decision Processes* 46:135–154.

Marwell, G., and D. R. Schmitt (1967). Dimensions of Compliance-Gaining Behavior: An Empirical Analysis. *Sociometry* 39:350–364.

Marwell, Gerald and David R. Schmitt (1990). An Introduction. In *Seeking Compliance: The Production of Interpersonal Influence Messages,* edited by James Price Dillard. Scottsdale, AZ.: Gorsuch Scarisbrick, pp. 3–5.

Masheter, Carol, and Linda M. Harris (1986). From Divorce to Friendship: A Study of Dialectic Relationship Development. *Journal of Social and Personal Relationships* 3:177–189.

Maslow, Abraham, and N. L. Mintz (1956). Effects of Esthetic Surroundings: I. Initial Effects of Three Esthetic Conditions upon Perceiving Energy and Well-Being in Faces. *Journal of Psychology* 41:247–254.

Matsumoto, David (1991). Cultural Influences on Facial Expressions of Emotion. *Southern Communication Journal* 56 (winter): 128–137.

Matsumoto, David (1994). *People: Psychology from a Cultural Perspective.* Pacific Grove, CA: Brooks/Cole.

Matsumoto, David (1996). *Culture and Psychology.* Pacific Grove, CA: Brooks/Cole.

Matsumoto, David and T. Kudoh (1993). American-Japanese Cultural Differences in Attributions of Personality Based on Smiles. *Journal of Nonverbal Behavior* 17:231–243.

May, Gerald G. (1988). *Addiction and Grace.* San Francisco: HarperSanFrancisco.

Maynard, Harry E. (1963). How to Become a Better Premise Detective. *Public Relations Journal* 19:20–22.

McBroom, William H. and Fred W. Reed (1992). Toward a Reconceptualization of Attitude-Behavior Consistency. Special Issue. Theoretical Advances in Social Psychology. *Social Psychology Quarterly* 55 (June): 205–216.

McCarthy, B., and S. W. Duck (1976). Friendship Duration and Responses to Attitudinal Agreement-Disagreement. *British Journal of Clinical and Social Psychology* 15:377–386.

McCornack, Steven A., and Malcolm R. Parks (1990). What Women Know That Men Don't: Sex Differences in Determining the Truth Behind Deceptive Messages. *Journal of Social and Personal Relationships* 7:107–118.

McCroskey, James C. (1993). *Introduction to Rhetorical Communication.* 6th ed. Englewood Cliffs, NJ: Prentice Hall.

McCroskey, James C., S. Booth-Butterfield, and S. K. Payne (1989). The Impact of Communication Apprehension on College Student Retention and Success. *Communication Quarterly* 37:100–107.

McCroskey, James C., and John Daly, eds. (1987). *Personality and Interpersonal Communication.* Thousand Oaks, CA: Sage.

McCroskey, James C., and Virginia P. Richmond (1983). Power in the Classroom I: Teacher and Student Perceptions. *Communication Education* 32:175–184.

McCroskey, James C. and Virginia P. Richmond (1990). Willingness to Communicate: Differing Cultural Perspectives. *Southern Communication Journal* 56 (fall): 72–77.

McCroskey, James, Virginia P. Richmond, and Robert A. Stewart (1986). *One on One: The Foundations of Interpersonal Communication.* Englewood Cliffs, NJ: Prentice Hall.

McCroskey, James, and Lawrence Wheeless (1976). *Introduction to Human Communication.* Boston: Allyn and Bacon.

McGill, Michael E. (1985). *The McGill Report on Male Intimacy.* New York: Harper and Row.

McKellen, Ian (1996). Out in Hollywood. *The Advocate* 703 (March 19): 43.

McLaughlin, Margaret L. (1984). *Conversation: How Talk Is Organized.* Thousand Oaks, CA: Sage.

McLaughlin, Margaret L., Michael L. Cody, and C. S. Robey (1980). Situational Influences on the Selection of Strategies to Resist Compliance-Gaining Attempts. *Human Communication Research* 1:14–36.

McLean, Paula A. and Brian D. Jones (1992). Machiavellianism and Business Education. *Psychological Reports* 71 (August): 57–58.

Mehrabian, Albert (1968). Communication Without Words. *Psychology Today* 2:53–55.

Mehrabian, Albert (1976). *Public Places and Private Spaces.* New York: Basic Books.

Mehrabian, Albert (1978). *How We Communicate Feelings Nonverbally.* A *Psychology Today* cassette. New York: Ziff-Davis.

Mencken, H. L. (1971). *The American Language.* New York: Knopf.

Mendoza, Louis (1995). Ethos, Ethnicity, and the Electronic Classroom: A Study in Contrasting Educational Environments. Paper presented at the 46th Annual Meeting of the Conferences on College Composition and Communication. Washington, D. C. (March 23–25).

Merton, Robert K. (1957). *Social Theory and Social Structure.* New York: Free Press.

Messick, R. M., and K. S. Cook, eds. (1983). *Equity Theory: Psychological and Sociological Perspectives.* New York: Praeger.

Metts, Sandra (1989). An Exploratory Investigation of Deception in Close Relationships. *Journal of Social and Personal Relationships* 6 (May): 159–179.

Metz, Michael E., B. R. Rosser, and Nancy Strapko (1994). Differences in Conflict Resolution Styles among Heterosexual, Gay, and Lesbian Couples. *Journal of Sex Research* 31:293–308.

Meyer, Janet R. (1994). Effect of Situational Features on the Likelihood of Addressing Face Needs in Requests. *Southern Communication Journal* 59 (spring): 240–254.

Midooka, Kiyoshi (1990). Characteristics of Japanese Style Communication. *Media, Culture and Society* 12 (October): 477–489.

Millar, Frank E. and L. E. Rogers (1987). Relational Dimensions of Interpersonal Dynamics. In *Interpersonal Processes: New Directions in Communication Research,* edited by Michael E. Roloff and Gerald R. Miller. Thousand Oaks, CA: Sage, pp. 117–139.

Miller, Casey, and Kate Swift (1976). *Words and Women: New Language in New Times.* Garden City, NY: Doubleday.

Miller, George A. and David McNeill (1969). Psycholinguistics. In Gardner Lindzey and Elliot Aronson, eds. *The Handbook of Social Psychology.* 2d ed. Vol. III. Reading, MA: Addison-Wesley, pp. 666–794.

Miller, Gerald R. (1978). The Current State of Theory and Research in Interpersonal Communication. *Human Communication Research* 4:164–178.

Miller, Gerald R. (1990). Interpersonal Communication. In *Human Communication: Theory and Research,* edited by G. L. Dahnke and G. W. Clatterbuck. Belmont, CA: Wadsworth, pp. 91–122.

Miller, Gerald R. and Judee Burgoon (1990). In DeVito and Hecht (1990), pp. 340–357.

Miller, Gerald R., and Malcolm R. Parks (1982). Communication in Dissolving Relationships. In *Personal Relationships 4. Dissolving Personal Relationships,* edited by Duck. New York: Academic Press, pp. 127–154.

Miller, J. G. (1984). Culture and the Development of Everyday Social Explanation. *Journal of Personality and Social Psychology* 46:961–978.

Miller, Mark J. and Charles T. Wilcox (1986). Measuring Perceived Hassles and Uplifts Among the Elderly. *Journal of Human Behavior and Learning* 3:38–46.

Miller, Rodney, A. Reynolds, and Ronald E. Cambra (1987). The Influence of Gender and Culture on Language Intensity. *Communication Monographs* 54:101–105.

Miller, Sherod, Daniel Wackman, Elam Nunnally, and Carol Saline (1982). *Straight Talk.* New York: New American Library.

Miner, Horace (1956). Body Ritual Among the Nacierma. *American Anthropologist* 58:503–507.

Mintz, N. L. (1956). Effects of Esthetic Surroundings: II. Prolonged and Repeated Experience in a Beautiful and Ugly Room. *Journal of Psychology* 41:459–466.

Mir, Montserrat (1993). Direct Requests Can Also Be Polite. Paper presented at the Annual Meeting of the International Conference on Pragmatics and Language Learning (Champaign, IL).

Moghaddam, Fathali M., Donald M. Taylor, and Stephen C. Wright (1993). *Social Psychology in Cross-Cultural Perspective.* New York: W. H. Freeman.

Mole, John (1990). *When in Rome. . . A Business Guide to Cultures and Customs in 12 European Nations.* New York: American Management Association.

Molloy, John (1988). The New *Dress for Success.* New York: P. H. Wyden.

Molloy, John (1996). *The New Woman's Dress for Success Book.* Chicago: Follet.

Molloy, John (1981). *Molloy's Live for Success.* New York: Bantam.

Montague, Ashley (1971). *Touching: The Human Significance of the Skin.* New York: Harper and Row.

Montgomery, Barbara M. (1981). The Form and Function of Quality Communication in Marriage. *Family Relations* 30:21–30.

Montgomery, M. (1986). *An Introduction to Language and Society.* New York: Methuen.

Moon, Dreama G. (1966). Concepts of 'Culture': Implications for Intercultural Communication Research. *Communication Quarterly* 44 (winter): 70–84.

Morales, Jorge (1995). London: Death by Outing. *The Advocate* 680 (May 2): 20–22.

Moriarty, Thomas (1975). A Nation of Willing Victims. *Psychology Today* 8:43–50.

Morland, David (1995). Paper delivered at the Academy of Management, cited in *Psychology Today* 28 (March/April): 16.

Morrill, Calvin (1992). Vengeance Among Executives. *Virginia Review of Sociology* 1:51–76.

Morris, Desmond (1967). *The Naked Ape.* London: Jonathan Cape.

Morris, Desmond (1972). *Intimate Behavior.* New York: Bantam.

Morris, Desmond (1977). *Manwatching: A Field Guide to Human Behavior.* New York: Abrams.

Morris, Desmond (1985). *Bodywatching.* New York: Crown.

Morris, Desmond, Peter Collett, Peter Marsh, and Marie O'Shaughnessy (1979). *Gestures: Their Origins and Distribution.* New York: Stein and Day.

Morrison, Terri, Wayne A. Conaway, and George A. Borden (1994). *Kiss, Bow, or Shake Hands: How to Do Business in Sixty Countries.* Holbrook, MA: Bob Adams, Inc.

Morrow, Gregory D., Eddie M. Clark, and Karla F. Brock (1995). Individual and Partner Love Styles: Implications for the Quality of Romantic Involvements. *Journal of Social and Personal Relationships* 12 (August): 363–387.

Motley, Michael (1988). Taking the Terror Out of Talk. *Psychology Today* 22:46–49.

Motley, Michael T. (1990a). On Whether One Can(not) not Communicate: An Examination via Traditional Communication Postulates. *Western Journal of Speech Communication* 54 (winter): 1–20.

Motley, Michael T. (1990b). Communication as Interaction: A Reply to Beach and Bavelas. *Western Journal of Speech Communication* 54 (fall): 613–623.

Mulac, A., J. M. Wiemann, S. J. Widenmann, and T. W. Gibson (1988). Male/Female Language Differences and Effects in Same-Sex and Mixed-Sex Dyads: The Gender-Linked Language Effect. *Communication Monographs* 55:315–335.

Mulac, Anthony, Lisa B. Studley, John W. Wiemann, and James J. Bradac (1987). Male/Female Gaze in Same-Sex and Mixed-Sex Dyads: Gender-Linked Differences and Mutual Influence. *Human Communication Research* 13 (spring): 323–344.

Murstein, Bernard I., Joseph R. Merighi, and Stuart A. Vyse (1991). Love Styles in the United States and France: A Cross-Cultural Comparison. *Journal of Social and Clinical Psychology* 10 (spring): 37–46.

Myers, Scott A. (1995). Student Perceptions of Teacher Affinity-Seeking and Classroom Climate. *Communication Research Reports* 12 (fall): 192–199.

Naifeh, Steven and Gregory White Smith (1984). *Why Can't Men Open Up? Overcoming Men's Fear of Intimacy.* New York: Clarkson N. Potter.

Naisbitt, John (1984). *Megatrends: Ten New Directions Transforming Our Lives.* New York: Warner.

Neimeyer, Robert A., and Kelly A. Mitchell (1988). Similarity and Attraction: A Longitudinal Study. *Journal of Social and Personal Relationships* 5 (May): 131–148.

Neimeyer, Robert A., and Greg J. Neimeyer (1983). Structural Similarity in the Acquaintance Process. *Journal of Social and Clinical Psychology* 1:146–154.

Neugarten, Bernice (1979). Time, Age, and the Life Cycle. *American Journal of Psychiatry* 136:887–894.

Newsweek (1992). The Wounds of Words: When Verbal Abuse Is as Scary as Physical Abuse. (October 12): 90–92.

Nichols, Ralph (1961). Do We Know How to Listen? Practical Helps in a Modern Age. *Communication Education* 10:118–124.

Nichols, Ralph and Leonard Stevens (1957). *Are You Listening?* New York: McGraw-Hill.

Nicotera, Anne Maydan and Andrew S. Rancer (1994). The Influence of Sex on Self-Perceptions and Social Stereotyping of Aggressive Communication Predispositions. *Western Journal of Communication* 58 (fall): 283–307.

Nierenberg, Gerald and Henry Calero (1971). *How to Read a Person Like a Book.* New York: Pocket Books.

Nierenberg, Gerald and Henry Calero (1973). *Metatalk.* New York: Simon and Schuster.

Noble, Barbara Presley (1994). The Gender Wars: Talking Peace. *New York Times* (August 14, 1994), p. 21.

Noelle-Neumann, E. (1973). Return to the Concept of Powerful Mass Media. In H. Eguchi and K. Sata, eds., *Studies in Broadcasting: An International Annual of Broadcasting Science.* Tokyo: Nippon Hoso Kyokai, pp. 67–112.

Noelle-Neumann, E. (1980). Mass Media and Social Change in Developed Societies. In G. C. Wilhoit and H. de Bock, eds., *Mass Communication Review Yearbook,* vol. 1. Thousand Oaks, CA: Sage, pp. 657–678.

Noelle-Neumann, Elisabeth (1991). The Theory of Public Opinion: The Concept of the Spiral of Silence. *Communication Yearbook/14,* edited by James A. Anderson. Thousand Oaks, CA: Sage, pp. 256–287.

Noller, Patricia (1982). Couple Communication and Marital Satisfaction. *Australian Journal of Sex, Marriage, and Family* 3:69–75.

Noller, Patricia (1993). Gender and Emotional Communication in Marriage: Different Cultures or Differential Social Power? Special Issue: Emotional Communication, Culture, and Power. *Journal of Language and Social Psychology* 12 (March–June): 132–152.

Noller, Patricia, and Mary Anne Fitzpatrick (1993). *Communication in Family Relationships.* Englewood Cliffs, NJ: Prentice Hall.

Noller, Patricia, and Harley Hiscock (1989). Fitzpatrick's Typology: An Australian Replication. *Journal of Social and Personal Relationships* 6:87–92.

Norton, Robert, and Barbara Warnick (1976). Assertiveness as a Communication Construct. *Human Communication Research* 3:62–66.

Notarius, Clifford I., and Lisa R. Herrick (1988). Listener Response Strategies to a Distressed Other. *Journal of Social and Personal Relationships* 5:97–108.

Oberg, K. (1960). Cultural Shock: Adjustment to New Cultural Environments. *Practical Anthropology* 7:177–182.

Obujinrin, O. (1993). Wife Battering in Nigeria. *International Journal of Gynaecology and Obstetrics* 41 (May): 159–164.

O'Hair, D., M. J. Cody, B. Goss, and K. J. Krayer (1988). The Effect of Gender, Deceit Orientation, and Communicator Style on Macro-Assessments of Honesty. *Communication Quarterly* 36:77–93.

O'Hair, D., M. J. Cody, and M. L. McLaughlin (1981). Prepared Lies, Spontaneous Lies, Machiavellianism, and Nonverbal Communication. *Human Communication Research* 7:325–339.

O'Hair, Mary John, Michael J. Cody, and Dan O'Hair (1991). The Impact of Situational Dimensions on Compliance-Resisting Strategies: A Comparison of Methods. *Communication Quarterly* 39 (summer): 226–240.

Olaniran, Bolanle A. (1994). Group Performance in Computer-mediated and Face-to-Face Communication Media. *Management Communication Quarterly* 7 (February): 256–281.

O'Neil, Barbara and Richard Phillips (1975). *Biorhythms: How to Live with Your Life Cycles.* Pasadena, CA: Ward Ritchie Press, 1975.

Otto, Herbert A., ed. (1972). *Love Today: A New Exploration.* New York: Delta.

Palmer, M. T. (1989). Controlling Conversations: Turns, Topics, and Interpersonal Control. *Communication Monographs* 56:1–18.

Papa, Michael J. and Elizabeth J. Natalle (1989). Gender, Strategy Selection, and Discussion Satisfaction in Interpersonal Conflict. *Western Journal of Speech Communication* 53:260–272.

Parks, Malcolm R. (1995). Webs of Influence in Interpersonal Relationships. In C. R. Berger and M. E. Burgoon, eds., *Communication and Social Influence Processes.* East Lansing: Michigan State University Press, pp. 155–178.

Parks, Malcolm R. and Kory Floyd (1996). Making Friends in Cyberspace. *Journal of Communication* 46 (winter): 80–97.

Parlee, Mary Brown (1979). The Friendship Bond. *Psychology Today* 13 (October): 43–54, 113.

Patterson, Brian, and Dan O'Hair (1992). Relational Reconciliation: Toward a More Comprehensive Model of Relational Development. *Communication Research Reports* 9 (December): 119–130.

Peabody, Susan (1989). *Addiction to Love: Overcoming Obsession and Dependency in Relationships.* Berkeley, CA: Ten Speed Press.

Pearce, W. Barnett and Steward M. Sharp (1973). Self-Disclosing Communication. *Journal of Communication* 23:409–425.

Pearson, Judy C. (1980). Sex Roles and Self-Disclosure. *Psychological Reports* 47:640.

Pearson, Judy C. (1993). *Communication in the Family.* 2d ed. New York: HarperCollins.

Pearson, Judy C., and Brian H. Spitzberg (1990). *Interpersonal Communication: Concepts, Components, and Contexts,* 2d ed. Dubuque, Iowa: William C. Brown.

Pearson, Judy C., Lynn H. Turner, and William Todd-Mancillas (1991). *Gender and Communication.* 2d ed. Dubuque, IA: William C. Brown.

Pearson, Judy C., Richard West, and Lynn H. Turner (1995). *Gender and Communication.* 3d ed. Dubuque, IA: Wm. C. Brown.

Pease, Allen (1984). *Signals: How to Use Body Language for Power, Success, and Love.* New York: Bantam.

Peck, Janice (1995). TV Talk Shows as Therapeutic Discourse: The Ideological Labor of the Televised Talking Cure. *Communication Theory* 5 (February): 58–81.

Penfield, Joyce, ed. (1987). *Women and Language in Transition.* Albany: State University of New York Press.

Pennebacker, James W. (1991). *Opening Up: The Healing Power of Confiding in Others.* New York: Morrow.

Peplau, Letitia Anne (1988). Research on Homosexual Couples: An Overview. In *Gay Relationships,* edited by John DeCecco. New York: Harrington Park Press, pp. 33–40.

Peplau, Letitia Anne, and Daniel Perlman, eds. (1982). *Loneliness: A Sourcebook of Current Theory, Research, and Therapy.* New York: Wiley/Interscience.

Perlman, Daniel, and Letitia Anne Peplau (1981). Toward a Social Psychology of Loneliness. In *Personal Relationships. 3: Personal Relationships in Disorder,* edited by Steve Duck and Robin Gilmour. New York: Academic Press, pp. 31–56.

Perse, Elizabeth M. and Rebecca B. Rubin (1989). Attribution in Social and Parasocial Relationships. *Communication Research* 16 (February): 59–77.

Petrocelli, William and Barbara Kate Repa (1992). *Sexual Harassment on the Job.* Berkeley, CA: Nolo Press.

Phlegar, Phyllis (1995). *Love Online: A Practical Guide to Digital Dating.* Reading, MA: Addison-Welsey.

Pilkington, Constance J., and Deborah R. Richardson (1988). Perceptions of Risk in Intimacy. *Journal of Social and Personal Relationships* 5:503–508.

Pilkington, Neil W. and Anthony R. D'Augelli (1995). Victimization of Lesbian, Gay, and Bisexual Youth in Community Settings. *Journal of Community Psychology* 23 (January): 34–56.

Pinker, Steven (1994). *The Language Instinct: How the Mind Creates Language.* New York: William Morrow and Co.

Pittenger, R. E., C. F. Hockett, and J. J. Danehy (1960). *The First Five Minutes.* Ithaca, NY: Paul Martineau.

Plutchik, R. (1980). *Emotions: A Psycho-Evolutionary Synthesis.* New York: Harper and Row.

Pollack, Andrew (1995). A Cyberspace Front in a Multicultural War. *New York Times* (August 7): D1, D4.

Pollack, Andrew (1996). Happy in the East (^—^) or smiling:—) in the West. *New York Times* (August 12): D5.

Pollack, David H. (1992). Forced Out of the Closet: Sexual Orientation and the Legal Dilemma of "Outing". *University of Miami Law Review* 46 (January): 711–750.

Porter, R. H. and J. D. Moore (1981). Human Kin Recognition by Olfactory Cues. *Physiology and Behavior* 27:493–495.

Potter, Ellen F., and Sue V. Rosser (1992). Factors in Life Science Textbooks That May Deter Girls' Interest in Science. *Journal of Research in Science Teaching* 29 (September): 669–686.

Prather, H., and G. Prather (1988). *A Book for Couples.* New York: Doubleday.

Pratkanis, Anthony and Elliot Aronson (1991). *Age of Propaganda: The Everyday Use and Abuse of Persuasion.* New York: W. H. Freeman.

Prins, K. S., B. P. Buunk, and N. W. Van Yperen (1993). Equity, Normative Disapproval, and Extramarital Sex. *Journal of Social and Personal Relationships* 10 (February): 39–53.

Prisbell, Marshall (1986). The Relationship Between Assertiveness and Dating Behavior Among College Students. *Communication Research Reports* 3 (December): 9–12.

Prosky, Phoebe S. (1992). Complementary and Symmetrical Couples. *Family Therapy* 19:215–221.

Prusank, Diane T., Robert L. Duran, and Dena A. DeLillo (1993). Interpersonal Relationships in Women's Magazines: Dating and Relating in the 1970s and 1980s. *Journal of Social and Personal Relationships* 10 (August): 307–320.

Purnell, Rosentene B. (1982). Teaching Them to Curse: A Study of Certain Types of Inherent Racial Bias in Language Pedagogy and Practices. *Phylon* 43 (September): 231–241.

Rabin, Claire, and Dvora Zelner (1992). The Role of Assertiveness in Clarifying Roles and Strengthening Job Satisfaction of Social Workers in Multidisciplinary Mental Health Settings. *British Journal of Social Work* 22 (February): 17–32.

Rabinowitz, Fredric E. (1991). The Male-to-Male Embrace: Breaking the Touch Taboo in a Men's Therapy Group. *Journal of Counseling and Development* 69 (July–August): 574–576.

Radford, Mark H, Leon Mann, Yasuyuki Ohta, and Yoshibumi Nakane (1993). Differences Between Australian and Japanese Students in Decisional Self-Esteem, Decisional Stress, and Coping Styles. *Journal of Cross-Cultural Psychology* 24 (September): 284–297.

Rancer, Andrew S., Roberta L. Kosberg, and Robert A. Baukus (1992). Beliefs About Arguing as Predictors of Trait Argumentativeness: Implications for Training in Argument and Conflict Management. *Communication Education* 41 (October): 375–387.

Rank, H. (1984). *The PEP talk: How to Analyze Political Language.* Park Forest, IL: Counter Propaganda Press.

Rankin, Paul (1929). Listening Ability. *Proceedings of the Ohio State Educational Conference's Ninth Annual Session.*

Rappaport, Herbert, Kathy Enrich, and Arnold Wilson (1985). Relation Between Ego Identity and Temporal Perspective. *Journal of Personality and Social Psychology* 48 (June): 1609–1620.

Raven, B., C. Centers, and A. Rodrigues (1975). The Bases of Conjugal Power. In *Power in Families,* edited by R. E. Cromwell and D. H. Olson. New York: Halsted Press, pp. 217–234.

Rawlins, William K (1983). Negotiating Close Friendship: The Dialectic of Conjunctive Freedoms. *Human Communication Research* 9 (spring): 255–266.

Rawlins, William K. (1989). A Dialectical Analysis of the Tensions, Functions, and Strategic Challenges of Communication in Young Adult Friendships. *Communication Yearbook/12,* edited by James A. Anderson. Thousand Oaks, CA: Sage, pp. 157–189.

Reardon, Kathleen K. (1987). *Where Minds Meet: Interpersonal Communication.* Belmont, CA: Wadsworth.

Reed, Warren H. (1985). *Positive Listening: Learning to Hear What People Are Really Saying.* New York: Franklin Watts.

Reichert, Elisabeth (1991). Perceptions of Domestic Violence Against Women: A Cross Cultural Survey of International Students. *Response to the Victimization of Women and Children* 14:13–18.

Reik, Theodore (1944). *A Psychologist Looks at Love.* New York: Rinehart.

Reisman, John (1979). *Anatomy of Friendship.* Lexington, MA: Lewis.

Reisman, John M. (1981). Adult Friendships. In *Personal Relationships. 2: Developing Personal Relationships,* edited by Steve Duck and Robin Gilmour. New York: Academic Press, pp. 205–230.

Remp, Richard (1974). The Efficacy of Electronic Group Meetings. *Policy Sciences* 5 (March): 101–115.

Rezabeck, Landra L. and John J. Cochenour (1994). Emoticons: Visual Cues for Computer-Mediated Communication. In *Imagery and Visual Literacy: Selected Readings from the Annual Conference of the International Visual Literacy Associaton* (Tempe, Arizona, October 12–16).

Rich, Andrea L. (1974). *Interracial Communication.* New York: Harper & Row.

Richards, I. A. (1951). Communication Between Men: The Meaning of Language. In *Cybernetics, Transactions of the Eighth Conference,* edited by Heinz von Foerster.

Richmond, Virginia P., L. M. Davis, K. Saylor, and J. C. McCroskey (1984). Power Strategies in Organizations: Communication Techniques and Messages. *Human Communication Research* 11:85–108.

Richmond, Virginia P., and J. C. McCroskey (1984). Power in the Classroom II: Power and Learning. *Communication Education* 33:125–136.

Richmond, Virginia P., and J. C. McCroskey (1989). *Communication: Apprehension, Avoidance, and Effectiveness.* 2d ed. Scottsdale, AZ: Gorsuch Scarisbrick.

Richmond, Virginia P. and James C. McCroskey (1996). *Communication: Apprehension, Avoidance, and Effectiveness.* 4th ed. Scottsdale, AZ: Gorsuch Scarisbrick.

Richmond, Virginia P., J. C. McCroskey, and Steven Payne (1987). *Nonverbal Behavior in Interpersonal Relationships.* Englewood Cliffs, NJ: Prentice Hall.

Riggio, Ronald E. (1987). *The Charisma Quotient.* New York: Dodd, Mead.

Roach, K. David (1991). The Influence and Effects of Gender and Status on University Instructor Affinity-Seeking Behavior. *Southern Communication Journal* 57 (fall): 73–80.

Robinson, W. P. (1972). *Language and Social Behavior.* Baltimore: Penguin.

Rodenburg, Frances A. and John W. Fantuzzo (1993). The Measure of Wife Abuse: Steps Toward the Development of a Comprehensive Assessment Technique. *Journal of Family Violence* 8 (September): 203–228.

Rodriguez, Maria (1988). Do Blacks and Hispanics Evaluate Assertive Male and Female Characters Differently? *Howard Journal of Communication* 1:101–107.

Roeher Institute (1995). *Harm's Way: The Many Faces of Violence and Abuse Against Persons with Disabilities.* North York (Ontario): Roeher Institute.

Roger, Derek and Willfried Nesshoever (1987). Individual Differences in Dyadic Conversational Strategies. A Further Study. *British Journal of Social Psychology* 26 (September): 247–255.

Rogers, Carl (1970). *Carl Rogers on Encounter Groups.* New York: Harrow Books.

Rogers, Carl, and Richard Farson (1981). Active Listening. In DeVito (1981), pp. 137–147.

Rogers, Everett M. (1983). *Diffusion of Innovations.* 3d ed. New York: Free Press.

Rogers, Everett M., and Rekha Agarwala-Rogers (1976). *Communication in Organizations.* New York: Free Press.

Rogers, L. E., and R. V. Farace (1975). Analysis of Relational Communication in Dyads: New Measurement Procedures. *Human Communication Research* 1:222–239.

Rogers-Millar, Edna and Frank E. Millar (1979). Domineeringness and Dominance: A Transactional View. *Human Communication Research* (spring): 238–246.

Rohlfing, Mary E. (1995). "Doesn't Anybody Stay in One Place Anymore?" An Exploration of the Under-Studied Phenomenon of Long-Distance Relationships. In Julia T. Wood and Steve Duck (1995). *Under-Studied Relationships: Off the Beaten Track.* Thousand Oaks, CA: Sage, pp. 173–196.

Rosenbaum, M. E. (1986). The Repulsion Hypothesis. On the Nondevelopment of Relationships. *Journal of Personality and Social Psychology* 51:1156–1166.

Rosenfeld, Lawrence (1979). Self-Disclosure Avoidance: Why I Am Afraid to Tell You Who I Am. *Communication Monographs* 46:63–74.

Rosenfeld, Lawrence, Sallie Kartus, and Chett Ray (1976). Body Accessibility Revisited. *Journal of Communication* 26:27–30.

Rosengren, Annika, et al. (1993). Stressful Life Events, Social Support, and Mortality in Men Born in 1933. *British Medical Journal* (October 19). Cited in Goleman (1995).

Rosenthal, Peggy (1984). *Words and Values: Some Leading Words and Where They Lead Us.* New York: Oxford University Press.

Rosenthal, Robert and L. Jacobson (1968). *Pygmalion in the Classroom.* New York: Holt, Rinehart and Winston.

Rosnow, Ralph L. (1977). Gossip and Marketplace Psychology. *Journal of Communication* 27 (winter): 158–163.

Rossiter, Charles M., Jr. (1975). Defining "Therapeutic Communication." *Journal of Communication* 25:127–130.

Rotello, Gabriel (1995). The Inning of Outing. *The Advocate* 679 (April 18): 80.

Rothblum, Esther D. and Lynne A. Bond (1996). *Preventing Heterosexism and Homophobia.* Thousand Oaks, CA: Sage.

Rothwell, J. Dan (1982). *Telling It Like It Isn't: Language Misuse and Malpractice/What We Can Do About It.* Englewood Cliffs, NJ: Prentice Hall.

Rowland-Morin, Pamela A. and J. Gregory Carroll (1990). Verbal Communication Skills and Patient Satisfaction: A Study of Doctor-Patient Interviews. *Evaluation and the Health Professions* 13:168–185.

Ruben, Brent D. (1985). Human Communication and Cross-Cultural Effectiveness. In Samovar and Porter (1985), pp. 338–346.

Ruben, Brent D. (1988). *Communication and Human Behavior.* 2d ed. New York: Macmillan.

Rubenstein, Carin (1993). Fighting Sexual Harassment in Schools. *New York Times* (June 10): C8.

Rubenstein, Carin, and Philip Shaver (1982). *In Search of Intimacy.* New York: Delacorte.

Rubin, Alan, Elizabeth Pearse, and Robert Powell (1985). Loneliness, Parasocial Interaction, and Local Television News Viewing. *Human Communication Research* 12:155–180

Rubin, D. C., E. Groth, and D. J. Goldsmith (1984). Olfactory Cues of Autobiographical Memory. *American Journal of Psychology* 97:493–507.

Rubin, Jeffrey, and Warren F. Shaffer (1987). Some Interpersonal Effects of Imposing Guilt Versus Eliciting Altruism. *Counseling and Values* 31 (April): 190–193.

Rubin, Rebecca B., C. Fernandez-Collado, and R. Hernandez-Sampieri (1992). A Cross-Cultural Examination of Interpersonal Communication Motives in Mexico and the United States. *International Journal of Intercultural Relations* 16:145–157.

Rubin, Rebecca B. and Elizabeth E. Graham. (1988). Communication Correlates of College Success: An Exploratory Investigation. *Communication Education* 37:14–27.

Rubin, Rebecca B. and M. M. Martin (1994). Development of a Measure of Interpersonal Communication Competence. *Communication Research Reports* 11:33–44.

Rubin, Rebecca and Michael McHugh (1987). Development of Parasocial Interaction Relationships. *Journal of Broadcasting and Electronic Media* 31:279–292.

Rubin, Rebecca B. and Randi J. Nevins (1988). *The Road Trip: An Interpersonal Adventure.* Prospect Heights, IL: Waveland Press.

Rubin, Rebecca B., Elizabeth M. Pearse, and Carole A. Barbato (1988). Conceptualization and Measurement of Interpersonal Communication Motives. *Human Communication Research* 14:602–628.

Rubin, Rebecca B. and Alan M. Rubin (1992). Antecedents of Interpersonal Communication Motivation. *Communication Quarterly* 40:3, 5, 317.

Rubin, Theodore Isaac (1983). *One to One: Understanding Personal Relationships.* New York: Viking.

Rubin, Zick (1973). *Liking and Loving: An Invitation to Social Psychology.* New York: Holt, Rinehart and Winston

Rubin, Zick and Elton B. McNeil (1985). *Psychology: Being Human.* 4th ed. New York: Harper & Row.

Ruesch, Jurgen and Gregory Bateson (1951). *Communication: The Social Matrix of Psychiatry.* New York: W. W. Norton.

Rundquist, Suellen (1992). Indirectness: A Gender Study of Fluting Grice's Maxims. *Journal of Pragmatics* 18 (November): 431–449.

Rusbult, Caryl E. and Bram P. Buunk (1993). Commitment Processes in Close Relationships: An Interdependence Analysis. *Journal of Social and Personal Relationships* 10 (May): 175–204.

Ryan, Kathryn M. (1995). Do Courtship-Violent Men Have Characteristics Associated with a "Battering Personality"? *Journal of Family Violence* 10 (March): 99–120.

Sabatelli, Ronald M., and John Pearce (1986). Exploring Marital Expectations. *Journal of Social and Personal Relationships* 3:307–321.

Saegert, Susan, Walter Swap, and Robert B. Zajonc (1973). Exposure, Context, and Interpersonal Attraction. *Journal of Personality and Social Psychology* 25:234–242.

Salminen, Simo and Timo Glad (1992). The Role of Gender in Helping Behavior, *Journal of Social Psychology* 132 (February): 131–133.

Samovar, Larry A., and Richard E. Porter, eds. (1985). *Intercultural Communication: A Reader.* 4th ed. Belmont, CA: Wadsworth.

Samovar, Larry A., and Richard E. Porter, eds. (1988). *Intercultural Communication: A Reader.* 5th ed. Belmont, CA: Wadsworth.

Samovar, Larry A. and Richard E. Porter, eds. (1991). *Communication Between Cultures.* Belmont, CA: Wadsworth.

Samovar, Larry A., Richard E. Porter, and Nemi C. Jain (1981). *Understanding Intercultural Communication.* Belmont, CA: Wadsworth.

Sanders, Judith A., Richard L. Wiseman, and S. Irene Matz (1991). Uncertainty Reduction in Acquaintance Relationships in Ghana and the United States. In *Cross-Cultural Interpersonal,* edited by Stella Ting-Toomey and Felipe Korzenny. Thousand Oaks, CA: Sage, pp. 79–98.

Sanford, John A. (1982). *Between People.* New York: Paulist Press.

Sapadin, Linda A. (1988). Friendship and Gender: Perspectives of Professional Men and Women. *Journal of Social and Personal Relationships* 5:387–403.

Sapir, Edward (1929). *Language: An Introduction to the Study of Speech.* New York: Harcourt, Brace and World.

Sargent, J. F., and Gerald R. Miller (1971). Some Differences in Certain Communication Behaviors of Autocratic and Democratic Leaders. *Journal of Communication* 21:233–252.

Sarwer, David B., Seth C. Kalichman, Jennifer R. Johnson, Jamie Earl, et al. (1993). Sexual Aggression and Love Styles: An Exploratory Study, *Achives of Sexual Behavior* 22 (June): 265–275.

Sashkin, Marshall, and William C. Morris (1984). *Organizational Behavior: Concepts and Experiences.* Reston, VA: Prentice Hall, Reston Publishing.

Satir, Virginia (1972). *Peoplemaking.* Palo Alto, CA: Science and Behavior Books.

Satir, Virginia (1983). *Conjoint Family Therapy.* 3d ed. Palo Alto, CA: Science and Behavior Books.

Saunders, Carol S., Daniel Robey, and Kelly A. Vaverek (1994). The Persistence of Status Differentials in Computer Conferencing. *Human Communication Research* 20 (June): 443–472.

Schachter, Stanley (1964). The Interaction of Cognitive and Physiological Determinants of Emotional State. In *Advances in Experimental Social Psychology,* vol. 1, edited by Leonard Berkowitz. New York: Academic Press.

Schaef, Anne Wilson (1986). *Co-Dependence.* New York: HarperCollins.

Schaef, Anne Wilson (1990). *Addictive Relationships.* New York: HarperCollins.

Schaefer, Charles E. (1984). *How to Talk to Children About Really Important Things.* New York: Harper and Row.

Schafer, R. B. and P. M. Keith (1980). Equity and Depression Among Married Couples. *Social Psychology Quarterly* 43:430–435.

Schatski, Michael (1981). *Negotiation: The Art of Getting What You Want.* New York. New American Library.

Schegloff, E. (1982). Discourses as an Interactional Achievement: Some Uses of "uh huh" and Other Things that Come Between Sentences. In *Georgetown University Roundtable on Language and Linguistics,* edited by Deborah Tannen. Washington, D.C.: Georgetown University Press, pp. 71–93.

Scherer, K. R. (1986). Vocal Affect Expression. *Psychological Bulletin* 99:143–165.

Schmidt, Tracy O. and Randolph R. Cornelius (1987). Self-Disclosure in Everyday Life. *Journal of Social and Personal Relationships* 4:365–373.

Schramm, Wilbur (1988). *The Story of Human Communication: Cave Painting to Microchip.* New York: Harper & Row.

Schwartz, Marilyn and the Task Force on Bias-Free Language of the Association of American University Presses (1995). *Guidelines for Bias-Free Writing*. Bloomington: Indiana University Press.

Seaver, W. B. (1973). Effects of Naturally Induced Teacher Expectancies. *Journal of Personality and Social Psychology* 28:333–342.

Sergios, Paul A., and James Cody (1985). Physical Attractiveness and Social Assertiveness Skills in Male Homosexual Dating Behavior and Partner Selection. *Journal of Social Psychology* 125 (August): 505–514.

Shannon, J. (1987). Don't Smile When You Say That. *Executive Female* 10:33, 43. Reprinted in DeVito and Hecht (1990), pp. 115–117.

Sharkey, William F. and Laura Stafford (1990). Turn-Taking Resources Employed by Congenitally Blind Conversers. *Communication Studies* 41 (summer): 161–182.

Shea, Virginia (1994). *Netiquette*. Albion Books.

Sheppard, James A. and Alan J. Strathman (1989). Attractiveness and Height: The Role of Stature in Dating Preferences, Frequency of Dating, and Perceptions of Attractiveness. *Personality and Social Psychology* 15 (December): 617–627.

Shimanoff, Susan (1980). *Communication Rules: Theory and Research*. Thousand Oaks, CA: Sage.

Shuter, Robert (1990). The Centrality of Culture. *Southern Communication Journal* 55 (spring): 237–249.

Siavelis, Rita L., and Leanne K. Lamke (1992). Instrumentalness and Expressiveness: Predictors of Heterosexual Relationship Satisfaction. *Sex Roles* 26 (February): 149–159.

Siegert, John R. and Glen H. Stamp (1994). 'Our First Big Fight' as a Milestone in the Development of Close Relationships. *Communication Monographs* 61 (December): 345–360.

Signorielli, Nancy and Margaret Lears (1992). Children, Television, and Concepts About Chores: Attitudes and Behaviors. *Sex Roles* 27 (August): 157–170.

Signorile, Michelangelo (1993). *Queer in America: Sex, the Media, and the Closets of Power*. New York: Random House.

Sillars, Alan L., and Michael D. Scott (1983). Interpersonal Perception Between Intimates: An Integrative Review. *Human Communication Research* 10:153–176.

Simpson, Jeffry A. (1987). The Dissolution of Romantic Relationships: Factors Involved in Relationship Stability and Emotional Distress. *Journal of Personality and Social Psychology* 53 (October): 683–692.

Singer, Marshall R. (1987). *Intercultural Communication: A Perceptual Approach*. Englewood Cliffs, NJ: Prentice Hall.

Siu, R. G. H. (1984). *The Craft of Power*. New York: Quill.

Slade, Margot (1995). We Forgot to Write a Headline. But It's Not Our Fault. *New York Times* (February 19): 5.

Small, Jacquelyn (1990). *Becoming Naturally Therapeutic*. New York: Bantam.

Smith, L. J., and L. A. Malandro (1985). *Courtroom Communication Strategies*. New York: Kluwer Law Book Publishers.

Smith, Stephen A. (1994). Communication and the Constitution in Cyberspace. *Communication Education* 43 (April): 87–101.

Snyder, C. R. (1984). Excuses, Excuses. *Psychology Today* 18:50–55.

Snyder, C. R., Raymond L. Higgins, and Rita J. Stucky (1983). *Excuses: Masquerades in Search of Grace*. New York: Wiley.

Snyder, Mark (1987). *Public Appearances, Private Realities*. New York: W. H. Freeman.

Solomon, Michael R. (1986). Dress for Effect. *Psychology Today* 20:20–28.

Sommer, Robert (1969). *Personal Space: The Behavioral Basis of Design*. Englewood Cliffs, NJ: Prentice Hall, Spectrum.

Sommer, Robert (1972). *Design Awareness*. Englewood Cliffs, NJ: Prentice Hall.

Spencer, Ted (1993). A New Approach to Assessing Self-Disclosure in Conversation. Paper presented at the Annual Convention of the Western Speech Communication Association, Albuquerque, New Mexico.

Spencer, Ted (1994). Transforming Relationships Through Everyday Talk. In *The Dynamics of Relationships*, Vol. 4, *Understanding Relationships*, edited by Steve Duck. Thousand Oaks, CA: Sage.

Spitzberg, Brian H. (1991). Intercultural Communication Competence. In Larry A. Samovar and Richard E. Porter, eds., *Intercultural Communication: A Reader*. Belmont, CA: Wadsworth, pp. 353–365.

Spitzberg, Brian H., and Michael L. Hecht (1984). A Component Model of Relational Competence. *Human Communication Research* 10:575–599.

Spitzberg, Brian H., and William R. Cupach (1984). *Interpersonal Communication Competence*. Thousand Oaks, CA: Sage.

Spitzberg, Brian H., and William R. Cupach (1989). *Handbook of Interpersonal Competence Research*. New York: Springer-Verlag.

Sprecher, Susan (1987). The Effects of Self-Disclosure Given and Received on Affection for an Intimate Partner and Stability of the Relationship. *Journal of Social and Personal Relationships* 4:115–127.

Sprecher, Susan and Sandra Metts (1989). Development of the "Romantic Beliefs Scale" and Examination of the Effects of Gender and Gender-Role Orientation. *Journal of Social and Personal Relationships* 6:387–411.

Stafford, L., and D. J. Canary (1991). Maintenance Strategies and Romantic Relationship Type, Gender, and Relational Characteristics. *Journal of Social and Personal Relationships* 8:217–242.

Staines, Graham L., Kathleen J. Pottick, and Deborah A. Fudge (1986). Wives' Employment and Husbands' Attitudes Toward Work and Life. *Journal of Applied Psychology* 71:118–128.

Steil, Lyman K., Larry L. Barker, and Kittie W. Watson (1983). *Effective Listening: Key to Your Success*. Reading, MA: Addison-Wesley.

Steiner, Claude (1981). *The Other Side of Power*. New York: Grove.

Steinfatt, Thomas M. (1987). Personality and Communication: Classic Approaches. In *Personality and Interpersonal Communication*, edited by James C. McCroskey and John A. Daly. Thousand Oaks, CA: Sage, pp. 42–126.

Stephan, Walter G. and Cookie White Stephan (1985). Intergroup Anxiety. *Journal of Social Issues* 41:157–175.

Stephens, Gregory K. and Charles R. Greer (1995). Doing Business in Mexico: Understanding Cultural Differences. *Organizational Dynamics* 24 (summer): 39–55.

Sternberg, Robert J. (1986). A Triangular Theory of Love. *Psychological Review* 93:119–135.

Sternberg, Robert J. (1988). *The Triangle of Love: Intimacy, Passion, Commitment*. New York: Basic Books.

Stillings, Neil A., et al. (1987). *Cognitive Science: An Introduction*. Cambridge, MA: MIT Press.

Strecker, Ivo (1993). Cultural Variations in the Concept of 'Face.' *Multilingua* 12:119–141.

Sunnafrank, Michael (1989). Uncertainty in Interpersonal Relationships: A Predicted Outcome Value Interpretation of Gudykunst's Research Program. In *Communication Yearbook 12*, edited by J. A. Anderson. Thousand Oaks, CA: Sage, pp. 355–370.

Swensen, C. H. (1973). *Introduction to Interpersonal Relations*. Glenview, IL: Scott, Foresman.

Swets, Paul W. (1983). *The Art of Talking so That People Will Listen*. Englewood Cliffs, NJ: Prentice Hall, Spectrum.

Szapocznik, Jose (1995). Research on Disclosure of HIV Status: Cultural Evolution Finds an Ally in Science. *Health Psychology* 14 (January): 4–5.

Tannen, Deborah (1990). *You Just Don't Understand: Women and Men in Conversation*. New York: Morrow.

Tannen, Deborah (1994a). *Gender and Discourse*. New York: Oxford University Press.

Tannen, Deborah (1994b). *Talking from 9 to 5*. New York: Morrow.

Taraban, Carolyn Beth and Clyde Hendrick (1995). Personality Perceptions Associated with Six Styles of Love. *Journal of Social and Personal Relationships* 12 (August): 453–461.

Taylor, D. M. and V. Jaggi (1974). Ethnocentrism and Causal Attribution in a South Indian Context. *Journal of Cross Cultural Psychology* 5:162–171.

Taylor, Dalmas A. and Irwin Altman (1987). Communication in Interpersonal Relationships: Social Penetration Processes. In *Interpersonal Processes: New Directions in Communication Research,* edited by M. E. Roloff and G. R. Miller. Thousand Oaks, CA: Sage, pp. 257–277.

Tersine, Richard J., and Walter E. Riggs (1980). The Delphi Technique: A Long-Range Planning Tool. In *Intercom: Readings in Organizational Communication,* edited by Stewart Ferguson and Sherry Devereaux Ferguson. Rochelle Park, NJ: Hayden Books, pp. 363–373.

Thayer, Stephen (1988). Close Encounters. *Psychology Today* 22:31–36. Reprinted in DeVito and Hecht (1990), pp. 217–225.

Thibaut, J. W., and H. H. Kelley (1959). *The Social Psychology of Groups.* New York: Wiley. Reissued (1986). New Brunswick, NJ: Transaction Books.

Thomas, Candice E., Melanie Booth-Butterfield, and Steve Booth-Butterfield (1995). Perceptions of Deception, Divorce Disclosures, and Communication Satisfaction with Parents. *Western Journal of Communication* 59 (summer): 228–245.

Thomlison, Dean (1982). *Toward Interpersonal Dialogue.* New York: Longman.

Thompson, Catherine A. and Donald W. Klopf (1991). An Analysis of Social Style Among Disparate Cultures. *Communication Research Reports* 8 (June–December): 65–72.

Thompson, Catherine A. and Donald W. Klopf (1995). Social Style Among North American, Finnish, Japanese, and Korean University Students. *Psychological Reports* 77 (August): 60–62.

Thompson, Catherine A., Donald W. Klopf, and Satoshi Ishii (1991). A Comparison of Social Style between Japanese and Americans. *Communication Research Reports* 8 (June–December): 165–172.

Thompson, S. C., and H. H. Kelley (1981). Judgments of Responsibility for Activities in Close Relationships. *Journal of Personality and Social Psychology* 41:469–477.

Thorne, Barrie, Cheris Kramarae, and Nancy Henley, eds. (1983). *Language, Gender, and Society.* Rowley, MA: Newbury House.

Ting-Toomey, Stella (1985). Toward a Theory of Conflict and Culture. *International and Intercultural Communication Annual* 9:71–86.

Ting-Toomey, Stella (1986). Conflict Communication Styles in Black and White Subjective Cultures. In Young Yun Kim, ed. *Interethnic Communication: Current Research.* Thousand Oaks, CA: Sage, pp. 75–88.

Tolhuizen, James H. (1986). Perceiving Communication Indicators of Evolutionary Changes in Friendship. *Southern Speech Communication Journal* 52:69–91.

Tolhuizen, James H. (1989). Communication Strategies for Intensifying Dating Relationships: Identification, Use, and Structure. *Journal of Social and Personal Relationships* 6 (November): 413–434.

Trager, George L. (1958). Paralanguage: A First Approximation. *Studies in Linguistics* 13:1–12.

Trager, George L. (1961). The Typology of Paralanguage. *Anthropological Linguistics* 3:17–21.

Trenholm, Sarah (1986). *Human Communication Theory.* Englewood Cliffs, NJ: Prentice Hall.

Trower, P. (1981). Social Skill Disorder. In *Personal Relationships* 3, edited by S. Duck and R. Gilmour. New York: Academic Press, pp. 97–110.

Truax, C. (1961). A Scale for the Measurement of Accurate Empathy. Wisconsin Psychiatric Institute Discussion Paper no. 20, Madison.

Tschann, J. M. (1988). Self-Disclosure in Adult Friendship: Gender and Marital Status Differences. *Journal of Social and Personal Relationships* 5:65–81.

Tubbs, Stewart L. (1988). *A Systems Approach to Small Group Interaction.* 3d ed. New York: Random House.

Tyler, Patrick E. (1996). Crime (and Punishment) Rages Anew in China. *New York Times* (July 11): A1, A8.

Ueleke, William, et al. (1983). Inequity Resolving Behavior as a Response to Inequity in a Hypothetical Marital Relationship. *A Quarterly Journal of Human Behavior* 20:4–8.

Ullmann, Stephen (1962). *Semantics: An Introduction to the Science of Meaning.* New York: Barnes and Noble.

VandeCreek, Leon and Lori Angstadt (1985). Client Preferences and Anticipations About Counselor Self-Disclosure. *Journal of Counseling Psychology* 32:206–214.

VanHyning, Memory (1993). *Crossed Signals: How to Say No to Sexual Harassment.* Los Angeles: Infotrends Press.

Varonis, Evangeline Marlos and Susan M. Gass (1985). Miscommunication in Native/Nonnative Conversation. *Language in Society* 14 (September): 327–343.

Veenendall, Thomas L. and Marjorie C. Feinstein (1995). *Let's Talk About Relationships: Cases in Study.* Prospect Heights, IL: Waveland Press.

Verderber, Rudolph F. and Kathleen S. Verderber (1989). *Inter-Act: Using Interpersonal Communication Skills.* Belmont, CA: Wadsworth.

Vernon, JoEtta A., J. Allen Williams, Terri Phillips, and Janet Wilson (1990). Media Stereotyping: A Comparison of the Way Elderly Women and Men Are Portrayed on Prime-Time Television. *Journal of Women and Aging* 4:55–68.

Victor, David (1992). *International Business Communication.* New York: HarperCollins.

Walster, E., and G. W. Walster (1978). *A New Look at Love.* Reading, MA: Addison-Wesley.

Walster, E., G. W. Walster, and E. Berscheid (1978). *Equity: Theory and Research.* Boston: Allyn and Bacon.

Walster, Elaine, G. W. Walster, and J. Traupman (1978). Equity and Premarital Sex. *Journal of Personality and Social Psychology* 36:82–92.

Walther, Joseph B. (1993). Impression Development in Computer-Mediated Interaction. *Western Journal of Communication* 57 (fall): 381–398.

Wardhaugh, R. (1985). *How Conversation Works.* New York: Basil Blackwell.

Watson, Arden K. and Carley H. Dodd (1984). Alleviating Communication Apprehension Through Rational Emotive Therapy: A Comparative Evaluation. *Communication Education* 33:257–266.

Watson, Kittie W. and Larry L. Barker (1984). Listening Behavior: Definition and Measurement. In *Communication Yearbook 8,* edited by Robert N. Bostrom. Thousand Oaks, CA: Sage, pp. 178–197.

Watzlawick, Paul (1977). *How Real Is Real? Confusion, Disinformation, Communication: An Anecdotal Introduction to Communications Theory.* New York: Vintage.

Watzlawick, Paul (1978). *The Language of Change: Elements of Therapeutic Communication.* New York: Basic Books.

Watzlawick, Paul, Janet Helmick Beavin, and Don D. Jackson (1967). *Pragmatics of Human Communication: A Study of Interactional Patterns, Pathologies, and Paradoxes.* New York: W. W. Norton.

Weber, Ann L. and John H. Harvey, eds. (1994). *Perspectives on Close Relationships.* Boston: Allyn And Bacon.

Webster, E. (1988). The Power of Negative Thinking: Twenty-two Convenient Ways to Bury an Idea. *Etc.: A Review of General Semantics* 45:246–249.

Weinberg, Harry L. (1959). *Levels of Knowing and Existence.* New York: Harper and Row.

Weiner, Bernard (1985). An Attributional Theory of Achievement, Motivation, and Emotion. *Psychological Review* 92:548–573.

Weiner, Bernard, J. Amirkhan, V. S. Folkes, and J. A. Verette (1987). An Attributional Analysis of Excuse Giving: Studies of a Naive Theory of Emotion. *Journal of Personality and Social Psychology* 52:316–324.

Weinstein, Eugene A. and Paul Deutschberger (1963). Some Dimensions of Altercasting. *Sociometry* 26:454–466.

Weitzman, Jennifer (1996). Drawing a Family History Out of Cyberspace. *New York Times* (June 13): C2.

Wells, Theodora (1980). *Keeping Your Cool Under Fire: Communicating XA*

Wertz, Dorothy C., James R. Sorenson, and Timothy C. Heeren (1988). Can't Get No (Dis) Satisfaction: Professional Satisfaction with Professional-Client Encounters. *Work and Occupations* 15 (February): 36–54.

Wessells, Michael G. (1982). *Cognitive Psychology*. New York: Harper & Row.

West, Candace and Don H. Zimmerman (1977). Women's Place in Everyday Talk: Reflections on Parent-Child Interaction. *Social Problems* 24 (June): 521–529.

Westefeld, J. S. and D. Liddell (1982). Coping with Long-Distance Relationships. *Journal of College Student Personnel* 23:550–551.

Westen, Robin (1996). The Real Slant on Gossip. *Psychology Today* 29 (July/August): 44–48, 80–81.

Westwood, R. I., F. F. Tang, and P. S. Kirkbride (1992). Chinese Conflict Behavior: Cultural Antecedents and Behavioral Consequences. *Organizational Development Journal* 10 (summer): 13–19.

Wetzel, Patricia J. (1988). Are "Powerless" Communication Strategies the Japanese Norm? *Language in Society* 17:555–564.

Wheeless, Lawrence R., and Janis Grotz (1977). The Measurement of Trust and Its Relationship to Self-Disclosure. *Human Communication Research* 3:250–257.

Wiemann, John M. (1977). Explication and Test of a Model of Communicative Competence. *Human Communication Research* 3:195–213.

Wiemann, John M., and P. Backlund (1980). Current Theory and Research in Communicative Competence. *Review of Educational Research* 50:185–199.

Wiemann, John M., A. Mulac, D. Zimmerman, and S. K. Mann (1987). Interruption Patterns in Same-Gender and Mixed-Gender Dyadic Conversations. Paper presented at the Third International Conference on Social Psychology and Language, Bristol, England. Cited in Mulac, Wiemann, Widenmann, and Gibson (1988).

Williams, Andrea (1985). *Making Decisions*. New York: Zebra.

Wilmot, William W. (1987). *Dyadic Communication*. 3d ed. New York: Random House.

Wilson, Glenn and David Nias (1976). *The Mystery of Love*. New York: Quadrangle/New York Times.

Wilson, R. A. (1989). Toward Understanding E-prime. *Etc.: A Review of General Semantics* 46:316–319.

Winhahl, Sven and Benno Signitzer with Jean T. Olson (1992). *Using Communication Theory: An Introduction to Planned Communication*. Thousand Oaks, CA: Sage.

Wolf, Florence I., Nadine C. Marsnik, William S. Tacey, and Ralph G. Nichols (1983). *Perceptive Listening*. New York: Holt, Rinehart and Winston.

Wolfson, Nessa (1988). The Bulge: A Theory of Speech Behaviour and Social Distance. In J. Fine, ed., *Second Language Discourse: A Textbook of Current Research*. Norwood, N.J: Ablex.

Wolpe, Joseph (1958). *Psychotherapy by Reciprocal Inhibition*. Stanford, CA: Stanford University Press.

Won-Doornink, Myong-Jin (1985). Self-Disclosure and Reciprocity in Conversation: A Cross-National Study. *Social Psychology Quarterly* 48:97–107.

Wood, John, ed. (1974). *How Do You Feel?* Englewood Cliffs, NJ: Prentice Hall.

Wood, Julia T. (1982). Communication and Relational Culture: Bases for the Study of Human Relationships. *Communication Quarterly 1* 30:75–83.

Wood, Julia T. (1994). *Gendered Lives: Communication, Gender, and Culture*. Belmont, CA: Wadsworth.

Wood, Julia T. and Steve Duck (1995). *Under-Studied Relationships: Off the Beaten Track*. Thousand Oaks, CA: Sage.

Wright, J. W. and L. A. Hosman (1983). Language Style and Sex Bias in the Courtroom: The Effects of Male and Female Use of Hedges and Intensifiers on Impression Formation. *Southern Speech Communication Journal* 48:137–152.

Wright, John W. (1995). *The Universal Almanac 1995*. Kansas City, MO: Andrews & McMeel.

Wright, Paul H. (1978). Toward a Theory of Friendship Based on a Conception of Self. *Human Communication Research* 4:196–207.

Wright, Paul H. (1984). Self-Referent Motivation and the Intrinsic Quality of Friendship. *Journal of Social and Personal Relationships* 1:115–130.

Wright, Paul H. (1988). Interpreting Research on Gender Differences in Friendship: A Case for Moderation and a Plea for Caution. *Journal of Social and Personal Relationships* 5:367–373.

Wright, Rex A., and Richard J. Contrada (1986). Dating Selectivity and Interpersonal Attraction: Toward a Better Understanding of the "Elusive Phenomenon." *Journal of Social and Personal Relationships* 3:131–148.

Yapko, Michael D. (1997). The Art of Avoiding Depression. *Psychology Today* 30 (May/June): 37, 75.

Yerby, Janet, Nancy Buerkel-Rothfuss, and Arthur P. Bochner (1990). *Understanding Family Communication*. Scottsdale, Ariz.: Gorsuch Scarisbrick.

Yogev, Sara (1987). Marital Satisfaction and Sex Role Perceptions Among Dual-Earner Couples. *Journal of Social and Personal Relationships* 4:35–45.

Yun, Hum (1976). The Korean Personality and Treatment Considerations. *Social Casework* 57.173–178.

Zajonc, Robert B. (1968). Attitudinal Effects of Mere Exposure. *Journal of Personality and Social Psychology Monograph* Suppl. 9, no. 2, pt. 2.

Zanden, James W. Vander (1984). *Social Psychology*. 3d ed. New York: Random House.

Zimbardo, Philip A. (1977). *Shyness: What It Is and What to Do About It*. Reading, MA: Addison-Wesley.

Zimmer, Troy A. (1986). Premarital Anxieties. *Journal of Social and Personal Relationships* 3:149–159.

Zimmerman, Don H. and Candace West (1975). Sex Roles, Interruptions and Silences in Conversations. In *Language and Sex: Differences and Dominance,* edited by B. Thorne and N. Henley. Rowley, MA: Newbury House.

Zuckerman, M., R. Klorman, D. T. Larrance, and N. H. Spiegel (1981). Facial, Autonomic, and Subjective Components of Emotion: The Facial Feedback Hypothesis Versus the Externalizer-Internalizer Distinction. *Journal of Personality and Social Psychology* 41:929–944.

Zunin, Leonard M. and Natalie B. Zunin (1972). *Contact: The First Four Minutes*. Los Angeles: Nash.

Index

A

Abarbanel, Albert, 487
accenting, 176, 191
accommodation, 36
acculturation, 48–50, 469
accuracy, of perception, 475
acknowledgement tokens, 277. *See also* backchanneling cues
active fighting, 382, 395
active listening, 87, 99, 127, 146–150, 151, 169, 343, 366, 381, 469. *See also* listening
Acuff, Frank L., 62, 485
Adams, Linda, 485
Adams, R. G., 398t, 485
Adams, Rebecca G., 339, 398t, 399, 406, 487
adaptors, 189t, 228t, 229–230, 245, 363, 365, 403, 412, 469
Addeo, Edmond G., 485
address, 204
adjustment, principle of, 34–36, 45, 469
Adler, Mortimer J., 485
Adler, Ronald B., 485
aesthetics, 469
affect displays, 207, 228t, 229, 245, 469
affection, 19f
affectional orientation, 201–202, 214, 374, 381,
affinity-seeking strategies, 305, 306t, 313, 469
affirmation, 343–344, 386, 469
affirmation value, 401, 415
Africa/Africans, 9, 183t, 255t, 355
African Americans, 21, 213, 250t, 376, 412
agape, 410, 411, 412, 413, 415
Agarwala-Rogers, Rekha, 502
agenda-setting, 144t
aggressiveness, 101, 102, 105, 363
Akert, Robin M., 485
Akin, J., 486
Akmajian, A., 485
Albert, Rosita, 36, 485
Albert, S. M., 398t, 485
Alberti, Robert E., 101, 485
Alberts, J. K., 485
Alessandra, Tony, 135t, 485
allness, 189t, 211t, 217–219, 225, 469
Alloway, T., 491
Altendorf, Dayle M., 317, 486
alter-adaptors, 230, 469
altercasting, 16, 376t, 469
Altman, Irwin, 252, 295, 296, 485, 504
altruism, 367t
Amato Paul R., 316
ambiguity, 469
American Indians, 21, 63, 182, 214, 255t

Amirkhan, J., 115, 505
Andersen, Peter, 56, 236, 237, 238, 239, 485, 493
Anderson, Carolyn M., 497
Anderson, J. A., 492, 500, 501, 504
Angier, Natalie, 161, 162, 240, 241, 485
Angstadt, Lori, 84, 505
animals, 161, 252
Aoki, Melanie F., 236, 488
Apache, 53, 245
apologies, 385
appeal for suspension of judgment, 281
apprehension, 92–96, 105, 166, 237 management, 96–99, 471
Arabs, 53, 155, 169, 257, 258, 259, 355
arbitrariness, 469
Archer, Richard L., 78, 486
Ardrey, Robert, 252, 485
argot, 469
argumentativeness, 104, 140–141, 381, 389–392, 395, 469
Argyle, Michael, 82, 230, 233, 234, 235, 241, 251, 338, 485, 492
Aries, E. J., 398t, 495
Arliss, Laurie P., 485
Armstrong, Cameron B., 147, 485
Arnold, Carroll C., 485, 487
Aronson, Elliot, 118, 119, 122, 144t, 305, 485, 487, 489, 498, 501
arrangement, of physical setting, 469–470
artifactual communication, 253–258, 263
Asch, Solomon, 485
Asians, 9, 21, 63, 139, 169, 185, 214, 255t, 274, 312, 355, 356, 376–376, 377, 381, 404, 412. *See also* specific countries
assertiveness, 100–105, 381, 423, 425, 470
assimilation, 470
association, 400, 415
Association of American University Presses, 203, 213, 503
attack, 144t, 385, 392
attention, 470
attitude, 36, 164, 171, 470
attitudinal positiveness, 164
attitudinal similarity, 470
attraction, 470
attraction theory, 302–305, 313, 326, 340, 404
attractiveness, 302–303, 310, 313, 326, 327f, 360, 361, 470
attribution theory, 110–111, 470
attribution errors, 117–120
attribution processes, 111–117, 129
Auerbach, A. H., 493
Auerbach, D., 398t, 491
Aune, R. Kelly, 36, 242, 485, 488
Australia/Australians, 51t, 73–74, 183t
Auter, Philip J., 294, 485
Authier, Jerry, 161, 485

autonomy, 291, 306t, 422, 424
avoidance, 382, 395, 470
Axtell, Roger E., 62, 167, 169, 182, 233, 485
Aylesworth, Thomas G., 485
Aylesworth, Virginia L., 485
Ayres, Debbie M., 97, 485, 486
Ayres, Joe, 94, 97, 337, 485, 486

B

Bach, George R., 486
Back, K. W., 303, 491
backchanneling cues, 137, 277–278, 279f, 365, 470
Backlund, P., 506
Backrack, Henry M., 486
balance, 203–205, 207
balanced split pattern, 427, 433
Balswick, Jack O., 486, 490
bandwagon, 144t
Banks, Stephen P., 317, 486
Barbato, Carole A., 19f, 147, 492, 502
bargaining, 381
Barker, Deborah Ann, 230, 233, 240, 256, 497
Barker, Larry, 132, 135f, 230, 233, 240, 256, 486, 497, 504, 505
Barker, Randolph T., 132, 486
Barna, LaRay M., 62, 63, 486
Barnlund, Dean C., 486
Baron, Robert, 206, 486
Barrett, Karen, 486
barriers, 210–225, 470
Barron, James, 486
Bartholomew, Kim, 486
Bartlett, K., 259, 497
Basso, K. H., 54, 245, 486
Bate, Barbara, 486
Bateson, Gregory, 37, 486, 504
Bateson, M. C., 496, 497
Baukus, Robert A., 391, 501
Bavelas, Janet Beavin, 33, 486
Baxter, Leslie A., 291, 293, 296, 298, 337, 339, 486, 490
BBS (bulletin board system), 204
Beach, Wayne A., 33, 486
Beattie, Melody, 95, 486
Beatty, Michael J., 486
Beavin, Janet Helmick, 31, 33, 37, 195, 505
Beck, A. T., 76, 210, 320, 486
Becker, Samuel L., 244, 486
Beebe, Steven A., 419t, 486
behavioral synchrony, 327f, 470
Beier, Ernst, 486
Belgians/Belgium, 51t, 257, 258, 269t
belief, 470
believability, 185–190, 191
Bell, Robert A., 293, 306t, 486
beltlining, 470
Bennett, Mark, 281, 486
Berg, J. H., 78, 82, 489
Berg-Cross, Linda, 78, 486

Berger, Charles R., 126, 177, 302, 303, 487, 488, 500
Berger, P. L., 487
Berkowitz, L., 495
Berkowitz, Leonard, 503
Berman, J. J., 308, 487
Bernstein, W. M., 487
Berry, John W., 50, 118, 381, 487
Berscheid, Ellen, 121, 304, 307, 487, 490, 505
Bibby, Cyril, 487
Bierhoff, Hans W., 412, 487
bilateral communication, 160
biological time, 260
biorhythms, 260
Birdwhistell, Ray L., 487
Bishop, Jerry E., 240, 487
Bitar, Nadine, 125, 491
Bitti, Pio Ricci, 230, 492
blame, 381, 383–384, 385, 395, 470
Blieszner, Rosemary, 339, 398t, 399, 406, 487
blind self, 72, 89, 476
blinking, 189t, 233
Blood, Jr., Robert O., 319, 487
Blue, Janet, 51, 495
Blumstein, Philip, 305, 321, 322, 323, 326, 415, 418, 487
Bochner, Arthur, 50, 56, 74, 84, 85, 419t, 487, 506
Bochner, Stephen, 59, 491
body movement, 159, 228–230, 245
Bolivia/Bolivians, 269t
Bond, Lynne A., 201, 502
Booth-Butterfield, Melanie, 504
Booth-Butterfield, Steve, 95, 498, 504
Borden, George A., 56, 487, 499
Borisoff, Deborah, 487
Borker, Ruth, 487
Bosmajian, Haig, 198, 487
Bostrom, Robert N., 489, 491, 495, 505
Boumil, Marcia Mobilia, 356, 491
boundary marker, 253, 263, 470
Bourland, Jr., D. David, 487
Bowers, John Waite, 485, 487
Bradac, James J., 36, 126, 234, 303, 487, 492, 499
Bravo, Ellen, 356, 358, 487
Brazil/Brazilians, 55, 413
breadth, 295–296, 302, 327f, 402, 470
breakdown phase, 317, 331
Brecher, Edward M., 487
Breidenstein-Cutspec, Patricia, 93, 487
Brock, Karla F., 412, 499
Brommel, Bernard, 196t, 419t, 421, 432, 487, 492
Brougher, Toni, 163, 487
Brown, Charles T., 274, 487
Brown, J. K., 376, 489
Brown, Penelope, 274, 487
Brownell, Judi, 135f, 487
Bruneau, Tom, 487
Bruning, Stephen D., 386, 494

Brunner, Claire C., 488
Buerkel-Rothfuss, Nancy L., 293, 419t, 486, 506
buffer zone, 250–251. See also personal distance; proxemics
Bugental, J., 73, 487
Bulgaria/Bulgarians, 303
Bull, Peter, 487
Bull, R., 310, 487
Buller, David B., 36, 185, 229, 230, 242, 250t, 251, 275, 278t, 363, 488
bulletin board system (BBS), 204
Bullis, C., 298, 486
Burger, Robert E., 485
Burgoon, Judee K., 185, 189, 229, 230, 237, 250t, 251, 275, 278t, 363, 488, 498
Burgoon, Michael, 354, 488, 500
Burks, D. M., 155, 493
Burns, D. D., 210, 488
Burr, Chandler, 215, 488
business, of conversation, 268, 283
Buss, David, 488
Butler, Pamela E., 75, 488
Buunk, Bram P., 328, 337, 501, 502
Byrne, Donn, 486

C
Cabello, B., 306, 488
Calabrese, Richard J., 302, 487
Calero, Henry, 499
Cambra, Ronald F., 499
Camden, C. T., 277, 488, 495
Campbell, J. C., 376, 489
Canada/Canadians, 51t, 60
Canary, Daniel J., 337, 488, 490, 504
cant, 470
Caplow, T., 413, 496
Cappella, Joseph N., 231, 488
Carducci, Bernardo J., 93, 95, 98, 488
Caribbean people, 269t
caring cluster, 406
Carlson, R. E., 155, 493
Carmin, Cheryl N., 96, 497
Caroll, John B., 57, 488
Carpenter, David, 488
Carr, Peggy, 78, 486
Carroll, J. Gregory, 167, 502
Cartwright, Dorwin, 491
Cartwright-Smith, J., 231, 496
Cassedy, Ellen, 356, 358, 487
Cate, R., 383, 488
causes, 111–120, 345. See also attribution
Cegala, Donald J., 488
censorship, 113, 324–325, 470
Centers, C., 359, 501
central marker, 253, 263, 470
certainty, 470
Chadwick-Jones, J. K., 306, 488
Chaffee, Steven H., 487, 488
Chaikin, A. L., 84, 488
Chandler, Teresa A., 386, 494
Chaney, Robert H., 236, 488

Chang, Hui-Ching, 24, 488
change, 422, 424
channel, 16, 25, 470
Chanowitz, B., 195, 488
character attack, 386
chat, 204
Chen, Guo-Ming, 164, 488
cherishing behaviors, 327f, 344, 470
Cherokee, 255t
Cherry, Kittredge, 84, 488
Chesebro, James, 488
Chicana/Chicano, 214. See also Latin Americans; Latina/Latino; Mexican/Mexican American
China/Chinese, 24, 60, 81, 121, 139, 185, 255t, 258, 273–274, 297, 354, 275, 286
Christie, Richard, 352, 354, 488
Christopher, R., 383, 488
chronemics, 258–262, 263, 470
Chua, Elizabeth, 53, 493
Cialdini, Robert T., 488
Civikly, Jean, 489
civil inattention, 235, 470
Clark, Eddie M., 412, 499
Clark, Herbert, 488
Clark, Leslie F., 329, 489
Clark, M. L., 375, 488
Clark, Ruth Anne, 30, 488
Clatterbuck, G. W., 498
clearance, 311
Clement, Donald A., 14, 488
clichÈ, 470
Cline, M. G., 232, 488
Cline, Rebecca J., 451, 488
Clinton, Bill, 147
closed-mindedness, 470
closedness, 291
closeness, 167, 235, 312, 313
closing, a conversation, 268–269, 270, 279–280, 283
clothing, 255–257, 263, 323, 412
clusters, 478
Cochenour, John J., 179, 501
code, 471
Cody, Michael J., 186, 189, 317, 368, 486, 489, 500
Cody, James, 303, 503
Cody, Michael L., 368, 498
coercive power, 360–361, 363, 369
cognitive disclaimers, 281
cognitive distortions, 210. See also barriers
cognitive restructuring, 96, 105
Cole, P., 492
collectivist culture, 50–52, 53, 54t, 67, 73–74, 100–101, 164, 354, 381, 385, 404, 412, 413, 422, 471, 475
Collett, Peter, 499
Collier, Mary Jane, 213, 376, 489, 493
Collins, B. E., 489
Collins, James E., 329, 489
Colombia/Colombians, 51t, 269t

color communication, 254–255, 263, 471
Comadena, Mark, 496
commitment, 34, 327f, 335–337, 406–408
communication adjustment, 471. *See also* adjustment
communication apprehension, 92, 471. *See also* apprehension
communicology, 471
comparison level, 307
competence, 12–13, 303, 381, 392, 471
competitive symmetry, 39
complementarity, 39, 305, 471
complementary relationship, 37, 38–40, 471
complementing, with nonverbal messages, 176, 191
complete (consummate) love, 408
compliance-gaining strategies, 104, 354, 361, 366–368, 369, 471
compliance-resisting strategies, 104, 366, 368, 369, 471
compliments, 164, 167, 171, 328
computers. See Internet; online communication,
Conaway, Wayne A., 56, 499
Condon, John C., 489
confidence, 104, 166, 171, 471
confidentiality, 471
confirmation, 195–197, 207, 385, 386, 412, 471
conflict, 372–373, 471
  avoidance, 423, 425
  content and relationship dimensions of, 42–43, 374–375, 427
  culture and, 375–377, 381
  in relationships, 296, 323, 326, 337, 404, 426, 427, 428, 431
  irreversibility and, 34
  listening and, 144t
  management, 376, 380–393, 394
  negative allness in, 477
  resolution, 42–43, 104, 343, 354, 377–380, 393–395
  silence and, 243
  status and, 165
  unproductive strategies, 484
congruence, 471
connection, 291
connotation, 179–180, 191, 471
Conrad, Anne B., 488
consensus, 115, 117, 119–120, 129
consistency, 115, 117, 119–120, 124, 129, 157, 471
contact cultures, 239
contact
  in relationship, 291, 292f, 299, 311–312, 313, 327f
content and relationship dimensions, 40–44, 45, 145, 188, 343, 471
context, 250t, 471–472
context references, 271
Contrada, Richard J., 311, 506

contradictory signals, 167–168, 176, 185–190, 191
control, 19f, 176, 191, 237, 376
controllability, 115–116, 117, 119–120, 129
controversy, 244
conversation, 472
  management of, 270–280, 472
  problems in, 280–283
  processes, 266–270, 283, 472
  maxims, 472
  turns in, 275–277, 278f, 283, 472
Cook, Anthony, 489
Cook, K. S., 307, 498
Cook, Mark, 489
Cook, S. W., 328, 491
Cooley, Charles Horton, 70, 489
cooperation, 472
cooperation principle, 272–275, 283, 472
Cornelius, Randolph R., 503
Cornell, C., 492
Costa Rica, 51t
Coulmas, Florian, 497
Counts, D. A., 376, 489
Courtright, John A., 487
Cozby, Paul, 84, 489
cracker, 204
Craig, Mary E., 383, 489
credentialing, 281, 283
credibility, 140, 181, 202, 242, 363, 427, 472
critical feedback, 14, 15
critical listening, 143, 146f
critical thinking, 128, 129, 472
criticism, 205, 206, 207, 479
Crohn, Joel, 376, 489
Cromwell, R. E., 501
Crouch, Isabel, 490
Crusco, April H., 237, 489
cues, 128, 341
cultural display, 255–256, 472
cultural identifiers, 213–214
cultural relativism, 50
cultural rules, 155, 472
cultural sensitivity, 155, 171
cultural time, 258–260, 263, 472
culture shock, 59–60, 67
culture
  apprehension and, 93–94
  attribution and, 118, 119, 121
  barriers to intercultural communication, 19, 36, 59–60, 470. *See also* ethnocentrism
  body and facial language, 229, 232
  clothing, 254–255
  collectivist. See collectivist culture,
  colors in, 255
  compliments and, 164
  conflict and, 375–377, 381
  conversation and, 268, 269t, 270, 273–274
  criticism and praise and, 206, 207
  directness and, 185

eye contact, 233
  family and, 421, 422
  friendship and, 404, 415
  gift giving and, 257–258
  high-context, 52–55, 67, 375
  individualistic. See individualistic culture,
  listening and, 139–140
  love and, 412, 415
  low-context, 52–55, 67
  nature of, 48–50
  nonverbal messages and, 36, 182
  perspective of, 17, 22–25
  relationships in context of, 293, 297, 308, 347–348, 349
  self-disclosure and, 81–82, 87
  silence and, 243–245
  social data and, 9
  status and, 165
  taboos. See taboos,
  time and, 259, 260
  touch communication and, 239
  U.S. demographics, 21f, 22
  uncertainty and, 126
Cupach, William R., 489
Cupach, William R., 12, 13, 166, 504

D

Dahnke, G. L., 498
Dainton, M., 337, 489
Daly, John, 95, 306t, 486, 498, 504
Daly, John A., 489
Dance, Frank E. X., 489
Danehy, J. J., 500
Dangello, Frank, 354, 491
Danks, Joseph H., 136, 492
Dasen, Pierre R., 50, 118, 381, 487
date, 472, 474
DíAugelli, Anthony R., 357, 489, 500
Davidson, A. G., 489
Davis, Flora, 489
Davis, Keith E., 406, 415, 489, 490, 495
Davis, L. M., 361, 501
Davis, M. H., 487
Davis, Murray S., 288, 297, 311, 412, 489
Davis, Ossie, 198, 489
Davitz, Joel R., 489
de Bock, H., 499
Deal, James E., 382, 383, 489
Dean, J., 251, 485
deBono, Edward, 489
DeCecco, John, 432, 489, 500
deception, 326, 327f, 331
decoder, 11, 472
decoding, 11–12, 472
decoration
  clothing and body, 255–257, 263
  space, 253–254, 263
Deetz, Stanley, 489
defensiveness, 327f, 472
DeFrancisco, Victoria, 277, 489
deintensifying, 231t

delayed feedback, 14, 15
delayed reactions, 472
Delia, Jesse G., 177, 489
DeLillo, Dena A., 291, 501
Demers, R. A., 485
denial, 472
Denmark/Danes, 51t, 56, 348
denotation, 178–180, 191, 472
depenetration, 296, 472
depression, 328–329, 331
depth, 143–145, 146f, 151, 295–296, 302, 327f, 402, 472
Derlega, V. J., 84, 488
Derlega, Valerian J., 82, 84, 489
describing, 9
descriptiveness, 162–163, 171
deterioration, relationship. See under Relationship,
determinism, principle of, 472
DeTurck, Mark A., 185, 189, 251, 383, 489, 491
Deutsch, Ronald M., 486
Deutschberger, Paul, 16, 505
DeVito, Joseph A., 10, 189, 260, 485, 487, 489, 490, 492, 493, 495, 498, 502, 503, 504
DeVries, Mary A., 62, 490
Dewey, John, 378
dialogic coversation, 472
dialogue, 196t, 472
Dickson-Markman, Fran, 84, 490
diffused time orientation, 259, 263
Dillard, James Price, 367t, 490
DiMichael, Eleanor, 139, 496
Dindia, Kathryn, 337, 344, 490
Dion, Karen K., 121, 412, 490
Dion, Kenneth L., 412, 490
direct messages, 183–185
direct speech, 139, 472
disabilities, people with, 65, 180, 310, 390
disagreement, 165
disclaimer, 16, 280–281, 283, 472
disclosure responses, 472
disconfirmation, 194–198, 201–202, 207, 243, 386, 412, 473
discriminating, 473
disengagement, 317
displaced time orientation, 258, 263
display rules, 139, 231t, 232
dissolution, relationship. See under Relationship
distinctiveness, 115, 117, 119–120, 129
Dodd, Carley H., 490, 505
Dodd, David H., 490
Dolgin, Kim G., 404, 490
domestic partnership, 289, 348, 418
dominance, 237. See also status
Donohue, William A., 385, 490
Dosey, M., 250, 490
Dosser, Jr., David A., 490
Douglas, William, 126, 490
Drass, Kriss A., 278, 490

Dresser, Norine, 23, 164, 207, 239, 255t, 376, 404, 422, 490
Dreyfuss, Henry, 255t, 490
Driscoll, R., 490
Drummond, Kent, 277, 490
Dubois, Betty Lou, 490
Duck, Steve W., 316, 411, 486, 490, 492, 493, 494, 495, 496, 498, 500, 501, 502, 504, 505, 506
Dullea, Georgia, 490
Duncan, Barry L., 344, 490
Duncan, Jr., S. D., 275, 490
Duran, R. L., 303, 490
Duran, Robert L., 291, 501
dyadic coalition, 7, 473
dyadic communication, 6–7, 10, 78, 81, 250t, 473
dyadic consciousness, 7, 403, 473
dyadic effect, 78, 473
dyadic phase, 316, 331
dyadic primacy, 7–8, 473
Dyer, Wayne, 147
dynamic tension, 291, 402

E
Eadie, W. F., 155, 493
Eakins, Barbara, 490
Eakins, R. Gene, 490
ear marker, 243, 263, 473
Earl, Jamie, 409, 503
Ebesu, Amy S., 185, 488
Ecuador, 51t
Eden, Dov, 490
Eder, D., 407, 490
Edgar, T., 490
Edwards, R., 132, 486
effect, 473
effective listening, 87. See also active listening; listening
effectiveness, 84, 473
effects, 12f, 18, 25
efficiency, 36
Egan, Gerard, 443, 490
ego-support value, 401, 415
Eguchi, H., 499
Egypt/Egyptians, 183t, 255t, 269t
Ehrenhaus, Peter, 243, 490
either-or fallacy. See polarization
Ekman, Paul, 186, 190, 228, 230, 232, 490, 491
Ellis, Albert, 76, 96, 406, 487, 491
Ellis, Donald, 411, 496
Ellsworth, Phoebe, 230, 491
Ellyson, S. L., 235, 365, 491
Elmes, Michael B., 154, 491
Eloy, Sylvia V., 242, 337, 488, 493
e-mail, 204
emblems, 228–229, 245, 473
Emmons, Michael L., 101, 485
emoticons, 35, 179, 204
emotion, 104, 166, 231, 236–237, 243, 473. See also feelings

emotional appeal, 221–222
emotional expression, 473
empathy, 142, 146f, 147, 151, 160–162, 171, 197, 473
empowerment,
empty love, 408
encoder, 11, 473
encoding, 473
encoding-decoding, 11–12
enculturation, 48, 473
England/English, 21, 259
Enke, J. L., 407, 490
Enrich, Kathy, 260, 501
e-prime, 473
Epstein, N., 320, 491
equality, 165, 171, 473
equality pattern, 426–427
equilibrium theory, 473
equity theory, 473
erotic love, 408, 411, 413, 415
escape, 19f
Escobedo, Emma, 412, 496
et cetera, 218–219, 473, 474
ethics, 18–192, 20–21, 25, 186–188, 221–222, 473
ethnocentrism, 220–222, 223t, 473
euphemism, 473
Europe/Europeans, 139, 255t, 412. See also Northern Europeans; Southern Europeans
evaluation, 135f, 137, 143, 151, 160, 161, 162–163, 171, 242, 473
excluding talk, 202–203, 207
excuse, 281–282, 283, 385, 473
Exline, R. V., 235, 365, 491
expectancy violations theory, 251, 263, 473
expectations, 319–321, 474
experiential limitation, 474
expert power, 361–362, 369
explaining, 9–10
expressiveness, 104, 168–170, 171, 403, 474
extensional devices, 474
extensional orientation, 211t, 212, 474
external causes, 111–120
eye avoidance, 235, 412
eye contact, 159, 167, 170, 233–236, 245, 249, 251, 275, 277, 278t, 311, 313, 323, 328, 364, 365, 403, 412
eye gaze, 474

F
Faber, Adele, 491
facesaving, 52, 54t, 55, 375, 381, 394
    detraction strategies, 385, 395
    enhancement strategies, 385, 395
facial communication, 35, 161, 170, 230–232
facial feedback hypothesis, 230, 474
facial management techniques, 230, 231t, 474

fact-inference confusion, 211t, 215–217, 225, 474
factual statement, 137, 215, 474. *See also* fact-inference confusion
Falk, Dennis R., 84, 491
family, 474
   communication patterns, 427–432, 433
   nature and characteristics, 418–426, 433
Fantuzzo, John W., 389, 501
FAQ (frequently asked questions), 204
Farace, R. V., 39
Farina, Amerigo, 166
Farrell, M. P., 398t, 491
Farson, Richard, 502
Fathi, Yousef, 489
fear appeal, 221–222, 474
feedback, 12f, 14–15, 35, 127, 137, 140, 268, 269, 270, 283, 474
   facial, 231, 234
feedforward, 12f, 15–16, 25, 157, 268, 269, 270, 283, 474
Feeley, Thomas H., 185, 189, 251, 491
feelings, 157, 160, 164, 170, 171, 196–197, 395. *See also* emotions; empathy
Feinstein, Marjorie C., 195, 505
Fengler, A. P., 415, 491
Ferguson, Sherry Devereaux, 504
Ferguson, Stewart, 504
Fernald, C. D., 64, 491
Fernandez-Collado, C., 19f, 502
Festinger, L., 303, 491
Field, R. H. G., 491
Fiji, 183t
Filley, Alan C., 491
Fine, J., 506
finger, 204
Fischer, C. S., 406, 491
Fisher, Donna, 365, 491
Fishman, Joshua A., 57, 491
Fiske, Susan T., 491
Fitzpatrick, Mary Anne, 308, 381, 382, 419t, 422, 427, 431, 344, 424–425, 490, 491, 500
flames, 159, 204, 276
Flanary, Rodney, 329, 493
Fleming, B., 320, 491
flexibility, 155, 156–157, 171, 474
flooding, 382
Floyd, James J., 142, 491
Floyd, Kory, 341, 500
Flynn, Teresa, 96, 497
Folger, Joseph P., 491
Folkes, V. S., 115, 505
Follingstad, Diane R., 383, 389, 489, 491
Foote, Franklin H., 413, 494
Forbes, Malcolm, 79
force, 382–383, 395, 474
formal time, 258, 263
Foster, M., 489
Fox, M., 398t, 491

France/French, 21, 51t, 229, 255t, 412
Frandsen, Kenneth D., 14, 488
Fraser, Bruce, 274, 491
Frazier, P. A., 328, 491
free information, 474
Freedman, Jonathan, 288, 321, 491
French, Jr., J. R. P., 359, 491
Frentz, Thomas, 368,, 491
frequently asked questions (FAQ), 204, 276
Frey, Kurt, 231, 496
Friedman, Joel, 356, 491
Friedman, Meyer, 491
friendship, 338–339, 398–406, 415, 474
Friesen, Wallace V., 228, 230, 490, 491
Frye, Jerry K., 491
Fudge, Deborah A., 321, 504
Fuller, Linda K., 310, 491
fundamental attribution error, 118–119, 129
Furlow, F. Bryant, 240, 241, 492
Furman, Mellie, 487
Furnham, Adrian, 59, 125, 398t, 491, 493
future orientation, 260, 263

G
Gable, Myron, 354, 491
Gabor, Don, 491
Gabrenya, Jr., W. K., 491
Gaines, C., 132, 486
Galbraith, J. K., 491
Galvin, Kathleen, 196t, 419t, 421, 432, 492
game, 474
Gangestad, S., 169, 492
Gao, Ge, 293, 492
Garner, Alan, 492
Gass, Susan M., 158, 505
gatekeeper, 113–114
gay men, 201, 202, 214, 303, 321–322, 323, 324–325, 374r, 381. *See also* affectional orientation; homosexual; lesbian
Geis, F. L., 488
Gelles, R., 383, 492
Gemmill, Gary, 154, 491
gender. *See also* sexism
   bias in language, 199–200
   body & facial language, 229, 230, 232
   conflict and, 375, 376, 381
   differences, 42–43, 160
   directness, 184–185
   expressiveness, 169, 244
   eye contact, 234
   interaction management, 167–168
   listening and, 140–141
   opening lines, 271–272
   politeness, 274–275
   power and, 355–356
   relationships, 303, 321, 322, 323, 328, 329, 341, 398t, 404–406, 413–415
   self-disclosure, 82, 87

   spatial distance and, 250t
   stereotypes, 125
   touch communication and, 237, 239
   turn-taking, 277, 278
general semantics, 474
generalization, 144t
generalized aggression, 101
generalized nonassertiveness, 101, 105
Gergen, K. J., 306, 492
Germany/Germans, 21, 53, 81, 82, 93, 259, 303
gestures, 170, 275, 403
Ghana, 255t
Gibb, Jack, 162, 492
Gibbs, M., 398t, 491
Gibson, T. W., 499, 506
gifts, 257–258
Giglioli, Pier Paolo, 486
Gilbert, Shirley, 84, 492
Giles, Howard, 36, 492
Gilmour, Robin, 490, 492, 493, 500, 501, 505
Givens, Carolyne A., 236, 488
Glad, Timo, 140, 502
Gladney, K., 132, 486
Gladstein, Gerald A., 492
Glucksberg, Sam, 136, 492
Goering, Elizabeth, 93, 487
Goffman, Erving, 235, 253, 492
Goldberg, A., 486
Goldberg, Philip, 492
Goldsmith, D. J., 240, 502
Goleman, Daniel, 161, 289, 382, 418, 492
Gombiner, Michael L., 236, 488
Gonzalez, Alexander, 260, 492
Goodwin, Robin, 81, 82, 492
Gordon, Thomas, 146, 492
Goss, Blaine, 189, 492, 500
gossip, 474
Gottman, John, 382, 492
Gottschalk, L. A., 493
Gould, Stephen Jay, 55, 492
Graham, E. E., 492
Graham, Elizabeth E., 13, 19f, 502
Graham, Jean Ann, 230, 492
granfallon, 144t
Grant, August E., 294, 492
grave-dressing phase, 317, 331
Gray, John, 147
Great Britain, 51t, 73–74, 81, 82
Greeks, 183t, 355
Green, Bonnie L., 389, 495
Greenberg, M. S., 306, 492
Greene, John O., 317, 486
Greenspan, Michael, 489
Greer, Charles R., 50, 504
Greif, Esther Blank, 278, 492
Grice, H. P., 272, 492
grief, 195–197
Griffin, Em, 28, 406, 492
Gross, Larry, 79, 492
Groth, E., 240, 502

Grotz, Janis, 82, 506
Grudzinskas, Gary, 97, 485
Gu, Yueguo, 273, 492
Guatemala, 51t
Gudykunst, William B., 50, 53, 54, 54t, 59, 62, 81, 94, 126, 158, 223t, 293, 492, 493, 495
Guerrero, Laura K., 236, 239, 337, 493
gunnysacking, 384, 395, 474
Gupta, U., 493
Gustafson, Kay, 161, 485
Guthrie, K. Kendall, 294, 492
hacker, 204

H
Haferkamp, Claudia J., 382, 493
Haga, Yasushi, 245, 493
Haggard, E. A., 231, 493
Hale, Jerold L., 251, 459, 488, 493
Hall, Edward T., 50, 54t, 55, 81, 169, 248, 258, 259, 493
Hall, J. A., 230, 493
Hall, Joan Kelly, 407, 493
Hall, Judith, 189, 233, 496
Hall, Mildred Reed, 50, 54t, 55, 81, 169, 259, 493
halo effect, 121, 124, 474
Halpern, Howard, 147
Halverson, Jr., Charles F., 490
Hamachek, Don E., 493
Han, Sang-pil, 52, 493
handle, 204
Haney, William, 216, 217t, 449, 493
haptics, 236–239, 245, 474
Harkins, S., 496
Harnish, R. M., 485
Harper, Robert A., 76, 96, 491
Harrell, W. Andrew, 323, 493
Harris, Judy, 159, 493
Harris, Linda M., 298, 498
Harris, Marvin, 493
Harris, R. M., 486
Hart, Fiona, 404, 493
Hart, R. P., 155, 493
Hart, Russell D., 65t, 493
Hartley, Karen C., 386, 494
Harvey, John H., 329, 336, 493, 496, 505
Hasart, Julie K., 257, 493
Hashimoto, T., 413, 497
Hastorf, Albert, 493
hate speech, 113, 147
Hatfield, Elaine, 24, 51, 304, 348, 355, 375, 376, 427, 493, 497
Hause, Kimberley S., 337, 488
Hayakawa, A. R., 493
Hayakawa, S. I., 493
Hayes, A. S., 496, 497
Hays, Robert B., 403, 404, 493
Hecht, Michael L., 189, 213, 412, 485, 487, 490, 492, 493, 495, 497, 498, 503, 504
hedging, 281, 283

Heeren, Timothy C., 13, 505
Hegstrom, Timothy, 493
Heiskell, Thomas L., 161, 493
helping, 18, 19f, 268
Henderson, M., 398t, 493
Henderson, Monika, 82, 338, 485
Hendrick, Clyde, 409, 413, 493, 493, 504
Hendrick, Susan, 409, 413, 493, 494
Henley, Nancy M., 199, 237, 494, 504
Henton, J., 383, 488
Hernandez-Sampieri, R., 19f, 502
Herrick, Lisa R., 148, 500
Hertzler, J. O., 494
Heseltine, Olive, 494
Hesketh, Beryl, 50, 56, 487
Hess, Eckhard H., 236, 494
Hess, Ursula, 231, 494
heterosexism, 201–202, 475
Heulip, J. W., 493
Hewitt, John, 281, 494
Hickson, Mark L., 494
hidden self, 73, 89, 476
Higgins, Mary Anne, 386, 494
Higgins, Raymond L., 282, 503
high-context culture, 52–55, 67, 475
high-monitored feedback, 14, 15
Hindu culture, 119, 255t
Hiscock, Harley, 422, 500
Hispanics, 21, 214, 233, 375. *See also* Chicana/Chicano; Latin America;Latin Americans; Mexicans/Mexican Americans
Hocker, Joyce L., 494
Hockett, Charles F., 494, 500
Hofstede, Geert, 50, 51, 55, 58, 59, 355, 494
Hoft, Nancy L., 255t, 494
Hoijer, Harry, 57, 494
Holden, Janice M., 38, 494
Hollender, Marc, 494
Holley, F., 132, 486
Holliday, Heithre, 407, 496
Hollon, Charles, 354, 491
Holmes, Janet, 274, 275, 494
Holt, G. Richard, 24, 488
home field advantage, 475
home territories, 475
homophobic language. See heterosexism
homosexual, 201, 202, 214, 236, 289, 321–322, 324–325, 348, 357, 374t, 418, 420. *See also* affectional orientation; gay men; heterosexism; lesbian
honest appraisal, 206, 207
Honeycutt, James, 304, 494
Hong Kong, 60
Hope, David, 79
Hopf, Tim, 94, 97, 485, 486
Hopper, Robert, 277, 411, 490, 494
Horvath, Cary L., 386, 494
Hosman, L. A., 281, 494, 506
Hovanitz, Christine, 389, 495
Huffines, LaUna, 494

Hull, W. F., 60, 496
humanistic approach, 158–165, 171, 366, 386
Hur, Gyeongho, 386, 494
Huston, Michelle, 288, 321, 427, 494
Hutchinson, Kevin L., 257, 493
Hymes, Dell, 494
hypertext, 204
hyphen, 474, 475

I
Iceland, 348
Ickes, W. J., 496
identity management, 368, 471
ideolect, 139
Illinois Coalition Against Sexual Assault, 383, 494
illustrators, 228t, 229, 245, 475
I-messages, 160, 170, 206, 343, 381, 475
immediacy, 36, 167, 171, 327f, 403, 404, 475
immediate feedback, 14, 15
impersonal encounters, 8–10
implicit personality theory, 120–121, 475
in-group talk, 475
inclusion, 19f, 202–203, 207, 475
independents, 426, 433
index, 222–223, 474, 475
India/Indians, 55, 56, 60, 304, 309t, 376, 415
indirect messages, 183–185
indirect speech, 139, 475
indiscrimination, 211t, 219–224, 225, 475
individualistic culture, 50–52, 53, 54t, 67, 73–74, 100, 354, 381, 385, 404, 412, 415, 422, 475, 476
Indonesia/Indonesians, 51t, 60, 64, 259, 303
inevitability, 33–34, 45, 475
Infante, Dominic A., 28, 30, 385, 386, 387, 389, 391, 392, 494
infatuation, 408
inferential statement, 137, 215, 475. *See also* fact-inference confusion
influencing, 18, 19f, 268
informal-time terms, 258, 263, 475
information (persuasion) power, 362–363, 369
information overload, 475
Ingham, Harry, 72f
Ingham, R., 233, 485
initiating relationships, 475
Insel, Paul M., 122, 494
insulation, 475
intensifying, 231t, 292
intensional orientation, 211t, 212–215, 225, 475–476
intensity, 36, 109
interaction management, 104, 167–168, 171, 476
interactional contact, 291, 299

intercultural communication, 59, 61–66, 67, 126, 127, 476. *See also* culture
internal causes, 111–120
Internet, 22–23, 25, 48, 79, 113–114, 159, 204, 276, 294, 310–311, 341
interpersonal communication, definitions, 6–10, 476
interpersonal conflict, 476
interpersonal deterioration, 292f, 296, 299
interpersonal perception, 476
interpersonal relationships. See relationships
interpersonal repair, 292f, 297, 299
interpersonal separation, 292f, 297, 299
interpretation, 196t, 476
interpretation-evaluation, 109–110, 129
interrupting, 104, 165, 277–278, 279f, 365, 392
intimacy, 36, 235, 251, 292f, 296–296, 299, 327f, 373, 403–404, 406, 476
intimacy claims, 319, 331, 476
intimate distance, 248–249, 263, 476
intonation, 275, 277
intrapersonal communication, 476
intrapersonal dissatisfaction, 292t, 296, 299
intrapersonal repair, 292f, 296–297, 299
intrapsychic phase, 316, 331
Inuit/Inuk, 214
involvement, in relationship, 291–293, 299, 327f
Iran/Iranians, 255t, 257, 258, 348, 376
Iraq, 269t
Ireland/Irish, 21, 51t, 255t
irreversibility, 34, 45, 86, 343, 476
Isaacs, K. S., 231, 493
Ishii, Satoshi, 100, 504
Israel, 93
Italy/Italians, 21, 52t, 63, 259, 355
Izard, C. E., 490

J
Jackson, Don D., 31, 33, 37, 195, 496, 505
Jacobson, L., 122, 502
Jacobson, Lenore F., 122, 494
Jacobson, W. D., 494
Jaggi, V., 118, 504
Jain, Nemi C., 503
Jaksa, James A., 18, 494
James, David L., 62, 494
James, Phil, 179, 276, 494
James, William, 195
Jandt, Fred E., 19, 60, 214, 487, 494
Janus, Cynthia L., 328, 494
Janus, Samuel S., 328, 494
Japan/Japanese, 23, 53–54, 55, 60, 81, 93, 139, 140, 167, 183t, 185, 229, 232, 233, 239, 245, 255t, 259, 269t, 273, 304, 375, 413
jargon, 476

Jaspers, Karl, 243
Jaworski, Adam, 243, 494
Jecker, Jon, 306, 494
Jensen, J. Vernon, 495
Johannesen, Richard L., 18, 495
Johari window, 71–73, 89, 476
Johnson, C. E., 363, 495
Johnson, F. L., 398t, 495
Johnson, Frank A., 495
Johnson, Jennifer R., 409, 503
Johnson, M. P., 495
Johnson, Otto, 495
Johnson, Patricia, 36, 492
Johnson, Scott A., 495
Johnson, Wendell, 495
Jones, Brian D., 352, 498
Jones, E. E., 166, 495
Jones, Stanley, 236, 239, 495
Jones, W. H., 495
Jordan, Felecia F., 386, 494
Jourard, Sidney M., 80, 81, 82, 239, 495
Joyner, Russell, 495
justification, 368, 471

K
Kalichman, Seth C., 383, 409, 489, 503
Kanner, Bernice, 255, 495
Kapoor, Suraj, 51, 495
Kappas, Arvid, 231, 494
Kartus, Sallie, 502
Kasian, Marilyn, 389, 495
Kasimatis, Margaret, 231, 496
Kazoleas, Dean, 495
Kearney, P., 361, 495
Keating, Carolinen F., 235, 495
Keenan, Elinor Ochs, 273, 495
Keith, P. M., 308, 503
Keller, Paul W., 487
Kelley, H. H., 83, 306, 495, 504
Kelly, Clifford, 487
Kelly, Erin, 97, 485
Kelly, L., 303, 490
Kemp, Anita, 389, 495
Kendon, A., 486
Kennedy, C. W., 277, 495
Kenyans, 257, 258
Kersten, K., 383, 495
Kersten, L., 383, 495
Key, M. R., 486
Keyes, Jr., Ken, 77t, 495
Keyes, Penny, 77t, 495
Kidd, Frank, 78, 486
Kidd, R. F., 496
Kiesler, Sara, 159, 495
Kikuchi, Toshiyuki, 36, 485
Kim, Min-Sun, 52, 495
Kim, Sung Hee, 394, 495
Kim, Young Yun, 50, 53, 94, 223t, 492, 495, 505
kinesics, 228–230, 476
King, Robert, 139, 496
Kirkbride, P. S., 56, 505
Kirkpatrick, C., 413, 496

Kleck, R. E., 231, 496
Klein, Renate, 412, 487
Kleinfield, N. R., 496
Kleinke, Chris L., 271, 363, 496
Klimoski, Richard J., 118, 497
Klineberg, O., 60, 496
Klopf, Donald W., 100, 504
Klorman, R., 231, 506
Knapp, Mark L., 189, 233, 283, 323, 335, 336, 411, 414, 494, 496
Knox, David, 488
Kochman, Thomas, 376, 496
Koester, Jolene, 58, 169, 497
Kolbe, Jim, 79
Kolt, Robert, 385, 490
Komarovsky, M., 82, 496
Korda, M., 496
Korea/Koreans, 51t, 53, 60, 78, 140, 155, 239, 255t, 269t
Korzenny, Felipe, 489, 495, 503
Korzybski, Alfred, 474
Korzybski, Alfred, 219, 496
Kosberg, Roberta L., 391, 501
Koval, J., 383, 488
Kramarae, Cheris, 199, 496, 504
Kramer, Ernest, 496
Krames, L., 491
Kraut, R., 185, 496
Krayer, K. J., 189, 500
Kristof, Nicholas D., 496
Krug, Linda, 496
Kudoh, T., 232, 498
Kurdek, Lawrence A., 335, 324, 496
Kurt, P. David, 485

L
LaBarre, W., 496
LaFrance, M., 496
Lahey, B. B., 109, 496
Laing, Milli, 407, 496
Laing, Ronald D., 126, 496
Lakoff, Robin, 496
Lambdin, William, 496
Lamke, Leanne K., 293, 503
Landy, David, 306, 494
Langer, Ellen J., 59, 154, 155, 488, 496
language fairness, 476
language relativity hypothesis, 57, 67, 476
Lanzetta, John T., 231, 494, 496
Larrance, D. T., 231, 506
Larsen, Randy J., 231, 496
Latane, B., 491, 496
Latina/Latino, 214
Latin America/Latin Americans, 53, 81, 182, 185, 255t, 258, 259, 404
Lea, Martin, 35, 310, 496
Leaper, Campbell, 407, 496
learning, 17, 19f, 268
Lears, Margaret, 503
Leathers, Dale G., 186, 189, 230, 496
leave-taking cues, 476
LeBlanc, Dee-Ann, 114, 179, 496

LeBlanc, Robert, 114, 179, 496
Lederer, William J., 319, 326, 344, 496
Lee, A. Russell, 126, 496
Lee, Alfred McClung, 144t, 496
Lee, Elizabeth, Briant, 144t, 496
Lee, Fiona, 275, 496
Lee, Iona Lee, 81, 82, 492
Lee, John Alan, 408, 409, 410, 496
legitimate power, 360, 361, 362, 369
Leibowitz, Ken, 237, 238, 485
Lenz, Elinor, 485
Leon, Joseph J., 412, 496
LePoire, Beth A., 242, 488
lesbians, 201, 202, 214, 321–322, 323, 324–325, 374t, 381
Leung, Kwok, 375, 381, 497
LeVay, Simon, 215, 497
leveling, 143, 476
Lever, Janet, 214, 497
Levine, D., 495
Levine, R, 259, 413, 497
Levinger, George, 497
Levinson, D., 375, 497
Levinson, S. C., 274, 487
Lewis, David, 363, 497
libel, 113
Libya, 269t
Liddell, D., 421, 505
Liddy, G. Gordon, 147
Lighthouse, Inc., 182
liking, 408
Limbaugh, Rush, 147
Lin, Yuan-Huei W., 497
Lindzey, Gardner, 487, 489, 498
linguistic relativity hypothesis, 57, 476
Lipetz, M. E., 490
Lips, H. M., 497
listener cues, 277–278, 279f
listening, 132–138, 476. *See also* active listening
listening power, 364–365, 369
Littlejohn, Stephen W., 28, 30, 126, 497
Lloyd, S., 383, 488
Loftus, Elizabeth F., 497
loneliness, 328–329, 331
Long, B., 235, 365, 491
Lorenz, Konrad, 497
loving, 243, 476
low-context culture, 52–55, 67, 476
low-monitored feedback, 14, 15
Lowell, James Russell, 243
Luce, Gay Gaer, 260, 497
Luckmann, T., 177, 487
ludus love, 409–410, 411, 413, 415
Luft, Joseph, 72, 497
Lujansky, H., 308, 497
Lukens, J., 223t, 497
Lundy, James C., 459, 493
Lurie, Alison, 256, 497
lurking, 204, 276
Lustig, Myron W., 58, 169, 497
lying, 186–187, 326
Lyman, Stanford M., 497

M
Ma, Karen, 232, 347, 497
Ma, Ringo, 185, 497
Machiavelli, Niccolo, 352
Machievallianism, 352–354, 476
MacLachlan, James, 242, 497
Mahl, George F., 497
Main, Frank, 38, 497
maintenance strategies, 476
maintenance, relationship. See under Relationship
Majeski, William J., 497
Malandro, Loretta A., 230, 233, 240, 256, 497, 503
Malaysia, 60, 73–74, 255t
Malinowski, Bronislaw, 15, 497
Mallardi, Vincent, 260, 497
Manes, Joan, 274, 497
manic love, 410, 411, 412, 413, 415
manipulation, 477
Mann, Leon, 74, 501
Mann, S. K., 506
Mann, Thomas, 243
manner maxim, 273, 276, 477
Mao, LuMing Robert, 274, 497
Margulis, Stephen T., 84, 489
markers, 253, 477
Markway, Barbara G., 96, 497
Marsella, Anthony J., 495
Marsh, Peter, 499
Marsh, Peter, 233, 237, 253, 497
Marshall, Eldon K., 485
Marshall, Evan, 233, 234, 236, 497
Marshall, Linda L., 382, 497
Marsnik, Nadine C., 506
Marston, P. J., 489
Marston, Peter J., 412, 497
Martel, Myles, 497
Martin, Matthew M., 19f, 157, 386, 494, 497, 502
Martin, Scott L., 118, 497
Marwell, Gerald, 367t, 497
Masheter, Carol, 298, 498
masking, 231t
Maslow, Abraham, 254, 498
Masterson, John T., 419t, 486
matching hypothesis, 304, 477
Matsumoto, David, 24, 168, 232, 235, 498
Matz, S. Irene, 53, 503
May, Gerald G., 498
Maynard, Harry E., 498
Mayo, C., 496
Mazlish, Elaine, 491
Mazur, Alan, 235, 495
McBroom, William H., 124, 498
McCarthy, B., 498
McConnell-Ginet, Sally, 487
McCornack, Steven A., 189, 498
McCroskey, James C., 92, 93, 95, 96, 361, 489, 495, 498, 501, 504
McGill, Michael E., 498
McHugh, Michael, 294, 502

McHugo, Gregory J., 231, 494
McKellen, Ian, 80, 498
McLaughlin, Margaret L., 16, 186, 266, 281, 283, 368, 492, 498, 500
McLean, Paula A., 352, 498
McNeil, Elton B., 502
McNeill, David, 57, 498
meaning interpretation, 158, 477
meaningfulness, 477
meanings, 176–180, 191, 206, 477
media, 244, 294, 335
mediation, 381
Mediterranean people, 259
Mehrabian, Albert, 189, 498
Meisels, M., 250, 490
Mencken, H. L., 498
Mendoza, Louis, 159, 498
Mercer, Alexander, 494
mere exposure hypothesis, 477
Merighi, Josepoh R., 412, 499
Merrill, Lisa, 487
Merton, Robert K., 122, 498
message-focused feedback, 14, 15
messages, 13–16, 343, 477
    characteristics of, 180–190, 191
    meanings of, 177–180, 191
    taste and smell, 240–241
Messick, R. M., 307, 498
metacommunication, 155–158, 171, 477
metacommunication, messages and, 190, 191
metalanguage, 477
metamessage, 14, 477
metaskills, 154–171
Metts, Sandra, 189, 415, 489, 498, 504
Metz, Michael E., 381, 498
Mexicans/Mexican Americans, 21, 53, 55, 81–82, 93, 250t, 258, 269t, 304, 376, 412
Meyer, Janet R., 385, 498
Meyer, Leslie, 404, 490
micromomentary expressions, 477
Middle Eastern cultures, 81, 183t, 375–376, 404
Midooka, Kiyoshi, 273, 498
Mikula, G., 308, 497
Millar, Frank E., 39, 498, 502
Miller, Casey, 498
Miller, George A., 57, 498
Miller, Gerald R., 8, 189, 323, 367t, 489, 492, 496, 498, 503, 504
Miller, J. G., 119, 498
Miller, Mark J., 407, 498
Miller, Rodney, 499
Miller, Sherod, 499
mindfulness, 154–155, 171, 477
mindlessness, 154, 477
Miner, Horace, 499
Mintz, N. L., 254, 498, 499
Mir, Montserrat, 184, 499
mirroring, 477
Mitchell, Kelly A., 304, 305, 499
mixed message, 161, 169, 180, 477

model, 477
Moghaddam, Fathali M., 9, 82, 297, 308, 316, 399, 499
Mole, John, 62, 499
Molloy, John, 256, 363, 499
Monahan, J., 497
Mongeau, Paul A., 459, 493
monochronic time orientation, 259, 263, 477
monologue, 196t, 477
monopoly pattern, 428, 433
Montague, Ashley, 499
Montgomery, Barbara M., 160, 499
Montgomery, M., 499
Moon, Dreama G., 24, 499
Moore, J. D., 241, 501
Moore, Roy L., 294, 485
moral appeals, 367t
Morales, Jorge, 79, 499
Morgan, J. L., 492
Morgan, Melinda, 329, 493
Moriarty, Thomas, 100, 499
Morland, David, 257, 499
Morrill, Calvin, 375, 499
Morris, Desmond, 255, 499
Morris, William C., 503
Morrison, Terri, 56, 499
Morrow, Gregory D., 412, 499
Moss, M., 398t, 485
Motley, Michael T., 33, 488, 499
Mulac, Anthony, 36, 234, 492, 499, 506
Murphy-Berman, V., 308, 487
Murstein, Bernard I., 412, 499
Muslims, 63, 214, 239, 255t
Myers, G., 486
Myers, Scott A., 306, 499

N
Naifeh, Steven, 82, 499
Naisbitt, John, 499
Nakane, Yoshibumi, 74, 501
name-calling, 144t
Natalle, Elizabeth J., 381, 500
National Council of Teachers of English (NCTE), 200
Native Americans. See American Indians
need, 308
negative allness, 477
negative feedback, 14, 477
negotiation, 368, 369, 471
Neimeyer, Greg J., 305, 499
Neimeyer, Robert A., 304, 305, 499
Nelson, Gayle L., 36, 485
Nesshoever, Willfried, 278, 501
Netherlands, 51t
netiquette, 159, 204, 276
Neugarten, Bernice, 259, 499
neutrality, 477
neutralized symmetry, 39
neutralizing, 231t
Nevins, Randi J., 502
 wbies, 276

newsgroups, 204, 341
Nias, David, 506
Nichols, Ralph, 499, 506
Nicotera, Anne Maydan, 391, 499
Nierenberg, Gerald, 499
Nigeria/Nigerians, 183t, 269t, 303
Nishida, T., 94, 492
Nizer, Louis, 372
Noble, Barbara Presley, 499
Noelle-Neumann, Elisabeth, 244, 499, 500
noise, 12f, 16–17, 25, 135f, 142, 477
Noller, Patricia, 308, 381, 382, 419t, 422, 427, 431, 500
nonallness, 218, 477
nonassertiveness, 101, 102–104, 105
noncontact cultures, 239
nondirective language, 477
nonjudgmental listening, 143, 146f, 151
nonnegotiation, 471, 478
nonverbal communication, 103, 104, 139, 167, 170, 176, 183f, 196t, 323, 327f, 403, 412, 478
  believability, 185–190
  rules for, 180–182, 183t
nonverbal dominance, 478
nonverbal encounter, 478
nonverbal power, 363–364
Norton, Robert, 102, 500
Norway/Norwegians, 53, 269t, 348
Notarius, Clifford I., 148, 500
Nothern Europeans, 155, 239
novelty, 109, 291
Nunnally, Elam, 499

O
Oberg, K., 60, 500
object language, 478
object-adaptors, 230, 363, 478
objectivity, 142–143, 146f, 151
Obujinrin, O., 500
offensive listening, 142
Ogden, C. K., 497
OíHair, Dan M., 186, 189, 368, 500
Ohta, Yasuyuki, 74, 501
OíKeefe, Barbara J., 177, 489
OíKeefe, Daniel J., 177, 489
Olaniran, Bolanle A., 500
Olds, S., 492
olfactics, 478
olfactory communication, 478
Oliker, S. J., 406, 491
Oliver, Ronald, 38, 497
Olson, D. H., 501
Olson, Jean T., 244, 506
omoiyari, 185
OíNeil, Barbara, 260, 500
online communication, 35, 147, 159, 204, 303, 310–311, 341, 348. See also Internet
open self, 71–72, 89, 476
opening lines, 271–272

opening, a conversation, 266–268, 269, 270, 271–272, 283
openness, 159–160, 167, 168, 171, 291, 327f, 343, 383, 386, 402, 403, 431, 478
opinion, 244, 427, 428, 478
OíShaughnessy, Marie, 499
other talk, 203–205, 207, 478
other-adaptors, 363
other-orientation, 170, 171, 327f, 343, 403, 478
other-references, 271
Otto, Herbert, 500
outcomes, maximizing, 59, 67
outing, 79–80, 478
overattribution, 201
oversimplification, 143
ownership of feelings, 160, 206, 343, 386, 403, 404, 478
packages, 180–181, 191, 363, 478, 481
packaging, 478, 481. See also reinforcement

P
Painter, Susan L., 389, 495
Pakistan/Pakistanis, 41t, 269t, 413
Palmer, J. C., 497
Palmer, M. T., 428, 500
Palmgreen, P., 492
Panama, 51t
Papa, Michael J., 381, 500
paralanguage, 241–242, 245, 478
paraphrasing, 148–149, 151, 158, 169
parasocial relationship, 294
Parks, Malcolm R., 189, 323, 341, 367t, 498, 500
Parlee, Mary Brown, 400, 500
Parra, Fernando, 412, 496
participatory listening, 141–142, 146f, 151
passion, 406
passion cluster, 406
passive listening, 141–142, 146f, 151, 478
past orientation, 260, 263
Patterson, Brian, 500
pauses, 478
Payne, S. K., 95, 498
Payne, Steven, 501
Peabody, Susan, 500
Pearce, John, 307, 502
Pearce, W. Barnett, 500
Pearse, Elizabeth, 147, 502
Pearson, Judy C., 42, 161, 196t, 275, 278, 278t, 281, 419t, 500
Pease, Allen, 500
Peck, C., 486
Peck, Janice, 294, 500
Penfield, Joyce, 200, 500
Pennebacker, James W., 84, 289, 500
people of color, 213–214
Peplau, Letitia Anne, 420, 500

perception, 108– 129, 478
  checking, 127–128, 129, 388, 478
  process, 108–110, 129
perceptual accentuation, 122–123, 478
perceptual contact, 291, 299
performance visualization, 97
Perlman, Daniel, 490, 495, 500
Perse, Elizabeth M., 19f, 294, 492, 500, 502
person-focused feedback, 14, 15
personal distance, 248f, 249, 263, 364, 374t, 478
personal rejection, 478
personality, 241–242, 250t
personality conflict, 381
persuasion, 242, 478
persuasion (information) power, 362–363, 369
Peru, 51t
Petrocelli, William, 356, 358, 500
phatic communication, 15, 266, 323, 478–479
pheromones, 240
Philbrick, Joseph L., 412, 496
Philippines/Filipinos, 55, 62–63, 269t
Phillips, Richard, 260, 500
Phillips, Terri, 125, 505
Phillipson, H., 126, 496
Phlegar, Phyllis, 310, 500
physical dimension, 17
physical noise, 16
Picard, Max, 243
Pilkington, Constance J., 295, 500
Pilkington, Neil W., 357, 500
Pinker, Steven, 500
pitch, 241, 479
Pittenger, R. E., 500
Plax, T. G., 361, 495
play, 18, 19f, 237, 268
pleasure, 19f
Pliner, P., 491
Plutchik, R., 500
Pocs, O., 492
Poland/Poles, 21
polarization, 210–212, 225, 479
Polefka, Judith, 493
politeness, 273–275
Pollack, Andrew, 48, 179, 500
Pollack, David H., 500
Pollard, C. Alex, 96, 497
Pollyanna effect, 123, 479
polychronic time orientation, 259, 263, 479
Poole, Marshall Scott, 491
Poortinga, Ype H., 50, 118, 381, 487
Porter, R. H., 241, 501
Porter, Richard E., 19, 485, 486, 487, 495, 502, 503, 504
positive feedback, 14, 479
positiveness, 164, 171, 383, 388, 402, 403, 404, 479
posting, 204
posture, 166, 278t, 312, 313, 365, 403
Potter, Ellen F., 199, 501

Pottick, Kathleen J., 321, 504
Powell, Robert, 294, 502
power, 352–359, 479
  in relationships, 323, 327f, 355–356, 374t, 383
power bases, 359–365, 479
power communication, 479
power distance, 55–57, 67
power play, 104, 358–359, 393, 427, 428, 479
pragma love, 410, 411, 413, 415
pragmatic approach, 166–171, 479
pragmatic implication, 216–217, 479
praise, 205, 206–207, 479
Prather, G., 501
Prather, H., 501
Pratkanis, Anthony, 144t, 501
predictability, 291
predicting, 9
premature self-disclosure, 479
present orientation, 260, 263
prestige, 360. See also status
Pretzer, J. L., 320, 491
previewing, 15–16
primacy, 479
primacy effect, 123–124, 479
primary affect displays, 479
primary relationship, 479
  communication patterns, 426–432, 433
  types and characteristics, 418–426
primary territory, 252, 479
Prins, K. S., 328, 501
Prisbell, Marshall, 102, 501
Pritchard, Michael S., 18, 494
private language, 327f
process, 479
productive conflict, 479–480
progressive differentiation, 480
projection, 473, 480
pronouncements, 480
Prosky, Phoebe S., 38, 501
prosocial behavior, 337
protection theory, 250–251, 263, 480
provisionalism, 162, 163–164, 171, 470
proxemic distance, 248–253, 263, 480
proxemics, 248, 476, 480
proximity, 109, 303, 313, 480
Prusank, Diane T., 291, 501
psychological data, 8–9
psychological noise, 16
psychological time, 260, 263, 480
public (social) separation, 292f, 297, 299
public distance, 248f, 249, 480
public territory, 252, 480
Puerto Rico
  Puerto Ricans, 81, 82, 93
Puhl, Carol A., 451, 488
punctuation, of communication, 37, 38f, 45, 142, 344–346, 480
punishment, 480
pupil dilation, 189t, 236, 245, 480
pupillometrics, 480
Purnell, Rosentene B., 198, 501
purpose, 17–18, 25

Pygmalion effect, 122, 480
Pygmalion gift, 257

Q
qualifiers, 311
quality maxim, 273, 283, 480
quantity maxim, 272–273, 276, 283, 480
queer, 198, 214–215. See also gay men; homosexual; lesbians
questions, 149–150, 151
quotes, 474, 480

R
Rabin, Claire, 102, 501
Rabinowitz, Fredric E., 237, 501
racism
  language, 197–199, 213, 480
  listening, 201–202
Radford, March, 74, 501
Rancer, Andrew, 28, 30, 385, 386, 391, 494, 499, 501
Rank, H., 501
Rankin, Paul, 132, 501
Rappaport, Herbert, 260, 501
Rapson, Richard L., 24, 51, 304, 348, 355, 375, 376, 427, 493, 497
rate, 36, 241, 242, 278t, 480
Raush, Harold L., 497
Raven, B. H., 359, 489, 491, 501
Rawlings, Edna I., 389, 495
Rawlins, William K., 402, 501
Ray, Chett, 502
real time, 204
Reardon, Kathleen K., 268, 491, 501
reasonableness, 432, 433
reasoning, 381
receiver, 480
receiving, 133–134, 151
recency, 479
recency effect, 123–124, 480
receptivity, 399–400, 415
reciprocity, 399, 415
reconciliation strategies, 480
reconstructive listening, 136
redundancy, 480
Reed, Fred W., 124, 498
Reed, Warren H., 50
referent power, 360, 363, 369
reflecting, 161, 196t
reflexiveness, 480
regulators, 228t, 229, 234, 245, 480
Reichert, Elisabeth, 375, 501
Reik, Theodore, 305, 501
reinforcement (packaging), 481
reinforcement theory, of relationships, 305–306, 313, 327f, 328, 340, 480
Reisman, John M., 399, 501
rejection, 195, 197, 381, 481
relation maxim, 273, 283, 481
relational communication, 481
relational references, 271
relationship dialectics theory, 291, 302, 481
relationship messages, 481

relationships, 288–290, 299
complementary, 38–40, 45
culture and. See culture
deterioration, 292f, 296, 299, 316–331
dimensions, 40–44, 45, 145, 188, 235
dissolution, 292f, 297, 299, 327f,
    328–330, 331, 481
improvement, 481
maintenace, 348, 476
primary. See primary relationship
as purpose of communication, 17–18,
    19f, 268
repair, 292f, 296–297, 299, 340–347,
    349481
spatial distance, 250t, 251
stimulation, 481
symmetrical, 37, 39–40, 45
touch in, 236
relaxation, 19f
remembering, 135–136, 151
Remp, Richard, 159, 501
Repa, Barbara Kate, 356, 358, 500
repair, of relationships. See under
    relationships,
repeating, 176, 191
research, 29, 30–31, 45
resemblance, 109, 481
responding, 135f, 137–138, 151
response, 481
reverse halo effect, 121, 124
reward power, 360, 361, 369
Reynolds, A., 499
Rezabeck, Landra L., 179, 501
rhythm, 241
Ribeau, Sidney, 213, 493
Rich, Andrea L., 197, 501
Richards, I. A., 15, 497, 501
Richardson, Deborah R., 295, 500
Richmond, Virginia P., 93, 95, 96, 361,
    495, 498, 501
Riddle, Bruce L., 386, 494
Riggio, Ronald E., 121, 213, 501
Riggs, Walter E., 504
rigid complementarity, 481
ritualistic touching, 237
Roach, K. David, 501
Robers, Tia, 412, 497
Roberts, Churchill L., 486
Robey, C. S., 368, 498
Robey, Daniel, 35, 503
Robinson, W. P., 501
Rock, Joseph W., 344, 490
Rock, Leslie, 495
Rockwell, Patricia, 185, 488
Rodenburg, Frances A., 389, 501
Rodrigues, A., 359, 501
Rodriguez, Maria, 501
Roeher Institute, 390, 501
Roger, Derek, 278, 501
Rogers, Carl, 76, 502
Rogers, Everett M., 502
Rogers, L. E., 39, 498
Rogers-Millar, Edna, 39, 502
Rohlfing, Mary E., 421, 502
Role, 419–420, 422, 425, 427, 481

Roloff, Michael E., 489, 498, 504
romantic rules, 339, 481
Rose, Patricia , 382, 497
Rosenbaum, M. E., 305, 502
Rosenberg, S. D., 398t, 491
Rosenfeld, Lawrence, 82, 485, 502
Rosengren, Annika, 289, 502
Rosenman, Ray, 491
Rosenthal, Peggy, 502
Rosenthall, Robert, 122, 502
Rosnow, Ralph L., 407, 502
Rosser, B. R., 381, 498
Rosser, Sue V., 199, 501
Rossiter, Jr., Charles M., 502
Rotello, Gabriel, 502
Rothblum, Esther D., 201, 502
Rothwell, J. Dan, 502
Rowland-Morin, Pamela A., 167, 502
Ruben, Brent D., 62, 63, 502
Rubenstein, Carin, 358, 502
Rubin, Alan M., 19f, 147, 485, 502
Rubin, D. C., 240, 502
Rubin, Jeffrey, 502
Rubin, Rebecca B., 13, 19f, 147, 157,
    294, 492, 500, 502
Rubin, Theodore Isaac, 502
Rubin, Zick, 502
Rudd, Jill E., 386, 389, 494
Ruesch, Jurgen, 502
rules theory, 10, 181–182, 302, 338–339,
    349, 399, 422, 481
Rumsey, N., 310, 487
Rundquist, Suellen, 185, 502
Rusbult, Caryl E., 337, 497, 502
Ryan, Kathryn M., 389, 502
Rychiak, Joseph F., 161, 493

S

Sabatelli, Ronald M., 307, 502
Sabourin, Teresa Chandler, 386, 389, 494
Saegert, Susan, 303, 502
Saline, Carol, 499
Salminen, Simo, 140, 502
Samovar, Larry A., 19, 485, 486, 487,
    495, 502, 503, 504
Sanders, Judith A., 53, 503
Sanford, John A., 503
Sapadin, Linda A., 405, 503
Sapir, Edward, 57, 503
Sapir-Whorf hypothesis. See language
    relativity hypothesis
Sargent, J. F., 503
Sarwer, David B., 409, 503
Sashkin, Marshall, 503
sassuru, 185
Sata, K., 499
Satir, Virginia, 421, 503
Sato, S., 413, 497
Saunders, Carol S., 35, 503
Savage, Grant T., 488
Saylor, K., 361, 501
Scandinavia, 289
Schachter, Stanley, 303, 491, 503
Schaef, Anne Wilson, 503
Schaefer, Charles E., 503

Schafer, R. B., 308, 503
Schatski, Michael, 503
Schegloff, E., 277, 503
Scherer, K. R., 503
Schlien, John M., 236, 494
Schmidt, Tracy O., 503
Schmitt, David P., 488
Schmitt, David R., 367t, 497
Schneider, David, 493
Schramm, Wilbur, 503
Schulze, Gene, 497
Schwartz, Janet, 404, 490
Schwartz, Marilyn, 203, 213, 503
Schwartz, Pepper, 288, 305, 321, 322,
    323, 326, 415, 418, 417, 487, 494
Scott, Lorel, 411, 494
Scott, Marvin B., 497
Scott, Michael D., 503
Seaver, W. B., 503
Sebeok, T. A., 496, 497
secondary territory, 252, 481
security value, 401, 415
Segall, Marshall H., 50, 118, 235, 381,
    487, 495
selective exposure, 109, 481
selective perception, 109
self-acceptance, 481
self-adaptors, 229, 363, 481
self-affirmation, 76
self-appreciation, 481
self-attribution, 481
self-awareness, 71–74, 89, 482
self-concept, 70–71, 89, 388–389, 482
self-disclosure, 73, 77–88, 89, 127,
    159–160, 161, 168, 203, 235, 237,
    354, 469, 482, 483
    guidelines, 482
    in relationships, 293, 296, 312, 319,
        323, 327f, 337, 344, 404, 412, 425,
        426, 427, 431, 433
self-esteem, 74–77, 89, 99, 102, 117,
    195, 282, 288, 318, 329, 366, 394,
    482
self-fulfilling prophecy, 122, 482
self-manipulations, 363
self-monitoring, 168, 169, 171, 353, 482
self-orientation, 170
self-references, 167, 271
self-serving bias, 117–118, 129, 482
self-talk, 482
Seltzer, Allan L., 236, 494
semantic noise, 16
semantics, 482
separates, 426, 433
Sergios, Paul A., 303, 503
sex role bias, 200
sexist language, 199–200, 482
sexist listening, 201–202
sexual assault, 383
sexual harassment, 356–358, 482
sexual orientation, 215. See also
    affectional orientation
sexual preferences, 215
sexual status, 215
Shaffer, Warren F., 502

Shannon, Elizabeth A., 386, 389, 494
Shannon, J., 168, 229, 503
sharing, 422, 424
Sharkey, William F., 52, 278, 495, 503
Sharp, Steward M., 500
sharpening, 482
Sharver, Kelley G., 495
Shaver, Philip, 502
Shavitt, Sharon, 52, 493
Shea, Virginia, 276, 503
Sheppard, James A., 228, 503
Shimanoff, Susan, 503
Shuter, Robert, 19f, 503
shyness, 159, 482. *See also* apprehension
Siavelis, Rita L., 293, 503
Siegert, John R., 375, 503
signal and noise, relativity of, 482
signal reaction, 482
signature, 204
Signitzer, Benno, 244, 506
Signorielli, Nancy, 503
Signorile, Michelangelo, 79, 503
silence, 243–245, 482
silencers, 384, 395, 482
Sillars, Alan L., 503
similarity, 303–305, 313, 405–406, 482
Simon, Eric P., 282, 486
Simpson, Jeffry A., 328, 503
sin licenses, 281, 283
Singapore, 81
Singer, Marshall R., 503
Singh, P., 308, 487, 493
Sissela, Bok, 407, 487
situational aggression, 101
situational nonassertiveness, 101, 102, 105
Siu, R. G. H., 503
skill acquisition, 97–98, 105
Slade, Margot, 282, 503
slander, 113
slang, 482
Slapion-Foote, Michelle J., 413, 494
Small, Jacquelyn, 503
smell, 240–241, 478. *See also* olfactics; olfactory communication
Smith, Gregory White, 82, 499
Smith, L. J., 503
Smith, Richard H., 394, 495
Smith, Stephen A., 113, 503
snail mail, 204
Snyder, C. R., 282, 503
Snyder, Mark, 169, 492
Snyder, Mark, 168, 503
sociability, 36
social (public) separation, 292f, 297, 299
social bonding, 292f, 293, 299
social clock, 259–260
social comparison processes, 288, 482
social Darwinism, 50
social data, 9
social distance, 248f, 249, 263, 483
social exchange theory, 306–307, 313, 328, 340, 355, 483
social network convergence, 341
social penetration theory, 296, 302, 482
social phase, 316–317, 331

social-psychological dimension, 17
Solomon, Michael R., 504
Sommer, Robert, 504
Sorenson, James R., 13, 505
source, 483
source-reciever, 10, 12f, 203–205
Southern Europeans, 64, 183t, 229, 239, 375
space, 420–421, 422, 424
space decoration, 253–254
Spain/Spaniards, 269t
spamming, 159, 276
Sparks, Glenn G., 406, 492
spatial distance, 248–253, 483
speaker apprehension, 483
speaker cues, 275–277
speaking power, 363, 369
Spears, Russell, 35, 310, 496
specificity, 127
speech, 139, 483
speech rate, 142, 483
Spencer, Ted, 78, 504
Spiegel, N. H., 231, 506
spiral of silence, 244
Spitzberg, Brian H., 12, 13, 27t, 62, 63, 166, 278, 278t, 504
spontaneity, 483
Sprecher, Susan, 82, 84, 85, 415, 504
Sproull, Lee, 159, 495
stability, 483
Stacks, Don W., 494
Stafford, Laura, 278, 337, 488, 489, 503, 504
Staines, Graham L., 321, 504
Stamp, Glen H., 375, 503
Stanley, Julia, 199
state apprehension, 92, 105, 483
static evaluation, 211t, 219, 225, 483
status, 237, 242, 250t, 253, 260–262, 405, 483
Steil, Lyman K., 135f, 504
Steiner, Claude, 358, 359, 504
Steinfatt, Thomas M., 352, 354, 504
Stephan, Cookie White, 62, 94, 504
Stephan, Walter G., 62, 94, 487, 504
Stephens, Gregory K., 50, 504
stereotype, 124–125, 198, 201, 222, 242, 321, 483
Sternberg, Robert J., 406, 415, 504
Stevens, Leonard, 499
Stevenson, Sheryl, 489
Stewart, J., 486
Stewart, Robert A., 498
Stillings, Neil A., 504
stimulation value, 401, 415
stimulus, 483
stimulus-response models, 344–346, 483
Stokes, Randall, 281, 494
storgic love, 410, 411, 412, 413, 415
Strapko, Nancy, 381, 498
strategy, 483
Strathman, Alan J., 228, 503
Strecker, Ivo, 274, 504
Stucky, Rita J., 282, 503

Studley, Lisa B., 234, 499
subjectivity, 483
submissive symmetry, 39
substituting, 176, 191
Sunnafrank, Michael, 59, 504
superiority, 483
supportive feedback, 14, 15
supportiveness, 162–163, 388, 402, 403–404, 483
surface listening, 143–145, 146f, 151
Swap, Walter, 303, 502
Sweden/Swedes, 51t, 53, 56, 348, 375, 418
Swensen, C. H., 504
Swets, Paul W., 504
Swift, Kate, 498
Switzerland/Swiss, 257, 258, 259
symmetrical relationship, 37, 39–40, 45, 483
sympathy, 160, 319
Sypher, H. E., 492
sysop (systems operator), 204
systematic desensitization, 97, 105
systems operator (sysop), 204
Szapocznik, Jose, 82, 504

T
taboo, 183t, 269t, 483
Tacey, William S., 506
tactile communication, 483
Taiwan/Taiwanese, 51t, 60, 93, 183t, 259, 376, 451
talk radio, 147
Tang, F. F., 56, 505
Tannen, Deborah, 140, 184, 185, 381, 503, 504
Taraban, Carolyn Beth, 504
task-related touching, 237, 239
taste messages, 240
Taylor, Barbara Ewert, 356, 491
Taylor, Dalmas, 295, 296, 485, 504
Taylor, Donald M., 9, 82, 118, 297, 308, 316, 399, 499, 504
Taylor, Eric H., 335, 336, 496
Taylor, Shelley E., 491
technical time, 258, 263
telephone communication, 159
temporal communication, 258–262, 263, 483
temporal dimension, of context, 17
temporal regularity, 422, 425
Terrell, R., 306, 488
territorial encroachment, 475, 483
territoriality, 252–253, 263, 484
Tersine, Richard J., 504
testimonial, 144t
testing, 291–292, 293
Thailand, 53, 60, 255t, 413
Thayer, Stephen, 504
theory, 28–30, 45, 484
Thibaut, J. W., 83, 306, 495, 504
Thomas, Candice E., 504
Thomlison, Dean, 504
Thompson, Catherine A., 100, 504

Thompson, M., 492
Thompson, S. C., 504
Thorne, Barrie, 199, 504
thread, 204
tie signs, 412
Ting-Toomey, Stella, 53, 375, 376, 489, 493, 495, 503, 504, 505
Todd-Mancillas, William, 281, 500
Tolhuizen, James H., 292, 296, 505
Tomkins, S. S., 490, 491
topics, 295–296
touch, 484
  avoidance, 237, 238, 323, 484
  communication, 236–239, 245
  rules, 484
Towne, Neil, 485
traditionalism, 422, 423–425
Trager, George L., 241, 505
trait apprehension, 92–93, 105, 484
transactional, 484
  process, 31–32, 45, 368
transition patterns, 39–40
Traupman, Jane, 308, 427, 493, 505
Trenholm, Sarah, 505
Trower, P., 339, 505
Truax, C., 505
Tschann, J. M., 83, 505
Tubbs, Stewart L., 505
Tumlin, S. A., 386, 494
turn-denying cues, 277, 279f, 283
Turner, Lynn H., 42, 161, 281, 500
turn-maintaining cues, 275, 279f, 283
turn-requesting cues, 277, 279f, 283
turn-yielding cues, 275–277, 279f, 283
Tyler, Patrick E., 505

U
Ueleke, William, 307, 505
Ullmann, Stephen, 505
unbalanced split pattern, 427–428, 433
uncertainty, 327f, 403, 422, 424
  avoidance, 57–59, 67, 126
  reduction, 302, 341, 484
understanding, 134, 135f, 149, 151, 169, 196t, 386
United Kingdom, 255t. *See also* Great Britain; Ireland
universals, 484
unknown self, 73–74, 89, 476
unproductive conflict strategies, 484
unrepeatability, 34, 45
utility value, 401, 415

V
valence, 81
validation, 384
value, 484
Van Yperen, N. W., 328, 501
VandeCreek, Leon, 84, 505
Vangelisti, Anita, 323, 496
VanHyning, Memory, 357–358, 505
Varonis, Evangeline Marlos, 158, 505
Vaverek, Kelly A., 35, 503
Veenendall, Thomas L., 195, 505

Venezuela, 51t
verbal abuse, 386–389, 484
verbal aggressiveness, 386, 389, 484
verbal encounter, 484
Verderber, Kathleen S., 505
Verderber, Rudolph F., 505
Verette, J. A., 115, 505
Verma, J., 413, 497
Vernon, JoEtta A., 125, 505
Victor, David, 53, 54t, 55, 56, 505
visual dominance, 234, 235, 484
vocal segregates, 241
vocalizations, 241, 275
voice, 241–242, 310, 412
volume, 241, 484
von Foerster, Heinz, 501
Vonnegut, Kurt, 144t
Vyse, Stuart A., 412, 499

W
Wabnik, A. I., 337, 493
Wackman, Daniel, 499
Wad, Lawrence M., 495
Wagner, Pat N., 84, 491
Wallace, Lise A., 337, 488
Walsh, R., 492
Walster, Elaine, 121, 304, 307, 308, 427, 487, 490, 505
Walster, G. W., 304, 307, 308, 427, 505
Walther, Joseph B., 341, 505
Wampler, Karen Smith, 382, 383, 489
Wang, Y. E., 491
Wardhaugh, R., 505
Warnick, Barbara, 102, 500
Watson, Arden K., 505
Watson, Kittie W., 135f, 504, 505
Watzlawick, Paul, 31, 33, 37, 195, 505
web browser, 204
Weber, Ann L., 336, 496, 505
Webster, E., 505
Weinberg, Harry L., 217t, 505
Weiner, Bernard, 115, 505
Weingarten, Jan, 179, 276, 494
Weinstein, Eugene A., 16, 505
Weitzman, Jennifer, 421, 505
Wells, Theodora, 505
Wenner, Jann, 79
Wertz, Dorothy C., 13, 505
Wessells, Michael G., 505
West, Candace, 278, 505, 506
West, Richard, 42, 161, 278, 500
Westefeld, J. S., 421, 505
Western, Robin 407, 505
Westwood, R. I., 56, 505
Wetzel, Christopher G., 237, 490
Wetzel, Patricia J., 274, 505
Wheeless, Lawrence, 82, 92, 498, 506
White, Jr., Raymond M., 490
Widenmann, S. J., 499, 506
Wiemann, J. M., 506
Wiemann, J. W., 234, 499
Wigley, C. J., 385, 387, 494
Wilcox, A. Kathlee, 97, 485
Wilcox, Charles T., 407, 498

Wilhoit, G. C., 499
Williams, Andrea, 506
Williams, Barbara A., 411, 496
Williams, David E., 65t, 493
Williams, J. Allen, 125, 505
Williams, K., 496
Willis, R. H., 306, 492
Wilmot, William W., 7, 8, 293, 486, 494, 506
Wilson, Ann, 488
Wilson, Arnold, 260, 501
Wilson, Glenn, 506
Wilson, Janet, 125, 505
Wilson, Timothy D., 485
Windahl, Sven, 244, 506
Winstead, Barbara A., 84, 489
Wiseman, Richard L., 53, 503
withdrawal, 323, 327f, 331
Wolf, Florence I., 506
Wolfe, Arnold, 51, 495
Wolfson, Nessa, 274, 275, 497, 506
Wolpe, Joseph, 97, 506
Womack, Deanna F., 28, 30, 494
Won-Doornink, Myong-Jin, 78, 506
Wong, Paul T. P., 489
Wood, John, 506
Wood, Julia T., 42, 494, 496, 502, 506
Woodall, W. Gill, 185, 229, 230, 242, 250t, 251, 275, 278t, 363, 488
World Wide Web, 204
Wright, John W., 281, 418, 506
Wright, Paul H., 399, 401, 406, 506
Wright, Stephen C., 9, 82, 297, 308, 316, 399, 499
Wyden, Peter, 486

Y
Yang, S., 94, 492
Yarbrough, A. Elaine, 236, 495
Yerby, Janet, 419t, 487, 506
Yogev, Sara, 321, 506
you-messages, 160, 381, 484
you-statements, 166
Yun, Hum, 155, 506

Z
Zajonc, Robert B., 303, 502, 506
Zanden, James W. Vander, 111, 506
Zander, Alvin, 491
Zelen, S., 73, 487
Zelner, Dvora, 102, 501
Ziglar, Zig, 147
Zimbardo, Philip G., 93, 95, 96, 98, 260, 488, 492, 506
Zimmer, Troy A., 293 506
Zimmerman, Don H., 278, 505, 506
Zuckerman, M., 231, 506
Zunin, Leonard M., 291, 506
Zunin, Natalie B., 291, 506